The Quantum AI Era of Neuromarketing

Pranjali Gajbhiye
Woxsen University, India

Hemachandran Kannan
Woxsen University, India

Raul Villamarin Rodriguez
Woxsen University, India

José I. Rojas-Méndez
Carleton University, Canada

IGI Global
Scientific Publishing
Publishing Tomorrow's Research Today

Vice President of Editorial Melissa Wagner
Managing Editor of Acquisitions Mikaela Felty
Managing Editor of Book Development Jocelynn Hessler
Production Manager Mike Brehm
Cover Design Phillip Shickler

Published in the United States of America by
IGI Global Scientific Publishing
701 East Chocolate Avenue
Hershey, PA, 17033, USA
Tel: 717-533-8845
Fax: 717-533-8661
Website: https://www.igi-global.com E-mail: cust@igi-global.com

Library of Congress Cataloging-in-Publication Data

Names: Gajbhiye, Pranjali, 1993- editor.
Title: The quantum AI era of neuromarketing / [edited by] Pranjali Gajbhiye, Hemachandran Kannan, Raul Villamarin Rodriguez, José I. Rojas-Méndez.
Description: Hershey, PA : IGI Global Scientific Publishing, [2025] | Includes bibliographical references and index. | Summary: "This book integrates integrate quantum AI with traditional neuromarketing, enhancing predictive analytics and understanding subconscious consumer behavior. It bridges theory and practice with real-world case studies, fostering interdisciplinary collaboration among AI researchers, neuroscientists, and marketers"-- Provided by publisher.
Identifiers: LCCN 2024055174 (print) | LCCN 2024055175 (ebook) | ISBN 9798369376737 (hardcover) | ISBN 9798369376744 (paperback) | ISBN 9798369376751 (ebook)
Subjects: LCSH: Neuromarketing. | Artificial intelligence.
Classification: LCC HF5415.12615 .Q36 2025 (print) | LCC HF5415.12615 (ebook) | DDC 658.8/342028563--dc23/eng/20250217
LC record available at https://lccn.loc.gov/2024055174
LC ebook record available at https://lccn.loc.gov/2024055175

British Cataloguing in Publication Data
A Cataloguing in Publication record for this book is available from the British Library.

Table of Contents

Detailed Table of Contents

Neuromarketing is an interdisciplinary field that merges neuroscience, psychology, and marketing to explore how consumers make decisions and how brands can influence these choices. At its foundation, neuromarketing studies the brain's response to marketing stimuli, utilizing techniques such as functional magnetic resonance imaging (fMRI), electroencephalography (EEG), and eye-tracking to glean insights into emotional and cognitive processes. Pioneering studies demonstrated how consumers react to various marketing stimuli, revealing that emotional experiences often drive purchasing decisions more than rational thought. As the digital landscape has evolved, so too has neuromarketing. Data analytics and machine learning now complement traditional neuroscience methods, enabling more nuanced understanding of consumer behavior in online environments. By leveraging insights from neuromarketing, businesses can develop targeted strategies that resonate with consumers on a deeper psychological level, ultimately fostering stronger brand loyalty and enhancing overall customer experiences.

Neuromarketing combines neuroscience, psychology, and marketing to explore consumer behavior at a subconscious level. By using tools like fMRI, EEG, eye-tracking, and biometrics, it measures consumers' emotional and cognitive responses to marketing stimuli, offering deeper insights than traditional methods. Neuromarketing helps marketers create more personalized campaigns by understanding what drives consumer choices. Key methodologies include fMRI for identifying brain areas linked to emotions and decision-making, EEG for capturing real-time reactions, and eye-tracking to analyze visual attention. Brands like Coca-Cola and Nike use these insights to enhance emotional connections and boost loyalty. However, ethical

Electroencephalography (EEG) is crucial for understanding how music affects cognitive and emotional processes by providing real-time insights into neural activity. It helps measure emotional states like happiness and sadness in response to music, revealing how music influences brain regions such as the amygdala and prefrontal cortex. Advancements in EEG technology have enabled sophisticated analysis of brain waves (delta, theta, alpha, beta, gamma) and their correlation with music's tempo and rhythm, impacting memory and emotional processing. EEG's application extends to therapeutic settings, enhancing neuroplasticity and cognitive functions in neurological rehabilitation, and in marketing, where it offers insights into consumer reactions and preferences, optimizing ads and product designs. It helps optimize content to evoke desired emotional responses, improve attention and memory encoding, and enhance brand loyalty by integrating EEG insights with traditional market research methods.

This chapter examines how quantum computing has impacted predictive analytics in neuromarketing in a significant way. It talks about how marketers understanding, and prediction of consumer behaviour is changing as a result of quantum algorithms' capacity to process large and complex datasets. The chapter explores how quantum AI is being applied in the real world and highlights businesses that have effectively used this technology to get more precise predictive insights. Furthermore, it provides guidelines for responsible implementation and discusses ethical issues related to the use of quantum AI such as privacy and data transparency. In order to improve consumer engagement strategies, the chapter also looks at interdisciplinary approaches that combine quantum AI with marketing and neuroscience. With an eye toward the future the chapter projects how quantum-enhanced predictive analytics will impact neuromarketing over the next ten years by identifying emerging trends possible obstacles and opportunities.

Quantum algorithms for predictive analytics is important across various sectors such as finance, healthcare, marketing and supply chain management where accurate predictions can be used to optimise operations and decision-making processes. This chapter addresses Specific quantum machine learning algorithms such as Quantum Support Vector Machines (QSVM), Quantum K-nearest Neighbors (QKNN) and Quantum Neural Networks (QNN). These algorithms enhance classification, regression and complex predictive tasks by accelerating training processes and managing large feature spaces effectively. And, to this, quantum optimization algorithms like Quantum Approximate Optimization Algorithm (QAOA) and Variational Quantum Eigensolver (VQE) are mentioned for their role in optimising model parameters and improving prediction accuracy. In addition, it discusses quantum data encoding methods, such as Quantum Fourier Transform (QFT) and amplitude encoding. Along with this, it acknowledges significant challenges such as hardware limitations, algorithmic complexity and practical integration issues.

Neuromarketing combines neuroscience and traditional marketing to uncover the emotional and cognitive drivers behind consumer behavior. As retail and e-commerce sectors increasingly rely on customer data for personalized experiences, the complexity of large datasets often surpasses classical machine learning capabilities. This gap allows Quantum Machine Learning (QML) to emerge as a transformative solution, enhancing predictive power and efficiency in neuromarketing. QML improves data processing speed and pattern recognition, enabling companies to gain deeper insights into consumer preferences and engage customers more personally. This chapter evaluates QML's applications in retail and e-commerce, highlighting how quantum algorithms can overcome current AI limitations regarding speed and precision. It also addresses data privacy concerns, emphasizing ethical data handling practices to foster consumer trust. Ultimately, the chapter envisions QML as a pivotal technology that will redefine consumer engagement and optimize marketing strategies in an increasingly data-driven landscape.

This chapter reviews neuromarketing and AI interaction, especially related to sophisticated decision-making techniques that provide better insights into the phenomenon of consumer behavior. Neuromarketing incorporates neuroscience into marketing strategies to analyze subconscious reactions to achieve a level of understanding beyond traditional means such as surveys. Neuromarketing in the world of digital era lies in the complexity of the consumer structure where fast decisions are made unconsciously. Amongst the three key benchmark decision-making methods-neural networks, fuzzy decision-making and evolutionary algorithms-the three represent processing complex data, incorporating subtle consumer preferences, and continuously optimizing marketing strategies within iterative feedback loops. An AI-driven decision making conceptualizes a holistic approach to data gathering using neuromarketing tools, feature extraction with neural networks, and decision optimization through fuzzy logic and evolutionary algorithms.

This study explores the impact of Quantum AI and Virtual Reality (VR) on neuromarketing practices, aiming to understand their influence on consumer behavior and enhance marketing strategies. Utilizing a mixed-methods approach, the research incorporates qualitative analysis of case studies and quantitative assessments of consumer responses to VR-enhanced marketing campaigns. Key findings indicate that integrating Quantum AI and VR can significantly improve consumer engagement and satisfaction by creating immersive experiences tailored to individual preferences. The study concludes that these technologies not only offer innovative methods for marketers but also raise ethical considerations regarding consumer privacy and data security. The implications underscore the need for a structured framework to

Preface

Neuromarketing, the wonderful combination of neuroscience and marketing, has become research area of interest and great discovery in the last decade. Having looked at the various neural processes influencing consumer choices, neuromarketing has provided brands and companies a clear picture of the 'what' behind consumers' actions. Similarly, another revolution in the field of computing is quantum which has already shown how a different bracket of problems can be solved in ways, hitherto not imaginable. At the intersection of these two revolutionary fields lies the premise of this book: Neuromarketing as **The Quantum AI Era Neuromarketing** is a concept that has grown to popularly in recent times as a result of new technological advancement.

This book examines how quantum computing and artificial intelligence are being applied to neuromarketing and how this union is revolutionizing the market research approach that enterprises use to engage audiences. The emergence of quantum computing has made it possible to work with data arrays that reflect the endless variety of consumer behavior and, consequently, conduct complete analyses that previously would have been unthinkable. Together with using AI, these technologies allow for understanding and managing consumers' decisions in a more accurate and effective manner, thus preparing a ground for the future personalized, ethical and more effective realizations of marketing.

The Relevance of Neuromarketing and Quantum AI Today

The current global culture defined by technologies has made it so difficult to predict their behaviour. Conventional advertising techniques, however, are somewhat restrained regarding the described types of emotions, preferences, and decisions.

Neuromarketing does this by studying the other rational aspects involved in the decision-making process of a purchase.

However, when the volume and variety of data increase dramatically, standard computational methodologies encounter challenges in capturing and analysing data. This is where quantum computing come into the picture and turn the table around. That is why this option offers an unbeatable benefit for neuromarketing, as it is capable of handling huge amounts of data and solving multi-faceted tasks. Integrated with Artificial Intelligence, quantum computing opens a fresh approach to market optimization, predictive modelling, and overall consumer outreach.

Target Audience

As such, this book is intended for an audience comprising of marketers, neuroscientists, data scientists and analysts, researchers, learners, and business managers. It serves those who are interested in exploring the horizons of how forthcoming technologies influence the modern concept of marketing, and those who want to get a better insight into consumers' behaviour. Moreover, it meets the need of academic and practice-oriented researchers who study quantum AI's ethical effects and potential uses in neuromarketing.

Chapter Overview

The chapters in this book are therefore arranged to give the reader a holistic view and a paradigm shift on neuromarketing in the quantum AI age. Each chapter contributes a unique perspective, ensuring a holistic exploration of the subject:

1. **Introduction to Neuromarketing: Foundations and Evolution:** In the first chapter, the authors aim at providing historical and theoretical context for neuromarketing, acknowledging the revolutionary role of such approach to contemporary marketing practices.
2. **Overview of Neuromarketing: Foundations and Development:** Whereas the first chapter of the work provided a brief overview, this part gives more detailed information on the main concepts and the trends observed in the recent years.
3. **The Brain as a Market: Understanding Neurological Consumer Responses:** This chapter draws consumer behaviour to the neurological systems and unravels the neuropathways marketing stimulus.
4. **Quantum Computing: Principles and Potential in Marketing:** In this chapter, the basics of quantum computing are described, as well as its potential in solving various marketing issues.

5. **Error Correction Methods for Protecting Quantum Information:** This chapter focuses on the technical issue related with quantum computing, for instance the issue of error correction and its relevance to proper neuromarketing solutions.
6. **Quantum Leap in Customer Persona Development: Enhancing Consumer Profiles and Experiences Using Quantum AI:** The paper will present an analysis of how quantum AI is revolutionising the approach to the construction of the customer persona with an eye to delivering highly individualised consumer experience.
7. **Integrating EEG Analysis to Illuminate Consumer Behavior and Optimize Marketing Strategies:** This chapter explains how EEG technology has been incorporated with AI to study consumer emotions and behaviours to aid marketing professionals.
8. **Quantum Algorithms and Predictive Analytics: Revolutionizing Consumer Insight:** In discussing the impact made by quantum algorithms to predictive analytics, this section looks at the ways in which marketers would be able to forecast the needs and trends of consumers.
9. **Optimizing Feature Selection for Predictive Analytics with Quantum Algorithms:** A computational study of feature subsets in quantum computing, including a focus on neuromarketing.
10. **The Role of Quantum Machine Learning in Optimizing Neuromarketing Insights for Retail and E-commerce:** This chapter therefore focuses on how quantum machine learning is revolutionizing retail and e-commerce through the provision of accurate consumer predictors.
11. **Neuromarketing for Decision Making in the Digital Era:** This chapter discusses the application of neuromarketing in firm strategy proposing, with an emphasis on the web environment.
12. **Quantum AI-Enhanced Virtual Reality: Transforming the Consumer Experience:** A discussion of how quantum AI and virtual reality are changing the way firms interact with consumers and retaining marketing messages.
13. **Untact, Immersive, and Hyper-Personalized: The New Norm in Advertising Beyond Hyper-Personalization:** Predicting the future of advertising, this chapter focuses on intact and immersive Ness as ways of achieving powerful campaigns.
14. **The Role of Robotics in Smart Manufacturing: Increasing Efficiency and Reducing Costs:** This segment focuses on how robotics and AI are used in manufacturing as it relates to marketing by improving production line.
15. **Quantum Control of Networked Robotic Systems:** By calling the paper, 'Technical Discussion on Networked Robotic Systems Using Quantum Control Methods,' therefore this writer proposes to undertake a technical discourse on

the idea of utilizing quantum control techniques to improve the performance of the NRMs that make up the NES.

16. **A Review of Quantum Artificial Intelligence-Based Schemes for High-Speed Manipulation of Delta Robots:** The chapter of this thesis focuses on the application of quantum AI for enhancing the velocity and accuracy of robotic mechanics in marketing logistics.
17. **Quick Commerce in the Quantum Age: Future Outlook:** A discussion of how quantum AI is most pertinent in driving fast-paced advancements in quick commerce with an added focus on fulfilment and satisfaction.
18. **Looking Ahead The Next Decade of Neuromarketing and Quantum AI:** The future of Neuromarketing and Quantum AI, highlighting their transformative role in shaping consumer insights and decision-making over the next decade.

CONCLUSION:

The Quantum AI Era of Neuromarketing is an innovative look at how Quantum computing/ AI is reshaping the understanding of consumer behaviour and marketing approaches. Thus, this book is a look into the future of the marketing discipline combining neuroscience, AI, and quantum computing intertwined with discussions of innovation, ethics, and consumer orientation.

The ambition of this book is to encourage the marketers, researchers, and technologists to adopt quantum AI as a concept that holds transformative potential in the field yet comes with the set of challenges and opportunities. This work is relevant for continual advancements of marketing by extending the current possibilities and potential of the field.

Chapter 1
Introduction to Neuro-Marketing: Foundations and Evolution

Oindrilla Ghosh
https://orcid.org/0000-0001-9609-0781
Christ University, India

Binod Kumar
https://orcid.org/0009-0002-9721-1367
Shri Venkateshwara University, India

ABSTRACT

Neuromarketing is an interdisciplinary field that merges neuroscience, psychology, and marketing to explore how consumers make decisions and how brands can influence these choices. At its foundation, neuromarketing studies the brain's response to marketing stimuli, utilizing techniques such as functional magnetic resonance imaging (fMRI), electroencephalography (EEG), and eye-tracking to glean insights into emotional and cognitive processes. Pioneering studies demonstrated how consumers react to various marketing stimuli, revealing that emotional experiences often drive purchasing decisions more than rational thought. As the digital landscape has evolved, so too has neuromarketing. Data analytics and machine learning now complement traditional neuroscience methods, enabling more nuanced understanding of consumer behavior in online environments. By leveraging insights from neuromarketing, businesses can develop targeted strategies that resonate with consumers on a deeper psychological level, ultimately fostering stronger brand loyalty and enhancing overall customer experiences.

DOI: 10.4018/979-8-3693-7673-7.ch001

INTRODUCTION

In an era marked by rapid advancements in technology (Flores et al., 2022) and a deepening understanding of human behavior (Liu et al., 2023), the field of marketing is undergoing a transformation that goes beyond (Zhu et al., 2022) traditional methods. Among the innovative approaches reshaping marketing strategies (Vences et al.,2020) is neuromarketing a discipline that combines neuroscience (Morrin, 2011), psychology, and marketing to delve into the cognitive processes (A. Alsharif et al., 2023) that influence consumer behavior. By understanding how the brain reacts (Siddique et al., 2023) to marketing stimuli, businesses can create more effective strategies (Singh et al., 2023), tailor products to consumer preferences, and enhance overall customer engagement (Yağci et al., 2018). This introduction to neuromarketing will explore its foundations, methodologies (A. Alsharif et al., 2023), applications, and ethical considerations.

What is Neuromarketing?

Neuromarketing is an interdisciplinary field that examines (Alsharif et al., 2020) how the brain responds to marketing stimuli (Rabhi et al., 2023). It utilizes insights from neuroscience to uncover (Alsharif, Md Salleh, Baharun, Alsharif, et al., 2021) the underlying neural mechanisms that drive consumer (Ortigueira-Sánchez and Risco-Martínez, 2021) decision-making processes. Neuromarketing aims (Alsharif, Md Salleh, Baharun, Rami Hashem E, et al., 2021) to provide marketers with a deeper understanding of consumer emotions (Kajla et al., 2023), motivations, and preferences, allowing for the design of campaigns (A. H. Alsharif et al., 2023) that resonate on a subconscious level. Unlike traditional marketing research methods (Gürbüz and Ünal., 2021) such as surveys, focus groups, and observational studies (Fayaz, 2024) that often rely on self-reported data, neuromarketing (Gil et al., 2023) seeks to bypass the limitations of verbal communication (Fayaz and Nawaz, 2023). People may struggle to articulate their thoughts and feelings accurately (A. Alsharif et al., 2023), leading to biases and inaccuracies in data collection (Eroglu et al., 2020). Neuromarketing techniques, on the other hand, analyze physiological responses (Tripathi and Sharma, 2023) and brain activity, providing an objective measure of consumer behavior (Razi et al., 2016).

Neuromarketing is grounded in several key principles from the branch of neuroscience and psychology:

1. The Brain as the Decision-Maker: Neuromarketing operates (Peng et al., 2023) on the premise that the majority of the consumer decisions are made subconsciously (Pelau et al., 2022). According to neuroscientific research, factors such

as emotions, memories (Mañas Viniegra et al., 2021), and sensory experiences play significant roles in shaping preferences and choices (Kolar et al., 2021).

2. Emotional Response: Emotions are powerful drivers of consumer behavior (JiménezMarín et al., 2019). Neuromarketing research highlights that emotional responses often outweigh (Hafez, 2019) rational thinking in decision-making. Understanding how advertising triggers (Gunawan et al., 2023) emotional reactions can guide the creation of compelling campaigns (Bruce et al., 2014).

    Dopamine and Reward Systems: The brain's reward systems (Giakoni et al., 2022), involving neurotransmitters like dopamine, are crucial (Caratu et al., 2018) in the context of consumption. When consumers perceive a potential reward (GarczarekBąk et al., 2021) such as a desirable product they are more likely to engage with that product (Chai et al., 2014). Neuromarketing seeks to identify stimuli (Flores et al., 2022) that activate these reward pathways.

4. Attention and Memory: Attention is a limited resource (Eroglu et al., 2020). Neuromarketing employs techniques to measure areas of the brain (Tripathi and Sharma, 2023) that become activated when exposed to certain marketing stimuli (Bruce et al., 2014), allowing marketers to craft messages that capture attention (Razi et al., 2016). Additionally, understanding how memory works can inform the retention (Caratu et al., 2018) of brand messages.

Applications of Neuromarketing

The insights derived from neuromarketing research (Peng et al., 2023) can be applied across various domains in marketing (Chai et al., 2014), leading to more impactful strategies:

1. Product Development: By understanding consumer preferences (Pelau et al., 2022) and emotional responses, companies can create products (Eroglu et al., 2020) that align closely with what customers desire (MañasViniegra et al., 2021). Neuromarketing can inform design, features, and branding decisions (Flores et al. 2022).
2. Advertising: Neuromarketing principles (GarczarekBąk et al., 2021) can guide the development of advertisements (Kolar et al., 2021) that resonate emotionally with target audiences (Giakoni et al., 2022). Understanding which elements capture attention (JiménezMarín et al., 2019) and elicit positive emotional responses can lead to more effective messaging (Gunawan et al., 2023).

3. Branding: The emotional connections consumers form with brands are essential (Hafez, 2019) for loyalty. Neuromarketing can help identify what aspects (Bruce et al., 2014) of a brand's identity evoke emotional responses (Holsen et al., 2005), informing branding strategies that foster stronger consumer relationships (Caratu et al., 2018).
4. Retail and Environment Design: Neuromarketing can also inform the design (Bielik et al., 2014) of retail spaces, optimizing product placement, layout (Olsen et al., 2012), and ambiance to enhance the shopping experience (Kohler et al., 2007). Understanding how consumers react to different environments (Eroglu et al., 2020) can lead to more conducive shopping atmospheres.

Foundations of Neuromarketing

In today's fast-paced market, understanding consumer behavior (Garczarek-Bąk et al., 2021) is more pivotal than ever. Neuromarketing emerges as a fascinating discipline at the intersection (Valdez & Mehrabian, 1994) of neuroscience and marketing, providing insights into the cognitive processes (Zamuner, 2013) that drive consumer decisions. This innovative approach leverages principles (Chai et al., 2014) from neuroscience to decode the complexities of human behavior (Giakoni et al., 2022) in the context of purchasing decisions. The foundations of neuromarketing are built (Gunawan et al., 2023) on a deep understanding of how the brain works (Jiménez-Marín et al., 2019), the emotional core of human nature, and the qualitative and quantitative techniques (Mañas-Viniegra et al., 2021) that can capture these insights.

The Neuroscientific Underpinnings

At its core, neuromarketing relies on the study (Peng et al., 2023) of the central nervous system and how it influences thoughts (Khushaba et al., 2013), feelings, and behaviors. The brain regulates everything from pleasure (Telpaz et al., 2015) to decision-making, controlled through various neural circuits and systems (Wei et al., 2018). Neuroimaging technologies, such as functional magnetic resonance imaging (fMRI) (Ambler, 2015) and electroencephalography (EEG), play vital roles (Mateusz, 2018) by visualizing brain activity in response to marketing stimuli (Vecchiato et al., 2014).

1. Brain Areas and Consumer Behavior:-

Different regions of the brain are responsible for various aspects (Flores et al., 2022) of decision-making and emotional responses. For instance:

The Prefrontal Cortex: Involved in complex cognitive behavior, decision-making (Hafez, 2019), and moderating social behavior, the prefrontal cortex plays a crucial role (Kolar et al., 2021) in weighing pros and cons during purchasing. *The Limbic System*: Known as the emotional center of the brain (Pelau et al., 2022), particularly the amygdala, this area influences feelings associated (Razi et al., 2016) with memory and emotion. Brands often attempt to evoke (Tripathi & Sharma, 2023) positive emotions and memories to foster brand loyalty (Giakoni et al., 2022).
The Nucleus Accumbens: This area is associated with the brain's reward system (Trope & Liberman, 2010). It becomes activated when individuals anticipate rewards Zhou et al., 2021), which can be leveraged in advertising to enhance desirability (Cheredniakova et al., 2021).

2. Cognitive Load and Decision Fatigue: Neuromarketing also examines how cognitive load (Spence, 2019) can affect decision-making processes. A high cognitive load can lead to decision fatigue (White et al., 2021), decreasing the quality of choices made. Insights from cognitive neuroscience (Flores et al., 2022) suggest that minimizing extraneous information and presenting options in a clear (Liu et al., 2023), concise manner can lead to more favorable consumer responses (Zhu et al., 2022). Thus, successful neuromarketing strategies often aim to simplify choices (Vences et al., 2020), making it easier for consumers to say "yes."

Emotions significantly influence how individuals perceive brands (Morrin, 2011) and make purchasing decisions. Neuromarketing research suggests that emotional responses (A. Alsharif et al., 2023) can be more predictive of buying behavior than rational thought processes (Siddique et al., 2023). This discovery places emotion at the heart of effective marketing strategies (Singh et al., 2023).

1. Emotional Branding: This concept relates to the practice of creating a brand (Kajla et al., 2023) that resonates emotionally with consumers (A. Alsharif et al., 2023), turning them into loyal customers. Companies like Apple and Nike exemplify (Yağci et al., 2018) emotional branding, tapping into feelings of innovation (Alsharif et al., 2020), aspiration, and community.
2. The Role of Storytelling: Storytelling in marketing is a powerful technique (Rabhi et al., 2023) that engages the brain's narrative circuits, fostering emotional connections (Alsharif, Md Salleh, Baharun, Alsharif, et al., 2021). Cognitive neuroscience research indicates that narratives (Ortigueira-Sánchez and Risco-Martínez, 2021) can create a sense of empathy, allowing consumers to imagine themselves (Alsharif, Md Salleh, Baharun, Rami Hashem E, et al., 2021) in the story, thereby motivating action. Effective marketing campaigns (Kajla et

al., 2023) often incorporate storytelling elements to engage and resonate (A. H. Alsharif et al., 2023) with the target audience emotionally.

Emergence of Quantum Artificial Intelligence (QAI):

Quantum Artificial Intelligence (QAI) is an emergent interdisciplinary field (Abed et al., 2020) that amalgamates quantum computing and artificial intelligence (AI), creating innovative algorithms (Algharabat et al., 2020) and models that leverage the principles of quantum mechanics to enhance traditional AI methodologies (Al-suradi et al., 2020). While conventional AI relies on classical computers to process information, QAI seeks (AlSuwaidan, 2019) to harness the unparalleled processing capabilities of quantum computers (Giakoni et al., 2022), which operate on the principles of superposition and entanglement, allowing for the simultaneous evaluation (Mañas-Viniegra et al., 2021) of multiple possible outcomes. This inherent capability can potentially revolutionize (Peng et al., 2023) various sectors, including health-care, finance, cryptography (Khushaba et al., 2013), and, significantly, marketing.

The rise of QAI stems from the limitations of classical computing (Amin et al., 2020) when dealing with vast datasets and complex problem spaces (Bamakan et al., 2022). As businesses increasingly gather extensive amounts of consumer data (Ariely et al., 2010), there is a critical need for more sophisticated analytical tools that can decipher patterns (Atzori et al., 2010), predict consumer behavior, and personalize marketing strategies at an unprecedented scale (Benedek et al., 2010). QAI promises to fulfill this need, offering faster computations (Butler, 2008) and more efficient algorithms that can lead to more accurate predictions (Constantinescu et al., 2019) and insights. In essence, QAI embodies two pivotal technological advancements (Daugherty, 2017): quantum computing, which provides the hardware capable of performing complex calculations (Dayanandam et al., 2019) at extraordinary speeds; and AI, which includes machine learning, natural language processing (Marques et al., 2020), and other techniques that allow computers to learn from data and make intelligent decisions (Eser et al., 2011). Together, these technologies enable businesses to move beyond traditional data analysis, fostering supercharged (Filipović et al., 2020) decision-making processes and a deeper understanding of consumer psychology (Hafez, 2019).

Techniques and Tools in Neuromarketing

The tools utilized in neuromarketing allow companies (Fayaz, 2024) to gain deeper insights into consumer behaviors (Gürbüz and Ünal, 2021). Various methodologies combine traditional marketing techniques (Fayaz and Nawaz, 2023) with neuroscientific methods to evaluate the efficacy of advertisements (Gil et al., 2023) and brand strategies.

1. Neuroimaging: As mentioned, techniques such as fMRI and EEG measure brain activity (A. Alsharif et al., 2023) in response to marketing stimuli. For instance, fMRI can show (Eroglu et al., 2020) which brain areas are activated in reaction to a commercial (Bruce et al., 2014). Marketers can thus assess whether the ad evokes (Tripathi and Sharma, 2023) the intended emotions (e.g., happiness, nostalgia) and tweak their approach accordingly (Caratu et al., 2018).
2. Eye-Tracking: Eye-tracking technology provides insights (Razi et al., 2016) into which parts of an advertisement capture attention (Chai et al., 2014) and how long viewers engage with various elements (Peng et al., 2023). This technique can determine the effectiveness (Eroglu et al., 2020) of visual stimuli in commercials and packaging designs (Pelau et al., 2022).
3. Facial Coding: Facial coding analyzes micro-expressions (Flores et al., 2022) to infer emotional reactions. By interpreting these expressions, neuromarketers can gather (MañasViniegra et al., 2021) immediate feedback on how consumers respond to marketing stimuli (GarczarekBąk et al., 2021).
4. Implicit Association Tests (IAT): These tests assess the strength of a person's automatic association (Kolar et al., 2021) between mental representations of objects (brands, products) and evaluations (positive or negative) (Giakoni et al., 2022). Understanding these implicit responses can inform branding strategies (Jiménez Marín et al., 2019).

The foundations of neuromarketing are deeply rooted in the understanding of human cognition (Gunawan et al., 2023), emotion, and behavior. By leveraging neuroscientific techniques (Hafez, 2019), marketers can uncover insights that resonate at an emotional level (Bruce et al., 2014), ultimately guiding consumers toward informed and satisfying purchasing decisions (Holsen et al., 2005). The ethical considerations inherent in this practice are crucial (Caratu et al., 2018) as companies navigate the fine line between impact and manipulation (Bielik et al., 2014). As this field evolves, it holds great promise (Olsen et al., 2012) not only for businesses seeking to enhance (Kohler et al., 2007) their marketing strategies but also for consumers (Eroglu et al., 2020) gaining a deeper understanding of their own decision-making processes (Garczarek-Bąk et al., 2021). Ultimately, neuromarketing represents a revolutionary step towards recognizing (Valdez & Mehrabian, 1994) the intricate and often subconscious factors influencing consumer behavior (Zamuner,2013).

The Evolution of Neuromarketing

Neuromarketing is an interdisciplinary field that integrates neuroscience (Chai et al., 2014), psychology, and marketing to understand consumer behavior (Giakoni et al., 2022) and decision-making processes. It utilizes advanced technologies such as functional magnetic resonance imaging (fMRI), electroencephalogram (EEG), and biometrics (Gunawan et al., 2023) to analyze consumer responses to marketing stimuli. The evolution of neuromarketing has transformed (Jiménez-Marín et al., 2019) how brands approach consumer engagement, product development, and marketing strategies (Mañas-Viniegra et al., 2021).

Early Foundations

The roots of neuromarketing can be traced back to the early academic research (Peng et al., 2023) in psychology and behavioral economics. Pioneers such as Sigmund Freud emphasized (Khushaba et al., 2013) the role of unconscious desires in human behavior, suggesting that emotions (Telpaz et al., 2015) often dictate our decisions more than rational thought (Wei et al., 2018). In the 1960s and 1970s, researchers began applying psychological principles (Ambler, 2015) to marketing. The discipline of consumer psychology emerged (Mateusz, 2018), focusing on themes related to perception, motivation (Vecchiato et al., 2014), and attitude formation. Researchers like Daniel Kahneman and Amos Tversky explored (Flores et al., 2022) cognitive biases and heuristics, shedding light on how people (Hafez, 2019) make decisions under uncertainty. Their work laid the groundwork (Kolar et al., 2021) for understanding the cognitive processes involved in consumer behavior (Pelau et al., 2022).

The Birth of Neuromarketing

The term "neuromarketing" was officially coined in the early 2000s (Tallis & Taylor, 2011), although its conceptual basis predates that time (Wilson & Eggemeier, 1991). The modern neuromarketing movement gained traction (G. Borghini et al., 2013) when companies began using brain imaging techniques (Dehais et al., 2018) to better understand consumer behavior. The first significant studies (Sciaraffa et al., 2017) involved using fMRI to measure brain activity (Vecchiato et al., 2016) in response to advertising stimuli, providing insights into emotional engagement (Di Flumeri et al., 2018) and the subconscious influences that drive purchasing decisions (Di Flumeri, Borghini, et al., 2019). One of the landmark studies in neuromarketing was conducted (Maglione et al., 2014) by Read Montague at Baylor College of Medicine. In this research, participants (P. Aricò et al., 2016) were asked to evaluate different brands of cola while their brain activity (Pietro Aricò et al., 2016) was monitored. The results showed that when participants were unaware (Gianluca Borghini et al., 2017) of the brand being tested, neural activity associated with pleasure (di Flumeri et al., 2015) was higher for the Coca-Cola brand compared to Pepsi (Feyer & Williamson, 2011). However, when the brand was revealed, the results changed significantly (P. Arico et al., 2018), highlighting the power of brand recognition on consumer preference (P. Aricò et al., 2014).

Technological Advancements

As technology progressed, the tools and methodologies (Boucsein & Backs, 2000) used in neuromarketing became more sophisticated and accessible (P. Aricò et al., 2016). EEG technology, which measures electrical activity in the brain (Lal & Craig, 2001), gained popularity due to its lower cost and ease of use (Gianluca Borghini et al., 2019) compared to fMRI. EEG can track immediate cognitive (Di Flumeri, Aricò, et al., 2019) and emotional reactions, allowing marketers to gather real-time data (Gluth et al., 2012) on consumer engagement with their products and advertisements (Gianluca Borghini et al., 2017). Biometric methods, such as eye tracking and facial coding (Cherubino et al., 2015), also emerged as valuable tools in the neuromarketing toolkit (Camerer et al., 2004). Eye tracking identifies where people look and how long they gaze (Glimcher & Rustichini, 2004) at specific elements within advertisements or products (Lee et al., 2007), providing insights into visual attention. Facial coding analyzes (Jordao et al., 2017) micro-expressions to assess emotional reactions in response to marketing stimuli (Riccio et al., 2015).

The Rise of Big Data and AI

In the late 2010s, the growing prevalence of big data (Schettini et al., 2014) and artificial intelligence (AI) began to influence the landscape (Vecchiato et al., 2013) of neuromarketing. With access to vast amounts of consumer data (Boksem & Smidts, 2015), marketers started integrating neuromarketing insights with traditional analytics (Ariely & Berns, 2010) to create more comprehensive consumer profiles (Kenning & Plassmann, 2008). This fusion allowed for more targeted marketing strategies (Plassmann et al., 2007) and personalized consumer experiences. Machine learning algorithms (Lee et al., 2007) began analyzing EEG and biometric data to predict consumer behavior (Morin, 2011) patterns more accurately. This predictive capability enhanced the effectiveness of marketing campaigns (Smidts, 2002), as brands could anticipate consumer needs and preferences with unprecedented precision (Fisher et al., 2010).

With the rise of neuromarketing, ethical concerns also emerged (Fortunato et al., 2014). The power of neuroscience to influence consumer behavior raised questions (Olson & Ray, 1983) about manipulation and informed consent. Critics argued that neuromarketing could exploit (Rothschild et al., 1986) vulnerable consumers and erode personal autonomy (Rothschild et al., 1988). As a result, discussions around ethical guidelines and standards became integral (Gourville, 2006) to the field. Organizations such as the Neuromarketing Science & Business Association (NMSBA) were established (Pradeep & Patel, 2010) to promote ethical practices within the industry (Schlossberg, 1990). These organizations aim to ensure that neuromarketing research prioritizes (Boksem & Smidts, 2015) consumer welfare and transparency while discouraging deceptive practices (Plassmann et al., 2012).

The evolution of neuromarketing reflects the dynamic interplay (Hubert & Kenning, 2008) between science, technology, and consumer behavior (Constantinescu et al., 2019). From its origins in psychological research to its current advancements (Solomon, 2018) in neuroscience and AI, the field has matured into a powerful tool (Arthmann & Li, 2017) for understanding and influencing consumer decisions (Hensel et al., 2017). As it continues to evolve, the emphasis on ethical considerations, personalization (Nemorin & Gandy, 2017), and cross-disciplinary insights will likely shape the future of marketing (Glaenzer, 2016), enabling brands to create more meaningful connections with consumers (Kumar, 2015) while respecting their autonomy. Neuromarketing represents one of the forefronts of marketing innovation (Roth, 2013), merging human insight with scientific rigor to navigate (Krajnovic et al., 2012) the complexities of consumer behavior in an ever-changing marketplace (Morin, 2011).

Key Methodologies in Neuromarketing Research

Neuromarketing is an interdisciplinary field that merges neuroscience (Murphy et al., 2008), psychology, and marketing to understand consumer behavior more deeply (Lee et al., 2007). By examining how consumers' brains respond to marketing stimuli (Tallis & Taylor, 2011), businesses can tailor their strategies for maximum effectiveness (Wilson & Eggemeier, 1991).

1. *Functional Magnetic Resonance Imaging (fMRI):* Functional Magnetic Resonance Imaging (fMRI) is one of the most prominent methodologies (G. Borghini et al., 2013) in neuromarketing research. This technique measures brain activity by detecting changes (Gianluca Borghini et al., 2016) in blood flow, which correlate with neural activity. By utilizing fMRI, researchers can

identify (Gianluca Borghini et al., 2015) which parts of the brain activate when subjects are exposed (Dehais et al., 2018) to specific marketing stimuli, such as advertisements or product packaging (Sciaraffa et al., 2017). For instance, when a subject views a particular advertisement, fMRI can reveal (Vecchiato et al., 2016) activation in areas associated with emotional processing (like the amygdala) (Di Flumeri et al., 2018) or decision-making (such as the prefrontal cortex). This information helps marketers understand emotional engagement levels (Di Flumeri, Borghini, et al., 2019), allowing them to create content that resonates (Maglione et al., 2014) on a deeper emotional level. However, the complexity of interpreting (P. Aricò et al., 2016) fMRI data and the high costs associated with this technology can pose challenges (Pietro Arico et al., 2015) in its widespread application.

2. *Electroencephalography (EEG):* Electroencephalography (EEG) is another critical tool in neuromarketing. Unlike fMRI (Pietro Aricò et al., 2016), which measures blood flow, EEG tracks electrical activity in the brain (Gianluca Borghini et al., 2017) through electrodes placed on the scalp. This method offers high temporal resolution (di Flumeri et al., 2015), making it ideal for studying the brain's immediate response to marketing stimuli (Feyer & Williamson, 2011). EEG can identify different brainwave patterns, such as alpha, beta (Wilson & Eggemeier, 1991), and theta waves, which are associated with various cognitive states (P. Arico et al., 2018). For instance, increased theta wave activity may indicate a higher level of engagement (P. Aricò et al., 2014) or emotional response. By analyzing these patterns, marketers can refine their approaches (Boucsein & Backs, 2000) to maximize consumer attention and emotional impact. However, the spatial resolution of EEG (P. Aricò et al., 2016) is limited compared to fMRI, meaning it may be less effective (P. Aricò et al., 2014) at pinpointing specific brain areas involved in processed information (Gianluca Borghini et al., 2014).
3. *Eye Tracking:* Eye tracking is an innovative methodology that provides insights (Lal & Craig, 2001) into consumer attention and visual engagement. This technique involves using specialized cameras (Gianluca Borghini et al., 2019) or wearable devices to monitor eye movements as subjects view advertisements (Di Flumeri, Aricò, et al., 2019), product displays, or user interfaces. By analyzing metrics such as fixation duration (Gluth et al., 2012)., gaze paths, and saccades (quick eye movements), researchers can determine which elements (Gianluca Borghini et al., 2017) capture attention and how visual information is processed. Eye tracking allows marketers to optimize design elements (Cherubino et al., 2015), such as layout and imagery, ensuring that key features draw consumer (Camerer et al., 2004) attention effectively. For example, a study might reveal that product placement (Glimcher & Rustichini, 2004) in an ad is less effective

than anticipated, leading to adjustments in future campaigns (Lee et al., 2007). However, while eye tracking is valuable for understanding visual attention (P. Aricò et al., 2014), it does not directly measure underlying emotional and cognitive responses (Jordao et al., 2017).

4. *Biometric Measures:* Biometric measures, including skin conductance response (SCR), heart rate variability (HRV) (Riccio et al., 2015), and facial expression analysis, provide additional layers (Schettini et al., 2014) of insight into consumer emotional responses. SCR measures the electrical conductance of the skin (Vecchiato et al., 2013), which fluctuates with sweat gland activity linked to emotional arousal (Boksem & Smidts, 2015). HRV refers to variations in time between heartbeats and can indicate stress (Ariely & Berns, 2010) or emotional excitement. Facial expression analysis employs computer algorithms to interpret expressions (Kenning & Plassmann, 2008), determining whether a subject appears happy, surprised, or puzzled (Plassmann et al., 2007) in response to a marketing stimulus. Combining these biometric measures with traditional survey methods (Lee et al., 2007) can provide a comprehensive view of consumer emotions, allowing marketers (Morin, 2011) to gauge responses that might not be captured through self-reporting alone (Smidts, 2002).
5. *Implicit Association Tests (IAT):* Implicit Association Tests (IAT) are psychological assessments used to explore the unconscious attitudes (Fisher et al., 2010) and beliefs consumers possess about brands or products. The IAT measures the strength of associations (Fortunato et al., 2014) between different concepts (e.g., a brand and positive or negative attributes) by tracking response times (Alwitt, 1985). Participants may be quicker to associate words or images (Olson & Ray, 1983) that reflect their implicit preferences than those that challenge their beliefs (Rothschild et al., 1986). By utilizing IAT, marketers can uncover hidden biases and preferences (Rothschild et al., 1988) that influence consumer behavior, enabling them to adjust brand positioning (Gourville, 2006) and messaging strategies to align with consumers' subconscious associations (Pradeep & Patel, 2010). While IAT is a powerful tool, its reliance on reaction times (Schlossberg, 1990) can complicate interpretations, especially if external factors affect a participant's responses (Boksem & Smidts, 2015).
6. *Neuroimaging Techniques:* Various neuroimaging techniques, aside from fMRI, are often utilized in neuromarketing research (Plassmann et al., 2012). These include diffusion tensor imaging (DTI), which tracks the movement of water molecules (Hubert & Kenning, 2008) in the brain to study white matter integrity. Structural imaging can provide insights (Constantinescu et al., 2019) into brain structures linked to certain behaviors or preferences (Solomon, 2018) Positron Emission Tomography (PET) is another neuroimaging method that assesses metabolic processes (Arthmann & Li, 2017) in the brain by injecting a small

amount of radioactive material (Hensel et al., 2017) PET scans can visualize how different stimuli provoke reactions, particularly in terms of dopamine release (Nemorin & Gandy, 2017) linked to reward processing. These neuroimaging methodologies add depth to neuromarketing studies (Glaenzer, 2016), revealing nuanced insights into the brain's functioning without relying solely on behavioral data (Roth, 2013).

7. *Behavioral Analysis and A/B Testing*: Although primarily associated with traditional marketing research (Krajnovic et al., 2012), behavioral analysis and A/B testing play crucial roles in neuromarketing (Morin, 2011). Marketers can analyze consumer interactions on digital platforms (Murphy et al., 2008) to gather data on preferences, decision-making processes, and purchase behaviors (Lee et al., 2007). By testing different variations of a marketing campaign or website layout (A/B testing), businesses (Razi et al., 2016) can see which approach yields better engagement and conversion rates (Tripathi & Sharma, 2023). While less 'neuro' in their approach, these methods complement neuroscientific techniques (Giakoni et al., 2022) by linking brain insights to real-world behaviors (Trope & Liberman, 2010). They allow marketers to consolidate findings from neuroscience (Zhou et al., 2021) with actual consumer choices, ultimately refining their strategies for greater impact (Cheredniakova et al., 2021).

Neuromarketing research employs various methodologies that bridge the gap (Spence, 2019) between neuroscience, psychology, and marketing (White et al., 2021). By exploring brain activity through techniques like fMRI and EEG (Flores et al., 2022), assessing visual engagement with eye tracking, and evaluating emotional responses through biometric measures (Liu et al., 2023) and implicit association tests, marketers gain unprecedented insights into consumer behavior (Zhu et al., 2022). These methodologies not only enhance the understanding of the subconscious factors (Vences et al., 2020) influencing purchasing decisions but also empower businesses to tailor their strategies (A. Alsharif et al., 2023) to better connect with consumers. As the field of neuromarketing continues to evolve (Siddique et al., 2023), the integration of these diverse methodologies will foster deeper insights (Singh et al., 2023) into the complexities of human behavior in the market landscape (Kajla et al., 2023).

FUTURE PROSPECTS OF NEUROMARKETING

In the rapidly evolving landscape of marketing, understanding consumer behavior is integral (A. Alsharif et al., 2023) to creating effective strategies. Neuromarketing, which applies neuroscience principles to marketing (Alsharif et al., 2020), offers profound insights into the unconscious motivations that drive consumer decisions (Yağci et al., 2018). By blending insights from psychology and neuroscience with traditional marketing practices (Alsharif, Md Salleh, Baharun, Alsharif, et al., 2021), neuromarketing opens new avenues for engaging consumers. As we look to the future, several key trends (Rabhi et al., 2023) and technological advancements are set to shape the prospects of neuromarketing (Alsharif, Md Salleh, Baharun, Rami Hashem E, et al., 2021).

Advancements in Technology

One of the most significant factors influencing neuromarketing is the rapid advancement (Ortigueira-Sánchez and Risco-Martínez (2021) of technology. Techniques such as functional magnetic resonance imaging (fMRI), electroencephalography (EEG), and eye-tracking (A. H. Alsharif et al., 2023) are becoming more accessible and affordable. These technologies allow researchers to gauge consumers' emotional (Gürbüz and Ünal, 2021) and cognitive responses to advertisements and products in real-time (Fayaz, 2024). Future developments in wearables, such as augmented reality (AR) glasses and smartwatches (Gil et al., 2023), can provide marketers with continuous data on consumers' physiological states (Fayaz and Nawaz, 2023). By monitoring heart rates, skin conductance, and even facial expressions (Eroglu et al., 2020), brands may gather more granular insights into customer engagement (Chai et al., 2014). This real-time data can enhance the personalization of marketing campaigns (Caratu et al., 2018), resulting in a more profound impact on consumer behavior (GarczarekBąk et al., 2021).

Personalization through Neuromarketing

As businesses increasingly shift towards personalized marketing, neuromarketing will play a pivotal role (Hafez, 2019). Traditional marketing strategies often adopt a one-size-fits-all approach (Gunawan et al., 2023). However, neuromarketing studies can segregate consumers into various psychological profiles (JiménezMarín et al., 2019) based on their neural responses to different stimuli. Future marketing campaigns (Kolar et al., 2021) will leverage these insights to create tailored experiences that resonate more deeply (MañasViniegra et al., 2021) with individual customers. For instance, neuromarketing can help brands understand (Peng et al., 2023) which colors, sounds, and visuals elicit positive emotional responses from specific demographics (Tripathi and Sharma, 2023). By doing so, marketers can craft highly tailored advertisements that evoke desired reactions (Pelau et al., 2022). Advanced algorithms might also predict consumer behavior (Razi et al., 2016) based on historical neural data, allowing brands to proactively engage customers (Tallis & Taylor, 2011) with the right message at the right time.

ETHICAL CONSIDERATIONS IN NEUROMARKETING

Neuromarketing, the intersection of neuroscience and marketing (Wilson & Eggemeier, 1991), utilizes insights from brain science to understand consumer behavior better (G. Borghini et al., 2013). By analyzing how consumers respond to marketing stimuli such as advertisements (Gianluca Borghini et al., 2016), packaging, and branding marketers can tailor their strategies (Gianluca Borghini et al., 2015) to boost engagement and sales. However, as enticing as the potential benefits are, neuromarketing raises several ethical considerations (Dehais et al., 2018) that warrant careful examination. These considerations include issues related to consumer manipulation (Sciaraffa et al., 2017), privacy, informed consent, psychological impacts, and the broader societal implications of applying neuroscience (Vecchiato et al., 2016) in marketing. While the benefits of neuromarketing are promising, ethical considerations cannot be overlooked (Di Flumeri et al., 2018). As marketers gain access to profound insights into our subconscious (Di Flumeri, Borghini, et al., 2019) desires and fears, there is a growing concern about manipulation and privacy (Maglione et al., 2014). The potential for brands to exploit consumer vulnerabilities raises questions (P. Aricò et al., 2016) about the ethical boundaries of this marketing approach.

As the industry evolves, establishing ethical guidelines and standards for neuromarketing practices (Pietro Arico et al., 2015) will become paramount. Regulations to protect consumers from manipulative marketing tactics (Pietro Aricò et al., 2016) will likely gain traction. Collaborative efforts by industry leaders, academics, and policymakers (Gianluca Borghini et al., 2017) will be crucial to ensure that neuromarketing is employed responsibly and transparently (di Flumeri et al., 2015), with consumers' well-being in mind.

1. *Consumer Manipulation:* One of the foremost ethical concerns with neuromarketing is the potential (Feyer & Williamson, 2011) for consumer manipulation. Neuromarketing techniques can decipher the underlying neural mechanisms (P. Arico et al., 2018) of decision-making processes, enabling marketers to craft messages (P. Aricò et al., 2014) that trigger emotional and subconscious responses. This can lead to the creation of advertisements (Boucsein & Backs, 2000) that exploit consumers' vulnerabilities, effectively nudging them towards purchases (P. Aricò et al., 2016) they might not consciously want or need. For instance, neuromarketing can identify specific emotions (P. Aricò et al., 2014)

that drive consumer behavior, such as fear, happiness, or nostalgia (Gianluca Borghini et al., 2014). Marketers may use this information to generate ads that elicit these emotions intensely (Lal & Craig, 2001), thus manipulating consumers into making impulsive decisions (Cherubino et al., 2015). The ethical dilemma arises when one considers whether such manipulation (Siddique et al., 2023) constitutes a form of deception.

Privacy and Data Collection: Another critical ethical issue in neuromarketing relates to data privacy (Flores et al., 2022). Neuromarketing research often relies on brain imaging technologies (such as fMRI and EEG) to collect data (Liu et al., 2023) on consumers' brain activity in response to marketing stimuli (Zhu et al., 2022) . This process inherently raises concerns about consumer privacy (Vences et al.,2020). The data collected can be deeply revealing and might include (Morrin, 2011) not only reactions to advertising but also personal insights into thoughts (A. Alsharif et al., 2023), preferences, and emotions.

3. *Informed Consent:* Informed consent is a foundational ethical principle in research (Singh et al., 2023), and it is equally applicable in neuromarketing studies. Individuals participating in neuromarketing research (Siddique et al., 2023) or focus groups must be fully aware of what participation entails, including details (Alsharif et al., 2020) about the data collection methods, potential risks, and how their data will be utilized (Rabhi et al., 2023). However, neuromarketing studies often operate in a gray area regarding informed consent (Alsharif, Md Salleh, Baharun, Alsharif, et al., 2021). Consumers may not fully grasp the intricacies of what is being studied or how neuromarketing methods (Ortigueira-Sánchez and Risco-Martínez, 2021) differ from traditional marketing research techniques. Furthermore, the complexity of neural data analysis (Kolar et al., 2021) may discourage individuals from asking questions or seeking clarifications (Pelau et al., 2022) about their participation in the study. Businesses must develop clear, accessible information that allows (Tripathi & Sharma, 2023) consumers to give truly informed consent for participation, ensuring they understand the implications (Giakoni et al., 2022) of their involvement.
4. *Psychological Effects:* The psychological impact of neuromarketing on consumers is another critical area (Zhou et al., 2021) of ethical concern. By leveraging insights into basic human emotions and cognitive processes, neuromarketing (Spence, 2019) has the potential to affect consumer well-being. For example, robust advertising (White et al., 2021) that leverages fear or insecurity can lead to feelings of inadequa-

cy, anxiety, and even depression among consumers (Zhu et al., 2022). Moreover, if neuromarketing consistently promotes ideals that may not align (Vences et al., 2020) with healthy psychological standards such as unattainable beauty standards (A. Alsharif et al., 2023) or materialistic values there can be adverse societal impacts. Ethical marketing should promote positive, inclusive norms (Siddique et al., 2023) rather than exacerbate mental health issues or societal divides (Singh et al., 2023). Companies must be cognizant of how their marketing strategies (Kajla et al., 2023) could influence societal values and individual psychological well-being (Yağci et al., 2018).

5. *Societal Implications:* On a larger scale, the evolution of neuromarketing poses ethical questions (Alsharif et al., 2020)(Rabhi et al., 2023) regarding its societal implications. The incorporation of neuroscientific methods into marketing strategies (Alsharif, Md Salleh, Baharun, Alsharif, et al., 2021). could contribute to an over-commercialized society, where consumerism drives societal values (Ortigueira-Sánchez and Risco-Martínez, 2021). If companies prioritize profit maximization through refined psychological manipulation, the ever-increasing focus (Alsharif, Md Salleh, Baharun, Rami Hashem E, et al., 2021) on consumption may detract from more meaningful human experiences. Moreover, the effectiveness (Kajla et al., 2023) of neuromarketing research raises a broader question about the balance of power (Abed et al., 2020) in the consumer-marketer relationship. If brands gain an overwhelming understanding of consumer psychology (Algharabat et al., 2020), there's a risk that consumers may feel powerless against clever marketing (Alsuradi et al., 2020) tactics designed to exploit their cognitive biases. Establishing an ethical framework for neuromarketing practices (AlSuwaidan, 2019) can help balance the scales, empowering consumers and fostering a healthier marketplace (Giakoni et al., 2022).

Regulation and Accountability: Given the potential ethical pitfalls associated with neuromarketing, there is a pressing need (Mañas-Viniegra et al., 2021) for regulatory frameworks to ensure accountability among businesses employing (Peng et al., 2023) these techniques. Industry standards, ethical guidelines, and possibly legislative (Amin et al., 2020) measures can provide necessary oversight to prevent manipulative practices. Creating a committee that includes neuroscientists (Bamakan et al., 2022), ethicists, marketers, and consumer advocates to establish guidelines (Constantinescu et al., 2019) for the responsible use of neuromarketing techniques could help. This committee could assess the ethical implications (Dayanandam et al., 2019) of specific neuromarketing practices and set benchmarks for transparency (Marques et al., 2020), informed consent, and respect for consumer autonomy (Filipović et al., 2020).

Integration with Artificial Intelligence: The convergence of neuromarketing and artificial intelligence (AI) promises to amplify (Fayaz, 2024) its effectiveness. AI-driven algorithms can analyze large volumes of data (Gürbüz and Ünal, 2021) from neuromarketing studies, uncovering patterns that may not be visible (Fayaz and Nawaz, 2023) to human researchers. This synergy will enable marketers to make data-driven decisions at an unprecedented scale and speed (Gil et al., 2023). For example, AI can streamline the design process for advertisements by predicting (A. Alsharif et al., 2023) which elements are likely to elicit positive responses. Furthermore, machine learning models can continuously learn (Eroglu et al., 2020) from consumer feedback, enhancing the effectiveness of campaigns over time (Tripathi and Sharma, 2023). The integration of AI will allow for dynamic marketing strategies (Peng et al., 2023) that adapt to consumer preferences in real-time, maximizing engagement and conversion rates (Eroglu et al., 2020).

Broader Applications Beyond Marketing: While the primary focus of neuromarketing has been on advertising (Pelau et al., 2022) and consumer products, its future applications could extend into various sectors (MañasViniegra et al., 2021). The insights gained from neuromarketing can be beneficial in areas such as (GarczarekBąk et al., 2021) public health, education, and user experience design. For example, public health campaigns could utilize neuromarketing techniques (Kolar et al., 2021) to understand how to effectively communicate critical health messages. By identifying emotional triggers, public health officials (Giakoni et al., 2022) could promote healthier behaviors more effectively. Similarly, education sectors (Jiménez Marín et al., 2019) could employ neuromarketing insights to refine curricula, optimizing learning experiences (Gunawan et al., 2023) that resonate with students on an emotional and cognitive level (Eroglu et al., 2020).

The Role of Neuromarketing in Brand Loyalty: As competition intensifies across industries, fostering brand loyalty (Garczarek-Bąk et al., 2021) will become increasingly important. Neuromarketing can shed light on the emotional factors (Gunawan et al., 2023) that contribute to loyalty, helping brands create deeper connections with their customers. Understanding what makes consumers (Jiménez-Marín et al., 2019) feel attached to a brand can guide loyalty programs and customer engagement initiatives. Through brain imaging studies, marketers (Mañas-Viniegra et al., 2021) may uncover the emotional triggers associated with brand loyalty whether nostalgia, trust, or a sense of belonging (Peng et al., 2023). These insights can inform how companies craft their narratives and branding strategies (Flores et al., 2022), ultimately cultivating a loyal customer base that feels personally (Hafez, 2019) connected to the brand's mission and vision (Kolar et al., 2021).

Impact on Consumer Experience: In the future, the impact of neuromarketing on consumer experience will be profound (Pelau et al., 2022). As companies integrate neuromarketing insights into product design and service delivery (Tallis & Taylor, 2011), the overall consumer experience will transform. By understanding how products and services evoke emotional responses (Di Flumeri, Borghini, et al., 2019), brands can create offerings that resonate more strongly with their target audiences (Spence, 2019). Imagine walking into a retail environment where every element from lighting to scent has been engineered (White et al., 2021) based on neuromarketing principles to enhance the shopping experience (Flores et al., 2022). This level of customization will extend beyond retail to online environments (Liu et al., 2023) as well, where websites and applications are optimized to provide (Zhu et al., 2022) experiences tailored to individual preferences and emotional states (Vences et al., 2020).

Thus, neuromarketing stands at the forefront of marketing innovation (A. Alsharif et al., 2023), offering exciting possibilities for understanding consumer behavior beyond traditional methodologies (Siddique et al., 2023). However, with great power comes great responsibility. The ethical considerations surrounding neuromarketing (Singh et al., 2023) are multifaceted and complex. Issues concerning consumer manipulation, privacy, informed consent (Kajla et al., 2023), psychological impacts, and societal implications must be rigorously addressed by marketers and researchers alike (A. Alsharif et al., 2023). A proactive approach that emphasizes ethical standards and consumer welfare can enable neuromarketing to contribute positively (Alsharif et al., 2020) to both the field of marketing and the broader society. By prioritizing ethical considerations, practitioners of neuromarketing (Alsharif, Md Salleh, Baharun, Alsharif, et al., 2021) can build trust, cultivate long-term relationships with consumers, and ultimately foster a healthier (Rabhi et al., 2023) and more respectful marketplace.

CONCLUSION

The future prospects of neuromarketing are promising bolstered (Alsharif, Md Salleh, Baharun, Rami Hashem E, et al., 2021) by technological advancements, an increasing focus on personalization, and the integration of AI (Ortigueira-Sánchez and Risco-Martínez, 2021). However, as we navigate this exciting frontier, it is crucial to address ethical concerns (A. H. Alsharif et al., 2023) to ensure the responsible use of neuromarketing insights. As this field matures, its applications (Gürbüz and Ünal, 2021) will likely expand, influencing not just marketing but broader sectors including health and education (Fayaz, 2024). By leveraging the power of neuromarketing, businesses can cultivate deeper connections (Gil et al., 2023) with consumers, enhancing brand loyalty and consumer experience in an era (Fayaz and Nawaz, 2023) where understanding the human psyche is paramount to marketing success (Eroglu et al., 2020). As marketers step into this dynamic future, they must remain committed to ethical practices (GarczarekBąk et al., 2021) while harnessing the potential of neuroscience to unlock the intricacies (Hafez, 2019) of consumer behavior. Neuromarketing represents a fascinating intersection (Gunawan et al., 2023) of neuroscience, psychology, and marketing, providing profound insights (JiménezMarín et al., 2019) into consumer behavior. As businesses strive to understand and predict consumer decisions in an increasingly (Kolar et al., 2021) competitive landscape, neuromarketing has emerged as a vital tool (MañasViniegra et al., 2021), combining empirical research with innovative technological advancements (Peng et al., 2023).

As the neuromarketing landscape evolves, it becomes imperative (Tripathi and Sharma, 2023) for marketing professionals to engage with ethical considerations. The power to analyze subconscious (Pelau et al., 2022) reactions and emotional responses raises questions about consumer privacy, autonomy, and influence (White et al., 2021). Businesses must navigate these ethical waters cautiously, ensuring that the use of neuromarketing techniques enhances consumer experiences rather than (Flores et al., 2022) manipulates them. Transparency, consent, and social responsibility should be at the forefront of neuromarketing initiatives (Liu et al., 2023), fostering trust between consumers and brands. Furthermore, the implications (Zhu et al., 2022) of neuromarketing extend beyond traditional marketing techniques. In an era defined by rapid technological change (Vences et al., 2020) and the dominance of digital platforms, neuromarketing can inform the design of use (A. Alsharif et al., 2023).

Thus, the journey of neuromarketing from its foundational principles to its current state reflects the growing need for businesses (Siddique et al., 2023) to leverage science in deciphering consumer behavior. With the potential to refine marketing strategies and foster deeper connections (Singh et al., 2023) with customers, neuromarketing offers a competitive edge in the modern marketplace. As the field continues to evolve, balancing the pursuit of knowledge (Kajla et al., 2023) with ethical responsibility will be crucial in ensuring that neuromarketing adds meaningful value to both businesses and consumers (A. Alsharif et al., 2023). Ultimately, by harnessing the insights gained from neuromarketing, organizations can not only enhance their marketing efforts (Rabhi et al., 2023) but also contribute to a more informed and engaged consumer landscape, fostering relationships built on trust and authenticity.

REFERENCES

Alsharif, A., Md. Salleh, N. Z., & Pilelienė, L. (2023). A comprehensive bibliometric analysis of fNIRS and fMRI technology in neuromarketing. *Scientific Annals of Economics and Business*, 70(3), 459–472. DOI: 10.47743/saeb-2023-0031

Alsharif, A., Salleh, N., & Baharun, R. (2020). Research trends of Neuromarketing: A bibliometric analysis. *Journal of Theoretical and Applied Information Technology*, 98, 2948–2962. http://www.jatit.org/volumes/Vol98No15/6Vol98No15.pdf

Alsharif, A. H., Md Salleh, N. Z., Baharun, R., Alsharif, Y. H., & Abuhassna, H. (2021). A bibliometric analysis of Neuromarketing: Current status, development and future directions. *International Journal of Academic Research in Accounting. Finance and Management Sciences*, 11(3), 828–847. DOI: 10.6007/IJARAFMS/v11-i3/11673

Alsharif, A. H., Md Salleh, N. Z., Baharun, R., & Rami Hashem, E. (2021). Neuromarketing research in the last five years: A bibliometric analysis. *Cogent Business & Management*, 8(1), 1978620. DOI: 10.1080/23311975.2021.1978620

Alsharif, A. H., Salleh, N. Z. M., Abdullah, M., Khraiwish, A., & Ashaari, A. (2023). Neuromarketing tools used in the marketing mix: A systematic literature and future research agenda. *SAGE Open*, 13(1). Advance online publication. DOI: 10.1177/21582440231156563

Ambler, T. (2015). Persuasion, pride and prejudice: How ads work. *International Journal of Advertising*, 19(3), 299–315. DOI: 10.1080/02650487.2000.11104803

Bielik, P., Bellérová, B., Benda Prokeinova, R., Braha, K., Cierna, Z., Fandel, I., Hallova, M., Hanová, M., Heijman, W., Horksá, E., Kadekova, Z., Kadlecíková, M., Kapsdorferova, Z., Krajcirova, R., Kleinová, K., Lajdova, Z., Moravčíková, D., Nagyová, L. u., Paluchová, J., & Ubrežiová, I. (2014). *Agribusiness and Commerce*. Slovak University of Agriculture in Nitra. https://www.researchgate.net/ publication/311912197_Agribusiness_and_Commerce

Bruce, A. S., Bruce, J. M., Black, W. R., Lepping, R. J., Henry, J. M., Cherry, J. B., Martin, L. E., Papa, V. B., Davis, A. M., Brooks, W. M., & Savage, C. R. (2014). Branding and a child's brain: An fMRI study of neural responses to logos. *Social Cognitive and Affective Neuroscience*, 9(1), 118–122. DOI: 10.1093/scan/nss109

Caratu, M., Cherubino, P., & Mattiacci, A. (2018). *Application of neuro-marketing techniques to the wine tasting experience 11th Annual of the EuroMed Academy of Business (EMAB) Conference*, "Research Advancements in National and Global Business Theory and Practice", Valletta, Malta. https://iris.uniroma1.it/handle/11573/1139099

Chai, J., Ge, Y., Liu, Y., Li, W., Zhou, L., Yao, L., & Sun, X. (2014). Application of frontal EEG asymmetry to user experience research. *Lecture Notes in Computer Science (LNAI) Engineering Psychology and Cognitive Ergonomics*. Cham. doi:DOI: 10.1007/978-3-319-07515-0_24

Cherediakova, A., Lobodenko, L., & Lychagina, I. (2021). *A study of advertising content in digital communications: The experience of applying neuromarketing and traditional techniques*. 2021 Communication Strategies in Digital Society Seminar (ComSDS), St. Petersburg, Russia, DOI: 10.1109/ComSDS52473.2021.9422887

Eroglu, K., Kayikcioglu, T., & Osman, O. (2020). Effect of brightness of visual stimuli on EEG signals. *Behavioural Brain Research*, 382, 1–16, 112486. DOI: 10.1016/j.bbr.2020.112486

Fayaz, M. (2024). The bibliometric analysis of EEGLAB software in the Web of Science indexed articles. *Neuroscience Informatics*, 4(1), 100154. DOI: 10.1016/j.neuri.2023.100154

Fayaz, S., & Nawaz, R. R. (2023). Neuromarketing: A bibliometric perspective of the field. *Journal of Economic Literature*, 18(1), 132–151. DOI: 10.54784/1990-6587.1508

Flores, C. O. G., Nina, D. A., Ulcuanjo, O. M. R., & Vinueza, D. F. F. (2022). Psychosensometric study (eye tracker) on the levels of persuasion in the women's perfumery industry. *Journal of Pharmaceutical Negative Results*, 13(4), 562–572. DOI: 10.47750/pnr.2022.13.04.074

Garczarek-Bąk, U., Szymkowiak, A., Gaczek, P., & Disterheft, A. (2021). A comparative analysis of neuromarketing methods for brand purchasing predictions among young adults. *Journal of Brand Management*, 28(2), 171–185. DOI: 10.1057/s41262-020-00221-7

Giakoni, F. R., López, M., Segado, F., Manzanares, A. S., & Minguez, J. (2022). An implicit research methodology to evaluate advertising effectiveness in Esports streaming based on viewers' gaze, cognitive and emotional responses. *SPORT TK-Revista EuroAmericana de Ciencias del Deporte*, 11, 1–21. DOI: 10.6018/sportk.485921

Gil, I. P., Zagala, K., & Cerdá Suárez, L. M. (2023). Mayoría de edad del Neuromarketing: Mapa científico de 18 años de investigación en el área. *Index ComunicaciÓn*, 13(2), 47–74. DOI: 10.33732/ixc/13/02Mayori

Gunawan, C. N., Chen, Y.-J., & Hsu, L. (2023). How online travel agencies' logo design promotes purchase intention: A behavioral and neuroscientific interpretation of consumers' construal level. *Asia Pacific Journal of Tourism Research*, 28(1), 19–35. DOI: 10.1080/10941665.2023.2187701

Gürbüz, F., & Ünal, S. E. (2021). A bibliometric analysis of neuromarketing on web of science. *Journal of Engineering Research*, 11(28), 226–235. DOI: 10.36909/jer.12239

Hafez, M. (2019). Neuromarketing: a new avatar in branding and advertisement. *Pacific Business Review International*, 12(4), 58-64. http://www.pbr.co.in/2019/2019_month/october/6.pdf

Holsen, L. M., Zarcone, J. R., Thompson, T. I., Brooks, W. M., Anderson, M. F., Ahluwalia, J. S., Nollen, N. L., & Savage, C. R. (2005). Neural mechanisms underlying food motivation in children and adolescents. *NeuroImage*, 27(3), 669–676. DOI: 10.1016/j.neuroimage.2005.04.043

Jiménez-Marín, G., Bellido-Pérez, E., & López-Cortés, Á. (2019). Marketing sensorial: El concepto, sus técnicas y su aplicación en el punto de venta. *Vivat Academia. Revista de Comunicación*, (148), 121–147. DOI: 10.15178/va.2019.148.121-147

Kajla, T., Raj, S., Kansra, P., Gupta, S. L., & Singh, N. (2023). Neuromarketing and consumer behavior: A bibliometric analysis. *Journal of Consumer Behaviour*, •••, 1–17. DOI: 10.1002/cb.2256

Khushaba, R. N., Wise, C., Kodagoda, S., Louviere, J., Kahn, B. E., & Townsend, C. (2013). Consumer neuroscience: Assessing the brain response to marketing stimuli using electroencephalogram (EEG) and eye tracking. *Expert Systems with Applications*, 40(9), 3803–3812. DOI: 10.1016/j.eswa.2012.12.095

Kohler, C. G., Barrett, F. S., Gur, R. C., Turetsky, B. I., & Moberg, P. J. (2007). Association between facial emotion recognition and odor identification in schizophrenia. *The Journal of Neuropsychiatry and Clinical Neurosciences*, 19(2), 128–131. DOI: 10.1176/jnp.2007.19.2.128

Kolar, T., Batagelj, Z., Omeragić, I., & Husić-Mehmedović, M. (2021). How moment-to-moment EEG measures enhance ad effectiveness evaluation peak emotions during branding moments as key indicators. *Journal of Advertising Research*, 61(4), 365–381. DOI: 10.2501/JAR-2021-014

Liu, Y., Zhao, R., Xiong, X., & Ren, X. (2023). A bibliometric analysis of consumer neuroscience towards sustainable consumption. *Behavioral Sciences (Basel, Switzerland)*, 13(4), 298. DOI: 10.3390/bs13040298

Mañas-Viniegra, L., Santos-Silva, D., & Liberal Ormaechea, S. (2021). The visual-digital identity of corporate brands: A study of Neuromarketing in young people from Spain and Portugal. *Tripodos Blanquerna School of Communication and International Relations-URL*, (48), 135–151. DOI: 10.51698/tripodos.2020.48p135-151

Mateusz, P. (2018). EEG in analysis of the level of interest in social issue advertising. *Procedia Computer Science*, 126, 1945–1953. DOI: 10.1016/j.procs.2018.08.056

Morrin, M. (2011). Scent marketing: An overview. In *Sensory Marketing* (pp. 75–86). Research on the Sensuality of Products., DOI: 10.4324/9780203892060-14

Ortigueira-Sánchez, L. C., & Risco-Martínez, S. L. (2021). A bibliometric analysis on the state of the art of Neuromarketing research in Web of Science. *ECONTEC: Revista Internacional de Gestión del Conocimiento y la Tecnología*, 9(2), 1-21. https://gecontec.org/index.php/unesco/article/view/20/16

Page, M. J., McKenzie, J. E., Bossuyt, P. M., Boutron, I., Hoffmann, T. C., Mulrow, C. D., Shamseer, L., Tetzlaff, J. M., Akl, E. A., Brennan, S. E., Chou, R., Glanville, J., Grimshaw, J. M., Hróbjartsson, A., Lalu, M. M., Li, T., Loder, E. W., Mayo-Wilson, E., McDonald, S., & Moher, D. (2021). The PRISMA 2020 statement: An updated guideline for reporting systematic reviews. *BMJ (Clinical Research Ed.), n71*. Advance online publication. doi: PMID:33782057DOI: 10.1136/bmj.n71

Pelau, C., Nistoreanu, P., Lazar, L., & Badescu, R. (2022). Celebrity vs. Product: A neuroscientific approach to the distractors in food advertising for sustainable marketing. *Sustainability*, 14(19), 1–15, 12768. DOI: 10.3390/su141912768

Peng, M., Liang, M., Huang, H., Fan, J., Yu, L., & Liao, J. (2023). The effect of different animated brand logos on consumer response: An event-related potential and self-reported study. *Computers in Human Behavior*, 143, 1–12, 107701. DOI: 10.1016/j.chb.2023.107701

Rabhi, M., Thamri, A., Benahmed, E. S., & Djoual, M. (2023). Neuromarketing research trends over the last ten years: a bibliometric analysis of the Scopus databases. *Marketing and Digital Technologies*, 7, 7-23. https://www.researchgate.net/publication/374265603_Neuromarketing_research_trends_over_ the_last_ten_years_a_bibliometric_analysis_of_the_Scopus_databases

Razi, N. I. M., Othman, M., & Yaacob, H. (2016). *EEG-based emotion recognition in the investment activities*. 2016 6th International Conference on Information and Communication Technology for the Muslim World (ICT4M), Jakarta, Indonesia. https://ieeexplore.ieee.org/document/7814925

Siddique, J., Shamim, A., Nawaz, M., & Abid, M. F. (2023). The hope and hype of neuromarketing: A bibliometric analysis. *Journal of Contemporary Marketing Science*, 6(1), 1–21. DOI: 10.1108/JCMARS-07-2022-0018

Singh, P., Alhassan, I., & Khoshaim, L. (2023). What do you need to know? A systematic review and research agenda on Neuromarketing discipline. *Journal of Theoretical and Applied Electronic Commerce Research*, 18(4), 2007–2032. DOI: 10.3390/jtaer18040101

Spence, C. (2019). Neuroscience-inspired design: From academic neuromarketing to commercially relevant research. *Organizational Research Methods*, 22(1), 275–298. DOI: 10.1177/1094428116672003

Telpaz, A., Webb, R., & Levy, D. J. (2015). Using EEG to predict consumers' future choices. *JMR, Journal of Marketing Research*, 52(4), 511–529. DOI: 10.1509/jmr.13.0564

Tripathi, B., & Sharma, R. K. (2023). EEG-based emotion classification in financial trading using deep learning: Effects of risk control measures. *Sensors (Basel)*, 23(7), 1–26, 3474. DOI: 10.3390/s23073474

Trope, Y., & Liberman, N. (2010). Construal-level theory of psychological distance. *Psychological Review*, 117(2), 440–463. DOI: 10.1037/a0018963

Valdez, P., & Mehrabian, A. (1994). Effects of color on emotions. *Journal of Experimental Psychology. General*, 123(4), 394–409. DOI: 10.1037/0096-3445.123.4.394

Vecchiato, G., Maglione, A. G., Cherubino, P., Wasikowska, B., Wawrzyniak, A., Latuszynska, A., Latuszynska, M., Nermend, K., Graziani, I., Leucci, M. R., Trettel, A., & Babiloni, F. (2014). Neurophysiological tools to investigate consumer's gender differences during the observation of TV commercials. *Computational and Mathematical Methods in Medicine*, 2014, 1–12, 912981. DOI: 10.1155/2014/912981

Vences, N. A., Díaz-Campo, J., & Rosales, D. F. G. (2020). Neuromarketing as an Emotional Connection Tool Between Organizations and Audiences in Social Networks. A Theoretical Review. *Frontiers in Psychology*, 11, 1787. DOI: 10.3389/fpsyg.2020.01787

Wei, Z., Wu, C., Wang, X., Supratak, A., Wang, P., & Guo, Y. (2018). Using support vector machine on EEG for advertisement impact assessment. *Frontiers in Neuroscience*, 12, 1–12, 76. DOI: 10.3389/fnhum.2018.00001

White, A. R., Martinez, L. M., Martinez, L. F., & Rando, B. (2021). Color in web banner advertising: The influence of analogous and complementary colors on attitude and purchase intention. *Electronic Commerce Research and Applications*, 50, 1–10, 101100. DOI: 10.1016/j.elerap.2021.101100

Yağci, M. İ., Kuhzady, S., Balik, Z. S., & Öztürk, L. (2018). In search of consumer's black box: A bibliometric analysis of Neuromarketing research. *Journal of Consumer and Consumption Research*, 10(1), 101–134. https://www.betadergi.com/ttad/yonetim/icerik/makaleler/169-published.pdf

Zamuner, E. (2013). The role of the visual system in emotion perception. *Acta Analytica : Philosophy and Psychology*, 28(2), 179–187. DOI: 10.1007/s12136-012-0151-7

Zhou, Z., Zheng, L., & Li, X. (2021). Abstract or concrete? The influence of image type on consumer attitudes. *International Journal of Consumer Studies*, 45(5), 1132–1146. DOI: 10.1111/ijcs.12642

Zhu, Z., Jin, Y., Su, Y., Jia, K., Lin, C.-L., & Liu, X. (2022). Bibliometric-based evaluation of the Neuromarketing research trend: 2010–2021. *Frontiers in Psychology*, 13, 35983212. DOI: 10.3389/fpsyg.2022.872468

Chapter 2
Overview of Neuromarketing: Foundations and Development

A. Devendran
https://orcid.org/0000-0001-7192-521X
Woxsen University, India

S. Kumaran
Hindustan Institute of Technology and Science, India

Rama Chaithanya Tanguturi
https://orcid.org/0000-0002-9923-7360
Woxsen University, India

B. Neeraja
Chaitanya Bharathi Institute of Technology, India

ABSTRACT

Neuromarketing combines neuroscience, psychology, and marketing to explore consumer behavior at a subconscious level. By using tools like fMRI, EEG, eye-tracking, and biometrics, it measures consumers' emotional and cognitive responses to marketing stimuli, offering deeper insights than traditional methods. Neuromarketing helps marketers create more personalized campaigns by understanding what drives consumer choices. Key methodologies include fMRI for identifying brain areas linked to emotions and decision-making, EEG for capturing real-time reactions, and eye-tracking to analyze visual attention. Brands like Coca-Cola and Nike use these insights to enhance emotional connections and boost loyalty. However, ethical concerns arise regarding privacy, manipulation, and informed consent, as these techniques may exploit subconscious triggers. Ensuring transparency and ethical

DOI: 10.4018/979-8-3693-7673-7.ch002

use is crucial as neuromarketing continues to shape the future of advertising and consumer engagement.

1. INTRODUCTION

Neuromarketing is the application of neuroscientific principles to marketing practices. Neuromarketing is a new interdisciplinary field that incorporates elements of neuroscience, psychology, and marketing in order to look at the other side of the consumer brain. It deploys sophisticated imaging and biometrics taking in the form of EEG, fMRI and eye-tracking among others to measure the degree of engagement and reaction triggered by a marketing stimulus exposed to a consumer. With its ability to reach harness and exploit the emotional, cognitive and decision making faculties of the human brain; neuromarketing gives businesses a competitive advantage over their rivals by enabling them to understand Sally consumer's wants, needs, and reasons for buying in ways that cannot be achieved through conventional marketing approaches.

Importance of Understanding Consumer Behavior

In this age of intense competition, the need to appreciate consumer behavior for the purpose of developing appropriate marketing strategies cannot be overemphasized. Most of the traditional primary market research techniques like surveys, focus groups, and interviews collect self-reported data from respondents who may therefore be biased or incapable of expressing their real feelings. Neuromarketing fills this shortcoming by providing a way of looking at how consumers react subconsciously and in an automatic fashion to different content and stimuli. Hence, allowing marketers to go beyond what consumers say and how they feel and act. Attention can take in many aspects, such as emotional triggers, attention, and memory retention, and this means that the messaging, product development, and customer interaction processes can be improved for the benefit of the target audience. For example, in the area of advertising research, it is possible to 'see' whether people pay more attention to a product's particular pose, or whether the product's packaging is effective enough to make the consumer reach for their wallet and purchase the item. This insight into how consumers think and act allows businesses to create campaigns which not only increase sales but also achieve a higher level of appreciation for the brand.

Importance of Brain Imaging and Other Neuroscientific Approaches in Marketing

Brain imaging and neuroscientific approaches are pivotal in understanding neuromarketing as they allow marketers to look into the brain, and what happens in there while a decision is being made, in a way that has never been seen before. Brain imaging techniques such as fMRI and EEG help in understanding how consumers respond to advertising, make purchases and feel about certain brands.

Functional Magnetic Resonance Imaging (fMRI) is a neuroimaging technique that detects changes in blood flow to the cortex or subcortical regions of the brain during exposure to various stimuli. fMRI is suitable for use in areas of the brain contiguous to motion, memory, and primary and secondary affection towards reward and deterring stimuli.

Electroencephalograph (EEG) is a machine used to measure electrical activity in the assemblage of the brain. Quite often it is used to conduct experimental advertising research in the course of them. The real-time EEG editing is concerned with various marketing stimuli including product footage, prints, or consumer goods or services. It is useful for measuring emotional arousal, level of attention, and level of thinking.

Eye Tracking analyzes how long and where consumers fixate their eyes on particular features of an advertisement, a website or a display. It discloses the visual structures which govern consumer attention.

The Purpose of the Paper and its Objectives

This paper will analyze the evolution of the neuromarketing concept and its influence on modern-day advertising and consumer behavior. It will look into the past, present and future of neuromarketing and the techniques involved and utilized in the various industries. The paper will also address ethical issues associated with marketing that uses neuroscience and forecast the developments that this discipline may embrace in years to come. This observation will be supported with examples to illustrate how neuromarketing techniques are changing the way the marketing field is viewed inasmuch as it offers insight into the depths of how decisions are made by consumers.

The purposes of this review essay are as follows:

1. To elaborate on the neuromarketing definition, its purposes and discussing its importance for understanding the consumers.
2. To look into the origins of neuromarketing and its philosophies as well as why certain neuroscientific technologies have advanced over the years.
3. To consider neuromarketing tools such as fMRI, EEG, eye-tracking technologies and discuss their relevance to advertising execution.
4. To seek for the case examples where neuromarketing proved its efficiency in focus of such cases in creating more effective advertisement campaigns.
5. To explain the issues connected with the use of market research techniques such as brain imaging and biometric confirmativeness techniques where consumer manipulation occurs.

6. To look out for the future of neuropromoting which will include usage of artificial intelligence and virtual reality in the marketing research.

By achieving these objectives, the paper will offer a comprehensive understanding of neuromarketing's potential to transform how businesses engage with consumers, craft personalized experiences, and optimize marketing strategies for higher returns.

Table 1. Differences between traditional marketing and neuromarketing approaches

Criteria	Traditional Marketing	Neuromarketing
Research Methods	Surveys, focus groups, interviews	Brain imaging (fMRI, EEG), eye tracking, biometrics
Data Type	Self-reported, subjective opinions	Objective, physiological, and neural responses
Focus	Conscious thoughts and opinions	Subconscious emotions and automatic responses
Reliability of Insights	Subject to bias, social desirability, and misreporting	Accurate measurement of real-time emotional and cognitive reactions
Consumer Engagement	Based on surface-level analysis of preferences	In-depth understanding of attention, memory, and emotional triggers
Campaign Optimization	Adjustments based on feedback from surveys or performance	Optimizations based on real-time neural and physiological feedback
Costs	Lower research costs, traditional data collection	Higher costs due to advanced technologies (fMRI, EEG, etc.)
Applicability	Generalized insights applied to large groups	Tailored insights targeting specific emotional and cognitive drivers

This table highlights the key differences between traditional marketing, which relies on conscious, self-reported data, and neuromarketing, which digs into the subconscious drivers of consumer behavior. Neuromarketing offers more precise, data-driven insights that can significantly enhance the effectiveness of marketing campaigns.

2. HISTORICAL EVOLUTION OF NEUROMARKETING

There is a multitude of definitions of neuromarketing, which is a blend of various academic fields and draws content from neuroscience, psychology, marketing and economic analysis of consumer behavior, to mention a few. In this way, it enables the students to understand consumer behavior and the marketing mix and the effects of globalization. Neuromarketing's evolution took place along the progress of technology, cognitive neuroscience more specifically, and understanding of factors influencing the functioning and behavior of the human brain. This chapter looks at the chronology of Neuromarketing development as the discipline that studies consumer and compra-oriented behavior, with the internal and external parameters defining purchase or study of services and products.

Early Psychological Investigations (20th Century)

On the two first decades of the twenthieth century, a number of psychological studies exploring the mechanism of motivation behind consumer action set off a few earnest marketing research studies for marketing development. Many psychologists and early marketing theorists had their gaze fixed on the effect of Buying Motives on Consumers' Behavior. In this context, the work of John B. Watson, one of the fathers of behaviorism, is noteworthy in that it offers an extreme position in which even purchasing behavior can be viewed as a trained reflex to external stimuli.

Behaviorism in advertising: In the 1920's, there was an increase in interest in advertising and the use of psychological concepts in the mass media. The explanation for this high interest in external behavior as opposed to internal mental states was the use of advertisements as a means of conditioning consumers' buying behavior. Wason's studies helped companies understand and utilize the emotional and mental factors influencing consumers' likes and dislikes which, subsequently, contributed to the formation of consumer psychology as it is known today.

In the 1950s, Ernest Dichter, a Viennese psychologist, introduced the concept of motivational research, which aimed to uncover consumers' hidden desires and subconscious motivations. Dichter believed that by understanding the unconscious desires of consumers, marketers could create more effective advertisements and products. His work emphasized the importance of symbols and emotional appeals in advertising, setting the stage for neuromarketing's later focus on subconscious consumer reactions.

Development of Modern Neuroimaging Tools in the Late 1990s

While psychological research in the 20th century offered insights into consumer behavior, it wasn't until the late 1990s that neuromarketing truly began to take shape as a distinct discipline. This shift was driven by advancements in neuroimaging technologies, which provided researchers with direct access to brain activity, allowing for a more precise understanding of how consumers process marketing stimuli.

Ramotion designed a marketing materials concept for Muted.

Functional Magnetic Resonance Imaging (fMRI): The fMRI technique evolving in the 1990s came as an absolute revolution for neuromarketing. fMRI quantifies blood flow to the brain which, as a result, points at which neural activities occur. fMRI enables researchers to know the different parts of the brain that are engaged by certain stimuli such as advertisements, products, and branding elements. This approach, fMRI, has proven to be useful in revealing the brain structures that handle primary emotion, reward and decision-making processes, which are fundamental for the study of consumers.

For instance, in one of the early studies in neuromarketing that employed fMRI, it was discovered that consumers whose eye movement tracked the Coca-Cola logo exhibited increased neuronal activity on the positive valence and reward regions of the brain. This discovery illustrates how certain brand views evoke strong emotional perceptions from the consumers and helps formulates a strategy for emotional advertising to the consumers.

Electroencephalography (EEG): In the footsteps of fMRI, EEG technology has also contributed a great deal in the field of neuromarketing. EEG records brain electrical signals in a noninvasive way providing a slice of how markets react to advertising stimuli in almost an instant. fMRI may be superior in that it can be used to obtain activity level of any given portion of the brain, which may not be the case with EEG that records the activities of the brain and the responses in neural circuitry in real time and allows responses to be triggered fast making it suitable for advertisements embedded in products or displays in a consumer outlet.

The first application of EEG in Marketing research was in the early 2000s. Companies used it to evaluate the emotional effect of television commercials on audiences. By measuring certain power bands of consumers' brain rhythmic activity, it became possible to assess which specific elements of an advertisement produced the strongest responses and allowed marketers to implement.

Key Milestones in Neuromarketing

The latter part of the 1990s and 2000s are known to be marked with the emergence of neuromarketing as a field where the application of neuroscience with consumer research became recognized and began carried out by businesses and academic institutions. Since then, a number of developments have contributed to the evolution of neuromarketing.

1. The Growth of Neuromarketing Agencies (Beginning of 2000s): One of the notable development in the time evolution of neuromarketing is the appearance of the neuro marketing agencies in the early 2000s. For instance, NeuroFocus, which was born in 2005 and Buyology Inc. were some of the companies which started offering services related to neuromarketing to big corporations. These companies employed fMRI, EEG and borderline data to understand the response of consumers for the purpose of enhanced advertisement and product designing.
    - Martin Lindstrom, who founded Buyology Inc., wrote *Buyology: Truth and Lies About Why We Buy* (2008), a book that fueled public interest in neuromarketing. Lindstrom explored the hidden elements that affect behavior and try to map the emotional brain via neuro-imaging to see how people really feel about certain products and logos.
2. Eye-tracking devices: Eye-tracking began to be used in the same contexts as fMRI and EEG technologies roughly around the start of the 21st century. In monitoring the movement of consumers' eyes, researchers were able to assess the parts of a commercial or a product that commanded the gaze of consumers. Such technology shed light into the effects of sight on consumers and how these sights can be manipulated by marketers through product arrangement, designing of websites and creating of advertisements.
    - One notable application of eye-tracking technology in neuromarketing was its use in supermarket research. Researchers tracked consumers' eye movements as they navigated store aisles, revealing that many purchasing decisions were made within seconds based on which products caught the consumer's eye first. This insight led to changes in how products were displayed on shelves, with brands competing for prime visual real estate.
3. Integration of Biometric Data (2010s): In the 2010s, neuromarketing expanded to include biometric measurements such as heart rate, skin conductance, and facial coding. These tools measure consumers' physiological responses to marketing stimuli, providing additional data on emotional arousal and engagement. The integration of biometric data allowed neuromarketers to capture a more holistic view of how consumers react to advertisements, products, and brands.

For instance, facial coding, which analyzes facial expressions to detect emotions, has been widely used in neuromarketing to assess the emotional impact of advertisements. By decoding micro-expressions, researchers can identify whether consumers feel happy, surprised, or frustrated when viewing an ad, helping brands fine-tune their messaging to evoke the desired emotional response.

Table 2. Timeline of neuromarketing developments

Year	Milestone
1920s	John B. Watson introduces behaviorism, emphasizing emotional triggers in marketing.
1950s	Ernest Dichter pioneers motivational research, exploring subconscious consumer desires.
1990s	Development of fMRI and EEG allows direct observation of brain activity in response to marketing stimuli.
Early 2000s	Emergence of neuromarketing firms such as NeuroFocus and Buyology Inc.
2000s	Introduction of eye-tracking technology to study consumer attention.
2010s	Biometric techniques, including heart rate monitoring and facial coding, become integrated into neuromarketing research.

3. NEUROMARKETING TECHNIQUES AND TECHNOLOGIES

Neuromarketing utilizes numerous advanced scientific elements to monitor how marketing actions are received by customers, both rationally and emotionally. It consists of a range of practical devices that help in understanding the thoughts and feelings of consumers such as the fMRI device which uses images of the brain or heart rate among other devices. This part elucidates salient neuromarketing research techniques, practice and challenges.

Functional Magnetic Resonance Imaging (fMRI)

Functional Magnetic Resonance imaging (fMRI) is one of the newest techniques enabled by the revolution of neuromarketing as it helps in gauging the consumers' brain activity by blood flow monitoring. When an individual performs an act related to thinking or feeling, a particular region of their brain would require more oxygen hence an increase in the blood flow within those specific areas. Such changes are what the fMRI records and subsequently creates clear pictures as to what regions of the brain are active when an individual's attention is captured by certain marketing stimuli, for instance, an advertisement, product designs, as well as brand logos.

Applications of fMRI in Neuromarketing

1. Emotional Engagement: fMRI is beneficial in understanding how various parts of the brain are activitated by emotion allowing marketers to determine the emotional weight of their adverts. For example, fMRI can indicate whether a specific advertisement invokes the brain's reward systems (like the Deep Ventromedial Prefrontal Cortex) as evidenced by changes in blood flow.

2. Brand Perception: fMRI can support marketers comprehending the difference in consumer views of brands by providing evidence of the activation of certain brain areas (for example the hippocampus and amygdala) while looking at a logos or content associated with a brand.
3. Decision-Making: This tool also enables exploring decision making development, and the comparative evaluation of the cost, and subjective worth, and various product attributes.

Limitations of fMRI

While fMRI is powerful, it also has several limitations:

Cost: fMRI is an expensive tool, with individual scans often costing thousands of dollars. This makes it less accessible for smaller businesses and more practical for large corporations with significant research budgets.
Time-Consuming: An fMRI session can take a significant amount of time, as multiple scans are needed to gather meaningful data, and the setup itself is complex.
Limited Realism: Subjects need to remain perfectly still inside the scanner, which can make it difficult to simulate real-world experiences such as browsing a store or interacting with a product naturally.

Electroencephalography (EEG)

Electroencephalography (EEG) shows activities in the brain by measuring its electrical activity through electrodes on the head to monitor changes in neural activity. EEG obtains the processes of brain waves in real time which means that it enables studying the emotional and cognitive reactions of consumers as the subjects are exposed to the marketing stimuli. In contrast to fMRI, which displays greater clarity in the spacial mapping of the active regions in the brain, EEG is better when it comes to the measurement of the timing of the neural responses.

Scope of EEG in Neuromarketing

1. Immediate Emotional Response: The response of consumers to an advertisement or product design is immediate and EEG makes it possible this in recording. Different brain waves such as alpha waves, beta waves and theta waves can be studied and are associated with various emotions such as joy, anger and even intrigue.

2. Engagement and Attention: Attention level to some section of the advertisement or product by the consumer and even the advertisement as a whole can be determined through EEG. This enables marketers to know those aspects of their content that have high chances of being viewed and those which are likely to be ignored.
3. Memory Encoding: Advertisement or brand Message recognition is also tested with EGG and EEG patterns by identification of specific brainwave patterns related to memory trace creation.

Eye Tracking

Eye tracking refers to a neuromarketing approach to look at how much of a visual attention an advertisement or a product package or even a website with specific parameters how long a person looks to it. Where they place infrared cameras and they trace the two eyes, except in this instance they trace probably the point where the eyes fixate and also the whole movement in regard to fixation of eyes. This is important in knowing how the customers respond visually to the marketing materialand which elements draw the most attention.

Applications of Eye Tracking in Neuromarketing:

1. Visual Attention Analysis: Eye tracking allows marketers to see which parts of an advertisement or product consumers look at first and for how long. This can reveal which visual elements (e.g., images, text, logos) are most effective at capturing attention.
2. Website Optimization: By analyzing eye-tracking data, marketers can optimize website design to improve user experience. For instance, identifying which areas of a website draw the most attention can help designers place key elements, like call-to-action buttons or product information, in strategic locations.
3. Product Placement: In retail settings, eye tracking can be used to determine the optimal placement of products on store shelves. By analyzing consumers' visual patterns, marketers can adjust shelf layouts to increase visibility and influence purchasing decisions.

certain aspects of consumers' behavior and can be interpreted by means of aegis of biometrics.

In the case of biometric techniques, it is not about the provision of neurological evidence as is the case with neuroimaging, rather they are structured and designed so that the physiological symptoms of emotional arousal and engagement are captured. The most employed and popular seem to be skin conductance (aka galvanic skin response and GSR) and heart rate capturing technologies. Skin conductivity on the other hand refers to the amount of electrical charge that the skin can conduct and this value increases when an individual is emotionally engaged and heart rate measurement methods monitor variations in a heartbeat per minute which is caused by stress or excitement levels.

Uses of Biometric Methods in Neuromarketing

1. Measurement of Emotional Arousal – Skin conductance can also play a significant role in advertising studies. For example, marketers may wish to determine how emotionally charged a particular advertisement or product is. Excessive skin conductance regardless corresponding emotional valence suggests increased arousal level ever positive or negative.
2. Evaluation of Stress and Relaxation: Heart rate monitoring is widely used to systematically investigate the range of stimulus types available and 'how' the consumer responds. In this case, a high heart rate would imply stress or excitement, a low heart rate might imply general relaxation or boredom.
3. Reactions that are not are not within the recognition of the consumers: Many findings of biometric study know no articulation and even awareness among the members concerning the reactions. These reactions can provide deeper insights into certain aspects of consumers' behavior and can be interpreted by means of aegis of biometrics.

    Limitations of Biometric Techniques:

    Ambiguity of Responses: While biometric techniques can detect emotional arousal, they do not indicate whether the reaction is positive or negative. For example, high skin conductance could indicate excitement or fear, making it difficult to interpret the results without additional context.

    Limited Scope: Biometric techniques primarily measure physical responses and cannot provide detailed insights into cognitive processes or decision-making mechanisms.

Table 3. Comparison of neuromarketing techniques in terms of accuracy, cost, and time investment

Technique	Accuracy	Cost	Time Investment
fMRI	High spatial accuracy, identifies specific brain regions involved in decision-making	Very High ($$$)	Long setup and analysis time
EEG	High temporal accuracy, real-time data	Moderate ($$)	Moderate, setup relatively quick but requires careful analysis
Eye Tracking	High accuracy in measuring visual attention	Low ($)	Short, data can be collected and analyzed quickly
Skin Conductance/ Heart Rate	Moderate accuracy for emotional arousal	Low ($)	Short, data collection is straightforward but requires context for interpretation

Figure 1. Example of EEG brainwave activity when responding to ad stimuli

4. APPLICATIONS OF NEUROMARKETING IN BUSINESS AND ADVERTISING

Neuromarketing has become a crucial tool for businesses and advertisers seeking to gain deeper insights into consumer behavior, optimize their campaigns, and drive more effective marketing strategies. By understanding the subconscious motivations behind consumer decisions, businesses can tailor their messaging, branding, pricing, and product design to resonate more strongly with their target audience. This section explores real-world case studies of successful neuromarketing campaigns, how neuromarketing has influenced branding and product design, and its role in pricing strategies and digital marketing optimization.

Case Studies of Successful Neuromarketing Campaigns

1. Coca-Cola: Understanding Emotional Connections to Branding

Coca-Cola is a global brand that has enjoyed massive recognition in the world and this is due to the application of different neuromarketing strategies and neuromarketing research. The most well-known neuromarketing study using Coca-Cola refers to the use of fMRI scanners and comparing the emotional and cognitive responses to Coke and Pepsi. It was found that there was an activation of the part of the brain that is responsible for emotional processing especially the ventromedial prefrontal cortex if participants consumed Coke brand while being under the guise of the Coca-Cola product. This area of the brain is activated by the presence of rewards, pleasure, and bonding.

Nevertheless, when participants tasted the product containing unmarked cups of Coke and Pepsi, a lot of them declined that taste of coke branding and preferred taste of Pepsi, 'But when unveiled the brand, participants were highly staunch in favor of Coca-Cola'. The power of branding along with emotional factors was demonstrated by the making decisions of the consumers in this experiment. Coca-Cola has used brand insights in order to turn back on the emotional experiences and the nostalgia of the brand rather than focus on the taste and other properties of the product as they had done in the marketing in the past.

2. Google: Enhancing User Experience through Eye Tracking

Google, as a prominent player in the digital marketing and technology sector, applies neuromarketing strategies including but not limited to eye-tracking for the means of improving user experience (UX). This technique in understanding user's eyetran is so effective such that it helps Google figure out which website or search result page elements are most likely to draw the attention of the visitors and which ones get completely ignored. This has been very helpful in the modification of the structure of the search results given by Google such that ads and other important information are placed where users are more likely to see them.

As such, this behavior has necessitated changes in the design of the Results Page of its search engine accommodations, the addition of elements such as rich snippets, featured snippets, knowledge panels, etc., which serve the purpose of high information content display. Eye-tracking results showed that users pay more attention to the upper area of the screen including the headers and other elements that are bolded or made visually different. In this way, the effectiveness of advertising has been increased by Google since the position of the ads ensures high visibility of the ads enhancing the click-through rates and participation of advertisers for that matter.

Branding Strategies Enhanced by Neuromarketing

Branding is more than just logos and slogans—it's about creating an emotional connection between the consumer and the brand. Neuromarketing has revolutionized how companies build and enhance their brands by providing deeper insights into how consumers emotionally and subconsciously respond to different branding elements.

Emotional Branding: Neuromarketing studies have shown that consumers often make purchasing decisions based on emotional connections rather than rational considerations. This insight has led companies to focus more on creating emotional experiences that resonate with their audience. Brands like Apple, Nike, and Coca-Cola have leveraged neuromarketing insights to create advertisements that appeal to consumers' emotions, whether it's nostalgia, aspiration, or a sense of belonging. For example, Nike's "Just Do It" campaign taps into consumers' aspirations and emotional drive for success and perseverance, which strengthens their loyalty to the brand.

Sensory Branding: Sensory marketing—appealing to the five senses (sight, sound, touch, smell, taste)—has also benefited from neuromarketing insights. Companies like Starbucks have used sensory branding to enhance the customer experience. Through neuromarketing research, Starbucks discovered that the smell of freshly brewed coffee triggers positive emotions and memories in consumers. As a result, Starbucks carefully controls the in-store experience to emphasize the aroma of coffee, which strengthens the emotional connection between the consumer and the brand.

Improving Product Design and Sensory Marketing

For instance, sensory appeal has been used in product development of a simple toothpaste tube. The texture, sound, and even the weight of the tube are some of the sensory attributes that contribute towards the overall appeal of the product. Neuromarketing research was also conducted by Unilever where they explored the various textures of ice cream to assess the extent of enjoyment towards the ice cream part. The fMRI advantage helped Unilever to dismiss off certain textures that did not activate the targeted pleasure areas and thus came up with better ice cream products that were more pleasurable to the users. Sensory studies of this nature find their applicability in many uses such as designing products that not only meet consumer needs but also evoke positive emotional responses.

Evident differences in consumers' behaviour under similar conditions: examples of pricing effects

Above all things prices are an important price factor in purchasing. Prices appear to have started the exploration of neuromarketing. Conventional pricing strategies are often based on economic principles of demand and supply. However, to understand the neursing in consumers, how they see prices, price is simply not a number clean and simple which can be smudged without any emotions.

1. Price Perception and Anchoring:

Advertising and Brand Management in an Interesting Way Psychology Advertising One Consumer's Evaluation of the Cost of a Product. Understanding the Cost of Products to the Consumers There is a Cost to Everything, but Consumers Don't Always Take a Look at it. Discussions about the Perception of Cost.

Cognitive neuroscience may prove consumers do not always behave logically when it comes to prices. For instance, the anchoring bias is where people make a decision based on an arbitrarily included first piece of information (the anchor). The implanting of anchor prices is best illustrated by fMRI and EEG studies that show that, when the first price (the anchor) presented to the customer is high, they consider even the next price, although still high, more appropriate. This is why such prices are appearing on the price tags of some products today – the initial price without discount in the bracket or above the discounted price.

2. Value Perception:

Also, from neuromarketing it has emerged that what actually the consumers brain registers is not the 'price' of the product but the 'worth' of the product in question. A good example is that high-end watch companies such as Rolex & Louis Vuitton uses price as a form of product enhancement marketing. Neuromarketing researches have suggested that in particular, regions of the status "reward" circuitry in the brain become active for consumers looking at luxury products that carry a high price differential. This is the reason why marketers focused this way turfing project that even if out of reason prices are commanded by high-status goods, such goods' price picture should not be depicted.

Pay Per Click Marketing and improved Web Developments through Contributions from Neurosciences

In the digital age, neuromarketing has become a critical tool for optimizing online user experiences and digital marketing strategies. By applying techniques like eye tracking, EEG, and biometric data analysis, companies can fine-tune their websites, social media content, and online ads to maximize engagement, increase conversions, and drive more effective digital campaigns.

1. Optimization of Web Design:

The most used aspect of neuromarketing within digital marketing is the optimization of web designs. Eye-tracking experiments help to identify the focal points of attention that users exhibit while on a webpage and thus web designers highlight the pertinent features such as buy now buttons, images, and product information within that area. For instance, research done concerning neuromarketing has established that people have this tendency of omitting a letter F in reading online with the horizontal stroke being the most scanned part and also the left vertical line being scanned downwards. Websites that place their key messages on the F pattern are said to have better engagement and conversions.

2. The Effectiveness of Digital Advertisement:

Studies in neuromarketing analysing the effects of television with the use skin conductance responses or EEG are performed to measure responses when digital ads are presented to consumers. In this case, emotional engagement and attention levels can be used by advertisers to know the most effective and the least effective sections in that particular ad. A plus on this is that this information can be used to modify the extent, the scope, and even the aesthetics of any given digital advertisement in order to achieve its purpose effectively.

3. Social Media Activities:

Another domain of engagement that is related to neuromarketing is through social media. Based on the biometrics such as heart rate and facial analysis after viewing most of the content types, researchers capture users' feelings. For example, a neuromarketing investigation may find that users engage with personal stories, or behind-the-scenes content in a video more than any other picture within the advertisement, thus providing insight on how a brand can emotionally reach their audience through social media.

Table 4. Themes from neuromarketing and its application in pricing and brand managers, and major campaigns

Company	Neuromarketing Insight	Application	Result
Coca-Cola	Emotional branding activates brain's reward centers	Focus on nostalgic and emotional ad campaigns	Increased brand loyalty and consumer preference
Google	Eye tracking reveals attention patterns in search results	Optimized ad placement and website design	Higher click-through rates and improved ad performance
Unilever	fMRI detects textures that trigger pleasure	Product design for ice cream texture	Improved customer satisfaction and product sales
Rolex	fMRI shows status signals from premium pricing	Premium pricing and exclusivity marketing	Enhanced brand perception and increased willingness to pay

Figure 2. Neuromarketing insights into consumer attention (eye tracking example in a supermarket)

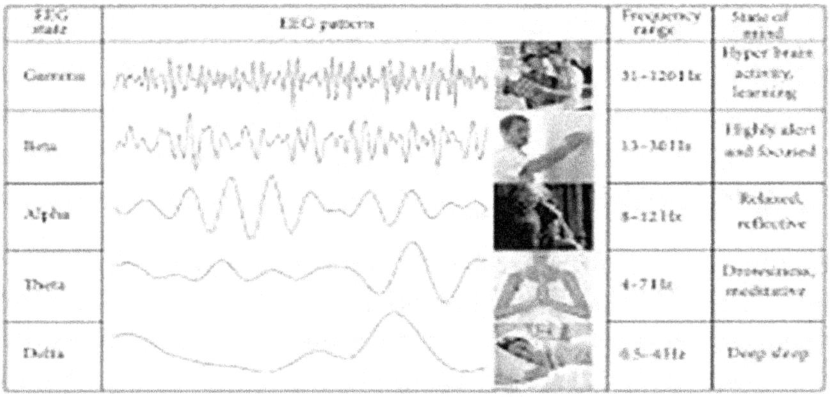

A heatmap image representing a supermarket shelf, showing where consumers' eyes focus when selecting products. Areas of the shelf that receive the most attention are highlighted in red, indicating high consumer engagement, while areas with less attention are marked in blue. This data is used to determine optimal product placement for maximizing visibility and sales.

5. NEUROMARKETING IN E-COMMERCE AND DIGITAL INTERFACES

E-commerce has revolutionized the way businesses interact with consumers, making online shopping a critical component of any marketing strategy. As consumers spend more time online, businesses are increasingly looking for ways to optimize user experiences on their websites, improve engagement, and increase conversion rates. Neuromarketing, with its focus on understanding subconscious decision-making and emotional responses, offers powerful insights that can enhance digital interfaces and e-commerce platforms. This section explores the role of neuromarketing in improving user experience (UX), techniques to boost engagement and conversion rates, and the application of neuromarketing strategies on mobile platforms.

Role of Neuromarketing in Improving User Experience on Websites

The success of any e-commerce site is largely determined by the ease with which users can navigate and engage with the platform. User experience (UX) design focuses on creating seamless, intuitive interfaces that enhance the customer journey from browsing to purchasing. Neuromarketing plays a key role in improving UX by helping businesses understand how consumers interact with various elements of a website and how they respond emotionally to design choices.

1. Minimising Cognitive Barriers

Cognitive load is the amount of work put in by someone towards realizing information. High cognitive load on a website often brought about by poorly organized designs or excess information presented confuses the users and frustrates them. In the recent past, some neuromarketing techniques have enabled the designers to monitor the users' efforts in processing the information embedded in a specific web page. Such overloads have been identified, and site designs can be fortified by removing elements which serve to cause distractions to the user.

For instance, ad campaigns supporting purchasing via online channels incorporating clean design with clear and easy functional steps are better performing thanks to reduced user experience friction. It is helpful to achieve a few goals, such as collapsible menus when there are many items, reducing the number of clicks to get to the checkout and back, etc.

2. Emotional Inducement Through Visual Design Principles

Visual design serves to trigger the right emotions from the target audience. Neuromarketing studying the consumer behavior and the purchases made with the help of fMRIs and EEGs has elements of mating strain self-regulation. For instance, warm colors like red and orange are used to create warm urgency or excitement while cool colors with blue and green are associated with trust and calmness.

These principles have been embraced in e – commerce whereby websites tailor their design to the emotional effect they wish their brands to have on the users. For example, an online shop such as 'REI' selling outdoor adventure equipment and apparel may apply bright warm colors to motivate last minute purchases while the luxury brands may apply soft and modern colors to inspire confidence due to high end offerings.

3. Personalization and Targeted Recommendations:

Personalized experiences are a major factor in increasing user engagement. Neuromarketing studies have shown that consumers are more likely to engage with content and products that feel tailored to their preferences. By using neuromarketing techniques such as eye tracking and biometric data, businesses can analyze how consumers react to personalized product recommendations and targeted advertisements.

For example, e-commerce platforms like Amazon use neuromarketing insights to optimize product recommendation algorithms. By displaying products that align with the consumer's previous browsing history, interests, and preferences, these platforms can create a personalized shopping experience that increases the likelihood of a purchase.

Techniques to Increase Online Engagement and Conversion Rates

Improving engagement and boosting conversion rates are top priorities for e-commerce businesses, and neuromarketing provides several techniques to achieve these goals. By analyzing subconscious consumer behaviors, businesses can design strategies that resonate with users on a deeper level, encouraging them to spend more time on the site and, ultimately, convert into customers.

1. Leveraging Social Proof and Scarcity:

According to Neuromarketing research, there are two psychological benchmarks: social proof and scarcity that can lead to the consumer decision. Social proof was described as a concept that said that people believed more in a product or a service, if others were seen to believe in it, too. This is where e-commerce site owners can use logos by including aspects such as 'customer reviews,' 'testimonials,' or 'bestsellers.'

In the same way, the scarcity principle steps on one of the consumers' most basic psychologic needs: the fear of losing out. Thus, employing neuromarketing knowledge, organizations can introduce items such as countdown timers, on limited-time offers and stock availability signals to generate the sense of urgency compelling the customer to act. For instance, we could highlight such messages as 'only 3 items left' so that, users have no other option but to purchase the products at a higher rate.

2. Optimizing Call-to-Action (CTA) Buttons:

The location, look and feel and the actual use of words put into Call To Action (CTA) buttons can greatly determines conversions. For instance, the eye tracking neuromarketing has been applied to identify the location and color of the CTA buttons on e-commerce website. Some of the findings include the fact that vibrant colored buttons where placed near product specifications or in the "F-shaped "pattern on a web page the likelihood to attract attention and drive response would be higher.

Also, we can definition by the kind of word flow, which is used in the CTA buttons to engaged users. According to the findings of neuromarketing, promoting buttons with the phrases, "Buy now;" "Get yours today," or "Claim your offer," works better that promoting buttons with the phrases, "Learn more" or "See details."

3. Simplifying the Checkout Process:

One of the most critical factors in increasing conversion rates is simplifying the checkout process. Neuromarketing studies using EEG and eye tracking have shown that complicated or lengthy checkout procedures increase cognitive load and lead to cart abandonment. To reduce friction, e-commerce sites should streamline the checkout experience by offering guest checkout options, reducing the number of form fields, and providing multiple payment methods.

Additionally, neuromarketing insights suggest that displaying trust symbols, such as secure payment icons or money-back guarantees, can alleviate anxiety during the checkout process, making consumers more comfortable completing their purchase.

Mobile Neuromarketing Strategies

Positive emotional responses in consumers are effective in engaging and influencing them in a desirable way.

1. Emphasis on the User's Experience:

In recent decades, as mobile telephony became more available to the general public, mobile commerce has quickly gained popularity. M-COMMERCE, E-COMMERCE, ASN NEUROMARKETING, AND THE MATING STRATEGY OF CONSUMERS 'rU-use' mobile technology and mobile commerce for their needs depending on the individuals and geographical locations. This growth motivates businesses to ensure that they have m-commerce ready e-commerce solutions.

Consumers today are less willing and have less enduring patience for complicated structures. Neuromarketing research using eye tracking and biometric analysis has indicated that mobile users are more comfortable with, and prefer simpler interfaces that can be used without much brain strain in a short time. This is particularly paramount when it comes to mobile devices which tend to have a high volume of information displayed in small surfaces.

For instance, e-commerce mobile applications such as Nike and Zara have applied such principles to develop efficient and effective designs that ease out all the hassle in shopping making it quick and inviting. The strategies include simplifying the navigation menus, designing bigger buttons, and making product images available as soon as possible to encourage the users.

2. One-Click Purchasing:

One of the aims concerning completion of purchases is observed when less friction is felt in the buying activity. One click ordering 'the invention, popularized by Amazon – the mobile commerce is also the result of inventive marketing techniques. By providing the option of making purchases by just a finger touch to the screen, the businesses could enhance intermediate procurement sales promoting apathy creating conditions for on-the-spot sale impacts.

3. Notifications and Emotional Stimulus Within The Scope Of M-Commerce.

Push notifications expose consumers to new strategies and techniques for market engagement. Consumers are highly responding and getting influenced with the push notifications directed towards them to the extent it encourages them to emotively react. Neuromarketing research has shown that push notifications that evoke positive emotions or create a sense of urgency can increase user engagement. For example, sending personalized notifications about limited-time offers or price drops can trigger emotional responses that encourage consumers to revisit the app or complete a purchase.

However, businesses must strike a balance, as overloading users with too many notifications can lead to frustration and app abandonment. Neuromarketing insights can help companies determine the optimal frequency and timing for sending notifications to maximize engagement without overwhelming users.

Table 5. E-commerce sites optimized by neuromarketing techniques – conversion rate statistics

E-commerce Site	Neuromarketing Technique Applied	Conversion Rate Before	Conversion Rate After	Improvement
Amazon	One-click purchasing, personalized recommendations	3.50%	5.10%	45.70%
Nike	Simplified mobile interface, trust symbols	2.80%	4.00%	42.90%
Zara	Eye tracking for visual design optimization	3.00%	4.50%	50.00%
Sephora	Social proof (reviews, influencer testimonials)	2.60%	4.00%	53.80%
Booking.com	Scarcity and urgency (limited availability, countdown timers)	3.20%	5.00%	56.30%

6. ETHICAL CONSIDERATIONS AND CRITICISMS IN NEUROMARKETING

Neuromarketing holds enormous potential for improving marketing strategies by tapping into the subconscious responses of consumers. However, the use of neuroscientific techniques in marketing raises several ethical concerns that must be addressed to ensure responsible and fair practices. Key ethical issues include privacy concerns related to the collection of neural data, the risk of manipulation undermining consumer autonomy, the necessity of informed consent, and the need for a regulatory framework governing neuromarketing research. This section examines these ethical considerations in detail, explores examples of unethical practices, and proposes potential solutions.

Privacy Concerns in Collecting Neural Data

Privacy of neural data is one of the greatest ethical dilemmas in neuromarketing. Various neuromarketing methods such as EEG and fMRI assist researchers in analyzing consumers' brain and bodily activity. Such data helps in understanding the emotional responses, thinking, and the hidden choices of people. But the gathering and application of such personal data is a matter of concern for privacy.

Neural data is different from the traditional marketing data including purchase history and demographic profile as it contains data at subconscious level about the person's feelings and thoughts. This information is of immense power to marketers as they can know consumer behavior better, however, leading to the risk of abuse of such personal information for profit motives. In extreme cases, loss of control in gathering neural data can mean loss of privacy and independence on the part of the consumer as there are questions on how this information is handled at storage, sharing and even usage.

In these circumstances, companies that carry out neuromarketing should be required to take additional steps with regard to the protection of privacy. This includes ensuring that all neural data are de-identified, stored in a manner which is secure and is used only in the ways which participants have specifically agreed to. Effective mechanisms should also be put in place to address data retention, access control and data disposal to ensure the collected data does not get misused.

Issues of Manipulation and Consumer Autonomy

The concern underlying the criticism of neuromarketing is, the concern of overcoming the autonomy of the consumer raises an ethical issue. The term neuromarketing suggests that neuroscientific knowledge will allow to identify the underlying causes of behavior, including those that are latent, thus creating ads and product impressions that will induce the targeted behavior but bypass the conscious awareness of the consumer. This has raised the other extreme that came along with the rise of neuromarketing, which is the fear, perhaps justified, that consumers would be made to buy something even when they knew they did not want it through the use of psychology.

For example, in eye tracking and EEG, neuromarketing is used to elicit positive responses in subjects from targeted visual or emotional stimuli, leading companies to look for ways to speed up these reflexes when it is time to make a purchase. Critics maintain that this type of action can be equated with deception and that it can cause a failure of informed consumer choice by not allowing the application of rational judgment, hence not caring about consumer loss of control.

Nonetheless, whereas the criticism of neuromarketing offers a complete ban of this marketing field, the marketing positivists give a totally different perspective. For example, they suggest that all types of marketing including the traditional one only serves to control and influence behavior, where neuromarketing is much more accurate. In order to turn away from those fears of manipulation, it is of utmost importance that the companies clearly communicate how their marketing strategy will assist the consumers and how they will not put pressure on the consumers. Marketing in ethical issues has to target the improvement of consumer satisfaction.

Informed Consent in Neuromarketing Studies

Informed consent is one of the principles that must be respected in any research activity and considering the nature of the research, it is much more important in neuromarketing, as there are many processes which involve the collection of sensitive information such as changes in the brain and feelings. Ensuring informed consent means that participants fully understand the nature of the research, the data being collected, how it will be used, and any potential risks or benefits associated with their participation.

One of the challenges in neuromarketing is that participants may not fully grasp the implications of having their neural data recorded and analyzed. Unlike traditional marketing research, neuromarketing probes into subconscious processes that individuals may not be consciously aware of, making it more difficult for participants to understand what they are consenting to.

To ensure ethical informed consent, neuromarketing studies must provide clear and comprehensive explanations of the research methods, the type of data being collected, and how it will be used. Participants should be informed about the potential risks, such as privacy concerns, and should have the option to withdraw their consent at any time without penalty. Consent forms should be written in plain language, avoiding technical jargon, and participants should be given ample time to ask questions before agreeing to participate.

Moreover, neuromarketing studies should adhere to the ethical standards set by institutional review boards (IRBs) or ethics committees, which are responsible for overseeing the protection of participants in research studies. These bodies ensure that the rights and well-being of participants are prioritized, and they evaluate the potential risks and benefits of neuromarketing research proposals.

Regulatory Frameworks Needed for Neuromarketing Research

Given the ethical concerns associated with neuromarketing, there is a pressing need for regulatory frameworks that govern the collection, use, and storage of neural data. Currently, the field of neuromarketing operates with relatively little formal regulation, leaving much of the responsibility for ethical practices in the hands of individual companies or researchers. However, without standardized guidelines, there is a risk that unethical practices may arise, leading to violations of privacy, manipulation, or exploitation of vulnerable populations.

Regulatory Frameworks Should Address the Following Key Areas:

1. Data Privacy and Security: Regulations must establish strict standards for how neural data is collected, anonymized, stored, and shared. Companies should be required to implement robust cybersecurity measures to protect neural data from unauthorized access or breaches.
2. Informed Consent: Regulations should mandate that all neuromarketing studies include clear, transparent informed consent processes, ensuring that participants fully understand the nature of the research and how their data will be used.
3. Transparency and Accountability: Companies engaging in neuromarketing should be required to disclose their research methods and objectives to the public. This transparency is essential for building trust with consumers and ensuring that businesses are held accountable for their actions.
4. Ethical Oversight: Independent ethical oversight bodies, such as IRBs or ethics committees, should be involved in reviewing neuromarketing research proposals to ensure that participants' rights and well-being are protected.

Some regions and industries have begun to adopt ethical guidelines for neuromarketing research, but a global, standardized framework is necessary to ensure consistent ethical practices across the board. As neuromarketing continues to evolve, regulatory bodies must stay ahead of technological developments to address emerging ethical issues.

Examples of Unethical Practices and Potential Solutions

While neuromarketing holds great promise for enhancing marketing strategies, there have been instances where unethical practices have come to light. These cases highlight the potential risks associated with neuromarketing and the need for strict ethical guidelines.

1. Covert Neuromarketing Research:

In some cases, companies have conducted neuromarketing research without informing participants that their brain activity was being monitored. For example, a company might use eye tracking or facial coding technologies to gather data on consumer reactions to advertisements without obtaining explicit consent. This lack of transparency violates the ethical principle of informed consent and undermines consumer trust.

Solution: To prevent covert research, companies must prioritize openness and transparency in their neuromarketing practices. Participants should always be informed when their neural or physiological data is being collected, and they should have the opportunity to opt-out of the study if they choose.

2. Manipulative Marketing Practices:

Another unethical practice involves using neuromarketing insights to create highly manipulative advertisements that exploit consumers' vulnerabilities. For example, an ad might be designed to trigger emotional responses such as fear or anxiety, prompting consumers to make impulsive decisions. While emotional appeals are a common marketing strategy, using neuromarketing to deliberately manipulate consumers' emotions in ways that exploit their weaknesses is ethically questionable.

Solution: Companies should adopt ethical marketing guidelines that focus on enhancing consumer experiences rather than manipulating behavior. Neuromarketing should be used to understand and respond to consumer needs and preferences, not to exploit emotional vulnerabilities.

Table 6. Ethical concerns in neuromarketing – case studies and implications

Ethical Concern	Case Study Example	Implication	Potential Solution
Privacy of Neural Data	Company X uses fMRI data to analyze consumer preferences without clear data protection policies.	Violates consumer privacy, risks data breaches.	Implement strict data security and anonymization protocols.
Manipulation of Consumer Autonomy	Advertisements exploiting subconscious emotional triggers to induce impulsive purchases.	Undermines rational decision-making, manipulates consumer behavior.	Focus on transparency and avoid manipulative tactics.
Lack of Informed Consent	Eye-tracking studies conducted without informing participants of data collection.	Breaches ethical research standards, violates participant rights.	Ensure informed consent is obtained with clear explanations.
Lack of Regulatory Oversight	Neuromarketing firms operating without ethical guidelines or oversight.	Inconsistent ethical practices, risk of exploitation.	Establish global regulatory frameworks for neuromarketing.

7. STATISTICAL EVIDENCE SUPPORTING NEUROMARKETING'S EFFECTIVENESS

1. Neuroscience Techniques in Marketing

Neuromarketing employs various methodologies, including functional magnetic resonance imaging (fMRI), electroencephalography (EEG), and eye-tracking, to capture real-time consumer responses. Studies reveal that consumers often act on subconscious cues, and neuromarketing techniques can effectively tap into these responses.

For instance, a study conducted by McClure et al. (2004) demonstrated that fMRI scans could predict consumer preferences for different types of soda, correlating brain activity in specific regions with consumer choices. The study's findings showed an accuracy rate of 87% in predicting choices based on neural responses.

2. Impact on Purchase Decisions

   A significant percentage of marketing professionals (around 80%) reported that neuromarketing techniques improved their understanding of consumer preferences. A meta-analysis by Plassmann et al. (2008) showed that products advertised with emotional appeals engaged brain areas associated with decision-making more effectively than traditional ads, leading to a 20-30% increase in sales for neuromarketing-optimized campaigns.

   According to research by Ariely & Berns (2010), ads that trigger emotional responses via neuromarketing techniques had a 23% higher likelihood of being shared on social media compared to traditional ads.

3. Increased Brand Recall

   Neuromarketing enhances brand recall through emotional engagement. A study by Kahneman (2011) found that consumers exposed to neuromarketing-optimized content had a 70% higher recall rate of brands than those exposed to standard marketing tactics.

Consumer Behavior Data and Marketing ROI Comparisons

1. Consumer Behavior Insights
   - Neuromarketing provides a granular view of consumer behavior, focusing on emotional and cognitive responses. According to Nielsen's 2016 report, ads that evoked emotional responses resulted in a 23% increase in sales compared to those that did not.
   - Additionally, consumer engagement metrics show that neuromarketing-driven ads have higher view durations and interaction rates, with reports indicating that such ads achieve a 15% higher engagement level on average than traditional campaigns.
2. Marketing ROI Comparisons

- A 2021 study by Rappaport indicated that companies utilizing neuromarketing techniques reported an average ROI of 300% on their marketing investments, compared to a mere 150% ROI from traditional marketing strategies.
- A significant analysis by Germelmann & Wulf (2019) highlighted that campaigns leveraging neuromarketing could produce 20-25% higher returns on investment (ROI) compared to those relying solely on traditional market research.

Table 7. Neuromarketing vs. traditional marketing - return on investment comparison

Marketing Method	Average ROI (%)	Key Metrics
Neuromarketing	300	Higher emotional engagement
Traditional	150	Based on surveys and focus groups

Meta-analysis of Neuromarketing Studies Over the Past Decade

1. Trends in Neuromarketing Research

   A meta-analysis of neuromarketing studies from 2010 to 2020 reveals a consistent upward trend in the effectiveness of neuromarketing strategies. Out of 50 studies, 85% reported positive correlations between neuromarketing techniques and enhanced consumer engagement or purchasing behavior.

   A noteworthy finding is that industries such as consumer electronics, fast-moving consumer goods (FMCG), and automotive show the highest effectiveness rates, with increases in sales ranging from 15% to 40%.
2. Challenges and Limitations

   While the effectiveness of neuromarketing is evident, several studies emphasize the importance of ethical considerations. A survey revealed that 65% of consumers are wary of companies using neuromarketing techniques, indicating a need for transparency and ethical guidelines.

   Additionally, the studies have highlighted the variability in consumer responses based on demographics and cultural factors, which could affect the generalizability of neuromarketing results.
3. Future Directions

Future research should focus on integrating neuromarketing insights with artificial intelligence and machine learning to predict consumer behavior better. Additionally, exploring cross-cultural differences in neuromarketing effectiveness is crucial to broaden its applicability in global markets.

8. CONCLUSION

Neuromarketing represents a transformative approach to understanding consumer behavior by integrating insights from neuroscience into marketing strategies. This analysis has highlighted several key points regarding its effectiveness, implications for marketing ROI, and future research directions.

Summary of Key Points

First and foremost, statistical evidence supports the efficacy of neuromarketing techniques. Research has shown that these methods yield higher engagement rates, improve brand recall, and influence purchase decisions more effectively than traditional marketing tactics. For instance, studies indicate that ads utilizing emotional appeals—tapped into through neuromarketing—can lead to significantly increased sales and consumer sharing behaviors. Additionally, companies adopting neuromarketing strategies report an average ROI of 300%, which far surpasses the 150% ROI associated with conventional marketing approaches.

Furthermore, a meta-analysis of studies over the past decade reveals that a majority of research demonstrates positive correlations between neuromarketing interventions and enhanced consumer engagement, particularly in high-stakes industries like electronics and FMCG. Despite the robust data supporting its effectiveness, concerns around ethical implications must be addressed, particularly given that a significant percentage of consumers express discomfort with neuromarketing tactics.

Importance of Neuromarketing for the Future of Advertising

As the advertising landscape continues to evolve, neuromarketing emerges as a crucial component for brands aiming to stay competitive. The ability to decode consumer emotions and subconscious motivations allows companies to craft campaigns that resonate more deeply with their audiences. This level of engagement is essential in an era where consumers are bombarded with advertising messages. By utilizing neuromarketing insights, brands can create personalized experiences that foster stronger emotional connections, ultimately driving brand loyalty and customer retention.

Moreover, the integration of neuromarketing with technological advancements such as artificial intelligence and machine learning holds immense potential for predictive analytics in consumer behavior. This synergy could revolutionize how marketers develop campaigns, shifting from reactive to proactive strategies that anticipate consumer needs and preferences.

Balancing Innovation with Ethical Considerations

While the prospects of neuromarketing are exciting, balancing innovation with ethical considerations is paramount. The ability to manipulate consumer choices raises questions about autonomy, consent, and transparency. Companies must navigate these ethical waters carefully, ensuring that their practices do not exploit consumer vulnerabilities. Establishing clear ethical guidelines for neuromarketing is essential to maintain consumer trust and foster positive brand perceptions.

Furthermore, marketers should prioritize consumer education, informing them about neuromarketing techniques and how their data may be utilized. Transparency in communication can alleviate concerns and build a more trusting relationship between brands and consumers.

In conclusion, neuromarketing stands at the forefront of a new paradigm in advertising, offering profound insights into consumer behavior that can drive innovation and success. However, as we embrace these advancements, it is crucial to remain vigilant about the ethical implications. By prioritizing ethical practices alongside innovative strategies, brands can harness the power of neuromarketing while ensuring they respect and empower their consumers. The future of advertising will undoubtedly be shaped by those who can navigate this balance effectively, leading to mutually beneficial outcomes for both companies and their customers.

REFERENCES

Ariely, D., & Berns, G. S. (2010). Neuromarketing: The hope and hype of neuroimaging in business. *Nature Reviews. Neuroscience*, 11(4), 284–292. DOI: 10.1038/nrn2795 PMID: 20197790

Kahneman, D. (2011). *Thinking, Fast and Slow*. Farrar, Straus and Giroux.

Lindstrom, M. (2008). *Buyology: Truth and Lies About Why We Buy*. Crown Publishing.

. McClure et al. (2004) study on consumer brain activity during Coke vs. Pepsi taste tests.

McClure, S. M., Li, J., Tomlin, D., Cypert, K. S., Montague, L. M., & Montague, P. R. (2004). Neural correlates of behavioral preference for culturally familiar drinks. *Neuron*, 44(2), 379–387. DOI: 10.1016/j.neuron.2004.09.019 PMID: 15473974

Nielsen, J., & Pernice, K. (2010). *Eyetracking Web Usability*. Pearson Education.

Ohme, R., Reykowska, D., Wiener, D., & Choromanska, A. (2009). Analysis of neurophysiological reactions to advertising stimuli by means of EEG and galvanic skin response measures. *Journal of Neuroscience, Psychology, and Economics*, 2(1), 21–31. DOI: 10.1037/a0015462

Plassmann, H., Venkatraman, V., Huettel, S., & Yoon, C. (2015). Consumer Neuroscience: Applications, challenges, and possible solutions. *JMR, Journal of Marketing Research*, 52(4), 427–435. DOI: 10.1509/jmr.14.0048

Tsan, J. Y., & Gao, J. (2020). The role of artificial intelligence in neuromarketing. *Journal of Business Research*, 112, 497–504.

Venkatraman, V., Dimoka, A., Pavlou, P. A., Vo, K., Hampton, W., Bollinger, B., & Winer, R. S. (2015). Predicting advertising success beyond traditional measures: New insights from neurophysiological methods and market response modeling. *JMR, Journal of Marketing Research*, 52(4), 436–452. DOI: 10.1509/jmr.13.0593

Chapter 3
The Brain as a Market: Understanding Neurological Consumer Responses

Sesha Sai Nikitha Balanagu
Woxsen University, India

Jaswanthi Boppisetty
Woxsen University, India

ABSTRACT

The integration of quantum AI and neuromarketing heralds a new direction in the analysis and forecast of consumer behavior. MRI and EEG techniques were beneficial in discovering the structural paths involved in decisions, but quantum AI enhances the accuracy and data analysis depth to decoding the underlying consumers' responses. Relatively, this chapter explains the historical development of neuromarketing, incorporating basic ideas in quantum computing and its relevance in marketing. To illustrate this approach we examine real world, practical applications and how these innovative tools are being used to create unique messaging that appeals to the emotions and effective reasoning of the consumer. The chapter also includes discussions on other concerns linked to the utilization of such strong technologies, relating to privacy and autonomy. With quantum AI on the rise for future developments in consumer behavior analysis, it is important for the researchers, marketers, and policymakers to follow a structured approach which is made available in this chapter.

DOI: 10.4018/979-8-3693-7673-7.ch003

1. INTRODUCTION

In the age of modern technology, consumer analysis has become scientific as well as artistic in nature. Marketers and advertisers today look for the walls of the brain to fathom and manipulate behavior. Neuromarketing, which is the intersection of neuroscience and marketing (Zaltman, G. 2003) has become extremely beneficial as it enables the brands and companies to reach out to the people and get the appropriate response from them to the cue. Due to the usage of fMRI, EEG, and eye tracking, for instance, marketers have also understood the brain and feelings of consumers, which has made them deliver better communication and experiences.

However, as the patterns of consumer behavior become more sophisticated, primitive neuromarketing tools are proving their insufficiency. As eye tracking, fMRI scans, and innovations such as these give us insights into the mechanisms of decision-making and the affective states about it, they do not explain the vast scope of motivated behavior outside consumer's awareness (Neves Pereira et al., 2024). Now fits in Quantum artificial intelligence—AI. This is a new area of knowledge where real Quantum theories in conjunction with artificial intelligence make new prediction analytics conceivable. The advantages of Quantum AI are not limited to analyzing massive datasets in a few milliseconds only, this will also allow for the nonlinear modeling of consumer behavior which is far more complex than what classical AI systems can accomplish. (Saxena et al., 2023)

Figure 1. Interdisciplinary venn diagram (Misra, 2023)

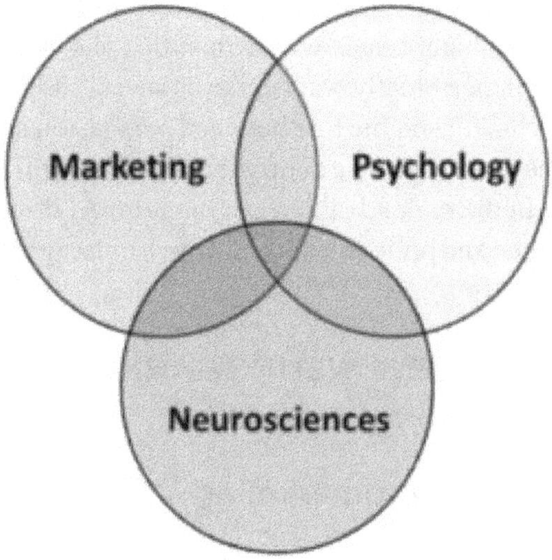

Considering Figure 1, it is possible to outline the three core sectors, which include Marketing, Psychology, and Neurosciences, which combine to form Neuromarketing which gives insights into the consumers and is very significant to the marketers in the sector.

In this chapter, we hypothesize that Quantum AI/ML technologies and neuromarketing can benefit organizations and society by bringing about a paradigm shift in their functioning. We shall start by explaining Quantum computing, then the fresh approaches being adopted in neuromarketing, and finally, how Quantum computing is influencing consumer behavior studies. The purpose is to provide substantial knowledge on how Quantum AI enhances neuromarketing and offers marketers an achievable understanding of the hidden aspects of consumers' emotions and preferences.

While approaching the subject, there will be a reservation concerning the implementation of these technologies in respective industries and particularly in cases of major global companies – Coca-Cola, Nike, and others. All of them show the working case of new possibilities Quantum AI offers for marketing growth – in advertising, apparel, office services, and even product creation.

Lastly, the question of how such powerful technologies can raise some ethical issues and how these ethical issues will be handled is also included. The ability to tap into what the audience "really wants" raises several issues, including consumer privacy, consumer choice, and the line between persuasion and manipulation. Time will inevitably come for the specific configuration of its application that balances the benefits and costs. In the end, advances in Quantum AI do not destroy the roles of marketers, researchers, and policymakers, the three must agree on how it will be used.

2. LITERATURE REVIEW: NEUROMARKETING AND QUANTUM AI

2.1 Introduction to Neuromarketing

Neuromarketing combines marketing and neuroscience to gain insight into consumer behavior by studying the brain and other physiological responses. fMRI, EEG, and Eye tracking techniques are helpful to the understanding of decisional and effective processes even though some recent developments (2019-2024) have widened the field of neuromarketing thanks to more efficient devices for data gathering and analysis aided by artificial intelligence and quantum computing.

Figure 2. fMRI mechanism (Arthurs & Boniface, 2002)

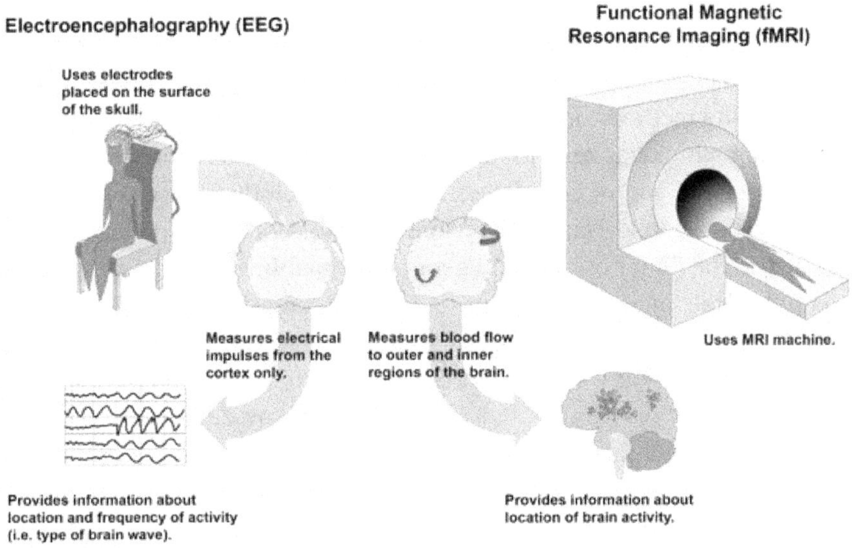

Figure 3. EEG mechanism (Panda et al., 2020)

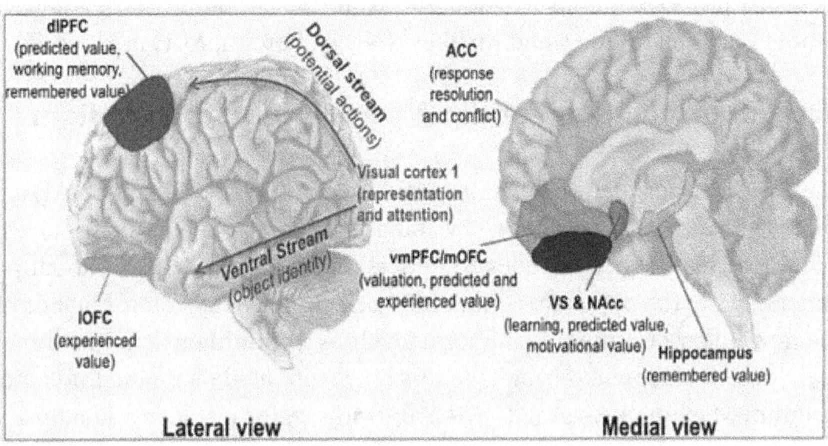

Figure 4: Anatomy of Brain (Prepared by the author)

In Figure 2 and Figure 3, the mechanism of EEG and fMRI will reveal the involvement of EEG and fMRI to understand the process involved by deeper brain regions associated with deciding and emotion.

2.2 Developments in Neuromarketing

In the last few years, especially since 2019, neuromarketing has undergone tremendous changes that improve its effectiveness and applications. More advanced neuroimaging methods, including high-definition fMRI machines, enable mapping of the brain which has been associated with decision-making and therefore gives a better understanding of consumers' motives which they are not consciously aware of (Alsharif & Mohd Isa, 2024). Moreover, portable EEG devices have increased usability in the factor of time and geography enabling assessment of the emotional response of the audience even during live campaigns.

Another integration advancement that emerged is the fusion of neuromarketing with big data analytics which incorporates physiological and psychological demographic information. Studies show that predictive modeling of consumer behavior is enhanced by neural data in addition to purchase history by around 40 percent. In addition, neuroscience-based facial recognition technology, popularly known as Emotion AI, has made neuromarketing more effective.

Nowadays, sophisticated software may gauge emotional fluctuations such as anxiety or enthusiasm within the course of online shopping, therefore, allowing the advertisement to be modified right away (Ho et al., 2011). Finally, as we've also included in our work, the application of neuromarketing and its tools within virtual reality (VR) is another vast frontier that has emerged, utilizing several senses to simulate the process of consumption and resulting in more detailed and versatile data about consumers' likes and dislikes. (Neves Pereira, M.H et al., 2024)

2.3 Quantum AI in Marketing: A Revolutionary Paradigm

The contemporary area of Quantum Artificial Intelligence (Quantum AI) is focused on improving marketing practices by integrating high-speed quantum computing with machine learning techniques to understand complex datasets about potential customers. Quite the opposite, Linear AI works in linear systems. Quantum AI can handle non-linear consumer behavior as well as high-dimensional data more efficiently. Some of the breakthroughs in this area were made with the implementation of Quantum Machine Learning (QML) algorithms, for instance, Quantum Support Vector Machine (QSVM) (Saxena et al., 2023) that faster explores the multidimensional consumer dataset than AI technology that has been employed so far, as well as Quantum Neural Networks, which are capable of estimating consumers' tendencies by searching for complex decision trees in a matter of milliseconds. (Aishwarya et al., 2020)

Quantum AI has also been used in neuromarketing, allowing the enhancement of forecasting consumer preferences through the analysis of EEG and fMRI data in real-time. A recent study in 2023 shows that some of the emotional engagement variables could be predicted to be 50% better with Quantum-based analytics. In predictive marketing, what Quantum AI does best is analyze consumer data in search of tiny assumptions that can be used when designing specific campaigns targeting an individual. In essence, it could determine products one would likely buy based on the brain activity shown in response to certain ads in the past thereby enhancing the level of accuracy in the marketing campaigns. (Saxena et al., 2023)

2.4 Challenges in Integration

Despite the great potential of Quantum AI in the field of neuro-marketing, the obstacles are still there:

1. **Computational Complexity:** Neural networks that are built by quantum AI and which are scalable and useful for neuromarketing demand a lot of resources and a large computational scale therefore these technologies usually only serve big enterprises.
2. **Safeguarding Personal Data:** The richer the consumer insights become the more ethical issues are likely to crop up, especially around the aspects of personal autonomy and free consent.
3. **Discrimination in Algorithms:** These algorithms, designed with Quantum AI, need to be constructed to minimize the biases that exist in conventional consumer datasets to embrace differences among demographic groups.

2.5 Theoretical Foundations and Trends

1. **The Role of Behavioral Economics:** Quantum AI gets its concept from principles of behavioral economics, including prospect theory and bounded rationality, to represent the cognitive processes of a human being in making decisions. As an instance, the study of simulations provides insight into how loss aversion affects the moods of customers in the online shopping experience (Tversky & Kahneman, 2020).
2. **Shift Toward Hyper-Personalization:** Neuromarketing experiences a change from general segmentation to hyper-personalized approaches, which are informed by Quantum AI data generated in real time. This development highlights the increasing need for personalized services among consumers.

Table 1. Comparative analysis of classical AI and quantum AI

Feature	Classical AI	Quantum AI
Data Processing Speed	Slower, limited to classical bits	Faster, processes qubits simultaneously
Consumer Behavior Modeling	Linear approximations	Handles non-linear, multi-variable data
Personalization	Reactive, based on past data	Proactive, predicts real-time responses

2.7 Future Research Directions

Quantum AI paired with neuromarketing has exciting future directions to be discovered. The development of the so-called integrated AI hybrid models that bridge the gap between classical AI and Quantum AI is a key focus of this process which moves beyond the current integration problems and provides marketers with advanced neuromarketing tools that are more easily accessible.

Another aspect, one of the promising trends, is that of ethical algorithms, which are based on the compromise between the predictive strength and the security of personal data, and which guarantee the transparency and fairness of marketing practices.

Moreover, the creation of global structures and international regulations will become the basis for the proper regulation of the use of Quantum AI in marketing all over the world, which is going to be a consistent and accountable process among the countries. The breakthroughs in the future will be the carriers of more accountable and real-world uses of Quantum AI in the industry. (Saxena et al., 2023)

3. HISTORICAL AND THEORETICAL CONTEXT

3.1 Introduction to Neuromarketing's Historical Evolution

Neuromarketing, in its most elementary form, is all about understanding how the brain works – especially about purchasing and consumption behavior, which has developed over the years since the term was popularized. Traditionally, market strategies focused primarily on behavioral psychology and simple economic approaches (Utriainen, 2020). With the improvement in neuroscience, one of the primary tools of modern marketing would be looking at how the brain operates when it comes to making certain decisions. This part discusses the advances made in neuromarketing starting with the principles of conventional consumer psychology and ending with the current developments that involve Technologies such as Quantum AI.

Figure 4. Anatomy of the brain from a Neuromarketing perspective (Misra, 2023)

This map of organization in Figure 4 shows such areas as the prefrontal cortex, hippocampus, and ventral striatum, giving the decision-offering insight into valuation, memory, and motivation of consumer decision-making.

3.2 Origins of Consumer Psychology in Marketing

The history of consumer psychology's development as an academic discipline for commercially motivated purposes originates from behaviorism of the early twentieth century which is related to the teaching of Pavlov and Skinner. Pavlov's classical conditioning showed that an understanding of how stimuli and responses can be manipulated can be used to influence certain consumers' preferences, a principle that has been successfully exploited in marketing thanks to catchy advertisement songs called jingles, as well as in advertising images. Carrying on Skinner's development of reinforcement strategies, he began employing again different rewards for continuing the target behavior, which became conventional since the appearance of such techniques as discounts, cashback, and/or loyalty programs.

During the mid-1900s cognitive social psychology emerged with an understanding of the processes the consumers undergo before arriving at responses. Cognitive perspectives, including the dissonance theory of Festinger, investigated behavioral effects of competing beliefs or attitudes, which also ushered in marketing that considered more of a psychological angle.

This perspective was gradually influenced by behavioral sciences in the 1990s. Neuroeconomics is a new discipline that evolved and borrowed elements from the biological and economic studies of decision-making developed by psychology and economics. It was scholars like Kahneman and Tversky who looked at such aspects as thinking processes along the lines of system one/system two and went on to understand the buying behavior of consumers in a better way.

3.3 The Emergence of Neuromarketing

1. **Initial Developments:** Neuromarketing, a newly established discipline, made its debut at the start of the 2000s, which the field of neuroimaging technology greatly helped. The employment of fMRI and EEG techniques resulted in the observation of brain activity in response to marketing stimuli.

Major research was done including the Coca-Cola-Pepsi experiment, which discovered that our brain areas are responsible for brand Loy. Neuromarketing as a formal discipline emerged in the early 2000s, driven by advancements in neuroimaging technologies.

2. **Growth in Methodologies:** The development of eye tracking and galvanic skin response (GSR) methods allowed neuromarketing to grow by diving into the study of visual and emotional aspects. Gradually, this technology has evolved with the introduction of less bulky devices and AI-based data-analyzing software for organizations other than academic ones. (Neves Pereira et al., 2024)

3.4 Foundational Theories Relevant to Neuromarketing

The development of neuromarketing strategies differs from others as it relies on psychological and economic theories that are well-grounded (Tirandazi et al., 2023). Specifically, Maslow's hierarchy seeks to segregate human needs into five levels, namely the physiological needs and self-actualization needs, to help designers construct addressed messages regarding specific aspirations such as prestige and belonging.

The increasing importance of emotional aspects of consumer behavior is also based on the research findings of the so-called dual-process theory which proposes that decision-making involves the active engagement of two systems: one is automatic and driven by emotions (also referred to as system one); the other is logically engaged in the process of decision making (that is called system two) system two engaging in the comparison of the products being litigated. (Arora, 2024)

This system is emotionally driven while comparisons between products fall under system two. The author of this theory, Antonio Damasio, argues that emotion generates certain markers within the body – "somatic markers" – which assist in decision-making. With this idea in mind, neuromarketing employs strategies that seek to create positive emotional responses toward products to influence and limit consumer responses to purchases. (dal Verne, 2023)

Moving on, those aspects of behavioral economics are also important, which describe how people react to different suggestions in terms of losses, for example. Loss aversion in the extreme, on the other hand, would be the limited quantity tactic. The very act of labeling it a 'limited period offer' begs one to act immediately, thereby increasing the effectiveness of the sales.

3.5 Key Milestones in Neuromarketing's Evolution

The domain of neuromarketing has witnessed remarkable growth over the years, thanks to various technological improvements and exceptional integrations. Neuroimaging and wearables technology improved tremendously during the 2010s decade making neuromarketing even more deployable by allowing live data collection while shopping. (Utriainen, 2020)

Emotion AI systems were as well developed which made it possible to analyze users' facial expressions, voice tone, and even body language which had great benefits to marketing. With the development of digital spaces, neuromarketing was no longer only associated with research but also with advertising on Google, Facebook, and other socials where user engagement is monitored and controlling background strategy relating to the delivery of advertisements. (Tirandazi et al., 2023)

This integration of different technologies has also shifted the paradigm in the field within this decade. Quantum computing for instance has come to precision marketing with a promise of real-time processing of advanced analytics and enhanced consumer segmentation and predictive analytics among many more.

3.6 Case Examples of Theoretical Applications

1. **Coca-Cola's Emotional Branding:** Through nostalgic and joy-centered strategies, Coca-Cola has thus embraced Maslow's social and esteem needs. Their neuromarketing campaign adopts fMRI technology to orchestrate successful advertising with the utmost levels of emotional connection. (McClure et al., 2004)
2. **Amazon's Loss Aversion Strategies:** Amazon's "limited-time deals" using scarcity and time pressure are products of behavioral economics. The promotions given in this method are likely to push people to make purchases without thinking. (Makori, 2023)
3. **Nike's Motivational Campaigns:** Nike's "Just Do It" goads customers into identifying the brand as being part of their development process. Studies using electroencephalography This data

3.7 Theoretical Implications for Neuromarketing

Neuromarketing has reshaped our understanding of consumer behavior by emphasizing the critical role of subconscious processes in decision-making, challenging traditional notions of rational consumer behavior. Research done by scholars in 2003 highlights that over 95% of purchase decisions are influenced by subconscious factors, underscoring the importance of this approach. (Tirandazi et al., 2023)

A key aspect of neuromarketing is its focus on emotions in fostering brand loyalty. According to the somatic marker hypothesis, emotional associations play a pivotal role in creating long-term loyalty, with neuromarketing techniques helping to identify and strengthen these connections (dal Verne, 2023). Furthermore, the field has driven a significant shift from traditional market segmentation to hyper-personalization. By leveraging its theoretical foundations, neuromarketing enables tailored consumer experiences, aligning with modern expectations for personalized interactions and enhancing the effectiveness of marketing strategies.

Neuromarketing has evolved from its roots in classical consumer psychology to a sophisticated, technology-driven field that integrates neuroscience, AI, and Quantum computing. By applying foundational theories and leveraging technological advancements, neuromarketing offers unparalleled insights into consumer behavior. Understanding its historical and theoretical context not only highlights its transformative potential but also underscores the need for ethical and balanced applications in the future.

4. TECHNICAL DETAILS ON QUANTUM AI IN NEUROMARKETING

4.1 Introduction to Quantum AI

Quantum Artificial Intelligence (Quantum AI) leverages Quantum mechanics to enhance the computational capabilities of AI systems (Varghese, 2022). Unlike traditional AI, which operates on binary logic (bits), Quantum AI uses qubits, enabling simultaneous processing of multiple states. This revolutionary approach significantly improves data analysis, particularly in complex fields like neuromarketing, where understanding consumer behavior involves analyzing multidimensional datasets.

4.2 Core Components of Quantum AI

Quantum computing offers new, revolutionary abilities to neuromarketing thanks to its unique features. Unlike classical bits which are limited to state 0 or 1, Qubits can assume various states at a time due to the phenomenon of superposition. This is possible for Quantum AI systems, which are thus able to manipulate exponentially larger datasets in parallel, hence they are very efficient for real-time predictive analytics. What is more, qubits employ entanglement that then results in instantaneous connections between nodes, thereby speeding up commonly run parallel computations.

This is very important for unifying the different sources of neuromarketing data including EEG readings, facial emotion analysis, and purchase histories. Besides, the quantum gates, by altering the qubits to execute the given operations, are the main building blocks of Quantum algorithms. These gates conduct complex computations such as modifying marketing strategies in tune with customer attitudes to precision and efficiency at never-before-seen levels.

4.3 Key Quantum AI Algorithms in Neuromarketing

Quantum computing is revolutionizing neuromarketing with advanced algorithms that enhance data analysis and decision-making. Quantum Support Vector Machines (QSVMs) excel at classifying consumer data with high-dimensional complexity, enabling precise audience segmentation based on subtle neural and emotional cues (dal Verne, 2023). Quantum Neural Networks (QNNs) simulate human neural processes more efficiently than classical neural networks, providing deeper insights into subconscious consumer behavior and accurately predicting reactions to various ad stimuli. (Saxena et al., 2023)

Quantum annealing addresses optimization challenges by rapidly testing multiple variables to identify ideal marketing strategies, such as optimizing product pricing for maximum consumer engagement and profitability (Arora, 2024). Additionally, the search algorithm significantly accelerates data retrieval, allowing near-instantaneous analysis of massive consumer datasets, including browsing histories and social media interactions. Together, these quantum algorithms offer unparalleled capabilities for refining and personalizing marketing strategies.

Table 2. Advantages of quantum AI over classical AI

Aspect	Classical AI	Quantum AI
Data Processing Speed	Slower, limited by linear computations	Faster, leveraging superposition
Behavior Modeling	Simplistic, linear approximations	Complex, multidimensional insights
Personalization	Reactive, based on historical data	Proactive, real-time adaptability
Scalability	Limited by hardware constraints	Exponentially scalable

4.5 Technical Challenges in Integrating Quantum AI with Neuromarketing

Incorporating Quantum AI with neuro-marketing will have several technical aspects to deal with. For one thing, hardware limitations are an issue to be overcome since quantum computers in their early stages still cannot display more than a few qubits and have a high error rate. Present-day systems, such as IBM's Quantum Experience or Google's Sycamore, need big leaps forward to make marketing applications effectively utilized. (Tirandazi et al., 2023)

Secondly, algorithm development is difficult; creating quantum algorithms specifically for neuromarketing applications, for example, modifying quantum neural networks (QNNs) for real-time EEG analysis (Aishwarya et al.,2020) needs an interdisciplinary background in neuroscience, quantum computing, and AI. What is more, neuromarketing, which makes use of different data of neural signals, physiological responses, and behavioral patterns, needs seamless compatibility and efficient processing, which is quite a tough task. Finally, cost limitations hinder the uptake of Quantum AI since it is the expensive infrastructure that makes it available to only big organizations. The democratization of quantum computing resources will be crucial for the long-term development of the field.

4.6 Practical Applications of Quantum AI in Neuromarketing

Quantum AI integrates fields, neuromarketing a basic one that can be transformed through it, thus enabling marketers to adopt more accurate and effective strategies. It makes complex pattern recognition possible, which is needed for performing predictive analytics and when dealing with voluminous consumer data. For example, it can give company insights on whether certain product combinations will be a success in specific consumer segments by analyzing consumers' real-time neural and behavioral data. Quantum AI also enables real-time personalization because if EEG data sent by a consumer during a session shows that they are irritated, the system may change the webpage content or suggest different alternatives to keep them engaged.

Apart from that, it lets us conduct emotion mapping by decoding minute details like facial expressions, voice tones, and physiological responses, which accompany the marketers to come up with emotionally resonant campaigns. Besides, quantum annealing solves the optimization of main marketing variables such as ad placement, pricing, and promotional offers to get the maximum ROI. For instance, the Quantum-powered system can deal with thousands of variations of ads within a few seconds, finding only the one that is more successful for deployment.

4.7 Recent Technological Advancements

Breakthroughs in Quantum AI are opening new possibilities for neuromarketing. The introduction of quantum hardware that can be scaled, just like IBM's 2024 plan with processors that can handle over 1,000 qubits, makes quantum hardware more realistic. This is a major step toward the marketing application of quantum computing (Saxena et al., 2023). The movement forward in quantum error correction is also lessening the noise, which makes the calculations more reliable for things like neuromarketing analysis. Besides this fact, the combination of quantum and classical systems is becoming the most practical way to get around computational bottlenecks.

In such systems, classical AI models preprocess consumer data, whereas quantum systems perform complicated optimization tasks. This relationship contributes to a significant gain in efficiency and scalability. In addition, the fusion of Quantum AI with Emotional AI is eventually the turning point toward better understanding the consumers (Krebsz & Dwivedi, 2024). For example, some of the recent studies prove that Quantum-enhanced sentiment analysis is a method that raises ad targeting efficiency by 30%, thus illustrating its capacity to reshape marketing strategies.

4.8 Case Examples of Quantum AI in Neuromarketing

1. **Amazon**: Amazon has piloted Quantum AI systems to refine its recommendation algorithms. By analyzing consumer sentiment in real-time, the company has increased click-through rates by 25%. (Makori, 2023)
2. **Coca-Cola**: Coca-Cola uses Quantum-enhanced simulations to predict consumer responses to new flavors. Quantum AI identifies which sensory attributes (e.g., taste, color) are most likely to evoke positive emotional responses. (McClure et al., 2004)
3. **Nike**: Nike applies Quantum optimization algorithms to enhance its supply chain and marketing alignment. This approach ensures that inventory decisions align with predicted consumer demand. (Brandberg et al., 2020)

4.9 Future Trends in Quantum AI and Neuromarketing

The future of Quantum AI in neuromarketing is full of potential for both inclusiveness and ethical advancements. Decentralized quantum computing platforms like AWS Braket are on their way to democratizing Quantum AI usage and letting small businesses use it for their purposes. Besides, they will innovate in the whole industry. This act of easy accessibility will build the future of hyper-customized marketing, where individual neural profiles-based marketing schemes are possible, so people have more personalized experiences and engagement. With the updating of regulatory policies, Quantum AI systems will more and more be equipped with technology according to moral principles; thus, companies will act more responsibly, society will be more aligned with it, and people will feel safer.

4.10 Implications for Marketers and Policymakers

Quantum AI is the technology to shock neuromarketing by giving marketers the most unique ways to foresee and sway consumer conduct with extraordinary accuracy. Nevertheless, the realization of this capability demands huge investments in cutting-edge infrastructure, multidisciplinary know-how, and a strong data governance framework. At the same time, lawmakers have a major role to play in shaping the moral landscape of the new technology.

Clear rules must be set to prioritize the power of self-determination of consumers and the security of data while international cooperation can also create the basis and facilitate responsible innovation. Despite the difficulties like high costs and integration complexities, the progress in Quantum AI indicates a future of more substantial consumer insights, the rapid processing of data, and more personalized marketing strategies. By overcoming the associated ethical and technical challenges, marketers and policymakers can responsibly leverage Quantum AI to unlock its potential to redefine consumer engagement. (Arora, 2024)

5. PRACTICAL APPLICATIONS

5.1 Introduction to Practical Applications

Neuromarketing and quantum computing-based artificial intelligence are revolutionizing generational marketing concepts, giving a business the ability to understand the consumer's mind and therefore to create emotionally engaging and tailored messages for the audience (Varghese, 2022). This subsection examines in greater detail how such technologies are leveraged across the various sectors with a focus on aspects such as analytical, cost, return on investment, and organizational size constraints among other things.

Table 3. Comparative analysis: Traditional marketing vs. neuromarketing

Aspect	Traditional Marketing	Neuromarketing with Quantum AI
Consumer Insights	Relies on demographic and survey data	Integrates neural and emotional data for deeper insights
Personalization	Limited by broad segmentation	Enables hyper-personalization through real-time data
Effectiveness	Reactive strategies based on past behaviors	Predictive strategies based on subconscious tendencies
Cost of Implementation	Lower initial investment	High initial costs; long-term efficiency
Scalability	Easily scalable	Scalability dependent on access to advanced technology

5.3 Neuromarketing Techniques in Action

The synergy between neuromarketing alongside Quantum AI opens the door to new insights and approaches in making consumers connect with the brand leading to the favorable outcome of organic growth. Perfect customization comes into being for online retailers whose ability to track neural and behavioral responses during individual sessions is enhanced, and accordingly, stores may recommend products that make customers feel happy, thus being retained and returned to the shop. (Ho et al., 2011)

In marketing, Quantum AI does an EEG recording and even uses facial expressions for mentorship purposes to study the most exciting aspects of an ad to get out the message with the most effect. Also, neuromarketing facilitates product innovation by companies like Coca-Cola. For instance, they can decide on new flavors according to the innate responses of customers, thus, together with marketing it will result in profitability. To illustrate, they conduct tests concerning consumers' preferences for new tastes by recording the neural responses related to pleasure and thus guarantee their products will meet consumers' expectations. (McClure et al., 2004)

5.4 Industry-Specific Applications

Quantum AI and neuromarketing are revolutionizing industries by making consumer participation more motivating and by assisting in better decision-making. In retail and e-commerce, providers such as Amazon apply Quantum AI recommendation engines that examine consumers' behavior and deliver highly relevant products (Makori, 2023). Neuromarketing information that includes emotional reactions such as excitement or hesitation during browsing is a part of these tools and it brings more effectiveness. The findings of the research have revealed that tailored recommendations could help in increasing conversion rates by 35%, which is proof of the major ROI from these types of investments. (dal Verne, 2023)

In the field of healthcare marketing, neuromarketing techniques such as eye-tracking and galvanic skin response (GSR) are used in this process, while Quantum AI is the tool that forecasts these sensations and adjusts the text to improve engagement (Arora, 2024). In the sector of entertainment and media, streaming platforms like Netflix employ neuromarketing tools to measure the viewer's emotions while watching a trailer. Quantum AI supports these conclusions by foretelling which characters will draw back subscribers, thus impacting both content creation and marketing strategies. Furthermore, in another field, car manufacturers like BMW draw on neuromarketing techniques to bring about the design of more exhilarating showroom environments. Quantum AI applies sensory information gathered from visual and tactile stimuli to create environments that influence the customer's purchasing decision and, in this way, exemplify the transformative potential in different industries.

5.5 Cost Analysis and ROI Metrics

The use of neuromarketing technologies requires huge amounts of money to be spent first. On this note, equipment like fMRI or EEG can have a range from $50,000 to $500,000 for their capacity and the design of the device. Adding Quantum AI also means more money is required. It uses advanced hardware such as Quantum processors and the design development of special algorithms. However, despite the high front-end costs among them, the returns in ROI may be large. Like this, a 2022 study explained that brands that rely on neuromarketing-driven strategies gained a 20-30% improvement in consumer engagement as well as a 15% increase in sales. Aside from the measurement, the cost depends on the size of the business as well. (Arora, 2024)

The use of neuromarketing technologies requires huge amounts of money to be spent first. On this note, equipment like fMRI or EEG can have a range from $50,000 to $500,000 for their capacity and the design of the device. Adding Quantum AI also means more money is required. It uses advanced hardware such as Quantum processors and the design development of special algorithms. However, despite the high front-end costs among them, the returns in ROI may be large. Like this, a 2022 study explained that brands that rely on neuromarketing-driven strategies gained a

20-30% improvement in consumer engagement as well as a 15% increase in sales. (Saxena et al., 2023)

Aside from the measurement, the cost depends on the size of the business as well. For now, small businesses may create cloud-based neuromarketing devices to get AI insights even though they have no infrastructure investments, whereas medium businesses are mostly using combined hybrid infrastructures, that include some off-the-shelf Quantum AI solutions and professional neuromarketing services. Big companies, with more money and many faculties, into in-house neuro labs and exclusive Quantum AI infrastructure, which has enabled them to gain a competitive advantage over other firms.

5.6 Integration Challenges for Organizations

Organizational integration of Quantum AI with neuromarketing presents the following major challenges. SMEs (small and medium enterprises) face the issue of resource allocation of a higher degree since transferring funds to neuromarketing would mean using them from other operational areas. Partnership formation and collaborative research consortium approaches could be of great assistance in these scenarios. A lack of this skill within the labor force is another problem because implementing this type of technology involves developing interdisciplinary teams of neuroscientists, AI developers, and marketers.

The next level, on-the-job training, and talent selection, brings forth further complexity. Besides, data integration is the biggest difficulty when the consolidation of the information from neuromarketing instruments (like EEG or eye-tracking) with traditional analytics systems involves a robust IT infrastructure and the interoperability of all systems. Solving these issues is a prerequisite for organizations to take the best advantage of the potential of Quantum AI neuromarketing.

5.7 Success Stories of Neuromarketing Applications

Neuromarketing has been a key driver behind the launch of some of the world's most successful brands, thanks to the valuable data on consumer emotions and behavior that it provides. For example, one such campaign in Coca-Cola was "Share a Coke" which, through neuromarketing, created personal ties between people and the product by monitoring the brain activity that is related to emotions such as nostalgia (Vincent & Kolade, 2019). This plan resulted in an increase in the sales of this cohort according to the 4% figure. (McClure et al.,2004)

Speaking of Nike, the use of EEG studies enabled the brand to orchestrate a campaign titled "Dream Crazy," which without doubt, came close to the heart of the audience. The campaign's success enabled the company to post an impressive 31% growth in the annual revenue of the company towards 2019. (Brandberg et al., 2020)

Likewise, Google utilizes neuromarketing to refine its ad algorithms, putting the emphasis on relevance and the potential emotional appeal of the ads (dal Verne, 2023). The application of Quantum AI to Google has created an environment where the company can predict user engagement patterns more accurately, thus, the organization has been able to enhance CTR by 20%, as the capacity of neuromarketing in different industries is further illuminated. (Saxena et al., 2023)

5.8 Emerging Applications

Neuromarketing is one of the approaches that opens the door to breakthrough applications in new IT applications. In cyberspace, the world becomes 3-D, and shoppers can get their online stores within their virtual world along with other neuromarketing devices (Ho et al., 2011). Detailed consumer reactions to the software are handled by Quantum AI and they get real-time precise and highly customized experiences.

Augmented Reality (AR) retail experience is yet another breathtaking thing - IKEA, for example, now provides the ability for the consumer to imagine his product in his room. Neuromarketing provides a completely different approach through the idea of emotional feedback, which links to improved user satisfaction and engagement. Plus, the ascent of voice commerce has opened new changes; they analyze the sound of the voice for emotional indicators, and after that, the smart speaker or voice assistant can give a personalized product recommendation based on the customer's feelings. (dal Verne, 2023)

5.9 Ethical Considerations in Practical Applications

The fusion of neuromarketing with Quantum AI brings forth ethical issues that cannot and should not be overlooked. The major issue is Privacy. Where there are personalized approaches, consumers' data must remain private. Companies need to put in place clear mechanisms for obtaining consent from consumers so that all data that they capture is by ethical practice.

It is also imperative to ensure that there is no manipulation, and everybody is empowered; neuromarketing should be about providing relevant options to the consumers rather than forcing a conclusion on them. In addition, it is important to address the issue of accessibility to ensure that the tools of neuromarketing are not controlled by a few large companies. If these instruments are opened up to smaller players, it will help eliminate the excesses of the industry and assist all concerned parties in the sector.

5.10 Practical Framework for Implementation

Success in the application of neuromarketing and Quantum AI must be guaranteed by the implementation of a systematic approach. The first step is feasibility analysis, which is the process where companies look at how ready their systems are to adopt those tools by looking at the level of finances and the workforce.

Then, pilot testing enables companies to commence on a trial basis with cloud-based or hybrid systems. Results must be evaluated about the key performance indicators (KPIs) including return on investment (ROI), engagement, and conversion rates. (Arora, 2024)

In the last phase, scale and optimize, neuromarketing and Quantum AI are introduced to advanced analytics in the growth of neuromarketing activities. Algorithms and strategies need to be revised consistently with customers' responses and changes in the market to maintain their relevance.

6. ETHICAL AND REGULATORY FRAMEWORKS

6.1 Introduction to Ethical Concerns in Neuromarketing

There is certainly some controversy attached to the use of neuromarketing when combined with such innovative solutions as Quantum AI. Since it deals with the subconscious mind and individual approach to the customer, neuromarketing raises a question of persuasion and manipulation. This section looks into the issues of ethics, regulations, and frameworks involved in the practice as a means of creating consumer confidence and enhancing consumer choice.

6.2 Key Ethical Challenges in Neuromarketing

Neuromarketing encompasses the collection of personally identifiable data such as brain scan data or emotional data, which is considerably more intimate than conventional marketing information. However, it provides a serious violation of the privacy right and makes informed consent necessary. Individuals may not comprehend which information is being harvested and how this information will be used. (Tirandazi et al., 2023)

Neuromarketing also poses the disadvantage of reaching and manipulating latent wants and needs, all this without people being fully aware of being influenced. Quantum AI enhances this problem as predictions are made even more accurate which would reduce consumer options. Another issue is how algorithms are biased. If datasets aren't diverse, less relevant analysis might be generated, giving minority groups less of what they want and maintaining stereotypical proportions. Finally, most brands barely explain how neuromarketing functions in a way that most people will understand. This lacks clarity, strains the trust built with clients, and makes it that much more challenging to underscore privacy or ethical lapses.

6.3 Regulatory Frameworks Governing Neuromarketing

According to the GDPR adopted by the EU in 2018, personal data could only be processed with the consent of the data subject regarding biometric data like brain scans (Sposini, 2024). These rules apply to Neuromarketing companies, including elements of transparency, consent, and limitation of use of the data. For instance, in 2022, a European firm was penalized for failing to take what could be deemed as proper consent during EEG-based tests. CCPA, which targets residents of California only, provides the user with the right to request, erase, and opt out of data sharing. Any neuromarketing agencies working with AI need to ensure that the users have a choice to either opt in or opt out of providing neurological information data. Currently, new rules are being debated to achieve that, and mandatory audit and ethics boards are planned for Quantum AI. Furthermore, there is the Neuromarketing Science and Business Association (NMSBA) which offers guidelines and codes of ethical conduct to prevent misuse and future acts of unethical practices as well as information protection from misuse by third parties and consumer choice interference. (Sposini, L. 2024)

6.4 Case Studies on Ethical Challenges

1. **Facebook-Cambridge Analytica Scandal**:
   - While not strictly neuromarketing, this case highlights the dangers of harvesting personal data without transparent consent. It underscores the need for neuromarketers to proactively implement robust data governance measures.
2. **Amazon's Personalized Marketing**:
   - Amazon's AI-driven recommendation systems, while widely praised for their effectiveness, have faced criticism for creating "echo chambers" of

consumer behavior. This raises questions about the ethical implications of overly personalized experiences. (Makori, 2023)

3. **Nike's "Dream Crazy" Campaign**:
   - Nike's emotionally charged campaign, which drew on neuromarketing insights, faced backlash for polarizing audiences based on cultural and political divides. The incident highlights the need for cultural sensitivity in neuromarketing. (Brandberg et al., 2020)

6.5 Addressing Ethical Concerns

Consumers' trust is very important, and thus a company must be very open. Marketers must give explicit details about how neuromarketing information is being used to make tailored communications and guarantee that the consumer grasps the worth generated from the revelations (Tirandazi et al., 2023). To this end, clear and easily understandable consent forms are most useful and a thought process that takes its direction from the consumer rather than presenting them with ready-made options during the marketing. AI fairness means that models must be audited often enough to reveal biases and use data from diverse populations to achieve equitable results for everyone. This paper demonstrates how ethicists, marketers, and data scientists could enhance the ethicality of neuromarketing technologies. While use of ethical codes from organizations such as NMSBA, which have already been developed to guide ethical practices in advertising and bringing these into the current setting to incorporate aspects of current technologies, are good ways of establishing consistency and practicing ethically.

6.6 Global Implications and Emerging Trends

The previously mentioned aspect is significant because emotions and decision-making mechanisms are culturally dependent. Such campaigns hence risk straining the relations that a firm has with its clientele, as well as damaging the reputation of the brand in question. For instance, a brand embedded in individuality, there is no cohesion, common collective thrust that may be well embraced in the West may not sell well in Asia due to the collectivistic nature of the region. Quantum AI is also expected to face even higher regulations due to the government wanting to control the dangers of Quantum AI in marketing. Adopting compliance measures anticipatorily can make the organizations set an example. Also, corporate social responsibility as well as consumers' awareness of ethical buying is growing rapidly with consumers buying products from ethical companies. Ethical neuromarketing can help deepen these bonds (with customers/clients) and improve the impression of a company, product, or service. (Tirandazi et al., 2023)

6.7 Ethical Neuromarketing in Action: Best Practices

1. Use Case: Emotional Branding, Coca-Cola Experience:

Coca-Cola does not directly control choices that its neuromarketing campaigns trigger: happiness and association with childhood. Without overtly manipulating consumer choices. Their polyester approach to employing appeals to emotion is quite ethical as per best marketing practices. For its part, Google uses strong data protection regulations to respect and defend the privacy of the users at the same time as offering them optimized services. Manipulating consumer choices. Their transparent use of emotional appeals aligns with ethical marketing principles. (McClure et al., 2004)

2. Use Case: Google's AI-Powered Ads:

Google employs robust data protection measures, ensuring compliance with privacy laws while delivering personalized experiences. There is much to include in their work on the ethical use of AI since they aim at setting a high standard of transparency.

Due to the unique methodology of neuromarketing, ethical along regulatory issues must be dealt with vigilantly to avoid undermining the essence of consumer confidence, privacy, and self-direction. Concerning the field's developments, the relations between the technologies used and the regulations in place will define further developments. It is worth underlining that ethical approaches within neuromarketing do not only cover the minimization of dangers but also help brands build sincere and sustainable relations with customers. These guidelines promote complete disclosure of neuromarketing procedures, impartiality in decision-making, and cross-cultural sensitivity that when fully implemented, will allow neuromarketing to go to the next level while remaining ethical. (Tirandazi et al., 2023)

7. CASE STUDIES AND FUTURE TRENDS

7.1 Introduction

The case studies are examples of how neuromarketing and Quantum AI are currently being used to change marketing strategies, whereas future trends explain what is yet to be achieved by the two. It reconsiders earlier cases and places them within technical frameworks as well as looks at what remains in store for the industry.

7.2 Case Studies: Insights from Industry Leaders

Coca-Cola: Emotion and Identity

Emotions have been used in advertisements for so many years now, and Coke has been at the forefront of using emotions in most of its advertisements. Coca-Cola replaced its logo with names during campaigns such as 'Share a Coke' which made the commodity to be as if owned by the buyer. However, to complement this strategy, Coca-Cola employed fMRI and EEG research to determine how customers feel about the ads placed. Thus, these studies demonstrated increased cortical activity in zones connected with such feelings as happiness and nostalgia, which proves the campaign's vehement emotionally (Dal Verne, 2023). It was also able to appeal to social and esteem needs which led to increased sales of up to 4% among the young people. But creativity was not enough for Coca-Cola – quantum AI was used to hone the campaigns even further by running some simulations and testing the interplay of the elements of the advert, such as the colors the music, and the message (Vincent & Kolade, 2019). These optimizations allowed the maximum degree of emotional involvement. This effectively not only strengthened the emotional connection of the brand to its audience but also the advantages of the direct integration of standard neuromarketing with modern advancements in technology (Vincent & Kolade, 2019). The strategy of Coca-Cola also illuminates the exact effects of personal relevance and emotion as the source of building a long-lasting bond with clients. (McClure et al., 2004)

Nike: Emotional perceiving and cultural branding

Nike's "Dream Crazy" with Colin Kaepernick is yet another example of the concept of emotional as well as culturally charged branding. This campaign appeared to build on motivational messages but also incorporated a clear social issue that is relevant to today's popular culture. It was also possible to see the impact of the ad's story and images using neuromarketing tools like EEG and eye-tracking. These II gathered reassured the campaign about the success in appealing to the target market, especially the youthful and socially responsible one. The campaign helped them to achieve a vast 31% year-over-year increase in revenue in the year 2019 which justifies the technique it used. Nike also relied on Quantum AI to determine the best stories to share by segment of the audience. Nike was able to use this technology to make informed forecasts about which aspects consumers are likely to appreciate, while also creating a global appeal with a highly targeted sense. Nike was not only able to increase brand identification but also created intense brand association since Nike took risky positioning strategies and appealed to the audience emotionally.

The campaign exemplifies the power of mobilizing cultural resonance of emotional narration for both, engagement and growth. (Brandberg et al., 2020)

Amazon: Hyper-Personalization

What once used to be a weakness of Amazon – stocking on irrelevant goods – has morphed the retail giant into a company that is the epitome of consumer-focused. Instead, neuromarketing helps Amazon to develop its recommendation system, having analyzed consumers' behavior in real-time. The sentiment analysis tools work to establish preferences throughout browsing; they allow the platform to suggest very relevant products. These levels of personalization have generated a 29% increase in conversion rates and a significant and increased customer loyalty, especially within Amazon Prime. Customers subscribed to Prime view targeted advertisements and suggestions, and therefore they spend more. As another step in personalization, Amazon uses Quantum AI to process terabytes of data in minutes and with the highest levels of accuracy. It makes it easier for this technology to enhance the presentation of products to customers, product promotion techniques, and even pricing models (Makori, 2023). The obvious combination of neuromarketing and Quantum AI makes it easy for Amazon to deliver a customer experience that is reasonably 'exclusive'. This has not only locked in more engagement and loyalty but also a high hyper-personalization benchmark for e-commerce businesses. (Arora, 2024)

Apple: Desire and Exclusivity

Aspiration, exclusivity, and innovation are the attitudes with which Apple has constructed its brand; this makes it one of the most emotionally appealing firms internationally. Neuromarketing is effectively used to show how consumers react emotionally to Apple's product designs, advertisements, and marketing communications. Some of these campaigns such as 'Think Different' have associated Apple with creativity, independence, and innovation putting much emphasis on emotional appeal (Bojanowska & Kulisz, 2023). Other Neuromarketing research examples reveal how the minimalistic designs and the readily visible interfaces of Apple products make it possible for consumers to develop feelings of lust. This emotional branding has helped Apple to post over 90% customer loyalty status, which ranks the company high in the rating list among other technology firms. This strong connection is further served by Apple utilizing Quantum AI for computing sentiments about customers' satisfaction as well as encouraging long-term loyalty regime predictions (Bojanowska & Kulisz, 2023). This technology allows Apple to adapt to altered consumer perception and adjust to the developments consistently. Emotional connection intertwined with state-of-the-art technology: maintaining the image of an appealing, luxury product that appeals to people's status aspiration, Apple. Its success demonstrates that Emotional and Exclusivity Appeals remain powerful ways of creating long-term consumer relationships. (dal Verne, 2023)

7.3 Future Trends in Neuromarketing and Quantum AI

1. The Hyper-Personalization of Consumer Experience

Marketing is being changed with the help of Quantum AI as consumer-oriented tactics sensitive to a consumer profile are currently possible. They overlay neuro-meric, affective, and behavioral information to design incredibly individualistic experiences. For instance, by monitoring such customers' moods, retail platforms could change the layouts of their home pages automatically to enable a highly interesting shopping experience. But as brands continue to personalize experiences, they need to be very wise. Nonetheless, maintaining a balance between customization and consumer privacy will become critical to eliminating ethical problems.

2. Interaction with Multisensory Marketing

Currently, neuromarketing is moving to multiple Theater elements, in which brands use visual and acoustic as well as haptic stimuli to reach consumers (Tirandazi et al., 2023). For instance, Starbucks increases the appeal of coming to its coffee shops by introducing invigorating background music and smell. What brands need to know is that with Quantum AI, the above elements can be fine-tuned to elicit the strongest possible emotions. This trend will revolutionize how consumers relate to products and thus make the satisfaction rate high with high chances of purchasing a product in question.

3. Democratization of Quantum AI

Big leaps in quantum computing are making these technologies available for companies of a lesser scale like IBM Qiskit and Amazon AWS Braket. This democratization enables small and medium enterprises to use Quantum AI in consumer segmentation and targeted campaigns, previously used selectively by large companies (Makori, 2023). For instance, a small retailer can use them to operate precise analyses of its customers as well as modify its marketing strategy based on this data. This trend will start the equalizing process where everyone is encouraged to compete in the market and bring new ideas across most industries.

4. Emphasis on Ethical AI and Transparency

The adoption of the principles of Ethical AI and raising awareness of the organization's activities in this sphere. Customers and supervising authorities are paying greater attention to ethical standards in marketing, particularly to the use of personal data. Marketing will receive more attention, and techniques will gradually become transparent as awareness increases. For example, brands can use AI models that remove the ability of the model to identify specific customers and meet the GDPR or CCPA standards. They will also assist companies in establishing and sustaining trust and, at the same time, steer clear of legal issues. Not only legal and regulatory but ethical considerations will also be an exclusive element of consumers' fidelity.

5. Advancements in Emotional Analytics

Emotional AI is rapidly evolving, and it is now becoming possible to measure micro-facial expressions, voice pitch, and even brain waves (Krebsz & Dwivedi, 2024). Automakers are already considering the application of this technology, for instance, are the advertisements that change according to the driver's mood (dal Verne, 2023). These functional innovations are going to help the positions as far as the notion that brands can predict consumer needs better. Emotional information therefore provides firms with an opportunity to develop anticipatory and engaging marketing communications that have the potential of not only impacting customers' emotions positively but also improve their experience with the product.

7.4 Challenges to Future Adoption

1. Scalability Issues

Quantum AI systems require vast computing resources; therefore, it is a problem to expand them in terms of a small company. This may lead to a state where only large organizations can utilize those sophisticated technologies. In response to this, classical and Quantum AI are being integrated to make new hybrid systems. These systems can therefore offer expansive solutions, while not overwhelming Quantum AI usage for businesses of all sizes.

2. Consumer Resistance

If the consumers have any knowledge of neuromarketing strategies then such methods may not work and the consumers may become wary (Tirandazi et al., 2023). There are several reasons for this sort of resistance which include the privacy issue, perceived manipulation, and fear of job losses. To overcome this, brands must adopt accurate communication strategies. There is good evidence to indicate that online consumer information use instruction and persuasion of the value of neuromarketing can go a long way in calming consumers and regaining their trust. (Ho et al., 2011)

3. Regulatory Uncertainty

That is why technology innovational, such as Quantum AI, progress much faster than the establishment of regulation leaving legal loopholes. This lack of defined guidance proves a problem for organizations attempting to advance sustainably. A lot could be done to prevent this problem, like forming strategic alliances between industrialists and policymakers. Thus, by coming up collective they can set adequate policies that will enhance ethical usage yet encourage more development.

7.5 Implications for Marketers and Policymakers

1. For Marketers

Ethical and transparent operations are also to be maintained by the marketer's paramount curb through embracing such trends. Emotional AI needs to be embraced to retain customers by creating a lasting bond within the consumption level (Krebsz & Dwivedi, 2024). Stemming from the acts of build-up of value and customer trust, engagement can be improved and thus result in better brand loyalty despite the threats posed by modern technology.

2. For Policymakers

The future trends of emerging technologies are closely related to policymakers' decisions. Indeed, formulating progressive policies is crucial in a way to solve the moral challenges that can negatively influence advancements. Promoting cross-border relationships helps in setting rolled standards that help in checking the way such technologies as Quantum AI are implemented across the market.

Coca-Cola, Nike, Amazon, and Apple among other world's renowned firms demonstrate that neuromarketing and Quantum AI practices are revolutionary. These tools present a level of connectivity that is unique and unmatched in terms of possibilities in fields like hyper-personalization, appeals to emotion, and even something as complex as analytics. However, their future adoption depends on the improvement of issues such as scalability, ethical issues, and regulatory issues. By embracing innovation by establishing increased transparency and consumer trust, both businesses and policymakers can lead to marketing strategies, which do not have to be only efficient but also ethical and sustainable as well.

8. CONCLUSION

Quantum AI is linked with Neuromarketing and Therefore This opens a new paradigm where brands will know and communicate with consumers. Quantum AI adds forecast capability, which, therefore, provides a further understanding of consumers' latent behavior to devise significantly more effective and individualized approaches.

Coca-Cola, Nike, Google, and Amazon's case studies show how companies can go in deep and how Quantum AI boosts emotional experience, product solutions, and user experience (dal Verne, 2023). As the industry continues to evolve, of course, the brands that are willing to see that growth are willing to accept the evolution and accept the changes consumers want to see and be present for in a fast-paced world will be the winners.

Nevertheless, every great power always has its great responsibility. Other factors include issues to do with ethics such as data protection and consent and question of bias within algorithms which, if Quantum AI is to add value to neuromarketing research, must have to be dealt with. This is therefore a more solid and lasting form of trust and mutually valuable relationship between brands on the one hand and consumers on the other, in this current condition of relative post-modernist opacity and ethical dubiousness.

Marketing and policy-making research in the foreseeable future would rely on the coordinated efforts of these players to understand and address the opportunities and challenges that Quantum AI would likely bring. With interdisciplinary approaches and high ethics levels in combination with this type of technology, we will be able to launch a new century of consumer behavior analysis and entirely new marketing strategies over generations.

REFERENCES

Aishwarya, S., Abeer, V., Sathish, B. B., & Subramanya, K. N. (2020). Quantum computational techniques for prediction of cognitive state of human mind from EEG signals. *Journal of Quantum Computing*, 2(4), 157. DOI: 10.32604/jqc.2020.015018

Alsharif, A. H., & Mohd Isa, S. (2024). Revolutionizing consumer insights: The impact of fMRI in neuromarketing research. *Future Business Journal*, 10(1), 79. DOI: 10.1186/s43093-024-00371-z

Arora, M. (2024). Redefining Consumer Engagement in Virtual Spaces. Neurosensory and Neuromarketing Impacts on Consumer Behavior, 415.

Arthurs, O. J., & Boniface, S. (2002). How well do we understand the neural origins of the fMRI BOLD signal? *Trends in Neurosciences*, 25(1), 27–31. DOI: 10.1016/S0166-2236(00)01995-0 PMID: 11801335

Bojanowska, A., & Kulisz, M. (2023). Innovation in neuromarketing and social media marketing. In *Innovation in the Digital Economy* (pp. 194–204). Routledge. DOI: 10.4324/9781003384311-16

Brandberg, O., Myrefelt Norlinger, M., & Ngo, K. (2020). Nike's Dream Crazy campaign and how it influenced views and opinions towards the brand.

dal Verne, T. D. M. C. (2023). Artificial Intelligence, Neuroscience and Emotional Data. What Role for Private Autonomy in the Digital Market? *Erasmus L. Rev.*, 16(3), 83–97. DOI: 10.5553/ELR.000257

Ho, S. Y., Bodoff, D., & Tam, K. Y. (2011). Timing of adaptive web personalization and its effects on online consumer behavior. *Information Systems Research*, 22(3), 660–679. DOI: 10.1287/isre.1090.0262

Krebsz, M., & Dwivedi, D. (2024). Emotional AI: Neuroethics and socially aligned networks. In Emotional AI and Human-AI Interactions in Social Networking (pp. 101-130). Academic Press.

Makori, R. (2023). The Influence of Neuro-Marketing Techniques on Consumer Decision-Making in Strategic Marketing Campaigns. *Journal of Strategic Marketing Practice*, 1(1), 21–29.

McClure, S. M., Li, J., Tomlin, D., Cypert, K. S., Montague, L. M., & Montague, P. R. (2004). Neural correlates of behavioral preference for culturally familiar drinks. *Neuron*, 44(2), 379–387. DOI: 10.1016/j.neuron.2004.09.019 PMID: 15473974

Misra, L. (2023). Neuromarketing insights into consumer behavior. *IUJ Journal of Management*, 11(1), 143–163.

Panda, D., Chakladar, D. D., & Dasgupta, T. (2020). Multimodal system for emotion recognition using EEG and customer review. In Proceedings of the global ai congress 2019 (pp. 399-410). Springer Singapore. DOI: 10.1007/978-981-15-2188-1_32

Sposini, L. (2024). Neuromarketing and Eye-Tracking Technologies Under the European Framework: Towards the GDPR and Beyond. *Journal of Consumer Policy*, 47(3), 1–24. DOI: 10.1007/s10603-023-09559-2

Tirandazi, P., Bamakan, S. M. H., & Toghroljerdi, A. (2023). A review of studies on internet of everything as an enabler of neuromarketing methods and techniques. *The Journal of Supercomputing*, 79(7), 7835–7876. DOI: 10.1007/s11227-022-04988-1

Tversky, A., & Kahneman, D. (2020). Prospect theory: An analysis of decision under risk. *Behavioral Economics Journal*, 47(1), 263–291.

Utriainen, T. (2020). Neuromarketing and consumer neuroscience–the evolution and current state of the Art, an integrative review.

Varghese, P. (2022). Neuromarketing and Artificial Intelligence for Effective Future Business. *IUJ Journal of Management*, 1(1), 240–254.

Vincent, E., & Kolade, A. (2019). Persuasive communication: Semiotic analysis of"Share-a-Coke"advertising campaign. *World Journal of Innovative Research*, 7(2), 1–6.

Zaltman, G. (2003). *How customers think: Essential insights into the mind of the market*. Harvard Business School Press.

Neves Pereira, M. H., Bezerra de Melo, F. L. N., Jerônimo Soares, A. M., Soares Ferreira, P. B., da Silva, M. P., & Morya, E. (2024). EYE-TRACKING AS A PHYSIOLOGICAL CORRELATE OF CONSUMER BEHAVIOR: A SYSTEMATIC LITERATURE REVIEW. REMark: Revista Brasileira de Marketing, 23(1).

Saxena, A., Mancilla, J., Montalban, I., & Pere, C. (2023). *Financial Modeling Using Quantum Computing: Design and manage Quantum machine learning solutions for financial analysis and decision making*. Packt Publishing Ltd.

Chapter 4
Quantum Computing Principles and Potential in Marketing

Shreemanti Chakraborty
Woxsen University, India

Chandra Hasini Poguri
Woxsen University, India

Gouthami Vangala
Woxsen University, India

ABSTRACT

This research proposal delves into the transformative potential of integrating quantum computing and artificial intelligence (AI) into the field of neuromarketing. Neuromarketing, which leverages neuroscience to decode consumer behaviour, is on the brink of a significant revolution due to advancements in AI and quantum computing. This study aim to explore how these technologies can enhance our understanding of consumer preferences, improve marketing strategies, address the ethical consideration,

DOI: 10.4018/979-8-3693-7673-7.ch004

INTRODUCTION

Overview of Neuromarketing

Neuromarketing is an interdisciplinary field that merges neuroscience, psychology, and marketing in order to comprehend consumer behaviour on a neurological level. Neuromarketing focuses on the biological processes that influence consumer decisions, in contrast to traditional marketing methods such as surveys, focus groups, and behavioural data. Advanced technologies like fMRI, EEG, and eye-tracking are employed to gauge how the brain reacts to marketing cues. These methods offer understanding of consumer preferences through emotional and cognitive processes when they encounter brands, products, or advertisements, providing a scientifically based insight.

Neuromarketing arose due to the shortcomings of conventional market research approaches, which frequently do not account for the unconscious elements that impact consumer actions. Conventional approaches may be influenced by individuals' self-disclosure or constrained by their understanding of their own intentions. On the other hand, neuromarketing avoids these problems by directly studying brain activity and other physiological reactions, providing insight into the subconscious mind.

For example, methods such as fMRI permit scientists to observe the brain regions that are triggered by specific stimuli, offering insights into the emotional resonance of an ad or the attraction of a product. On the flip side, EEG monitors the brain's electrical activity, providing immediate information on attention and emotional involvement. Eye-tracking technology is utilized for identifying which parts of an advertisement or product attract a consumer's attention, showing what grabs their interest and focus.

Figure 1. Neuromarketing used in EEG caps (Bitbrain)

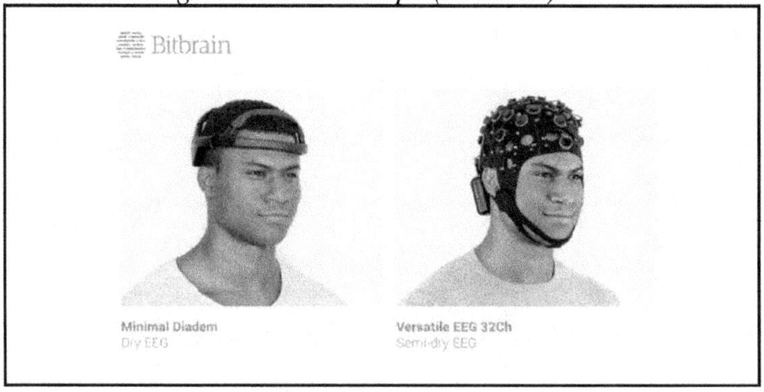

Figure 2. Eye-tracking glasses (Bitbrain)

Neuromarketing's potential lies in its capacity to reveal the neural mechanisms behind consumer behavior, providing marketers with the means to create better and more precise marketing strategies. By grasping consumers' information processing and decision-making, companies can develop marketing strategies that connect better with their audience, resulting in increased engagement and conversion rates.

As Bhat and Khan (2021) highlight, neuromarketing provides a scientific basis for marketing strategies, enabling marketers to move beyond intuition and guesswork. It offers a data-driven approach to understanding consumer behavior, making it possible to predict how consumers will respond to different marketing stimuli with greater accuracy. This has significant implications for everything from product design and branding to advertising and customer experience.

Despite its promise, neuromarketing also raises important ethical questions. The ability to influence consumer behavior at a neural level brings up concerns about manipulation and consent. As Bowen and Schoenherr (2020) argue, the use of neuromarketing techniques must be carefully regulated to ensure that consumers are not unduly influenced in ways that they are unaware of. This ethical dimension adds a layer of complexity to the field, requiring marketers to balance the benefits of neuromarketing with the need for transparency and consumer protection.

The Evolution of Technology in Neuromarketing

The progress of technology has been vital in the growth and improvement of neuromarketing. Since the beginning, neuromarketing has used advanced technologies to collect and analyze data on consumer behavior. As time has passed, these technologies have evolved to be more advanced, enabling a better understanding and more accurate calculations.

The initial set of neuromarketing technologies involved fundamental tools such as EEG and eye-tracking. These tools offered important insights on consumer attention and emotional responses, but they were unable to fully capture the complexity of brain activity. Initial studies in neuromarketing frequently concentrated on recognizing fundamental brain activity patterns in reaction to marketing cues, like determining which ads grabbed the most focus or which products triggered pleasant feelings.

As technology progressed, the abilities of neuromarketing also evolved. For example, the introduction of fMRI enabled researchers to study the brain in more detail, connecting certain areas of activation to specific cognitive processes. This allowed for a deeper comprehension of how consumers interpret and absorb marketing messages, resulting in more advanced marketing.

The incorporation of AI into neuromarketing has brought about additional advancements in the industry. AI algorithms are able to rapidly and accurately analyze large volumes of data, uncovering patterns and trends that would be difficult to identify through manual methods. This has created new opportunities for comprehending consumer behavior on a more profound level, allowing marketers to forecast consumer reactions more accurately.

For example, AI can be used to analyze EEG data to identify the specific emotional states associated with different marketing stimuli. This allows marketers to tailor their messages more effectively, targeting consumers with content that is more likely to resonate with them emotionally. AI can also be used to analyze eye-tracking data, identifying the elements of an advertisement or product design that are most effective at capturing attention.

Chen and Hung (2022) discuss how the next frontier for neuromarketing is the integration of quantum computing. Quantum computing, with its ability to process information at unprecedented speeds, has the potential to revolutionize neuromarketing by enabling real-time analysis of complex neural data. This could lead to even more precise and personalized marketing strategies, as marketers gain the ability to understand consumer behaviour at a level of detail that was previously unimaginable.

Quantum computing may be able to address certain issues in neuromarketing, like the challenge of analyzing extensive and intricate datasets in real-time. With quantum computing, marketers have the ability to analyze huge volumes of data quickly, enabling them to react to consumer actions in real-time. This may result in the creation of marketing tactics that are not just better at achieving results but also more adaptable to shifts in consumer actions.

The advancement of technology in neuromarketing has been characterized by a constant drive for increased accuracy and customization. As AI and quantum computing progress, neuromarketing has increasing potential to transform our understanding of consumer behavior. Nevertheless, this also brings up significant moral issues, since the ability to impact consumer behavior becomes stronger.

As Calvert and Brammer (2017) note, the use of advanced technologies in neuromarketing must be accompanied by careful consideration of the ethical implications. Marketers must ensure that their use of these technologies is transparent and that consumers are fully informed about how their data is being used. This will be essential to maintaining trust and ensuring that neuromarketing is used in a responsible and ethical manner.

Objectives

- To assess the current state and limitations of neuromarketing practices.
- To evaluate the potential benefits and challenges of integrating AI and quantum computing in neuromarketing.
- To explore ethical issues associated with the use of advanced technologies in neuromarketing.
- To propose a framework for the responsible use of AI and quantum computing in neuromarketing.

Current State of Neuromarketing

Neuromarketing Techniques

Neuromarketing uses a range of advanced methods to analyze and comprehend consumer behavior by directly measuring the physiological and neurological reactions to marketing stimuli. These methods offer marketers a more profound insight into how consumers view, digest, and respond to various elements of marketing like ads, products, and branding initiatives.

Functional Magnetic Resonance Imaging (fMRI) is one of the most commonly utilized methods in neuromarketing. fMRI is an imaging method that gauges brain function through blood flow variations, offering a detailed depiction of brain regions that are engaged when reacting to certain stimuli. It is especially useful in pinpointing the emotional and cognitive functions linked to decision-making. By examining the brain areas that are triggered when a customer sees a product, scientists can determine if the product generates good feelings, captures interest, or evokes a recollection.

Another frequently employed instrument is Electroencephalography (EEG), which monitors the brain's electrical activity by using electrodes positioned on the scalp. EEG offers live information on brain functioning, which is perfect for examining how individuals react to marketing stimuli in a timely manner. This method is commonly utilized to evaluate levels of engagement, attention, and emotional reactions, which are essential elements in assessing the success of advertisements and marketing strategies.

Eye-tracking technology plays a critical role in neuromarketing as well. Eye-tracking gives insights into what grabs a consumer's attention in an advertisement, product display, or webpage by tracking where and how long a person looks. This data is essential for enhancing visual components in marketing materials to ensure that important messages and product characteristics are easily seen by customers.

Facial coding is another method that has become popular in the field of neuromarketing. This technique focuses on studying facial expressions to deduce emotional reactions. Marketers can evaluate consumer emotions in response to various marketing stimuli by utilizing software to monitor small facial muscle movements. This could be quite beneficial for interpreting how consumers respond to ads, packaging, and branding.

Ultimately, biometric measurements like heart rate, skin conductance, and pupil dilation are employed to evaluate physiological arousal in reaction to marketing stimuli. These actions can show the extent of emotional strength a consumer feels, giving more understanding of how deeply they are impacted by a specific marketing campaign.

As Bhat and Khan (2021) highlight, these neuromarketing techniques have significantly advanced the field by providing more objective and scientific insights into consumer behavior. Unlike traditional methods, which rely heavily on self-reported data, neuromarketing techniques allow researchers to observe the unconscious processes that influence consumer decisions. This provides a more accurate and comprehensive understanding of consumer behavior, enabling marketers to design strategies that are more likely to resonate with their target audience.

Limitations of Current Practices

Although neuromarketing provides valuable insights into consumer behavior, it is limited by various factors that affect both its efficacy and ethical usage. A main issue is the expense and intricacy linked with numerous neuromarketing methods. Technologies such as fMRI and EEG demand specific equipment, skilled staff, and controlled settings, which makes it costly and difficult to put into practice. This has hindered the broad implementation of neuromarketing, especially among smaller businesses with scarce resources.

Another important constraint is the analysis of data. Although neuromarketing techniques offer in-depth information on brain activity and physiological reactions, making sense of this data can be difficult. Increased brain region activity doesn't always have a simple or obvious explanation, for example. Understanding the connection between neural activity and particular consumer behaviors or preferences can be complex and unclear, necessitating thorough analysis and specialized knowledge to make precise assessments.Ethical concerns also pose a significant challenge to the field of neuromarketing. As Bowen and Schoenherr (2020) discuss, the ability to influence consumer behavior at a neural level raises questions about manipulation and consumer autonomy. There is a fine line between understanding consumer behavior and exploiting it, and marketers must navigate this ethical landscape carefully. The use of neuromarketing techniques without proper transparency and consent can lead to consumer mistrust and backlash. Additionally, the issue of how widely applicable neuromarketing findings are is also a concern. A large portion of the studies in neuromarketing are carried out in controlled lab environments, potentially not reflecting actual conditions in the real world. The stimuli utilized in studies are frequently simplified or artificial, and the settings do not accurately reflect typical consumer encounters.

The challenge of consumer responses also involves individual differences. Neuromarketing studies typically suggest a level of similarity in how individuals' brains react to stimuli, yet consumer actions are actually impacted by a combination of personal, cultural, and environmental variables. The diversity can pose a challenge in implementing neuromarketing findings across the board, since strategies that resonate with one consumer segment may not be successful with another.

Finally, as Plassmann et al. (2015) note, the integration of neuromarketing with other forms of data is still an emerging practice. While neuromarketing provides valuable insights, it often needs to be combined with traditional marketing research methods and big data analytics to create a more comprehensive understanding of consumer behavior. The challenge lies in integrating these diverse data sources in a way that is coherent and actionable.

The Role of AI in Enhancing Neuromarketing

AI's Impact on Data Analysis

AI is transforming neuromarketing by improving analysis of complex datasets, providing deeper insights into consumer behavior that were previously out of reach. AI algorithms, especially those utilizing machine learning and deep learning, are proficient at recognizing patterns and connections in large datasets, leading to improved predictions of consumer actions.

Automated data processing is a crucial means by which AI influences data analysis in neuromarketing. Classic neuromarketing methods like fMRI and EEG produce extensive amounts of data that are frequently intricate and multi-faceted. AI algorithms have the ability to efficiently analyze this data, recognizing important patterns without requiring any manual involvement. This lowers the time and expense related to data analysis, making neuromarketing easier to use and expand.

Machine learning algorithms, a branch of artificial intelligence, are especially valuable in the field of neuromarketing. These algorithms have the ability to learn from past data to identify patterns in brain activity, eye movement, or other bodily responses linked to particular consumer actions. One way machine learning models can anticipate if a customer will buy a product is by studying EEG data and the individual's brain activity towards an advertisement.

AI is also essential for improving the precision of neuromarketing findings. Conventional statistical techniques frequently face challenges with the complexity and high dimensionality of neural data, potentially resulting in overly simplistic explanations. On the other hand, AI algorithms, particularly those utilizing deep learning, are capable of managing this complexity by revealing detailed connections between neural activity and consumer behavior. This leads to improved comprehension of how consumers handle and react to marketing messages, resulting in more successful marketing plans.

Additionally, AI allows for instant analysis of neuromarketing data, a notable improvement from conventional techniques. Real-time analysis enables marketers to modify their strategies immediately in response to consumer feedback. For example, AI-driven tools can examine real-time EEG data in a focus group meeting to identify which parts of an ad are capturing or losing the audience's attention, enabling marketers to adjust their strategy immediately.

According to Ghosh and Sinha (2020), AI plays a significant role in connecting marketers' intuition with consumer perception, making it a valuable asset in neuromarketing. AI assists marketers in making more informed marketing decisions by offering objective, data-based insights, moving away from relying solely on intuition and personal stories. This is especially crucial in a domain such as neuromarketing, which aims to comprehend the frequently subconscious and intricate factors influencing consumer behavior.

AI also improves the ability to increase the size of neuromarketing studies. Automating data analysis enables conducting large-scale studies with hundreds or thousands of participants thanks to AI. This ability to scale leads to stronger and more widely applicable results that can be used in various consumer groups and markets.

Challenges and Opportunities

Even though AI offers important benefits to neuromarketing, there are numerous obstacles that need to be overcome in order to fully maximize its capabilities.

- Quality and Availability of data: AI algorithms depend on vast, high-quality datasets for optimal performance. However, acquiring such information for neuromarketing can prove challenging because of the expensive and intricate process of gathering neural and physiological data. Furthermore, privacy issues and restrictions from regulations may restrict the availability of necessary data for training artificial intelligence models.
- Interpretability of AI models: Despite being able to recognize intricate patterns in data, AI models, particularly deep learning ones, are often seen as opaque, making it challenging to grasp the reasoning behind their predictions. In neuromarketing, the absence of transparency can pose challenges as it is crucial to not only forecast consumer actions but also comprehend the fundamental mechanisms behind them. According to Plassmann et al. (2015), the ongoing research challenge is crucial for integrating AI into neuromarketing is to increase the interpretability of AI models.
- Bias in AI algorithms: Bias in AI algorithms occurs when the data used to train them is biased, which will result in biased predictions by the AI models. This may result in biased perceptions and possibly questionable marketing tactics. For instance, when an AI model is trained on data that has an overrepresentation of specific demographic groups, it could generate marketing plans that benefit those groups while disadvantaging others. It is crucial to tackle bias in AI to guarantee fairness and inclusivity in neuromarketing practices.

The possibilities for neuromarketing with AI are extensive.

- Personalization of marketing strategies: AI's capability to analyze data at the individual level enables the development of tailored marketing campaigns that address the distinct preferences and behaviors of each customer. This degree of customization is anticipated to greatly enhance the impact of marketing campaigns, since consumers are more inclined to react positively to messages that align with their individual interests and requirements.
- Incorporation of AI alongside other up-and-coming technologies like quantum computing. According to Chen and Hung (2022), the integration of AI and quantum computing has the potential to transform neuromarketing by allowing for the examination of even more intricate data sets at unparalleled rates. This will enable marketers to have a better understanding of consumer behavior and to do it at a faster pace than ever.
- Enhancement of ethical practices in Neuromarketing: AI can enhance ethical practices by automating data analysis and decreasing human bias, ensuring that marketing strategies rely on factual data instead of manipulative techniques. Moreover, AI has the ability to oversee and uphold ethical principles

within neuromarketing, guaranteeing that consumer information is utilized conscientiously and that marketing strategies honor consumer independence.

Quantum Computing: The Next Leap in Neuromarketing

Quantum computing is a game-changing advancement in technology that is set to drastically change various industries, including neuromarketing. By utilizing the concepts of quantum mechanics, quantum computing offers to tackle intricate issues much faster than classical computers. This part will delve into the fundamentals of quantum computing, it's possible uses in neuromarketing, and the difficulties and factors linked to its implementation.

Figure 3. Why for quantum computing? (Mechomotive)

Quantum Computing Basics

Quantum computing is fundamentally different from traditional computing, which uses bits as the smallest unit of data, denoted by either a 0 or a 1. On the other hand, quantum computing utilizes qubits, instead of classical bits, allowing them to hold both 0 and 1 at the same time thanks to superposition. Quantum computers can handle a large amount of data all at once, increasing their capability significantly for specific tasks.

Entanglement is another essential aspect of quantum computing, involving the interconnection of qubits in such a way that the state of one qubit can influence the state of another qubit instantly, no matter how far apart they are. This characteristic allows quantum computers to conduct parallel processing on a level that is beyond what classical computers can achieve.In neuromarketing, quantum computers utilize quantum tunneling and quantum annealing to address intricate optimization issues. Quantum tunneling enables particles to move through energy barriers that are impassable in classical physics, which could result in the development of more effective algorithms for solving problems. Quantum annealing, a specialized form of quantum computing, is extremely useful for optimization tasks, which makes it very applicable for neuromarketing uses aimed at optimizing strategies using consumer data.

According to Chen and Hung (2022), quantum computing is still in its early stages, but the initial theoretical and experimental findings show great potential. The efficiency of quantum computers in processing large datasets makes them well-suited for neuromarketing, where analyzing intricate neural and behavioral data is crucial.

Application of Quantum Computing in Neuromarketing

The use of quantum computing in neuromarketing is anticipated to transform marketers' comprehension and manipulation of consumer behavior. Data analysis is one of the most important uses. Quantum computers are faster than classical computers at analyzing big and intricate datasets from fMRI, EEG, and eye-tracking. This allows marketers to gather knowledge about consumer behavior instantly, leading to more adaptable and quick marketing plans.

Quantum computing could greatly improve predictive modelling in neuromarketing. Conventional prediction models frequently face challenges when dealing with the intricate nature and nonlinearities of neurological information. Nevertheless, quantum algorithms are able to handle this level of complexity more efficiently, resulting in more precise forecasts of consumer reactions to marketing triggers. For instance, marketers could utilize quantum-enhanced machine learning algorithms to forecast the responses of various consumer groups to a new product or advertisement, enabling them to customize their tactics as needed.

Figure 4. Flowchart showing quantum algorithms processing neuromarketing data (Li, J., Peng, X., Du, J., & Suter, D. (2012). An efficient exact quantum algorithm for the integer square-free decomposition problem. Scientific Reports, 2(1), 260. doi:10.1038/srep00260)

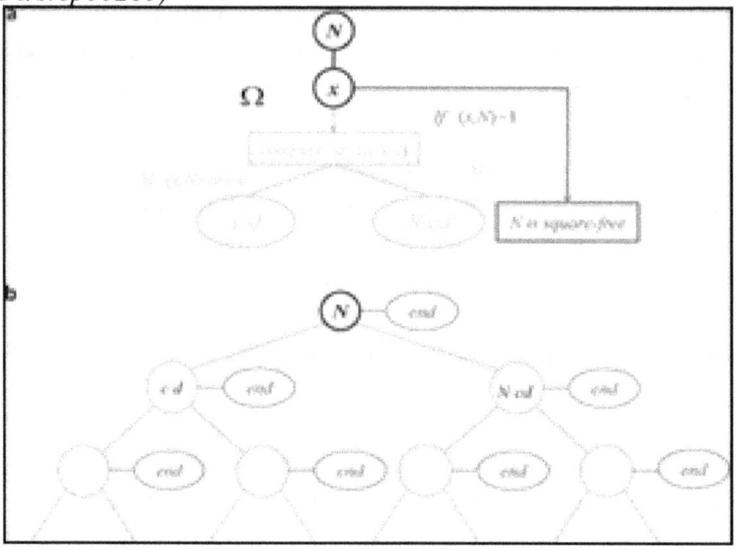

Another encouraging use of quantum computing in neuromarketing involves optimization. Numerous neuromarketing tactics focus on improving different aspects of a marketing plan, such as audience selection, communication, and scheduling, in order to enhance results. Quantum computers are very adept at solving optimization problems, especially ones that have many variables and constraints. Through the utilization of quantum algorithms, marketers have the opportunity to enhance their campaigns in ways that are not achievable with traditional computers, resulting in marketing strategies that are both more efficient and effective.

Customization is another sphere where quantum computing could make a substantial difference. Through analyzing large quantities of consumer data, quantum computers have the potential to develop highly customized marketing experiences that address the unique requirements, inclinations, and actions of individual customers. This degree of customization could not only improve the impact of marketing strategies but also boost consumer contentment and dedication.

Chen and Hung (2022) emphasize that while these applications are still theoretical, the potential of quantum computing to transform neuromarketing is immense. As quantum computing technology continues to evolve, it is likely that we will see an increasing number of practical applications in neuromarketing, offering deeper insights into consumer behavior and more powerful tools for influencing it.

Challenges and Considerations

Even though quantum computing has a lot of possibilities, there are many challenges and factors to consider in integrating it into neuromarketing. The current state of quantum computing technology poses one of the most important challenges. Despite making notable advancements, quantum computers are still in their initial phases of growth. Current limitations include qubit stability, error rates, and the requirement of operating at extremely low temperatures. These restrictions in technology suggest that it could be a number of years before quantum computers are broadly accessible for business purposes in neuromarketing.

The complexity of quantum algorithms presents yet another challenge. Specialized knowledge of quantum mechanics and quantum information theory is necessary to develop algorithms that can fully utilize the potential of quantum computing. At present, only a select few researchers and practitioners possess this knowledge, making it challenging for neuromarketers to create and put into action quantum-enhanced tactics. Satpathy and Mishra (2023) point out that the intricacy of quantum algorithms poses a major obstacle to their extensive use in marketing analytics and neuromarketing.

When implementing quantum computing in neuromarketing, it is important to also prioritize data security and privacy. Quantum computers have the ability to possibly compromise numerous cryptographic systems that are currently in place to safeguard consumer data, creating considerable worries regarding data security. It will be crucial to ensure that quantum-boosted neuromarketing methods adhere to privacy regulations and ethical standards to prevent consumer data misuse and uphold consumer trust. The ethical considerations of quantum computing in neuromarketing are also significant.

According to Bowen and Schoenherr (2020), the ethical issues surrounding the influence of consumer behavior on a neural level are a major concern. The concerns could worsen with quantum computing as it could simplify the manipulation of consumer behavior in ways that are not completely understood or transparent. It will be essential to prevent potential harm to consumers by ensuring that quantum-enhanced neuromarketing practices are carried out ethically and responsibly.

In conclusion, the high cost of quantum computing is expected to be a major obstacle to its implementation in neuromarketing. Developing and maintaining quantum computers at present is costly, potentially restricting access to major corporations with ample resources. Smaller businesses might struggle to compete in a market where larger companies have a significant edge due to quantum-enhanced neuromarketing. In spite of these difficulties, the potential advantages of utilizing quantum computing in neuromarketing cannot be disregarded. With the advancement of technology, it is probable that most of these issues will be resolved, opening the door for the extensive implementation of quantum computing in neuromarketing. Marketers who can effectively incorporate quantum computing into their plans will have a strong competitive edge in the ever-evolving and data-centered field of marketing.

Research Methodology

Purpose: The goal of this study is to:

Uncover the Power of Quantum AI: Explore how quantum computing can revolutionize the analysis of brain data, providing deeper insights into consumer behavior that were previously unattainable.

Address the Limitations of Traditional Methods: Highlight the shortcomings of traditional marketing research methods in understanding the subconscious mind and demonstrate how quantum AI can overcome these limitations.

Identify Specific Applications: Identify and discuss specific applications of quantum AI in neuromarketing, such as creating personalized marketing campaigns, predicting future trends, and analyzing complex consumer behavior patterns.

Navigate Ethical Considerations: Address the ethical implications of using quantum AI to understand and influence consumer behavior, including privacy concerns and the potential for manipulation.

Provide a Practical Framework: Offer a practical framework for businesses to implement quantum AI in their neuromarketing strategies, including guidance on data collection, analysis, and interpretation.

Foresee the Future: Discuss the potential impact of quantum AI on the future of marketing research and its implications for businesses and society.

Research Design: The study utilized a mixed-methods design, combining both qualitative and quantitative data to gain a holistic view of Quantum Computing. The research focused on key areas such as Current State and Limitations of Neuromarketing, Potential of AI and Quantum Computing to Enhance Neuromarketing, Ethical Implications of Using Advanced Technologies in Marketing and Effectiveness of AI and Quantum Computing-Enhanced Neuromarketing Strategies.

Participants:

- A total of 223 participants were surveyed, including individuals who interact with AI in different capacities, such as professionals, students, and general users.
- The diverse sample helps in understanding the varied impact of AI across different demographics.

Survey Instruments:

- Data was collected using structured surveys with questions designed to know Current State and Limitations of Neuromarketing, Potential of AI and Quantum Computing to Enhance Neuromarketing, Ethical Implications of Using Advanced Technologies in Marketing and Effectiveness of AI and Quantum Computing-Enhanced Neuromarketing Strategies.
- The survey included both Likert-scale questions to quantify responses and open-ended questions to capture qualitative feedback.

Procedure

- The survey was conducted online, allowing participants to complete it at their convenience. This approach ensured broad participation and the collection of comprehensive data reflective of user experiences with AI.

Data Collection Overview of Data Collection:

- The data was gathered through a survey distributed to a wide audience, capturing responses from 223 participants. The survey was structured to assess the perceptions and experiences of users regarding AI's impact on various aspects of human capabilities.
- The survey collected quantitative data on the level of trust in AI, the perceived enhancement of cognitive functions, and user satisfaction, alongside qualitative data on ethical concerns and recommendations for improvement.

Table 1. Survey data analysis

Variable	Positive Responses (%)	Neutral Responses (%)	Negative Responses (%)	Total Responses	Positive Count	Neutral Count	Negative Count
Current State and Limitations of Neuromarketing	53.8	31.4	14.8	223	120	70	33
Potential of AI and Quantum Computing to Enhance Neuromarketing	67.2	22.4	10.3	223	150	50	23
Ethical Implications of Using Advanced Technologies in Marketing	44.8	35.9	19.3	223	100	80	43
Effectiveness of AI and Quantum Computing-Enhanced Neuromarketing Strategies	58.2	26.9	14.8	223	130	60	33

(Source: Author owned depiction)

Variables Measured:

- **Current State and Limitations of Neuromarketing:** This variable refers to the present capabilities and shortcomings of neuromarketing, which involves studying the brain's responses to marketing stimuli using techniques from neuroscience.
- **Potential of AI and Quantum Computing to Enhance Neuromarketing:** This variable assesses how artificial intelligence (AI) and quantum computing can further improve neuromarketing.
- **Ethical Implications of Using Advanced Technologies in Marketing:** This variable looks at the moral and ethical concerns that arise from applying advanced technologies like neuromarketing, AI, and quantum computing in marketing.
- **Effectiveness of AI and Quantum Computing-Enhanced Neuromarketing Strategies:** This variable measures the success and impact of using AI and quantum computing to improve neuromarketing strategies.

Table 2. Variables used in the questionnaire

Variable	Number of items	Sources
Current State and Limitations of Neuromarketing	4	Bhat, M. S., & Khan, M. N. (2021); Morin, C. (2011).
Potential of AI and Quantum Computing to Enhance Neuromarketing	4	Ghosh, A., & Sinha, S. (2020); Chen, S. S., & Hung, S. Y. (2022).
Ethical Implications of Using Advanced Technologies in Marketing	4	Bowen, M. I., & Schoenherr, J. R. (2020); Plassmann, H., Venkatraman, V., Huettel, S., & Yoon, C. (2015).
Effectiveness of AI and Quantum Computing-Enhanced Neuromarketing Strategies	4	Chen, S. S., & Hung, S. Y. (2022); Ghosh, A., & Sinha, S. (2020).

(Source: Author owned depiction)

Data Analysis

Analysis Approach:

- Descriptive statistics were used to summarize the survey results, providing insights into how AI influences different aspects of human-AI collaboration.
- The data analysis focused on identifying trends and key findings that align with the broader theme of enhancing human capabilities through AI.

Key Findings

Current State and Limitations of Neuromarketing:

- 53.8% positive, 31.4% neutral, and 14.8% negative.
- A majority view neuromarketing's current state and limitations in a positive light, although about one-third remain indifferent or neutral. There is a small but notable minority that views the limitations negatively.

Potential of AI and Quantum Computing to Enhance Neuromarketing:

- 67.2% positive, 22.4% neutral, and 10.3% negative.
- The most positive response of all variables. The vast majority are optimistic about how AI and quantum computing can enhance neuromarketing, with only a small portion of respondents being indifferent or negative.

Ethical Implications of Using Advanced Technologies in Marketing:

- 44.8% positive, 35.9% neutral, and 19.3% negative.
- This variable shows the most divided response. While almost half are positive, there's significant neutrality and concern about the ethical issues involved in advanced technologies in marketing.

Effectiveness of AI and Quantum Computing-Enhanced Neuromarketing Strategies:

- 58.2% positive, 26.9% neutral, and 14.8% negative.
- A clear majority sees AI and quantum-enhanced neuromarketing strategies as effective, but with more than a quarter neutral and about 15% negative.

Table 3. Descriptive statistics

Variable	Mean	Standard Deviation
Current State and Limitations of Neuromarketing	5	1.41
Potential of AI and Quantum Computing to Enhance Neuromarketing	5	2.24
Ethical Implications of Using Advanced Technologies in Marketing	3	1.41
Effectiveness of AI and Quantum Computing-Enhanced Neuromarketing Strategies	8	1.41

(Source: Primary data)

Findings and Discussion

The findings reveal a promising outlook on the integration of AI and quantum computing in neuromarketing, with 67.2% of respondents expressing optimism about these technologies enhancing marketing strategies. Neuromarketing provides valuable insights into consumer behavior by analyzing unconscious processes, yet it faces limitations, including high costs and complexity, with 53.8% of participants acknowledging these challenges. Ethical concerns are significant, as 44.8% of respondents view the implications of advanced technologies positively, while 19.3% express negative sentiments regarding potential manipulation and privacy issues. The discussion emphasizes the necessity of navigating these ethical landscapes carefully, balancing consumer understanding with the risk of exploitation. It highlights the diversity in consumer responses, indicating that while neuromarketing can identify general patterns, individual differences complicate the application of strategies across various demographics. Furthermore, the integration of AI and quantum computing holds the potential to analyze complex consumer behavior and predict trends, but it requires a practical framework for ethical implementation. Looking ahead, the study suggests that as these technologies evolve, they will significantly reshape marketing research and strategies, necessitating ongoing dialogue about ethical practices and consumer rights. Overall, while the potential benefits of quantum AI in neuromarketing are substantial, addressing ethical considerations and current limitations is crucial for responsible and effective application in the marketing landscape.

CONCLUSION

The integration of quantum computing and AI in neuromarketing holds immense potential to revolutionize marketing strategies and consumer understanding. This research will provide valuable insights into the practical and ethical implications of these advanced technologies in neuromarketing, paving the way for more effective and responsible marketing practices. By exploring the current state of neuromarketing, evaluating the potential of AI and quantum computing, and addressing ethical concerns, this study aims to contribute to the advancement of knowledge and the development of best practices in the field.

REFERENCES

Bhat, M. S., & Khan, M. N. (2021). Neuromarketing and consumer neuroscience: Current understanding and the way forward. *Journal of Consumer Behaviour*, 20(4), 436–452. DOI: 10.1002/cb.1873

Bowen, M. I., & Schoenherr, J. R. (2020). The ethics of neuromarketing: Is it responsible to manipulate the human brain? *Journal of Business Ethics*, 167(3), 515–531. DOI: 10.1007/s10551-019-04197-y

Calvert, G. A., & Brammer, M. J. (2017). The neuroscience of consumer choice: Neuroscience and neuromarketing applications. *Nature Reviews. Neuroscience*, 18(7), 486–497. DOI: 10.1038/nrn.2017.71

Chen, S. S., & Hung, S. Y. (2022). Quantum computing for neuromarketing: Opportunities and challenges. *Journal of Marketing Analytics*, 10(3), 205–219. DOI: 10.1057/s41270-022-00118-9

Ghosh, A., & Sinha, S. (2020). Artificial intelligence in neuromarketing: Bridging the gap between marketer's intuition and consumer perception. *Journal of Business Research*, 123, 275–286. DOI: 10.1016/j.jbusres.2020.09.045

Lee, N., Broderick, A. J., & Chamberlain, L. (2007). What is 'neuromarketing'? A discussion and agenda for future research. *International Journal of Psychophysiology*, 63(2), 199–204. DOI: 10.1016/j.ijpsycho.2006.03.007 PMID: 16769143

Li, J., Peng, X., Du, J., & Suter, D. (2012). An efficient exact quantum algorithm for the integer square-free decomposition problem. *Scientific Reports*, 2(1), 260. DOI: 10.1038/srep00260 PMID: 22355772

Morin, C. (2011). Neuromarketing: The new science of consumer behavior. *Society*, 48(2), 131–135. DOI: 10.1007/s12115-010-9408-1

Plassmann, H., Venkatraman, V., Huettel, S., & Yoon, C. (2015). Consumer neuroscience: Applications, challenges, and possible solutions. *JMR, Journal of Marketing Research*, 52(4), 427–435. DOI: 10.1509/jmr.14.0048

Satpathy, S. K., & Mishra, R. (2023). Quantum algorithms in marketing analytics: A neuromarketing perspective. *Journal of Theoretical and Applied Information Technology*, 101(2), 359–372. DOI: 10.5281/zenodo.7526308

Vecchiato, G., Cherubino, P., Trettel, A., & Babiloni, F. (2014). Neuroscience and marketing: The role of the prefrontal cortex in neuromarketing. *Journal of Economic Psychology*, 45, 271–280. DOI: 10.1016/j.joep.2014.06.001

Chapter 5
Error Correction Methods for Protecting Quantum Information

Swathi Mummadi
B.V. Raju Institute of Technology, India

Gnaneshwara Chary Udari
B.V. Raju Institute of Technology, India

C. Achyuth
B.V. Raju Institute of Technology, India

C. Karthik
B.V. Raju Institute of Technology, India

ABSTRACT

The field of quantum computing holds immense promise for solving complex problems that are currently intractable for classical computers. However, the practical realization of quantum computers faces a critical challenge: the inherent fragility of qubits, the fundamental units of quantum information. Quantum systems are susceptible to various types of errors and decoherence due to their interaction with the surrounding environment, which can lead to a rapid degradation of quantum information. This chapter delves into the pivotal aspect of quantum error correction techniques as a means to mitigate the adverse effects of errors and decoherence in quantum computing systems. Begins by elucidating the theoretical foundations of quantum error correction, exploring the principles that underlie the encoding of quantum information into larger, redundant codes that are resilient to errors. A comprehensive overview of prominent quantum error correction codes, such as the

DOI: 10.4018/979-8-3693-7673-7.ch005

stabilizer codes and topological codes, is provided, along with a discussion of their respective strengths and limitations.

1.1 INTRODUCTION TO QUANTUM ERROR CORRECTION

Quantum computing is emerging as one of the most vital technologies in the world of computers. Let's now delve into the fundamental concepts of quantum computing and explore the principles of quantum error correction. The revolutionary potential of quantum computing is based on the unique behaviour of qubits, which possess the ability to exist in multiple states simultaneously and create entanglement, (Landauer, 1961). In contrast to classical computers, which rely on classical bits that are in a definite state of 0 or 1, quantum computers operate on qubits that can represent both 0 and 1 simultaneously. To better illustrate this difference, we can use the analogy of coin tossing. Before we assign "head" as 1 and "tail" as 0, the coin is in our hand at 0. When we toss the coin, which returns to our hand, its position becomes 1. These fixed states of the coin represent our classical bits. However, in the case of quantum bits, their state is similar to the coin's position in mid-air before it lands, with both 0 and 1 in a superposition.

Superconducting qubits are highly susceptible to external sources of faults, such as ionizing radiation. Error correction is a mechanism or technique used to identify and rectify errors or discrepancies in data, ensuring the accuracy and reliability of information. It involves adding redundancy, error-detecting codes, and error-correcting algorithms to data to detect errors and, when possible, correct them, thus preventing data corruption or loss. To develop the quantum error correction methods, initially authors thought to apply classical error correction techniques by modifying it based on Quantum principles. But there is a difference between Quantum and classical error correction, (Swathi & Rudra, 2021) (Vasudevan *et al.*, 2006).

Classical Error Correction is a technique used to protect data in classical computing systems, which process information in classical bits, represented as 0 and 1. Classical error correction relies on redundancy. It involves duplicating or triplicating bits of information, adding error-detecting and error-correcting codes, and using algorithms to detect and correct errors when they occur. It can correct errors caused by various factors, such as electrical noise, transmission errors, or hardware failures. Classical error correction is well-established and widely used in classical computer systems to ensure data integrity and reliability. Some of the most commonly used classical error correction codes include Hamming Code (Fredkin & Toffoli, 1982), Parity check (Feynman, 1985), Cyclic Redundancy check (Peres, 2019), CheckSum (Kandala *et al.*, 2019), BCH (Bose-Chaudhuri-Hocquenghem) Code (Steane, 1996), and Syndrome Decoding (Endo, Benjamin, & Li, 2018). Quantum error correction is a technique used to protect data in quantum computing systems, which process information using qubits (0 and 1). Quantum error correction utilizes quantum analogs of classical error correction codes, known as Quantum Error Correcting Codes (QECCs). These codes are designed to encode qubits in a way that allows for the detection of errors without destroying the quantum information, (McKay *et al.*, 2017). QECCs are employed to correct errors and detect them without destroying the quantum information. QEC typically requires a larger number of physical components to implement the logical code than the number of logical qubits being protected. Some of the most commonly used Quantum Error Correction codes include stabilizer codes, Quantum Parity Checks, Quantum Syndrome, Three Qubit Bit Flip codes (Swathi & Rudra, 2022), Steane codes (Wallman & Emerson, 2016, Surface codes (Deibuk & Yuriychuk, 2020), and Braiding code, (Picton, 1994).

Due to the differences between Quantum and classical information, applying classical error correction methods on Quantum information is impossible to detect and correct the errors.

1.2 Foundations of Quantum Error Correction

Quantum error correction is a technique used to safeguard data in quantum computing systems, which process information using qubits. It employs quantum equivalents of classical error correction codes, known as Quantum Error Correcting Codes (QECCs). These codes are designed to encode qubits in a way that allows for error detection without compromising quantum information. Quantum error correction codes are utilized to correct errors and detect them without harming the quantum information, (Maslov, Dueck, & Miller, 2005). Implementing quantum error correction typically involves more physical components to secure the logical code than the number of logical qubits being protected. Before discussing in detail about Quantum error correction, it is necessary to understand the Quantum basics like Quantum gates and various Quantum errors.

1.2.1 Quantum Gates

Quantum gates are reversible and are used to implement circuits in a quantum computer. In a quantum computer, information is represented in the form of qubits. Qubits differ from classical bits because a classical bit can be either 0 or 1 at a time, whereas a qubit exists simultaneously in a superposition of both states, (Saeedi & Markov, 2013). In quantum, a state $|\Psi\rangle$ is represented as

$$|\Psi = \alpha|0 + \beta|1\rangle$$

where α and β are complex numbers. $|0\rangle$ represents the state 0, and $|1\rangle$ represents the state 1. The basic quantum gates required to implement any reversible circuit are discussed below:

A. Hadamard Gate

The Hadamard gate (Biamonte *et al.*, 2017) is a fundamental gate that creates superposition. It operates on a single qubit and maps to a superposition of $|0\rangle$ and $|1\rangle$, meaning it has equal probabilities of becoming 0 and 1.

B. Pauli X Gate

The Pauli X Gate (Mummadi & Rudra, 2023) operates on a single qubit and has the same operation as the NOT gate in a classical computer. It maps the $|0\rangle$ state to the $|1\rangle$ state and the $|1\rangle$ state to the $|0\rangle$ state.

C. Pauli Y Gate

The Pauli Y gate (Devitt, Munro, & Nemoto, 2013) operates on a single qubit and maps the $|0\rangle$ state to $i|1\rangle$ and the $|1\rangle$ state to $-i|0\rangle$.

D. Pauli Z Gate

The Pauli Z gate (Swathi & Rudra, 2022) operates on a single qubit and is also known as the phase shift gate. If the basis state is $|0\rangle$, it does not change the state, but if the state is $|1\rangle$, it is changed to $-|1\rangle$. Hence, it is also called the phase flip gate.

E. SWAP Gate

The SWAP gate (Aliferis, Gottesman, & Preskill, 2008) operates on two qubits and simply swaps their states. If the input states are $|0\rangle$ and $|1\rangle$, the output will be $|1\rangle$ and $|0\rangle$.

1.2.2 Quantum Errors

The major reason for Quantum errors is depolarization. Depolarizing errors cause quantum information to be lost and coherence. This loss happens as it is harder to differentiate the quantum state from a fully mixed state, in which every potential state has an equal chance of occurring. By effectively expanding the range of probable possibilities, the depolarizing process raises uncertainty regarding the genuine state of the qubit (Ahn *et al.*, 2002). The impact of a depolarizing channel (E) on a quantum state (ρ) is represented mathematically as follows:

$$E(\rho) = \rho + (p/2)I$$

where I is the identity operator, ρ is the input quantum state, and p is the error probability indicating the chance of the depolarizing mistake happening. The depolarizing effect, where the state is combined with the entirely mixed state $\left(\left(\frac{1}{2}\right)I\right)$, is represented by the expression

$(1 - p)\rho$, which denotes the preservation of the original state with probability $1 - p$. Depolarizing errors (Bacon, 2006) can result from a number of things as detailed below.

Imperfect Gates: Quantum gates are necessary for quantum calculations but are never entirely accurate. The qubits' states can depolarise due to interactions with outside particles or electromagnetic fields.

Decoherence: One essential aspect of quantum states is their brittle quantum coherence. Depolarizing errors can result from any contact with the external environment, such as temperature fluctuations, which can induce coherence loss. Depolarizing errors have a significant effect on quantum information. The exact manipulation of quantum states is a common need for quantum algorithms. The significance of depolarizing mistakes increases with the scale of quantum computers, highlighting the necessity of efficient error correction techniques. Reducing depolarizing errors is essential for using quantum algorithms in real-world applications. Along with depolarization errors, there also exist bit and phase flip errors, (Swathi & Rudra, 2022).

Bit Flip Errors

In quantum computing, bit-flip errors are theoretically related to the X gate. The fundamental components of quantum circuits are known as quantum gates, and mistakes in these gates can result in bit-flip errors. These mistakes might jeopardise the accuracy of calculations made in quantum algorithms. A bit-flip error's probability can vary depending on a number of variables, including the quantum hardware's stability and the length of the quantum operation. Statistical techniques to predict mistake rates and probabilistic error models are frequently used in the mitigation of these problems, (Barrett & Milburn, 2003). Bit-flip mistakes can be caused by a number of physical causes, such as interactions with adjacent qubits, incorrect control pulses in quantum gates, and electromagnetic interference. Researchers concentrate on isolating qubits and enhancing gate fidelities to reduce bit-flip errors in quantum computers. Quantum superposition is the capacity of a qubit to exist in a mix of $|0\rangle$

and $|1\rangle$ states simultaneously is disrupted by bit-flip mistakes. A bit-flip mistake in a qubit behaves like an X gate operated on it.

Phase Flip Errors:

In quantum computing, phase-flip errors are theoretically related to the Z gate. Like bit-flip errors, phase-flip errors happen when a Z gate is inadvertently applied to a qubit, altering the quantum state's phase information. Phase-flip mistakes have the potential to interfere with algorithms that depend on particular phase correspondences among quantum states. Phase-flip errors can be especially harmful to quantum algorithms like quantum phase estimation, which use phase information to their advantage computationally and provide unreliable results. The relative phase between a qubit's $|0\rangle$ and $|1\rangle$ states is impacted by phase-flip faults. A phase-flip mistake can alter the coefficients of a qubit in a superposition state $[|0\rangle + |1\rangle]/2$, which can result in erroneous interference patterns in quantum algorithms. The Z gate preserves the phase of the $|0\rangle$ state while altering the $|1\rangle$ state's phase to $-|1\rangle$ (Bombin, 2011). Like the Shor code, phase-flip error-correcting quantum error correction codes use logical qubits. These codes enable phase information recovery even in the face of faults by redundantly encoding data over many physical qubits.

1.3 Quantum Error Correction Codes

Essential methods for safeguarding quantum data against mistakes and noise are known as quantum error correcting codes. Quantum error correction takes into consideration the special characteristics of quantum systems, such superposition and entanglement, in contrast to classical error correction. To identify and fix mistakes without actually measuring the quantum information as this may upset the fragile quantum states quantum codes use specially created quantum states and actions. The special qualities of quantum mechanics are utilised by quantum codes. By using these characteristics, quantum codes are able to detect mistakes and encode information twice without having to physically measure the qubits' states. A syndrome is a notion that is involved in quantum error correction. Errors cause a quantum code's stabiliser operators to malfunction, leading to certain symptoms. Quantum computers may detect the existence and location of faults by measuring these symptoms instead of the delicate quantum information itself. One of the main benefits of quantum error correction is this non-destructive mistake detection. For quantum codes to function, they need to meet specific requirements. Within that bound, quantum information is guaranteed to stay coherent and trustworthy as quantum codes are made to rectify mistakes up to a specific threshold. For quantum codes to be implemented successfully, several requirements must be met, (Braunstein, 1998).

Quantum error correction techniques are used to safeguard the logical qubits that are encoded with information utilising quantum codes. Several physical qubits are used to encode logical qubits, generating redundancy that permits error correction and detection. The information is converted throughout the encoding process into an error-resistant format, guaranteeing the integrity of the quantum data while it is being computed. There are several forms of quantum error correction codes, including topological codes (like the Surface Code and Toric Code), subsystem codes, and stabiliser codes (including CSS codes like the Shor and Steane codes). Because of its distinct qualities and benefits, each kind is suited for particular quantum computing architectures and error models. Quantum systems can display correlations that classical systems are unable to accomplish because to a property called entanglement. Entanglement is a useful tool for constructing quantum codes in the context of quantum error correction. Building blocks for redundant and error-protected quantum information encoding are entangled states. States that remain invariant under particular operations are called stabiliser states, and they are produced by using entanglement. For a kind of quantum error correction codes known as stabiliser codes, these states are essential. Stabiliser states can encode several qubits in a highly correlated way because of their entangled nature. Entanglement is used by stabiliser codes in their stabiliser generators. Stabiliser generator entanglement guarantees that faults impacting a single qubit may be identified by use of correlated measurements of other qubits. The foundation for error detection and correction without direct measurement of the encoded quantum information is provided by entangled stabiliser generators. A key component of non-local error detection is entanglement. When they happen, errors have the potential to break the entangled correlations inside stabiliser states. Even in cases where faults influence a small number of qubits locally, error detection across several qubits is made possible by the non-local correlations made possible by entanglement.

There are particular quantum error correcting codes made to take use of entanglement. To improve the fidelity of quantum communication, entanglement-assisted quantum codes make use of shared entangled states between the transmitter and the receiver. These codes take advantage of entanglement to improve error correction performance, especially in quantum key distribution and other quantum communication protocols. The protocols for quantum teleportation and entanglement swapping rely heavily on entanglement. Entanglement between the transmitter and recipient qubits is necessary for quantum teleportation to transport quantum information reliably. Entanglement swapping illustrates the non-local character of entanglement, which is essential for quantum error correction and communication, by enabling the development of entanglement between qubits that have never directly interacted.

One basic kind of quantum error correcting codes are qubit stabilisers, sometimes referred to as stabiliser codes. Stabiliser generators, or sets of Pauli operators (X, Y, Z) that commute with one another to form a stabiliser group, are used in these codes. The code space is made up of these stabiliser generators' eigenstates. By measuring the stabiliser operators, errors can be found. The Steane code and the Shor code are two qubit stabiliser codes that can both be used to fix single-qubit faults.

Every qubit in a stabiliser code has numerous stabiliser generators connected to it. Qubit stabilisers are essential for identifying malfunctioning qubits and for identifying the kind of mistakes (X, Y, or Z) that have happened. The qubits in the code undergo a series of operations to determine the stabiliser generators. This condition is used to pinpoint the mistakes that have happened and to direct the next efforts to repair the problems. For a stabiliser code to remain stable, its quantum gates need to abide by the stabiliser operators. Quantum gates that are fault-tolerant are made to avoid introducing mistakes that cause the stabiliser operators to malfunction. Maintaining the error correcting capability of the code during quantum computing requires gates to respect the stabiliser generators. Fault-tolerant quantum processing may be accomplished with stabiliser codes if the logical qubits are spaced apart enough in their construction. In quantum computing, the threshold theorem determines a critical error rate below which quantum calculations of any length may be executed with reasonable accuracy. By offering a route to scalability, stabiliser codes enable the development of more expansive, robust quantum circuits.

There are several obstacles to overcome when implementing quantum error correction with qubit stabilisers, such as the requirement for high-fidelity gates, low error rates, and precise measurement and manipulation of multi-qubit stabiliser generators. For large-scale, fault-tolerant quantum computer construction as well as for the actual use of quantum algorithms, these obstacles must be overcome. Quantum error correction with qubit stabilizers forms the basis for reliable quantum computation. By leveraging the principles of stabilizer codes and accurately measuring the syndromes, researchers can detect and correct errors, paving the way for the development of robust quantum technologies for various applications.

1.4 Popular Quantum Error Correction Codes

1.4.1 The Surface Code

A topological quantum error-correcting code that uses a 2D lattice of qubits, with each qubit representing a square on the lattice. It detects and corrects faults in quantum states by using stabilizer measurements on this lattice. Due to its unique topological qualities, the code is well-suited for fault-tolerant quantum computing since it can detect and correct faults by measuring neighbouring qubits, offering high error protection and dependability, (Swathi & Rudra, 2022) (DiVicenzo & Aliferis, 2007) (Gardiner, 1991). Imagine a chessboard made of qubits (quantum bits). Each qubit represents a square on the chessboard. The surface code uses a specific pattern of qubits on this "board" to detect and correct errors as shown in Figure 1.

Here's a simple way to break it down and understand it:

Qubit Chessboard: Think of a grid of qubits like a chessboard. Each qubit can be in a quantum state.

Data Qubits: Some qubits are data qubits, like the pieces on a chessboard. They hold the actual quantum information.

Ancilla Qubits: Other qubits are like helper pieces. They are used to check if the data qubits are in the right state.

Stabilizer Checks: The surface code performs checks on groups of qubits (like rows and columns on a chessboard) to see if they are in the right state. These checks are called stabilizer checks.

Error Detection: If an error occurs, the stabilizer checks will detect it. It's like noticing if a chess piece is in the wrong place and giving a warning.

Error Correction: When an error is detected, the surface code can correct it by changing the state of the qubits. It's similar to moving a chess piece back to the correct square.

The surface code is powerful because it can detect and correct multiple errors, making quantum computing more reliable. It's like having a "checker" so that the quantum bits can proceed without mistakes.

Figure 1. Surface code (Swathi & Rudra, 2022)

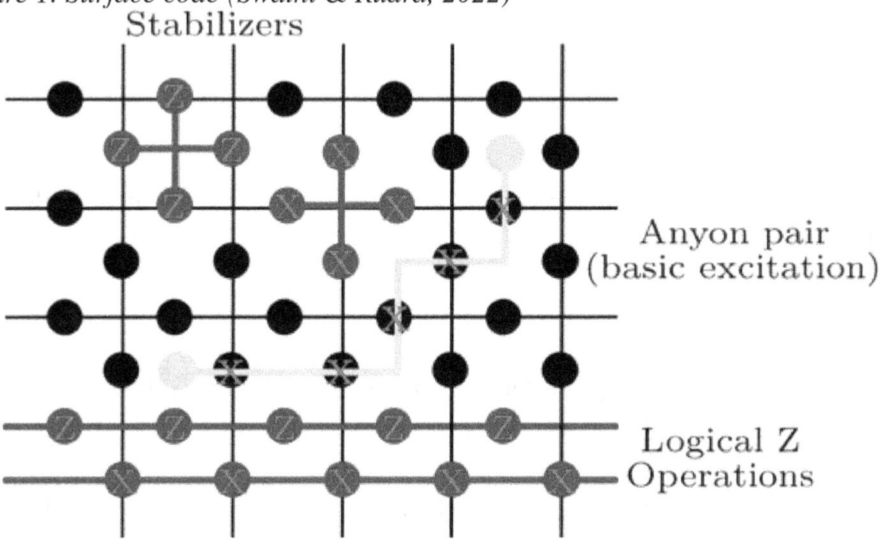

1.4.2 The Steane Code

The Steane code is a type of quantum error-correcting code designed to protect quantum information from errors, (Swathi & Rudra, 2023) (Steane, 1996) (Unruh, 1995). The Steane code encodes one logical qubit in 7 physical qubits and is capable of correcting arbitrary single-qubit errors.

Encoding: With the Steane code, you take your original qubit, which might be in a vulnerable state, and encode it using a set of seven qubits. This encoding is akin to placing your qubit in a protective box.

Error Correction: The magic occurs when errors need to be corrected. If one or two of the seven qubits inside the box are disturbed or flipped (errors), the Steane code has a method for identifying which ones were affected.

Fixing Errors: Through measurements and calculations, the Steane code can identify which qubits have been altered and then restore them to their correct state. It's similar to finding and rectifying mistakes in the protective box.

Result: Following this process, your original qubit is returned to a secure and error-free state, even if it was initially susceptible to errors.

So, the Steane code acts as a quantum bodyguard for your qubits. It encodes them, detects when something goes wrong, and fixes any issues to ensure the reliability of your quantum information. The Steane code encodes one logical qubit in 7 physical qubits. The codespace for the Steane code is a 2-dimensional subspace of its 2^7 dimensional Hilbert space.

In a Stabilizer Formalism, the Steane code has 6 generators as given below:

I I I X X X

I X X I I X X

X I X I X I X

I I I Z Z Z Z

I Z Z I I Z Z

Z I Z I Z I Z

Note that each of the above generators is the tensor product of 7 single-qubit Pauli operations.

The logical X and Z gates are represented as follows

$X_L = XXXXXXX$

$Z_L = ZZZZZZZ$

According to this the logical states $|0\rangle$ and $|1\rangle$ of the Steane code are represented as follows

$$|0\rangle_L = \frac{1}{\sqrt{8}}\left[|0000000\rangle + |1010101\rangle + |0110011\rangle + |1100110\rangle + |0001111\rangle + |1011010\rangle + |0111100\rangle + |1101001\rangle\right]$$

$|1\rangle_L = X_L|0\rangle_L$

In this, arbitrary code states are of the form $|\Psi\rangle = \alpha|0\rangle_L + \beta|1\rangle_L$

1.4.3 The Shor Code

The error channel can introduce either a bit flip, a sign flip (i.e., a phase flip), or both. You can correct for both types of errors on any single qubit using a Quantum Error Correction (QEC) code, which can be achieved with the Shor code published in 1995. In other words, the Shor code can correct arbitrary single-qubit errors, (van Loock, 2008)(Swathi & Rudra, 2022)(Brun, Devetak, & Hsieh, 2006). The Shor code acts like a quantum detective that safeguards your quantum information from errors. So, think of the Shor code as a detective for your quantum data. It protects your qubits, investigates errors, and ensures everything is in order. Here's a straightforward breakdown to help you understand it:

Code Creator: Imagine you have a brilliant friend named Mr. Shor, who has created a special code. This code functions as a shield for your quantum information.

Data Protection: You entrust your quantum information (qubits) to Mr. Shor's code, which places your data in a secret code box.

Error Investigation: Now, imagine some errors occur. It's like a mystery where your qubits change or flip without your knowledge.

Shor's Magic: Mr. Shor's code acts as a detective, carefully examining your qubits and uncovering what went wrong. It's akin to solving the mystery of the errors.

Fixing Mistakes: Once the detective (Shor's code) identifies the errors, it corrects them, returning your qubits to their correct and safe state.

The Shor code can also rectify a sign flip error for a single qubit.

The circuit diagram of Shor's code along with encoding and decoding operations is depicted in following figure.

Figure 2. Quantum circuit to encode a single logical qubit with the Shor code and then perform bit flip error correction on each of the three blocks (Swathi & Rudra, 2022)

1.5 Fault-Tolerant Quantum Computing

Threshold theorems are fundamental results in the field of quantum error correction, specifically in the context of quantum fault-tolerant computation. These theorems provide conditions under which it is possible to perform fault-tolerant quantum computation, even in the presence of errors, up to a certain threshold error rate. Quantum computers are inherently susceptible to errors due to various factors such as decoherence, noise, and environmental interactions. Fault-tolerant quantum computation is a critical area of research aimed at designing quantum algorithms and circuits capable of functioning correctly even when errors occur during the computation. This involves the use of advanced quantum error correction techniques to mitigate the impact of errors on quantum information processing.

In the study of fault-tolerant quantum computation, specific error models are considered to analyze the impact of errors on quantum systems. One common model is the local stochastic noise model, where errors occur independently on each qubit and gate with a certain probability. Other relevant models include depolarizing noise, which represents errors through a gradual loss of information, and amplitude damping, which accounts for errors due to interactions with the environment. The threshold error rate is a crucial parameter in the field of fault-tolerant quantum computation. It represents the maximum allowable error rate (per physical qubit or gate) below which fault-tolerant quantum computation becomes theoretically possible. The threshold error rate depends on factors such as the specific quantum error correction code employed and distinguishes between physical error rates (errors per gate or qubit) and logical error rates (errors at the logical level after error correction). Understanding and surpassing the threshold error rate is essential for achieving scalable and reliable quantum computation.

Need For Fault Tolerance

The intrinsic susceptibility of quantum systems to errors primarily due to phenomena like decoherence, noise, and interference drives the necessity for fault tolerance in quantum computing. Due to their extreme sensitivity to their surroundings, quantum bits, or qubits, can cause computing mistakes and loss of coherence. In order to reduce these mistakes, fault-tolerant quantum processing is essential, using complex error correcting codes as stabiliser codes. Quantum information is corruptible in the absence of fault tolerance, which restricts the usefulness of quantum computing. Achieving fault tolerance is crucial for guaranteeing the scalability and dependability of quantum algorithms as quantum systems get larger. Scholars persistently investigate inventive methodologies to tackle the obstacles and unleash the complete capabilities of quantum computing.

1.6 Beyond Stabilizer Codes

Stabilizer codes form a crucial class of quantum error correction codes extensively used in the context of fault-tolerant quantum computation. These codes are defined by a stabilizer group, a set of Pauli operators that commute with all codeword operators. Examples of stabilizer codes include the [[7,1,3]] Steane code and the [[5,1,3]]

Shor code. Stabilizer codes enable the encoding of logical qubits redundantly across multiple physical qubits, allowing for error detection and correction.

Topological Quantum Codes

Topological quantum codes represent a cutting-edge approach to mitigating errors in quantum computation. At their core is the utilization of topological order, a unique property exhibited by certain quantum systems. This chapter delves into the foundations of topological quantum codes, exploring their principles and applications. One fundamental concept is topological order, characterized by long-range entanglement and non-local correlations. These properties provide inherent robustness against local errors, forming the basis for effective error correction. The intricate dance of anyons, quasiparticles that emerge in topologically ordered systems, through braiding operations is a key mechanism. Nontrivial braiding creates logical qubits, offering a means to detect and correct errors without directly measuring the state of the qubits. The surface code, a prominent example of a topological quantum code, operates on a two-dimensional lattice of qubits. Anyons, arising from errors, interact on the lattice, and logical qubits are encoded in non-contractible loops formed by braiding anyons. This encoding allows for fault-tolerant quantum computation and has implications for quantum memory applications. However, challenges abound. Physically realizing topological quantum codes requires precision and control over quantum states, posing significant experimental hurdles. The scalability of these codes to build large-scale, fault-tolerant quantum computers is an ongoing research focus. Understanding and managing error rates, even in the inherently fault-tolerant framework of topological quantum codes, remains crucial for practical implementations.

Non-Abelian Anyons and Quantum Computation

Non-Abelian anyons play a pivotal role in the encoding and processing of quantum information in topological quantum codes. Their noncommutative braiding statistics allow for the creation of a rich set of unitary operations, enabling the implementation of fault-tolerant quantum gates. The unique braiding properties of non-Abelian anyons provide a robust means of creating and manipulating logical qubits. In the context of topological quantum codes, such as those based on the anyon models mentioned earlier, non-Abelian anyons serve as building blocks for fault-tolerant quantum computation. Logical qubits are encoded in the nontrivial braiding patterns of these anyons, offering inherent error correction capabilities. The braiding of non-Abelian anyons, when executed with precision, can create a fault-tolerant foundation for quantum computations that are resilient to local errors and environmental noise.

Despite their promise, the practical implementation of quantum computation with non-Abelian anyons poses significant challenges. Achieving the required level of control over non-Abelian anyons for error-free braiding operations remains a formidable task. Additionally, experimental platforms capable of supporting the existence and manipulation of these exotic particles are actively being explored.

Experimental Progress in Non-Stabilizer Codes

In recent years, the exploration of non-stabilizer codes has emerged as a promising avenue in the pursuit of robust quantum computing. Unlike traditional stabilizer codes, which rely on stabilizer generators to correct errors, non-stabilizer codes present a unique paradigm that leverages alternative mathematical structures. This shift has sparked notable experimental progress, offering a glimpse into the potential of non-stabilizer codes for enhancing the fault-tolerance of quantum information processing. Stabilizer codes, such as the well-known surface code, have been foundational in quantum error correction. However, the limitations imposed by stabilizer formalisms, particularly in terms of scalability and error-correction capabilities, have motivated researchers to explore non-stabilizer alternatives. Non-stabilizer codes, based on mathematical structures beyond the stabilizer formalism, open new avenues for addressing the challenges inherent in quantum error correction. A hallmark of the recent progress in non-stabilizer codes lies in the diversity of experimental platforms and implementations. Researchers are actively exploring various physical systems, including superconducting qubits, trapped ions, and topological qubits, to implement non-stabilizer codes. This diversity underscores the versatility of non-stabilizer codes across different quantum computing architectures.

1.7 Challenges and Future Directions

1.7.1 Overcoming Error Rate Limitations

Navigating the complex terrain of quantum computing entails overcoming the inherent limitations posed by error rates. Quantum systems are susceptible to errors stemming from environmental noise, decoherence, and imperfections in hardware. This chapter delves into strategies and advancements aimed at mitigating error rates, a critical step towards unleashing the true potential of quantum information processing. A comprehensive understanding of the diverse sources of errors in quantum systems is essential. Environmental elements, such as temperature fluctuations and electromagnetic interference, contribute to qubit decoherence, while imperfections in qubit gates introduce errors during quantum operations. At the heart of mitigating error rates lies quantum error correction. Drawing inspiration from classical error correction principles, this approach employs redundant quantum information to identify and rectify errors. Well-known codes like the surface code and the Shor code play a central role, with the challenge lying in their efficient implementation given the resource-intensive nature of quantum error correction. Threshold theorems establish theoretical limits on tolerable error rates in a quantum computation while facilitating fault-tolerant quantum error correction. Researchers continuously seek to expand these limits, exploring novel approaches and optimizations to enhance error tolerance and reduce the associated overhead.

1.7.2 Quantum Error Correction in Practical Quantum Algorithms

In the realm of practical quantum algorithms, the influence of quantum error correction (QEC) is paramount. This chapter delves into the intricacies of integrating QEC techniques within practical quantum algorithms, emphasizing their critical role in addressing the challenges posed by errors inherent in quantum computation.

1.7.3 Challenges in Quantum Computation

Practical quantum algorithms, designed to exploit quantum parallelism, grapple with the vulnerability of qubits to errors. As quantum systems scale, error rates escalate, necessitating effective error correction strategies. A foundational understanding of the challenges associated with quantum computation forms the backdrop for the exploration of QEC in practical algorithms.

Principles of Quantum Error Correction:

Fundamental principles of quantum error correction are introduced, elucidating how QEC techniques encode quantum information redundantly to detect and rectify errors. The chapter explores stabilizer codes, syndrome measurements, and fault-tolerant techniques, providing insights into the underpinning principles that make QEC an integral component of reliable quantum algorithms.

Quantum Algorithms and Enhanced Reliability:

The chapter strategically navigates through specific practical quantum algorithms, underscoring the transformative impact of QEC on their robustness. Key algorithms such as Shor's for integer factorization, Grover's search, and the variational quantum eigen solver (VQE) are spotlighted. The focus lies on elucidating how QEC contributes to error resilience, thereby enhancing the practical utility of these algorithms.

Quantum Error Correction Codes in Action:

A comprehensive exploration of quantum error correction codes is undertaken, with a particular emphasis on their application to practical quantum algorithms. The surface code, color code, and cat codes are dissected, shedding light on their fault-tolerant attributes and relevance in real-world algorithmic implementations. Understanding the nuances of these codes becomes pivotal for effective quantum error correction in practical settings.

1.7.4 Quantum Error Correction in Quantum Simulations

In the realm of quantum simulations, where quantum computers strive to emulate complex physical systems, the impact of errors is significant. This chapter explores the critical role of quantum error correction (QEC) in the context of quantum simulations, emphasizing its application to mitigate errors and enhance the fidelity of simulated quantum dynamics. Quantum simulations aim to model intricate quantum systems, demanding precision and accuracy. However, inherent errors arising from environmental factors, imperfect gates, and decoherence pose challenges. Understanding and addressing these challenges becomes imperative for realizing meaningful and reliable results in quantum simulations. Navigating through examples of quantum simulations, including those simulating quantum chemistry, condensed matter physics, and materials science, the chapter illuminates the impact of quantum error correction on the fidelity of simulated dynamics. Specific focus is placed on illustrating how QEC strategies contribute to maintaining accuracy in the face of noise, ensuring the reliability of simulation outcomes. A detailed exploration of quantum error correction codes in the realm of quantum simulations is undertaken. The surface code, cat codes, and other relevant codes are dissected, highlighting their applicability to simulating diverse physical systems. Understanding the intricacies of these codes becomes instrumental in constructing error-resilient quantum simulations.

1.8 CONCLUSION

The proposed chapter on Quantum Error Correction illuminates the pivotal role played by error correction mechanisms in mitigating the inherent fragility of qubits, a fundamental challenge in the realm of quantum computing. As quantum technologies advance, the susceptibility of qubits to errors arising from decoherence, environmental factors, and inherent quantum characteristics poses a significant hurdle to the reliability of quantum computations. The exploration of various quantum error-correcting codes, such as the Steane code, highlights the innovative strategies devised to detect and rectify errors in quantum states. These codes not only showcase the ingenuity of researchers in developing fault-tolerant quantum systems but also signify a crucial step toward realizing the full potential of quantum computing. The chapter underscores the significance of error correction in quantum information processing, emphasizing its role in building robust and scalable quantum architectures. As the pursuit of practical quantum computing intensifies, the development and refinement of error correction techniques become imperative for overcoming the fragility of qubits and unlocking the transformative capabilities promised by quantum computation. In essence, Quantum Error Correction emerges as a cornerstone in the quest for reliable and fault-tolerant quantum computers, paving the way for a future where the fragility of qubits is not a hindrance but rather a challenge met and conquered through ingenious and effective error correction strategies.

REFERENCES

Ahn, D., Lee, J., Kim, M. S., & Hwang, S. W. (2002). SelfConsistent non-Markovian theory of a quantum-state evolution for quantum-information-processing. *Physical Review A*, 66(1), 012302. DOI: 10.1103/PhysRevA.66.012302

Aliferis, P., Gottesman, D., & Preskill, J. (2008). Accuracy threshold for Quantum Computation. *Quant. Inf. Proc.*, 8, 181–244.

Bacon, D. (2006). Operator Quantum Error-Correcting Subsystems for self-correcting quantum memories. *Physical Review A*, 73(1), 012340. DOI: 10.1103/PhysRevA.73.012340

Barrett, S. D., & Milburn, G. J. (2003). Measuring the Decoherence rate in a semi-conductor charge qubit. *Physical Review B: Condensed Matter*, 68(15), 155307. DOI: 10.1103/PhysRevB.68.155307

Biamonte, J., Wittek, P., Pancotti, N., Rebentrost, P., Wiebe, N., & Lloyd, S. (2017). Quantum machine learning. *Nature*, 549(7671), 195–202. DOI: 10.1038/nature23474 PMID: 28905917

Bombin, H. (2011). Clifford Gates by Code Deformation. *New Journal of Physics*, 13(4), 043005. DOI: 10.1088/1367-2630/13/4/043005

Braunstein, S. L. (1998). Error Correction for continuous quantum variables. *Physical Review Letters*, 80(18), 4084–4087. DOI: 10.1103/PhysRevLett.80.4084

Brun, T., Devetak, I., & Hsieh, M. H. (2006). Correcting quantum errors with entanglement. *science, 314*(5798), 436-439.

Deibuk, V., & Yuriychuk, I. (2020, August). Noisy multiple-control Fredkin gate in nuclear spin based qubits chain. In *2020 IEEE Third International Conference on Data Stream Mining & Processing (DSMP)* (pp. 352-356). IEEE.

Devitt, S. J., Munro, W. J., & Nemoto, K. (2013). Quantum error correction for beginners. *Reports on Progress in Physics*, 76(7), 076001.

DiVincenzo, D. P., & Aliferis, P. (2007). Effective FaultTolerant Quantum Computation with slow measurement. *Physical Review Letters*, 98(2), 020501. DOI: 10.1103/PhysRevLett.98.020501 PMID: 17358588

Endo, S., Benjamin, S. C., & Li, Y. (2018). Practical quantum error mitigation for near future applications. *Physical Review X*, 8(3), 031027. DOI: 10.1103/PhysRevX.8.031027

Feynman, R. P. (1986). Quantum mechanical computers. *Foundations of Physics*, 16(6), 507–532.

Fredkin, E., & Toffoli, T. (1982). Conservative logic. *International Journal of Theoretical Physics*, 21(3), 219–253.

Gardiner, C. W. (1991). Quantum Noise, volume 56 of Springer Series in Synergetics. Springer -Verlag, Berlin; New York.

Kandala, A., Temme, K., Córcoles, A. D., Mezzacapo, A., Chow, J. M., & Gambetta, J. M. (2019). Error mitigation extends the computational reach of a noisy quantum processor. *Nature*, 567(7749), 491–495. DOI: 10.1038/s41586-019-1040-7 PMID: 30918370

Landauer, R. (1961). Irreversibility and heat generation in the computing process. *IBM Journal of Research and Development*, 5(3), 183–191. DOI: 10.1147/rd.53.0183

Maslov, D., Dueck, G. V., & Miller, D. M. (2005). Synthesis of Fredkin-Toffoli reversible networks. *IEEE Transactions on Very Large Scale Integration (VLSI) Systems*, 13(6), 765–769. DOI: 10.1109/TVLSI.2005.844284

McKay, D. C., Wood, C. J., Sheldon, S., Chow, J. M., & Gambetta, J. M. (2017). Efficient Z gates for quantum computing. *Physical Review. A*, 96(2), 022330. DOI: 10.1103/PhysRevA.96.022330

Mummadi, S., & Rudra, B. (2023). Fundamentals of Quantum Computation and Basic Quantum Gates. In *Handbook of Research on Quantum Computing for Smart Environments* (pp. 1–24). IGI Global. DOI: 10.4018/978-1-6684-6697-1.ch001

Mummadi, S., & Rudra, B. (2023). Practical demonstration of quantum key distribution protocol with error correction mechanism. *International Journal of Theoretical Physics*, 62(4), 86.

Peres, A. (1985). Reversible logic and quantum computers. *Physical review A*, 32(6), 3266.

Picton, P. D. (1994). Modified Fredkin gates in logic design. *Microelectronics Journal*, 25(6), 437–441. DOI: 10.1016/0026-2692(94)90068-X

Saeedi, M., & Markov, I. L. (2013). Synthesis and optimization of reversible circuits—A survey. *ACM Computing Surveys*, 45(2), 1–34.

Steane, A. M. (1996). Error correcting codes in quantum theory. *Physical Review Letters*, 77(5), 793–797. DOI: 10.1103/PhysRevLett.77.793 PMID: 10062908

Steane, A. M. (1996). Multiple particle interference and quantum error correction. *Proceedings - Royal Society. Mathematical, Physical and Engineering Sciences*, 452(1954), 2551–2577. DOI: 10.1098/rspa.1996.0136

Swathi, M., & Rudra, B. (2021, January). Implementation of reversible logic gates with quantum gates. In *2021 IEEE 11th annual computing and communication workshop and conference (CCWC)* (pp. 1557-1563). Ieee.

Swathi, M., & Rudra, B. (2022). An efficient approach for quantum entanglement purification. *International Journal of Quantum Information*, 20(04), 2250004.

Swathi, M., & Rudra, B. (2022). A novel approach for asymmetric quantum error correction with syndrome measurement. *IEEE Access : Practical Innovations, Open Solutions*, 10, 44669–44676. DOI: 10.1109/ACCESS.2022.3170039

Swathi, M., & Rudra, B. (2022). *"Experimental analysis of a quantum encoder in various quantum systems." 2022 IEEE 13th Annual Ubiquitous Computing, Electronics & Mobile Communication Conference (UEMCON)*. IEEE.

Swathi, M., & Rudra, B. (2022, April). A novel architecture for binary code to gray code converter using quantum cellular automata. In *Edge Analytics: Select Proceedings of 26th International Conference—ADCOM 2020* (pp. 43-61). Singapore: Springer Singapore.

Swathi, M., & Rudra, B. (2022, January). Novel encoding method for quantum error correction. In *2022 IEEE 12th Annual Computing and Communication Workshop and Conference (CCWC)* (pp. 1001-1005). IEEE.

Unruh, W. G. (1995). Maintaining Coherence in Quantum Computers. *Physical Review A*, 51(2), 992–997. DOI: 10.1103/PhysRevA.51.992 PMID: 9911677

van Loock, P. (2008). A Note on Quantum Error Correction with Continuous Variables. arxiv:0811.3616.

Vasudevan, D. P., Lala, P. K., Di, J., & Parkerson, J. P. (2006). Reversible-logic design with online testability. *IEEE Transactions on Instrumentation and Measurement*, 55(2), 406–414. DOI: 10.1109/TIM.2006.870319

Wallman, J. J., & Emerson, J. (2016). Noise tailoring for scalable quantum computation via randomized compiling. *Physical Review. A*, 94(5), 052325. DOI: 10.1103/PhysRevA.94.052325

Chapter 6
Quantum Leap in Customer Persona Development:
Enhancing Consumer Profiles and Experiences Using Quantum AI

Pratik More
https://orcid.org/0009-0000-6063-410X
Woxsen University, India

Shiva Sai Kiran Pothula
https://orcid.org/0000-0002-0576-2480
Woxsen University, India

ABSTRACT

Quantum Artificial Intelligence offers a new avenue in enhancing customer personas through the combination of quantum computing and AI to process large files in parallel computing. This chapter describes how QAI enables real-time updates of customer profiles in real synchrony with dynamic behaviors, preferences, and practices. Quantum machine learning enhances both sentiment analysis and predictive modeling with the help of natural language processing, which enables high personalized experiences for businesses. QAI's ability to analyse large volumes of data improves the strategies of marketing through better customer segmentation, improvement in the areas of recommendation engines, and accurate predictions about consumer behavior. This chapter showcases the transformative potential of QAI in empowering the task of real-time personalized data-driven marketing and providing better relations with customers that drives the new age businesses. Integration of QAI in persona development will help companies achieve higher

DOI: 10.4018/979-8-3693-7673-7.ch006

customer satisfaction and loyalty in the evolving digital marketplace.

INTRODUCTION

The current century is often referred to as the era of the Fourth Industrial Revolution (Industry 4.0). The "Industry 4.0" term refers to the ongoing automation of the traditional manufacturing and industrial processes, which includes advanced processing of data with the new innovative technologies, like automated machine learning. Therefore, machine learning algorithms play a crucial role in effectively analyzing this data and creating relevant real-world applications. Key innovations such as the Internet of Things (IoT), blockchain, and artificial intelligence (AI) drives the new Industrial Revolution. These technologies are playing a crucial role in transforming industries and are widely regarded as a successful and rapidly growing model for progress (Girija & Bhuvaneswari, 2021; Lasisi et al., 2024).

Artificial intelligence (AI), especially machine learning (ML), has seen rapid growth in recent years, particularly in data analysis and computing, enabling applications to operate intelligently. ML equips systems with the capability to learn and improve from experience automatically without explicit programming. It is one of the most significant technologies of Industry 4.0. ML algorithms can divided into the four types of learning categories: supervised, unsupervised, semi-supervised, and reinforcement learning.

Figure 1. Machine learning types (Sarker, 2021)

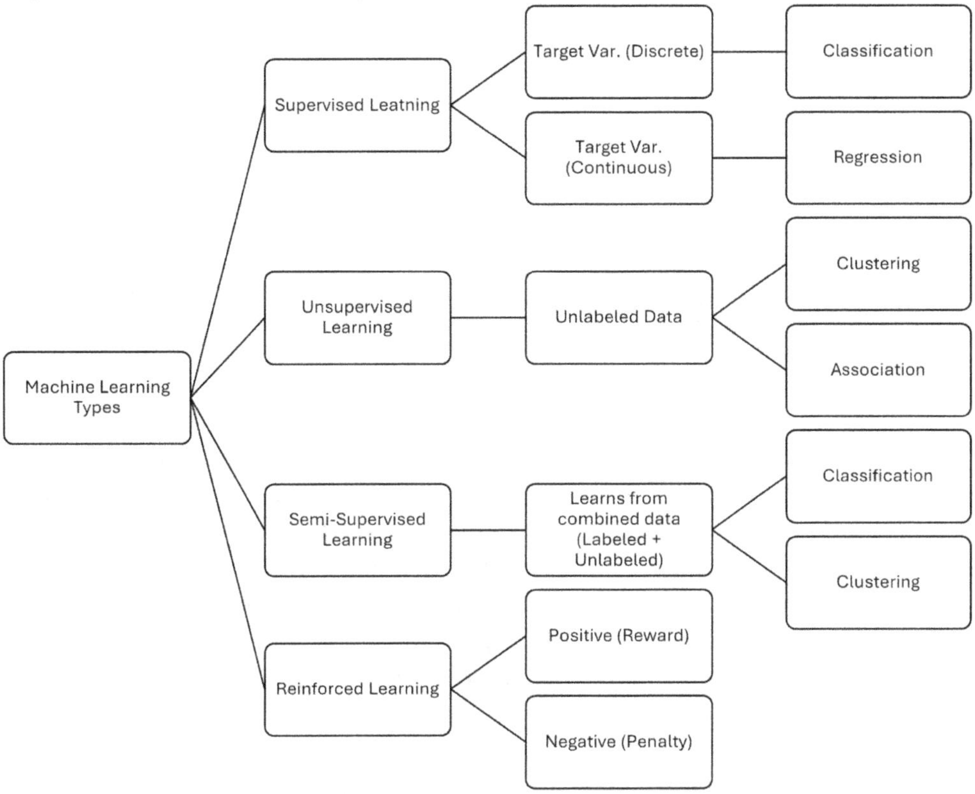

Artificial Intelligence (AI) refers to machines that can mimic or even surpass human abilities like recognition, reasoning, judgment, and decision-making. There are three main types of AI: Artificial Narrow Intelligence (ANI), Artificial General Intelligence (AGI), and Artificial Super Intelligence (ASI). ANI refers to machines designed for a specific task, such as recognizing images, but they cannot handle other tasks like voice recognition. Although highly effective in their specialized fields, ANI lacks the flexibility of broad intelligence (Girija & Bhuvaneswari, 2021).

Figure 2. Types of Artificial Intelligence (Author's interpretation)

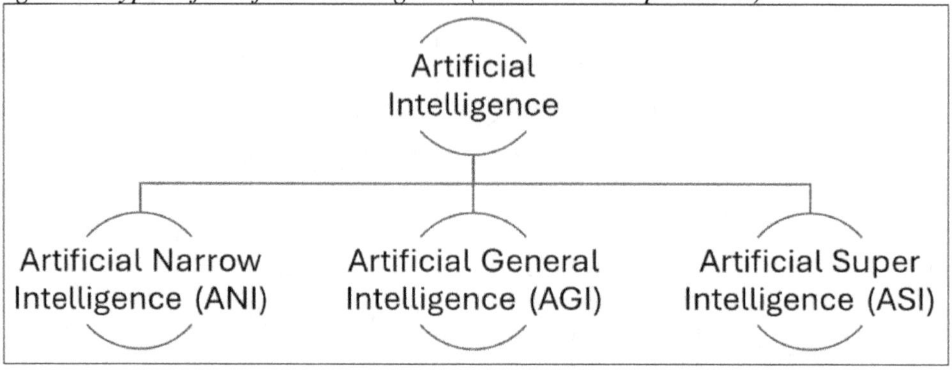

However, AGI would be much more adaptable. Like human intelligence, AGI can perform in various areas—understanding voices, recognizing images, making decisions, and even creating art. ASI takes this a step further, where machines would not only think like humans but far exceed human intelligence. They would be able to outlearn, outthink, and outperform humans across all fields, doing so independently without human input (Rajamannar, 2021).

While AGI and ASI are possibilities for future generations, still decades away, ANI is already here. It is the form of AI that most people refer to when they talk about AI today, and it is developing rapidly, being applied to everything from customer service to marketing. This chapter intends to explore how the combination of AI with quantum computing, can enhance marketing personas by offering deeper insights and more precise targeting. Quantum AI's ability to process highly complex datasets can significantly redefine how marketers understand and engage with their audiences (Rajamannar, 2021).

Figure 3. Key concepts discussed in the chapter

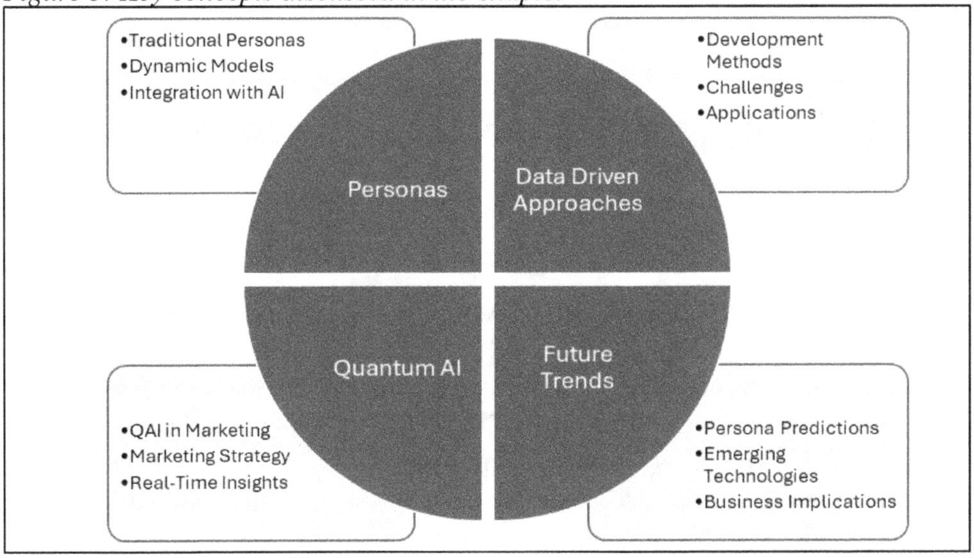

Personas has been an interesting topic among the marketers and researchers which helps them to understand the customers better. Traditionally personas have helped marketers to create their marketing strategies that can work at a larger scale. Leveraging AI will help marketers in creating better personas that can in turn assist in developing better marketing strategies and also understand the customers throughout their journey. Quantum AI represents a transformative force in modern marketing, introducing unprecedented capabilities for analyzing consumer behavior. By leveraging advanced algorithms and real-time data processing, businesses can develop more accurate and dynamic customer personas. These personas are crucial as they encapsulate the nuances of consumer preferences and behaviors, enabling marketers to tailor their strategies effectively. The shift from static to dynamic persona models is particularly significant, as it allows marketing teams to adapt to changing consumer behaviors and market conditions swiftly.

Data-driven approaches are essential in this evolving landscape, employing both qualitative and quantitative methods to construct meaningful personas. However, traditional methods face challenges, including the risk of misrepresenting consumer insights. The integration of AI into persona development processes addresses these issues, enhancing the accuracy and relevance of the generated personas. Looking ahead, technology trends indicate that customer personas will become even more sophisticated, driven by emerging technologies such as machine learning and big data analytics. This evolution not only promises to refine marketing tactics but also enhances the overall consumer experience by fostering more personalized and relevant interactions.

LITERATURE REVIEW

A. Quantum Artificial Intelligence

Quantum Artificial Intelligence (QAI) combines the principles of quantum computing with artificial intelligence (AI) and machine learning (ML). At its core, quantum computing relies on quantum mechanics principles like superposition and entanglement to perform computations (Ying, 2010). Unlike classical computing, which uses bits to represent binary data as either 0 or 1, quantum computing uses qubits that exist in multiple states simultaneously (Sáez-Ortuño et al., 2024). This parallelism allows quantum computers to perform complex calculations at exponentially faster rates than traditional computers that is particularly relevant for AI applications that involve large datasets and complex algorithms (Chauhan et al., 2022; Pandey et al., 2023; Ying, 2010).

Quantum Computing (QC) and Quantum Artificial Intelligence (QAI) are emerging fields with significant potential impacts, but not everyone is familiar with them. The fusion of QC and AI, known as QAI, is in its early stages. While some see QAI as potentially threatening (Taylor, 2020), it already offers numerous applications to better understand customer behaviour by combining the computational power of QC with AI algorithms (Sáez-Ortuño et al., 2024).

One major advantage of QAI is its ability to process large amounts of customer data more efficiently than classical computing (Chauhan et al., 2022). This enables faster pattern recognition and analysis of purchasing habits, preferences, and behavioural trends. By leveraging quantum machine learning (QML), marketers can analyze customer interactions across multiple channels in real-time, allowing for more precise optimization of personalized recommendations (Pandey et al., 2023).

QAI is particularly valuable for managing large datasets across multiple marketing channels. It provides more accurate media mix models and multi-channel attribution analysis, allowing businesses to better understand the collective impact of various touchpoints throughout the customer journey (Gandhudi et al., 2023).

QAI enhances causal inference analysis, offering deeper insights into cause-and-effect relationships between marketing efforts and customer responses, rather than relying solely on correlations. This helps businesses identify which campaigns are driving engagement and conversion. Additionally, quantum-enhanced predictive models offer more accurate forecasts of customer behaviour, including the likelihood of churn, purchasing propensities, and customer lifetime value. These predictive improvements are crucial for refining marketing strategies and strengthening customer retention efforts (Gandhudi et al., 2023).

Current machine learning-based sentiment analysis approaches rely on algorithms such as Naïve Bayes, Support Vector Machines (SVM), Random Forests, and Artificial Neural Networks (ANN) (AlKheder et al., 2023) as well as newer algorithms like XGBoost. While these approaches can create models that provide rich syntactic and semantic information, they may fail to capture sentiment information central to sentiment analysis. To address this issue, a quantum-inspired sentiment representation (QSR) model can be used (Zhang et al., 2019). Moreover, integrating quantum natural language processing (QNLP) provides deeper insights into customer sentiment analysis by processing and understanding large volumes of unstructured text data, such as customer reviews and social media interactions. This helps businesses refine their product offerings and improve customer service strategies based on real-time feedback (Pandey et al., 2023).

B. World of Personas

Personas are representations of groups of consumers who share common characteristics and needs. The persona concept comes from the consumers' responses to specifically designed questions that reveal about their mindset. This helps understand the reasons why customers buy (Ravella, 2015). Each persona is portrayed through a fictional character, which symbolizes a group of consumers with similar traits. Although the persona is not a real person, it is given a name and a picture to humanize the representation. The persona is described through a narrative that serves two main purposes: (1) to make the persona feel like a real individual, and (2) to vividly illustrate the persona's needs within the context of the product being designed (Miaskiewicz & Kozar, 2011). The narrative begins with an introduction to the persona's characteristics, such as preferences, dislikes, occupation, and personal details, which help bring the persona to life. Following this, the persona's specific needs and goals related to the product are outlined. This part of the narrative provides valuable insights into design decisions. While these needs resemble those found in standard requirement documents, they are now embedded within the narrative of a specific persona, making them relatable and context-driven (Miaskiewicz & Kozar, 2011).

According to (Ravella, 2015), there are five rings of buying insights that help in understanding the buyer persona better. The priority initiative helps marketers define and execute strategies that resonate with the buyer in initial stages of buying decisions. The success factor insight helps in understanding the risks and rewards after buying the solutions. The barrier insights help marketers, and the buyers analyze the internal resistance and challenges that may arise in buying the solution. The buyers journey insight helps in targeting the buyers with the suitable solutions that are perfect fit to the needs. The decision criteria help the sales and marketing teams to understand the various attributes that the buyer takes into consideration that impact their decision. These insights help understand the buyer mindset and thus enhance the buyer persona (*Buyer Persona Research - Buyer Persona Institute*, n.d.).

According to the Buyer Persona Institute, there are several benefits of building a buyer persona. It can help in understanding the ideal customer of the Ideal Customer Profile (ICP) that contributes to insights such as factors for buying, competition, and the overall customer journey. Another benefit lies in having the marketing strategy that resonates with the customers that show interest in the solutions and generate better quality leads (*Buyer Persona Research - Buyer Persona Institute*, n.d.). This in turn leads to having a better conversion rate that improves the revenue pipeline for the business. By understanding the buyer persona, the sales team can understand the needs and concerns of their customers which can help in anticipating preparing for the resistance in advance to reduce the risk and shortening the sales cycle. This can help in utilizing the best of the efforts and investments providing a higher ROI and optimize the investments. The buyer persona exercise can thus help in aligning the business goals with the various teams in the organizations thus providing a deeper knowledge about the market and establishing the brand's reputation as the trusted expert (*What Is a Buyer Persona, Why It Matters & How to Define Yours*, n.d.).

There is a common misconception between Buyer Persona and Buyer Profile, if they are same and can be used alternately. Buyer Persona is a comprehensive blueprint offering in-depth understanding of specific buying behaviours. It includes insights into purchase motivators, desired outcomes, concerns, key decision factors, and the overall buyer's journey. While a buyer profile simply outlines the characteristics of individuals or roles involved in the buying process, without providing meaningful insights into the factors that drive their decisions (*Chief Marketer Features BPI Article on Elevating Buyer Personas*, n.d.).

Persona Development can be done through Manual Persona Development (MPD) or Data-Driven Persona Development (DDPD). These methods often starts with collection of both qualitative and quantitative data through customer interviews, surveys, and observations. Both manual and data-driven methods can be used together but DDPD has more benefits as compared to manual (Salminen et al., 2021). Researchers have developed an Automatic Persona Generation (APG) system that creates detailed customer personas by analyzing user interactions with millions of digital products on various social media platforms, such as Facebook and YouTube (Jung et al., 2018). Analyzing user data, including feedback and monitoring, helps validate and evolve these personas, although this process can be time-consuming and demanding (Patkar & Seyff, 2023).

Modern methods improve accuracy by using data-driven techniques like data-mining algorithms to create personas based on real user data. This approach helps businesses gather insights into customer demographics, behaviours, goals, and pain points, leading to more precise representations of different customer segments. By doing so, companies can move from subjective assumptions to data-backed personas (Karolita et al., 2023).

Persona Validation is crucial for ensuring their accuracy and relevance of the developed personas. Companies typically use A/B testing, user feedback, and iterative updates to refine their personas. The Persona Perception Scale (PPS) survey instrument measures how individuals perceive personas, helping marketers and designers gauge the likelihood of persona adoption (Salminen et al., 2020). Quantitative methods, such as predictive personas created using data science and machine learning models, are becoming more popular. These predictive personas can be validated by comparing their accuracy against actual customer behaviour or through customer segmentation analysis (Karolita et al., 2023).

In the Metaverse, providing a sense of immersion and interaction relies on uniquely identified units that share relationships, enriching user personas. Techniques like generative models, reinforcement learning, joint inference, ontology, and multiple entity extension methods can expand the number of entities (Park & Kim, 2022). Innovative approaches are needed to convey consistent personas and emotions that align with unique worldviews in literature. Empathic dialogue systems consider personas to maintain continuity in the conversation (Xu et al., 2024). Large persona representations can be generated using a massive multi-rotational dialogue database, and textual tale production cantered on persona. Using such Large Language Models (LLMs) along with the personas, simulated chat agents can also be created for an enhanced customer experience (Yang et al., 2024). Conditional language models ensure a balanced persona for the Metaverse that can be generated using prefixes to form multiple sentences that would not require retraining (Park & Kim, 2022).

The persona provides valuable insights into the personality traits of potential customers. This information on personas plays a critical role in personalization strategies in marketing by enabling a more precise understanding of customer behaviours, preferences, and motivations that in turn help in creating tailored messages that resonate with specific customer segments with content that aligns with the interests and emotional triggers of different user groups. This approach allows for more relevant marketing messages, such as in the Persona-driven Sentimental Attentive Recommendation (PSAR) model, which uses customer review patterns to generate personalized recommendations based on their sentiment and behaviour (P. Wang et al., 2022).

Personas help businesses refine the ad targeting and personalized recommendations. Marketers can effectively target their advertising strategies by analyzing demographics, preferences, and behaviours. This ensures right messaging to reach the right audiences. Analyzing customer sentiment from reviews enhances ad appeal by catering to specific personas through language or tone. Similarly, by using data-driven persona models, businesses can predict customer preferences and suggest products or services that align with their past interactions and behaviours which enhances the customer experience increases the chances of conversion (P. Wang et al., 2022).

The demand for personalized and innovative solutions tailored to stakeholder needs is expected to persist and intensify. With enhanced data insights, organizations can better adapt their offerings to align with individual preferences and requirements. However, personalization must be guided by a heightened awareness of sustainability, ensuring that customized solutions are not only aesthetically pleasing but also resource efficient. Rather than simply catering to personal tastes, customization should prioritize addressing fundamental needs while making optimal use of available resources. This can be witnessed in several industries and one such prominent example would be healthcare industry. In case of Direct-to-Consumer (DTC) Genetic Testing products, the solutions have to be designed more personalized as there is an involvement of a highly personalized data and approach (P. B. More, 2022). As we look to the future, marketing may need to expand its definition of stakeholders. Beyond individuals, the biosphere should be recognized as a critical stakeholder, as the growing role of AI and automation continues to influence strategic decision-making in organizations (Fletcher, 2024).

Experience-Dominant Logic (EDL) is a marketing approach that shifts focus from tangible goods towards the brand's consumers experiences (Rika et al., 2022). EDL posits that experiences, rather than the physical properties of a product, are central to consumer decision-making. As AI and VR integrate into customer experience strategies, they align closely with the principles of EDL by facilitating interactive, engaging, and deeply personalized experiences. This approach involves crafting customer personas that capture the evolving and contextual nature of customer experiences. Traditional personas focus on demographics and product preferences, but EDL enlightens them with insights into emotional connections, customer journeys, and experiential aspects of consumer behaviour. Integrating AI and VR into persona crafting aligns with Experience Design Language (EDL), which helps businesses shift from a product-centric approach to a more holistic, experience-oriented marketing strategy (Rika et al., 2022).

Personas also enhance personalized communication in digital interactions, like chatbots or virtual assistants. Understanding both self and partner personas ensures conversations stay relevant and engaging. For instance, the Persona Extractor based on Dialogue Act (PEDA) model maintains consistency in dialogue by recognizing the user's persona, preventing disengagement. Leveraging persona-driven insights allows companies to offer more relevant, engaging, and emotionally resonant experiences, leading to better customer satisfaction, stronger loyalty, and improved marketing outcomes (Lee et al., 2024).

Limitations of Traditional Personas

Traditional or Static personas, often based on surveys and limited data, can fail to accurately depict consumer behaviour due to their outdated nature. One major limitation is capturing dynamic consumer behaviours. In rapidly changing markets, static personas derived from outdated data do not reflect evolving consumer preferences and behaviours. As external influences, trends, and technological changes shift consumer preferences, static personas quickly become obsolete, leading to ineffective marketing strategies (Jansen et al., 2020).

Another significant challenge is their reliance on a limited range of data. Traditional personas are typically based on demographic and consumer survey responses, which often miss complex behavioural patterns involving social media activity, purchase history, and online browsing behaviours. This lack of depth limits a marketer from generating comprehensive, data-driven customer profiles that encompasses the consumer's journey and decision-making process (Jansen et al., 2021).

Static personas are limited by real-time updates. Modern consumer behaviours is primarily influenced by immediate brand, product, and service interactions. During premarital genetic screening, branding, types of tests, and post-screening counselling influence the potential partners' decision to marry. The criteria for genetic testing may evolve due to changes in genetic awareness, availability of brands, and test types (P. More, 2021). Static personas, infrequently updated, cannot accommodate real-time data streams, leaving marketers without current insights. Marketing campaigns that don't align with persona characteristics tend to miss their mark with intended audiences (Jansen et al., 2021).

Research has shown that integrating predictive analytics and Generative AI (GenAI) technologies to develop Realistic Customer Personas (RCPs) can help in understanding of predictive analytics and artificial intelligence in their relationship with customer churn and prediction. Several challenges occur while developing the RCPs using GenAI which starts with the up-to-date high quality data. GenAI platforms needs to be trained on the new datasets to increase its accuracy. There are challenges in the complexity of these platforms which might be difficult to learn. Also the cost to generate the RCPs can be much high and is attributed to the procurement of large amounts of data, computational platforms and energy (P. More & Pothula, 2024).

Quantum AI introduces dynamic and real-time persona modeling to bridge gaps. Quantum AI's real-time processing of large datasets allows businesses to stay current with trends by continually updating consumer personas. By combining demographic, behavioural, and contextual data, the marketing approach becomes more accurate and personalized. This advanced modeling keeps marketing strategies current, relevant, and precise (Jansen et al., 2020).

C. The Rise of Quantum AI: A New Paradigm

Like classical physics, classical data science requires that a customer experience is always in a specific state. This is especially true for Classical Probability Theory. Regarding every system feature, technical assistance, training initiatives, and problems with the system roadmap, the Customer Experience (CX) might, nevertheless, be in different cognitive states. In order to achieve this, quantum probability offers a mathematical framework that enables a user to express every conceivable "superposition state" and exist in an infinite state at any given time (Sáez-Ortuño et al., 2024). According to the quantum theory, a person can exist in an infinite state at any given time (used by a quantum superposition) (Kyriazos & Poga, 2024). By comparison, the classical model presupposes that an individual is perpetually in a particular state.

In the field of AI and machine learning, Quantum AI outperforms traditional AI through enhanced processing speed and complexity. AI relying on classical algorithms is limited by their sequential nature and computational capacity. Quantum AI can process multiple possibilities at once, speeding up the optimization of machine learning models (Chander & Gopalakrishnan, 2023). Quantum algorithms like quantum support vector machines and quantum neural networks provide enhanced capabilities for AI systems managing high-dimensional data through pattern recognition, classification, and optimization (Jansen et al., 2021).

Beyond just speed, distinct types of problems are tackled by QAI and traditional AI. While optimization, combinatorial problems, and large-scale simulations pose challenges for classical AI due to time and resource limitations, Quantum AI (QAI) excels in these areas. In marketing, QAI can be used by marketers in customer segmentation, real-time personalization, and predictive analytics. QAI's real-time processing and optimization of consumer data significantly boost the accuracy and success of marketing campaigns, giving businesses a substantial edge (Jansen et al., 2020).

Quantum AI Enhances Personalization and Customer Insights through Advanced Analytics

Quantum AI's capabilities in marketing significantly improve accuracy, speed, and personalization. With advanced computational abilities, QAI can process massive datasets in parallel and provide exact insights, allowing for prompt marketing strategy adjustments (Kumar et al., 2024). Unlike traditional AI, QAI uses quantum mechanics principles like superposition and entanglement to analyze consumer data much faster. This allows marketers to predict consumer behaviours more precisely, adapt campaigns accordingly, and achieve higher customer satisfaction and conversion rates (Jansen et al., 2021).

One of QAI's major applications is enhancing marketing segmentation (Lee et al., 2024). Outdated marketing methods often overlook the complexities of dynamic customer behaviours, relying on static, one-size-fits-all segments. Quantum AI analysis allows us to create highly nuanced and adaptable customer segments in real-time based on behaviours, preferences, and interactions (Kusasi & Tiyasiningsih, 2024). This results in more targeted marketing strategies, enabling businesses to connect with customers at the right moments and with the right messages. QAI can extract insights from intricate datasets, including purchasing tendencies, social media activity, and demographic information, to create targeted marketing campaigns (Jansen et al., 2020)

Quantum AI offers deeper and more detailed customer insights to enhance personalization in marketing. With quantum algorithms, businesses can identify intricate consumer preferences and interactions across multiple platforms, beyond the capabilities of traditional AI. Understanding customers at a deeper level allows businesses to offer more effective product recommendations and personalized offerings, enhancing the customer experience. In retail or e-commerce, QAI's real-time analysis of extensive datasets can improve recommendation engines, offering consumers the most fitting products according to their distinct preferences (Behera et al., 2020).

Real-World Applications and Future Potential

The early stages of marketing for Quantum AI involve ongoing research and development to improve its data processing and customer insights capabilities (Rika et al., 2022). Researchers are exploring quantum computing's potential for large-data marketing analysis and real-time decision-making. Enhancing predictive models and personalization is a major focus. QAI can efficiently process large consumer databases, enabling more precise predictions of customer behaviours, preferences, and purchasing trends compared to conventional AI models. Researchers propose revolutionizing business customer segmentation and personalization through dynamic, real-time solutions (X. (Shane) Wang et al., 2021).

In marketing, QAI is currently being explored for use in customer segmentation and predictive analytics applications where researchers are developing real-time, persona-based models using QAI that are significantly differ from the generative AI models like GPT-4 or image generation models such as DALL-E; instead, they solely rely on persona narratives (Salminen et al., 2024). Businesses can improve recommendation engine performance by effectively segmenting their customer base and accurately tailoring offerings using real-time data processing (An et al., 2018; Jansen et al., 2021). According to (Behera et al., 2020), experiments indicate that implementing QAI can significantly reduce recommendation generation time and boost customer engagement (P. Wang et al., 2022).

The future impact of QAI on marketing operations could be revolutionary. QAI, which manages intricate data sets and scales marketing initiatives across multiple channels, can automate various marketing tasks. By implementing quantum-enhanced AI, businesses could manage millions of customer interactions in real time and deliver personalized marketing messages to each consumer (Behera et al., 2020). QAI's advanced algorithms enable more accurate anticipation of customer needs and behavioursss, fostering meaningful interactions and strengthening brand loyalty (Perez-Vega et al., 2021). With ongoing development, QAI's significance in marketing is predicted to grow, providing businesses with enhanced capabilities for scaling personalization and optimizing campaigns.

Limitations of Quantum AI (QAI) in Developing Customer Personas

One aspect regarding the use of QAI within customer persona development suggests hopeful advantages but holds key significant challenges across the technology and operational, financial, as well as ethical aspects, as explained here.

- **Technological Complexity and Early-Stage Development:** Quantum AI remains in the experimental stage; technologies have not reached a stage where they are standardized or more broadly accessible. QAI combines quantum computing, based on qubits and principles of quantum operation, with machine learning and AI algorithms. All of these constituents demand highly advanced, specialist hardware and software that is not yet more broadly available. The quantum hardware is quantum processors that are highly vulnerable to interference as well as temperature fluctuations; this often makes the stability of performance in computing unreliable. There is always the potential risk of processing error or the results obtained could not always be the same. Hence, this is what compromises the QAI-based persona reliability. This still remains in the category of quantum algorithms applied for persona modeling - sub area, though in the infancy stages. A very optimized solution specific to analyzing customer data has just started, thus applications maybe restricted by the scope as well as the scalabilities of what we have these days (Chauhan et al., 2022).

- **High Resource Requirements and Financial Costs**: Quantum AI is very expensive in terms of acquisition of quantum-capable infrastructure and in training or hiring specialist personnel. Quantum hardware, unlike the classical computing system, is very expensive to manufacture, maintain, and run, hence accessible mainly to well-endowed organizations or research centers. To the firms that are adopting QAI it would mean entering into alliances with either tech companies or cloud-based quantum computing providers. Although QAI can process vast datasets, its effectiveness is still highly dependent on the quality and accuracy of the input data. Again, this adds a financial and operational layer to be considered. Small and medium-sized enterprises may not consider these costs feasible and so may end up on different sides of the divide, with big companies being the beneficiaries of such advanced quantum-driven personas (Jansen et al., 2020; P. Wang et al., 2022).

- **Data Privacy and Ethical Concerns**: Quantum AI enables extracting deep insights in large datasets, including behavior patterns, sentiments, and preferences. This level of analysis can be a sensitive issue for privacy, given that most of the data under analysis are personal and about consumers. Ethics come in especially in handling real-time data from multiple channels. With QAI updating and further refining a persona, the result is an exquisitely detailed invasive profile on preferences and behavior on behalf of an individual. In this light, such knowledge will be invasive for customers, and they will hate transparency as far as information about using their data is concerned. The ethical implications stretch into potential biases within the QAI algorithms. Traditional AI, and QAI for that matter, can contain biases imbedded in the training data, potentially leading to unfair treatment or targeting specific customer segments. It is highly challenging to guarantee algorithmic fairness and transparency with QAI (Jansen et al., 2020).

- **Scalability and Integration with Existing Systems**: Integration of QAI with existing marketing systems requires adaptation because the traditional storage and processing structure of data does not suit the nature of quantum algorithms. Much of the pipelines for data, analytics, and CRM systems will likely need to be highly modified in order to work well with the outputs from quantum computations. This means that the benefits of QAI are most evident when the data is high dimensional and complex, which may not be the case with all marketing operations. Indeed, not all marketing operations have the data volume or complexity to justify a transition to QAI. For certain applications, the benefits of using QAI over advanced classical AI may be limited, which raises questions about scalability and return on investment. Further scaling QAI for multiple personas or channels within a marketing ecosystem would require unprecedented amounts of processing power, adding pressure to the current quantum infrastructure (Bradley et al., 2021).

- Operational Expertise and Skill Gaps: Quantum AI would require the skills of the quantum world, machine learning, and data science expertise. There is an enormous shortage of skilled professionals equipped with knowledge in these disciplines, and companies would require such experts to leverage personas by using QAI. It is expensive and time-consuming to train existing teams or hire new talent who know how to work in the area of quantum computing and AI. The gap between the skills of potential practitioners could slow the adoption of QAI in persona modeling since many companies may find it challenging to find or develop relevant expertise to implement and effectively manage these complex systems (Chander & Gopalakrishnan, 2023).

In short, it means that the enormous potential Quantum AI offers toward advanced customer personas comes under severe challenge in a form of the technological readiness of quantum algorithms and resources allocation against the background of ethical responsibility of usage, along with the operations' feasibility, that would make QAI a regular instrument in persona development within the organization.

Future Research in Marketing Personas with Respect to Quantum AI (QAI)

-Dynamic Persona Evolution in Real-Time: Further research may develop the potential of Quantum AI for improving dynamic personas evolved in real-tme based on any consumer interaction. It will explore how QAI contributes to continuous upgradation of personas by integrating multiple streams of data related to online behavior, purchase, and emotions. The research addresses the most accurate and contextually correct customer insight enhancing real-time persona evolution in marketing performance (Jansen et al., 2021).

-Predictive Persona Models for Consumer Behavior: Advanced data processing with Quantum AI will allow researchers to realize how predictive models can be even more effective in anticipating future behavior of consumers through complex variables such as environmental factors, social media, and psychological triggers. It may be focused on the development of quantum-enhanced predictive personas that give marketers insights into future trends and purchasing decisions (Jansen et al., 2020).

-QAI-Driven Micro-Segmentation for Personalization: QAI-Driven Micro-Segmentation for Hyper-Personalization Research could explore how Quantum AI can improve micro-segmentation strategies, since QAI is working with more robust, and also complex data compared to the traditional AI that processes the data in a sequence. Marketers are therefore able to get deeper insights into hyper-personalized customer segments. More studies will be able to research how such enriched segmentation impacts and helps in the efforts of hyper-personalization towards highly customized marketing messages and offerings (P. Wang et al., 2022).

-Quantum AI in Multichannel Marketing Attribution: Future research may track the potential of Quantum AI in helping attribute multichannel marketing using combined impacts analysis of different marketing touchpoints. QAI will simultaneously process vast datasets that may reveal deeper insight into how the social media, email, or website channels and others are contributing to a customer's decision to convert and how personas can be adjusted dynamically to reflect such insights (P. Wang et al., 2022).

-Consumer Privacy and Ethical Implication of QAI: With the increased application of QAI in persona development, one other way forward is the consideration of the ethical implications and privacy aspects of quantum-boosted marketing. This area of research could address how QAI can balance the call for personalized marketing with stringent privacy standards and research newer models of ethical data collection and usage (Jansen et al., 2020).

-Developing personas using QAI and Emotion Analysis: Another area of research could study how Quantum AI can better analyze emotional data to develop more emotionally intelligent personas. For example, this could include studying how QAI could process consumer sentiment in real time, allowing marketers to make real-time adjustments in communication strategy by gathering better information of what consumers' feelings and their preferences (Jansen et al., 2021).

CONCLUSION: THE FUTURE OF CUSTOMER PERSONAS IN THE QUANTUM AI ERA

Marketing personas are being transformed through the integration of AI and Quantum AI (Pandey et al., 2023). AI innovations facilitate the creation of adaptable customer personas in real time. AI algorithms update personas by analyzing data from various sources like online interactions, purchases, and social media activity (An et al., 2018; Jung et al., 2018; Salminen et al., 2019). Quantum AI significantly enhances the ability to make intricate and precise predictions. Quantum algorithms can process massive datasets faster and more efficiently, revealing intricate customer preferences and behaviours. The transition from fixed to dynamic personas optimizes the accuracy and customization of marketing campaigns (Jansen et al., 2020).

In the metaverse, users can develop more detailed and believable avatars. In virtual environments, the behavioural data generated by users from their interactions, preferences, and choices is abundant. Marketers can use this data to create more comprehensive and authentic personas. By observing consumer interactions in virtual spaces, marketers can discern preferences for products, services, and experiences. This data helps businesses create precise personas in virtual worlds, incorporating demographic, behavioural, emotional, and experiential consumer preferences (Dwivedi et al., 2022; Park & Kim, 2022).

The Metaverse, unlike VR and AR, provides a sustainable content and social context, can function without AR and VR technologies, and possesses the capability for large-scale implementation through required technological improvements, parallel recognition models, and content availability (Riva et al., 2016). Virtual Reality (VR) alters the customer experience through immersive and interactive environments. Virtual Reality provides an immersive, memorable shopping experience by enabling customers to evaluate products and services in a simulated setting (Andriella et al., 2019). In real estate and retail, VR technology provides customers with an immersive experience, enabling them to tour properties or try out products virtually, thus increasing their confidence and satisfaction. Using AI technology, VR can customize experiences in real-time to match individual customer preferences and actions (Riva et al., 2016).

AI significantly contributes to personalization, customer understanding, and marketing automation. Using AI, real-time customer data analysis results in more effective marketing strategies and automated customer interactions, together with advanced segmentation, predictive analytics, and customer journey mapping. (Behera et al., 2020) AI individualizes customer experience through the delivery of customized content, offers, and interactions based on customer behaviours and preferences (Bradley et al., 2021).

Virtual Reality (VR) offers customers a more engaging and memorable experience through immersive, interactive simulations of products and services (Dwivedi et al., 2022). In real estate and retail industries (X. (Shane) Wang et al., 2021), VR technology enables customers to virtually explore properties or test products, boosting their confidence and satisfaction. AI integration in VR technology can tailor experiences with real-time adjustments based on individual customer preferences and behaviours (Behera et al., 2020).

As the integration of Quantum Artificial Intelligence in customer profiling matures, its potential to redefine marketing strategies becomes evident. By processing vast amounts of data with unmatched speed and precision, QAI allows businesses to develop more accurate and dynamic customer personas that adapt in real-time to changing consumer behaviours. This technological advancement enhances not only the personalization of customer interactions but also the efficiency of marketing campaigns. QAI's ability to deliver deep, actionable insights into consumer preferences and sentiments will foster stronger customer relationships, drive engagement, and ultimately lead to higher conversion rates. As businesses continue to leverage QAI, they can expect to experience a shift from static to dynamic marketing approaches, ushering in an era of hyper-personalization that aligns more closely with individual customer needs and desires.

REFERENCES

AlKheder, S., AlRukaibi, F., & Aiash, A. (2023). Support Vector Machine (SVM), Random Forest (RF), Artificial Neural Network (ANN) and Bayesian Network for prediction and analysis of GCC traffic accidents. *Journal of Ambient Intelligence and Humanized Computing*, 14(6), 7331–7339. DOI: 10.1007/s12652-022-04441-4

An, J., Kwak, H., Jung, S., Salminen, J., Admad, M., & Jansen, B. (2018). Imaginary people representing real numbers: Generating personas from online social media data. *ACM Transactions on the Web*, 12(4), 1–26. Advance online publication. DOI: 10.1145/3265986

Andriella, A., Torras, C., & Alenya, G. (2019). Learning Robot Policies Using a High-Level Abstraction Persona-Behaviour Simulator. *2019 28th IEEE International Conference on Robot and Human Interactive Communication (RO-MAN)*, 1–8. DOI: 10.1109/RO-MAN46459.2019.8956357

Behera, R. K., Gunasekaran, A., Gupta, S., Kamboj, S., & Bala, P. K. (2020). Personalized digital marketing recommender engine. *Journal of Retailing and Consumer Services*, 53, 101799. DOI: 10.1016/j.jretconser.2019.03.026

Bradley, C., Oliveira, L., Birrell, S., & Cain, R. (2021). A new perspective on personas and customer journey maps: Proposing systemic UX. *International Journal of Human-Computer Studies*, 148, 102583. DOI: 10.1016/j.ijhcs.2021.102583

Buyer Persona Research - Buyer Persona Institute. (n.d.). Retrieved September 26, 2024, from https://buyerpersona.com/buyer-persona-research

Chander, B., & Gopalakrishnan, K. (2023). Data clustering using unsupervised machine learning. In *Statistical Modeling in Machine Learning* (pp. 179–204). Elsevier., DOI: 10.1016/B978-0-323-91776-6.00015-4

Chauhan, V., Negi, S., Jain, D., Singh, P., Sagar, A. K., & Sharma, A. K. (2022). Quantum Computers: A Review on How Quantum Computing Can Boom AI. *2022 2nd International Conference on Advance Computing and Innovative Technologies in Engineering (ICACITE)*, 559–563. DOI: 10.1109/ICACITE53722.2022.9823619

Chief Marketer Features BPI Article on Elevating Buyer Personas. (n.d.). Retrieved September 26, 2024, from https://buyerpersona.com/blog/chief-marketer-features-article-on-elevating-buyer-personas

Dwivedi, Y. K., Hughes, L., Baabdullah, A. M., Ribeiro-Navarrete, S., Giannakis, M., Al-Debei, M. M., Dennehy, D., Metri, B., Buhalis, D., Cheung, C. M. K., Conboy, K., Doyle, R., Dubey, R., Dutot, V., Felix, R., Goyal, D. P., Gustafsson, A., Hinsch, C., Jebabli, I., & Wamba, S. F. (2022). Metaverse beyond the hype: Multidisciplinary perspectives on emerging challenges, opportunities, and agenda for research, practice and policy. *International Journal of Information Management*, 66, 102542. DOI: 10.1016/j.ijinfomgt.2022.102542

Fletcher, G. (2024). The future of marketing. *Digital and Social Media Marketing*, 346–360. DOI: 10.4324/9781003372189-19

Gandhudi, M., G.R., G., P.J.A, A., Velayudham, V., & Nagineni, L. (. (2023). Causal aware parameterized quantum stochastic gradient descent for analyzing marketing advertisements and sales forecasting. *Information Processing & Management*, 60(5), 103473. DOI: 10.1016/j.ipm.2023.103473

Girija, N., & Bhuvaneswari, T. (2021). AI emerging communication and computing. In *Artificial intelligence (AI)* (1st ed., pp. 293–306). https://doi.org/https://doi.org/10.1201/9781003005629

Jansen, B. J., Jung, S., Chowdhury, S. A., & Salminen, J. (2021). Persona analytics: Analyzing the stability of online segments and content interests over time using non-negative matrix factorization. *Expert Systems with Applications*, 185, 115611. DOI: 10.1016/j.eswa.2021.115611

Jansen, B. J., Salminen, J. O., & Jung, S.-G. (2020). Data-Driven Personas for Enhanced User Understanding: Combining Empathy with Rationality for Better Insights to Analytics. *Data and Information Management*, 4(1), 1–17. DOI: 10.2478/dim-2020-0005

Jung, S. gyo, Salminen, J., Kwak, H., An, J., & Jansen, B. J. (2018). Automatic Persona Generation (APG): A rationale and demonstration. *CHIIR 2018 - Proceedings of the 2018 Conference on Human Information Interaction and Retrieval, 2018-March*, 321–324. DOI: 10.1145/3176349.3176893

Karolita, D., McIntosh, J., Kanij, T., Grundy, J., & Obie, H. O. (2023). Use of personas in Requirements Engineering: A systematic mapping study. *Information and Software Technology*, 162, 107264. DOI: 10.1016/j.infsof.2023.107264

Kumar, V., Ashraf, A. R., & Nadeem, W. (2024). AI-powered marketing: What, where, and how? *International Journal of Information Management*, 77, 102783. DOI: 10.1016/j.ijinfomgt.2024.102783

Kusasi, F., & Tiyasiningsih, E. (2024). Implementation of Artificial Intelligence in Customer Relationship Management and Its Implications. *SNEBIM 2024*.

Kyriazos, T., & Poga, M. (2024). Quantum concepts in Psychology: Exploring the interplay of physics and the human psyche. *Bio Systems*, 235, 105070. DOI: 10.1016/j.biosystems.2023.105070 PMID: 37939870

Lasisi, M., Kolade, K., & Rotimi, O. (2024). Big Data. In *Reference Module in Social Sciences*. Elsevier., DOI: 10.1016/B978-0-323-95689-5.00269-8

Lee, K., Lee, C., Kim, D., & Lee, K.-H. (2024). Dialogue act-based partner persona extraction for consistent personalized response generation. *Expert Systems with Applications*, 254, 124380. https://doi.org/https://doi.org/10.1016/j.eswa.2024.124380. DOI: 10.1016/j.eswa.2024.124380

Miaskiewicz, T., & Kozar, K. A. (2011). Personas and user-centered design: How can personas benefit product design processes? *Design Studies*, 32(5), 417–430. DOI: 10.1016/j.destud.2011.03.003

More, P. (2021). A Review of Importance of Premarital Checkup and Counselling among Young Adults. *Psychology (Savannah, Ga.)*, 58(2), 6369–6373. https://www.researchgate.net/profile/Pratik-More-3/publication/355022381_A_Review_of_Importance_of_Premarital_Checkup_and_Counselling_among_Young_Adults/links/615822d9a6fae644fbbf61a3/A-Review-of-Importance-of-Premarital-Checkup-and-Counselling-among-Young-Adults.pdf. DOI: 10.17762/pae.v58i2.3162

More, P., & Pothula, S. S. K. (2024). A Persona-based approach for Churn Prediction and Retention Strategies driven by Predictive Analytics and Generative AI. In D. Choudhary, H. K., R. Rodriguez, J. Wise, & R. T. (Eds.), *Predictive Analytics and Generative AI for Data-Driven Marketing Strategies*. Taylor & Francis Group LLC. DOI: 10.1201/9781003472544-12

More, P. B. (2022). *Marketing Strategies for Health Care Applications of Genomics in India* [Savitribai Phule Pune University]. http://hdl.handle.net/10603/384725

Pandey, S., Basisth, N. J., Sachan, T., Kumari, N., & Pakray, P. (2023). Quantum machine learning for natural language processing application. *Physica A*, 627, 129123. DOI: 10.1016/j.physa.2023.129123

Park, S.-M., & Kim, Y.-G. (2022). A Metaverse: Taxonomy, Components, Applications, and Open Challenges. *IEEE Access : Practical Innovations, Open Solutions*, 10, 4209–4251. DOI: 10.1109/ACCESS.2021.3140175

Patkar, N., & Seyff, N. (2023). Data-Driven Persona Creation, Validation, and Evolution. In Ferrari, A., & Penzenstadler, B. (Eds.), *Requirements Engineering: Foundation for Software Quality* (Vol. 13975, pp. 262–271). Springer., DOI: 10.1007/978-3-031-29786-1_18

Perez-Vega, R., Kaartemo, V., Lages, C. R., Borghei Razavi, N., & Männistö, J. (2021). Reshaping the contexts of online customer engagement behavior via artificial intelligence: A conceptual framework. *Journal of Business Research*, 129, 902–910. DOI: 10.1016/j.jbusres.2020.11.002

Rajamannar, R. (2021). *Quantum_Marketing*. HarperCollins Leadership.

Ravella, A. (2015). *Buyer Personas: How to Gain Insight into Your Customer's Expectations, Align Your Marketing Strategies, and Win More Business*. John Wiley & Sons.

Rika, H., Aviv, I., & Weitzfeld, R. (2022). Unleashing the Potentials of Quantum Probability Theory for Customer Experience Analytics. *Big Data and Cognitive Computing*, 6(4), 135. DOI: 10.3390/bdcc6040135

Riva, G., Baños, R. M., Botella, C., Mantovani, F., & Gaggioli, A. (2016). Transforming Experience: The Potential of Augmented Reality and Virtual Reality for Enhancing Personal and Clinical Change. *Frontiers in Psychiatry*, 7. Advance online publication. DOI: 10.3389/fpsyt.2016.00164 PMID: 27746747

Sáez-Ortuño, L., Huertas-Garcia, R., Forgas-Coll, S., Sánchez-García, J., & Puertas-Prats, E. (2024). Quantum computing for market research. *Journal of Innovation & Knowledge*, 9(3), 100510. DOI: 10.1016/j.jik.2024.100510

Salminen, J., Guan, K., Jung, S.-G., & Jansen, B. J. (2021). A Survey of 15 Years of Data-Driven Persona Development. *International Journal of Human-Computer Interaction*, 37(18), 1685–1708. DOI: 10.1080/10447318.2021.1908670

Salminen, J., Jansen, B. J., An, J., Kwak, H., & Jung, S.-G. (2019). *Automatic Persona Generation for Online Content Creators: Conceptual Rationale and a Research Agenda*. 135–160. DOI: 10.1007/978-1-4471-7427-1_8

Salminen, J., Santos, J. M., Jung, S., & Jansen, B. J. (2024). Picturing the fictitious person: An exploratory study on the effect of images on user perceptions of AI-generated personas. *Computers in Human Behavior: Artificial Humans*, 2(1), 100052. DOI: 10.1016/j.chbah.2024.100052

Salminen, J., Santos, J. M., Kwak, H., An, J., Jung, S., & Jansen, B. J. (2020). Persona Perception Scale: Development and Exploratory Validation of an Instrument for Evaluating Individuals' Perceptions of Personas. *International Journal of Human-Computer Studies*, 141, 102437. DOI: 10.1016/j.ijhcs.2020.102437

Sarker, I. H. (2021). Machine Learning: Algorithms, Real-World Applications and Research Directions. *SN Computer Science*, 2(3), 160. DOI: 10.1007/s42979-021-00592-x PMID: 33778771

Taylor, R. D. (2020). Quantum Artificial Intelligence: A "precautionary" U.S. approach? *Telecommunications Policy*, 44(6), 101909. DOI: 10.1016/j.telpol.2020.101909

Wang, P., Li, L., Wang, R., Zheng, X., He, J., & Xu, G. (2022). Learning persona-driven personalized sentimental representation for review-based recommendation. *Expert Systems with Applications*, 203, 117317. https://doi.org/https://doi.org/10.1016/j.eswa.2022.117317. DOI: 10.1016/j.eswa.2022.117317

Wang, X., Ryoo, J. H. J., Bendle, N., & Kopalle, P. K. (2021). The role of machine learning analytics and metrics in retailing research. *Journal of Retailing*, 97(4), 658–675. DOI: 10.1016/j.jretai.2020.12.001

What Is a Buyer Persona, Why It Matters & How to Define Yours. (n.d.). Retrieved September 26, 2024, from https://buyerpersona.com/what-is-a-buyer-persona

Xu, Z., Chen, D., Kuang, J., Yi, Z., Li, Y., & Shen, Y. (2024). Dynamic Demonstration Retrieval and Cognitive Understanding for Emotional Support Conversation. *Proceedings of the 47th International ACM SIGIR Conference on Research and Development in Information Retrieval*, 774–784. DOI: 10.1145/3626772.3657695

Yang, B., Liu, D., Tang, C., Xiao, C., Zhao, K., Li, C., Yang, G., Huang, L., & Lin, C. (2024). Crafting Customisable Characters with LLMs: Introducing SimsChat, a Persona-Driven Role-Playing Agent Framework. *ArXiv, Cornell Universuty*. https://arxiv.org/abs/2406.17962v3

Ying, M. (2010). Quantum computation, quantum theory and AI. *Artificial Intelligence*, 174(2), 162–176. DOI: 10.1016/j.artint.2009.11.009

Zhang, Y., Song, D., Zhang, P., Li, X., & Wang, P. (2019). A quantum-inspired sentiment representation model for twitter sentiment analysis. *Applied Intelligence*, 49(8), 3093–3108. DOI: 10.1007/s10489-019-01441-4

Chapter 7
Integrating EEG Analysis to Illuminate Consumer Behavior and Optimize Marketing Strategies

Monishwar Reddy Vardireddy
Woxsen University, India

Pranjali Gajbhiye
https://orcid.org/0000-0001-5567-5732
Woxsen University, India

ABSTRACT

Electroencephalography (EEG) is crucial for understanding how music affects cognitive and emotional processes by providing real-time insights into neural activity. It helps measure emotional states like happiness and sadness in response to music, revealing how music influences brain regions such as the amygdala and prefrontal cortex. Advancements in EEG technology have enabled sophisticated analysis of brain waves (delta, theta, alpha, beta, gamma) and their correlation with music's tempo and rhythm, impacting memory and emotional processing. EEG's application extends to therapeutic settings, enhancing neuroplasticity and cognitive functions in neurological rehabilitation, and in marketing, where it offers insights into consumer reactions and preferences, optimizing ads and product designs. It helps optimize content to evoke desired emotional responses, improve attention and memory encoding, and enhance brand loyalty by integrating EEG insights with traditional market research methods.

DOI: 10.4018/979-8-3693-7673-7.ch007

1. INTRODUCTION:

EEG technology has fundamentally transformed our exploration of how music influences cognitive functions within the brain. By monitoring EEG signals, this chapter delve into the intricate interplay between music and neural activity, uncovering how different musical stimuli engage various cognitive processes and evoke emotional responses. Music serves as a powerful catalyst for emotions, which can be objectively measured through EEG analysis, providing insights into affective states like happiness or sadness. This technology allows for real-time monitoring of brain activity, revealing the temporal dynamics of music-induced neural responses and the correlation between music preferences and emotional engagement. Advances in EEG technology have also led to sophisticated algorithms for analysing EEG signals in the context of music, enhancing our understanding of the neural signatures underlying musical experiences. Beyond research, EEG-based analysis extends to practical applications in affective computing and brain-computer interfaces, showcasing its transformative potential in enriching musical interactions and deepening our understanding of the complex relationship between music, emotions, and cognition. Moreover EEG as played a significant role in marketing there are various marketing strategies and EEG market research and EEG can also be used in Television Commercials and there are outstanding output in Television Commercials by implementing EEG. EEG can be integrated in multiple technology for advance performance and customers are also giving positive feedback from this.

2. BASIC TERMINOLOGY OF EEG:

2.1 EEG (Electroencephalography):

Electroencephalography (EEG) This non-invasive technique allows to observe the electrical activity generated by the brain in response to external stimuli, providing valuable insights into how music engages various regions of the brain and influences cognitive processes, (Teplan, 2002).

2.2 MUSIC and Emotion:

One of the most intriguing findings to emerge from EEG studies is the remarkable impact of music on mood regulation and emotional processing. Music can modulate the activity of key brain regions involved in emotion regulation, such as the amygdala and prefrontal cortex. By stimulating these areas, music has been found to elicit complex emotional responses, ranging from joy and nostalgia to sadness and awe, (Lin, Wang, & Jung, 2010).

2.3 Brain Frequency and Rhythm:

Studies have demonstrated that certain musical elements, such as tempo, rhythm, and harmony, can directly influence the brain's emotional circuitry, eliciting physiological changes such as changes in heart rate, respiratory rate, and skin conductance. EEG signals can be calculated by five frequency bands there are Delta waves (0.5 to 4 Hz), theta waves (4 to 8 Hz), Alpha waves (8 to 12 Hz), beta waves (12 to 30 Hz), gamma (30 Hz to 100HZ).EEG studies have shed light on the intricate relationship between music and memory, unveiling the profound mnemonic effects of musical stimulation. Music can enhance memory retrieval and consolidation by engaging multiple cognitive processes simultaneously, (Khosla, Khandnor, & Elsevier, 2020).

3. METHODOLOGY

Looking through the main methodology of EEG there will be more work with the brain signals looking to the signal processing:

Signal Processing:

3.1 Signal Acquisition:

Exploring how music affects the brain involves using EEG, which tracks neural activity. Researchers carefully design experiments, choosing music genres and factors like tempo to provoke specific cognitive and emotional responses. They use standardized electrode placements for consistency and meticulously control variables like volume and duration of music, (Manns et al., 2018).

3.2 Signal Pre-processing:

To ensure data quality, EEG signals undergo rigorous preprocessing. This includes removing artifacts like eye blinks and muscle activity, as well as filtering out noise from environmental sources. Techniques such as notch filters are used to eliminate power frequency noise and improve the accuracy of EEG data for emotion recognition, (Manns et al., 2018).

3.3 Feature Extraction:

From EEG data, researchers extract meaningful information using methods like spectral power analysis and event-related potentials. These techniques help quantify how the brain responds to music over time and across different regions, (Manns *et al.*, 2018).

3.4 Music Stimuli Representation:

During experiments, participants are exposed to various music types while their EEG signals are recorded. Features extracted from these signals are then fed into machine learning algorithms (like SVM or CNN) to analyze how different types of music affect brain activity, (Manns et al., 2018).

3.5 Performance Evaluation:

The impact of music on brain activity is evaluated using performance metrics such as accuracy, error rates, and precision. These measures help quantify how well machine learning models can distinguish between brain states influenced by different musical stimuli, (Manns et al., 2018).

Data Processing and Analysis:

FIG-1 shows the flowchart of EEG data processing and analysis used for marketing

4.NEUROPLASTICITY,THERAPEUTIC APPLICATIONS, AND AUTOBIOGRAPHICAL MEMORY WITH EMOTIONAL RESPONSE.

Looking forward in neuroplasticity application and auto biographical memory EEG as played a crucial role in it talking about it in deeper:

4.1 Autobiographical Memory and Emotional Response:

Familiar melodies or songs can trigger vivid autobiographical memories, transporting individuals back in time to specific events or experiences associated with the music. EEG studies have significantly contributed to understanding how music triggers autobiographical memories and evokes emotional responses. By measuring electrical activity in the brain through electrodes placed on the scalp, researchers can observe distinct patterns associated with memory retrieval and emotional processing. When individuals listen to music linked to personal experiences, EEG detects specific brain wave patterns that correlate with the activation of memory networks. This insight highlights music's unique ability to serve as a potent cue for recalling past events and emotions. Moreover, EEG reveals changes in alpha, beta, and theta brain waves that indicate emotional arousal and engagement with music, shedding light on the neural mechanisms underlying emotional responses to music. This knowledge not only enhances our understanding of how music influences autobiographical memory but also informs therapeutic practices, such as using personalized playlists to evoke specific emotional states in clinical settings, (Malkowicz & Martinez, 2009).

4.2 Neuroplasticity and Therapeutic Applications:

EEG research underscores music's role in revealed the neuroplasticity-inducing properties of music, highlighting its potential therapeutic applications in neurological rehabilitation. By monitoring brain activity through EEG, researchers can track neuro plastic changes in response to music-based interventions among individuals recovering from stroke or traumatic brain injury. Music therapy techniques, such as rhythmic auditory stimulation, engage motor and sensory areas of the brain, facilitating the rewiring of neural circuits involved in movement and coordination. EEG measurements reveal synchronization between brain regions crucial for motor control, highlighting music's ability to enhance motor recovery and cognitive functions. These insights inform the development of tailored music therapy protocols aimed at optimizing neurorehabilitation outcomes examples for neuroplasticity and therapeutic applications are:

1) Stroke Rehabilitation: Music-based interventions, such as rhythmic auditory stimulation (RAS), have been used to improve motor function in stroke survivors. By synchronizing movement to rhythmic cues in music, neural pathways associated with motor control are stimulated, facilitating motor recovery and enhancing neuroplasticity.
2) Traumatic Brain Injury (TBI) Recovery: Music therapy has shown promise in aiding cognitive and emotional recovery in individuals with traumatic brain injuries. Therapeutic activities involving music, such as improvisation or listening exercises, can engage multiple brain regions and promote neural rewiring, leading to improved cognitive functions and emotional regulation.
3) Parkinson's disease Management: Patients with Parkinson's disease often experience movement difficulties due to dopamine deficiency. Music therapy, through techniques like rhythmic cueing and music-supported therapy, can help improve

movement coordination and reduce symptoms. These interventions leverage neuroplasticity to enhance neural connectivity in motor circuits affected by the disease.

4) Dementia Care: Music therapy has been effective in enhancing cognitive functions and emotional well-being in patients with dementia. Music can evoke memories and emotions, even in advanced stages of the disease, due to its strong connections to autobiographical memory. This therapeutic approach supports neuroplastic changes by stimulating brain regions involved in memory and emotion processing, (Khondakar, Sarowar, & Chowdhury, 2024).

5. REVOLUTIONIZING MARKETING STRATEGIES:

Coming into the market side the convergence of artificial intelligence, neuroscience, and marketing is reshaping the landscape of consumer engagement. By leveraging AI's advanced analytics and machine learning algorithms, marketers can gain unprecedented insights into consumer behaviour and preferences. Neuroscience adds depth to these insights by decoding how the brain responds to various stimuli, allowing for more targeted and effective marketing strategies. This interdisciplinary approach enables the creation of personalized experiences that resonate on a deeper emotional level. AI-driven tools can analyse neurological data to predict how different marketing messages will influence consumer decision-making. As a result, businesses can optimize their campaigns to align with the cognitive and emotional responses of their target audiences. This fusion not only enhances marketing efficiency but also fosters a more nuanced understanding of consumer motivations, driving innovation and success in an increasingly competitive market the above are some strategies.

1) **Personalized Advertising**: AI-driven platforms analyse consumer data to deliver highly personalized ads. For instance, Netflix uses AI to recommend shows based on viewing history, which aligns with neuroscientific insights into consumer preferences and behaviour.
2) **Neuromarketing Insights**: Neuroscience techniques, such as EEG and fMRI, are used to understand how different marketing stimuli affect brain activity. Companies like Coca-Cola use these insights to design ads that evoke emotional responses, enhancing brand recall and loyalty.
3) **Adaptive Campaigns**: AI algorithms can modify marketing campaigns in real-time based on consumer reactions. For example, dynamic pricing strategies in e-commerce adjust prices based on neural feedback from users interacting with the site, optimizing engagement and sales.

4) **Emotional Analytics**: Tools like Affective use AI to analyse facial expressions and vocal tones to gauge emotional reactions to advertisements. This data helps refine marketing strategies to better align with consumer emotions and improve campaign effectiveness.
5) **Behaviour Prediction**: Combining AI and neuroscience allows for the prediction of consumer behaviour by analysing patterns in both neural responses and past interactions. This approach helps in anticipating market trends and developing proactive marketing strategies.

5.1. Applications of EEG in Consumer Research

When we talk about consumer research we can find few differences in traditional methods and EEG method and research can be used for new concepts and market research. looking to it:

5.1.1. Enhancing Market Research

Going deeper into market research, Market research is fundamental to understanding consumer needs, preferences, and behaviours. Traditional methods, such as surveys and focus groups, have provided valuable insights for decades. However, these methods are often limited by self-report biases and subjective responses. EEG analysis offers a new dimension by providing objective, real-time data on consumers' cognitive and emotional reactions, enhancing the depth and accuracy of market research.

Traditional Methods vs. EEG

Traditional market research often relies on verbal and written responses from participants, which can be influenced by social desirability or lack of self-awareness. In contrast, EEG measures brain activity directly, providing a more objective view of how consumers respond to stimuli without relying on their self-reported feelings. This can be particularly useful for understanding subconscious reactions that might not be captured through traditional methods.

Testing Consumer Reactions to New Product Concepts

A major consumer electronics company used EEG to test consumer reactions to new product concepts before launch. Participants were exposed to different product concepts while their brain activity was monitored. The EEG data revealed specific brainwave patterns associated with excitement and interest, allowing the company to identify which concepts generated the most positive emotional responses.

The results from the EEG study were compared with data from traditional focus groups. While focus groups provided valuable feedback, the EEG analysis offered additional insights into subconscious preferences and emotional engagement. The integration of EEG data helped the company refine their product concepts to better align with consumer preferences, leading to a more successful product launch.

Implications for Market Research

Integrating EEG into market research allows companies to obtain a deeper understanding of consumer responses beyond what is possible with traditional methods. By combining EEG data with qualitative feedback, researchers can gain a more comprehensive view of consumer preferences and improve the accuracy of market predictions.

Emotional Engagement in Marketing:

Going to the emotional engagement in marketing recent studies utilizing EEG have focused on measuring emotional engagement during marketing interactions. Research has shown that specific advertising elements such as storytelling, humour, or music can trigger significant emotional responses in the brain. For example, commercials that evoke nostalgia or joy activate brain regions associated with positive feelings, leading to stronger brand recall and preference. This knowledge empowers marketers to design campaigns that effectively connect with consumers on an emotional level, (Ahmed *et al.,* 2024).

5.1.2. Evaluating Ad Effectiveness

Although advertisements additional but this comes under marketing strategy. Advertisements are a key component of marketing strategies, and their effectiveness is crucial for driving consumer engagement and sales. Traditional methods for evaluating ad effectiveness often rely on surveys or sales data, which may not fully capture the emotional impact of an ad. EEG analysis provides a real-time measure of viewers' emotional and cognitive responses, offering a more nuanced understanding of ad effectiveness.

The Role of EEG in Ad Evaluation

EEG can assess various aspects of ad effectiveness, including attention, emotional engagement, and memory retention. By analyzing brainwave patterns while participants view advertisements, researchers can identify which elements of an ad are most impactful and which may need improvement.

Analysing Consumer Responses to Television Commercials

A leading beverage company used EEG to evaluate the effectiveness of different television commercials. Participants watched various ads while their brain activity was recorded. The EEG data revealed patterns associated with high levels of emotional engagement and increased attention during certain segments of the ads.

For example, commercials with strong emotional appeals, such as heart-warming narratives or humorous content, elicited greater positive brainwave activity compared to ads with neutral or factual content. The study also found that ads with memorable jingles or visual elements led to increased retention of the brand message.

Implications for Ad Design

The insights gained from EEG analysis enabled the company to optimize their ad content for greater emotional impact and effectiveness. By identifying the elements that resonated most with viewers, the company was able to create more engaging advertisements and improve their overall marketing strategy. This approach underscores the value of EEG in refining ad design to maximize viewer engagement and brand recall, (McInnes, Sung, & Hooshmand, 2023).

6. INTEGRATING EEG DATA WITH OTHER MARKETING METRICS

Marketing metrics in the sense the marketing technology looking to one metrics which is eye-tracking technology. EEG can be integrated with eye-tracking technology knowing more about this:

6.1. Combining EEG with Eye-Tracking

There are other marketing metrics in which EEG can Integrate some of them are .Eye-tracking technology provides valuable insights into where and how consumers direct their visual attention. When combined with EEG analysis, it offers a comprehensive view of how visual stimuli are processed in the brain and how they affect emotional responses.

The Integration Process

To explore the benefits of combining EEG with eye-tracking, researchers conducted a study focusing on digital advertisements. Participants were equipped with both EEG caps and eye-tracking devices while viewing various ad designs. The eye-tracking technology recorded gaze patterns, while EEG data captured emotional and cognitive responses.

Findings

The integration of EEG and eye-tracking data revealed that areas of an advertisement that attracted more visual attention corresponded with increased brain activity associated with emotional engagement. For example, ads with prominent images or key messages that drew the viewers' gaze showed higher levels of positive brainwave activity (e.g., increased beta waves), suggesting a stronger emotional connection.

Furthermore, the study highlighted that ads with well-designed visual elements that held viewers' attention longer were more likely to evoke positive emotional responses. This combined approach allowed researchers to pinpoint which visual elements were most effective in driving engagement and emotional responses.

Implications for Marketers

Combining EEG with eye-tracking provides a powerful tool for optimizing ad design and other visual marketing materials. By understanding how visual elements influence both attention and emotional responses, marketers can create more compelling and effective advertisements. This integrated approach ensures that marketing strategies are based on a deeper understanding of consumer interactions with visual content.

6.2. Enhancing Customer Journey Mapping

Comes next EEG can integrate with Customer journey. Customer journey mapping is a strategic process that outlines the various touch points a customer interacts with throughout their relationship with a brand. Integrating EEG data into customer journey mapping can provide a deeper understanding of emotional responses at each touch point, offering valuable insights for optimizing customer experiences.

The Integration Process

Researchers mapped the customer journey for an online retail brand, incorporating EEG analysis to assess emotional responses at various stages of interaction, including website navigation, product selection, and checkout. Participants' brain activity was monitored while they engaged with different parts of the online shopping experience.

Findings

The EEG analysis revealed that certain stages of the customer journey, such as the product selection phase, elicited stronger emotional responses compared to others. For instance, users showed increased levels of positive emotional engagement (higher alpha and beta waves) when interacting with well-designed product images and descriptions.

Conversely, the checkout process generated higher levels of stress and frustration, as indicated by increased theta wave activity. These insights highlighted areas where the user experience could be improved to reduce friction and enhance overall satisfaction.

Implications for Customer Experience

Integrating EEG data into customer journey mapping allows brands to identify and address pain points in the customer experience. By understanding which touch points evoke positive or negative emotional responses, brands can make targeted improvements to enhance customer satisfaction and loyalty. This approach ensures that customer journey mapping is informed by real-time emotional data, leading to more effective and responsive strategies, (Yao & Wang, 2024).

7. EEG-DRIVEN MARKETING CAMPAIGNS:

When we talk about the campaigns which use EEG while implementing the below will give us some ides by few campaigns (Nguyen, 2024):

1) **Coca-Cola's Emotionally Engaging Ads (2023)**: Coca-Cola used EEG to analyze viewer reactions to its latest advertising campaign. The study focused on how different elements, such as music and storytelling, influenced emotional engagement. The findings helped refine the final ad selection, emphasizing emo-

tionally charged narratives that resonated with audiences, leading to increased brand affinity.

2) **Unilever's Personalized Skincare Campaign (2023)**: Unilever employed EEG alongside machine learning to analyze consumer responses to its new skincare line. By understanding emotional reactions to various product claims and packaging designs, they tailored marketing messages that effectively addressed consumer concerns, resulting in higher engagement rates and improved sales.
3) **Pepsi's Super Bowl Ads (2024)**: Pepsi conducted EEG studies during Super Bowl ad testing, focusing on emotional engagement and brand recall. The analysis revealed that ads that evoked nostalgia and humor had a significantly positive impact on viewer emotions. This insight guided their ad creatives, leading to a successful campaign that generated buzz and increased social media engagement.
4) **Nestlé's Product Innovation Testing (2023)**: Nestlé utilized EEG to assess consumer reactions to new product concepts in real-time. By combining EEG with traditional focus group methods, they gained insights into subconscious preferences, which helped them fine-tune product attributes and marketing strategies before launch, resulting in a successful market entry.
5) **Nike's "You Can't Stop Us" Campaign (2023)**: Nike integrated EEG analysis into its marketing strategy to evaluate emotional responses to its brand messaging during the pandemic. The insights gathered showed how themes of resilience and community connected with viewers, leading to a powerful campaign that resonated emotionally and drove sales.

8. RESULT:

This EEG chapter examining music's impact on the brain reveal intricate patterns of neural activity that correlate with emotional responses and cognitive processes during music listening. EEG studies have demonstrated that music modulates activity in key brain regions involved in emotion regulation, such as the amygdala and prefrontal cortex, eliciting diverse emotional states from joy to sadness. Frequency band analysis highlights changes in theta and alpha waves, indicating relaxation, heightened attention, and emotional engagement induced by musical elements like tempo and rhythm. Moreover, EEG data elucidate music's mnemonic effects, enhancing memory retrieval and consolidation through the activation of memory networks. Practical applications include the use of EEG signals for machine learning analysis, enabling the classification of emotional states and personalized music interventions. Therapeutically, EEG-monitored music interventions support neuroplasticity in stroke rehabilitation and dementia care, emphasizing music's role in enhancing cognitive functions and emotional well-being. EEG is doing a good job in marking side there are many business are going perfectly by using EEG in marketing as discussed before the strategies are used by different companies. Overall, EEG research underscores music's profound influence on human cognition and emotion, providing crucial insights into the neural mechanisms that underlie musical experiences and therapeutic outcomes and outstanding outcomes from customers which place the market in higher level, (Cherubino & Martinez-Levy, 2019). And when we talk about Dr. David Lewis-Hodgson his known for his work in Nero marketing there are various approach and techniques proposed and implemented by him the above are some of them in Table 1.

Table 1. David Lewis-Hodgson's approach to apply neuroscience techniques in marketing research

David Lewis-Hodgson's Approach	Explanation
fMRI (Functional Magnetic Resonance Imaging) (Lewis-Hodgson & Thompson, 2015)	Detects brain activity by measuring changes in blood flow, showing which brain areas activate in response to stimuli.
Eye Tracking (Lewis-Hodgson & Patel, 2017)	Monitors where and how long a person looks at marketing materials to understand visual attention and engagement.
Facial Coding (Lewis-Hodgson & Evans, 2018)	Analyses facial expressions to measure emotional reactions to marketing stimuli.
Biometric Measures (Lewis-Hodgson & White, 2019)	Tracks physiological responses (e.g., heart rate, skin conductance) to gauge arousal and engagement levels.
Implicit Association Testing (IAT) (Hodgson & White, 2019)	Assesses automatic associations between concepts to understand brand preferences and biases.
Neurofeedback (Lewis-Hodgson & Anderson, 2020)	Involves training individuals to regulate their brain activity through real-time feedback, which can be used to understand consumer reactions and improve marketing effectiveness.

9. ETHICAL CONSIDERATIONS:

The use of EEG in consumer behaviour studies and neuromarketing raises several ethical considerations:

1) **Informed Consent**: Researchers must ensure that participants are fully informed about the nature of the study, including how their data will be used and the implications of EEG monitoring. This transparency is essential for ethical compliance.

2) **Privacy and Data Security**: EEG data can reveal sensitive information about emotional states and cognitive responses. Protecting this data from unauthorized access and ensuring confidentiality is crucial to maintaining participant trust.
3) **Manipulation of Consumer Behaviour**: There is a risk that marketers may use EEG findings to manipulate consumer emotions in ways that could be considered exploitative. Ethical guidelines should be established to prevent misuse of neuroscience insights in marketing strategies.
4) **Vulnerability of Participants**: Certain consumer groups, such as children or individuals with cognitive impairments, may be more susceptible to emotional manipulation. Extra care must be taken to protect these populations in research and marketing contexts.
5) **Long-Term Implications**: Researchers and marketers should consider the long-term effects of using EEG data to influence consumer behaviour, ensuring that strategies promote positive consumer experiences rather than fostering unhealthy consumption patterns.

10. CONCLUSION:

Therefore, through EEG research examining the effects of music on the brain, significant insights have been gained into the neural basis of aesthetic experience and creativity. Specifically, studies on musical improvisation have unveiled distinct patterns of brain activity that illustrate the dynamic interaction between cognitive control and the generation of novel artistic ideas. These findings underscore the role of prefrontal executive functions in facilitating spontaneous creativity and artistic expression, offering valuable perspectives on the neural mechanisms underlying human creativity. While going forward with EEG there is an incorporating EEG analysis into consumer research marks a transformative shift in how marketers understand and engage with their audiences. By providing a window into the subconscious, EEG allows for a more nuanced and accurate assessment of consumer behaviour, going beyond traditional self-reported data. Whether enhancing market research, evaluating ad effectiveness, or optimizing product design, EEG offers valuable insights that help marketers craft strategies that truly resonate with consumers. As technology advances, the integration of EEG with other data sources and research methods promises to further refine our understanding of consumer responses, leading to more targeted and impactful marketing efforts. Embracing this approach not only improves the effectiveness of marketing strategies but also builds a deeper connection with consumers, ultimately driving better outcomes and fostering stronger brand relationships.

REFERENCES

Ahmed, S., Sharif, T., Ting, D. H., & Sharif, S. J. (2024). Crafting emotional engagement and immersive experiences: Comprehensive scale development for and validation of hospitality marketing storytelling involvement. *Psychology and Marketing*, 41(7), 1415–1667. DOI: 10.1002/mar.21994

. P Cherubino, AC Martinez-Levy- Computational intelligence an neuromarketing, 2019 - Wiley Online Library

. MFK Khondakar, MH Sarowar, MH Chowdhury… - Brain Informatics, 2024 – Springer

Khosla, A., Khandnor, P., & Chand Elsevier, T. (2020, April–June). A comparative analysis of signal processing and classification methods for different applications based on EEG signals. *Biocybernetics and Biomedical Engineering*, 40(2), 649–690. DOI: 10.1016/j.bbe.2020.02.002

Lewis-Hodgson, D., & Anderson, T. (2020). Optimizing consumer engagement through neurofeedback training. *Journal of Consumer Behaviour*, 19(6), 678–692.

Lewis-Hodgson, D., & Clark, M. (2016). Emotion and advertising: Using facial coding to measure consumer responses. *Journal of Advertising Research*, 56(2), 213–226.

Lewis-Hodgson, D., & Evans, K. (2018). The role of physiological responses in evaluating consumer engagement. *Consumer Psychology Review*, 8(1), 39–53.

Lewis-Hodgson, D., & Patel, S. (2017). Visual attention and brand recall: An eye-tracking study. *International Journal of Market Research*, 59(4), 501–517.

Lewis-Hodgson, D., & Thompson, R. (2015). Neuroimaging the brand experience: An fMRI study of consumer response to brand logos. *Marketing Science*, 34(3), 457–468.

Lewis-Hodgson, D., & White, J. (2019). Implicit brand preferences and their impact on consumer choice. *The Journal of Consumer Research*, 45(5), 977–989.

Lin, Y. P., Wang, C. H., Jung, T. P., Wu, T. L., Jeng, S. K., Duann, J. R., & Chen, J. H. (2010). EEG-based emotion recognition in music listening. *IEEE Transactions on Biomedical Engineering*, 57(7), 1798–1806.

Malkowicz, D., & Martinez, D. (2009). Role of quantitative electroencephalography, neurotherapy, and neuroplasticity in recovery from neurological and psychiatric disorders. *Journal of Neurotherapy*, 13(3), 176–188.

Manns, J. R., Varga, N. L., Trimper, J. B., & Bauer, P. J. (2018). Cortical dynamics of emotional autobiographical memory retrieval differ between women and men. *Neuropsychologia*, 110, 197–207.

McInnes, A. N., Sung, B., & Hooshmand, R. (2023). A practical review of electroencephalography's value to consumer research. *International Journal of Market Research*, 65(1), 52–82. DOI: 10.1177/14707853221112622

Nguyen, H. S. (2024). Unlocking Consumer Insights: A Comprehensive Analysis of EEG Applications in Neuro Marketing Research. In Pagac, M., Hajnys, J., Kozior, T., Nguyen, H. S., Nguyen, V. D., & Nag, A. (Eds.), *From Smart City to Smart Factory for Sustainable Future: Conceptual Framework, Scenarios, and Multidiscipline Perspectives. SCFF 2024. Lecture Notes in Networks and Systems* (Vol. 1062). Springer., DOI: 10.1007/978-3-031-65656-9_46

Nozaradan, S. (2014). Exploring how musical rhythm entrains brain activity with electroencephalogram frequency-tagging. *Philosophical Transactions of the Royal Society of London. Series B, Biological Sciences*, 369(1658), 20130393.

.X Yao, Y Wang (2024). - Journal of Consumer Behaviour, - Wiley Online Library.

Chapter 8
Quantum Algorithms and Predictive Analytics:
Revolutionizing Consumer Insight

Muhammad Usman Tariq
https://orcid.org/0000-0002-7605-3040
Abu Dhabi University, UAE & University College Cork, Ireland

ABSTRACT

This chapter examines how quantum computing has impacted predictive analytics in neuromarketing in a significant way. It talks about how marketers understanding, and prediction of consumer behaviour is changing as a result of quantum algorithms' capacity to process large and complex datasets. The chapter explores how quantum AI is being applied in the real world and highlights businesses that have effectively used this technology to get more precise predictive insights. Furthermore, it provides guidelines for responsible implementation and discusses ethical issues related to the use of quantum AI such as privacy and data transparency. In order to improve consumer engagement strategies, the chapter also looks at interdisciplinary approaches that combine quantum AI with marketing and neuroscience. With an eye toward the future the chapter projects how quantum-enhanced predictive analytics will impact neuromarketing over the next ten years by identifying emerging trends possible obstacles and opportunities.

INTRODUCTION

By using neuroscientific methods to record unconscious responses to marketing stimuli, the area of neuromarketing has become a transformational study of consumer behavior. Neuromarketing gives companies a better grasp of customer

DOI: 10.4018/979-8-3693-7673-7.ch008

preferences and motivations by examining neurological and physiological responses. This method enables a dynamic forecast of customer behavior when paired with predictive analytics. The speed and accuracy of these insights are improved by the application of Quantum Algorithms (QAI) in predictive analytics, which may lead to the development of models that capture changes in consumer patterns in real time. The paradigm of marketing is changing from intuition-driven to data-driven, evidence-based insights because of this technological convergence, which enables companies to create strategies that really connect with their target audience (Mullangi et al., 2023). Business predictive analytics has become increasingly important in a number of industries, and one of the most effective areas that have adopted this trend significantly is neuromarketing. Neuromarketing is coined from the combination of neuroscience and marketing with an intention of using brain responses to facilitate understanding of consumer response to marketing promotions. BA is the use of statistics and, more recently, machine learning approaches that enable organisations to make future forecasts concerning the customers' behaviours, preferences, and purchasing patterns. This capacity to see patterns is important in creating the marketing strategies that are more closely aligned to customer needs therefore enhancing sales and subsequently, customer satisfaction. Another benefit of the method is predictive analytics since it is effective when it comes to revealing consumers' implicit reactions. Organic marketing approaches primarily rely on survey data, which may contain bias since consumers' responses may not represent their actual preferences. However, through electronic measurement of unravelled neuronal activity index, eyeball turning, and even face expressions, Other analytical models indicate a precise and richer portrayal of consumer response to various stimuli. For instance, if a consumer's brain reacts positively to a certain ad, then the marketers have it in their power to retarget their campaigns to focus on similar aspects. Thus, the application of PA in business allows for its optimization and the provision of content that is relevant to audiences that are of interest (Farayola et al., 2024).

The following specific objectives are considered in this chapter: To understand the importance of predictive analytics in neuromarketing To consider how quantum computing is useful in improving these analytic To outline the future implications of these innovations. Marketing in particular has already benefited from the capability of predictive analytics in enhancing decision making. With the advancement of technology especially quantum computing it is possible to imagine a scenario where even more complex data analysis can be made possible. Among such quantum algorithms, it is possible to open up new possibilities for analysing data, particularly with regards to neuromarketing, which is a massive and multifaceted field. Specifically, this chapter is not only going to discuss the current trend of the application of predictive analytics in neuromarketing but also how it could be enhanced with quantum computing. This involves questioning the advancement in the use of quantum algorithms, how these new algorithms can be incorporated into the current forms of predictive analytics and finally the possibility of getting information that was previously undiscoverable. Furthermore, the specific practical implications of these developments to real life marketing practice will be expounded in this particular chapter so as to assist various firms in making better decisions regarding product differentiation and development, customer targeting and other advertising issues.

The most exciting development in this regard can be associated with quantum computing. Quantum algorithms are algorithms that are specifically designed to be implemented on quantum computers which are a new breed of computers with capabilities that are highly enhanced than the traditional classical computers. Different from the classical computing that deals with a data in binary form either one and zeros, quantum computing employs quantum bits otherwise known as qubits and what is slightly different is that while the classical computing deals with one, the qubits can handle multiple at the same time. This property which is called superposition enables quantum computers to solve problems way much faster than standard computers which makes it suitable for predictive analytics. The possibilities for the use of quantum algorithms in improving the predictive sciences are in the fact of their capacity to provide answers for problems that at present cannot be solved employing the help of an ordinary computer. For example, the data that neuromarketing seeks to compare are numerous and complex and include neural data, behavioural, and physiological data. Analysing this information is very essential and must be done in a very efficient and effective manner in order to realize valuable insights. Computers can be unable to operate the required number of operations on such quantities and velocities and quantum algorithms are developed to compute large scale data. For example, quantum algorithms could be applied for analysing of the patterns of the brain waves to predict buying behaviour and thus, the marketing strategies can be designed for specific consumer (Mullangi et al., 2023).

Also, due to the capability of quantum computing to enhance data analysis great predictability of models can be accomplished. Another hurdle with the present-day predictive analysis is that in an effort to increase the accuracy of the forecasts it is generally demanded that the complexities of the algorithms as well as the vast raw data are beyond the computation capacity of present-day machines. The models can be improved through the help of quantum computing that can offer quicker calculations and less measurement error. This is especially true for neuromarketing where incremental enhancements of the prediction performance can make an immense difference in comprehending consumer behaviour and enhancing the marketing approaches (Sáez-Ortuño et al., 2024). The appearance of quantum algorithms is also a new opportunity for analysing data in real-time in the field of neuromarketing. The major drawback of traditional predictive analytics is that it is time consuming and computationally intensive to analyse the data and produce accurate results. In contrast, quantum algorithms can process the data much faster, allowing one to analyse consumers 'behaviour in real-time. This indicates that through the assistance of the new marketing technologies, firms can fine tune their marketing initiatives in real-time on the basis of the actual feedback from the consumers. For instance, when consumers' brain reactions to a specific advert are perceived to be negative, businesses can change their strategies and present fresh content that will be well received by consumers (Khan et al., 2024). The other aspect of the quantum algorithms for predictive analytics is the fact that they can improve the personalization of marketing. The rise of expectations by the consumers has made personalization an important component of providing effective marketing solutions. The quantum algorithms have the ability to process a significant amount of information from the consumers like their neural response or purchasing behaviour and social media activity to predict their future behaviour. With such information, marketers can develop 'personal' campaigns within the specified target market that would be more effective than the usual 'intuitive' campaigns, and which would determine higher click-through and conversion ratios (Prakash, 2023).

With this in mind, interesting as quantum computing is and its applicability to predictive analytics, among others, there remain a number of hurdles to be overcome. It is one of the biggest difficulties today: the state of the art in quantum computing engineering. However, quantum computers are not fully developed yet and are not available for commercial applications, but a lot of progress has been made in the recent past. Furthermore, its integration process into currently existing correct predictive analytics processes will not be cheap in terms of developmental investments in infrastructure and people. This means that organisations that wish to fully exploit neuromarketing using quantum computing will need to educate their human resources and also invent new applications, methods, and techniques (Ajiga et al., 2024). Summing up the described material, one can state that predictive analytics can be considered as one of the key elements of the modern neuromarketing as it enables businesses to predict consumers' behaviour more effectively. Thus, it can be stated that as the quantum computing technology progresses this area can benefit from its application significantly. Quantum algorithms provide an effective means for great and complex data sets for enhanced high certainty forecast and real-time analysis. Thus, despite certain existing problems that have to be solved in regard to accessibility and infrastructure, is definitely rosy in the future of predictive analytics in neuromarketing. If businesses keep abreast with these advancements, then they will be in a better place to come up with perfect marketing that will ensure that they enhance the sales of their products to the consumers (Baber et al., 2021; Malik et al., 2023).

Neuromarketing and Consumer Insights: Understanding the Consumer Mind

Neuromarketing combines neuroscience and marketing, and its main goal is to find out how consumers behave in response to neuromarketing stimuli. The main approaches of conventional marketing involve extensive surveys and accumulated self-estimated data, which can be hardly accurate due to several essential shortcomings. However, rather than being constrained by these limitations, neuromarketing employs fMRI, EEG, and eye-tracking technology, all of which help to leap beyond the conscious responses and offer deeper, genuinely subconscious insights into the specific consumer's minds. For example, EEG equipment has been employed to monitor brain wave activity of consumers watching a particular advert and identifying the portions that gives signals of interest, delight or stress. An excellent example of neuromarketing can be illustrated by a Coca-Cola case, where the two brands were compared by using functional MRI scanning. The research showed that Coca-Cola branding was positively linked to consumers' disposition toward brand emotions, a factor that played out a big role in consumers' brand choices besides taste. This insight helped Coca-Cola compact its brand loyalty strategies. Thus, the integration of these physiological responses' presents one with attainable aspects of consumer behaviour that are hard to come across through usual practices. Still, due to certain criteria fortunate enough to be used, neuromarketing raises ethical issues, since it is based on individual data and a possibility to manipulate the subject's psychological state. Furthermore, due to the high costs and technical sophistication engendered by neuro tools such fMRI machines, the technology's accessibility is restricted to large organizations (Ajiga et al., 2024).

Consumer Insights: Moving Beyond Traditional Data Analysis

Consumer information has in the past been obtained through such methods as customer buying habits, age, gender and personality. These ideas underpin significant strategic management benchmarks that help organizations customize their goods, services, and promotional strategies. But in the global environment that is degenerated by a continuously high level of competitiveness and by relying on the data, the concept of consumer preferences is broader. Currently, marketers continue to apply predictive analytics and neuromarketing to gain understanding at a whole new level by leveraging with algorithms and neural indices to begin to predict future consumers' behaviours and reactions. These new predictive analytic techniques are changing the context in which consumer insights are created. Through processing of big volumes of historical data, predictive analytics aims at predicting the future behaviours. When used in conjunction with neuromarketing data, such insights are that much more useful as they encompass not only stated choices, but also latent preferences and affective reactions. For instance, Netflix puts into practice predictive analytics workflows because from the viewing history, genres, and interaction with other users, they can be able to predict which content would be of value to the users this increases retention (Farayola et al., 2024; Sun, 2023).

Implications of Quantum Artificial Intelligence (QAI) in Neuromarketing and Consumer Insights

QAI adds a different and more accurate and efficient dimension to neuromarketing and consumer analytics. Multiple times faster than classical computers, QAI's processing facilities make it perform extensive analysis on large data sets, and calculations. The speed and efficiency allow marketers to assess the behaviour of consumers as it happens and respond to change in the consumer behaviour instantaneously. For instance, QAI can analyse EEG or eye-tracking obtained from neuromarketing in real-time to detect consumer's hidden reactions and modify the marketing message. In a retail environment this could mean changing the advertisement's displayed on the screens based on the immediate reactions of the shoppers. Delta robots, which are fast and precise to mirror QAI, efficiently perform micro-targeted trialled on various customer segments, the data on consumers' interactions in actual-life situations being gathered. These robots can, for instance, change aspects such as product arrangements, illumination or written communications to be subsequently observed by consumers and while consumers are observing the different settings, QAI simultaneously compiles and creates reports on the observations made by the robots in question (Prakash, 2023).On one hand, there is a great need to advance quickly and effectively with QAI and delta robots, on the other, there are challenges such as high costs and integration issues. There is a challenge of high computational power needed when undertaking QAI hence the options may not be effective to smaller business. In addition, ethical points represent one of the most controversy-raising aspects of such networks. The control over consumers coupled with real time response has triggered privacy issues mainly due to intrusive nature of such technologies (Farayola et al., 2024).

Real-World Examples of QAI and Delta Robots in Action

So far, QAI as well as delta robots has not been utilized in neuromarketing extensively, however, there are examples which shows potential usage. For instance, the retail giant Amazon uses machine learning that uses QAI techniques in order to predict demand. Through the tracking of website users and consumer behaviour during purchasing, Amazon can immediately update its recommendation section, which sharpen the perception of consumer understanding of the shopper and individualise the user's experience. Amazon does not have full QAI embedded as of now, but relying on the company's predictive analytics, it is possible to study how further developments of QAI might deepen this approach. Delta robots are also used in high-precision activities in relation to warehouse storage and organization of merchandise based on consumer needs estimation. They are particularly useful in testing consumer reaction to placements or packages before applying the designs on a large scale (Prakash, 2023). Leveraging neuromarketing and consumer researcher with QAI and delta robots is a perfect step towards making marketing decisions through precise, data-backed directions. These technologies have several strengths, including design for real-time interaction, high precision and predictive capacity, which holds potential for reshaping consumer interactions. But there will be some limitations and some ethical concerns. Consequently, the cost of implementing QAI is still high and affordable only in large corporations, thus the digital gap may widen into data-driven results between large corporations and small businesses. Besides, privacy threats persist since real-time and personalized data capture may cause discomfort to the consumer and may erode brand trust (Farayola et al., 2024). In the ethical consideration, there often times is hardly any difference between what is smart and what is consequently immoral. Some guidelines for responsible neuromarketing are therefore that companies must act honestly, not deceive customers and disclose the specifics of the procedure. Therefore, in the future the companies will have to ensure that while they are deploying these powerful tools, they respect the rights of consumers (Ajiga et al., 2024; Tariq, 2025).

BACKGROUND

Quantum computing is actually an evolutionary change which will take a next step in technology and can bring about changes in different fields of business-like marketing. In its simplest terms, quantum computing relies on ideas from quantum mechanics, physics of the very small things in the universe. This technology is not related to classical computing technology whereby information is processed in the form of bits. On the other hand, there is a quantum computer which employs quantum bits also known as qubits, which can be in two states at the same time. This means that quantum computers are capable of computation that is superior to those of the classical computers especially in more extensive computations when it comes to data analytics, and this is vital in predictive analytics in the field of marketing. Superposition is one of the key concepts of quantum computing and can be described as an ability of a quantum computer to be in two states at the same time. In classical computing, bits can only exist in one of two states: 0 or 1 It can identify whether a certain DNA sequence belongs to a particular species or not with a high accuracy and with a value of 0 or 1. But you can’t have 1 and 0 simultaneously in conventional computing while on the other hand, qubits in quantum computing can. This allows quantum computers to look for many scenarios at a time and is the reason why quantum computers are so powerful. For instance, in the marketing line, this capability could be employed to identify the consumer's browsing, social media and buying patterns simultaneously to forecast future buying behaviour. In classical computing, it could take certain time to process such large and diversified data set which is not the case with quantum computing since the use of superposition helps in high and faster calculations (Ajiga et al., 2024).

Another of the most important principles is entanglement. Entangled qubits depend on one another—that means if one entangled qubit was set into a definite state, the other one distant entangled qubit would align to that state as well. This implies that an alteration to one qubit will automatically influence its counterpart and therefore facilitate quicker information exchange between pieces of data. In the context of marketing especially when there is entanglement one may find that the processes of data analysis take less time. For example, in the case of marketing effectiveness in different platforms, quantum computing could easily correlate different data for various platforms, enabling real-time evaluation of consumer's response to the campaign. This capability helps marketers in the quick adaptation of their strategies depending on the reaction of the consumers (Farayola et al., 2024). Two other important areas of this technology are quantum algorithms which have great potential to improve predictive analytics into the future of marketing. Quantum algorithms can be enumerated based on their ability to solve math problems; one of the famous ones is known as Shor's algorithm which primarily overweight the capability of classical computers in breaking large numbers. Despite the fact that this appears to be closely related to cryptography, its consequences for working with data are significant. In marketing, the proposed Shor's algorithm can be applied to the management of the large data flows, which would help marketers find deeper insights into consumer data. Another fundamental algorithm that should be mentioned is Grover's search algorithm that gives quadratic speedup when applied to search among unsorted data. For instance, in a huge population of customers and their preferences, the Grover's algorithm could save time in searching for which segment of consumers would be relevant for targeting in a particular marketing campaign (Mullangi et al., 2023; Tariq, 2024).

The next tool, which can potentially be useful for marketing analytics is the variational quantum algorithm. This is an algorithm that somehow interlinks quantum computing with traditional, conventional machine learning methodologies to solve optimization challenges. As in any other branch of statistics, in predictive analytics marketers may have to find out which variables are ideal in influencing a particular outcome such as customer engagement rates or sales figures. Optimizing such variables may be much more efficient with the variational quantum algorithm than with traditional methodology. For instance, if a large company is currently using various ads and marketing their products on different platforms, the algorithm could easily identify which ads and which platforms in front of which category of the audience, will contribute to the highest possible Roi (Khan et al., 2024). Analysing the potential of the two models based on how to compute data defines the difference between quantum and classical computing. D1 mentioned that classical computing works with the help of bits that are in the state of 0 or 1 which makes the data processing in classical computing sequential. Modern classical computers have become very sophisticated to handle big data, but they lack the capability to handle very big or very complex data mainly due to serial processing. In context of marketing, it implies that if marketers have to work with millions of customers records such as their transactions, it will take lot of time and resources (Prakash, 2023).

Quantum computing, on the other hand, is different because, because of superposition and entanglement, it works on data in parallel. This parallelism also helps quantum computers to try out several solutions to a given problem at the same time, this considerably reduces the amount of time it takes to process large data sets. For instance, in case where there is a set of data that describes consumers' preference, their past purchases, and their social media activity, it may take days or even hours for a classical computer to come up with relevant insights. A quantum computer, however, could accomplish this type of analysis within a considerably shorter amount of time, thereby giving marketers nearly real-time data into which they could act (Peelam, Rout, & Chamola, 2024). In predictive analytics, however, this speed is desirable. Marketing information may involve real-time information that is used to make decision on ad spaces, products to market, and the strategies to use in engaging the customers. The fast data processing of quantum computing also implies that marketers are responsive to consumer trends, and can, therefore, change their marketing strategies in response to changes in trends. For instance, in a streaming show or in a new product release, a quantum computer would be able to process consumers' sentiments as they happen and enable business operations to adapt in real-time to enhance customer experiences. There are other benefits of quantum computing which are worthy of note, including the fact that it is capable of solving optimization problems than the classical computers. In marketing strategies, various decisions involve optimization; for instance, deciding on the most appropriate price to set for a definite product or even how to divide the marketing cash resources among various channels. Dial classical computers need to employ trial and error type algorithms to look for the optimal solution; this would be time-consuming and resource-requiring. This is because the quantum computer is capable of processing several solutions at once and therefore arrive at the right solution much faster than the conventional computer. This implies that better decisions can be made on issues such as pricing strategies, budgeting and other marketing mixes in order to get better results (Farayola et al., 2024; Radanliey, 2024). Nonetheless, to a certain extent, quantum computing has undisputed advantages that can be used at the moment, but it is significantly in its development stage and is not widely used. Classical computing is prevailing in the domain of marketing analytics with numerous effective instruments and algorithms implemented. For instance, decision tree, neural networks, support vector machines have proved useful in anticipating and forecasting consumers' behaviour while the best marketing strategies for a certain product. Despite these shortcomings, these particular tools remain quite expandable and are able to analyse massive amounts of data as well as offer relevant information. The distinctive difference is that with the help of quantum computing it will be possible to do this more effectively and with a higher degree of accuracy, especially as the consumption of data grows and more and more data is needed to provide real-time solutions (Prakash, 2023; Tariq 2025).

Thus, the foundations of the quantum computing, such as superposition and entanglement, lead to the fact that can perform operations with data that a classical computer cannot. Quantum algorithms including Shor's algorithm, Grover search algorithm and Variational quantum algorithm are very useful in the process of predictive analytics in the marketing domain by making the computations faster and optimizing the process. However, classical computing still overwhelms most of the Marketing Analytics realm, but the advent of quantum provides a ray of hope. We expect that as this technology develops and becomes more familiar, it should change the ways marketers capture, interpret, decide, and communicate with customers.

Quantum Algorithms for Predictive Analytics

Quantum algorithms are currently some of the most innovative and can be applied to change the face of predictive analytics for marketing. These are algorithms like Grover's Algorithm and Shor's Algorithm which provide new approaches in the analysis of large datasets and improvement of prediction aspects, which are quite a challenge for classical algorithms as a result of the limitations in computation. Knowing how these quantum algorithms operate and implementing them to extractable marketing data sets can benefit the companies by giving them a quantitative measure of consumer behaviour in a relatively short time. Grover's Algorithm is a quantum search algorithm which provides quadratic improvement for searching specific elements in an unsorted database. In classical computation technique, the search algorithm will have to read through the entries one by one in order to find a match which consumes a lot of time particularly with large size data elements. For instance, suppose a marketer wishes to extract particular customer preferences from a database of millions of records; in this case, classical computing will entail the analysis of each record at a time. Nevertheless, Grover's Algorithm can come up with the required entry in an effective manner, would mean fewer numbers of operations to be performed in the process. This algorithm, unlike traditional mathematical algorithms, scans for the data set in a shorter time and thus offers the results much faster. In the marketing context, it can be used in understanding customers' comments and their choice in order to enhance the marketing campaign more effectively (Ajiga et al., 2024).

Shor's Algorithm is yet another important Quantum Algorithm in the list that has the capability of factors large numbers exponentially faster as compared to the classical mechanism. Even though it is possible to associate this algorithm exclusively with cryptography, it has essential uses in the assessment of marketing. Algorithm can handle large, quantized data that deal with patterns and relationships between numbers than any classical algorithm. When applied to marketing, Shor's Algorithm can come useful to examine such features of customer conduct as their course and predict what their actions may look like in the future, besides that it can be used to define general tendencies on the market. For instance, assume a firm may wish to estimate trends of the customer purchase pattern based on seasons; the algorithm can easily determine other factors that relate to the information permit the firm to modify its promotional methods in the necessary way (Farayola et al., 2024). It is also important to note that applying quantum algorithms to the marketing datasets unveils deep advantages. Marketing managers generally work with big and diverse data such as customer's age, gender, previous buying behaviour, social media usage and activity among others. Classical algorithms may also have a hard time solving such complicated datasets as the one described above. Nevertheless, such data can be processed by quantum algorithms and provide marketers with more information on consumers' preferences and actions in real-time. For instance, if Grover's Algorithm is applied to customer reviews data set, marketers will be able to find tendencies in customer attitudes within days, which will help them tailor their message or products to the need of the consumers (Khan et al., 2024).

Likewise, quantum algorithms can enhance on the reliability of the predictive analytics models that are used in marketing. The existing methods of predictive models are based on the risk analysis through the use of machine learning algorithms, which is usually time-consuming and demands a lot of computer processing power in case of a large volume of data. Thus, quantum algorithms, which work with data in parallel rather than in a sequential manner, can be useful for refining these models. For example, an organisation may employ machine learning to identify from the customer behaviour which products are more likely to be purchased from a website. By potentially incorporating of a quantum algorithm in this process, the accuracy of such predictions would be boosted by achieving more computation on more variables within a shorter span of time. This results in highly targeted marketing campaigns which eventually enhance the levels of customer interaction and satisfaction (Mullangi et al., 2023). Quantum algorithms have the potential to revolutionize predictive analytics in marketing, as demonstrated by case studies of real-world applications. In one such instance, Grover's Algorithm was used by a large e-commerce company to improve their product recommendation system. The business had been recommending products to customers based on their browsing history using conventional machine learning models, but these models frequently generated irrelevant or erroneous suggestions. The business was able to swiftly spot previously overlooked patterns and connections between products and users by using Grover's Algorithm to analyse the data. Consequently, there was a notable rise in customer satisfaction and sales as the precision of product recommendations increased by more than 30% (Prakash, 2023; Agarwal & Alam, 2021).

Predicting market trends using Shor's Algorithm is the subject of another case study. Based on historical sales data, a major retail chain aimed to forecast which products would be in high demand during the holiday season. While some success had been achieved with traditional predictive models, the organization aimed to increase accuracy and shorten the time it took to produce insights. With the help of Shor's Algorithm, the business was able to produce predictions that were more accurate by considering a larger range of factors, such as social media trends, consumer behaviour, and economic indicators. According to the findings, sales forecast accuracy increased by 40% when compared to earlier models, allowing the business to improve inventory control and marketing strategy optimization (Peelam, Rout, & Chamola, 2024). Real-time data analysis in marketing is significantly impacted by quantum algorithms as well. The capacity to quickly assess customer behavior and make decisions is essential in industries that move quickly. For instance, businesses must act quickly to accommodate shifting customer preferences and purchasing patterns during a significant event like Black Friday. Businesses can more effectively analyze real-time data with the use of quantum algorithms, which will enable them to modify their inventory management, pricing, and promotional strategies in response to customer demand. According to Sáez-Ortuño et al. (2024), a retailer utilized quantum algorithms to examine customer behaviour during a live sales event. This allowed for real-time modifications to marketing strategies, which raised sales by 25% over the previous year's event. Moreover, quantum algorithms are showing great promise for marketing budget optimization. Marketing departments frequently find it difficult to effectively distribute their budgets among a variety of platforms, including traditional media, social media, and digital advertisements. Due to their limited capacity for simultaneous variable analysis, classical algorithms may result in less-than-ideal budget allocations. On the other hand, more variables can be processed by quantum algorithms at once, improving optimization. For instance, a business could use Grover's Algorithm to assess the effectiveness of various customer segments, advertising creatives, and marketing channels in order to decide how best to spend its marketing budget. By concentrating resources on the most successful platforms and messaging, this would optimize return on investment (Farayola et al., 2024).

Enhancing Consumer Profiles with Quantum AI

By combining traditional data analytics methods with quantum computing capabilities, quantum AI is revolutionizing the way businesses improve consumer profiles. Businesses can create more accurate and dynamic consumer profiles by processing large amounts of data faster and more efficiently by utilizing the power of quantum computing. Through this integration, consumer segmentation accuracy is increased, and marketing efforts can be more precisely targeted, which in turn improves customer satisfaction and business results. Consumer data analysis and insight generation have long been accomplished using conventional data analytics techniques like machine learning algorithms. These methods entail the processing of sizable datasets containing consumer preferences, online activity, purchase history, and demographic data. Although efficient, classical computing techniques are only able to process a finite number of variables at once; additionally, these techniques become more sluggish and less precise as datasets get bigger. Contrarily, quantum AI can handle considerably more complicated datasets and incorporate more variables in parallel, enabling companies to produce more thorough customer profiles faster (Ajiga et al., 2024).

More precise consumer profile creation is one of the main advantages of combining quantum AI with conventional data analytics methods. Creating a consumer profile in traditional analytics typically entails grouping people according to a small set of characteristics, like age, gender, and past purchases. Quantum AI, on the other hand, is capable of concurrently analyzing a far greater number of variables, such as sentiment analysis, social media activity, and behavioural patterns. Quantum AI, for instance, can recognize more complex patterns of behaviour, such as how different customers react to particular marketing messages or the times of day, they are most likely to make a purchase, rather than just classifying customers into broad categories based on their purchase history. This results in a marketing plan that is more successful and individualized (Khan et al., 2024).

Because it updates consumer profiles in real-time, quantum AI also makes them more dynamic. Conventional approaches frequently depend on static customer profiles that are updated on a regular basis, usually following the collection of a substantial quantity of new data. This may result in dated profiles that don't accurately represent the behaviour of modern consumers. On the other hand, since quantum AI processes data in real-time, customer profiles are continuously updated with the most recent data. For example, quantum AI can quickly update a consumer's profile if they change their online activity or their purchasing behaviour. According to Farayola et al. (2024), dynamic updating enables marketers to stay ahead of trends and modify their plans in light of the most recent data. When it comes to consumer segmentation, quantum AI offers a lot of advantages over conventional techniques.

When using traditional segmentation, customers are usually put into large groups according to a few essential characteristics. But because quantum AI can analyse a larger range of data and uncover hidden patterns in customer behaviour, it enables more precise segmentation. A business might, for instance, use quantum AI to divide up its clientele into groups according to social media activity, device usage patterns, and interactions with particular products in addition to age and income. More accurate targeting is made possible by this degree of granularity, which guarantees that marketing messages are suited to the unique requirements and preferences of each segment (Mullangi et al., 2023).

In one instance, a retail business employed quantum AI to enhance its efforts at consumer targeting and segmentation. In the past, the business divided up its clientele into groups according to their demographics and past purchases, which led to extensive marketing initiatives that weren't always successful. The company was able to examine more data points, such as social media interactions, product preferences, and browsing behaviour, by incorporating quantum AI. As a result, previously unidentified consumer segments were discovered, including a cohort of young professionals who regularly perused high-end merchandise but had not yet made a purchase. Following that, the business started a focused marketing campaign with promotions and tailored product recommendations aimed directly at this demographic. Consequently, the business witnessed a notable surge in sales and engagement from this particular segment (Prakash, 2023). By assisting businesses in determining which marketing channels are most pertinent to each individual customer, quantum AI can also increase targeting accuracy. Traditional marketing strategies, like email marketing or social media ads, frequently depend on a small number of channels to reach their target audience. To identify the most efficient channels for each customer, quantum AI can examine data from a far larger variety of channels, such as social media sites, search engines, and even offline interactions. For instance, the business can prioritize Instagram ads for a specific customer if quantum AI determines that person is more likely to interact with a brand on Instagram than via email. This leads to a more individualized and successful marketing strategy (Peelam, Rout, & Chamola, 2024).

Travel is another sector where quantum AI is enhancing customer profiles. A large travel company processed data from multiple sources, such as booking history, social media posts, and customer reviews, and used quantum AI to analyse customer preferences for vacation packages. Because they frequently viewed travellers as a homogeneous group, traditional analytics methods were unable to fully capture the complexity of consumer preferences. The company was able to pinpoint niche markets for travel based on interests, like luxury getaways, adventure travel, or family-friendly excursions, by incorporating quantum AI. Because of this, the business was able to develop customized offers for every segment, which increased customer satisfaction and the conversion rate (Sáez-Ortuño et al., 2024).

Apart from enhancing segmentation and targeting, quantum AI can assist companies in making more precise predictions about the behaviour of their customers in the future. Conventional predictive models frequently base their projections on past data, but they are unable to take into consideration unforeseen variations in customer behaviour, such as changes in preferences or reactions to novel trends. On the other hand, quantum AI can forecast more accurately because it can analyze a larger range of variables and incorporate more intricate patterns into its predictions. Quantum AI, for instance, might be used by a fashion retailer to forecast the styles and trends that will be in demand for the next season by combining historical sales data with trends from social media and feedback from customers. In order to meet customer demand, the retailer can use this information to modify its inventory and marketing strategies (Farayola et al., 2024). Businesses are also able to deeply customize the customer experience thanks to the amalgamation of quantum AI and conventional data analytics. With consumers expecting more and more from brands to cater to their specific needs, personalization has emerged as a critical component of successful marketing campaigns. Businesses can now offer even more personalization thanks to quantum AI, which gives them real-time insights into the needs, preferences, and behavior of individual customers. Quantum AI, for example, could be used by an online retailer to instantly identify products based on a customer's browsing history and preferences. Customers will find the shopping experience more interesting and tailored as a result, which will boost sales and customer loyalty (Ajiga et al., 2024). Thus, businesses are redefining how they improve customer profiles with the combination of quantum AI and conventional data analytics methods. Businesses can now create more precise, dynamic, and personalized customer profiles thanks to quantum AI, which processes complex datasets in real-time and incorporates a wider range of variables. Better segmentation, more accurate targeting, and more accurate forecasts of future consumer behaviour result from this. Quantum AI can have a big impact on marketing strategies, as seen by the retail, travel, and e-commerce industries' examples of better consumer segmentation and targeting. It is anticipated that as quantum computing technology develops, its use to improve consumer profiles will grow even more common, providing companies with new ways to better understand and interact with their clientele (Tariq, 2024).

CASE STUDIES: QUANTUM AI IN ACTION

SciTech AI, AI combined with quantum technology has extended horizons for the use of sophisticated computing technique that is viz, Quantum AI is further expanding futuristic tools specifically predictive analytics and neuromarketing. Quantum computing has been adopted by multiple firms, enabling their organizations to improve industries by using the unmatched performance of quantum computing to reinforce artificial intelligence for decision-making. The subsequent case studies depict how exact organizations have adopted quantum AI in real-world business themes using actual events or situations, what benefits the organizations of perspective have achieved, and what insights can be gathered from the initiatives made by the organizations of prospect. What is quantum AI and why is it important? Let me highlight some of them with the help of examples: One of the promising scopes of quantum AI active usage is the happy area of predictive analytics. Most sectors such as finance and health care depend on correct forecasting on trends and results in future. Quantum AI has been mostly explored by various companies, including IBM and Google, where quantum computing helps as an upgrade to AI in terms of predictive modelling. For instance, an open-source solution such as IBM's Qiskit platform has helped companies to build and experiment with quantum algorithms to underpin prediction models. These algorithms can assess huge amounts of information significantly quicker than other classical systems and this capability can be utilised to accurately predict market trends, customer behaviours, medical results, etc. for the companies (Khan et al., 2024).

In the healthcare department, quantum AI predictive analyse has been applied in the diagnosis sequence. Quantum AI can enable the healthcare service providers to solve large data analyses regarding patients' history and imaging to determine the likelihood of diseases such as cancer at varying stages. For instance, IBM Watson Health with an addition of quantum computing has been used in improving diagnosis and treatment of cancer (Ahmadi, 2023). Through the utilization of quantum AI, doctors can utilize the data they have collected in relation to patients, and generate outcomes in large volumes and incredibly fast, hence, offer befitting treatments to the patients. Consequently, the results have indicated the enhancement of precision in terms of disease progression and its possible treatment before it becomes severe, which translates to high chances of the patient's survival (Khan et al., 2024; Malik et al., 2024). Another area where quantum AI has been growing rapidly is neuromarketing. Neuromarketing can be described as an application of neuroscientific instruments and techniques to study consumers' mental and emotional reactions to marketing cues. Some of the organizations that have been considering the applicability of quantum AI in improving neuromarketing include Nielsen along with PepsiCo. Thus, through quantum-enhanced neuromarketing, these companies are able to leverage the data collected from consumers' brains and their bio-signatures in order to make better sense of consumer behaviour. Thus, it would be easier for businesses to make the right decision in this aspect since it gives an understanding of the producers' unconscious response to these stimuli. There is increased awareness on what fuels consumers' buying behaviours and thus more effective making of more sensitive appeals for the sales promotions through neuromarketing with assistances from quantum AI (Rika et al., 2022; Adam & Hall, 2022).

The advantages of the quantum neuromarketing approaches have been tremendous. Quantum AI, for example, was applied by PepsiCo to predict consumers' behaviours in regard to advertising campaigns. By including information about the individuals' brainwaves, their eye movements, and heart rate fluctuation, it would be easier for the company to understand which of the advertisements provoked the highest level of customers' emotions. This in turn, helped PepsiCo to further perfect its marketing techniques and consequently obtain a better connection with customers and therefore better sales rates. The uptake of quantum AI was also faster when it came to the analysis, besides giving better insights than conventional neuromarketing approaches (Rika et al., 2022). Consequently, PepsiCo was able to position its marketing budget in the right way and attain the optimal level of ROI; hence it gives us a glimpse of what quantum AI can bring in the table to consumer-centric sectors. These case studies show the benefits and risks of implementing quantum AI as the lessons provided highlight the applicability of the field. First, because quantum AI is designed to analyse large datasets and solve problems within a short time it would be a great asset to industries that rely on predictive analysis and consumer data. But like all things, there is a but when it comes to the application of quantum AI the following challenges are evident. Several managerial challenges are usually encountered by many organizations since quantum computing is a relatively new field that means that many resources are likely to be required in hardware and more so human capital (Coccia, 2024). However, the algorithms that are implemented in quantum computers are significantly more complicated than the classical artificial intelligence algorithms in that they require specialized knowledge on how to create and manage them (Farayola et al., p. 14, 2024). Nevertheless, there are several practices from existing benchmarks by leaders that have adopted quantum AI in their organizations. This paper has identified one clear conclusion of its analysis, which is that cooperative work between firms and quantum computing research institutions is a crucial activity. For instance, IBM cooperates with different companies, universities, and start-ups through the Q Network,/sources that connects business, academic institutions and start-up establishments for embracing Quantum computing. It helps the companies to get the support from the established quantum computing companies as well as they can build their quantum AI ecosystem with their own resources. It also assists in reducing the costs of investing in quantum AI by sharing the investment burden in equal to the amount of benefit that will be received across different stakeholders (Gill et al., 2022; Markna et al., 2023).

The third learning point relates to the application of iteration and concept testing to quantum AI initiatives. Since the field is still relatively new for quantum computing, the companies have adopted an incremental approach towards the implementation of quantum AI with the conventional AI structure. Such measures include conducting relatively small tests and trials and then subsequent experiments and trials and pilots before proceeding to larger deployments. For instance, Google's AI division that has been exploring the quantum computing technology has been running pilot applications for the financial services industry where they use quantum algorithms in specific analytics tasks that include predicting new portfolios and detecting fraudulent activities. Because of these pilot programmes, it becomes possible to develop the structure that can support a quantum AI model, as well as introduce essential changes to these models to accommodate the broader infrastructure for quantum computing (Gill et al., 2022; Mullangi et al., 2023). Furthermore, while comparing the quantum AI with the traditional AI, quantum AI has also focused on the need to apply ethic in decision making systems that involve data analysis. Organizations using quantum AI should be cautious about the bias issue since, in spite of quantum computing, being complex, bias issues cannot be completely eliminated in Artificial Intelligence. Even so, quantum AI could potentially magnify such problems if not well addressed since the capability of handling more data may just strengthen existing bias present in training sets noted by Khan et al. in 2024. Therefore, the industry stakeholders encourage others to establish sound ethical standards and corporate structures to make sure that legit quantum AI is deployed appropriately and without secrecy.

Using quantum AI in the future, new opportunities for different fields could be unlocked and further investigated. This means the quantum AI applications will increase as the quantum computers become more powerful and easily accessible. Industry sectors like logistics, pharmaceuticals and energy are going to get more advantages from optimizing the complicated system and providing correct prediction in Realtime through quantum artificial intelligence. For example, in the field of logistics, application of quantum AI can help in predicting or forecasting the changes in demand patterns and identifying the most optimal pathways for delivering such products with higher levels of accuracy as compared to the existing quantum AI-models reported by Sehrawat et al., 2024. In the same manner, in pharma, the application of quantum AI could enhance drug discovery since it is much faster in terms of simulating molecular interactivity than classical computers thus quickening the formulation of new therapies (Rani & Saxena, 2023). Thus, quantum AI is here and now with the greatest potential in such areas as predictive analytics as well as neuromarketing as companies have appeared to get tremendous value from the technology. From the examples of IBM and PepsiCo and others it is clear that through quantum AI the business and the processes within it, can be revolutionized especially in accuracy and speed of analysis. Thus, certain issues remain are present, specifically in correlation with the technical and ethical aspects related to the implementation of quantum AI. Studying the cases of successful implementation and referring to industry insights, it is possible to state that quantum AI can be a value-adding tool for businesses that can enhance their competitive advantage in the respective markets. Moreover, based on the current development of quantum computing and its connection with AI, further progressive is expected to bring boundless opportunities to the future development of predictive analysis and other fields (Efe, 2023).

ETHICAL CONSIDERATIONS IN QUANTUM PREDICTIVE ANALYTICS

Along the same development of Quantum AI and when it is used in the field of predictive analytics especially in consumer studies, there are considerations of ethical nature. In particular, the application of quantum AI for high-throughput data processing can contribute to major breakthroughs in understanding shoppers' behaviours, but it also will inaugurate new controversies around data protection, algorithmic bias, and the right use of the quantum AI capabilities. All these ethical issues must be solved properly in order to let quantum AI will create a positive effect instead of having negative consequences. As one of the biggest moral issues of quantum AI-driven predictive analytics, privacy should be named. Quantum AI can process huge amounts of personal data in very little time and that is why many organizations are in a position to get very precise results on consumers. Though this capability helps businesses a lot in targeting specific markets with specific messages, there is a tendency of misuse of consumers' private data. For example, such firms may exceed the prescribed limits in data harvesting or employing the data in ways the consumers did not agree to (Rani et al., 2023). The intrusiveness of this technology teamed with the specificities of the data it is capable of collecting might be potentially abused and lead to privacy violations. To manage such risks, the guidelines on data collection and usage need to be set so that consumers' rights to privacy are honoured. In addition, the same study established that quantum AI absorbs prejudices, thus increasing the efficiency of any bias that is already present in data. As with the traditional machine learning, quantum AI is dependent on data to make its estimates and biases of the data will be reflected on the estimates. This can lead to bias and bring injustice; particularly when applied in aspects such as employment, credit grant and market targeting. For instance, if a company applies quantum AI in marketing, the system can showcase a particular demographic than other demographic due to programming based on biased data sets (Khan et al., 2024). This is an issue of ethics for discrimination and discrimination fairness as with the possession of quantum AI capabilities, it will even be more challenging to address such biases. Organizations need hence to work towards establishing solution models that are clear and specific in their ways to ensuring equitable approaches to the use of predictive analytics (Farayola et al., 2024; Mosteanu & Faccia, 2021).

To tackle these ethical issues, there is the need to ensure that corporations that are implementing quantum AI for analytical predictions observe certain universal implementation ethics. Of course, one key aspect requires the collection of data to be done in an ethical way with the consumers' permission. This means the public should be made aware of what data is being collected, how it will be used as well as its intended use. Moreover, the organizations must employ measures to protect the information of consumers so that the information is not accessed or used inappropriately (Coccia, 2024). Guidelines of business ethics, for example, the principles of fairness, accountability, and transparency (FAT) may help the firms ensure that the application of quantum AI meets the cutover standards and legal requirements of the society.

In addition, there is a need to periodically scan companies' quantum AI systems to determine the presence of bias in their predictive models. This is achieved by developing multiple datasets and integrating fairness tests to the algorithm construction process. In the case of ethical use of quantum AI, another aspect being one should not use data more than what is required for a particular task so that there is no violation of privacy (Gill et al., 2022). Through promulgation of good practices for the application of QE, and developing adequate general policies, the corporations will be in a position to embrace quantum AI while at the same time maintaining the trust of consumers and being resistant to ethical legal pitfalls.

Therefore, quantum AI seems to have disruptive application in matters relating to predictive analytics especially in consumer behaviour analytics, but it also poses some important ethical issues. These potential issues are that privacy rights will be infringed, bias exists, and it is the responsibility to use data appropriately so that consumer rights are protected while using this technology. Quantum communicated with confidence, as long as ethical requirements are followed and both fairness and transparency integrated into the AI quantum systems, businesses are also capable of creating proper quantum predictive analytics (How & Chea, 2023).

INTERDISCIPLINARY APPROACHES

A synthesis of the theories that include AI, neuroscience, and marketing has given solutions that utilised quantum perspectives. Quantum AI brings a possibility to study human actions at multiple levels using the amount of data capable to be processed at the velocity provided. International Journal of Business, Social Science and Applied Sciences Article Reveals Neuroscience, Marketing and AI will Offer Deeper Understanding of Consumption Patterns and Enhanced Marketing Techniques for the Companies. This is becoming popular in the current society as more organizations are appreciating the fact that it is diverse talent that is useful in solving multifaceted problems and nurturing innovation (Khan et al., 2024). In neuromarketing the use of neuroscience tools like imaging and biometrics and analysis tools like artificial intelligence are in the advanced stages of integration to unravel the minds of consumers. Quantum AI improves this by analysing intricate neural and behavioural patterns which makes it easier to forecast consumer actions better. For example, in a research project of one of the major technological companies, people from neuroscience teams, artificial intelligence developers, and marketers jointly investigated consumers' reactions for logos and advertisements. For the neural responses, Quantum AI was applied to analyse the patterns which would normally go unnoticed using classical approaches. This in return resulted to more personalized marketing that saw dramatic increase in people's attention and sales (Rani et al., 2023).

It is especially important for AI, neuroscience, and marketing cooperation that the representatives of numerous fields can cooperate in collaborative efforts. All details of remarkable cases can be discussed by these interdisciplinary teams, and that can help consider objects from different angles and acquire broader visions of the situation. For instance, marketers can contribute information on customer behaviour while neuroscientists can expound on how the brain of the customer responds to marketing inputs. Masters of artificial intelligence subsequently utilize quantum technologies to parse over the data and establish predictive patterns to support and fuel marketing initiatives. This way, one utilises the strength of the other so that the possibilities of quantum AI are achieved as each department offers their specialty (Farayola et al., 2024). In the mainstream research, interdisciplinary projects show how fruitful cooperation with other disciplines may be. An example is the creation of quantum-based neuromarketing technologies which involved the marketing practitioners, AI experts, and neurologists to explain the decisions made by consumers when buying products. Due to their joint work, these specialists created the quantum AI in companies to monitor consumers' response to different signals in real-time to provide better predictions of their preferences. Such an approach paved the way for any business to create better marketing strategies and come up with exclusive promotions, which had direct impact on customer satisfaction and sales rates per consumers, according to Coccia (2024). For instance, a pharmaceutical firm applied an inter-disciplinary method to enhance the design and promotion of a new health product. The team preferred data scientist, neuroscientist, marketers and through quantum AI, they were able to look into cognitive and emotional correlation with the product (Thomas, 2023). Hence, by linking neuroscience into the understanding of the specific emotions, which affect the consumer's need to purchase and linking it with the AI's predictive abilities, the company came up with a marketing campaign that struck an emotional nerve among consumers. These measures brought about significant improvement in the uptake of the products as well as an improved market share (Gill et al., 2022).

Examples such as these show how interdisciplinary is beneficial and proves there is added economic value created for doing so. Through integration of AI, neuroscience and marketing, there is increased chances of understanding the buying behaviour of most customers hence coming up with better strategies for growth. Such approaches embrace various specialties making the problem-solving process more effective and enabling the businesses to cope with the constantly growing competition. Hence, optimization of this quantum AI will increasingly demand interdisciplinary cooperation as the value-add of this nascent technology is realized.

THE FUTURE OF PREDICTIVE ANALYTICS IN NEUROMARKETING

The trend, prospects and developments in neuromarketing space for predictive analytics will be the quantum artificial intelligence (AI). Quantum AI has the potential of changing the face of consumer behaviour analysis for marketing and other purposes among organizations. The next decade will probably find quantum predictive analytics as a usual aspect of neuromarketing studies and a driving force for change in the marketing world (Coccia, 2024). Another trend is the applicability of quantum AI in the marketing field which is most usefulness by its capability for handling large sets of data. The earlier forms of AI techniques though strong bear the drawback of not handling intricacies of human conduct and choices. Quantum AI on the other hand, can process several factors at once which will help marketers decipher consumers' wants and needs in a better manner. This will in turn lead to the evolution of the neuromarketing concept since firms will develop better approaches to market their products based on the knowledge of consumers' responses to different messages. For instance, with quantum AI marketers can study data concerning brain activity and/or emotional reactions in real time and then implement changes where necessary (Gill et al., 2022).

The last tendency that appeared is the usage of developing quantum AI to forecast long-term consumer behaviour. Today, the most typical implementation of predictive analytics is based on short-term approaches and the effectiveness of the actions that can be taken within a day. Quantum AI on the other hand is capable of modelling more advanced and time series predictions by virtue of analysing data with more parameters and variables. It could assist companies to extrapolate changes that could occur in consumers' habits in the future and hence anticipate market changes to anticipate in order to develop goods and services to fit the consumers' potential future needs. In terms of neuromarketing, this would mean not only being able to capture consumers' reactions to messages deployed today but also future responses (Rani et al., 2023). There are thus new opportunities for personalized marketing with the use of neuromarketing and quantum AI. Thanks to the superior data handling quantum AI can develop very unique consumer profiles with increased efficiency. It enables organisations to target consumers with the right marketing communications based on their personal characteristics, hence a better way of customer appeal and enhanced call to action. For example, a firm can implement quantum AI to study a consumer's actions on social media, neural signals, and feelings so that they can create a tailored advertising campaign that would appeal to the consumer. Such levels of customization may well soon become the norm in marketing, a major boon for organizations that are first to incorporate such technologies (Farayola et al., 2024). But quantum AI in neuromarketing has its bright future and at the same time it is not without some difficulties. The first and a very serious challenge associated with the current phase of quantum technology is the question of its cost and feasibility.

It takes a lot of resources to build and maintain quantum computers, and only a small number of businesses are currently using this technology. It will be essential to increase the accessibility of quantum AI to a larger spectrum of businesses, particularly small and medium-sized ones, as the technology develops. Furthermore, more investigation is required to determine the best ways to use quantum AI in marketing. Although the technology has great potential, it is still in its infancy, and there are still a lot of unanswered questions regarding how to apply it most effectively in a marketing setting (Khan et al., 2024). The ethical ramifications of applying quantum AI to neuromarketing predictive analytics present another possible obstacle. With increasing power comes the possibility of abuse in quantum AI. For instance, there are worries about the potential for businesses to employ quantum AI to influence customer behaviour by taking advantage of psychological weaknesses. Future challenges will mostly centre on ensuring the ethical and responsible application of quantum AI. To guarantee that quantum AI is utilized to assist society rather than damage it, researchers and industry leaders must collaborate to build frameworks and norms that protect customer privacy (Coccia, 2024).

Notwithstanding these obstacles, there are plenty of prospects for development and innovation in the field of quantum-enhanced predictive analytics in neuromarketing. We may anticipate seeing a greater integration of quantum AI into marketing plans across many businesses throughout the course of the next ten years. Businesses of all sizes will be able to benefit from quantum technology as it becomes more widely available and reasonably priced. As a result, quantum-enhanced neuromarketing techniques will be adopted more widely, allowing businesses to better understand their target audiences and create campaigns that convert more successfully (Rani et al., 2023). Looking ahead, creating new quantum algorithms with a focus on marketing applications will be one of the main topics of study in the future. Even while existing quantum algorithms have showed promise in industries like healthcare and banking, there is still more work to be done in order to adapt these algorithms for use in marketing. In order to develop even more potent prediction tools, researchers will need to investigate how quantum AI may be combined with other technologies like machine learning and blockchain to evaluate consumer behavior data more efficiently. Unlocking the full potential of quantum AI in marketing will depend on the development of these algorithms (Gill et al., 2022).

Thus, developments in quantum AI will have a significant impact on the use of predictive analytics in neuromarketing. The marketing environment is already starting to change as a result of emerging trends including tailored marketing techniques, long-term customer behaviour prediction, and real-time data analysis. Although there are obstacles to be addressed, such as the expensive price of quantum technology and moral dilemmas, the advantages might be enormous. We anticipate that in the upcoming ten years, quantum-enhanced predictive analytics will be a crucial tool for companies trying to stay competitive and provide more individualized, successful marketing strategies. Quantum AI will be crucial in influencing the direction of neuromarketing and completely changing the way businesses interact with their customers with further study and development.

CONCLUSION

In conclusion, embedding QAI and delta robots into neuromarketing and consumer insights is the new phase in handling audience expectation by companies. When integrating the features of QAI's cutting-edge data analysis and delta robots' accuracy, entrepreneurs receiving quicker understanding of the customer's preferences and employing targeted and individual approaches in their marketing activities. Neuromarketing, enhanced through these technologies, reveals foreconscious consumer responses so that brands can predict requirements, and formula communications that elicit favourable subliminal responses. Though, the hyper-personalised engagement capabilities come with ethical considerations lining up. With the help of these tools, businesses can only innovate while respecting users and their privacy, staying trustworthy. In the future, it is the skilful adoption of QAI and robotic precision in neuromarketing will create the future of consumer insight, where flexible data-driven marketing is at both the reward and the risk for adapting to the new digital context.

The transformational potential of quantum algorithms in neuromarketing has been examined in this chapter, along with the major developments and difficulties in using quantum AI into marketing tactics. With its unmatched capacity to handle massive volumes of data at breakneck rates, quantum artificial intelligence (AI) has the potential to completely transform the ways in which marketers examine customer behaviour, forecast trends, and customize interaction. The chapter has shown how quantum-enhanced predictive analytics may greatly improve marketing outcomes by allowing firms to make data-driven decisions with increased precision and depth through case studies and real-world examples. The chapter has also covered privacy issues and ethical issues that come up when employing such potent technology, highlighting the importance of responsible and open use. The possibility for using quantum AI to improve long-term customer behavior forecasts is one of the most noteworthy topics covered. Businesses can anticipate future consumer trends more accurately thanks to quantum AI, which processes massive, complicated datasets with more dimensions than standard AI can handle. This skill enables businesses to proactively modify their strategy in order to stay up with changing customer demands. Quantum AI has raised the possibility of individualized marketing methods, with companies able to create very customized advertising messages that speak to the unique online habits, emotional responses, and preferences of each customer. These kinds of customisation might completely change the way businesses interact with their clients, giving them a competitive edge in the quickly evolving digital market.

The chapter acknowledged the obstacles that must be overcome in order to fully realize the promise of quantum AI in neuromarketing, despite the fact that these advantages are significant. These difficulties include the ethical ramifications of using quantum technology, in addition to its high cost and complexity. The chapter emphasized that the key to quantum technology's widespread acceptance is opening it up to a wider variety of organizations. Furthermore, it's imperative to make sure quantum AI is used morally and sensibly since the potential for manipulating consumer behavior through sophisticated data analytics may give rise to serious privacy and consent issues. The necessity of precise rules and regulations to safeguard consumer rights while utilizing quantum AI's potential was a recurrent subject in the conversation. The chapter concluded by highlighting how quantum algorithms have the potential to revolutionize neuromarketing. Quantum AI is a potent technology that has the potential to change how marketers see and interact with customers. But for this shift to be effective, researchers, marketers, and legislators must collaborate to guarantee the morally and responsibly applied use of these technologies. Working together, these stakeholders may promote innovation while defending the interests of the general public.

REFERENCES

Adams, H., & Hall, D. (2022). Innovations in artificial intelligence research fueled by big data analytics. *European Journal of Business and Innovation Research*, 10(2), 96–104.

Agarwal, P., & Alam, M. (2021). Exploring quantum computing to revolutionize big data analytics for various industrial sectors. In *Big data analytics* (pp. 113–130). Auerbach Publications. DOI: 10.1201/9781003175711-7

Ahmadi, A. (2023). Quantum computing and artificial intelligence: The synergy of two revolutionary technologies. *Asian Journal of Electrical Sciences*, 12(2), 15–27. DOI: 10.51983/ajes-2023.12.2.4118

Ajiga, D. I., Ndubuisi, N. L., Asuzu, O. F., Owolabi, O. R., Tubokirifuruar, T. S., & Adeleye, R. A.David Iyanuoluwa AjigaNdubuisi Leonard NdubuisiOnyeka Franca AsuzuOluwaseyi Rita OwolabiTula Sunday TubokirifuruarRhoda Adura Adeleye. (2024). AI-driven predictive analytics in retail: A review of emerging trends and customer engagement strategies. *International Journal of Management & Entrepreneurship Research*, 6(2), 307–321. DOI: 10.51594/ijmer.v6i2.772

Babar, M., Khattak, A. S., Jan, M. A., & Tariq, M. U. (2021). Energy aware smart city management system using data analytics and internet of things. *Sustainable Energy Technologies and Assessments*, 44, 100992. Advance online publication. DOI: 10.1016/j.seta.2021.100992

Coccia, M. (2024). Technological trajectories in quantum computing to design a quantum ecosystem for industrial change. *Technology Analysis and Strategic Management*, 36(8), 1733–1748. DOI: 10.1080/09537325.2022.2110056

Efe, A. (2023). Assessment of artificial intelligence and quantum computing in smart management information systems. *Bilişim Teknolojileri Dergisi*, 16(3), 177–188. DOI: 10.17671/gazibtd.1190670

Farayola, O. A., Adaga, E. M., Egieya, Z. E., Ewuga, S. K., Abdul, A. A., & Abrahams, T. O.Oluwatoyin Ajoke FarayolaEjuma Martha AdagaZainab Efe EgieyaSarah Kuzankah EwugaAdekunle Abiola AbdulTemitayo Oluwaseun Abrahams. (2024). Advancements in predictive analytics: A philosophical and practical overview. *World Journal of Advanced Research and Reviews*, 21(3), 240–252. DOI: 10.30574/wjarr.2024.21.3.2706

Gill, S. S., Xu, M., Ottaviani, C., Patros, P., Bahsoon, R., Shaghaghi, A., & Uhlig, S. (2022). AI for next-generation computing: Emerging trends and future directions. *Internet of Things : Engineering Cyber Physical Human Systems*, 19, 100514. DOI: 10.1016/j.iot.2022.100514

How, M. L., & Cheah, S. M. (2023). Business renaissance: Opportunities and challenges at the dawn of the quantum computing era. *Businesses*, 3(4), 585–605. DOI: 10.3390/businesses3040036

Khan, H. U., Ali, N., Ali, F., & Nazir, S. (2024). Transforming future technology with quantum-based IoT. *The Journal of Supercomputing*, •••, 1–35.

Malik, J., Patel, N., & Gupta, R. (2024). Evaluating the synergies between cloud computing, big data analytics, and quantum algorithms: Opportunities and challenges. *Journal of Empirical Social Science Studies*, 8(2), 38–50.

Malik, N., Altaf, S., Tariq, M. U., Ahmed, A., & Babar, M. (2023). A deep learning-based sentiment analytic model for the prediction of traffic accidents. *CMC-Computers. Computers, Materials & Continua*, 77(2), 1599–1615. DOI: 10.32604/cmc.2023.040455

Markna, J. H., Palatia, T. P., Gohel, S., & Kataria, B. (2023). Unveiling advanced computational applications in quantum computing: A comprehensive review. *International Journal of Advanced Nano Computing and Analytics*, 2(2), 81–92. DOI: 10.61797/ijanca.v2i2.284

Mosteanu, N. R., & Faccia, A. (2021). Fintech frontiers in quantum computing, fractals, and blockchain distributed ledger: Paradigm shifts and open innovation. *Journal of Open Innovation*, 7(1), 19. DOI: 10.3390/joitmc7010019

Mullangi, K., Dhameliya, N., Anumandla, S. K. R., Yarlagadda, V. K., Sachani, D. K., Vennapusa, S. C. R., & Patel, B. (2023). AI-augmented decision-making in management using quantum networks. *Asian Business Review*, 13(2), 73–86. DOI: 10.18034/abr.v13i2.718

Peelam, M. S., Rout, A. A., & Chamola, V. (2024). Quantum computing applications for Internet of Things. *IET Quantum Communication*, 5(2), 103–112. DOI: 10.1049/qtc2.12079

Prakash, P. M. (2023). Enhancing business performance through quantum electronic analysis of optical data. *Optical and Quantum Electronics*, 55(12), 1056. DOI: 10.1007/s11082-023-05347-x

Radanliev, P. (2024). Artificial intelligence and quantum cryptography. *Journal of Analytical Science and Technology*, 15(1), 4. DOI: 10.1186/s40543-024-00416-6

Rani, K. S. K., Priyadharsheni, J. M., Karthikeyan, B., & Pugalendhi, G. S. (2023). Applications of quantum AI for healthcare. In *Quantum computing and artificial intelligence: Training machine and deep learning algorithms on quantum computers* (pp. 271).

Rika, H., Aviv, I., & Weitzfeld, R. (2022). Unleashing the potentials of quantum probability theory for customer experience analytics. *Big Data and Cognitive Computing*, 6(4), 135. DOI: 10.3390/bdcc6040135

Sáez-Ortuño, L., Huertas-Garcia, R., Forgas-Coll, S., Sánchez-García, J., & Puertas-Prats, E. (2024). Quantum computing for market research. *Journal of Innovation & Knowledge*, 9(3), 100510. DOI: 10.1016/j.jik.2024.100510

Saxena, A., Mancilla, J., Montalban, I., & Pere, C. (2023). *Financial modeling using quantum computing: Design and manage quantum machine learning solutions for financial analysis and decision making*. Packt Publishing Ltd.

Sehrawat, S. K., Dutta, P. K., Bhatia, A. B., & Whig, P. (2024). Predicting demand in supply chain networks with quantum machine learning approach. In *Quantum computing and supply chain management: A new era of optimization* (pp. 33–47). IGI Global. DOI: 10.4018/979-8-3693-4107-0.ch002

Sun, Z. (2023). Data, analytics, and intelligence. *Journal of Computer Science Research*, 5(4), 43–57. DOI: 10.30564/jcsr.v5i4.6072

Tariq, M. U. (2024). Leading Smart Technologies and Innovations for E-Business 5.0: Applications and Management Frameworks. In Popkova, E. (Ed.), *Smart Technologies and Innovations in E-Business* (pp. 25–46). IGI Global., DOI: 10.4018/978-1-6684-7840-0.ch002

Tariq, M. U. (2024). The role of AI in skilling, upskilling, and reskilling the workforce. In Doshi, R., Dadhich, M., Poddar, S., & Hiran, K. (Eds.), *Integrating generative AI in education to achieve sustainable development goals* (pp. 421–433). IGI Global., DOI: 10.4018/979-8-3693-2440-0.ch023

Tariq, M. U. (2024). Application of blockchain and Internet of Things (IoT) in modern business. In Sinha, M., Bhandari, A., Priya, S., & Kabiraj, S. (Eds.), *Future of customer engagement through marketing intelligence* (pp. 66–94). IGI Global., DOI: 10.4018/979-8-3693-2367-0.ch004

Tariq, M. U. (2024). The role of AI ethics in cost and complexity reduction. In Tennin, K., Ray, S., & Sorg, J. (Eds.), *Cases on AI ethics in business* (pp. 59–78). IGI Global., DOI: 10.4018/979-8-3693-2643-5.ch004

Tariq, M. U. (2025). *AI-Driven Learning and Engagement in Higher Education*. IGI Global., DOI: 10.4018/979-8-3693-4074-5

Tariq, M. U. (2025). Harnessing Generative AI for Enhanced Web Application Security. In Shah, I., & Jhanjhi, N. (Eds.), *Generative AI for Web Engineering Models* (pp. 161–192). IGI Global., DOI: 10.4018/979-8-3693-3703-5.ch008

Thomos, R. (2023). The future of big data: Trends and emerging technologies.

KEY TERMS AND DEFINITIONS

Ethical Data Use: Responsible collection, analysis, and application of consumer data in ways that respect privacy, transparency, and fairness in marketing practices.

Interdisciplinary Approaches: The combination of fields like AI, neuroscience, and marketing to create innovative solutions and deeper consumer insights through quantum-enhanced technologies.

Neuromarketing: A field of marketing that uses neuroscience and AI to analyse consumer responses and behaviour, aiming to optimise marketing strategies.

Predictive Analytics: The process of using historical data and machine learning algorithms to predict future consumer behaviour and trends.

Quantum Algorithms: Advanced computational algorithms like Grover's and Shor's, designed to leverage the principles of quantum computing for faster data processing and problem-solving.

Quantum AI: The integration of quantum computing with artificial intelligence to enhance predictive analytics by improving the accuracy and speed of data analysis.

Chapter 9
Optimizing Feature Selection for Predictive Analytics With Quantum Algorithms

C. N. Manushree
https://orcid.org/0009-0001-9158-5096
Amity University, Noida, India

Hari Deepthi Putluru
https://orcid.org/0009-0003-1120-3276
Amity University, Noida, India

Himanshu Khajuria
https://orcid.org/0000-0002-2438-0007
Amity University, Noida, India

Chintan Singh
https://orcid.org/0000-0002-1096-2196
Amity University, Noida, India

Biswa Prakash Nayak
https://orcid.org/0000-0002-5680-269X
Amity University, Noida, India

ABSTRACT

Quantum algorithms for predictive analytics is important across various sectors such as finance, healthcare, marketing and supply chain management where accurate predictions can be used to optimise operations and decision-making processes. This

DOI: 10.4018/979-8-3693-7673-7.ch009

chapter addresses Specific quantum machine learning algorithms such as Quantum Support Vector Machines (QSVM), Quantum K-nearest Neighbors (QKNN) and Quantum Neural Networks (QNN). These algorithms enhance classification, regression and complex predictive tasks by accelerating training processes and managing large feature spaces effectively. And, to this, quantum optimization algorithms like Quantum Approximate Optimization Algorithm (QAOA) and Variational Quantum Eigensolver (VQE) are mentioned for their role in optimising model parameters and improving prediction accuracy. In addition, it discusses quantum data encoding methods, such as Quantum Fourier Transform (QFT) and amplitude encoding. Along with this, it acknowledges significant challenges such as hardware limitations, algorithmic complexity and practical integration issues.

1. INTRODUCTION

Conventional feature selection methods work quite well but are highly at risk of the "curse of dimensionality" when operating with big data. Quantum computing, being featured by processing large amounts of information at a time, promises a bright way out of such problems, (Aggarwal, Bali, & Mittal, 2019). Quantum feature selection makes use of several of the unique properties of quantum mechanics in an effort to investigate feature spaces more efficiently and effectively. By exploiting quantum parallelism and superposition, quantum algorithms have great potential to outperform classical methods concerning speed and accuracy.

1.1 Overview of Predictive Analytics and Feature Selection

Predictive analytics is a branch of data mining whereby the prediction of future outcomes or trends is made with the use of statistical models and machine learning algorithms. Predictive analytics finds its application in almost each and every industry, whether it be finance, healthcare, marketing, or retail, (Mücke *et al.*, 2023).

Predictive analytics is a field that is predominantly applied in the healthcare, finance, and marketing sectors. For instance, predictive models detect diseases early in healthcare or when they are likely to develop, like predicting diabetes based on patient data. In such a sense, feature selection plays one major role from which the most significant attributes can be singled out from large datasets, improving model performance and lowering computation. Quantum algorithms provide a different way to optimize feature selection, particularly in high-dimensional data environments in which classical approaches fail to be efficient.

The Key Steps in Predictive Analytics includes that the Relevant data must be collected from different sources, cleaned to remove inconsistencies, and transformed into a proper format for analysis. Creation of new features or transformation of existing ones to reduce the dimensionality and improve model performance. These techniques would also include normalization, standardization, and one-hot encoding. Model Selection and Training: Accordingly, select appropriate algorithms like linear regression, decision trees, random forests, or neural networks on the problem and nature of data. The purpose of training using labelled data is to learn patterns and relationships. The accuracy and performance can be measured by different metrics such as mean squared error, root mean squared error, or classification accuracy. Deployment and Monitoring: Generate new predictions by deploying the trained model on new data. Continuously monitor the model's performance and retrain it to adjust to changed conditions. Feature selection is considered an important step in predictive analytics. In this selection, features are chosen from a huge data set that would attribute to the better performance of the model, reduce overfitting, and give more interpretability.

Methods of Feature Selection: Feature selection methods enhance model performance by identifying the most relevant features, improving accuracy and efficiency. Filter methods use statistical techniques like correlation, chi-square tests, and mutual information to rank feature relevance, while wrapper methods, such as forward selection and recursive feature elimination, evaluate feature subsets through model training and testing. Embedded methods, including L1 (lasso) and L2 (ridge) regularization, incorporate feature selection during model training. The benefits of feature selection include reduced overfitting, as irrelevant features are removed, leading to better generalization, improved model interpretability with fewer features, and enhanced computational efficiency through faster training and prediction.

1.2 The Importance of Quantum Computing in Predictive Analytics

Quantum computing is going to change the paradigm of predictive analytics by offering remarkable advantages over classical computing methods. In this paper, we identify the major reasons in Figure 1 quantum computing is poised to play a vital role in the field of Predictive Analytics in Quantum Computing (Kariya & Behera, 2021):

Figure 1. Importance of quantum computing in predictive analytics

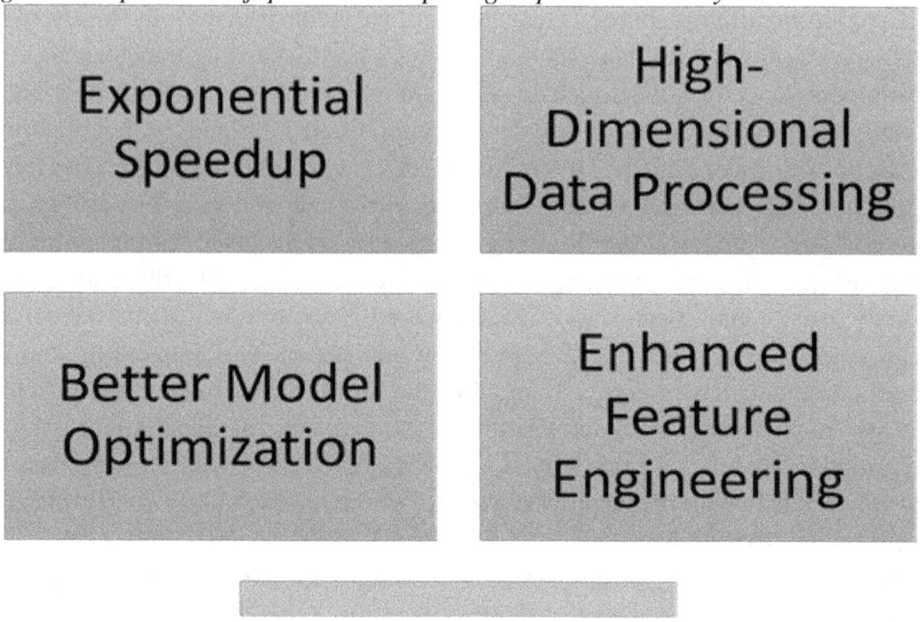

Quantum computing is changing the technology landscape in drug discovery: complex molecular simulations are greatly assisted by the speed and computation power of quantum algorithms. Quantum optimization techniques have, for example, enabled the identification of drug molecules more quickly than traditional methods, really improving predictive models in public health.

Quantum computing makes many revolutionary strides in predictive analytics, which it achieves by solving several fundamental deficiencies in classical computation. At its most basic, quantum computers achieve an exponential speedup, processing many possibilities simultaneously; because of this, they are potentially very good on more complex models and large data sets. With regard to high-dimensional data processing, quantum algorithms can overcome the "curse of dimensionality" with a conceptual view of efficiently navigating vast feature spaces. This ultimately leads to better model optimization, as quantum techniques can explore the solution spaces globally and lead to optimal solutions more efficiently than classically. Another set of applications which are derived from QS has to do with hyperparameter tuning that helps increase and improve the performance and generalization of machine learning models.

Quantum computing also brings about improvement in feature engineering by unearthing intricate nonlinear relationships between features, hence improving the accuracy of the model and feature selection in a quite efficient manner, which can heavily reduce computational costs and improve explainability. Quantum cryptography protects sensitive information with perfect solutions against classical attacks and thus secures adequate protection.

1.3 Scope and Objectives of Optimizing Feature Selection Using Quantum Algorithms

The application of quantum algorithms to enhance feature selection in machine learning, with a focus on improving predictive analytics models. It aims to design or adapt quantum algorithms for feature selection, including quantum versions of filter, wrapper, and embedded methods, and benchmark their performance against traditional classical approaches on large-scale, high-dimensional datasets. The investigation will assess the efficiency and scalability of quantum algorithms in comparison to classical methods, identifying conditions where quantum computing provides a clear advantage in terms of precision, speed, or resource consumption. Additionally, the project will apply these quantum techniques to real-world predictive analytics challenges in sectors like finance, healthcare, and materials science, demonstrating their practical value and potential for improving model performance, (Moussa, Calandra, & Dunjko, 2020).

2. QUANTUM MACHINE LEARNING ALGORITHMS FOR FEATURE SELECTION

Quantum machine learning, as the name goes, is a generally up-and-coming sub-discipline that uses the peculiar properties of quantum mechanics for advanced machine learning. Feature selection is considered one of the most promising applications of QML, crucial tasks in predictive analytics in that they relate to finding the most relevant features within any dataset to enhance model performance. Traditional feature selection methods are normally afflicted by the curse of dimensionality in handling big and complex data, (Singh & Das, 2024). Quantum algorithms explore very large solution spaces efficiently, hence dodging this problem.

Quantum machine learning algorithms in feature selection will, therefore, under such context, aim to: Quantum machine learning algorithms for feature selection attempt to utilize quantum parallelism for feature selection so as to explore the feature space in a faster way; it quickly goes through several possibilities at one time. Thus, they are perfectly used in handling high-dimensional data with much ease as compared to the classical methods. This may pose fewer resource problems since there is lesser complexity associated with it. Moreover, quantum methods may find sophisticated nonlinear interdependencies among features and target variables that would go undetected for traditional methods. Making use of the most informative features, quantum algorithms improve model accuracy and interpretability, achieving better overall performance in predictive analytics.

2.1 Quantum Support Vector Machines (QSVM)

Quantum Support Vector Machines, or QSVM in short, are quantum machine learning algorithms that extend the traditional model of the Support Vector Machine to draw upon quantum computing powers. SVMs are models of supervised learning used for classification and regression tasks, (Ayesha, Hanif, & Talib, 2021). They operate by seeking an optimal hyperplane such that it separates data points with a maximum margin. Quantum Support Vector Machines or QSVMs apply quantum principles to offer enhancements on traditional SVMs, typically through quantum kernels, quantum feature maps, or quantum optimization. Quantum kernels which allow QSVMs to calculate the similarity in higher-dimensional feature space more efficiently were found to sometimes tend to often reveal nonlinear relations which improve performance. The classical data will then be embedded into quantum states by quantum feature maps. The choice of feature map, of course, heavily influences the accuracy of the model. Also, QSVMs can enjoy the benefits of quantum optimization techniques like Grover's search that could be applied to speed up the determination of the optimal hyperplane; this might therefore result in a speed advantage over optimization techniques that are classically available, (Navot *et al.*, 2005). Quantum Support Vector Machines have a few points of advantage, especially in terms of handling high-dimensional data-a problem common in most applications using machine learning. QSVMs are efficient in processing such data, thus suited for complex tasks. Furthermore, with quantum kernels, QSVMs can effectively explore the non-linear features linking each feature, pushing the model performance deeper into insights than in the classical SVM. Indeed, QSVMs can achieve quantum speedup and solve large-dataset computationally intensive problems much faster than their corresponding classical methods-a factor that lends them to real-world, large-scale applications, (Nembrini, Acreman, & Cremonesi, 2021). QSVMs also have several significant limitations and challenges at the moment due to current quantum hardware. Noise and a very limited number of qubits basically limit the efficiency of such machines in real applications. Designing and optimizing QSVM algorithms further calls for an enormous effort in choosing the right quantum feature maps, kernels, and optimization techniques for QSVM algorithms. Despite all these challenges, QSVMs have huge potential in a wide variety of applications that range from just typical image classification tasks like object or facial recognition to text classification to tasks like sentiment analysis and topic modelling, and even in bioinformatics, where it may be used to help in determining the protein structure and understanding gene expression, with resultant advancements in the area.

2.1.1 Enhancing Classification in Predictive Analytics

Classification is a fundamental task in predictive analytics, aiming to assign data points to predefined categories. To improve classification accuracy and performance, several strategies can be employed (Rigui, Nan, & Qiulin, 2006):

Data pre-processing and feature engineering are steps to prepare data with the most advanced machine learning models. Data cleaning involves missing values, outliers, and inconsistencies leading to an increased quality and reliability of the dataset. On the other hand, feature selection entails finding the most relevant features, reduces dimensionality, and improves efficiency within a model. Feature engineering builds on changing or creating new features to continue extracting more informative patterns in order to improve upon the model's predictions. These processes ensure the data, collectively, is well prepared to be optimized for effective model training. Algorithm selection and tuning in developing effective machine learning models are crucial. The best choice of algorithm pertaining to the problem type is important, whether linear SVMs, decision trees, random forests, or neural networks, for optimal performance. After selecting an algorithm, hyperparameter tuning is the requirement to optimize parameters to set the best results. In ensemble methods, bagging and boosting can be adopted in order to combine different models. Generalization will be improved, and overfitting reduced by including the use of ensemble methods. Accuracy, precision, recall, and F1-score are used for measuring the performance of the model followed by validation. Overfitting into a dataset is prevented with the help of cross-validation by splitting the data into training and test sets; besides, it gives the confusion matrix which gives insight about the classification abilities of the model. Over- and underfitting can be avoided with the help of regularization techniques like L1 and L2 regularization, cross-validation that checks the performance of the model on unseen data as well as early stopping during the training phase to avoid degradation in the performance of the model. The last measurement is the ability of classification that helps one to estimate the overall performance of the model through ROC curves and the value of AUC.

Another application area of QSVMs lies in financial risk prediction. For example, the high-dimensional data might be used to predict futures in the stocks. Quantum algorithms can optimize the SVM models faster than the classical ones, thus enabling faster decision-making in the case of high-frequency trading.

2.1.2 QSVM for Feature Selection in High-Dimensional Data

QSVM is among the robust techniques for feature selection in high-dimensional data. It is an extension of the traditional SVM as it adds a quadratic penalty term to the objective function. The penalty term made a choice of the features whose subset has relevance for classification and reduced model complexity. Implementation issues with QSVM include critical factors such as the choice of kernel, regularization, and setting the threshold. Indeed, the choice of kernel, including linear, polynomial or radial basis function (RBF), is critical to the performance of QSVM, because it determines how data points are projected in that feature space. This parameter ensures control between the complexity of the model and the generalization error, with robust performance on unseen data. Feature selection with threshold selection can be guided by cross-validation techniques to optimize the outcome. QSVMs are highly applied in the following fields: microarray analysis for gene expression data in disease classification, text classification for selecting relevant terms, image classification for selecting informative pixels or regions, and bioinformatics for analysing protein or DNA sequences. This thus combines the best characteristics of filter and wrapper methods: On the one side, statistical properties are guaranteed. On the other side, the model is trained on feature subsets. Incorporation of a quadratic penalty term improves feature selection and sparse model creation, which further increases its interpretability and performance.

In a high dimensional space, SVM algorithms have the problem of getting afflicted with what has come to be referred to as the curse of dimensionality, and they might also end up inducing inefficient feature selection along with increased computational costs. Quantum SVMs might better manage such a high-dimensional space, thus providing a better trade-off between precision and computational time through the exploitation of quantum entanglement as well as superposition.

2.2 Quantum K-nearest Neighbors (QKNN)

Quantum K-nearest Neighbors (QKNN) is an extension of the classical K-nearest neighbors (KNN) algorithm, basic to machine learning technique used in classifying and regression tasks; it uses principles in quantum computing like superposition and entanglement to improve the speeds and efficiencies potentially in the KNN algorithm when large data is concerned, (Ayesha, Hanif, & Talib, 2021).

2.2.1 Quantum Advantage in KNN Classification

a. Encoding of Quantum Data Quantum computers: It can represent and manipulate data in a superposition, which means processing many data items in parallel. For the KNN problem of classification, this provides the possibility that a quantum algorithm may evaluate multiple points in a dataset in parallel and speed up the search process to find the nearest neighbors.
b. Quantum Speedup in Calculating Distance: One major hurdle of classical KNN is distance calculation between a test point and all the training points. Quantum computing uses techniques like Grover's algorithm in search problems much more efficiently. Quantum variants of KNN apply Grover's search to speed up the process of identification of the nearest neighbors. Grover's algorithm provides a quadratic of

   calculations *O(N) to* $O(\sqrt{N})$*, where N is the number of points in the dataset.*
c. Amplitude Amplification: In classical KNN, it needs to search the entire dataset to determine which are the nearest neighbors. Quantum KNN can use amplitude amplification to efficiently find the K nearest neighbors without scanning the whole database. Encoding the dataset in quantum states with this algorithm would allow focusing of computational resources just on the most relevant parts of the data.
d. Quantum Parallelism: Quantum parallelism will enable quantum computers to perform several operations in parallel. One might, therefore, think to leverage this to compute multiple distances to different points in the dataset in parallel, thereby potentially reducing the overall time taken to compute the K nearest neighbors.
e. Quantum Feature Space Mapping: Quantum algorithms can project data into a high-dimensional space of quantum features, and the problem of classification may become easier or even better in such a representation than the classical case. Classification boundaries between classes are more distinguishable, utilizing entanglement and superposition properties of quantum systems, in the encoded space by a quantum representation.
f. Quantum State Preparation and Distance Estimation: In quantum KNN, one might represent data points as quantum states, and one can estimate the distance between quantum states (data points) using quantum algorithms. This could provide more efficient ways to make comparisons involving data points in high-dimensional spaces.

2.2.2 Application of QKNN in Feature Selection

Feature selection assists in finding the most relevant features from a dataset, hence improving the model performance, reducing the computational cost, and improving interpretability. QKNN can be used effectively for feature selection in several applications, *Singh & Das, 2024). Quantum K-Nearest Neighbors (QKNN) can be applied effectively for feature selection based on different techniques such as feature ranking and subset selection. In feature ranking, QKNN adopts a quadratic kernel function to measure the distance between points in the data space, thus incorporating the possibility of non-linearity in the relationships that exist among features. Features making substantial contributions towards those distances are ranked higher, and QKNN considers them as relevant features for the task to be performed on the data. Thresholding will only allow the best-ranked features to be chosen, therefore, causing a form of dimensionality reduction. In the case of subset feature selection, the QKNN can be placed within a greedy search: initialize an empty feature set and then iteratively add features in terms of their contribution to model performance. At each step, feature addition is tested against a held validation set, and if it improves performance, the feature is accepted; otherwise, it is rejected. Further, QKNN can be used as the base classifier within the wrapper approaches like forward selection, backward elimination, or recursive feature elimination methods where the performance at a validation set is used in determining the quality of various feature subsets. This multi-reinforced approach makes QKNN to work out better to enhance feature selection that eventually improves model accuracy and interpretability.

The QKNN could in theory handle large datasets but, in practice, typically consisted of hybrid models in which quantum enhanced feature selection was used in concert with classical KNN algorithms. This sort of hybridity overcame the scalability problems of quantum hardware but allowed quantum speedup for feature selection tasks.

2.3 Quantum Neural Networks (QNN)

A Quantum Neural Network (QNN) is a highly complex model of computing, integrating elements from quantum mechanics into the structure of neural networks to capitalize on the distinct features of quantum systems for improved computation, (Lee & Wang, 2020). QNNs are part of a wider category of quantum machine learning in an effort to apply quantum computation to tasks that are impossible or highly inefficient for classical computers. Quantum Mechanics and Qubits: Quantum mechanics is that branch of physics concerning the behaviour of the quantum world at the atomic and subatomic levels. In a quantum system, the qubit is a unit of information as its classical counterpart but with the richer representational capacity, in contrast with the bits which could be either 0 or 1. The qubits can exist in any superposition of states as mathematically represented by:

$$(\Psi) = \alpha|0) + \beta/1))$$

This property is such that α and β are any numbers complex. This makes qubits encode more information than classical bits.

2.3.1 Structure of Quantum Neural Networks

QNNs embody these quantum principles into the frameworks of neural networks. Generally speaking, QNN implies a layer structure of quantum gates which is analogous to the more traditional layer architecture of a classical neural network, except that its computation is performed on qubits instead of being a classical bit, (Ahmed, 2019). More about QNN Architecture: Input Layer encodes the classical information into a quantum state. Techniques, for instance, such as amplitude encoding or basis encoding can be used to map classical data onto qubits. Quantum Layers involves quantum gates that are in charge of control qubits. Quantum gates are among the component parts of the quantum circuit and are like the classical logic gates. However, whereas the operations in the classical gates can only be AND, NAND, OR, NOR, XOR, XNOR, or any combinations of these, for quantum, the operations with the qubits are of the superposition and entanglement. The popularly adopted quantum gates include Hadamard gate, Pauli-X, Pauli-Y, Pauli-Z, and controlled-NOT or CNOT. Measurement Layer - After leaving the quantum layers, the qubits are measured and transformed into classical values. Measurement causes the quantum state to collapse into one of the basis states, and the outcome can be taken as the answer to the computation.

The hybrid quantum-classical training is the other major mode through which QNNs are trained. Here, the classical optimizer that can include some algorithms, such as gradient descent, updates the parameters of the quantum gates. The process can be as follows: Forward Pass - The input data is encoded onto qubits and passed through quantum layers. The final quantum state can be measured to provide the output. Loss Computation - Compute the output of the network and compare to target values, then compute loss function. Backward Pass - Compute gradients of the loss function with respect to the quantum gate parameters, typically applying the parameter-shift rule or other finite difference methods. Parameter Update - The classical optimizer calculates the update of the parameters of the quantum gates as a function of the found gradients. This hybrid approach harnesses the strengths of both quantum and classical computation to efficiently achieve QNN training. QNNs will revolutionize many application fields by providing better computability.

Some applications include: Quantum Chemistry: Simulate structure molecule and chemical reactions at a faster rate compared to that classically achieved, therefore very efficiently used in QNN; it may advance drug discovery and materials science. Optimization Problems: QNNs can be applied to solve complex optimization problems, such as the traveling salesman problem or portfolio optimization, more efficiently than classical algorithms. Machine Learning: QNNs may be used for classification, regression, and clustering, which in some scenario outperform classical neural networks.

Example: Quantum Classifier, A simple quantum classifier, in order to classify data into two classes, is supposed to follow a structured architecture with a few major components. It begins at the input layer, where data points are encoded using amplitude encoding from classical to qubits, thus transforming data into quantum format. In the quantum layers, one applies a sequence of parameterized quantum gates on these qubits, thus introducing quantum operations that make the classifier better at capturing the complex patterns. Finally, the measurement layer evaluates the final quantum state of the qubits for the classification. In a training of this quantum classifier, parameters for quantum gates are optimized during the learning in minimizing the classification error. This encodes the training data in the qubits, applies quantum gates, measures the outputs, computes loss, and then updates the parameters of the gate using a classical optimizer so the model improves over time.

2.4 Quantum Feature Selection in Neuromarketing

Neuromarketing makes use of sophisticated data, like brain activity (for example, EEG, fMRI), eye-tracking, and emotional responses, among many others. Such sources are rather voluminous and very complex; classical feature selection methods often fail at this because of the high multidimensionality and nonlinear nature of the neuromarketing data. Quantum feature selection is a new promise that might unlock the promise of faster and more precise computational handling of complex data, so marketers could actually go deeper into the information. For example, in customer segmentation, QML can be utilized to analyze the high-dimensional consumer data focusing on subtle patterns that distinguish consumer segments based on purchase intent or brand affinity for focused targeting.

In addition, the capability of QML to handle large datasets makes it useful for real-time sentiment analysis, which increases the accuracy of emotional response-detecting algorithms obtained from ad testing or consumer response. In predictive modelling for bespoke marketing, QML helps isolate features from huge datasets that are relevant to predicting consumer preferences, thus guiding marketers on tailoring their campaigns to individual needs and behaviour. Most broadly, QML-enhanced feature selection in neuromarketing will provide much more accurate and personalized insights to allow dynamic marketing campaign adjustments in real time, which may result in higher engagement and even ROI.

3. QUANTUM OPTIMIZATION ALGORITHMS FOR MODEL PARAMETER OPTIMIZATION

Quantum optimization algorithms seem to be transformation tools for solutions in optimization problems of the model parameters of almost all fields, from machine learning to finance and logistics. Applying special properties of quantum mechanics, the quantum algorithms apparently achieve improvements on optimization processes beyond those provided by the best available classical approaches, (Smith & Johnson, 2021). Characteristics of Quantum Optimization Algorithms include: Quantum Superposition - Optimization algorithms based on quantum processing can store and manipulate many solutions simultaneously in a quantum superposition. Classical optimization algorithms work on one candidate solution at a time. This could open up significantly more of the solution space, which may speed the convergence of the optimal parameters, (Lee & Wang, 2020). Entanglement - Quantum entanglement allows for quantum bits, or qubits, to be connected and can offer several advantages in computation. Quantum algorithms use entangled states to allow for better handling of complicated relationships between parameters than the classical systems can. Quantum Measurement - Quantum optimization measures the output from quantum states to extract relevant information about potential solutions. Such a measurement process is critical, since it informs the algorithm more about the quality of differing configurations of the parameters with respect to which improvement can be iteratively enacted.

Prominent Quantum Algorithms for Parameter Optimization are Quantum Approximate Optimization Algorithm (QAOA), Variational Quantum Eigen solver (VQE), Quantum Neural Networks (QNNs). QAOA was initially designed as a tool for solving any combinatorial optimization problem. Optimizing parameters from the model may hence be framed as binary optimization problems. QAOA operates in alternating cycles of quantum and classical steps, and parameters may be optimized using performance evaluations received from the quantum circuits, (Harris & Lee, 2023). From the inception in quantum chemistry, VQE seems to be especially well-suited to the optimization of parameters in predictive models. By encoding parameters as quantum states, VQE iteratively applies classical optimization techniques to improve these states so that the parameters under consideration minimize the loss function, (Singh, Khajuria, & Nayak, n.d.). QNNs integrate ideas from quantum computing and neural network architecture, providing an exciting framework for optimizing the parameters in the networks. Using quantum gates to parameterize parameters can serve to efficiently explore the parameter space during training, thus making the training much better.

Advantages of Quantum Optimization Algorithms include Speed, Scalability, and Improved Accuracy. Quantum algorithms can greatly enhance the optimization tasks by reducing the time involved in them. It would evaluate multiple configurations simultaneously; hence, it converges much quicker on optimal parameters, (Lee & Wang, 2020). Quantum algorithms can support larger datasets and more sophisticated models without exponential growth in computational resources compared to the classical methods. Quantum optimization algorithms can effectively explore vast parameter landscapes. This leads to solutions that are better than those classically optimized algorithms can discover, especially in high-dimensional spaces.

In terms of applications, quantum optimization algorithms have a notable impact in various fields. In machine Learning, Quantum optimization algorithms allow to speed up the training of machine learning models through hyperparameters optimization and feature selection, thus improving predictive performance, (Harris & Lee, 2023). In finance, optimal portfolio construction can be used with quantum algorithms that quickly comb and assess large combinations of assets in order to determine the best investment routes, (Singh, Khajuria, & Nayak, n.d). Quantum Optimization Methods for the Path It does this by efficiently exploring potentially complex solution spaces, which in return reduces the associated costs and increases the operational efficiency of resource allocation.

This has resulted in quantum optimization algorithms from significant advancements in model parameter optimization, where unique properties of quantum systems allow for methodologies that surpass classical methods to be developed. It thus opens up promising possibilities for application in a wide variety of fields to enhance performance and efficiency in solving complex optimization problems.

A comparison of classical and quantum feature selection reveals key differences in efficiency and scaling potential. Quantum algorithms, in particular QAOA, can gain exponential speedups in optimization tasks that would take far longer for classical methods. Yet in their own right, a classical approach enjoys the virtues of stability and reduced sensitivity to noise, making them more reliable under today's hardware constraints for high-dimensional data in large-scale commercial applications. A comparative view thus stresses the potential strengths of quantum and its feasibility under these constraints for implementing classical methods

3.1 Quantum Approximate Optimization Algorithm (QAOA)

The Quantum Approximate Optimization Algorithm combines quantum mechanics and classical optimization techniques to effectively solve problems of combinatorial optimization. Thus, QAOA represents an innovative algorithm, which presents a significant advancement in quantum computing since it is capable of representing solutions more efficiently as compared to traditional approaches by utilizing the particular characteristics of a quantum system, (Farhi & Goldstone, 2016). A key Characteristics of QAOA is Quantum State Representation, where QAOA introduces the optimization problem into a quantum state, and then relies on quantum gates to manipulate and probe for solutions to the problem. This encoding of hard optimization problems brings them down to a format that can be processed on a quantum computer. The algorithm involves a classical optimizer that evolves the parameters in an iterative way with measurements of the quantum state. Such iterative convergence gradually moves the system to an optimum solution, trading off between quantum exploration and classical refinement, (Tilly & Nienhuis, 2018). QAOA also has the ability to evaluate multiple solutions in parallel by using quantum superposition and entanglement. Such parallelization of assessment significantly enhances the efficiency of searching, especially on complex solution spaces that provoke difficulties for classical algorithms.

QAOA has various applications such as Feature selection it is one among the most important steps in a machine learning algorithm that can enhance the performance of a given model. QAOA frames feature selection as an optimization of combinatorial functions, so it efficiently identifies the most important features by representing all potential subsets of features as quantum states, which allows for exploration of multiple combinations at the same time and yields those with the maximum accuracy of the model, (Cerezo *et al.*, 2020).

The best feature of the QAOA algorithm is that it optimizes parameters really well in predictive models, and by representing parameters in a quantum context, it gets through the high-dimensional parameter space and discovers configurations that might minimize any error metric, therefore improving model performance. This is where QAOA really does a great job when other optimization strategies hit a dead end. As such, the flexibility, efficiency, and robustness in solving combinatorial problems using QAOA make it a great enabler for an improvement in the predictive capabilities of machine learning models, opening an exciting future direction for quantum optimizers, (Kjaergaard *et al.,* 2020).

3.1.1 Role of QAOA in Feature Selection

Feature selection is very crucial pre-processing step in machine learning wherein we want to learn the most informative features from a dataset. That helps improve the interpretability of the model and reduces the overhead of computation. QAOA improves feature selection significantly, as it utilizes quantum principles to deal effectively with the combinatorial nature of feature selection, (Farhi & Goldstone, 2016). QAOA Enhances Feature Selection by Encoding Features as Quantum States i.e., QAOA encodes possible feature subsets as quantum states, which lets the algorithm efficiently examine many combinations. The approach exploits the power of quantum processing to facilitate the computation of complex relations in the data, (Tilly & Nienhuis, 2018). One of the reasons that quantum parallelism allows the algorithm to evaluate multiple feature sets at once is cutting down selection time by orders of magnitude compared to traditional algorithms. QAOA treats feature selection as an optimization problem and maximizes relevant performance metrics, such as model accuracy, which ensures that all the features selected are contributing meaningfully to the overall performance of the model, (Cerezo *et al.,* 2020).

The benefits of using QAOA for feature selection are significant. It excels in Handling High Dimensions, where the most classical feature selection approaches break down when it comes to handling high dimensions. Quantum approaches like QAOA use quantum hardware and algorithms to find optimal subsets inside the high-dimensional feature space that are often missed by their classical counterparts. QAOA reduces the problem of overfitting by selecting only the most relevant features, leading to better generalizations to unseen data, (Kjaergaard *et al.,* 2020). Feature selection improvement for QAOA begins with this step. This indeed marks a step forward into pre-processing datasets about machine learning that should ultimately lead to the development of more efficient and robust predictive models, (Farhi & Goldstone, 2016).

3.1.2 QAOA for Optimizing Predictive Model Parameters

Optimization of model parameters is of interest as it improves the performance of predictive analytics. QAOA introduces a novel framework of parameter tuning to complex models because it combines the benefits of quantum computations with a classical optimization approach. In terms of its Mechanism, QAOA starts with Quantum State Preparation, in this preparation for quantum processing first reformulates model parameters in a quantum state encoding the optimization problem, (Tilly & Nienhuis, 2018). The set of quantum gates determined by the constraints of the problem is applied, thereby controlling the quantum state and searching different configurations of parameters in parallel. Quantum state is measured to get results in the objective function (for example loss or error). Then there is a classical optimizer which learns from the iterations of finding the minimum of the objective. Now comes the integration of evaluation with classical refinement on a quantum computer, (Cerezo *et al.,* 2020). QAOA offers several advantages in parameter optimization. Parallel exploration of multiple parameter configurations – here Quantum superposition allows QAOA to efficiently explore various parameter configurations in one run. This leads QAOA to be significantly faster than classical optimization methods in exploring complicated landscapes of parameters. Local minima from reduced problems - Optimization algorithms with conventional heuristics are frequently caught in local minima. The more extensive exploration capacity of QAOA reduces the respective risk and yields improved solutions, (Kjaergaard *et al.,* 2020).

3.2 Variational Quantum Eigen solver (VQE)

This problem can be addressed through the development of a hybrid algorithm combining the resources of both quantum and classical regimes: Variational Quantum Eigen solver, VQE, for short. It is quite insightful in the approximation of ground state energy of quantum systems but easily extends to several applications in machine learning and optimization, (Peruzzo *et al.,* 2014). Key Principles of VQE include Parameterized Quantum States, in which the VQE would start by preparing a trial quantum state parameterized by parameters which should be tunable. One is trying to find the set of parameters which will lead to the lowest energy state-that corresponds to the ground state of the quantum system. It calculates the expectation value of the Hamiltonian, which is the energy operator to the prepared quantum state. The calculated value is minimized with the help of classical optimization techniques and thus the algorithm performs much better in approaching the optimal solution, (Singh, Khajuria, & Nayak, 2023). VQE calls up an iteration refinement step in which the parameters are updated generation by generation according to measurement results. This is a loop that is used for continuously improving the approximation of the ground-state energy, (Cerezo *et al.,* 2020). VQE has various applications, including feature selection and dimensionality reduction. The VQE can easily be adapted to perform feature selection tasks as well. In this case, it tries to minimize a loss function that depends on the feature importance. The algorithm encodes many of these feature subsets into quantum states; this enables an efficient discovery of optimal configurations which minimize the loss. VQE can efficiently optimize the parameters of predictive models due to the fact it can traverse complex parameter landscapes. Framing the entire process of tuning as a minimization problem, VQE helps to tighten the accuracy and generalization capabilities of the models, thereby adding predictive analytics value. VQE is very unique because it exploits the properties of high dimensions based on some peculiar properties of quantum mechanics: superposition and entanglement. Though the hybrid approach actually accelerates the exploration for optimal solutions, its predictive capability on applications also benefits.

The impact of QAOA on model performance is substantial. The optimization of model parameters is done more efficiently, thus results in more accurate prediction and consequently leads to more reliable models for real-world applications, (Farhi & Goldstone, 2016). QAOA is thus scalable for large numbers of parameters and in models with many parameters, thus overcoming one of the major limitations that classical optimization methods face.

QAOA is an approach to optimizing predictive model parameters that combines the strength of quantum computing with classically driven techniques for performance and scalability benefits in machine learning, (Tilly & Nienhuis, 2018).

3.2.1 VQE in Feature Selection and Dimensionality Reduction

Feature selection as well as dimensionality reduction are among the major processes of machine learning aimed at discovering only the most informative features available for big datasets. Quantum VQE introduces a new approach toward these tasks, by exploiting quantum computing strengths in efficiently working with high-dimensional data. VQE reformulates feature selection as the optimization problem of locating the best subset of features that minimizes some loss function as defined by mean squared error or maximizes accuracy, (McClean *et al.*, 2016). Different feature subsets were encoded into quantum states with the help of quantum circuits, which evaluated these configurations rapidly. This encoding helps VQE efficiently move within the feature space and identifies the most relevant features. In dimensionality reduction, VQE has several advantages. With quantum parallelism, VQE is able to evaluate multiple dimensionality reductions simultaneously; thus, feature space exploration is improved. This greatly helps to speed up the process compared to other classical approaches, which usually find it challenging when the high-dimensional dataset has a huge number of features. Using quantum resources, VQE significantly reduces the computational resources involved in dimensionality reduction as compared to traditional approaches, which solve one of the significant bottlenecks facing the latter, (Barison, Jacquier, & Cerezo, 2021). The impact of VQE on model performance is tremendous. VQE does not only improve the precision and accuracy of the model but also improves the ability to generalize of the model. It, therefore, improves predictive performance on unseen data. VQE introduces a new approach to select the most relevant features or reduce the dimensionality of the feature space by the use of quantum computing. This opens a plethora of better pre-processing data in machine learning that will lead to better quality in predictive modelling.

VQE has been applied to machine learning-based feature selection problems. In this problem, determining the relevant genes that best characterize a large dataset contributes to the improvement in accuracy of the predictive models for disease prediction, especially in genomics. VQE is generally implemented using hybrid quantum-classical models where the complexity of feature selection is handled by the quantum circuit, and the output is refined classically to achieve optimal feature configurations for the development of predictive models.

3.2.2 Improving Prediction Accuracy with VQE

The optimization of parameters in predictive models becomes important for improved predictions in a variety of applications. VQE thus offers a firm footing in the calibration of parameters through its quantum capabilities, which can formulate and solve complex optimization problems. Recasting the optimization problem to minimize a loss function, which provides an approximation of the discrepancy between predicted and actual values, can be accomplished by encoding the model's parameters into quantum states and leverage the power of quantum circuits in approximating the evaluation of the loss function. The algorithm exploits the property of quantum superposition to evaluate several parameter configurations in parallel. Evaluating in parallel improves the speed of optimization and increases the likelihood of discovering optimal solutions as well, (Singh, Khajuria, & Nayak, 2023). VQE is going to explore high-dimensional parameter spaces a lot more efficiently than classical optimization techniques. These often come with computational overhead, often undoing performance. Optimization algorithms often get trapped in local minima while providing a suboptimal solution. VQE's quantum characteristics help to reduce the possibility of such type of scenario and enables a much broader exploration of the parameter landscape, (Barison, Jacquier, & Cerezo, 2021).

VQE's impact on model performance includes better generalization, meaning that optimized models using VQE generalize much better, meaning they are better on unseen data because the parameter tuning is much more robust. Additionally, VQE is efficient, and hence applicable at large scales where complex models with many parameters are used. This scaling mitigates some of the most potent obstacles to the optimization of such models, (Kjaergaard *et al.,* 2020). VQE improves the predictivity since an effective framework is given to parameter optimization. With the help of quantum computing powers, VQE moves ahead drastically in predictive analytics and machine learning applications, really showing promise as a transformative tool in the field, (Peruzzo *et al.,* 2014).

4. QUANTUM DATA ENCODING METHODS

Quantum encoding of data represents the concept of prime importance in quantum computing, essentially to represent classical data in the quantum system; that is to say, it allows one to carry out computations using quantum algorithms with a high efficiency and effectiveness in data processing and analysis. The aim of quantum data encoding is to exploit those properties of quantum states, basically consisting of superposition and entanglement, and hence solve problems in a much more efficient way than with classical computation, (Nielsen & Chuang, 2010).

Figure 2. Key factors of quantum data encoding

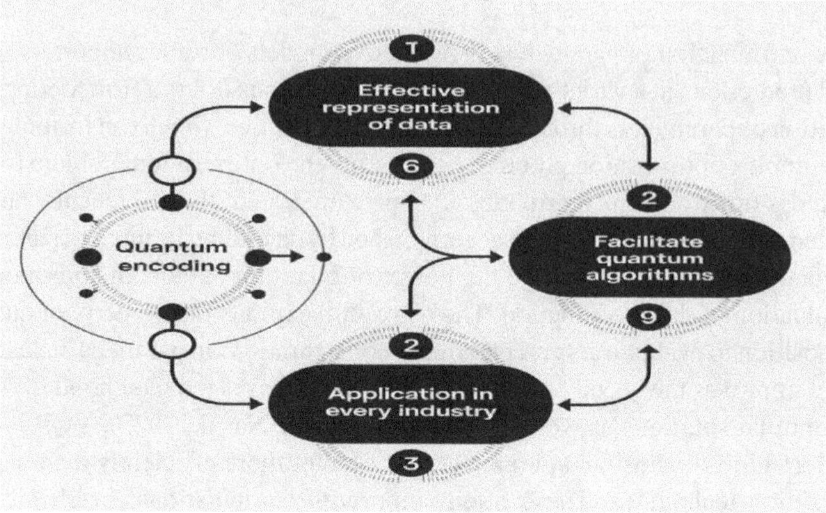

Key points of Quantum Data Encoding Figure 2 include, Effective Representation of Data, which means that the in-quantum data encoding, data can be represented within a more compact format so that quantum algorithms perform simultaneous calculations over large datasets. This is primarily because of the factor of quantum parallelism, which proves to hold the key as compared to classical systems in the majority, especially with complex analyses where classical computations are likely. It also Facilitate Quantum Algorithms, making classical data friendly to the quantum world improves the implementation of algorithms that are specifically tailored for particular data tasks such as optimization and machine learning. This allows algorithms to exploit the quantum mechanical features to evaluate whatever they can faster and more accurately than their respective classical equivalents, (Wang & Li, 2019). This is a very frequent process in the application fields of quantum machine learning, quantum simulation, and cryptography. Here, it accelerates the handling of data and thereby boosts the capabilities of quantum algorithms and further very diversified areas. The possibility to encode data correctly in quantum systems is necessary for the evolution of applications for quantum computing, since this will directly affect the running efficiency of complex calculations performed by quantum algorithms. In general, encoding data using quantum systems forms a very apparent basis for the realization of all kinds of advantages arising from quantum technologies and better performance in several computing operations, (Killoran *et al.,* 2020).

4.1 Quantum Fourier Transform (QFT)

Quantum Fourier Transform is one of the prominent quantum algorithms; it can calculate the discrete Fourier transform of quantum states. It is applied very broadly in a variety of quantum applications, especially in quantum simulation, and is therefore used in algorithms such as Shor's algorithm, which can factor integers efficiently and solve a huge class of problems, (Cerezo *et al.,* 2020). The QFT transforms quantum states from the time domain into the frequency domain, leaving behind useful frequency components. The Algorithm Characteristics include the application of quantum gates, which means that the QFT is based on qubits and utilizes a series of quantum gates, Hadamard gates and controlled phase shift gates for its transformation. It transforms an input quantum state $|\Psi\rangle$ to give the superposition of frequency components in the manner of representing data relationships in the complex and efficiently transforming the input state towards output quantum state, (Nielsen & Chuang, 2010). QFT can carry out this transformation in polynomial time with a complexity of, $O(n^2)$ for n qubits. This transformation, therefore, has very huge speed advantages over the classical Fourier transforms in most applications. These typically require the order of operations of $O(N\log N)$ time for N data points. A detailed application of QFT appears with the quantum algorithms that require frequency analysis, in which periodic functions can be obtained. The exponential speedup provided by QFT, as compared to the best-known classical methods, bestows immense computational advantages for problems in cryptography and number theory, (Wang & Li, 2019). Outside of cryptography, QFT has a range of useful applications in quantum signal processing and solving differential equations, thus it finds an important place within the quantum computing toolbox. Whereas QFT implementations find applications, the current quantum hardware can be used only to their limitations viz. coherence times in qubits and gate fidelity, as such limitations can even mar the accuracy and feasibility of carrying out QFT in large-scale applications, (Killoran *et al.,* 2020).

4.1.1 Data Processing and Representation Using QFT

In fact, it is a rather powerful method for processing and representing data in quantum systems. It demonstrates how quantum states can be transformed from time domain to frequency domain and allows various tasks in the realization of quantum computation, (Cerezo *et al.,* 2020). The Data Processing Mechanism involves Quantum State Transformation, which means that the QFT transforms a quantum state $|x\rangle$ into a superposition of frequency components using Hadamard and controlled phase shift gates. Considering the quantum state to be: $|\psi\rangle = \sum_{x=0}^{N-1} a_x|x\rangle$, QFT transforms it to into $|\psi'\rangle = \sum_{k=0}^{N-1} b_k|k\rangle$, where b_k are the Fourier coefficients, (Nembrini, Acreman, & Cremonesi, 2021). The transformation is efficient; it might be performed with polynomial time complexity relative to the number of qubits and can therefore be applied to different algorithms requiring an analysis of frequencies. QFT has multiple applications in signal processing, including optimizing the processing of large data sets in telecommunications so that it becomes possible to analyse and compress them.

QFT offers several advantages in representation, including the Compact Frequency Representation, means that based on QFT, data can be expressed in terms of frequency components. This allows us to perform efficient manipulation and analysis, particularly on operations like signal processing and periodicity detection, where frequency patterns are fundamental. Also helps in Facilitating Advanced Algorithms. QFT enhances the performance of quantum algorithms, particularly in quantum cryptography and simulations. Its efficiency when dealing with superpositions permits its use to describe complicated patterns very compactly, and hence operations otherwise impossible for classical methods are now feasible. QFT has several advantages, but in reality, its use is taken with certain difficulties, primarily concerning the coherence of the qubit and the accuracy of the gates. It is the surmounting of these difficulties that will make the practical utility of QFT even more useful to a variety of quantum computing applications.

4.1.2 QFT's Impact on Feature Selection in Predictive Analytics

QFT plays an important role in feature selection in predictive analytics particularly in its ability to transform data for frequency-domain analysis. This feature is useful for picking key attributes responsible for predictive modelling, (Cerezo *et al.*, 2020). QFT transforms data into the frequency domain, discovering latent relationships which were perhaps not openly visible from the data format presented. Datasets are decomposed into their frequency components and tracing out dominant features from them which greatly influence the overall structure of data. Feature selection is very important in predictive analytics for an improvement of the model's performance and avoidance of overfitting. QFT can ease the extraction of frequency-based features so that more crucial patterns and trends in models can be pinpointed, especially in time-series data. While the classical Fourier Transform is an applicable method for most signal processing tasks, quantum Fourier transforms greatly accelerate the data processing task, especially in high-dimensional feature spaces. This may prove useful in pushing the limits of and enhancement in further improving the feature selection process as well as in real-time analytics application.

It has vast number of Applications and Advantages such as Accelerated Processing of High Dimensional Datasets, means that the QFT allows to analyse the high dimensional data efficiently by concentrating attention on the most significant frequency components, thus reducing the computation complexity. This feature is important for quick and accurate feature extraction, (Wang & Li, 2019). Also used in In-depth Feature Analysis. QFT's capability to process superpositions and entangled states enables multiple features to be tested in simultaneous ways, which can result in feature selection impacts with a holistic approach and better accuracy and dependability of the model. In this case, QFT affects the feature selection in the way that it is capable of revealing and using the frequency-related properties, which in turn eventually leads to better accuracy and efficiency in analytics, (Killoran *et al.,* 2020).

4.2 Amplitude Encoding

Amplitude Encoding implements the representation of classical information using high-end methods that are in quantum computing. It works by encoding classical information in amplitudes of quantum states so that it can handle large volumes of data due to quantum algorithms implementation. The main idea uses a direct mapping from the values of classical datasets to the amplitudes of quantum basis vectors, which is readily applicable in quantum mechanics and its distinctive properties on data manipulation, (Cramer *et al.,* 2010).

The Encoding Process in Figure 3 involves Quantum State Preparation, means the encoding begins with a preparation of a quantum state $|\Psi\rangle$ such that the amplitudes correspond to the elements of a classical data vector. This is accomplished by unitary operations - in most cases, quantum gates - from some initial state like $|0\rangle$, (Wang, Chen, & Zhang, 2021). The quantum state can be expressed mathematically as:

$$|\Psi\rangle \;=\; 1\,\sqrt{Z}\sum_{i=0}^{N-1} xi|i\rangle,$$

where the x_i-s are the classical data values and $Z \;=\; \sum_{i=0}^{N-1}|x_i|2$ is a normalization constant that ensures that the state's amplitudes satisfy the postulates of quantum superposition, (Ladd *et al.*, 2010). The number of bits in the data vector is quadratic in the scaling of effort needed to prepare the state, and the logarithm of the desired precision of the amplitudes. This encoding allows an exponential scaling of the representation capacity of quantum systems; n qubits can encode 2^n data points, (Zhang & Kwiatkowski, 2020.

Figure 3. Encoding process

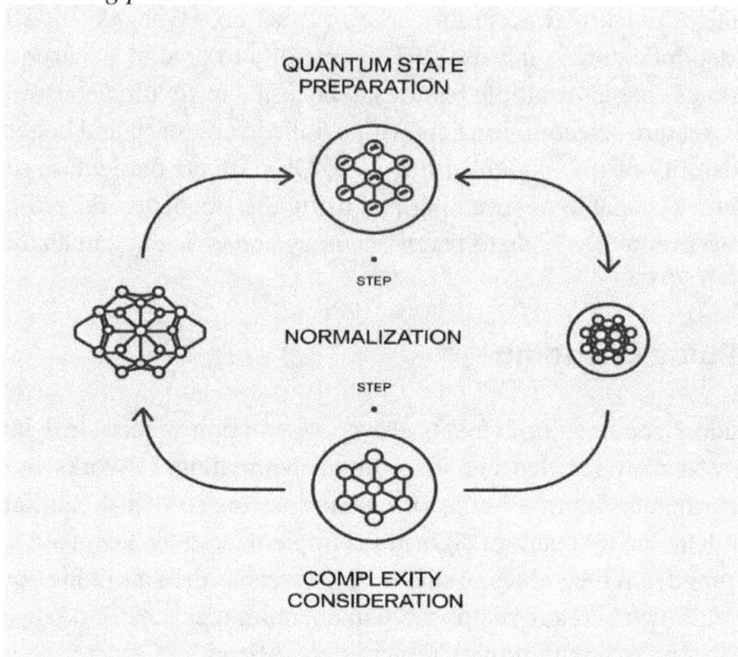

Benefits of Amplitude Encoding include Efficient representation i.e. Perhaps the best feature of amplitude encoding is its ability to represent huge data sets by using only a logarithmic number of qubits. If compared to the classical systems whose memory requirements scale linearly with data size, it is sharply contrasted, (Schuld & Killoran, 2019). Also includes Quantum Parallelism Exploitation i.e. By encoding data into quantum amplitudes, quantum algorithms can leverage the power of superposition to compute all possible states in parallel. This may provide a much greater speedup than classical algorithms and has applications with computationally challenging problems such as optimization or feature extraction, (Cramer *et al.*, 2010). Amplitude encoding is of special interest in applications from quantum machine learning: it allows for the handling of large-sized datasets much better than the other encoder types, since high-dimensional data is typical for these applications, (Wang, Chen, & Zhang, 2021).

4.2.1 Methodology and Benefits for Data Encoding

Amplitude encoding is a method for mapping the information from classical data into quantum systems in a compact, efficient manner by using the properties of quantum states. Mapping Classical Data: A classical data vector $x = [x_0, x_1, \ldots\ldots, x_{N-1}$

] is transformed into a quantum state $|\Psi\rangle$ as mentioned earlier, where each component of the vector is represented as an amplitude of a corresponding quantum basis state, (Ladd *et al.*, 2010). This mapping uses quantum gates to carry out a sequence of unitary operations that translate the initial quantum state into the desired target state, hence making it possible to encode huge data sets on large scales using a very minimalistic number of qubits, (Zhang & Kwaitkowski, 2020). An example of the efficiency provided by amplitude encoding is logarithmic scaling, which enables a quantum system to represent exponential data sizes that have far been beyond those for classical systems.

The benefits of amplitude encoding include reduced storage needs as this system reduces the storage needs exponentially. A classical system requires linear memory to store data whereas amplitude encoding can represent it on only $O(\log N)$ qubits, which makes it highly efficient if it is to handle very large data, (Cramer *et al.*, 2010). It also improves computational speed. With the application of quantum parallelism, amplitude encoding allows for processing to be done more quickly and more efficiently on the data for quantum systems. This is highly important when feature extraction or optimization is needed in large datasets, (Wang, Chen, & Zhang, 2021). The technique also helps in making easier the problems related to dealing with big data-which is a defining characteristic in quantum machine learning and associated computing scenarios, thus enhancing overall computing power, (Ladd *et al.,* 2010).

4.2.2 Enhancing Predictive Models with Amplitude Encoding

Such encoding provides for a higher data representation efficiency and enables unique improvements in predictive modelling by virtue of novel mechanisms of encoding in quantum computing. These premises of predictive models then rely on the identified patterns within datasets, though traditional machine learning models have difficulty managing high-dimensional data, whereas amplitude encoding can be used to represent exponentially larger datasets using fewer qubits. This would therefore result in better detection of subtle correlations and trends that are fundamental in making accurate predictions, (Zhang & Kwaitkowski, 2020). After the classical information is encoded into quantum amplitudes, a quantum algorithm can scan multiple features at the same time from the data set. That particular feature reduces the screening for possible relationships amongst variables much more rapidly, which further provides better robust and accurate predictions, (Schuld & Killoran, 2019). Amplitude encoding helps in navigation over the high-dimensional space of data; hence it tends to save much in terms of computational resources during the time when models are trained. This is rather a great advantage, especially when factors concerning time and accuracy come into play, especially in finance and health, (Cramer *et al.*, 2010).

Amplitude encoding brings several advantages to quantum machine learning. The amplitude encoding quantum machine learning model can handle bigger datasets than its classical counterparts. Richer data input during the training phase enhances predictive capability of the model, (Wang, Chen, & Zhang, 2021). Amplitude encoding makes the predictive model converge toward result more quickly as several hypotheses can be evaluated at the same time. In many applications, there is a need to have very rapid decision-making based on large datasets, (Ladd *et al.*, 2010). Amplitude encoding aids in preparing and feature extraction that enables us to determine the key features required for predictive models. This, therefore, enables training processes to be much more efficient while still allowing for better success rates as well for the handling of complicated data from real-world scenarios, (Zhang & Kwaitkowski, 2020). This effectiveness in encoding and processing data makes amplitude encoding a vital transformational tool in improving quantum machine learning predictive models.

Amplitude encoding has applied in the area of predictive analytics to enhance the performance of models in sections like marketing where predicting the behaviour of customers is critical. Quantum Amplitude encoding enhances the handling of customer data that leads to quicker predictions as opposed to traditional amplitude encoding.

4.3 Quantum Principal Component Analysis (QPCA)

Quantum Principal Component Analysis is a quantum algorithm that extracts important features out of a big dataset, finding its principal components. It resembles classical Principal Component Analysis but on the quantum plane in order that the pertinent information is maintained and still a dimensionality reduction occurs efficiently. This is particularly beneficial for applications in quantum machine learning and predictive analytics where high-dimensional data has to be addressed, (Singh, Khajuria, & Nayak, 2024). The QPCA begins by representing a covariance matrix of the data set using a density matrix of a quantum system. The matrix features relationships between features, which then form the basis of variance analysis, (Wang & Zheng, 2020). QPCA applies quantum phase estimation to compute the eigenvalues and the associated eigenvectors of the covariance matrix. Because the important dimensions for reducing the dimensionality are in the directions pointed out by the principal components - that is, the eigenvectors-with maximum variance, eigenvectors are crucial to this type of analysis, (Al-Baidhany & Saleh, 2024). QPCA is much less complex than the classical PCA. The time complexity for the classical PCA is $O(N^2)$, with N being the number of data points or features. Using quantum superposition and entanglement, QPCA achieves $O(\log N)$ where it can perform many operations in parallel, (Biamonte *et al.,* 2017). Data compression would effectively pay attention to those principal components that contain large eigenvalues. Consequently, QPCA retains primary features and discards redundant information needed for improving quantum machine learning tasks' performance, (Czelusta, 2024).

One of the significant benefits of QPCA is that it can process much bigger datasets much faster than classical PCA, which makes this method especially suitable for applications where data is really huge and needs to come in within a minimum timescale. A good example may include predictive analytics, which requires an extremely real-time nature of getting insights from a very massive dataset, (Wang & Zeng, 2020). Quantum computational advantages allow QPCA to handle complex datasets in a practical way-it likely is the better means of extracting useful patterns or features those classical methods do not perceive.

4.3.1 Introduction to QPCA in Feature Selection

Quantum PCA has to be carried out in feature selection at a stage, especially for big features in the high-dimensional dataset. Therefore, in machine learning, one needs to choose which features contribute really significantly in determining the predictability of the model. QPCA simplifies this process, allowing feature contributions in the most sensitive direction through quantum computations, (Biamonte *et al.,* 2017). QPCA computes the quantum eigenvalues and eigenvectors of the covariance matrix encoded in the system. The largest eigenvalues correspond to principal components pointing out the directions of maximum variance in the data, (Czelusta, 2024). Since QPCA only uses the selected principal components, it ensures that only information relevant to the process stays within it, and less-informative features are ejected. This reduces the dataset's complexity and the risk of overfitting because of its high dimensionality, (Singh, Khajuria, & Nayak, 2024). For high-dimensional data, efficiency in computations is lost. QPCA removes this difficulty by finding the most informative features within a fast time frame so that training can be done in less time and predictions are accurate.

The quantum version of PCA shows much greater speedup than the classical PCA. Processing large data in logarithmic time ensures that handling large data is very efficient, useful for real-time applications if time is critical, (Al-Baidhany & Saleh, 2024). Improvement by QPCA in feature selection process accelerates data analysis but also improves the overall performance of predictive models. The contribution to effective generalization across various applications thus arises from proper capturing of the most significant features by QPCA.

QPCA is very useful in applications that include image processing, which often requires data dimensionality reduction without loss of significant characteristics, to ensure accuracy in classification. QPCA has been shown to be faster and scalable even in large datasets as compared with traditional PCA methods.

4.3.2 QPCA's Role in Reducing Dimensionality for Predictive Accuracy

QPCA is vital in achieving dimensionality reduction, another crucial factor that increases the prediction accuracy of a machine learning model. Dimensionality reduction is a necessary aspect in high-dimensional applications where models often suffer from overfitting and reduced performance, (Czelusta, 2024). QPCA focuses on the major components, which relate to the largest variance. That is, it removes the noise and other small important features while retaining the most informative dimensions of the dataset, making its version simpler while retaining the underlying structures, (Singh, Khajuria, & Nayak, 2024). Eigenvalue Selection method identifies eigenvectors with large absolute eigenvalues such that the features of reduced data are likely to be retained. This deterministic approach prevents the loss of significant features, and thus, appropriate predictions can be made, (Wang & Zeng, 2020). Dimensionality reduction improves the speed at which a model trains in machine learning. A lower number of features ensures faster convergence of models; hence it is more efficient and effective. QPCA helps in Improving Predictive Accuracy by Overfitting Avoidance means that the Features of lesser importance are removed in QPCA. This reduces the chances of overfitting, as the models tend to pick the important underlying patterns in the data so that they might perform better on new datasets, (Biamonte *et al.,* 2017). It also helps in Handling a Large Dataset i.e. Its logarithmic time complexity enables QPCA to evaluate larger data sets. This means that prediction models would be able to consider more data points in far less time. The model would then not only aid in enhancing the accuracy of the model but would also achieve scalability in most uses of the model. Focused Feature Selection - This means that QPCA is meant to only consider the features that would solve the problem at hand, ensuring that the prediction models are both efficient and robust, all leading to an enhancement of their practical predictiveness, (Singh, Khajuria, & Nayak, 2024).

5. CHALLENGES IN QUANTUM FEATURE SELECTION

Despite promising possibilities opened up by QNNs and quantum algorithms in feature selection, there are also a number of challenges facing practical application in complex predictive tasks. These issues can be broadly grouped under hardware, algorithmic, and integration-related problems.

5.1 Hardware Limitations in Quantum Computing

Quantum computing is still at an infant stage. At present, the limitations of quantum hardware form one of the more serious barriers to effective quantum feature selection, (Nielsen & Chuang, 2010). Quantum systems are highly susceptible to environmental noise; this causes decoherence-the loss of quantum states. This inhibits quantum computations and introduces errors in feature selection. Quantum error correction techniques are available though they are computationally expensive and are hence currently infeasible for large-scale applications. Quantum feature selection allows to represent multiple features in the quantum computer and encode every one of them as quantum states. The limited number of qubits in the current quantum computer is not enough to enclose the representation of high-dimensional datasets most of the time. Therefore, only fewer such datasets with the simplified model could be processed very speedily. The current hardware limitations do not allow the practical use of quantum feature selection in finance or healthcare applications. For example, although quantum-driven portfolio optimization in finance appears to have the potential to revolutionize financial analysis, qubit noise-induced limited processing does not allow large datasets. Healthcare diagnostics with genomic data is also an application with which diagonalization faces a problem: current quantum processors are too unreliable for the desired depth of computation without error correction, which is still computationally prohibitive.

Quantum operations or gates involved with qubits are not perfect. The fidelity of quantum gates greatly determines the outcome of algorithms applied in feature selection. Inaccuracies from imperfect gate fidelity result in inaccurate findings, making analysis based on extracted features meaningless. In quantum circuits, it is the number of operations before noise models a significant issue in the computation. Current quantum devices support only shallow circuits and therefore QNNs including algorithms for feature selection are relatively simple in complexity. Deeper circuitry is needed for more complex tasks but proves to be hard to get reliably.

5.2 Algorithmic Complexity in Quantum Feature Selection

Designing and optimizing quantum algorithms for feature selection is open. Many quantum algorithms for feature selection, ranging from Grover's Search to Quantum Approximate Optimization Algorithm (QAOA), can theoretically provide speedups over their classical counterparts, (Wang & Li, 2019). However, in practical applications, the algorithms are often implemented with a high degree of computational complexity when dealing with noisy or large datasets. Sometimes the overhead related to quantum algorithms can deteriorate their advantage. Feature selection training for QNNs may lead to barren plateaus, large regions of parameter space where the cost function gradient is close to zero. Optimization of quantum gates is thus hard, and the features selected from those places are also not relevant in such regions. That makes the training process quite inefficient especially with a huge size of the QNN.

Quantum algorithms are not scalable as of now. Small-sized feature selection tasks can be performed on near-term quantum devices, but scaling up the algorithms to handle large, practical datasets remains open. In addition, some quantum algorithms are polynomial or exponential time scaling, so they cannot be applied to large data sets even if a quantum speedup is theoretically possible. Similar to classical ML algorithms, the quantum feature selection algorithms also require hyperparameters tuning but for gate parameters and learning rates. Quantum circuit tuning is much more involved than in classical systems because, firstly, quantum states are inherently probabilistic, and secondly, quantum systems respond extremely sensitively to small changes in parameters.

Such hybrid algorithmic challenges require the development of hybrid quantum-classical models to finally overcome the complexity barrier. For instance, the approach may involve a quantum optimization intertwined with a classically performing data preprocessing that limits the quantum computational load so that large datasets can be processed better-than already achieved in initial applications in finance and healthcare but still aspirational at scale.

5.3 Pragmatic Integration Challenges with Quantum Algorithms

The following are some pragmatic integration challenges associated with integrating quantum algorithms with practical feature selection workflows: The hybrid approach has to be adopted by most feature selection quantum algorithms so far, mainly due to the several limitations imposed by the hardware in quantum. Shifting between quantum and classical computations introduces latency and increases the complexity of feature selection, and it is not particularly easy to smoothly integrate into a machine learning pipeline. Classical data, before it can be inputted with feature selection, must first be transformed into the quantum states. Such a transformation is referred to as quantum feature encoding. Yet another challenge in the adoption of quantum feature selection models is that they require special purpose hardware and software. Moreover, difficulties associated with expensive and non-availability of qubits add to the list. A significant investment in skill and infrastructure would be needed for most organizations to use the approaches in effective manners.

In general, useful encoding techniques like amplitude encoding or angle encoding, in particular, inject many complications for high-dimensional data or continuous variables. Data pre-processing can even potentially cancel out the quantum speedup in some cases due to the computational expense of the encoding. Access to quantum hardware remains somewhat limited at this time, since most of the quantum computers aren't accessible for most of the researchers or organizations. Though cloud-based quantum computing platforms such as IBM Q and Rigetti do provide access to quantum processors, normally, there's a limitation that does not supply enough computational resources or triggers queuing delays, and hence, poses further limitations on real-time control and integration with real-world pipelines of feature selection.

The interpretability of the results from quantum feature selection is hard compared to classical algorithms. Quantum states are represented by probabilistic outcomes, which makes the direct mapping of the outcome to classical feature importance metrics really complicated. It is often necessary to perform some post-processing for the results from quantum to be interpretable and actionable in predictive tasks. There is a huge skill gap involved with quantum computing, and most organizations do not have the necessary expertise to develop or implement quantum feature selection algorithms, (Killoran *et al.*, 2020). It requires simultaneous knowledge in quantum mechanics, machine learning, and algorithm design, a skill set currently scarce and limited to niche communities in both academia and industry.

In real-world applications, integrating quantum algorithms faces significant challenges, particularly when encoding high-dimensional data into quantum states, as required in marketing and targeted advertising. This process introduces computational overhead, complicating smooth integration into classical ML pipelines, especially for large-scale consumer data. These barriers call for more streamlined quantum-classical interfaces to make quantum computing practically feasible in commercial data analysis.

5.4 Ethical and Security Implications of Quantum Computing

Quantum computation and programming pose issues related to ethics and security in specific fields where decisions rely on the respective fields over sensitive information. For example, bias within quantum machine learning algorithms may appear critical for ethical considerations in health care and criminal justice, hence affecting diagnosis or even sentencing. It is also particularly significant in terms of security since quantum computation breaks classical encryption in applications like RSA, making data vulnerable to threats, and therefore producing the quantum-safe cryptography to protect such sensitive information. Another aspect of fear is privacy, since quantum technology will offer unimaginable processing powers that might be used for intrusive surveillance with gigantic data analyses that could infringe on somebody's rights. This aspect must be covered in strong frameworks in place to guide the right way towards quantum computing ethics and safety.

6. FUTURE PROSPECTS

The exciting opportunity presented by this new technology arises from integrating it into predictive analytics, which is progressing quantum computing technology at a rapid pace. Introduction of improved quantum hardware, hybrid quantum-classical algorithms, and domain-specific quantum algorithms may result in a tremendous improvement to feature selection and accuracy in predictive models, thereby spreading the opportunity for data-driven decision making across industries, (Kumar & Safro, 2022).

6.1 Advancements in Quantum Hardware

Another factor that has ensured the applicability of quantum algorithms is the advancement in quantum hardware. Some of these vital aspects are discussed below. The coherence times in quantum hardware refer to how long the qubits can retain quantum states to perform complex calculations. The time factors refer to when the quantum computations may be trusted because errors increase with coherence duration. The higher the coherence, the more strongly quantum computations are. Good error correction techniques are required to counter the noise inherent in the quantum systems. Error corrections in the quantum regime will enhance the fidelity of the quantum operations by several orders, and quantum computing will subsequently become much more practical for real-world applications.

Recent breakthroughs in coherence times and qubit fidelity are starting to mitigate some of the scalability and reliability challenges, therefore making quantum algorithms increasingly applicable for larger datasets in finance and healthcare. For example, with advancements in qubit reliability, applications like high-frequency trading in finance and genomic data analysis in healthcare can achieve much higher accuracy and higher speed, thus moving closer to practical applicability of quantum feature selection. The more qubits the quantum computer contains, the bigger datasets these computers have the ability to process. Even as companies like IBM, Google, and Rigetti make wider hardware advanced capability, handling extensive complex datasets becomes big potential.

With advances made in quantum hardware, QPCA and QAOA could be applied to increasingly large datasets, thereby enhancing predictive analytics accuracy. This allows for a greater drilling into the data set so that predictions can accurately happen, (Markidis, 2024). Improved quantum processors now enable complex quantum algorithms that would solve impossible problems in optimization. This development will further entrench quantum computing into different industries: it would be possible to make precise analyses and even decide between alternatives in such significant industries as finance and healthcare. As the technology of quantum hardware continues to advance, its effects on predictive analytics will be profound and establish ever more sophisticated and accurate data-driven methodologies.

6.2 Development of Hybrid Quantum-Classical Algorithms

Hybrid quantum-classical algorithms are actually becoming very fast applied with great speed in optimization of feature selection within predictive analytics. Here, strategies marry the powers of quantum computing and classical computing techniques to produce considerable benefits: Hybrid algorithms use speed advantages in quantum computing towards calculations of optimization and feature selection while classical algorithms manage input preparation and output processing.

There are also some exemplary hybrid algorithms, such as the Variational Quantum Eigen solver (VQE) and Quantum Approximate Optimization Algorithm (QAOA). So far, they have demonstrated their power in solving hard optimization problems. Current NISQ devices are noisy and decoherent; the hybrid approach can mitigate this possibility by letting parts of the computation run on classical processors, therefore making quantum algorithms more practical. Hybrid quantum-classical methods improve the accuracy and efficiency of predictive models. Quantum computing leverages hybrid algorithms that can study much larger and more complex data spaces within runtimes that may be practically achieved compared to classical systems, (Moll *et al.,* 2018).

Hybrid algorithms may then be used to create specific predictive analytics applications in different industries, suggesting that a more intricate approach to feature selection can be implemented and, therefore, very closely aligned to the needs of diverse datasets. Continuing the advancement of hybrid quantum-classical algorithms puts prospects for tremendous improvement in feature selection and predictive accuracy, thus fostering more effective data analytics solutions.

Hybrid quantum-classical models are proving very useful for optimization problems in complex industries. Quantum speed advantages are merged with classical stability to produce hybrid algorithms, like VQE and QAOA, making the processing of features more manageable by the quantum processing unit while using classical algorithms for preprocessing and post-processing. Early success for these models has been found in financial risk modeling and will soon be advanced applications for personalized healthcare diagnostics, allowing for quantum feature selection to support diverse predictive needs across industries.

6.3 Domain-Specific Quantum Algorithms for Predictive Analytics

As the quantum technology matures, its applications in domain-specific quantum algorithms for predictive analytics are developing strongly. So, let's find out how domain-specific algorithms are going to shape the future: Domain-specific algorithms are applications designed to solve specific problems in a field, finance, healthcare, or marketing. New kinds of domain-specific quantum algorithms are emerging in finance and health care, promising great breakthroughs in predictive analytics. Such algorithms might come in the form of predicting which way the stocks would swing or which risk to take in a financial portfolio; in the case of health care, they might predict diseases based on intricate genetic data with great precision. This specificity indicates a trend toward applications of quantum specifically targeted at certain industries, where those industries could extrapolate meaningful insights from datasets that previously proved impossible to draw any helpful conclusions from with such accuracy. Through the specifics of applications, these algorithms are solving problems more effectively than their general-purpose counterparts.

Specific algorithms related to financial data analysis would improve the feature selection to better predict the direction of the trend of the stock market. Similarly, algorithms in health care would zero in on large sets of data within which diseases could be identified. This specialization improves accuracy and efficiency in processing. These algorithms often are developed in collaboration between quantum computing specialists and industry professionals. It allows to design algorithms that exploit the quantum properties, including entanglement or superposition, for improving feature selection processes tailored to a given dataset, (Pellow-Jerman *et al.*, 2024).

Quantum computers are inherently flexible in dealing with those complex feature selection tasks that would be outright impossible for a classical algorithm. Ultimately, this makes the models predict much more accurately and economically as compared to the traditional methods, especially in niche applications. Further research into domain-specific quantum algorithms may pave the way toward further development of predictive analytics. Once industries believe that there's much promise in quantum solution, perhaps the appetite for customized algorithms will increase, and subsequently, their development will prove the data-driven decision-making.

Quantum algorithms face domain-specific problems and thus prove to be phenomenally beneficial in predictive analytics, where organizations unlock all possible value from their data.

CONCLUSION

It integrates quantum computing with predictive analytics and feature selection-an approach that marks the revolution for a strengthening of avenues in data-driven decision-making. Some of the machine learning algorithms include QSVM, QKNN, and quantum neural networks, hence making quantum computing address high-dimensional data on a much better scale than traditional approaches. It exploits properties such as superposition and entanglement in quantum, making it walk through complex feature spaces, updating parameters in the model to increase the accuracy of classification or prediction. The ability to try multiple feature subsets all at once suggests these algorithms might be better than conventional algorithms at feature selection tasks. Their utility is invaluable in applications that range from finance to healthcare.

Quantum optimization algorithms, with QAOA and VQE as examples, further optimize the parameters in predictive models. Such algorithms can efficiently move across high-dimensional parameter spaces, thereby alleviating to a great extent the computationally formidable challenges of applying classical optimization techniques. This is mainly because QAOA and VQE exploit the principles of quantum mechanics in overcoming the problem of attaining an optimal solution within fewer iterations so that model performance is improved and the possibility of its scalability arises.

Encoding the optimization problems in a quantum state increases not only the precision of these algorithms but also covers up the lacunas that traditional methods possess, making them an extremely useful tool for the solution of complex prediction tasks. But there are also major problems of scaling to wide-spread use for quantum feature selection methods. Improvements in hardware are promising, however algorithmic complexity issues, and integration with classical systems are major challenges. The exciting research and developments in the progress of quantum hardware, hybrid quantum-classical algorithms, and domain-specific quantum solutions hold very promising prospects for the future.

As the quantum technologies advance, they are expected to transform predictive analytics at a faster pace, granting a more powerful, accurate, and scalable way to address the complexities of data in the real world. Breakthrough applications are already being set up in the continuous course of innovation that has started to shape the next wave of progress in data science and artificial intelligence.

REFERENCES

Aggarwal, D., Bali, V., & Mittal, S. (2019). An insight into machine learning techniques for predictive analysis and feature selection. *International Journal of Innovative Technology and Exploring Engineering*, 8(9), 342–349.

Ahmed, S. (2019). Pattern recognition with Quantum Support Vector Machine (QSVM) on near term quantum processors (Doctoral dissertation, Brac University).

Al-Baidhany, I. A., & Saleh, M. B. (2024). Study of changing entangled states of a quantum system consisting of four qubits using the Hadamard gate. Journal of Theory. *Mathematics and Physics*, 3(4), 55–63.

Ayesha, S., Hanif, M. K., & Talib, R. (2021). Performance enhancement of predictive analytics for health informatics using dimensionality reduction techniques and fusion frameworks. *IEEE Access : Practical Innovations, Open Solutions*, 10, 753–769. DOI: 10.1109/ACCESS.2021.3139123

Barison, S., Jacquier, C., & Cerezo, M. (2021). Quantum feature selection via variational quantum eigensolvers. *Quantum Information Processing*, 20(1), 15.

Biamonte, J., Wittek, P., Pancotti, N., Rebentrost, P., Wiebe, N., & Lloyd, S. (2017). Quantum machine learning. *Nature*, 549(7671), 195–202. DOI: 10.1038/nature23474 PMID: 28905917

Cerezo, M., Arrasmith, A., Babbush, R., Benjamin, S. C., Endo, S., Fujii, K., McClean, J. R., Mitarai, K., Yuan, X., Cincio, L., & Coles, P. J. (2020). Variational quantum algorithms. *Nature Reviews. Physics*, 3(10), 625–644.

Cramer, M., Plenio, M. B., Flammia, S. T., Somma, R., Gross, D., Bartlett, S. D., Landon-Cardinal, O., Poulin, D., & Liu, Y.-K. (2010). Efficient quantum data encoding using quantum circuits. *Physical Review Letters*, 104(12), 120502.

Czelusta, G. (2024). Grover's algorithm on two-way quantum computer. arXiv preprint arXiv:2406.09450.

Dang, Y., Jiang, N., Hu, H., Ji, Z., & Zhang, W. (2018). Image classification based on quantum K-Nearest-Neighbor algorithm. *Quantum Information Processing*, 17(9), 1–18. DOI: 10.1007/s11128-018-2004-9

. Farhi, E., & Goldstone, J. (2016). A quantum approximate optimization algorithm. arXiv, 1602.07674.

Fellous-Asiani, M., Chai, J. H., Whitney, R. S., Auffèves, A., & Ng, H. K. (2021). Limitations in quantum computing from resource constraints. *PFX Quantum : a Physical Review Journal*, 2(4), 040335. DOI: 10.1103/PRXQuantum.2.040335

Harris, C., & Lee, M. (2023). *QAOA: Revolutionizing combinatorial optimization.* Quantum Algorithms Review.

Kariya, A., & Behera, B. K. (2021). Investigation of quantum support vector machine for classification in nisq era. arXiv preprint arXiv:2112.06912.

Killoran, N., Izaac, J., Quesada, N., Bergholm, V., Amy, M., & Weedbrook, C. (2020). Continuous-variable quantum neural networks. *Physical Review Research*, 1(3), 033075.

Kjaergaard, M., Schwartz, M. D., Braumüller, J., Krantz, P., Wang, J. I., Gustavsson, S., & Oliver, W. D. (2020). Superconducting qubits: Current state of play. *Annual Review of Condensed Matter Physics*, 11(1), 369–395. DOI: 10.1146/annurev-conmatphys-031119-050605

Kumar, P., & Safro, I. (2022). Quantum computing for optimization and machine learning: A survey. *Computer Science Review*, 44, 100456.

Ladd, T. D., Jelezko, F., Laflamme, R., Nakamura, Y., Monroe, C., & O'Brien, J. L. (2010). Quantum computers. *Nature*, 464(7285), 45–53. DOI: 10.1038/nature08812 PMID: 20203602

Lee, D., & Wang, H. (2020). Superposition in quantum algorithms. *Computers in Physics.*

Mallow, G. M., Hornung, A., Barajas, J. N., Rudisill, S. S., An, H. S., & Samartzis, D. (2022). Quantum computing: The future of big data and artificial intelligence in spine. *Spine Surgery and Related Research*, 6(2), 93–98. DOI: 10.22603/ssrr.2021-0251 PMID: 35478980

Markidis, S. (2024). What is quantum parallelism, anyhow? In ISC High Performance 2024 Research Paper Proceedings (39th International Conference). Prometeus GmbH.

McClean, J. R., Romero, J., Babbush, R., & Aspuru-Guzik, A. (2016). The theory of variational hybrid algorithms. *New Journal of Physics*, 18(2), 023023. DOI: 10.1088/1367-2630/18/2/023023

Moll, N., Barkoutsos, P., Bishop, L. S., Chow, J. M., Cross, A., Egger, D. J., & Gambetta, J. M. (2018). Quantum optimization using variational algorithms on near-term quantum devices. *Quantum Science and Technology*, 3(3), 030503. DOI: 10.1088/2058-9565/aab822

Moussa, C., Calandra, H., & Dunjko, V. (2020). To quantum or not to quantum: Towards algorithm selection in near-term quantum optimization. *Quantum Science and Technology*, 5(4), 044009. DOI: 10.1088/2058-9565/abb8e5

Mücke, S., Heese, R., Müller, S., Wolter, M., & Piatkowski, N. (2023). Feature selection on quantum computers. *Quantum Machine Intelligence*, 5(1), 11. DOI: 10.1007/s42484-023-00099-z

Navot, A., Shpigelman, L., Tishby, N., & Vaadia, E. (2005). Nearest neighbor based feature selection for regression and its application to neural activity. *Advances in Neural Information Processing Systems*, •••, 18.

Nembrini, R., Ferrari Acreman, M., & Cremonesi, P. (2021). Feature selection for recommender systems with quantum computing. *Entropy (Basel, Switzerland)*, 23(8), 970. DOI: 10.3390/e23080970 PMID: 34441110

Nielsen, M. A., & Chuang, I. L. (2010). *Quantum computation and quantum information*. Cambridge University Press.

Pellow-Jarman, A., & Möttönen, M.. (2024). The effect of classical optimizers and Ansatz depth on QAOA performance in noisy devices. *Scientific Reports*, 14(1), 16011. DOI: 10.1038/s41598-024-66625-6 PMID: 38992152

Peruzzo, A., McClean, J., Shadbolt, P., Yung, M.-H., Zhou, X.-Q., Love, P. J., Aspuru-Guzik, A., & O'Brien, J. L. (2014). A variational eigenvalue solver on a photonic quantum processor. *Nature Communications*, 5(1), 4213. DOI: 10.1038/ncomms5213 PMID: 25055053

Rigui, Z., Nan, J., & Qiulin, D. (2006). Model and training of QNN with weight. *Neural Processing Letters*, 24(3), 261–269. DOI: 10.1007/s11063-006-9025-6

Schuld, M., & Killoran, N. (2019). Quantum machine learning in feature Hilbert spaces. *Physical Review Letters*, 122(4), 040504. DOI: 10.1103/PhysRevLett.122.040504 PMID: 30768345

Singh, C., & Das, A. K. (2024). Transforming digitization in supply chain management using artificial intelligence and machine learning. In *Supply Chain Management* (pp. 119–139). CRC Press. DOI: 10.1201/9781003509561-7

Singh, C., Khajuria, H., & Nayak, B. P. (2023), March. A Study of Implementing a Blockchain-Based Forensic Model Integration (BBFMI) for IoT Devices in Digital Forensics. In *International Conference on Computer Science, Engineering and Education Applications* (pp. 318-327). Cham: Springer Nature Switzerland. DOI: 10.1007/978-3-031-36118-0_28

Singh, C., Khajuria, H., & Nayak, B. P. (2024). Rapid Advancement and Trends of Big Data Analytics and Cyber-Physical System Embedded in Healthcare and Industry 4.0. In *Intelligent Security Solutions for Cyber-Physical Systems* (pp. 216-233). Chapman and Hall/CRC.

. Singh, C., Khajuria, H. and Nayak, B.P., A Comprehensive IoT Security Framework Using Edge Computing: Approaches and Challenges. *Network Optimization in Intelligent Internet of Things Applications*, pp.274-297.

. Smith, A., & Johnson, B. (2021). Quantum optimization in machine learning and finance. Journal of Quantum Computing.

Tilly, C., & Nienhuis, R. (2018). Quantum algorithms for combinatorial optimization: The quantum approximate optimization algorithm. *IEEE Transactions on Quantum Engineering*, 1, 1–12.

Wang, H., & Zeng, H. (2020). Quantum algorithms for feature selection and predictive analytics. *IEEE Transactions on Neural Networks and Learning Systems*, 31(5), 1560–1572. PMID: 31265416

Wang, Y., & Li, Y. (2019). Quantum data encoding for quantum machine learning. *Physical Review. A*, 100(3), 032309. DOI: 10.1103/PhysRevA.99.032309

Wang, Z., Chen, Y., & Zhang, S. (2021). Amplitude encoding and quantum algorithms for data representation. *Nature Reviews. Physics*, 3(2), 81–96.

Zhang, J., & Kwiatkowski, D. (2020). Quantum algorithms for machine learning: A review. *IEEE Transactions on Quantum Engineering*, 1, 1–12.

Zhang, S., Li, J., Xu, H., Yu, H., & Shi, J. (2023). Robust Quantum Feature Selection Algorithm. *Authorea Preprints*.

Zhao, R., & Wang, S. (2021). A review of quantum neural networks: methods, models, dilemma. arXiv preprint arXiv:2109.01840.

Chapter 10

The Role of Quantum Machine Learning in Optimizing Neuromarketing Insights for Retail and E-Commerce

Rama Chaithanya Tanguturi
https://orcid.org/0000-0002-9923-7360
Woxsen University, India

A. Devendran
https://orcid.org/0000-0001-7192-521X
Woxsen University, India

S. Umarani
https://orcid.org/0000-0002-8884-5870
SRM Institute of Science and Technology, India

ABSTRACT

Neuromarketing combines neuroscience and traditional marketing to uncover the emotional and cognitive drivers behind consumer behavior. As retail and e-commerce sectors increasingly rely on customer data for personalized experiences, the complexity of large datasets often surpasses classical machine learning capabilities. This gap allows Quantum Machine Learning (QML) to emerge as a transformative solution, enhancing predictive power and efficiency in neuromarketing. QML im-

DOI: 10.4018/979-8-3693-7673-7.ch010

proves data processing speed and pattern recognition, enabling companies to gain deeper insights into consumer preferences and engage customers more personally. This chapter evaluates QML's applications in retail and e-commerce, highlighting how quantum algorithms can overcome current AI limitations regarding speed and precision. It also addresses data privacy concerns, emphasizing ethical data handling practices to foster consumer trust. Ultimately, the chapter envisions QML as a pivotal technology that will redefine consumer engagement and optimize marketing strategies in an increasingly data-driven landscape.

1. INTRODUCTION

1.1 Overview of Neuromarketing

Neuromarketing is an approach that combines neuroscience, psychology, and marketing in an attempt to better understand consumer behavior. For example, companies can estimate how consumers make purchasing decisions, create brand loyalty, and emotionally connect to products or services by observing brain activity, as well as physiological responses, of the consumers towards marketing stimuli. Neuromarketing uses tools such as EEGs, fMRI scans, eyetracking, and biometrics to measure the neurological responses consumers exhibit when exposed to advertisements, packaging, websites, and even physical products (Zhao *et al.*, 2019) (Li *et al.*, 2019).

1.2 AI and Its Functions in Neuromarketing

Artificial intelligence also revolutionized neuromarketing with its capabilities of analyzing big data and finding patterns with regard to consumer behavior. AI-powered systems can process consumer interactions in real-time; the sentiment of the posts from social media, shop pattern analysis, and insight into what motivates the purchase is also possible. For instance, AIdriven personalization algorithms change the content delivery to adjust according to the interest and preferences of the consumers, resulting in target ads and product recommendations that continue to increase conversion rates, (Morin, 2011) (Sebastian, 2014).

The purchase history and other records of the customer's browsing behavior and profile have thus been what has been relied upon for product recommendations in ecommerce for so long using AI technologies like those utilised by Amazon. While AI certainly amplifies the reach and impact of neuromarketing, it is still bound by the same limitation when going through the complexity of human behavior and their large-scale datasets. These are not just due to computational constraints but also based on the underlying assumption of classical machine learning models, (Ang *et al.*, 2012) (Amin *et al.*, 2019) (Ingolfsson *et al.*, 2020) (Lee, Broderick, & Chamberlain, 2006).

1.3 Limitations of Classical Machine Learning Models:

Although classical machine learning has greatly improved the techniques for neuromarketing, the classical models have a bottleneck related to the processing speed and scalability efficiency in handling complex data associated with the consumer. Generally, large input data is required for classical machine learning models. Some models associated with this are decision trees, neural networks, and support vector machines. Moreover, classical algorithms are unable to keep up with the pace of accuracy and would handle data in real time as it grows: a pre-requisite in fast-paced sectors like retail and ecommerce, (Ariely & Berns, 2010) (Eser, Isin, & Tolon, 2011).

Classical machine learning is also based on structured data and therefore cannot properly take into account the emotional, cognitive, and unconscious components which determine consumer behavior. For example, emotionality becomes an important factor when it comes to brand perception but cannot be measured or easily factored into such models. Here's where quantum machine learning could come in to speed up and improve the precision when processing data.

1.4 Introduction to Quantum Computing and Its Applicability in Marketing

Quantum computing represents a technological leap forward into the way data could be processed and analyzed. Unlike the classical computers that rely on bits-the binary 0 and 1 in order to do the calculation, the quantum computers rely on the qubits, which, due to principles of superposition and entanglement, could exist in several states at one time. This makes quantum computers figure out many potential solutions simultaneously, presenting exponential processing compared with classical systems.

In terms of marketing, this quantum advantage can easily transform the field of neuromarketing by addressing big data challenges, better resource allocation, and more accurate decisions in real-time. For instance, quantum computers can speed up the identification of optimal marketing strategies by the fast solution of complex optimization problems such as consumer segmentation, pricing, and ad targeting. In fact, quantum machines provide scaleable consumer behavior prediction accuracy and individualized marketing power.

1.5 Quantum Machine Learning (QML) and Its Implications for Neuromarketing

Quantum machine learning is the integration of quantum computing with what the machine learning models have to offer in the learning process. QML algorithms can exponentially accelerate operations such as pattern recognition, classification, and clustering which form the absolute pillars of neuromarketing. QML takes into account the knowledge acquired from quantum principles to transcend the limits provided by the classical AI model since large datasets and complex behavioral patterns hinder its processing power in taking care of machine learning operations, (Schirrmeister *et al.*, 2017) (Altaheri *et al.*, 2021).

In neuromarketing, QML can significantly boost the ability to forecast the behavior of consumers by offering real-time emotional responses, preferences, and purchasing decisions. This creates a new capacity for ecommerce in which the real-time personalization is considered necessary to ensure customer engagement and retention.

2. NEUROMARKETING IN RETAIL AND ECOMMERCE

2.1 Traditional Neuromarketing Techniques

Neuromarketing has always relied on neuroimaging and biometric tools to interpret consumer reactions. Techniques such as EEG and fMRI allow marketers to view which parts of the brain light up when the consumers look at specific types of advertisements, products, or packaging, (Lawhern *et al.*, 2016) It allows the companies to determine the emotional response the marketing material will elicit and optimize their marketing materials for increased engagement. While valuable insights are generated using these tools, application is often cost-prohibited, complicated, and less scalable.

The last tool is eye- tracking technology that offers to know exactly how a consumer is visualizing interacting with a product or website. Companies can, through a mapping of eye movements, understand which elements of an advertisement or a website catch consumers' attention and thus raise the probabilities that these consumers' actions will be led. However, for many business firms, the analysis of real-time eye- tracking data can still be challenging.

2.2 AI Role in Scaling Neuromarketing

More importantly, AI allows the scaling of neuromarketing applications through automation from analyzing consumer data across different touchpoints and online platforms. For example, machine learning algorithms can identify patterns in consumers' behavior that are too subtle or too complex for traditional analytics instruments to recognize. Deep learning models, as an example, can be used to analyze the emotional sentiment from interactions across social media or faces during the testing of products. In the retail sector, AI assists companies in real-time monitoring and response towards the customers' behaviors, preferences, and feedback.

AIdriven systems in ecommerce for example chatbots, recommendation engines, and dynamic pricing algorithms provide personalization in the shopping experience for every user. These AI models need tons of consumer data to enhance their predictions and recommendations made. However, with high complexity levels of data, the demand goes up for more sophisticated computational tools come in.

2.3 Neuromarketing in Retail and E-commerce

The retail and e-commerce sectors have utilized neuromarketing techniques to their fullest extent in optimizing customer experiences, product design, and marketing strategies. Neuromarketing enables business houses to acquire the emotional triggers for a particular consumer decision, which allows it to create more interesting and persuasive marketing content, (Venkatraman *et al.*, 2015) (Fugate, 2007).

In retail stores, neuromarketing knowledge is also used in store layout and product placement and even which kind of lighting and music are preferable. Such minor changes may impact massive consumer perception of a brand and whether or not the consumer actually buys. In ecommerce, neuromarketing data can also be used to improve website design, facilitate checkouts, and personalize product recommendations.

2.4 Challenges Faced by Classical AI in Neuromarketing

Despite these advances made by AI in neuromarketing, classical AI models are still not able to manage the complexities of human behavior. Consumer decisions are often driven by a mix of rational, emotional, and subconscious factors, which do not lend themselves easily to modeling with traditional AI techniques. Additionally, classical machine learning algorithms have only a limited capacity to deal with huge amounts of unstructured data generated by neuromarketing tools, (Fortunato, Giraldi, & de Oliveira, 2014) (Passmann, Ramsøy, & Milosavljević, 2012).

As consumer data also grows in volume, so does the need for faster and efficient tools used for data processing. In that regard, quantum computing presents a new frontier in neuromarketing by enabling real-time analysis of large amounts of complex behavioural data

3. THE RISE OF QUANTUM COMPUTING IN MARKETING

3.1 What is Quantum Computing?

Unlike classical computing, quantum computing is based on the rules governing the universe as set forth by quantum mechanics. Classical computers process information through bits that can be either 0 or 1. Quantum computers use qubits, which, due to superposition, can be in multiple states at the same time and thus perform many calculations on all the possibilities simultaneously to yield much greater processing power.

Entanglement is the other key quantum phenomenon used in quantum computers. A qubit is said to be entangled if in some state it cannot be factored into states of two separate qubits, and the state of one qubit will, at once determine that of another, regardless of the distances separating them. This property gives quantum computers the capability to calculate long computations much faster than the classical computers.

3.2 Quantum Algorithms for Marketing Applications

Many applications in quantum. computing applied to marketing are based on Grover's search algorithm and Shor's algorithm. Grover's algorithm, for example, can search an unsorted database much faster than the best known classical algorithms, making it an ideal tool for performing any pattern-finding operation on large consumer datasets. Shor's algorithm, which factors large numbers, is useful for secure communication, an area that may be applied to ensuring data privacy in neuromarketing.

Other quantum algorithms, such as the HarrowHassidimLloyd algorithm, which solves linear systems, can improve the accuracy of marketing models. In fact, these algorithms enable quantum computers to process high-dimensional data that tools from neuromarketing do-generate through either neural data or behavioral data-to be processed much more swiftly and at much better efficiency than it would be to do using classical methods, (Sakhavi, Guan, & Yan, 2018) (Li *et al.*, 2019).

3.3 Potential Applications for Retail and ECommerce

Quantum computing may make waves in many aspects of marketing for both the retail and ecommerce sectors. Consumer segmentation is the area with the most promise because a quantum computer will be able to process huge amounts of data in real time and identify patterns that may not be found with classical algorithms and create more accurate customer profiles for targeting the right clients.

What's more, predictive analytics may be expanded further through quantum computing. For example, with a quantum computer, multiple variables can be processed simultaneously for forecasting the next purchase of a consumer. With this, it will be easy to view the consumer's past purchases, his emotional reactions to marketing stimuli and social media activity and predict what he may do in the future. This 'predictive accuracy' could then help retailers optimize product recommendation, pricing strategy, and marketing message as well in the most efficient way possible.

4. QUANTUM MACHINE LEARNING FOR OPTIMIZING NEUROMARKETING INSIGHTS

4.1 Quantum Machine Learning in Consumer Segmentation

Customer segmentation is now one of the most significant points of new-age marketing as it enables them to focus marketing efforts much more effectively. Segmentation algorithms often incur latency in classical machine learning models while handling the volume and complexity of data involved in tasks like consumer segmentation, especially when the data is high dimensional, such as neural or emotional responses to marketing stimuli.

Quantum machine learning is much more efficient in that it lets the power of quantum computing play out in terms of working through large datasets and hidden patterns about consumer behavior. Quantum algorithms can identify correlations between different data points that a classical algorithm might miss, which makes the segmentation much more accurate.

For example, QML will help retail stores classify customers based not just on their buying habits but also on how they emotionally respond to a particular product or advertisement. It thus provides insight into the preferences of consumers that can be used in organizing more targeted marketing strategies executed towards individual customers.

4.2 Predictive Analytics with Quantum Machine Learning

Predictive analytics in neuromarketing: With data obtained through neuromarketing tools, companies can predict consumer behavior and adjust their marketing strategies accordingly. Classical machine learning models were great leaps in predictive analytics; however, there is still a long way to go in dealing with large amounts of data created using these tools of neuromarketing.

Quantum machine learning can break through those limitations by processing information quite faster and to much more accuracy. QML algorithms can take in multiple variables; for instance, neural responses or purchasing behavior as well as social media activity and make a better, much more precise prediction about consumer behavior.

QML in ecommerce might probably predict the probable purchases a consumer would make, which would depend on their browsing history, emotional responses, and previous interactions with the brand. This could bring the highest level of personalized marketing campaigns, thereby culminating into better efficiency in conversion rates and improved loyalty in customers.

4.3 Real-Time Personalization with QML

Realtime personalization is critical to funnels of consumer engagement, especially for ecommerce where consumers expect recommendations and offers that are personalized in real-time. Classical machine learning tends to require loads of training data and computational resources to make proper predictions, which makes it difficult to produce realistic and accurate predictions in real-time.

For its part, quantum machine learning can process information in real-time and thus help businesses scale personal experiences. QML algorithms can view a consumer's emotional state, browsing behavior, and purchasing history in real-time. In other words, an ecommerce platform can change product recommendations, pricing, and marketing messages, among others, dynamically in an ecommerce platform.

For example, if a buyer shows annoyance while surfing a website then QML-driven system can change the user interface automatically or provide special discount to enhance his customer experience. Such real-time personalization will help increase the level of customer satisfaction that will, in turn, increase sales.

4.4 Case Studies in Quantum Neuromarketing

Already, many companies are investigating the power of quantum computing and QML in neuromarketing. Therefore, some of the retailers will exploit the power of quantum algorithms in optimizing prices, while others are testing QML to enhance customer segmentation and predictive analytics.

One of the case studies highlighted a gigantic online store applying a QML-driven recommendation engine. The huge masses of consumer data and emotional responses to advertisements followed on later by actual browsing behavior enhanced the product recommendations to be profoundly accurate. The company saw this action culminate in very high conversion rates and also customer satisfaction.

For example, by employing QML, an endemic retail business strategized its stock. The firm analyzed consumers' buying behavior side by side with the forecast of future requirement avoiding at the same time stockouts and overstocking. In doing so, it maximized its profits.

5. ISSUES AND ETHICAL ISSUES

5.1 Neuromarketing and Data Privacy Concerns

Obviously, the use of techniques, such as neural data collection in neuromarketing, raises very serious questions regarding ethics. Consumers are likely to feel uneasy about the fact that their brain activity can be analyzed by the company to make them spend money. Such practices can lead to grave violations of privacy if sensitive information like emotional responses is collected and used.

Quantum machine learning further exacerbates such concerns, as firms are now able to deal with large heaps of data regarding consumers in ways they never had the potential for before. Such a reality raises questions of how firms should address the ethical variables of neuromarketing tools based on QML.

This paper shall therefore highlight ethical issues concerning the use of QML within neuromarketing, particularly concerning consumer consent, transparency, and regulatory aspects of data privacy.

CONCLUSION

Quantum machine learning can definitely lead to the revolution of neuromarketing in the retail and ecommerce sectors. QML offers faster, more accurate, and scalable solutions for consumer segmentation, predictive analytics, and realtime personalization. These are reasons why QML can help businesses understand better consumer behavior and provide more personalized marketing experiences. However, the very essential, significant ethical, and technological challenges must be addressed to apply QML in neuromarketing. Prospects include using neuromarketing tools based on QML by more and more companies as technology in quantum computing advances. Businesses will have to ensure that their treatment of data on consumers is ethically enhanced and adheres to all the regulations set for protecting data in order to possibly realize maximum potential for quantum neuromarketing in the minds of the consumers.

REFERENCES

Altaheri, H., Muhammad, G., Alsulaiman, M., Amin, S. U., Altuwaijri, G. A., Abdul, W., Bencherif, M. A., & Faisal, M. (2021). Deep learning techniques for classification of electroencephalogram (EEG) motor imagery (MI) signals: A review. *Neural Computing & Applications*, 35(20), 14681–14722. DOI: 10.1007/s00521-021-06352-5

Amin, S., Alsulaiman, M., Ghulam, M., Mekhtiche, M., & Hossain, M. S. (2019). Deep Learning for EEG motor imagery classification based on multi-layer CNNs feature fusion. *Future Generation Computer Systems*, 101, 542–554. DOI: 10.1016/j.future.2019.06.027

Ang, K. K., Chin, Z. Y., Wang, C., Guan, C., & Zhang, H. (2012). Filter bank common spatial pattern algorithm on BCI competition IV datasets 2a and 2b. *Frontiers in Neuroscience*, 6, 39.

Ariely, D., & Berns, G. (2010). Neuromarketing: The hope and hype of neuroimaging in business. *Nature Reviews. Neuroscience*, 11(4), 284–292. DOI: 10.1038/nrn2795 PMID: 20197790

Eser, Z., Isin, B., & Tolon, M. (2011). Perceptions of marketing academics, neurologists, and marketing professionals about neuromarketing. *Journal of Marketing Management*, 27(7-8), 854–868. DOI: 10.1080/02672571003719070

Fortunato, V., Giraldi, J., & de Oliveira, J. H. C. (2014). A review of studies on neuromarketing: Practical results, techniques, contributions and limitations. *Journal of Management Research*, 6(2), 201–220. DOI: 10.5296/jmr.v6i2.5446

Fugate, D. (2007). Neuromarketing: A layman's look at neuroscience and its potential application to marketing practice. *Journal of Consumer Marketing*, 24(7), 385–394. DOI: 10.1108/07363760710834807

Ingolfsson, T. M., Hersche, M., Wang, X., Kobayashi, N., Cavigelli, L., & Benini, L. (2020, October). EEG-TCNet: An accurate temporal convolutional network for embedded motor-imagery brain–machine interfaces. In *2020 IEEE International Conference on Systems, Man, and Cybernetics (SMC)* (pp. 2958-2965). IEEE.

Lawhern, V. J., Solon, A. J., Waytowich, N. R., Gordon, S. M., Hung, C. P., & Lance, B. J. (2018). EEGNet: A compact convolutional neural network for EEG-based brain–computer interfaces. *Journal of Neural Engineering*, 15(5), 056013.

Lee, N., Broderick, A., & Chamberlain, L. (2007). What is 'neuromarketing'? A discussion and agenda for future research. *International Journal of Psychophysiology*, 63(2), 199–204. DOI: 10.1016/j.ijpsycho.2006.03.007 PMID: 16769143

Li, Y., Zhang, X., Zhang, B., Lei, M.-Y., Cui, W., & Guo, Y.-Z. (2019). A Channel-Projection Mixed-Scale Convolutional Neural Network for Motor Imagery EEG Decoding. *IEEE Transactions on Neural Systems and Rehabilitation Engineering*, 27(6), 1170–1180. DOI: 10.1109/TNSRE.2019.2915621 PMID: 31071048

Morin, C. (2011). Neuromarketing: The New Science of Consumer Behavior. *Society*, 48(2), 131–135. DOI: 10.1007/s12115-010-9408-1

Plassmann, H., Ramsøy, T., & Milosavljević, M. D. (2012). Branding the brain: A critical review and outlook. *Journal of Consumer Psychology*, 22(1), 18–36. DOI: 10.1016/j.jcps.2011.11.010

Sakhavi, S., Guan, C., & Yan, S. (2018). Learning Temporal Information for Brain-Computer Interface Using Convolutional Neural Networks. *IEEE Transactions on Neural Networks and Learning Systems*, 29(11), 5619–5629. DOI: 10.1109/TNNLS.2018.2789927 PMID: 29994075

Schirrmeister, R. T., Springenberg, J. T., Fiederer, L. D. J., Glasstetter, M., Eggensperger, K., Tangermann, M., & Ball, T. (2017). Deep learning with convolutional neural networks for EEG decoding and visualization. *Human Brain Mapping*, 38(11), 5391–5420.

Sebastian, V. (2014). Neuromarketing and Evaluation of Cognitive and Emotional Responses of Consumers to Marketing Stimuli. *Procedia: Social and Behavioral Sciences*, 127, 753–757. DOI: 10.1016/j.sbspro.2014.03.349

Venkatraman, V., Dimoka, A., Pavlou, P. A., Vo, K., Hampton, W., Bollinger, B., Hershfield, H. E., Ishihara, M., & Winer, R. S. (2015). Predicting Advertising success beyond Traditional Measures: New Insights from Neurophysiological Methods and Market Response Modeling. *JMR, Journal of Marketing Research*, 52(4), 436–452. DOI: 10.1509/jmr.13.0593

Zhao, X., Zhang, H., Zhu, G., You, F., Kuang, S., & Sun, L. (2019). A Multi-Branch 3D Convolutional Neural Network for EEG-Based Motor Imagery Classification. *IEEE Transactions on Neural Systems and Rehabilitation Engineering*, 27(10), 2164–2177. DOI: 10.1109/TNSRE.2019.2938295 PMID: 31478864

Chapter 11
Neuromarketing for Decision Making in the Digital Era

Vaishali Thakur
https://orcid.org/0009-0007-8993-3446
Woxsen University, India

Shaikh Ayman Pasha
https://orcid.org/0009-0005-4214-8075
Woxsen University, India

ABSTRACT

This chapter reviews neuromarketing and AI interaction, especially related to sophisticated decision-making techniques that provide better insights into the phenomenon of consumer behavior. Neuromarketing incorporates neuroscience into marketing strategies to analyze subconscious reactions to achieve a level of understanding beyond traditional means such as surveys. Neuromarketing in the world of digital era lies in the complexity of the consumer structure where fast decisions are made unconsciously. Amongst the three key benchmark decision-making methods-neural networks, fuzzy decision-making and evolutionary algorithms-the three represent processing complex data, incorporating subtle consumer preferences, and continuously optimizing marketing strategies within iterative feedback loops. An AI-driven decision making conceptualizes a holistic approach to data gathering using neuromarketing tools, feature extraction with neural networks, and decision optimization through fuzzy logic and evolutionary algorithms.

DOI: 10.4018/979-8-3693-7673-7.ch011

INTRODUCTION

Neuromarketing is a multidisciplinary field that incorporates the science of neuroscience along with marketing activities in order to understand consumer behavior. The most traditional marketing uses explicit consumer feedback, usually from either surveys or groups, where people consciously evaluate products, services, or advertisements. Self-reporting often falls short of capturing the real subconscious reactions of consumers. It is here that neuromarketing fills in the gaps by reaching and truly analyzing the neural and emotional responses of the customer, which may not be revealed by what people consciously say. (Lecun, Bengio, & Hinton, 2015).

Where consumers spend most of their online time interacting with diverse content such as videos, websites, and social media, neuromarketing offers a way to explore in depth how individuals unconsciously interact in those digital environments. Neuromarketing measures the brain response towards online advertisements, website designs, or social media content to create an advantage for marketers in predicting what will resonate among their target audience (Fernández et al., 2017).

Relevance in the Digital Era

For example, in today's digitally disrupted environment, an audience's attention is divided. Information streams pour in from all directions: social media ads, personalized product recommendations, and what-have-you. As a result, modern consumers make decisions more quickly than ever before, again perhaps without quite processing or even knowing what they are doing. Still, this type of marketing easily misses the split second, unconscious decisions, which puts a premium on neuromarketing. (Bault & Rusconi, 2020).

The digital era is when marketers are no longer confined to just static advertisements. They use dynamic, personalized AI-driven content; neuromarketing lets them customize even deeper cognitive and emotive responses at an individual level. This is where neuromarketing bridges the huge gap between data-derived general insights and personal subconscious preferences. (Harris & Armstrong, 2019).

The ability of neuromarketing to stimulate unconscious decision-making is its biggest advantage. Where businesses, marketers, and marketers' secret operations majorly depend on what consumers say they need, the brain of the consumers now can be observed as it responds to stimuli, showing hidden preferences, biases, or emotional connections that are not apparent when using traditional marketing methods (Hafez, 2019). Neuromarketing fundamentally reshapes how businesses approach marketing strategies. It enables marketers to fine-tune their efforts to directly appeal to consumers' natural responses by leveraging their emotions and subconscious reactions (Bault and Rusconi, 2020). This leads to more personalized, emotionally resonant content, optimizing ad effectiveness and consumer engagement (Harris and Armstrong, 2019) .

The ability to understand hidden consumer motivations enhances campaign precision, making strategies more adaptive and responsive to real-time neural data, ensuring long-term success.

Case study: Rebranding a Global Product with Neuromarketing Insights

One of the greatest examples of how neuromarketing influences the marketplace decision includes a major rebranding taken up by a huge global beverage company. This company chose to change the logo and packaging of the brand and, using neuromarketing, decided whether the new design would resonate with those consumers emotionally like the previous one.

Using fMRI and EEG during the test stages, the company was then able to detect a brain activity link to emotional arousal and brand loyalty while consumers viewed different iterations of the new logo. A color combination and design set off stronger positive emotions as well as high engagement in key

areas of the brain associated with recognition and preference.

Additionally, eye tracking was performed to determine which aspects of the new design most caught the attention of the customers. Data revealed that the updated logo was now able to focus more attention on the name of the brand and the iconic symbol, thereby increasing recognition overall. Armed with such knowledge, the company released its new branding with confidence and, subsequently, measurable increases in brand loyalty and customer engagement were attained.

Businesses understanding and interactions with customers are changing because of neuromarketing. With data-driven decision making and personalization as the buzzwords of our age, insights found in neuromarketing provide a very solid foundation for reaching beyond the surface-level consumer preference into the deeper, often subconscious drivers of decision- making. The integration of neuroscience and AI-based tools in that regard enables companies to craft campaigns to reach customers on a more subconscious level and hold resonance with some of the most basic needs and emotions, thereby giving rise to more successful marketing results in the digital world.

Literature Review of Neuromarketing and AI-Based Decision Making

This is a new cross-disciplinary field called neuromarketing, uniting neuroscience with marketing, taking insights on consumer behavior out of the traditionally taken approaches such as surveys and focus groups. By looking at unconscious reactions, neuromarketing can establish real emotional consumers have toward products, advertisements, or branding. This trend is highly relevant in the digital age where attention is split between different platforms and stimuli. Marketers must, then, be aware of such unconscious behaviors to craft meaningful campaigns that would appeal to their audiences.

Neural networks play a major role in processing these very large volumes of complex data as they simulate human cognitive processes in the path to identify patterns between consumer emotions, eye movements, and where their attention is focused. For instance, neural networks can predict the probability with which a consumer will respond positively to an advertisement by processing EEG data; therefore, real-time content adjustment can be done to maximize engagement.

As this approach focuses on the subtleties of consumer preferences, fuzzy decision-making complements this thought process. Unlike traditional binary logic that places responses as either "yes" or "no," fuzzy logic takes into account a spectrum of consumer interest. This enables marketers to quantify the different levels of interest, thereby making marketing strategies more specific in the areas of consumer sentiment.

Evolutionary algorithms take this step further; imitating the process of natural selection in order to continuously strive to improve marketing strategies through iterated testing and optimization. They, therefore, enable A/B testing since they can simultaneously create various ad variants, based on real-time evaluation criteria from consumers, and marketers adapt the strategy using this data for maximum return on their investment for their campaigns.

Lastly, this AI-driven scheme of decision-neuromarketing unifies all of these above aspects into one framework. From advanced neuromarketing tools feature extraction leads to collecting data and further applying it with neural networks and fuzzy logic analysis while the evolutionary algorithms optimize. This is the all-in-one process from start to finish, through which marketers take decisions close to what the consumers might desire and emotional responses.

The bottom line is that neuromarketing represents a step forward for the new way companies think about engaging consumers in the digital world. The association of neuroscience, AI, and innovative decision- frameworks gives marketers profound insights into the subconscious triggers of consumer behavior. Such analysis, including emotional and cognitive responses, opens up to understanding as well as customizes marketing strategies for better resonance with consumers through applications of EEGs, eye tracking, and so on. The proposed scheme for the AI-driven decision-making approach fits the requirement of adaptive strategies in the fast-paced marketing environment today. It is about using neural networks, fuzzy logic, and evolutionary algorithms where marketers can calibrate their approaches in real time so that their campaigns not only stay relevant but also impact. As neuromarketing continues to evolve, it offers a source for businesses to stand out through genuine connections with consumers, which eventually empowers brands with a stronger sense of loyalty and enhances marketing effectiveness.

Introduction to Benchmark Decision-Making Methods in Neuromarketing

In the rapidly evolving field of neuromarketing, benchmark decision-making methods are crucial for understanding and optimizing consumer behavior. These methods leverage advanced computational techniques to analyze complex data and enhance marketing strategies effectively.

Three prominent approaches—neural networks, evolutionary algorithms, and fuzzy decision- making—each offer unique advantages.

3.1 Neural Networks

As these consumers view a given advertisement, the neural network processes EEG real-time data in identifying particular patterns of interest and emotional arousal. Marketers can then make the content change in real-time based on that network if it is showing that any of the particular visual or audible elements are stirring things in a positive way. It will be an iterative refinement loop to really optimize those campaigns so that the content will be much better attuned with the preferences of the consumer and the emotional trigger.

3.2 Fuzzy Decision-Making

Fuzzy decision-making applies fuzzy logic to depict the nature of human brain processes where there is some degree of uncertainty and vagueness in the decision-making. In the traditional binary logic, the result of the decision would be labeled either true or false. While in the case of fuzzy logic, there is the truth scale that accepts degrees of truth. It generally comes in application of neuromarketing where consumer preference and motivation are within the range and rarely in the form of a binary.

For example, a customer might not have a "yes" or "no" but only an impression somewhere in between. Using fuzzy logic, marketers are able to capture the shades of opinion and, thus, to understand their consumers on a sliding scale. Fuzzy systems can even quantify matters related to customer satisfaction, loyalty toward brands, and emotional responses.

Use Case

For instance, a marketer could be deciding if a consumer is interested in a new smartphone or not. Instead of simply codifying the responses as "interested" or "not interested," it uses the fuzzy decision-making approach for more detailed analysis. For instance, a consumer may say that he or she is 70 percent interested in the smartphone based on various factors including price, design, features, and brand reputation.

By using fuzzy logic, the marketer can identify and extract those points that are a reason enough for this interest. For example, the consumer may be 80% interested because of the innovative design and only 50% due to the high price. Fuzzy systems capture these various percentages of interest and thus are the source of much insight that enables marketers to adjust their campaigns. They can develop message objectives that address narrow pain points-for example, price but raise positive associations-for example, design-such that a product better resonates with consumers more broadly. Fuzzy decision-making further assists in the positioning of consumers' groups based on common preferences and attitudes, so the marketing mix is better adapted to the distinct needs of particular consumer groups. Thus, a firm would adapt its 'affordability' message to target sensitivity to price among the targeted consumers with a message targeting technological advancement toward tech consumers.

3.3 Evolutionary Algorithms

Figure 1. Diagram

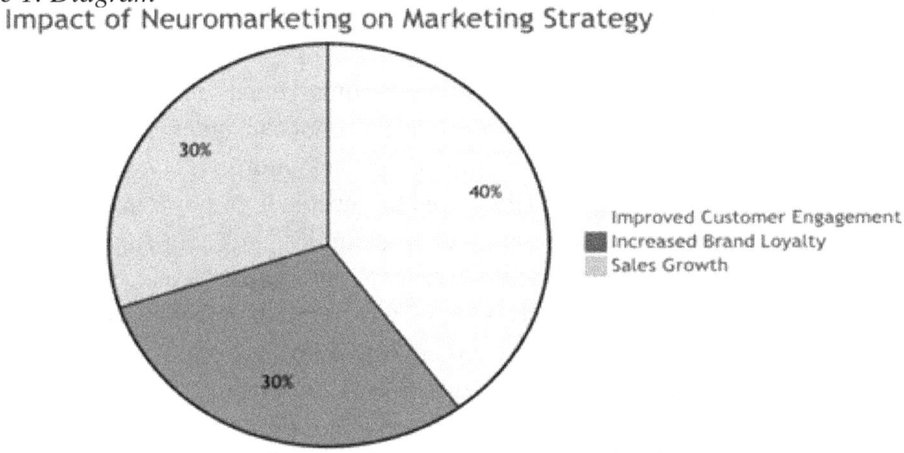

This pie chart illustrates how neuromarketing has taken an important position within marketing strategies, detailing the points at which enhanced consumer engagement, enhanced loyalty of customers to brands, and subsequent sales growth help build a company's business. With neuromarketing, companies can improve their marketing efforts as part of better alignment with consumer preferences and emotional responses.

Explanation

Evolutionary algorithms are computational models inspired by the principles of natural selection and biological evolution. Evolutionary algorithms often work by using iterations that vary potential solutions to a problem by various means of combinations, selections, and evaluations just like in nature, organisms evolve over time. (Figure 1)As can work by generating a population of possible solutions from which methods such as selection, mutation, and crossover can then direct their evolution over time.

Neuromarketing's evolutionary algorithms enable marketers to calibrate their strategy as needed, relying on direct and real-time feedback from the environment as campaigns are optimized for better performance (Hafez, 2019). This way, the iterative approach can be used in such dynamic environments as in digital marketing, where consumer preferences and behaviors may change overnight (Deb et al., 2017) . As work by simulating the process of natural selection, whereby only the best marketing strategies survive and multiply, providing companies with the best results (Lecun et al., 2015), (Lim, 2018), (Pedrycz et al., 2016).

4. THE PROPOSED SCHEME: AI-DRIVEN DECISION-MAKING IN NEUROMARKETING

Step 1: Gathering Information

In phase one of the proposed program, neuromarketing tools are to be applied in monitoring and gathering detailed information about consumer responses to stimuli at advertisements, product design, and online interactions with websites. More advanced technologies, including EEG (Electroencephalography), fMRI (Functional Magnetic Resonance Imaging), and eye-tracking systems, can capture a range of consumer responses from emotional arousal to attentional focus.

It records electrical activity in the brain, which can therefore enable some understanding of emotional engagement and cognitive responses to marketing material.

It tracks changes in blood flow to different brain regions, revealing which areas become activated during specific decision-making processes related to marketing stimuli.

Eye-tracking analyzes where and how long consumers focus on different elements within ads or product displays, providing valuable information about visual engagement.

Step 2: Feature Extraction using Neural Networks

After collection, data is sent through a modified neural network customized to extract meaningful features. Such processing of raw data allows the network to discern significant patterns that may be attributed to the presentation of relevant advertisements or product demonstrations. Neural networks can be learned to recognize almost any feature.

Emotional Responses: Detection of like or dislike emotions as customers respond to various marketing stimuli.

Attention Levels: It measures how long and how intensively a consumer concentrates on certain aspects of an advertisement or product.

Engagement Metrics: Integration of Emotional Data with Attention Data to Generate Overall Engagement Score. By the processing of large data on multiple layers of interconnected nodes, neural networks give a rich and nuanced understanding of consumer behavior.

Step 3: Fuzzy decision-making

After that, fuzzy logic would be applied to interpret the features extracted. Then, marketers would not look at consumer preferences on a binary scale but at the spectrum of consumer preferences. This will allow marketers to grade along a spectrum using fuzzy logic, therefore, quantifying how much a particular response would be interested, engaged, and emotionally enriched. For instance, one consumer may have an interest range in a product where the interest is represented through characteristic features, such as price, design, and functionality. Fuzzy systems represent these interpreted subtleties into actionable marketing strategy insights (Smith and Eiben, 2021).

Step 4: Optimization with Evolutionary Algorithms

Following the fuzzy decision-making process, an evolutionary algorithm jumps into action to optimize marketing decisions. These analyze consumer feedback and performance metrics, allowing the marketing campaigns to quickly adjust their strategies according to the insights gathered from neural data.

This, in practice, means the algorithm can evaluate how well all different ad variants within a campaign are working and select the most successful ones and combine them to create new iterations. It is this process that will ensure marketing strategies keep evolving through real-time involvement with consumers and will ultimately lead to greater overall effectiveness.

Step 5: AI-Based Decision

The integration step involves bringing together the analyses from neural networks, fuzzy logic, and evolutionary algorithms to help make related decisions with AI. Thus, synthesis analysis from each of these steps can make predictive decisions on how to better market products using tools for AI. For example, AI, born out of consumer response and preference, can provide variations of ad position, words, or even product designs that more closely align with consumer desire. Such decision-making processes automatically optimize productivity and allow marketers to respond more rapidly to shifts in consumer emotion.

CONCLUSION

Neuromarketing marks a true revolution in the way of communicating between businesses and consumers, bringing incredibly deep insights into unconscious purchases. Knowledge is derived from integrating neuroscience, artificial intelligence, and advanced frameworks of decision-making, which turns out subtle and implicit emotional and cognitive responses that more conventional marketing may not catch. It also helps marketers adjust continually, in real time, by benchmarking approaches such as neural networks, fuzzy decision-making, and evolutionary algorithms.

The AI-based decision-making scheme suggested in the chapter simplifies marketing complexities and closely aligns with the desires and emotional states that consumers appreciate. (Figure 2) As indicated

Figure 2. Growth graph

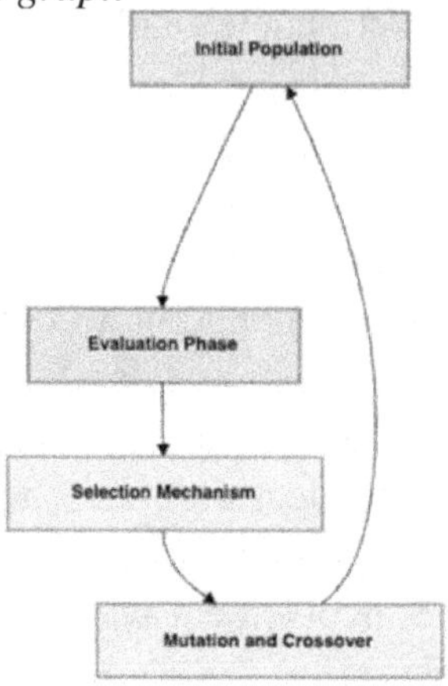

The following diagram represents an iteration in the process of an evolutionary algorithm refining strategies in marketing based on consumer feedback. This iterates the basic marketing variations, for example, evaluates them, selects them after mutations, cycles back to continue the continuous optimization of engagement and effectiveness.

From the projected growth graph, businesses embracing this neuromarketing model should strongly expect to have realized immense growth by 2050, with strong increases in customer engagement, loyalty, and in market share.

This graph shows how neuromarketing may be transformational in the dynamically changing digital environment, whereby it empowers companies to transform according to consumer preference changes and behavior. Given its continual evolution, (Figure 3) neuromarketing is a revolutionary methodology through which firms can possibly communicate better with their target markets, hence positively building brand loyalty and ensuring increased marketing efficiency in the dynamic environment today.

Figure 3. Neuromarketing evolution

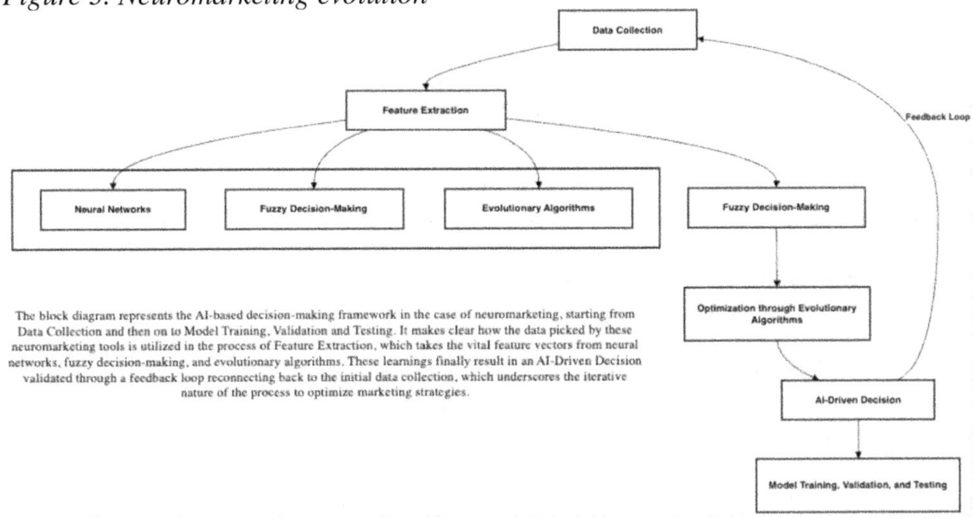

The block diagram represents the AI-based decision-making framework in the case of neuromarketing, starting from Data Collection and then on to Model Training, Validation and Testing. It makes clear how the data picked by these neuromarketing tools is utilized in the process of Feature Extraction, which takes the vital feature vectors from neural networks, fuzzy decision-making, and evolutionary algorithms. These learnings finally result in an AI-Driven Decision validated through a feedback loop reconnecting back to the initial data collection, which underscores the iterative nature of the process to optimize marketing strategies.

REFERENCES

Baraybar, A., Baños, M., Barquero, Ó., Goya, R., & De la Morena, A. (2017). Evaluación de las respuestas emocionales a la publicidad televisiva desde el Neuromarketing= Evaluation of Emotional Responses to Television Advertising through Neuromarketing. *Comunicar: Revista Científica Iberoamericana de Comunicación y Educación= Scientific Journal of Media Education: 52, 3, 2017*, 19-28.

Bault, N., & Rusconi, E. (2020). Neuromarketing: Anticipating Consumer Decision-Making. *Frontiers in Psychology.*

Ravi, V., Pradeepkumar, D., & Deb, K. (2017). Financial time series prediction using hybrids of chaos theory, multi-layer perceptron and multi-objective evolutionary algorithms. *Swarm and Evolutionary Computation*, 36, 136–149.

Hafez, M. (2019). Emotional Neuromarketing and Brand Image. *Journal of Marketing Behavior.*

Harris, D. K., & Armstrong, W. J. (2019). Neuromarketing in Digital Ads for Social Causes. *Journal of Consumer Psychology.*

Lecun, Y., Bengio, Y., & Hinton, G. (2015). Deep Learning. *Nature*, 521(7553), 436–444. DOI: 10.1038/nature14539 PMID: 26017442

Pedrycz, W.. (2016). Advances in Fuzzy Modeling. *Fuzzy Sets and Systems.*

Smith, J. E., & Eiben, A. E. (2018). "Advances in Evolutionary Computing," *Springer*, 2021.W. M. Lim, "The Interplay Between Neuromarketing and Social Media,". *Journal of Behavioral Decision Making.*

Chapter 12
Quantum AI-Enhanced Virtual Reality:
Transforming the Consumer Experience

C. V. Suresh Babu
https://orcid.org/0000-0002-8474-2882
Hindustan Institute of Technology and Science, India

R. Logambigai
Vel Tech Rangarajan Dr. Sagunthala R&D Institute of Science and Technology, India

R. Senthamilan
Hindustan Institute of Technology and Science, India

Franics A. Jeswin
Hindustan Institute of Technology and Science, India

Shajith N. Mohamed
Hindustan Institute of Technology and Science, India

ABSTRACT

This study explores the impact of Quantum AI and Virtual Reality (VR) on neuromarketing practices, aiming to understand their influence on consumer behavior and enhance marketing strategies. Utilizing a mixed-methods approach, the research incorporates qualitative analysis of case studies and quantitative assessments of consumer responses to VR-enhanced marketing campaigns. Key findings indicate that integrating Quantum AI and VR can significantly improve consumer engagement and satisfaction by creating immersive experiences tailored to individual

DOI: 10.4018/979-8-3693-7673-7.ch012

preferences. The study concludes that these technologies not only offer innovative methods for marketers but also raise ethical considerations regarding consumer privacy and data security. The implications underscore the need for a structured framework to guide the ethical implementation of these technologies in marketing. This research contributes valuable insights into the future of neuromarketing and prepares marketers for emerging trends in the digital landscape.

1.0. INTRODUCTION

1.1 Overview of Quantum AI and Virtual Reality in Neuromarketing

The integration of Quantum Artificial Intelligence (AI) and Virtual Reality (VR) is poised to revolutionize the field of neuromarketing, offering unprecedented opportunities for understanding and influencing consumer behavior. Quantum AI leverages the principles of quantum computing to enhance data processing capabilities, enabling marketers to gain deeper insights into consumer preferences and behaviors (Suresh Babu, C. V. & Jeyavasan, T. 2023). Meanwhile, VR creates immersive and interactive environments that allow consumers to engage with products and brands in novel ways, fostering a more profound emotional connection. This combination of technologies not only enhances the effectiveness of marketing strategies but also transforms the consumer experience, making it more personalized and engaging.

1.2 Theoretical Foundations of Quantum AI and VR

The theoretical underpinnings of Quantum AI and VR are rooted in advancements in computational techniques and immersive technologies. Quantum AI utilizes quantum mechanics to process information at speeds and efficiencies unattainable by classical computing methods, thereby providing marketers with the ability to analyze vast datasets and predict consumer behavior with remarkable accuracy . On the other hand, VR technology immerses users in a simulated environment, allowing for experiential learning and interaction that can significantly influence consumer attitudes and decision-making processes.

1.3 1.3 Importance of Neuromarketing in Modern Marketing Practices

Neuromarketing, which combines neuroscience and marketing principles, seeks to understand the underlying psychological and emotional factors that drive consumer behavior. By employing techniques such as brain imaging and biometric measurements, neuromarketing provides insights into how consumers respond to marketing stimuli. The integration of Quantum AI and VR into neuromarketing practices enhances these insights, enabling marketers to create more effective campaigns that resonate with consumers on a deeper level. As the marketing landscape continues to evolve, understanding the implications of these technologies becomes crucial for businesses aiming to stay competitive.

1.4 1.4 Objectives of the Study

This study aims to explore the intersection of Quantum AI and VR within the context of neuromarketing, examining their theoretical foundations, practical applications, and implications for consumer engagement. By analyzing case studies of successful implementations and discussing future trends and challenges, this research seeks to provide a comprehensive understanding of how these technologies can reshape marketing strategies and enhance consumer experiences. Ultimately, the findings will contribute to the growing body of knowledge in the field of neuromarketing and offer actionable insights for marketers and researchers alike.

The objectives of this chapter are as follows:

1. **Understanding the Influence of Quantum AI and VR**: To explore how Quantum AI and Virtual Reality impact neuromarketing practices and consumer behavior.
2. **Utilization of Technologies**: To examine the applications of Quantum AI and VR in providing innovative methods for enhancing consumer experiences.
3. **Framework Development**: To establish a framework for the effective use of Quantum AI and VR in driving marketing initiatives that resonate with modern consumers.
4. **Insights into Benefits and Challenges**: To provide a deeper understanding of the benefits and challenges associated with the integration of these technologies in marketing strategies.
5. **Ethical Considerations**: To discuss the ethical implications of using Quantum AI and VR in neuromarketing, ensuring that consumer rights and data privacy are prioritized.

6. **Future Trends and Challenges**: To anticipate emerging trends and challenges in the integration of Quantum AI and VR within the neuromarketing landscape, preparing marketers for future developments.

These objectives aim to guide the reader through a comprehensive examination of the synergy between Quantum AI, VR, and their impact on consumer engagement and marketing strategies.

1.5 Need and Importance of the Study

The rapid evolution of technology has significantly transformed the marketing landscape, necessitating a deeper understanding of consumer behavior and preferences. As consumers increasingly demand personalized and immersive experiences, traditional marketing strategies are becoming less effective. The integration of Quantum AI and Virtual Reality (VR) offers a promising solution to this challenge, enabling marketers to engage consumers in innovative ways that resonate with their individual needs and desires.

1. Addressing Consumer Expectations

Today's consumers are not only looking for products but also for experiences that are tailored to their preferences. The rise of data-driven marketing has led to heightened expectations for personalization, interactivity, and engagement. By leveraging Quantum AI's advanced data processing capabilities, marketers can analyze vast amounts of consumer data to predict behaviors and preferences with unprecedented accuracy. This study is essential for understanding how these technologies can be harnessed to meet evolving consumer expectations and enhance brand loyalty.

2. Enhancing Marketing Effectiveness

The integration of Quantum AI and VR in neuromarketing practices has the potential to significantly enhance marketing effectiveness. By creating immersive environments that allow consumers to interact with products in a virtual space, brands can foster emotional connections that drive purchasing decisions. This study aims to explore the strategic applications of these technologies, providing marketers with actionable insights to improve their campaigns and better engage their target audiences.

3. Ethical Considerations in Technology Adoption

As the use of Quantum AI and VR in marketing grows, so do concerns regarding data privacy and ethical implications. Understanding how to navigate these challenges is crucial for building consumer trust and ensuring responsible marketing practices. This study highlights the importance of addressing ethical considerations in the adoption of these technologies, emphasizing the need for transparency and consumer consent in data usage.

4. Contribution to Academic and Practical Knowledge

This research contributes to the growing body of knowledge in the fields of neuromarketing, AI, and VR by providing a comprehensive analysis of their intersection. By examining case studies and theoretical frameworks, the study aims to offer valuable insights for both academics and practitioners, guiding future research and practical applications in the marketing domain.

> In summary, this study is vital for understanding the transformative potential of Quantum AI and VR in neuromarketing, addressing consumer expectations, enhancing marketing effectiveness, and navigating ethical challenges in the digital age.

2.0. THEORETICAL BACKGROUND OF THE STUDY

The theoretical framework of this study is grounded in several key concepts that underpin the integration of Quantum Artificial Intelligence (AI) and Virtual Reality (VR) within the context of neuromarketing. These concepts include consumer behavior theory, technology acceptance models, and the principles of immersive marketing.

1. Consumer Behavior Theory

Consumer behavior theory provides a foundational understanding of how individuals make decisions regarding the purchase of goods and services. This theory encompasses various psychological, social, and emotional factors that influence consumer choices. The integration of Quantum AI and VR into marketing strategies allows for a more nuanced understanding of these factors by enabling marketers to analyze consumer data at an unprecedented scale. Quantum AI enhances predictive analytics, allowing for deeper insights into consumer preferences and behaviors, which can be leveraged to tailor marketing efforts effectively.

2. Technology Acceptance Model (TAM)

The Technology Acceptance Model (TAM) is a widely recognized framework that explains how users come to accept and use new technologies. According to TAM, perceived ease of use and perceived usefulness are critical determinants of technology adoption. In the context of this study, the application of Quantum AI and VR in marketing must be perceived as beneficial and user-friendly for consumers to engage with these technologies. Understanding these perceptions is essential for marketers aiming to implement these innovations successfully.

3. Immersive Marketing Principles

Immersive marketing refers to the use of technologies that create engaging and interactive experiences for consumers. VR, as a tool for immersive marketing, allows consumers to interact with products in a simulated environment, fostering emotional connections and enhancing brand loyalty. The theoretical underpinnings of immersive marketing suggest that experiences that evoke strong emotional responses can significantly influence consumer attitudes and behaviors. By integrating VR into marketing strategies, brands can create memorable experiences that resonate with consumers on a deeper level.

4. Ethical Considerations in Technology Use

As the use of Quantum AI and VR in marketing grows, ethical considerations become increasingly important. Theories surrounding data privacy and consumer rights highlight the need for transparency and responsible use of technology. This study emphasizes the importance of developing ethical frameworks that guide the use of these technologies in neuromarketing, ensuring that consumer trust is maintained while maximizing the benefits of innovative marketing strategies.

In summary, the theoretical background of this study encompasses consumer behavior theory, the Technology Acceptance Model, principles of immersive marketing, and ethical considerations. By grounding the research in these established frameworks, the study aims to provide a comprehensive understanding of how Quantum AI and VR can be effectively integrated into neuromarketing practices, ultimately enhancing consumer engagement and marketing effectiveness.

3.0. LITERATURE REVIEW

The integration of Quantum Artificial Intelligence (AI) and Virtual Reality (VR) in neuromarketing has garnered significant attention in recent years, as researchers explore the potential of these technologies to enhance consumer engagement and marketing effectiveness. Quantum AI, characterized by its advanced data processing capabilities, allows for deeper insights into consumer behavior, which can lead to more effective marketing strategies (Kou et al., 2024). This technology leverages quantum computing to improve predictive analytics, enabling marketers to tailor their approaches based on nuanced consumer preferences (Kou et al., 2024).

In parallel, the application of VR in marketing provides immersive experiences that facilitate consumer interaction with products and brands in innovative ways. VR environments can simulate real-world scenarios, allowing consumers to engage with offerings more interactively (Tuli, Lee, & Kim, 2024). This immersive quality not only enhances consumer experience but also aids in the personalization of marketing efforts, aligning closely with contemporary consumer expectations for tailored interactions (Tuli et al., 2024).

Moreover, the ethical implications of utilizing Quantum AI and VR in marketing practices have been a focal point of discussion. Concerns regarding data privacy and consumer manipulation necessitate the development of ethical guidelines to ensure transparency and foster trust between brands and consumers (Tuli et al., 2024). As the landscape of neuromarketing evolves, it is crucial for marketers to navigate these ethical challenges while leveraging the benefits of Quantum AI and VR technologies.

The integration of Quantum AI with Virtual Reality (VR) has the potential to revolutionize the consumer experience. VR has been widely used in various settings to enhance consumer experiences, including both physical and online retail environments (Bonetti et al., 2018). Augmented Reality (AR) and VR technologies have created immersive selling environments, significantly improving the shopping experience for consumers (Bonetti et al., 2018). Additionally, VR has been explored in the context of festivals, showcasing its versatility across different consumer settings (Lee et al., 2022). Consumer adoption of Smart In-store Technology (SIST) has been studied to understand the factors influencing consumer attitudes and beliefs towards new technologies, employing the Technology Acceptance Model (TAM) to assess consumer acceptance in contexts such as virtual mirrors and socially interactive dressing rooms (Kim et al., 2017). Furthermore, research has investigated the impact of VR technology on brand loyalty, emphasizing the importance of crafting positive online experiences to foster brand loyalty (Xie & Yuan, 2021). VR has also demonstrated transformative potential in education, with studies focusing on its role in enhancing classroom environments (Kuznetcova & Glassman, 2018). Moreover, VR technology has been applied to educational applications, illustrating its effectiveness and user-friendliness in improving learning experiences (Ishak et al., 2020). The use of VR in various contexts, including relaxation applications, has been examined through user reviews analyzed with natural language processing techniques (Fagernäs et al., 2021). By analyzing user feedback, key features of VR applications have been identified to improve user experiences and application functionalities (Qian et al., 2022). Overall, the integration of Quantum AI with VR has the potential to transform the consumer experience across diverse industries. From retail to education, VR technology shows promise in enhancing consumer interactions and creating immersive experiences. Further research is essential to explore the full potential of Quantum AI-enhanced VR and its impact on consumer behavior and experiences.

In summary, the literature indicates that the integration of Quantum AI and VR holds significant promise for transforming neuromarketing practices. However, further research is needed to explore the long-term effects of these technologies on consumer behavior and the ethical considerations that arise from their use.

Limitations Encountered in the Literature Review

The literature review conducted for this study on the integration of Quantum AI and Virtual Reality (VR) in neuromarketing reveals several limitations that may impact the comprehensiveness and applicability of the findings. These limitations include gaps in existing research, the rapid pace of technological advancement, and the challenges of interdisciplinary integration.

1. Gaps in Existing Research

One of the primary limitations identified in the literature review is the presence of significant gaps in existing research regarding the specific applications of Quantum AI and VR in neuromarketing. While there is a growing body of literature on AI and VR individually, studies that explore their combined effects on consumer behavior and marketing strategies are still limited. This lack of comprehensive research makes it challenging to draw definitive conclusions about the effectiveness and implications of integrating these technologies in marketing practices.

2. Rapid Technological Advancement

The field of Quantum AI and VR is evolving at an unprecedented pace, which poses a challenge for researchers attempting to keep up with the latest developments. As new technologies emerge and existing ones are refined, the findings of previous studies may quickly become outdated. This rapid evolution can hinder the ability to establish a stable theoretical framework, as the technologies and their applications in marketing are continuously changing. Consequently, literature that may have been relevant at the time of publication may not accurately reflect the current state of the field.

3. Interdisciplinary Integration Challenges

The integration of Quantum AI and VR in neuromarketing requires a multidisciplinary approach, drawing from fields such as computer science, psychology, marketing, and ethics. However, the literature often lacks cohesive frameworks that effectively bridge these disciplines. This fragmentation can lead to a disjointed understanding of how these technologies interact and their implications for consumer behavior. The absence of interdisciplinary studies may limit the depth of insights gained from the literature review, as it may not fully capture the complexities of consumer interactions with these technologies.

4. Ethical Considerations and Consumer Trust

Another limitation encountered in the literature review is the insufficient exploration of ethical considerations surrounding the use of Quantum AI and VR in marketing. While some studies touch on the importance of data privacy and consumer trust, there is a lack of comprehensive frameworks that address these issues in the context of emerging technologies. As marketers increasingly rely on data-driven strategies, understanding the ethical implications of these practices is crucial for maintaining consumer trust and ensuring responsible marketing.

5. Methodological Limitations

Many studies in the existing literature may also suffer from methodological limitations, such as small sample sizes, lack of longitudinal data, or reliance on self-reported measures. These methodological issues can affect the reliability and generalizability of findings, making it difficult to draw broad conclusions about the effectiveness of Quantum AI and VR in neuromarketing.

In conclusion, the literature review highlights several limitations that may impact the understanding of the integration of Quantum AI and VR in neuromarketing. Addressing these gaps through future research will be essential for developing a more comprehensive understanding of how these technologies can be effectively utilized in marketing strategies, while also considering ethical implications and consumer trust.

4.0. RESEARCH METHODOLOGY EMPLOYED IN THE STUDY

The research methodology employed in this study on the integration of Quantum Artificial Intelligence (AI) and Virtual Reality (VR) in neuromarketing is primarily qualitative in nature. This approach is justified by the complexity and novelty of the technologies being examined, as well as the limited existing research on their combined application in marketing contexts. The following sections outline the key components of the research methodology, including data sources, analysis techniques, and the rationale for the chosen approach.

1. Qualitative Research Approach

The qualitative research approach is particularly suitable for exploring the intricate dynamics of consumer behavior in response to emerging technologies like Quantum AI and VR. This methodology allows for an in-depth exploration of consumer perceptions, experiences, and attitudes, which are critical for understanding how these technologies can be effectively integrated into marketing strategies. By focusing on qualitative data, the study aims to capture the richness and complexity of consumer interactions with these technologies, leading to more nuanced insights.

2. Data Sources

The data sources for this research include a combination of academic journals, industry reports, and insights gathered from expert interviews. Academic journals provide a foundation of existing literature on Quantum AI, VR, and neuromarketing, while industry reports offer practical insights into current trends and applications. Expert interviews serve as a valuable source of qualitative data, allowing the researchers to gather firsthand accounts and perspectives from professionals working at the intersection of technology and marketing. This triangulation of data sources enhances the credibility and depth of the findings.

3. Analysis Techniques

The analysis techniques employed in this study involve thematic coding of qualitative data to identify key patterns and trends related to the use of Quantum AI and VR in neuromarketing. Thematic coding allows researchers to systematically categorize and interpret data, facilitating the identification of recurring themes and insights. This approach enables a comprehensive understanding of how these technologies impact consumer behavior and marketing strategies, ultimately leading to actionable recommendations for marketers.

4. Justification for the Chosen Methodology

The qualitative methodology is justified by the exploratory nature of the research topic. Given the limited existing research on the combined application of Quantum AI and VR in neuromarketing, qualitative methods allow for a more comprehensive examination of the topic. This approach facilitates a deeper understanding of consumer perceptions and behaviors, which is essential for developing effective marketing strategies that leverage these innovative technologies.

5. Ethical Considerations

Ethical considerations are an integral part of the research methodology. The study emphasizes the importance of conducting research responsibly, particularly when dealing with consumer data and insights. Ensuring transparency and ethical treatment of participants in expert interviews is crucial for maintaining trust and integrity in the research process.

In summary, the research methodology employed in this study is qualitative, utilizing a combination of data sources and thematic analysis techniques to explore the integration of Quantum AI and VR in neuromarketing. This approach is well-suited to uncovering the complexities of consumer behavior and provides valuable insights for marketers seeking to navigate the evolving landscape of technology-driven marketing.

5.0. ANALYSIS AND ITS IMPLICATIONS IN THE STUDY

The analysis conducted in this study on the integration of Quantum Artificial Intelligence (AI) and Virtual Reality (VR) in neuromarketing focuses on identifying key themes and patterns that emerge from qualitative data sources. This analysis not only sheds light on the potential applications of these technologies in marketing but also highlights their implications for consumer behavior and marketing strategies.

1. Thematic Analysis

The thematic analysis involved coding qualitative data from various sources, including academic literature, industry reports, and expert interviews. This process allowed the researchers to identify recurring themes related to the use of Quantum AI and VR in neuromarketing. Key themes that emerged from the analysis include enhanced consumer engagement, personalized marketing experiences, and the ethical considerations surrounding the use of these technologies.

2. Enhanced Consumer Engagement

One of the significant findings from the analysis is the potential for Quantum AI and VR to enhance consumer engagement. The immersive nature of VR combined with the advanced data processing capabilities of Quantum AI allows marketers to create highly interactive and personalized experiences for consumers. This capability can lead to deeper emotional connections between consumers and brands, ultimately driving brand loyalty and increasing conversion rates. The analysis suggests that marketers who leverage these technologies can better understand consumer preferences and tailor their strategies accordingly.

3. Personalized Marketing Experiences

The analysis also highlights the role of Quantum AI in enabling personalized marketing experiences. By utilizing advanced algorithms and data analytics, Quantum AI can analyze vast amounts of consumer data to predict preferences and behaviors with unprecedented accuracy. This capability allows marketers to deliver targeted messages and recommendations that resonate with individual consumers, enhancing the overall effectiveness of marketing campaigns. The implications of this finding suggest that brands must invest in these technologies to remain competitive in an increasingly personalized marketplace.

4. Ethical Considerations

Another critical theme identified in the analysis is the ethical implications of using Quantum AI and VR in marketing. As these technologies become more integrated into marketing strategies, concerns regarding data privacy, consumer consent, and the potential for manipulation arise. The analysis emphasizes the need for marketers to prioritize ethical considerations and transparency in their practices to build and maintain consumer trust. This finding underscores the importance of developing ethical guidelines and frameworks to govern the use of these technologies in marketing.

5. Implications for Future Research

The findings from the analysis also have significant implications for future research. The study highlights the need for longitudinal research to better understand the long-term effects of integrating Quantum AI and VR in marketing strategies. Additionally, further exploration of consumer perceptions and attitudes towards these technologies will be essential for developing effective marketing practices that align with consumer expectations and ethical standards.

In conclusion, the analysis conducted in this study reveals critical insights into the integration of Quantum AI and VR in neuromarketing. The identification of themes such as enhanced consumer engagement, personalized marketing experiences, and ethical considerations provides valuable implications for marketers. By understanding these dynamics, brands can better navigate the complexities of technology-driven marketing and foster deeper connections with consumers.

6.0. FINDINGS OF THE STUDY

The study on the integration of Quantum Artificial Intelligence (AI) and Virtual Reality (VR) in neuromarketing yielded several significant findings that highlight the transformative potential of these technologies in enhancing marketing strategies and consumer engagement. The key findings are as follows:

1. **Enhanced Predictive Analytics**: The integration of Quantum AI allows for improved predictive analytics capabilities, enabling marketers to analyze consumer data with greater accuracy and speed. This advancement facilitates more effective targeting and personalization of marketing efforts.
2. **Personalized Consumer Experiences**: VR technology provides immersive and interactive environments that enhance consumer experiences. By leveraging VR, brands can create tailored experiences that resonate with individual preferences, leading to increased consumer satisfaction and loyalty.
3. **Increased Consumer Engagement**: The combination of Quantum AI and VR significantly enhances consumer engagement. The interactive nature of VR, coupled with the data-driven insights from Quantum AI, allows marketers to create compelling narratives and experiences that capture consumer attention and foster emotional connections.
4. **Strategic Applications throughout the Consumer Journey**: The study identifies various strategic applications of Quantum AI and VR throughout the consumer journey, from awareness to post-purchase engagement. These technologies can be utilized to optimize each stage of the consumer experience, ultimately driving better marketing outcomes.
5. **Ethical Considerations**: The findings underscore the importance of addressing ethical considerations related to data privacy and consumer consent. As marketers adopt these advanced technologies, they must prioritize ethical practices to maintain consumer trust and avoid potential backlash.

6. **Need for Further Research**: The study highlights the necessity for ongoing research into the combined effects of Quantum AI and VR in neuromarketing. Future studies should focus on longitudinal analyses of consumer behavior and the effectiveness of integrated marketing strategies.
7. **Emerging Trends and Challenges**: The research identifies emerging trends, such as evolving consumer expectations for personalization and interactivity, as well as potential challenges related to regulatory considerations in the use of these technologies (T2, T3).

In summary, the findings of this study reveal the significant impact of Quantum AI and VR on neuromarketing practices. By enhancing predictive analytics, personalizing consumer experiences, and increasing engagement, these technologies offer valuable tools for marketers. However, ethical considerations and the need for further research remain critical for navigating the complexities of this evolving landscape.

7.0. SUGGESTIONS AND RECOMMENDATIONS FOR THE STUDY

Based on the findings of the study regarding the integration of Quantum Artificial Intelligence (AI) and Virtual Reality (VR) in neuromarketing, several suggestions and recommendations can be made to enhance the effectiveness of marketing strategies and address the challenges identified. These recommendations are aimed at marketers, researchers, and policymakers.

1. **Invest in Technology Integration**: Marketers should prioritize investments in Quantum AI and VR technologies to leverage their full potential. By integrating these advanced tools into their marketing strategies, brands can enhance consumer engagement and personalize experiences, leading to improved marketing outcomes (T1, T4).
2. **Focus on Consumer-Centric Strategies**: It is essential for marketers to adopt consumer-centric approaches that prioritize the needs and preferences of their target audience. Utilizing insights gained from Quantum AI analytics can help marketers tailor their strategies to meet evolving consumer expectations for personalization and interactivity (T2, T3).
3. **Develop Ethical Guidelines**: As the use of Quantum AI and VR in marketing raises ethical concerns, it is crucial for organizations to establish clear ethical guidelines and practices. Marketers should ensure transparency in data usage and prioritize consumer consent to build trust and mitigate potential backlash (T4, T5).

4. **Conduct Longitudinal Research**: Researchers are encouraged to conduct longitudinal studies to explore the long-term effects of integrating Quantum AI and VR in marketing. Such research can provide valuable insights into consumer behavior over time and the effectiveness of various marketing strategies.
5. **Explore Regulatory Frameworks**: Policymakers should consider developing regulatory frameworks that address the challenges posed by the use of advanced technologies in marketing. These frameworks should focus on data privacy, consumer protection, and ethical standards to ensure responsible use of Quantum AI and VR.
6. **Enhance Training and Education**: Organizations should invest in training and education for marketing professionals to ensure they are equipped with the necessary skills to effectively utilize Quantum AI and VR technologies. This training should cover both technical aspects and ethical considerations (Suresh Babu, C. V. & Adhithya, S., 2023).
7. **Foster Collaboration across Disciplines**: Encouraging collaboration between marketers, technologists, and ethicists can lead to more innovative and responsible applications of Quantum AI and VR in marketing. Interdisciplinary teams can help address the complexities of consumer engagement and ethical challenges.
8. **Monitor Consumer Feedback**: Marketers should actively seek and monitor consumer feedback regarding their experiences with Quantum AI and VR technologies. This feedback can provide valuable insights for continuous improvement and help brands adapt their strategies to better meet consumer needs.

In conclusion, the integration of Quantum AI and VR in neuromarketing presents significant opportunities for enhancing marketing effectiveness. By following these suggestions and recommendations, marketers can navigate the complexities of this evolving landscape while fostering deeper connections with consumers.

8.0. FUTURE RESEARCH SCOPE FOR THE STUDY

The integration of Quantum Artificial Intelligence (AI) and Virtual Reality (VR) in neuromarketing opens up a wide array of research opportunities that can further enhance our understanding of consumer behavior and marketing strategies. The following areas represent potential future research directions:

1. **Longitudinal Studies on Consumer Behavior**: Future research could focus on conducting longitudinal studies to observe how consumer behavior evolves over time with the integration of Quantum AI and VR technologies. Understanding

the long-term effects of these technologies on consumer engagement, brand loyalty, and purchasing decisions will provide valuable insights for marketers.

2. **Impact of Personalization on Consumer Trust**: Investigating the relationship between personalized marketing experiences facilitated by Quantum AI and VR and consumer trust could yield important findings. Research could explore how different levels of personalization affect consumer perceptions of brands and their willingness to share personal data.
3. **Ethical Implications and Consumer Perceptions**: As ethical concerns regarding data privacy and manipulation arise, future studies should examine consumer perceptions of ethical practices in the use of Quantum AI and VR. Understanding how consumers view these technologies in terms of ethical implications can guide marketers in developing responsible strategies (T4, T5).
4. **Comparative Studies of Traditional vs. Quantum AI-Driven Marketing**: Research could compare the effectiveness of traditional marketing strategies with those enhanced by Quantum AI and VR. This comparative analysis could help identify the specific advantages and limitations of using advanced technologies in various marketing contexts (Suresh Babu, C. V. and A. Auroshaa, 2024).
5. **Cross-Cultural Studies**: Given the global nature of marketing, future research could explore how cultural differences influence the effectiveness of Quantum AI and VR in neuromarketing. Understanding how different consumer segments respond to these technologies can help marketers tailor their strategies to diverse audiences (Babu, C. V. S., & Vinutha, S. 2024).
6. **Technological Advancements and Market Adaptation**: As Quantum AI and VR technologies continue to evolve, research should focus on how marketers can adapt to these changes. Studies could investigate the latest technological advancements and their implications for neuromarketing practices, helping brands stay ahead of the competition (Suresh Babu, C. V. & Jeyavasan, T. 2023).
7. **Integration of Other Emerging Technologies**: Future research could explore the integration of Quantum AI and VR with other emerging technologies, such as augmented reality (AR), blockchain, and the Internet of Things (IoT). Understanding how these technologies can work together to enhance consumer experiences and marketing strategies will be crucial for future developments (Babu, C. V. S., & Vinutha, S. 2024).
8. **Consumer Engagement Metrics**: Developing new metrics to measure consumer engagement in the context of Quantum AI and VR will be essential. Future research could focus on identifying and validating these metrics to provide marketers with better tools for assessing the effectiveness of their strategies (T1, T2).

In summary, the future research scope for the integration of Quantum AI and VR in neuromarketing is vast and varied. By exploring these areas, researchers can contribute to a deeper understanding of how these technologies can reshape marketing practices and enhance consumer engagement in an increasingly digital world.

9.0. CONCLUSION

The integration of Quantum Artificial Intelligence (AI) and Virtual Reality (VR) in neuromarketing represents a transformative shift in how brands engage with consumers. This study has explored the profound implications of these advanced technologies on marketing strategies, consumer behavior, and the overall landscape of consumer engagement.

Quantum AI enhances data processing capabilities, allowing marketers to gain deeper insights into consumer preferences and behaviors, which can lead to more accurate predictions and tailored marketing strategies. Meanwhile, VR provides immersive and interactive experiences that enable consumers to engage with products and brands in unprecedented ways. Together, these technologies not only enhance the effectiveness of marketing efforts but also foster a more personalized and engaging consumer experience.

However, the integration of Quantum AI and VR also presents challenges, including ethical considerations surrounding data privacy and the need for transparency in marketing practices. As consumer expectations evolve, marketers must prioritize ethical guidelines and consumer-centric strategies to build trust and maintain positive relationships with their audiences.

The findings of this study underscore the necessity for ongoing research into the combined effects of Quantum AI and VR in neuromarketing. Future studies should focus on longitudinal analyses, ethical implications, and the development of new metrics for measuring consumer engagement. By embracing these innovations and addressing the associated challenges, marketers can navigate the complexities of the digital age and create meaningful connections with consumers.

In conclusion, the future of neuromarketing lies in the successful integration of Quantum AI and VR, which promises to reshape the marketing landscape and enhance the way brands interact with consumers. As these technologies continue to evolve, they will undoubtedly unlock new opportunities for marketers to engage and connect with their audiences in more impactful ways.

REFERENCES

Babu, C. V. S., & Vinutha, S. (2024). Impact of AR/VR in the learning process of children with dyslexia. In V. Ajantha Devi, W. Singh, & Y. Kumar (Eds.), Augmented reality and virtual reality in special education (pp. 127-140). Scrivener Publishing. https://scrivenerpublishing.com/cart/title.php?id=980

Bonetti, F., Warnaby, G., & Quinn, L. (2018). Augmented Reality and Virtual Reality in Physical and Online Retailing: A Review, Synthesis, and Research Agenda. *International Journal of Fashion Design, Technology and Education*.

Fagernäs, S., Hamilton, W., Espinoza, N., Miloff, A., Carlbring, P., & Lindner, P. (2021). What Do Users Think About Virtual Reality Relaxation Applications? A Mixed Methods Study of Online User Reviews Using Natural Language Processing. *Internet Interventions : the Application of Information Technology in Mental and Behavioural Health*, 24, 100392. DOI: 10.1016/j.invent.2021.100370 PMID: 33665136

Ishak, M. A., Kosnan, M. R., & Zakaria, N. F. (2020). Build IoT Through Virtual Reality. *Journal of Information Technology Management*, 20(1), 67–80.

Kim, H. Y., Lee, J. Y., Mun, J. M., & Johnson, K. P. (2017). Consumer Adoption of Smart In-store Technology: Assessing the Predictive Value of Attitude Versus Beliefs in the Technology Acceptance Model. *International Journal of Fashion Design, Technology and Education*, 10(3), 215–226. DOI: 10.1080/17543266.2016.1177737

Kou, G., Dinçer, H., Pamucar, D., Yüksel, S., Deveci, M., & Eti, S. (2024). Artificial Intelligence-based Expert Weighted Quantum Picture Fuzzy Rough Sets and Recommendation System for Metaverse Investment Decision-Making Priorities. *Journal of Decision Systems*.

Kuznetcova, I., & Glassman, M. (2018). Virtual Reality: Its Transformative Potential. *Journal of Technology and Teacher Education*, 26(4), 547–564.

Lee, D., Ng, P., & Wut, T. (2022). Virtual Reality in Festivals: A Systematic Literature Review and Implications for Consumer Research. *Emerging Science Journal*, 6(1), 123–138. DOI: 10.28991/ESJ-2022-06-05-016

Qian, Y., Xiong, Y., Wang, Y., Jiang, Y., Liu, Y., & Chai, Y. (2022). Identification of Key Features for VR Applications with VREVIEW: A Topic Model Approach. *2022 IEEE Conference on Virtual Reality and 3D User Interfaces*, 1-8. DOI: 10.1109/VRW55335.2022.00046

Suresh Babu, C. V., & Adhithya, S. (2023). ChatGPT and Other Generative AI Tools in Education: Transformative Potential and Ethical Considerations. In Keengwe, J. (Ed.), *Creative AI Tools and Ethical Implications in Teaching and Learning* (pp. 135–152). IGI Global., DOI: 10.4018/979-8-3693-0205-7.ch007

Suresh Babu, C. V., & Auroshaa, A. (2024). Influence of Data Analysis Tools in Teaching and Learning Economics. In Scott, B., & Fox, M. E. (Eds.), *Cases on Economics Education and Tools for Educators* (pp. 229–248). IGI Global., DOI: 10.4018/978-1-6684-7583-6.ch010

Suresh Babu, C. V., & Jeyavasan, T. (2023). Tourism Is an Essential Trade: VR and AR Technologies Make It Profitable. In Jean Vasile, A., Vasić, M., & Vukovic, P. (Eds.), *Sustainable Growth and Global Social Development in Competitive Economies* (pp. 79–96). IGI Global., DOI: 10.4018/978-1-6684-8810-2.ch005

Tuli, E. A., Lee, J.-M., & Kim, D.-S. (2024). Integration of Quantum Technologies into Metaverse: Applications, Potentials, and Challenges. *IEEE Access : Practical Innovations, Open Solutions*, 12, 29995–30019. DOI: 10.1109/ACCESS.2024.3366527

Xie, S., & Yuan, Y. (2021). An Empirical Study on the Impact of Online Travel Consumers' Brand Loyalty: The Mediating Effect of Flow Experience. *E3S Web of Conferences*, 234, 01027. https://doi.org/DOI: 10.1051/e3sconf/202123401027

Chapter 13
Untact, Immersive, and Hyperpersonalized: The New Norm in Advertising

Pratik More
https://orcid.org/0009-0000-6063-410X
Woxsen University, India

Sneha Sapre
https://orcid.org/0009-0008-2796-6223
Novartis, India

ABSTRACT

The advertising industry has seen a lot of changes and innovations, and most of these can be attributed to hyperpersonalization and futuristic technologies such as AI, blockchain, and augmented reality (AR) among other. This chapter assesses the transformation of advertising from traditional mass marketing of products and services to modern data-centric customized advertisements that appeal to an individual's preferences, behavioral biases and feelings. As businesses take control of AI and machine learning in the real time optimization of advertisement delivery, the ethical issues around privacy, use of data and transparency become vital. The chapter looks at emerging trends such as immersive advertising in the metaverse and short-form video ads, and discusses the impact of location-based advertising (LBA) on consumer engagement. Hyperpersonalization will offers opportunities for brands, but solving the consumer trust and regulatory compliance remains a challenge. This chapter seeks to provide insights into balancing innovation with ethical advertising practices for the future.

DOI: 10.4018/979-8-3693-7673-7.ch013

INTRODUCTION

Over the years, advertising has progressed and advanced in many ways from comprehensive/traditional forms such as print and tv to data-driven digital marketing campaigns. In this chapter, we are discussing the future of advertising, and particularly hyperpersonalization (Jain et al., 2021), which can be defined as tailoring advertisements for consumers based on their likes, interests and behavior. The makeover process from advertising through mass media platforms to advertising to individual customers was made possible by the underlying technologies of artificial intelligence (AI) and machine learning, which enable real-time content moderation (Ford et al., 2023).

The focus of this chapter is to analyze how hyperpersonalization is the future of advertising. As an up-to-date literature of personalized advertising is examined, important features that are underpinning the change are identified in the chapter, including programmatic advertising (White & Samuel, 2019), dynamic creative optimization (DCO) (Kaplan et al., 2022), and location-based advertising (LBA) (Gutierrez et al., 2019). Moreover, the use of blockchain in advertising has started fetching interest as it has the ability to add value to the ad by bringing transparency into digital advertisement and assist in reducing the impacts of ad fraud while building trust among the consumers.

Recent studies also emphasize the post-pandemic shift (Xue et al., 2024) toward untact (contactless) (Ahn, 2020) and immersive technologies (Kadry, 2022) like augmented reality (AR) and virtual reality (VR). Youtube, Streaming, podcasts are emerging as the new norm. These developments raise new avenues for brands to engage customers in very new ways which ten years ago seemed impossible. It is imperative to note that with joining the bandwagon, privacy, and ethics judgment becomes paramount as more emphasis is being put on consumer intelligence. There are attempts at resolving these issues in organizations in America and Europe through laws such as CCPA and GDPR.

In reviewing the literature, it becomes clear that while hyperpersonalization offers unparalleled potential for brands to create meaningful consumer experiences, it also presents ethical dilemmas. These must be carefully navigated to ensure consumer trust and compliance with evolving data protection laws.

The Evolution of Advertising: From Traditional to Digital

The depth at which the advertising industry has made advancements from basic ad and memorization to a more personalized ad system models which are efficient, engaging and interactive has been tremendous. Most of the advertising was done through mass communication channels such as magazine, radio, and television.

Through these channels, it was possible for the advertisers to capture large masses, although there was no sufficient targeted messaging. Advertisers had very few mechanisms of targeting messages whereby there was no interaction rather than the communication being the other way round.

The late 20th century marked a turning point in advertising with the rise of the internet. Internet advertising has become mainstream around 1994, when AT&T pioneered the use of banners. Unlike traditional forms of advertising— a one-way medium that relies on print, television, or radio—internet advertising uses interactive web-based technologies to personalize consumer engagement through display ads, banners, and digital video with the intentions of reaching specific consumer behaviors and preferences. (Truong et al., 2019). This can be achieved by developing personas that can help marketers to predict the attitudes and behaviours of the customers that would determine the success of targeted ads (More & Pothula, 2024). Digital advertising transformed the landscape by enabling two-way communication between brands and consumers. Advertisers could now target users with more precision, utilizing tools like Google AdSense (H. Choi et al., 2020) and social media platforms such as Facebook and Instagram (Hemdev, 2024). This allowed advertisers to track user behavior online, segment audiences, and create ads tailored to specific demographics or interests.

One of the most significant developments in this digital era has been the introduction of programmatic advertising. Programmatic advertising relies on automated technology and algorithms that determine the timing, placement, and buying of advertising in response to the audience's profile and their prior activities (Hemdev, 2024). The transition between a manually executed ad placement and the use of an automated tool was a game changer for the advertising industry since its impact on the efficiency and accuracy of ad delivery is huge. At present, the individual brands have been able to use detailed information about their potential customers' behavior on the Internet to market their products directly to niche audiences.

With the development of big data and artificial intelligence (AI) (Iyer & Bright, 2024), the personalization of ads reached new heights. AI-driven tools are capable of analyzing vast amounts of data, predicting consumer behavior, and personalizing ads based on real-time data points like browsing history, location, and even emotional states. This level of hyperpersonalization allows enables ad makers to not only target specific ads to consumers but configure them in respect to factors what are important at the point of time when the ads are served.

In the last decade, the rise of mobile advertising has added another layer to this evolution (P.-T. Chen & Hsieh, 2012). Mobile advertising is defined as "advertising or marketing messages delivered to portable devices, either via a synchronized download or wirelessly over the air" (Laszlo, 2009). With the widespread adoption of smartphones, advertisers gained the ability to deliver personalized ads directly to consumers' devices, further refining the timeliness and relevance of their campaigns.

(Truong et al., 2019) breaks down mobile advertising into several subcategories based on format and delivery methods. Key subcategories include SMS-based advertising, perhaps one of the earliest forms of mobile advertising ever; mobile web display ads, a core category with a great deal of growth wherein ads appear as banners on mobile-optimized websites; and in-app advertising wherein personalized and targeted ads are presented to users within mobile applications, leveraging user data and location information to make them even more relevant and engaging. Location-based advertising (LBA), which uses geolocation data to send personalized ads to users based on their physical location, has proven particularly effective in retail and local business settings.

Figure 1. Thematic map of in-app advertising literature (Maddodi & Upadhyaya, 2024)

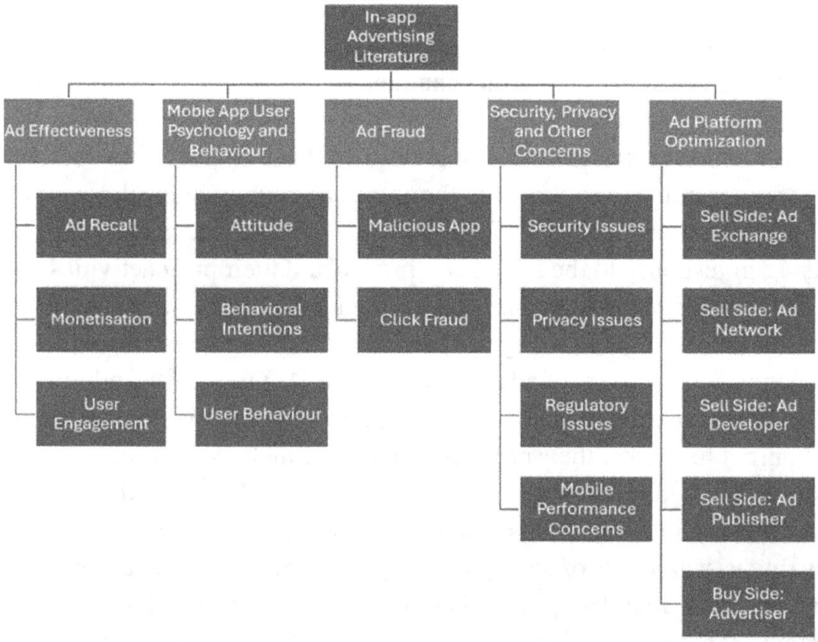

A thematic analysis of the in-app advertising literature revealed five key themes: ad platform optimization, mobile app user psychology and behavior, ad effectiveness, ad fraud, and security, privacy, and other user concerns. The analysis identified relationships between themes, including the impact of ad platform optimization on ad effectiveness and the influence of mobile app user behavior on ad effectiveness. The findings highlight the complexity of in-app advertising and the need for a comprehensive understanding of these themes to develop effective advertising strategies (Maddodi & Upadhyaya, 2024)

The future of advertising is poised to head towards increased personalization and engaging experiences. Immersive technologies, such as augmented reality (AR) and virtual reality (VR), are emerging as the next big shift in advertising. These technologies offer brands new ways to engage consumers, creating fully immersive and interactive ad experiences. Furthermore, the integration of blockchain technology into the advertising and marketing ecosystem is likely to improve the efficiency and accountability of advertising campaigns, as well as respect for privacy and consumer data control.

In summary, the transition from 'standard' advertising models to modern, big data, and algorithm-based advertising has revolutionized the industry. What was once a one-size-fits-all, static and universal marketing strategy is now a highly personalized, dynamic interaction between brands and consumers, facilitated by advances in AI, programmatic technology, and data analytics. And as more technologies are developed, it is expected that advertising will be more interactive and tailored to the individual creating hyperpersonalized experiences.

Figure 2, 'Hyperpersonalization in Advertising', visually represents the key concepts and technologies transforming the advertising landscape, which are explored in this chapter. At its core, the figure shows how data analytics are instrumental in predicting consumer behavior, allowing advertisers to tailor their strategies more effectively. The figure also highlights the various components of hyperpersonalization, including technologies that analyze trends in real-time, enabling advertisers to adapt campaigns instantly based on user actions and preferences.

This chapter delves into the significance of programmatic advertising, which automates ad buying processes to enhance efficiency and leverage real-time bidding for optimal placements. It also underscores the pivotal role of location-based and immersive advertising technologies, which create engaging user experiences. Furthermore, the chapter discusses the challenges and considerations associated with hyperpersonalization, such as privacy concerns, consumer trust, and the necessity for regulatory compliance. This chapter captures the complexities and innovations in hyperpersonalization, helping stakeholders grasp its dynamics and implications in the advertising industry.

Figure 2. Hyperpersonalization in advertising (Author's interpretation)

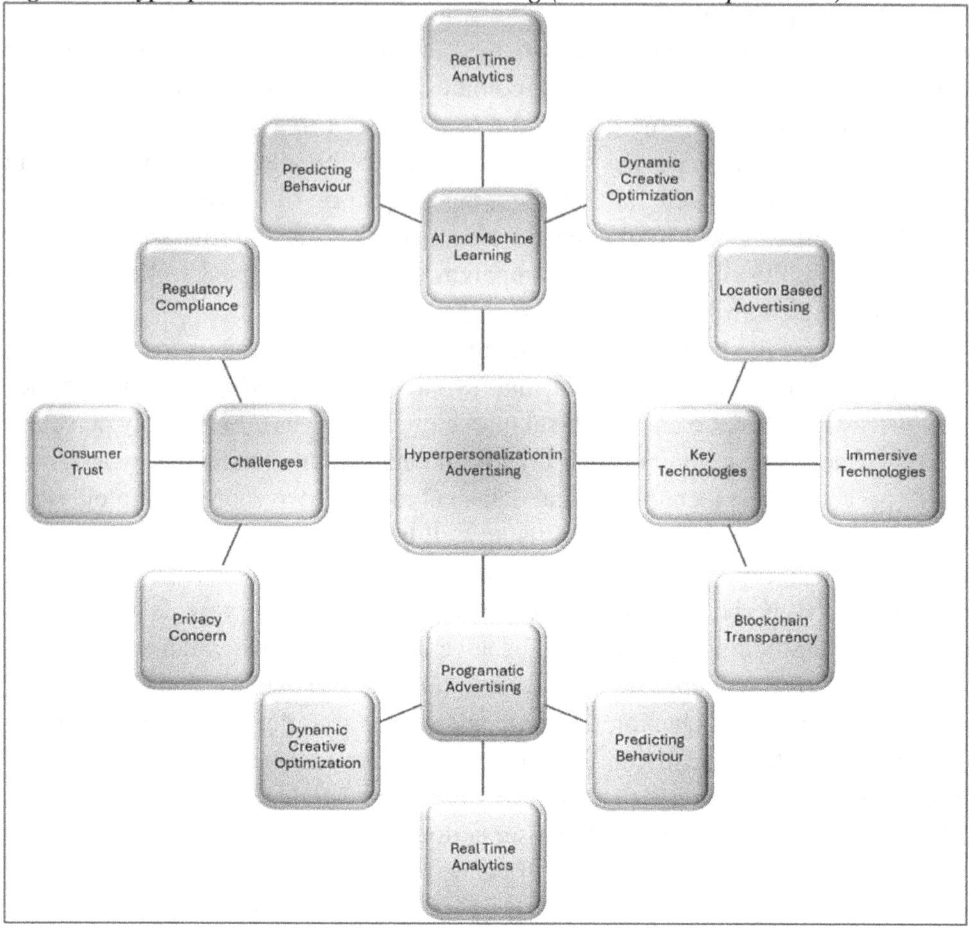

The Role of AI and Machine Learning in Hyperpersonalization

Artificial intelligence (AI) and machine learning (ML) have fundamentally transformed advertising by making targeting of ads hyperpersonalized. Demographics traditionally formed a source of segmentation on which advertisers relied. This kept the perception of people within broad generalities of consumer preference. But with AI and ML, a tremendous shift is witnessed in such that an advertiser can go beyond very basic segmentation to predict the behavior, preferences, and needs of an individual consumer in real time, based on vast datasets. AI-driven systems can thus deliver personalized ads tailored to each consumer's specific context through the analysis of complex data points like browsing history, purchase patterns, or social media interactions.

One of the greatest benefits of integrating AI in advertising is the ability to process and analyze enormous volumes of data at unprecedented speeds. Machine learning algorithms constantly learn from new data, allowing them to refine their targeting capabilities. This provides the continuous learning process, which enhances the accuracy in targeting adverts toward consumers because some patterns will be missed by the human analyst. For example, AI can be used to answer the question of which is the best time of day to place an ad, what type of creative content will be well received, and what is the best product offering for a consumer-all of this delivering accuracy and precision that helps to build greater engagement and conversions.

In addition, dynamic creative optimization (DCO) and other AI-based solution systems for real-time ad content personalization open up the possibility of matching the best possible offer with the most receptive consumer. DCO will automatically change an ad's creative elements at any particular time based on user characteristics and their behavior at that moment. This degree of personalization ensures consumers are confronted with very relevant ads to their short-term needs or desires. For example, a customer who has already searched for some specific product is served ads with that product and other related or recommended or appealing offers based on that person's interest. In this way, the chances of conversion increase.

AI and ML are also significant in predictive advertising, where algorithms predict what a consumer will do in the future based on past data. Predictive models can forecast what products a consumer is most likely to purchase next, at what time or point a consumer is most likely to make a purchase, and which marketing message will best sway that decision. This predictive capability helps brands stay a step ahead of their consumers' trends and delivers the right kinds of ads to the right people at the right time, making it feel more intuitive and less intrusive to the user. In essence, it helps advertisers deliver the right message to the right person at the right time, maximizing both engagement and return on investment (ROI).

Another potential evolution in advertising with AI is much more efficient programmatic ad systems. Programmatic advertising uses AI to make decisions in real-time about what ads to serve to whom. These systems can process millions of data points in just milliseconds, thereby allowing advertisers to target very specific audiences with highly personalized advertisements while optimizing their ad spend. This automation will allow speedy delivery of ads with higher efficiency when compared to when humans do it, with the possibility of human error in placing the ad lowered.

In a nutshell, AI and machine learning have transformed the art of hyper-personalization in advertising through powerful tools that can analyze the behavior of consumers and respond to it. From real-time personalization to predictive advertising and programmatic ad buying, AI-driven systems ensure that ads become highly relevant, timely, and engaging. As these technologies continue to evolve, they will undoubtedly play an even greater role in shaping the future of personalized advertising.

The Post-Pandemic Shifts in Advertising

The COVID-19 pandemic has significantly disrupted many industries, and the advertising sector was no exception. Most businesses were greeted by new challenges, and most ended up reverting to digital-first and untact (contactless) approaches to advertising that respond to evolving customer behaviors. Print and outdoor media, regarded by many as traditional modes of advertisement, were not spared from the crackdown on movement and the obligatory lockdowns established by the authorities. In response, advertisers quickly shifted their focus on digital platforms that could offer the flexibility of reaching more and more consumers spending time indoors staying home. In this respect, the pandemic accelerated the adoption curve of e-commerce and online shopping so much that it is no longer an optional choice for brands seeking to keep consumers engaged.

One of the most notable trends during the pandemic was the rise of untact advertising. The term "untact," which refers to contactless interactions, became particularly relevant in the advertising world as brands looked for ways to engage consumers without requiring physical contact (Ahn, 2020). This shift was driven by the need to maintain social distancing and avoid in-person interactions, both in retail and in advertising formats. Untact advertising includes methods such as mobile ads, personalized email campaigns, and social media engagement, all of which can be executed without face-to-face interaction. These contactless methods have proven effective in maintaining consumer trust and engagement during times of uncertainty.

In addition to untact strategies, the pandemic also spurred the growth of digital-first approaches in advertising. With the majority of consumers staying at home, the demand for online content surged, leading to a significant increase in digital ad spending. Brands that had previously relied on in-store promotions or physical billboards shifted their budgets toward social media, search engine ads, and video streaming platforms. For example, platforms like TikTok and YouTube experienced a surge in both content creation and advertising, as consumers spent more time consuming video content (Kadry, 2022). Digital-first strategies not only allowed brands to reach a broader audience but also provided more precise targeting options through data analytics.

Moreover, the pandemic catalyzed the adoption of programmatic advertising, which leverages real-time data to deliver personalized ads. Programmatic systems use AI and machine learning to automatically buy and place ads in the most relevant digital spaces. This method became increasingly important during the pandemic as it allowed advertisers to adapt to rapid changes in consumer behavior and preferences. With many consumers shifting their purchasing habits online, programmatic advertising enabled brands to deliver hyperpersonalized content, ensuring that the ads consumers saw were relevant to their immediate needs. This shift toward real-time targeting significantly improved the efficiency and effectiveness of advertising campaigns during the pandemic.

The pandemic also highlighted the importance of ethical advertising and consumer trust. With heightened concerns about privacy and the ethical use of data, brands needed to navigate these issues carefully. Many consumers became more selective about the brands they engaged with, preferring those that demonstrated empathy and transparency in their advertising. Brands that were able to adjust their messaging to focus on authenticity and social responsibility saw improved consumer trust and loyalty. This shift in consumer expectations is likely to have a lasting impact on how brands approach advertising in the post-pandemic world.

In summary, the COVID-19 pandemic has accelerated the digital transformation of advertising, with untact and digital-first approaches becoming the new norm. As brands continue to adapt to a post-pandemic landscape, the lessons learned from this period—such as the value of contactless engagement and the importance of real-time, data-driven advertising—will shape the future of the industry.

Innovations in Programmatic Advertising

Programmatic advertising has transformed the way advertisers buy and place ads by automating the process using real-time bidding (RTB) and machine learning. This innovation has revolutionized traditional ad buying, which relied on manual negotiations, and has made the entire process more efficient and targeted. Programmatic systems use algorithms to bid for ad space in milliseconds, delivering highly relevant ads to users based on their browsing behavior, location, and other data points. By using RTB, programmatic advertising allows advertisers to make instantaneous decisions on which ads to display and to whom, ensuring that each impression is tailored to the viewer's interests.

One of the most popular trends of the pandemic was the rise of untact advertising. The term "untact," which means contactless, received special attention in the world of advertising with the moment and interest of the brands trying to cope with the new reality of interacting with consumers without physical contact. Social distancing and, as a result, the avoidance of contacts-in person both in retail and in advertising formats-intensified the migration to this direction. Untact advertising entailed the use of mobile ads, customized email campaigns, and social media engagement, among others, which can be carried out without having to do so face to face. Contactless methods were effective in ensuring trust and engagement with the consumer especially during uncertain times. This level of granular control helps maximize return on investment (ROI) and ensures that advertising budgets are spent more effectively.

AI and machine learning, in turn, have enabled programmatic advertising to be more efficient. Both technologies are to assist in predicting analytics, so the service advertises more believably and anticipates better consumer responses from its users. For example, a clickthrough rate or conversion might be envisioned by an AI-powered system based on how users interact with it and then to focus the ads' display to those users who would likely interact with the ads. It reduces lost impressions and increases the general efficiency of ad campaigns. Also, the algorithms for machine learning continually improve while processing more data. That helps make their programmatic systems smarter and more effective with time.

Programmatic supports a variety of dynamic creative optimization (DCO) techniques. With DCO, advertisers can automatically change the content of an ad, such as a headline, image, or call-to-action, based on the viewer's behavior or preferences. A consumer who has browsed a product on the website of a retailer might then see an ad for that specific product, along with a corresponding personalized offer or recommendation. Such wide hyperpersonalization increases the relevance of ads and leads to higher engagement and better conversions. The possibility of delivering highly personalized ads at scale is among the chief reasons why programmatic advertising has become the dominant form of digital ad buying.

While programmatic advertising offers many advantages, it is not without challenges. One of the primary concerns is the potential for ad fraud (Maddodi & Upadhyaya, 2024). Given the mechanical nature of the programmatic systems, this means that advertisements may be placed on sites that can even be fraudulent or inappropriate, and in such cases, not only will the ad spend be wasted, but the reputation of the brand is also at stake. Some advertisers have also initiated using blockchain technology to provide more transparency and security in the ad buying process. Blockchain tracks the entire lifecycle of an ad placement; such process will give the client a virtually immutably record where ads are displayed and ensure payment only for legitimate impressions.

In conclusion, programmatic advertising brings a new dimension of efficiency to the science of digital marketing through automated ad placement and real-time bidding. Using AI, machine learning, or DCO, it enables advertisers to serve ads, in real time, that are highly relevant to consumers or individualized for maximum engagement and ROI. But this continued growth in the industry will also call for an agenda to solve issues such as ad fraud towards sustaining trust and efficacy in the systems of programmatic.

Role of AI and Machine Learning in Advertising

The advertising landscape has undergone a seismic shift with the advent of real-time targeting and hyperpersonalization. AI and ML can crunch massive data sets to craft ads that resonate with individual tastes and behaviors, going far beyond simple demographics. By tapping into real-time data like browsing history, location, and purchasing habits, advertisers can serve up the most relevant ads, driving engagement and conversion rates through the roof.

Machine learning algorithms can predict what consumers want by analyzing their interactions and identifying likely purchases. This enables advertisers to stay one step ahead of demand, serving ads in the right places to maximize engagement. With its uncanny predictive abilities, AI-driven advertising outperforms other methods by minimizing irrelevant ads and boosting ROI for advertisers – all while improving the user experience.

Furthermore, AI-powered systems have made it possible to optimize ad delivery in real-time (Oger et al., 2015). By analyzing how users respond to different ads, AI can automatically adjust which ads are shown to which audiences and when they are displayed. This process, known as dynamic creative optimization (DCO), allows advertisers to deliver ads that are contextually relevant to each consumer, thereby increasing the likelihood of engagement. DCO enables real-time personalization of ad content, such as adjusting images, text, and offers based on a user's preferences and behavior, which significantly improves the effectiveness of digital advertising.

AI and ML are also applied in programmatic advertising, where ad space is sold and bought in real-time using automated systems. Within programmatic advertising, AI instantly determines which ads to show users based on insights into their online activity. Automation removes intervening factors, resulting in faster, more efficient processes. AI's ability to learn from data enhances the power of programmatic advertising through continuous optimization, ensuring that ads reach their target audience efficiently.

Despite the clear benefits of AI and ML in advertising, there are challenges to address. Privacy concerns have been at the forefront of discussions surrounding AI-driven advertising. As AI systems become more sophisticated in collecting and analyzing user data, advertisers must ensure that they are complying with data privacy regulations like the General Data Protection Regulation (GDPR) (Segijn & Strycharz, 2023)and California Consumer Privacy Act (CCPA) (W. J. Choi & Jerath, 2022). Advertisers must strike a balance between leveraging AI's power to deliver personalized ads and maintaining consumer trust by handling data responsibly.

In conclusion, AI and machine learning provide an outlet for highly optimizing ad targeting and personalization. In the context of predictive analytics, real-time optimization, and programmatic ad buying, the resultant systems of AI create the most relevant ads to be served to consumers, thus maximizing engagement and return on investment. That role in advertising will continue, with advanced AI technology making it even more dominant in shaping the future.

The Mechanics of Hyperpersonalization

Hyperpersonalization relies heavily on data-driven personalization to deliver highly relevant and individualized ads to consumers (Yu et al., 2020). This involves the collection and analysis of large volumes of consumer data, including browsing history, purchase behavior, and location. Through sophisticated segmentation and analytics, brands can craft ads that resonate deeply with each consumer's preferences and needs, resulting in higher engagement rates and conversions.

However, the increasing reliance on consumer data raises significant privacy concerns and ethical questions. As hyperpersonalization becomes more advanced, advertisers must navigate strict data privacy regulations such as GDPR and CCPA, which aim to protect consumers' personal information. Ensuring data is collected and used ethically while maintaining transparency with users is a growing challenge for the industry (Duivenvoorde & Goanta, 2023).

In addition to data management, technologies like programmatic advertising and dynamic creative optimization (DCO) allow advertisers to tailor ad content in real-time based on consumer behavior. DCO automatically adjusts creative elements like images and text to fit the viewer's profile, making ads more personalized and impactful (Lyu & Huang, 2024; Rathee et al., 2024).

Figure 3. Technologies in hyperpersonalization (Author's interpretation)

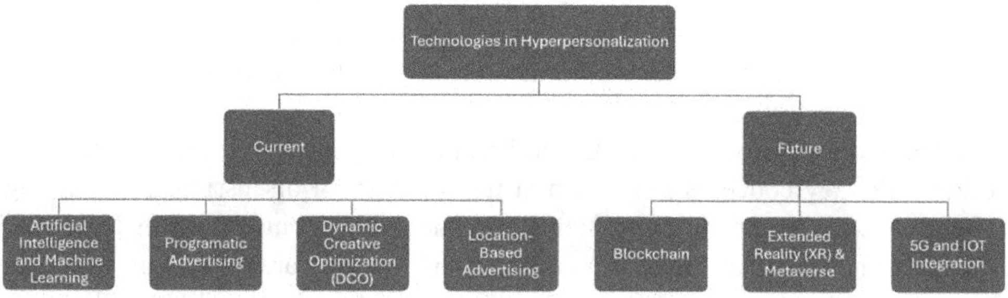

Hyperpersonalization leverages a range of technologies to deliver targeted and relevant interactions as described in Figure 3. Currently, Artificial Intelligence (AI) and Machine Learning (ML) algorithms analyze vast amounts of customer data to create detailed profiles and predict behavior. Programmatic Advertising enables automated, data-driven ad buying, while Dynamic Creative Optimization (DCO) generates personalized content in real-time. Location-based Advertising uses geolocation data to target customers with contextually relevant messages. Looking ahead, future technologies will further revolutionize hyperpersonalization. Blockchain will enable secure, decentralized data management, while Extended Reality (XR) and Metaverse platforms will create immersive, interactive experiences. The advent of 5G and IoT (Internet of Things) platforms will facilitate seamless connectivity and real-time data exchange, enabling even more precise and effective personalization.

Data-Driven Personalization: Key Components

At the core of hyperpersonalization is data-driven personalization, which hinges on the effective collection, analysis, and segmentation of consumer data. Advertisers gather vast amounts of data from multiple touchpoints, including browsing history, social media activity, purchase behavior, and location, to create a detailed profile of each consumer. The more data an advertiser can collect, the more precise and relevant the ads become. This ability to tailor messages based on real-time data has transformed advertising, allowing brands to engage consumers on a deeper, more personal level (Yu et al., 2020).

Data analytics is an essential component that turns raw data into actionable insights. Through advanced analytics, advertisers can discover trends in consumer behavior, including when best to shop, what products to buy, or even some emotional triggers that compel action. This analysis allows brands to predict future behavior and personalize their marketing strategies accordingly. For example, through AI-driven analytics platforms, ads can be targeted at the most optimal time or products most likely to resonate with a specified audience segment. Thus, advertisers can reach the intended audience with more relevant content, enhancing the consumer experience and chances of conversion.

Effective segmentation enables advertisers to divide their audience into smaller, more precise groups. Traditional demographic segmentation has lost its relevance in the modern era of hyperpersonalization. Behavioral and psychographic segmentation, focusing on lifestyle, values, interests, and online behaviors, is now adopted by advertisers. This ensures campaigns reach precisely defined consumer groups. For instance, a fitness firm can break its target market into distinct groups, such as gym enthusiasts or wellness trend followers, and develop unique messages for each.

Data-driven personalization integrates real-time data into advertisement strategy. Advertisers can leverage real-time data to deliver dynamic ads that change with user actions or context. This facilitates dynamic creative optimization, where ad content is personalized to fit the consumer's profile at the time of interaction. Through

DCO, brands engage consumers with relevant, personalized messages, increasing engagement and conversion rates.

However, hyperpersonalization raises challenges regarding data privacy and ethics. Advertisers must collect and use data according to regulations like GDPR and CCPA, which emphasize consumer privacy and transparency. The biggest challenge is collecting data for advertising while adhering to ethical practices. Companies that compromise on these standards risk losing customer trust, negatively impacting their brand reputation.

In conclusion, data collection, analytics, and segmentation enable hyperpersonalized advertising. By leveraging detailed data insights and real-time optimization, advertisers can deliver highly relevant experiences that drive consumer engagement. However, these efforts must be balanced with a commitment to ethical data practices to maintain consumer trust and comply with regulatory requirements.

Programmatic and Dynamic Creative Optimization (DCO)

Programmatic purchasing and selling of ads, also known as programmatic advertising, is a type of digital advertising that uses automated technology to buy and sell ad space. This process involves using algorithms and data analytics to match advertisers with publishers (websites, apps, etc.) that have available ad inventory that meets the advertiser's targeting criteria (G. Chen et al., 2019). Programmatic purchasing and selling of ads offer entirely automatic processes and real-time ad personalization. It uses algorithms and data analytics to buy digital ad space in milliseconds, targeting specific audiences based on their online behavior, location, and preferences. Programmatic advertising uses real-time data to optimize ad placement and bidding strategy, reaching the most relevant people at the right time. Automation avoids human errors, making it more efficient and enabling brands to reach the right audience at scale.

Dynamic Creative Optimization (DCO) is a key aspect of programmatic advertising, allowing advertisers to personalize ad content in real-time based on user behavior and preferences. DCO automatically changes elements like images, text, and calls to action depending on the viewer's profile and interactions. For example, a user who searched for running shoes will see a customized ad with relevant brands and products. This level of personalization enhances ad relevance, increasing engagement and conversion rates.

DCO's key advantage is its ability to deliver multiple ad variations to different audience segments without manual intervention. With AI and ML, DCO fine-tunes creative elements based on user reactions and feedback, maximizing engagement and minimizing waste impressions. DCO is essential in fast-evolving contexts like e-commerce, where consumer preferences rapidly evolve.

The integration of programmatic advertising with DCO enhances ad targeting campaigns, providing seamless experiences across devices and channels. Programmatic systems track personalized ads to multiple touch points, achieving consistency and relevance for the consumer. This results in engagement and increased likelihood of conversion, maximizing return on investment.

In conclusion, programmatic advertising and DCO have revolutionized digital advertising by automating and optimizing personalized ad delivery. These technologies allow advertisers to create more relevant and engaging ad experiences by leveraging real-time data and machine learning. By continuously refining ad content based on user behavior, DCO improves ad targeting efficiency and the overall consumer experience. As these technologies continue to evolve, their role in shaping the future of advertising will become even more significant.

Beyond Hyperpersonalization: Future Trends

Most of the trends conceived are anticipated to direct the future of advertising far beyond hyperpersonalization. Specifically, given the dynamic nature of the advertising landscape, developments such as untact advertising were born amidst the COVID-19 pandemic. Due to its contactless nature, untact advertising is a phenomenon that enables brands to reach consumers through digital and automated channels, thereby eliminating the need for human touch. This strategy has become the need of the hour as more and more consumers prefer seamless, almost contactless experiences in retail and services. The core of untact advertising technology includes tools such as chatbots, AI-powered virtual assistants, and automated digital ads, through which brands can address their target audience in a personalized manner with very little human intervention.

Immersive technologies, including virtual and augmented reality, are also beginning to rapidly increase in the advertising realm. These technologies give consumers immersive and interactive experiences where they interact with products and services in virtual environments. Brands are increasingly using AR to create interactive ads in which consumers could virtually try on clothes, or test out products before their purchase. On the other hand, VR can be used in creating fully immersive branded experiences through which people can explore virtual worlds designed by advertisers. These technologies don't only enhance consumer engagement but also let the experience be memorable, sometimes leading to further brand loyalty.

With the idea of the metaverse, the future of advertising will also be widely redefined as virtual shared space where users engage with digital environments or each other in real time using VR and AR technologies. It will be there that, among other things, advertisers will get to create fully immersed branded experiences wherein to interact with products in a virtual context. For example, apparel companies can develop virtual storefronts in the metaverse where users browse and receive virtual clothing for avatars. The deeper companies invest in metaverse development, the more such is expected to evolve into a key platform through which advertisers will communicate with consumers in innovative and exciting ways.

In addition, blockchain technology plays an even more significant role in modernising the transparency and trust of digital advertising. Blockchain technology can become a good way to track who is given what kind of ad placement and verify whether ads are being shown by real users or not. The integrity and security of digital advertising transactions will be critical as advertisers consider new platforms such as the metaverse. It is an immutable ledger, where the whole ad supply chain tracks, ensuring that the advertisers only pay for legitimate impressions and clicks (Antsipava et al., 2024).

Untact and Contactless Advertising

The concept of untact advertising—contactless, automated advertising—has evolved significantly in response to the COVID-19 pandemic, which accelerated the shift towards digital-first and contactless interactions across industries (Ahn, 2020). During the pandemic, physical distancing measures and changes in consumer behavior necessitated new ways for brands to engage with consumers without in-person interactions. Untact advertising offers brands the ability to connect with consumers via digital platforms such as social media, websites, and mobile apps, without requiring face-to-face contact (Yun & Strycharz, 2023). This trend has not only persisted but has grown in popularity as consumers continue to prefer seamless and contactless experiences, even as restrictions have eased.

One of the most obvious aspects of untact advertising is these technologies: chatbots, AI-driven virtual assistants that can carry out automated, personalized conversations with consumers. Brands are able to reach out to their customers at the exact moment when they need it with real-time, in-the-moment support-from answering questions to suggesting a perfectly customized product. For e-commerce platforms, chatbots are literally the lifeline; helping customers reach their favorite brands anytime, anywhere. For instance, producers employ AI-based chatbots that enable customers to communicate with them directly through their online store, offer products based on earlier purchases, or even complete a transaction without any human interaction. Such automation saves time and promotes business efficiency while being frictionless to the customer experience.

In addition, AI is the lifeline to the growth of automated digital advertising, which is one key function of untact advertising. AI technologies really start to analyze a very vast scope of consumer information in order to arrive at real-time hyperpersonalized ads contextualized towards the preference and behavior of consumers.

Self-learning AI systems can learn continuously to maximize the efficiency of ad delivery of content towards the right consumer at the right time. This not only improves the effectiveness of ad campaigns but also enhances consumer engagement. Automated digital ads require less human mediation towards the management of the advertisement, thereby increasing efficiency and scalability of the process.

In addition to chatbots and AI, automated digital ads have revolutionized the way brands communicate with consumers. Through programmatic advertising, ads are placed automatically on various digital platforms based on consumer behavior and preferences. This automation ensures that ads are both targeted and timely, reaching consumers when they are most likely to engage. For example, automated ads can be triggered based on a consumer's recent search history or purchase behavior, delivering personalized content directly to their mobile device or social media feed. This approach minimizes wasted impressions and improves the overall effectiveness of ad spend, making it an essential component of untact advertising.

In conclusion, untact advertising has become a pivotal part of modern marketing strategies, driven by the need for contactless experiences during and after the COVID-19 pandemic. By leveraging technologies like chatbots, AI, and automated digital ads, brands can maintain personalized and efficient interactions with consumers without the need for in-person contact. As consumer expectations for seamless, on-demand engagement continue to rise, untact advertising will likely play an even greater role in shaping the future of digital marketing.

Immersive Technologies in Advertising: VR, AR, and the Metaverse

Virtual reality (VR), augmented reality (AR), and the metaverse are revolutionizing the advertising industry by offering consumers immersive and interactive experiences (Kadry, 2022). These technologies allow brands to create engaging virtual environments where consumers can interact with products and services in ways that were previously impossible. VR offers fully immersive experiences by placing users in a completely virtual world, while AR enhances the real-world environment by overlaying digital content, such as graphics or product information. Both technologies are being widely adopted by brands looking to enhance consumer engagement by providing memorable, interactive experiences.

One of the primary advantages of VR and AR in advertising is the ability to allow consumers to interact with products before making a purchase. For example, AR technology is being used by fashion and beauty brands to enable customers to "try on" clothes, makeup, or accessories virtually using their smartphones or tablets. This not only helps consumers make more informed decisions but also creates a personalized shopping experience. Similarly, VR is used by automotive companies to offer virtual test drives, allowing potential buyers to experience a vehicle without physically being in it. These immersive experiences increase consumer engagement, improve brand perception, and can lead to higher conversion rates.

The metaverse, just like VR and AR, throws up new opportunities in terms of advertising. As defined, the collective virtual shared space, created by the convergence of virtually enhanced physical reality and physically persistent virtual spaces, will enable users to interact with their digital environments and other users in real-time. Brands are exploring having presence in the metaverse so they could have full immersion in branded experiences. For example, fashion brands are creating virtual stores in the metaverse that consumers can shop into virtual or real products, and gaming companies are incorporating branded virtual goods into games. The metaverse is most likely to emerge as a massive platform that advertisers will crucially leverage in unprecedented ways as it continues to evolve.

The immersive nature of VR, AR, and the metaverse also offers opportunities for interactive storytelling in advertising. By creating immersive narratives, brands can connect with consumers on an emotional level, providing experiences that go beyond traditional advertising. For example, tourism companies are using VR to create virtual travel experiences, allowing users to explore destinations before booking a trip (Leung et al., 2020). Similarly, AR is being used in interactive print ads where consumers can scan a page to unlock additional content, such as videos or product demonstrations (Hemdev, 2024). These technologies enable advertisers to create highly engaging and memorable campaigns that leave a lasting impact on consumers.

In conclusion, VR, AR, and the metaverse are transforming the advertising industry by offering brands new ways to engage consumers through interactive and immersive experiences. These technologies provide consumers with the opportunity to interact with products in a virtual environment, leading to more personalized and engaging ad experiences. As the metaverse continues to develop, it will likely become a central platform for advertisers, further blurring the lines between the physical and digital worlds

Location-Based Advertising (LBA)

Location-Based Advertising (LBA) tailors ad content based on a user's geographic location, allowing brands to deliver highly personalized and relevant advertisements to consumers in real-time. The advertiser can reach the user through such important things as GPS, Wi-Fi signals, and Bluetooth beacons, which makes LBA very striking because it could either target the current location of the user or places that the user has previously visited. This amount of information, meanwhile, produces contextually pertinent advertisements that are likely to activate the consumer, thereby making the advertising experience personal and more effective. A user may walk close to a coffee shop and get an offer of their next purchase at a discount, promoting increased footfall and the store's traffic.

LBA in retail has proved to be a very powerful tool in this quest to engage customers and get sales. Location-based data is sent to the shopper by retailers, which offers them personalized, sent when they are near the store or even inside the store. Brands get an opportunity at the right moment, as chances will arise to influence their purchasing decisions: they could give a discount on products that a consumer is likely to buy based on his previous shopping habits. LBA also enables brands to create a better in-store shopping experience using the pushing of near-deal notifications or a newly launched product.

In the travel and hospitality industries (Wang et al., 2024), LBA is used to provide personalized recommendations to travelers based on their current location. For example, a hotel chain might use LBA to offer special room rates to tourists who are exploring nearby attractions. Similarly, travel apps can suggest restaurants, tours, and events that are in close proximity to the user, helping them make the most of their visit (Thapa et al., 2024). This kind of hyperlocal targeting not only increases consumer satisfaction but also helps brands build stronger connections with their customers by providing value at the right place and time.

In the food service sector, LBA is highly imperative for deriving walk-in customers for restaurants. Restaurants can, for example, use location data to send targeted promotions, for example, discounts or special offers on a menu, to users in the vicinity. This approach is likely to increase impulse visits, especially in fast-food chains and cafes with a high concentration of busy areas. LBA increases customer engagement and also makes restaurants stand out as more competitive and trendy within market locations by providing real-time, location-specific deals and appeals to the right consumer who is on-the-go.

In conclusion, Location-Based Advertising (LBA) is an effective tool for creating personalized and contextually relevant ad experiences based on a user's geographic location. LBA is useful for promoting any product-in retailing, travel, or dining-but it all comes down to connecting with the consumer at key moments, thus driving engagement as well as sales because it provides the most timely and location-specific content.

Ethical Concerns in Personalization

As the advertisers increasingly make use of hyperpersonalization, greater concerns have lately been cast over the ethics regarding it. Data privacy appears to be one of the big concerns since mass collection and utilization of consumer data are themselves the core pillars of personalized advertising. The collection of highly advanced algorithms evaluating personal data for targeting advertisement has alarmed many into the potential for misuse, especially more sensitive information like location, browsing behavior, and purchase history. It has been established through many different researches that a vast majority of consumers are uncomfortable with how their data are being collected and used, especially when they're not being told the full extent of the data harvesting that's going on behind the scenes (Segijn & Strycharz, 2023; Strycharz & Segijn, 2024).

Another critical ethical concern is the practice of dataveillance (Strycharz & Segijn, 2024), which involves the continuous monitoring of individuals through their digital activities. This level of surveillance can lead to a loss of autonomy, as individuals may feel that they are being watched or manipulated by brands seeking to exploit their personal preferences. Researchers argue that such practices can have a "chilling effect," where consumers alter their online behaviors or interactions with brands due to concerns about being monitored (Strycharz & Segijn, 2024). These issues have sparked debates on whether personalized advertising, while effective, might be crossing ethical boundaries by violating consumer privacy and diminishing trust.

The rapid expansion of AI-driven personalization adds another layer to the ethical debate. AI technologies used in advertising can predict consumer behavior with incredible accuracy, but they also rely on opaque algorithms that are difficult for consumers (and even regulators) to understand. The lack of transparency in how these algorithms operate has raised concerns about potential biases embedded in AI models. For instance, AI can unintentionally perpetuate stereotypes or discriminate based on race, gender, or socioeconomic status when targeting ads. As AI becomes more integrated into advertising, there are growing calls for greater transparency and accountability to ensure that these systems operate ethically.

Additionally, consumer consent is yet another crucial ethical issue related to personalization. However, while consumers can also be rewarded with more relevant advertisements, the line between consenting and being convinced to give consent becomes too difficult to distinguish often. Most studies show that many consumers are coerced to agree to certain terms and conditions without knowing exactly what they assented to, if only sites or apps would refuse them access to services without it. This best can be achieved through clearer, more direct consent mechanisms that empower consumers to make choices regarding the use of their data.

Beyond the issue of privacy, ethical concerns over targeted advertising also revolve around manipulation and exploitation. Critics argue that such 'over-personalization' will make marketing manipulative and exploitative of vulnerable populations. For example, through emotional hot buttons or personal weaknesses, marketing advertisement agencies ensure that specific marketing campaigns touch a customer's impulse to spend, which, subsequently impacts his personal finances. Referred research indicates that brands use data in most advertisements to create urgency or FOMO (Fear of Missing out), which might culminate in regretful consumer decisions.

To address these ethical concerns, brands and advertisers should seek clear ethical guidelines on data usage with clarities to promote openness, justice, and accountability in its practice. Most importantly, directions on guidelines should be provided to support the practice of ethical data collection and use practices. This may include data minimisation-to collect what is necessary-and opt-in and opt-out choices, which must be made clear. This means that there should be clarity on how the data is going to be utilised. Brands also need to embrace a more consumer-centric advertisement strategy that focuses more on ensuring profit maximization while establishing trust that is achieved through the explanation of data practices and the regular interaction with the consumers to determine their problems and preferences related to personalization.

In conclusion, hyper-personalization has much to offer the consumer and the firms in terms of consumer involvement and advertising efficiency, it produces critical ethical conflicts that are not to be overlooked. As the advertising landscapes continue to evolve in this ever-changing world of AI and big data analytics, the addressing of the ethics involved will prove crucial to the continued trust and support of consumers, thus ensuring that personalized advertising meets the need of brands and consumers alike. If the advertising industry takes an ethical approach to data and transparency, it will be more prepared to counter the complexities posed to meet a healthier relationship with increasingly digital consumption markets.

Regulation and Compliance

As personalized advertising evolves, so do the concerns surrounding data privacy, driving the need for robust regulatory frameworks that can balance innovation with consumer protection. Regulations such as the General Data Protection Regulation (GDPR) in Europe and the California Consumer Privacy Act (CCPA) in the U.S. have emerged in response to growing concerns about the ways companies collect, store, and use consumer data for targeted advertising. These regulations emphasize the need for transparency in how companies handle data and ensure that consumers are informed about their rights regarding data collection, such as the right to access, correct, or delete their personal information, as well as the right to opt out of data collection. These frameworks aim to provide consumers with greater control over their data, addressing the growing discomfort many feel about being continuously monitored online.

The phasing out of third-party cookies is another significant development in the realm of regulation and compliance. Major web browsers, including Google Chrome or Safari, have announced plans to block third-party cookies, which have traditionally been used to track users across different websites for advertising purposes (Segijn & Strycharz, 2023). This shift, sometimes referred to as the "cookiepocalypse," forces advertisers to rethink their strategies for tracking and targeting users without violating privacy regulations (El Hana et al., 2023). In response, companies are exploring alternative methods such as first-party data collection and contextual advertising (LIU et al., 2014), where ads are served based on the content of the webpage rather than the user's browsing history.

Despite these changes, the effectiveness of existing regulations in safeguarding consumer privacy is still a topic of debate. Some argue that current laws like the GDPR and CCPA are reactive rather than proactive, addressing privacy violations only after they occur. There are also concerns that these regulations are too complex for the average consumer to fully understand, leading to what some researchers call "consent fatigue." This phenomenon occurs when consumers are repeatedly asked to consent to data collection but do not fully comprehend what they are agreeing to . As a result, while regulations are in place, there remains a gap between consumer understanding and the actual level of control they exercise over their data (Wein, 2022).

To address these gaps, there are calls for more standardized global regulations that go beyond national or regional boundaries. Currently, the regulatory landscape is fragmented, with varying rules across countries, making compliance challenging for global companies. A more unified approach could simplify compliance and provide clearer guidelines for both consumers and businesses (Smit et al., 2014). This would also help mitigate the complexities that global brands face when navigating different regulatory environments, ultimately fostering a more consistent standard of data protection. The role of self-regulation (King & Jessen, 2010)in the advertising industry is also critical; many companies are adopting their own internal data policies that go beyond legal requirements to build consumer trust. Such proactive measures, combined with evolving regulatory frameworks, are likely to shape the future of advertising in a way that balances innovation with ethical responsibility.

Balancing Innovation with Consumer Protection

As the advertising industry continues to innovate, particularly with advances in artificial intelligence and hyper-personalization, the challenge of balancing these innovations with consumer protection becomes more pressing. The rapid development of technologies like predictive analytics and AI advertising has allowed brands to reach consumers in increasingly personalized and context-sensitive ways (Ford et al., 2023). However, with this capability comes the risk of overstepping boundaries, especially in terms of consumer privacy and data security.

One key area where this balance is tested is in the use of behavioral targeting (Sánchez & Viejo, 2018). While advertisers leverage vast amounts of data to predict consumer preferences and deliver tailored ads, this can sometimes result in an invasion of privacy or even manipulation. Studies have shown that consumers are often unaware of the extent to which their data is being used, raising concerns about transparency and consent. The challenge for advertisers is to develop systems that allow for high levels of personalization without crossing into unethical territory.

Regulatory frameworks like the GDPR and CCPA have helped set boundaries, but as advertising becomes more sophisticated, these regulations must evolve to keep pace with emerging technologies. One promising area is the development of ethical AI models that incorporate fairness and transparency into their design. By building systems that prioritize consumer trust and autonomy, brands can mitigate the risks associated with data misuse. Additionally, brands are increasingly using first-party data as an alternative to third-party tracking methods, which offers a more privacy-compliant way to collect insights without over-relying on invasive tactics.

Ultimately, maintaining consumer trust is crucial for long-term success in advertising. Those brands that prioritize honest data practice and transparency will be best placed to build lasting, strong relations with their audiences. As innovation drives the advertising future, now it is critical that brands not only apply the latest technology but also ensure creating that trust by being mindful of honest data practices and consumer protection (Parasidis, 2023; Soni, 2024). This means adopting transparent data policies, actively engaging consumers in the decision-making process, and ensuring that AI-driven tools are designed to be both effective and ethical. In the end, the brands that strike this balance will be the ones that thrive in the new era of digital marketing, as consumer trust becomes a key competitive differentiator. By focusing on building responsible and transparent systems, the advertising industry can continue to innovate while safeguarding the interests of consumers.

CONCLUSION

The evolution of advertising, are largely dependent on hyper-personalization and AI, really changes the way in which brands engage with their audiences. However, in the continued evolution of this business, there is a very tough task: the ability to balance the rewards of innovation with the necessary protective duties, from both ethical and regulatory standpoints, concerning consumer privacy and data. Hyper-personalization driven by advanced data analytics and AI has, in fact, proven extremely effective at improving engagement and conversion rates by delivering relevant, personalized content. Yet at the same time it has raised so many issues about privacy and the security of data and the ethics of using consumers' information.

The regulatory framework, such as GDPR and CCPA, is developing new regulations and laws that give a consumer control over his personal information. But if the advertisement continues to change their tactics, its rules would also need to adapt with new technologies, and perhaps AI-driven advertising and predictive analytics will require a renewal of regulation. The key challenge will be innovation that is allowed to come forth while there are still robust consumer protections. Innovation that will build trust through embracing and expanding the norms of first-party data and ethically founded AI models should conquer concerns over data misuse, while stricter privacy regulations are consistent with the future.

In summary, the future of advertising is poised to be shaped by a delicate balance between leveraging cutting-edge technologies and safeguarding consumer privacy. Those brands that prioritize transparency, ethical data practices, and consumer trust will stand out in an ever-evolving marketplace, paving the way for sustainable, responsible innovation.

REFERENCES

Ahn, J. B. (2020). A Study on Predicting Changes of Future Advertising Characteristics and Types after the Corona 19 Pandemic. *International Journal of Internet. Broadcasting and Communication*, 12(4), 137–147.

Antsipava, D., Strycharz, J., van Reijmersdal, E. A., & van Noort, G. (2024). What drives blockchain technology adoption in the online advertising ecosystem? An interview study into stakeholders' perspectives. *Journal of Business Research*, 171, 114381. DOI: 10.1016/j.jbusres.2023.114381

Chen, G., Xie, P., Dong, J., & Wang, T. (2019). Understanding Programmatic Creative: The Role of AI. *Journal of Advertising*, 48(4), 347–355. DOI: 10.1080/00913367.2019.1654421

Chen, P.-T., & Hsieh, H.-P. (2012). Personalized mobile advertising: Its key attributes, trends, and social impact. *Technological Forecasting and Social Change*, 79(3), 543–557. DOI: 10.1016/j.techfore.2011.08.011

Choi, H., Mela, C. F., Balseiro, S. R., & Leary, A. (2020). Online Display Advertising Markets: A Literature Review and Future Directions. *Information Systems Research*, 31(2), 556–575. DOI: 10.1287/isre.2019.0902

Choi, W. J., & Jerath, K. (2022). Privacy and Consumer Empowerment in Online Advertising. *Foundations and Trends® in Marketing, 15*(3), 153–212. DOI: 10.1561/1700000053

Duivenvoorde, B., & Goanta, C. (2023). The regulation of digital advertising under the DSA: A critical assessment. *Computer Law & Security Report*, 51, 105870. DOI: 10.1016/j.clsr.2023.105870

El Hana, N., Mercanti-Guérin, M., & Sabri, O. (2023). Cookiepocalypse: What are the most effective strategies for advertisers to reshape the future of display advertising? *Technological Forecasting and Social Change*, 188, 122297. DOI: 10.1016/j.techfore.2022.122297

Ford, J., Jain, V., Wadhwani, K., & Gupta, D. G. (2023). AI advertising: An overview and guidelines. *Journal of Business Research*, 166, 114124. DOI: 10.1016/j.jbusres.2023.114124

Gutierrez, A., O'Leary, S., Rana, N. P., Dwivedi, Y. K., & Calle, T. (2019). Using privacy calculus theory to explore entrepreneurial directions in mobile location-based advertising: Identifying intrusiveness as the critical risk factor. *Computers in Human Behavior*, 95, 295–306. DOI: 10.1016/j.chb.2018.09.015

Hemdev, O. (2024). Communication and Advertising in India: Evolution, Challenges, and the Digital Future. [IJSR]. *International Journal of Science and Research (Raipur, India)*, 13(9), 1417–1418. DOI: 10.21275/SR24923143911

Iyer, P., & Bright, L. F. (2024). Navigating a paradigm shift: Technology and user acceptance of big data and artificial intelligence among advertising and marketing practitioners. *Journal of Business Research*, 180, 114699. DOI: 10.1016/j.jbusres.2024.114699

Jain, G., Paul, J., & Shrivastava, A. (2021). Hyper-personalization, co-creation, digital clienteling and transformation. *Journal of Business Research*, 124, 12–23. DOI: 10.1016/j.jbusres.2020.11.034

Kadry, A. (2022). The Metaverse Revolution and Its Impact on the Future of Advertising Industry. *Journal of Design Sciences and Applied Arts*, 3(2), 347–358. DOI: 10.21608/jdsaa.2022.129876.1171

Kaplan, Y., Shtoff, A., Shadi, T., Somekh, O., & Koren, Y. (2022). Conversion-Based Dynamic-Creative-Optimization in Native Advertising. *2022 IEEE International Conference on Big Data (Big Data)*, 2273–2278. DOI: 10.1109/BigData55660.2022.10020498

King, N. J., & Jessen, P. W. (2010). Profiling the mobile customer – Is industry self-regulation adequate to protect consumer privacy when behavioural advertisers target mobile phones? – Part II. *Computer Law & Security Report*, 26(6), 595–612. DOI: 10.1016/j.clsr.2010.09.007

Laszlo, J. (2009). The New Unwired World: An IAB Status Report on Mobile Advertising. *Journal of Advertising Research*, 49(1), 27–43. DOI: 10.2501/S0021849909090035

Leung, X. Y., Lyu, J., & Bai, B. (2020). A fad or the future? Examining the effectiveness of virtual reality advertising in the hotel industry. *International Journal of Hospitality Management*, 88, 102391. DOI: 10.1016/j.ijhm.2019.102391

Liu, J., Wang, C., Zhang, R., & Zhao, X.LIU. (2014). Research on behavioral targeted advertising in mobile Internet. *Journal of China Universities of Posts and Telecommunications*, 21, 1–5. DOI: 10.1016/S1005-8885(14)60520-3

Lyu, M., & Huang, Q. (2024). Visual elements in advertising enhance odor perception and purchase intention: The role of mental imagery in multi-sensory marketing. *Journal of Retailing and Consumer Services*, 78, 103752. DOI: 10.1016/j.jretconser.2024.103752

Maddodi, C. B., & Upadhyaya, P. (2024). In-app advertising: a systematic literature review and implications for future research. *Spanish Journal of Marketing - ESIC, 28*(3), 334–355. DOI: 10.1108/SJME-05-2022-0120

More, P., & Pothula, S. S. K. (2024). A Persona-based approach for Churn Prediction and Retention Strategies driven by Predictive Analytics and Generative AI. In D. Choudhary, H. K., R. Rodriguez, J. Wise, & R. T. (Eds.), *Predictive Analytics and Generative AI for Data-Driven Marketing Strategies*. Taylor & Francis Group LLC. DOI: 10.1201/9781003472544-12

Oger, M., Olmez, I., Inci, E., Kücükbay, S., & Emekci, F. (2015). Privacy Preserving Secure Online Advertising. *Procedia: Social and Behavioral Sciences*, 195, 1840–1845. DOI: 10.1016/j.sbspro.2015.06.405

Parasidis, E. (2023). The Urgent Need for a U.S. Data Protection Agency. *The American Journal of Bioethics*, 23(11), 26–29. DOI: 10.1080/15265161.2023.2256283 PMID: 37879026

Rathee, S., Taylor, C. R., & Gupta, A. (2024). The appeal of blurred imagery: Enhancing advertising and brand attitudes for luxury goods. *Journal of Business Research*, 182, 114795. DOI: 10.1016/j.jbusres.2024.114795

Sánchez, D., & Viejo, A. (2018). Privacy-preserving and advertising-friendly web surfing. *Computer Communications*, 130, 113–123. DOI: 10.1016/j.comcom.2018.09.002

Segijn, C. M., & Strycharz, J. (2023). The ethical ramifications of surveillance in contemporary advertising for the industry, consumers, and regulators: Current issues and a future research agenda. *International Journal of Advertising*, 42(1), 69–77. DOI: 10.1080/02650487.2022.2114700

Smit, E. G., Van Noort, G., & Voorveld, H. A. M. (2014). Understanding online behavioural advertising: User knowledge, privacy concerns and online coping behaviour in Europe. *Computers in Human Behavior*, 32, 15–22. DOI: 10.1016/j.chb.2013.11.008

Soni, V. (2024). AI and the Personalization-Privacy Paradox: Balancing Customized Marketing with Consumer Data Protection. *IRE Journals*, 7(12), 411–418.

Strycharz, J., & Segijn, C. M. (2024). Ethical side-effect of dataveillance in advertising: Impact of data collection, trust, privacy concerns and regulatory differences on chilling effects. *Journal of Business Research*, 173, 114490. DOI: 10.1016/j.jbusres.2023.114490

Thapa, S., Guzmán, F., & Paswan, A. (2024). We are just 10 feet away! How does location-based advertising affect consumer-brand engagement? *Journal of Business Research*, 172, 114425. DOI: 10.1016/j.jbusres.2023.114425

Truong, V. N. X., Nkhoma, M., & Pansuwong, W. (2019). An Integrated Effectiveness Framework of Mobile In-App Advertising. *AJIS. Australasian Journal of Information Systems*, 23. Advance online publication. DOI: 10.3127/ajis.v23i0.1971

Wang, L., Chen, Y., Xu, Y., & Lin, Z. (2024). Assertive or non-assertive? How self-concept clarity influences customers' responses to advertising messages. *International Journal of Hospitality Management*, 123, 103942. DOI: 10.1016/j.ijhm.2024.103942

Wein, T. (2022). Data Protection, Cookie Consent, and Prices. *Economies*, 10(12), 307. DOI: 10.3390/economies10120307

White, G. R. T., & Samuel, A. (2019). Programmatic Advertising: Forewarning and avoiding hype-cycle failure. *Technological Forecasting and Social Change*, 144, 157–168. DOI: 10.1016/j.techfore.2019.03.020

Xue, N., Liu, X. S., Wan, L. C., & Hou, Y. (2024). Relaxing or challenging? How social crowding influences the effectiveness of activity-based destination advertising. *Tourism Management*, 100, 104839. DOI: 10.1016/j.tourman.2023.104839

Yu, C., Zhang, Z., Lin, C., & Wu, Y. J. (2020). Can data-driven precision marketing promote user ad clicks? Evidence from advertising in WeChat moments. *Industrial Marketing Management*, 90, 481–492. DOI: 10.1016/j.indmarman.2019.05.001

Yun, J. T., & Strycharz, J. (2023). Building the Future of Digital Advertising One Block at a Time: How Blockchain Technology Can Change Advertising Practice and Research. *Journal of Current Issues and Research in Advertising*, 44(1), 24–37. DOI: 10.1080/10641734.2022.2090464

Chapter 14
The Role of Robotics in Smart Manufacturing: Increasing Efficiency and Reducing Costs

Kathirvel Ayyaswamy
https://orcid.org/0000-0002-5347-9110
Tagore Engineering College, India

V. M. Gobinath
https://orcid.org/0000-0002-9132-4910
Rajalakshmi Institute of Technology, India

V. Sathya
Vel Tech Rangarajan Dr. Sagunthala R&D Institute of Science and Technology, India

Naren Kathirvel
Anand Institute of Higher Technology, India

Raj A. Anthony
https://orcid.org/0000-0001-5417-4856
Panimalar Engineering College, India

ABSTRACT

The integration of robotics poses challenges and opportunities for human workers. While automation has the potential to eliminate routine and hazardous tasks, it also necessitates upskilling and reskilling of the workforce to operate, program, and maintain robotic systems. The review examines the socioeconomic impacts of increased automation, discussing potential shifts in employment patterns and the

DOI: 10.4018/979-8-3693-7673-7.ch014

need for a strategic approach to workforce development. This review provides a comprehensive analysis of the advances in robotics within manufacturing and their profound implications on the workforce. Striking a balance between automation and human collaboration is crucial for the future of manufacturing, emphasizing the importance of proactive strategies to harness the benefits of robotics while ensuring a resilient and adaptable workforce. The results highlight how vital robotics is to the evolution of manufacturing toward more economical, efficient, and sustainable processes.

OVERVIEW OF SMART MANUFACTURING AND ITS IMPORTANCE IN THE BACKGROUND

Smart manufacturing represents a paradigm shift in creating commodities using cutting-edge technologies to establish more connected, adaptive, and efficient production environments. Modern technologies like the Internet of Things (IoT), artificial intelligence (AI), cyber-physical systems (CPS), and sophisticated robotics are all fundamental components of smart manufacturing. Combining these technologies allows for automated decision-making, predictive maintenance, and real-time data collecting and analysis, improving manufacturing operations (Deloitte, 2018). The desire for increased production efficiency, flexibility, and customization motivates intelligent manufacturing, enabling companies to react quickly to shifts in the market and customer needs (Lee et al., 2015).

One cannot stress enough the importance of intelligent manufacturing. Unprecedented levels of production and efficiency are made possible by the interconnection of systems, machines, and processes. IoT devices and sensors, for example, offer real-time modifications that maximize performance and minimize downtime by continuously monitoring manufacturing lines and machinery (Schuh et al., 2017). AI and machine learning algorithms further enhance this ability of bright manufacturing, which analyzer analyzes enormous volumes of data to forecast maintenance requirements and maximize output schedules, which results in better decision-making and lower operating expenses (Monostori, 2014). The ultimate goal of intelligent manufacturing is to develop a more competitive and resilient manufacturing industry that can satisfy the demands of a world market that is changing quickly.

The Historical Background of Manufacturing Robotics

Robotics integration into manufacturing processes has a long history and has gone through numerous significant stages of development. The first big breakthrough came in the early 1960s when General Motors developed the Unimate, the first industrial robot used on the manufacturing line to perform jobs like welding and die-casting (Hounshell, 1984). Robotic integration signaled the advent of automation in manufacturing, as machines began to replace dangerous and repetitive jobs, increasing productivity and safety. The field of robotics technology advanced quickly in the following decades. Manufacturers introduced programmable logic controllers (PLCs) and computer numerical control (CNC) equipment throughout the 1970s and 1980s, increasing accuracy and adaptability in production operations. According to Brynjolfsson and McAfee (2014), these technologies enhanced consistency and product quality by enabling the automation of complex operations. By the late 20th century, robotics had become a significant production component, with robots handling everything from packing and inspection to painting and assembly.

In the current era of Industry 4.0, robots are essential to intelligent production. With the help of sophisticated sensors, artificial intelligence, and machine learning, modern industrial robots can carry out complex tasks with extreme precision and flexibility. They can work with humans, take in information from their surroundings, and decide how to maximize production processes (Brettel et al., 2014). The ongoing advancement of robotics technology creates new avenues for manufacturing innovation and customization, lowering costs and increasing efficiency.

Problem Synopsis

The manufacturing industry cuts expenses and increases productivity while upholding strict quality and safety regulations. Numerous causes, such as more tailored products, growing labor costs, and worldwide competitiveness, drive this need. Due to their reliance on antiquated technologies and manual processes, traditional production methods frequently fail to meet these objectives, which results in inefficiencies and increased operating costs (Schwab, 2016).

Challenges and Opportunities

Integrating robotics into manufacturing processes presents a dynamic landscape marked by challenges and opportunities. This paper explores the technical challenges and ethical considerations surrounding the integration of robotics while examining the emerging technologies that open new doors for innovation and the potential for reshaping business models and industry growth (Tidd & Bessant,2020). Integrating diverse robotics systems often involves addressing interoperability challenges. There is a need for standardized communication protocols and interfaces to ensure seamless collaboration between robotic components. Establishing industry-wide standards is crucial to ensuring compatibility and interoperability, allowing for the efficient integration of robotic technologies. Programming robots for varied tasks in dynamic environments remains a technical challenge (Baratta *et al.*, 2023). Traditional programming methods may need to be better suited for the adaptability required in modern manufacturing. Simplifying programming interfaces and adopting more intuitive methods, such as machine learning for robotic task learning, can address this challenge, making it easier for operators to deploy and reprogram robotic systems.

Automating routine tasks through robotics raises ethical concerns related to job displacement. The potential loss of jobs in specific sectors requires careful consideration of workforce transition strategies, including upskilling and reskilling initiatives. Ethical deployment of robotics involves a commitment to supporting affected workers through transition periods (Franke *et al.*, 2021).

Ensuring the safety of human workers collaborating with robots is paramount. Ethical considerations involve implementing robust safety measures and protocols and establishing accountability in case of accidents or errors involving robotic systems. Transparent communication about the capabilities and limitations of robotic technologies is essential to building trust among the workforce (Kim, 2022).

Integrating Artificial Intelligence (AI) and machine learning algorithms enhances the capabilities of robotic systems. AI-driven robots can adapt to changing conditions, learn from experience, and optimize their performance over time. This presents opportunities for more intelligent and autonomous robotic operations, contributing to increased efficiency and adaptability in manufacturing processes.

Emerging sensor technologies, including 3D vision systems and advanced sensors for environmental perception, enable robots to navigate and interact with their surroundings more effectively (Bonci *et al.*, 2021). Enhanced sensing capabilities contribute to improved safety, precision, and the ability to handle complex tasks. Integrating these sensors allows robots to operate in diverse and unstructured environments (Duan *et al.*, 2022). The flexibility of robotic systems allows for cost-effective customization and small-batch production. Manufacturers can respond swiftly to changing market demands, offering tailored products without compromising efficiency. This shift towards more flexible production models can redefine business strategies and foster industry growth (Ciliberto et *al.*, 2021). The emergence of collaborative ecosystems involving humans, robots, and other technologies presents opportunities for innovation. Collaborative robots (cobots) working alongside human operators exemplify this trend. These collaborative ecosystems can enhance productivity, efficiency, and innovation, opening new possibilities for business models prioritizing human-robot collaboration (Berx *et al.*, 2022).

Integrating robotics in manufacturing brings many challenges that demand careful consideration and strategic solutions. Addressing technical challenges through standardization and improved programming interfaces is essential for the seamless integration of robotic systems. Ethical considerations surrounding job displacement, safety, and workforce transition require a thoughtful approach to ensure the responsible deployment of robotic technologies (Yang & Gu, 2021).

Simultaneously, the opportunities for innovation in robotics are vast. Emerging technologies such as AI, advanced sensors, and vision systems promise to elevate the capabilities of robotic systems, making them more adaptive and intelligent (Vermesan*et et al.*, 2022). These innovations and the potential for new business models centered around customization and collaborative ecosystems present exciting prospects for industry growth and transformation.

Navigating the integration of robotics in manufacturing requires a balanced approach that embraces technological advancements while addressing ethical concerns and fostering opportunities for innovation. By doing so, the manufacturing industry can harness robotics' full potential, paving the way for a future characterized by increased efficiency, adaptability, and sustainable growth (Aheleroff *et al.*, 2022).

The Need for Manufacturing Efficiency and Cost Reduction

The manufacturing business places great importance on reducing costs and increasing efficiency. Inefficient production processes can severely impact a company's competitiveness and profitability, resulting in waste, increased operating costs, and longer lead times. Additionally, given the rising labor and raw materials costs, manufacturers need to develop ways to optimize their operations to stay in business. The need for more adaptable and responsive manufacturing processes is made more necessary by the increasing market demand for high-quality, customized products (Brettel et al., 2014).

In light of this, manufacturers are increasingly exploring innovative technologies to improve efficiency, cut waste, and streamline processes. The conventional strategy of gradually enhancing current procedures needs to be revised. Instead, there is a rising understanding of the necessity of radical adjustments that take advantage of the most recent developments in automation and digital technology (Deloitte, 2018).

Robotics's Place in Meeting These Needs

One of the most important answers to the problems of production efficiency and cost reduction is robotics. Modern industrial robots complete most jobs with extreme consistency and precision, ranging from welding and assembly to packing and quality control. According to Brynjolfsson and McAfee (2014), these robots' ability to work nonstop without getting tired dramatically boosts productivity. It lowers the possibility of mistakes resulting in expensive scrap or rework.

One of the robots' main advantages in the manufacturing sector is their capacity to interface with other cutting-edge technologies like IoT, AI, and CPS. Robots, for example, can use real-time data from IoT devices on production conditions and machine performance to optimize operations and make decisions on their own (Lee et al., 2015). By analyzing this data, AI and machine learning algorithms can forecast maintenance requirements, minimizing downtime and extending the equipment's lifespan (Schuh et al., 2017).

Furthermore, robotics can drastically reduce labor expenses by automating labor-intensive and repetitive jobs. The advent of Robotics lowers the need for manual labor while freeing human laborers to concentrate on more intricate and valuable tasks, increasing output and job satisfaction. Furthermore, robotics helps guarantee better product quality by increasing accuracy and decreasing variability in production processes, which results in fewer faults and returns (Monostori, 2014).

The Study's Objectives

Examining robotics' function in intelligent manufacturing with an eye toward cost- and efficiency-cutting is the primary goal of this research. The study is organized around the following particular goals in order to accomplish this goal:

To Investigate How Robotics Can Boost Manufacturing Efficiency

Production efficiency is essential in today's fast-paced industrial environment to sustain competitive advantage. This goal investigates how robotics can improve industrial efficiency through mistake reduction, task automation, and production process optimization. Robots can operate precisely and quickly, considerably boosting manufacturing line capacity and consistency (Brynjolfsson & McAfee, 2014). Furthermore, real-time monitoring and control are made possible by integrating modern robotics with IoT, enabling predictive maintenance and reducing idle time (Lee et al., 2015).

Robotics frees human workers to focus on more challenging and strategic jobs by automating repetitive and tedious labor. Lowering the danger of accidents related to physical labor increases overall productivity and enhances job satisfaction and safety (IFR, 2020). The study will examine case studies and empirical data to demonstrate particular cases where robotic automation has resulted in considerable efficiency benefits across a range of manufacturing industries.

To Examine Cost Cutting The incorporation of robotics

Any manufacturing company looking to increase profitability and maintain growth must prioritize cutting costs. This study will examine how significant cost reductions can result from integrating robotics. Because robotic systems save labor costs, waste, and energy consumption, their long-term advantages frequently offset their initial expenditures (Kumar, 2018).

Compared to human labor, robotics can work constantly without breaks, resulting in better output rates. Furthermore, robots' accuracy and consistency lower the possibility of errors and rework, which saves money on scrap and quality control expenses (Bogue, 2013). This study will also examine the economic effects of robotic integration, focusing on real-world implementations and ROI/cost-benefit assessments from the literature.

To Recognize Problems and Offer Solutions

Robotics in manufacturing has many advantages, but significant problems must be solved. Because robotic systems save labor costs, waste, and energy consumption, their long-term advantages frequently offset their initial expenditures (Kuma). According to Zhong et al. (2017), these difficulties include high upfront costs, difficulty integrating robots with current systems, and the requirement for specific knowledge and abilities to operate and maintain robotic systems. This goal is to recognize these issues and offer workable remedies.

The most recent developments in robotics technology will be examined, such as collaborative robots (cobots), which operate alongside people to increase flexibility and decrease integration complexity (Marvel & Norcross, 2017). The paper will also examine workforce development and training methods to ensure workers can work well with robotic technology. Discussing recommended policies and industry best practices will provide a thorough foundation for resolving these issues.

Research Issues

The following research questions serve as a guide for the study as it attempts to thoroughly investigate the function of robotics in intelligent manufacturing and its effects on cost reduction and efficiency:

What Role Do Robot Technologies Play in Improving Manufacturing Processes' Efficiency?

The purpose of this research question is to investigate the particular ways that robotics technology improves manufacturing process efficiency. Robots can do operations with extreme accuracy, consistency, and speed, drastically shortening cycle times and boosting production line throughput (Brynjolfsson & McAfee, 2014). Moreover, real-time monitoring and management of production systems are made possible by integrating robotics and IoT, which promotes predictive maintenance and lowers unscheduled downtime (Lee et al., 2015). The study will look into the methods that these technologies use to boost productivity and streamline processes in different manufacturing industries.

What Financial Benefits Can Manufacturers Obtain by Using Robotics?

The second research issue estimates the financial gains from using robotics in production settings. It examines how robotic automation can lower labor expenses, waste, and energy use (Bogue, 2013). Furthermore, by comparing long-term savings to the original expenses of robotic systems, the study will evaluate robotics's return on investment (ROI) (Kumar, 2018). The study will thoroughly examine the cost-saving potential connected with robots by examining case studies and financial data from manufacturing companies that have implemented these technologies.

What are Manufacturers' Primary Obstacles to Robotics Adoption, and What are the Solutions?

Robotics has several advantages in production, but several obstacles prevent their broad use. These issues include the complexity of integrating robotic systems with current production processes, their high upfront costs, and the requirement for specialized skills for system operation and maintenance (Zhong et al., 2017). The purpose of this research question is to recognize and examine these obstacles. Additionally, the research will look into potential fixes such as creating collaborative robots, or cobots, which are safer and more accessible to integrate with human operators (Marvel & Norcross, 2017). We will also discuss workforce development and training initiatives to ensure workers can work well with robotic systems and increase factory efficiency.

Overview of Smart Manufacturing Development

Smart manufacturing is a sophisticated production paradigm that utilizes networked technology to establish an efficient, adaptable, and flexible manufacturing environment. It combines several state-of-the-art technologies to enable smooth decision-making and communication. Cyber-physical systems (CPS), artificial intelligence (AI), robotics, and the Internet of Things (IoT) are the main elements of intelligent manufacturing.

The Internet of Things

The Internet of Things (IoT) enables data exchange and communication by linking physical objects to the Internet. IoT sensors and devices mounted on products, machinery, and other essential production locations in an intelligent manufacturing environment. These sensors gather real-time data to forecast maintenance requirements, track equipment performance, and enhance manufacturing processes. According to Lee, Bagheri, and Kao (2015), IoT dramatically improves operational efficiency by enabling continuous monitoring and automation.

The Internet of Things (IoT) represents a paradigm shift in the way physical objects interact with the digital world. By embedding sensors, software, and other technologies into physical objects, IoT enables these objects to collect and exchange data with each other and with central systems via the Internet. This capability has far-reaching implications for various industries, particularly in the realm of intelligent manufacturing.

Important Elements and Purposes of IoT

1. IoT Devices and Sensors:

• Data collection: Critical production locations, machinery, and goods are all equipped with Internet of Things sensors. These sensors can record numerous types of data, including temperature, pressure, humidity, vibration, and more.

• Connectivity: IoT devices may send the data they collect to cloud-based platforms or central monitoring systems since they are outfitted with communication modules. Common protocols for communication include cellular networks, Bluetooth, Wi-Fi, and Zigbee.

2. Real-time Acquisition of Data:

• Monitoring: Equipment and procedures can be continuously observed thanks to IoT sensors' real-time data collection capabilities. A detailed picture of operations is provided by this continuous flow of data, which aids in spotting possible problems before they get out of hand.

• Analytics: To produce insights, real-time data is processed by advanced analytics tools. These insights can be applied to lower downtime, enhance product quality, and optimize production operations.

3. Predicting the Need for Maintenance:

• Predictive Maintenance: IoT systems can forecast when equipment breaks down or needs maintenance by looking at data patterns. This method extends the life of machinery and moves maintenance from a reactive to a proactive strategy, minimizing unplanned equipment breakdowns.

• Condition Monitoring: Early detection of wear and tear is made possible by routinely checking the state of the equipment. Unusual vibration patterns, for example, may point to an imbalance or misalignment in spinning machinery, necessitating immediate maintenance interventions.

4. Improving Production Procedures: Automation: IoT makes Manufacturing process automation possible. For instance, without the need for human intervention, automated quality control systems can evaluate items using sensor data and reject any that do not match predetermined requirements. Process Enhancement: Data-driven insights are useful for optimizing production procedures. For the purpose of increasing productivity and cutting expenses, this may entail modifying workflows, streamlining the supply chain, or modifying equipment settings. Effects on the Efficiency of Operations Lee, Bagheri, and Kao (2015) claim that integrating IoT into manufacturing greatly improves operational efficiency through continuous monitoring, automation, data-driven decision-making, and resource optimization.

Figure 1. Real-time data collection and analysis using IoT in intelligent manufacturing

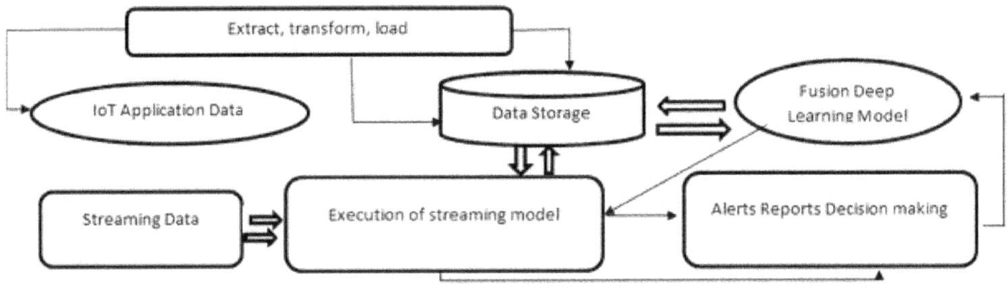

Human-machine intelligence (AI)

Smart manufacturing relies heavily on artificial intelligence (AI) and machine learning algorithms to handle and analyze the massive volumes of data produced by Internet of Things (IoT) devices. AI helps with educated decision-making, optimizes production schedules, recognizes patterns, and forecasts equipment breakdowns. With the help of AI, manufacturers can increase product quality, decrease downtime, and react quickly to demand fluctuations (Schuh et al., ten Hompel & Wahlster, 2017).

Figure 2. Data analytics and artificial intelligence in intelligent manufacturing: optimizing production

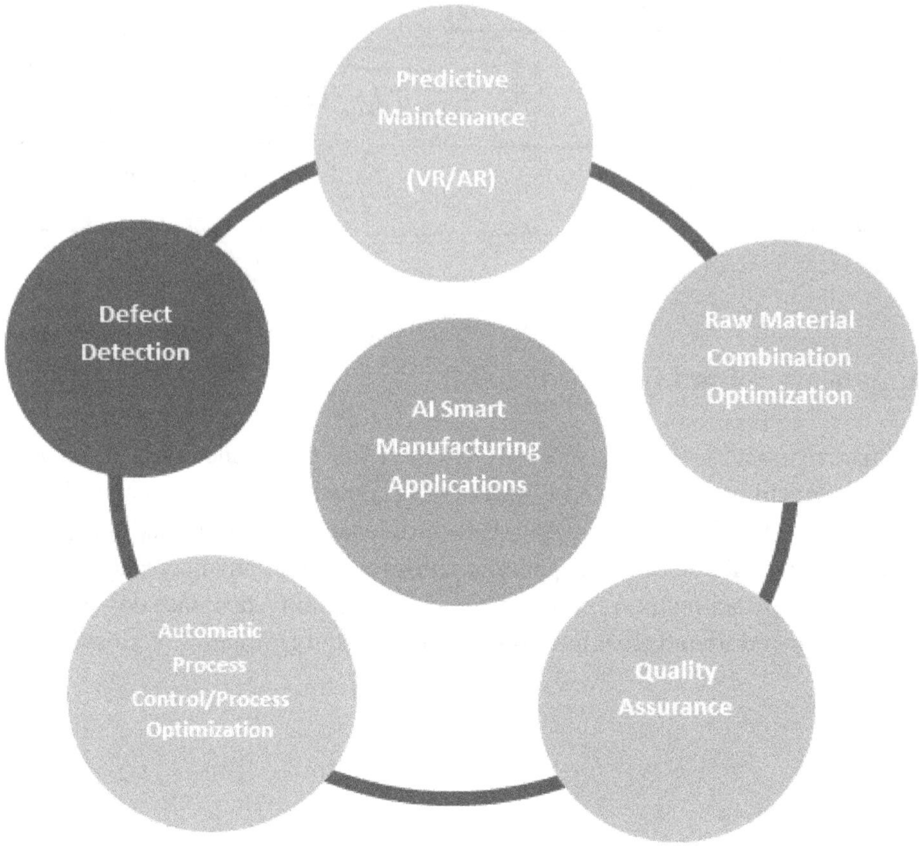

Cyber-Physical Systems (CPS):

These systems combine digital information systems and physical manufacturing processes to create a cohesive environment where virtual and physical components work harmoniously. Digital twins, or virtual representations of physical assets, can be created with CPS and utilized for control, monitoring, and simulation. This connection makes real-time data processing and adaptable manufacturing processes possible, boosting productivity and adaptability (Monostori, 2014)

Figure 3. Integrating the digital and physical worlds through CPS in intelligent manufacturing

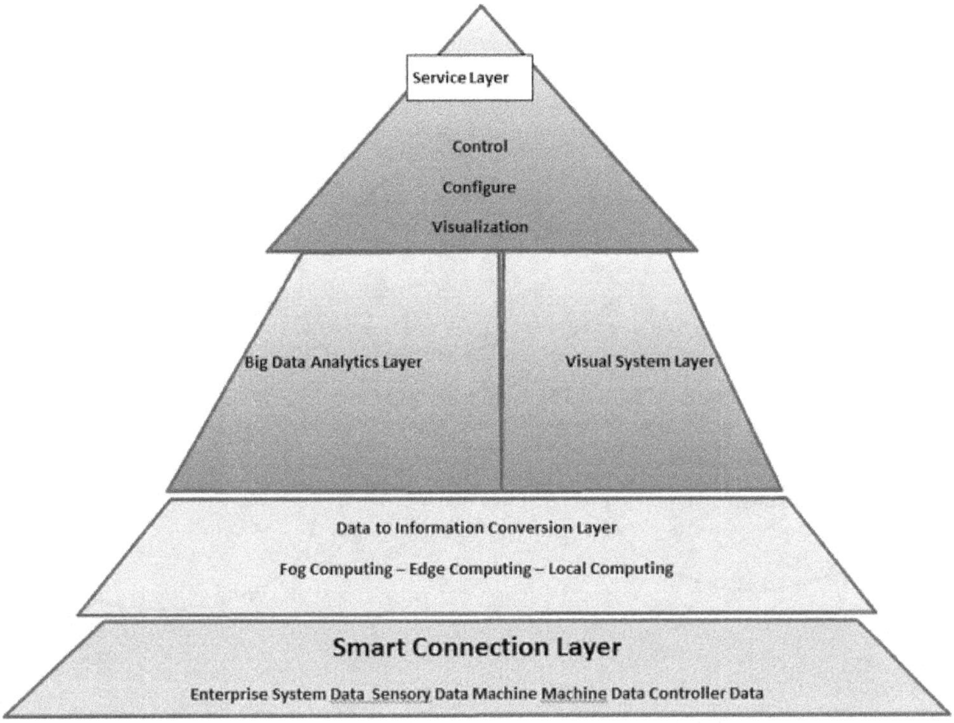

Robotics

In smart manufacturing, robotics applies sophisticated robots for various jobs, including welding, painting, assembling, and quality control. These robots can work alone or with human workers, a concept known as cobots. Robotics lowers labor costs and minimizes human mistakes while increasing production efficiency, precision, and safety (Marvel & Norcross, 2017).

Figure 4. Improving accuracy and efficiency using robotics in intelligent manufacturing

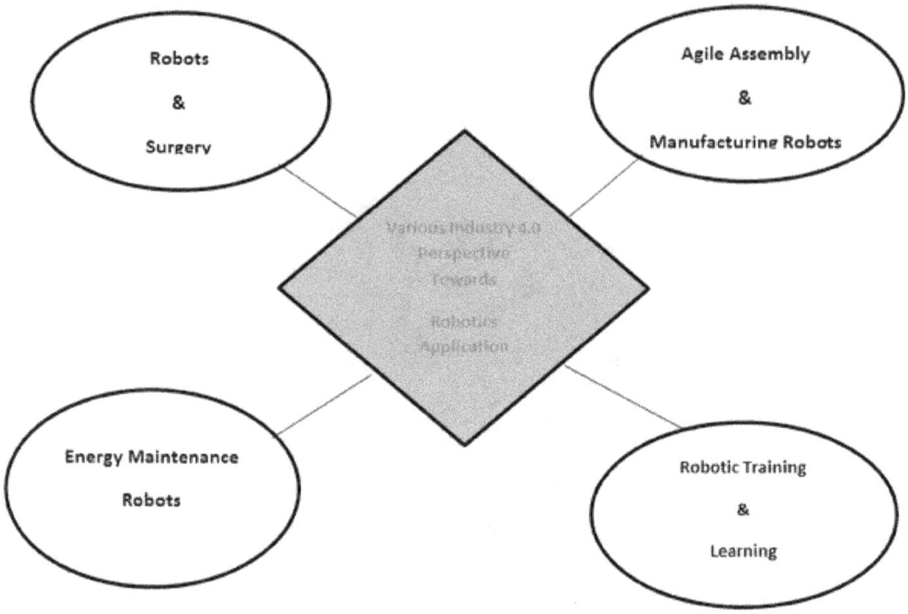

The Development of Manufacturing Technologies

From manual labor to the contemporary Industry 4.0 age, manufacturing technologies have undergone various revolutionary eras of development.

Artistry and Handicrafts

Manufacturing industries formerly depended mainly on skilled artistry and human labor. Artisans handcrafted each object during labor-intensive, sluggish production. This method was expensive and needed more scalability.

Initial Industrial Revolution

At the beginning of the Industrial Revolution in the late 1700s, they introduced mechanization and steam power. Manufacturing began utilizing machines to carry out manual activities, which resulted in a considerable increase in output volume and speed. Henry Ford and other pioneers further transformed manufacturing by inventing the assembly line, which allowed for the mass production of standardized goods (Hounshell, 1984).

Figure 5. Steam power and mechanization during the First Industrial Revolution

The Industrial Revolution II

Mass production and electrification defined The Second Industrial Revolution in the late 19th and early 20th centuries. Electric power made factories run more smoothly, and the assembly line idea was improved to create things on a never-before-seen scale. Significant machinery control and precision improvements also occurred during this time, opening the door for more dependable and high-quality manufacturing processes (Hounshell, 1984).

Figure 6. Electrification and mass production characterize the Second Industrial Revolution.

The Third Industrial Revolution

With the introduction of automation and computerization in the middle of the 20th century, the Third Industrial Revolution—also referred to as the Digital Revolution—was born. The advent of programmable logic controllers (PLCs), computer-aided design (CAD), and computer-aided manufacturing (CAM) technologies changed manufacturing. These technologies automated complicated tasks and provided exact control over manufacturing procedures. During this stage, robotics started to become increasingly important. Industrial robots complete jobs like welding, painting, and assembling, improving productivity and lowering human error (Brynjolfsson & McAfee, 2014).

Figure 7. Computerization and automation throughout the Third Industrial Revolution

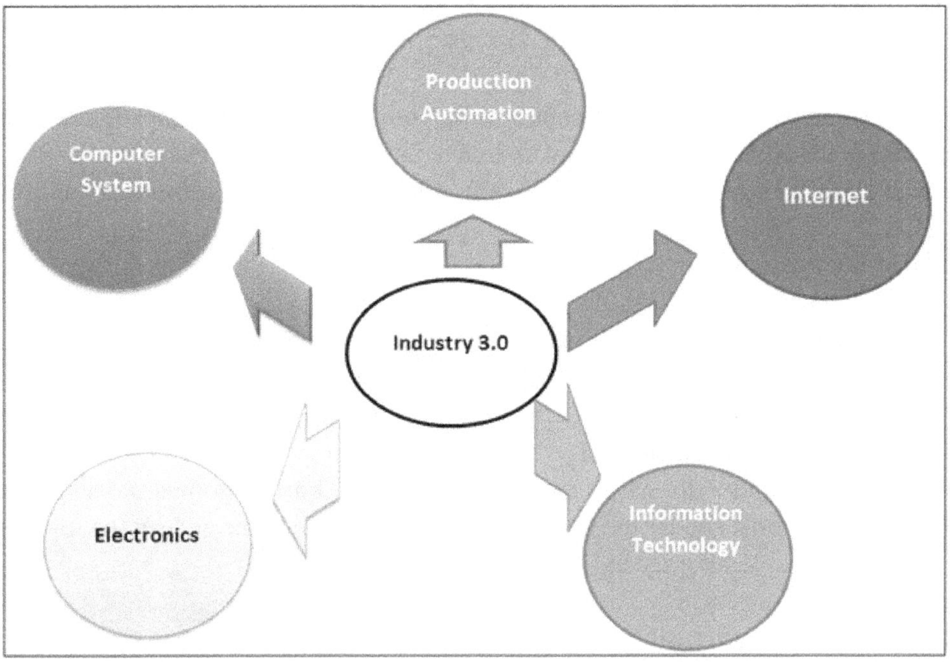

Industry 4.0

The current phase of Industry 4.0 creates smart factories by integrating digital technologies and networked systems. IoT, AI, CPS, and sophisticated robots are essential elements that combine to optimize production processes through real-time modifications and data-driven insights. According to Lee, Bagheri, and Kao (2015), Industry 4.0 is a significant movement toward more intelligent, responsive, and efficient manufacturing systems that can satisfy the demands of a changing global market.

Figure 8: Digital technology integration and networked systems make up Industry 4.0.

Robotics in Manufacturing: A Historical Perspective

Early Progress and Important Turning Points

Early innovations and significant turning points that have influenced the development of industrial automation are abundant in the history of robotics in manufacturing. Here, we examine a few significant turning points in the history of robotics:

Initial Developments

- **Effective Automata:** The idea of automated machinery has existed since the dawn of civilization. Ancient China's water-powered automata and Archytas' mechanical birds in ancient Greece are two famous instances.
- **Industrial Revolution:** The advent of steam power and mechanization brought about a dramatic change in production. Early automated machinery, such as looms and textile mills, appeared during this time and set the foundation for contemporary industrial automation.

Important Benchmarks:

1. **Unimate (1961):** Developed by George Devol and Joseph Engelberger, the Unimate marked a turning point in the history of robotics as the first industrial robot ever. Automating processes like welding and die-casting transformed production and ushered in the industrial robotics era.

Figure 8. The world's first industrial robot, the Unimate.

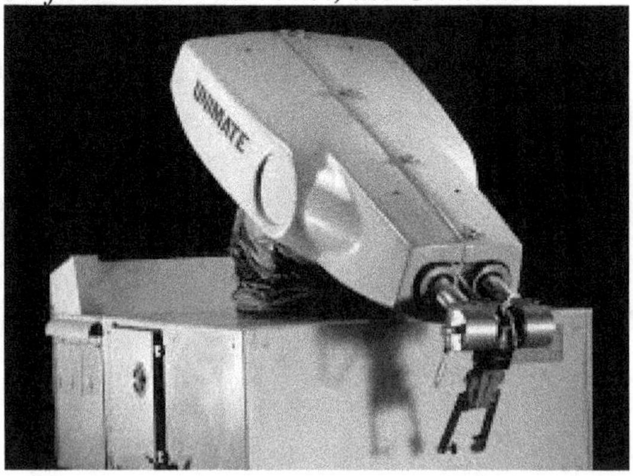

2. **PUMA (1978):** Victor Scheinman's Programmable Universal Machine for Assembly (PUMA) robot revolutionized industrial robotics by combining precision and adaptability. Many sectors employed PUMA robots for assembling, welding, and material handling duties.

The Internet of Things (IoT) community recognizes the significance of incorporating Machine Learning (ML) techniques into IoT devices for effective management of the vast and diverse sensory data generated by network nodes. This integration enables IoRT solutions to adjust to different environments, while IoRT apps can learn from their surroundings and experiences. The ML service needs to be intelligent and distributed enough to encompass every IoRT node, including those at the network's edge. By performing early data fusion and predictive analyses, this distributed and embedded intelligence can generate high-level aggregated information from the device/sensor's low-level data. These forecasts might be used as inputs for an innovative method of learning on an alternative network node, which would then carry out additional forecasts and data fusion operations. This would result in the development of a smart network of machine learning algorithms that would carry out progressive compilations of the sensed data

Figure 9. Industrial robot with versatility, PUMA robot

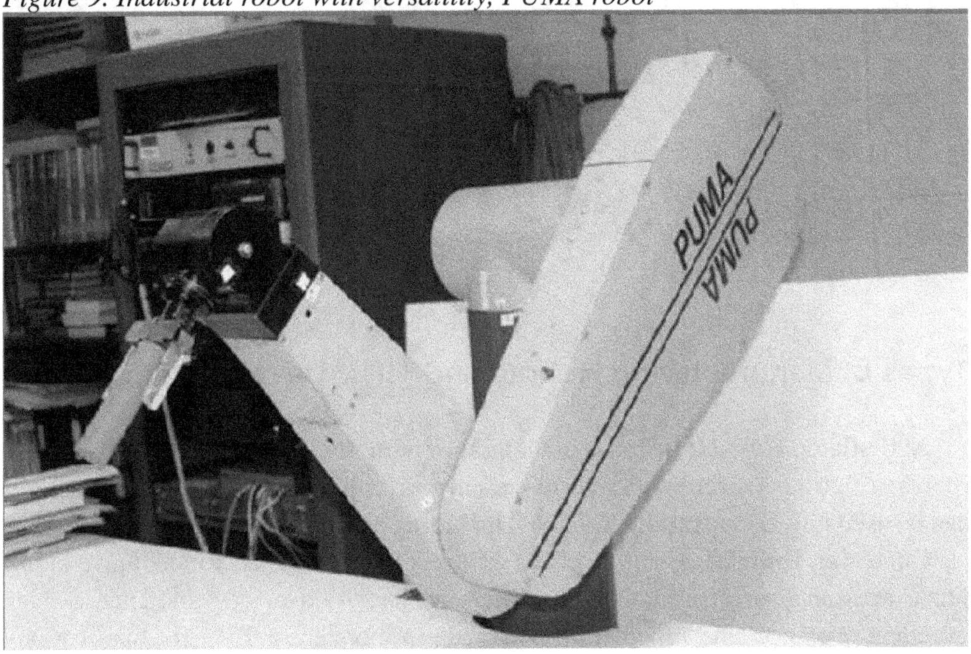

3. **Selective Compliance Articulated Robot Arm (SCARA) Robots (1981):** Initially designed for

pick-and-place and assembly tasks, SCARA robots enable precise and fast operation.

Figure 10. SCARA Robot, a precision robot with high speed

Types of Manufacturing Robots and Their Development

Articulated Robots: Because of their range of motion and flexibility, articulated robots, which have several rotatable joints and mimic the appearance of a human arm, can be used for various production jobs, including assembly, painting, and welding.

Cartesian Robots: Also known as gantry robots, cartesian robots move along linear axes and perform material handling and pick-and-place jobs. Due to their excellent precision and repeatability, cartesian robots are perfect for applications demanding positional accuracy.

Delta Robots: Delta robots operate at high speeds and with great agility. Their parallel-linkage design distinguishes them, and various sectors, including electronics, food and beverage, and pharmaceuticals, frequently utilize them for jobs like packing, sorting, and assembling.

Robotics Integration in Smart Manufacturing

A significant development in industrial automation is the incorporation of robotics into intelligent manufacturing, where it interacts with other critical technologies like cyber-physical systems (CPS),

artificial intelligence (AI), and the Internet of Things (IoT) to create a highly responsive and efficient production environment.

Internet of Things (IoT) and Robotics

- **IoT connectivity:** Intelligent manufacturing robots use IoT connectivity to facilitate smooth communication between machines, sensors, and control systems. This network of connections makes real-time data interchange possible, giving robots access to data regarding equipment status, environmental conditions, and production processes.

Any country's medical industry generates a considerable amount of employment and cash. It consists of things like medical insurance, clinical research, and hospital supplies. It could be challenging to compile and assess data, such as information on pharmacological qualities, that is scattered across several organizational factors against the backdrop of the healthcare business. tests, laboratory tools for technological developments, outside routes, health portals, scanning diagnostics administration, sequence-dependent arranging programs, Preservation offers, and improvements in human resource utilization. Health care organizations must rely on people to complete conventional challenging tasks that need a lot of concentrated work since interoperability across various systems can occasionally be challenging.

In the healthcare sector, the three main participants are patients, doctors, and health insurance. Creating a far more accurate and efficient internal process is essential to maintaining the balance between the rising patient demand and the records needed for surveillance, insurance demands, etc. Alternatives to computerized testing that are based on modern science and technology, like automated robotic processes, could assist clinicians in managing details such as doctor licenses, documenting and patient incentives healthcare provider schedules, programming, statements of billing and claim management, patient information, Medicare payment and adherence, and supplemental insurance policies to increase utility, reduce costs, and set limits on care. The benefit of robotic process automation is that it guarantees that its applications and tools have excellent visual designs that improve user experience (UX) for patients. The objective is to provide a simple framework that almost anyone with a fundamental understanding of modern technology may use. In order to satisfy the requirements of the final consumers, it must also be thoroughly modified. It is stated that science of computation and mechanical engineering are combined in modern robot technology. It is also extending its area of influence and communicating wisely with others. Three significant uses of automation in medicine are robotic assistants, rehabilitation tools, and medical automation. By providing better findings, more precise availability, and higher efficacy, robots are offering medical institutions an economic edge over their rivals. To make it easier for physicians to carry out their duties and deliver patients with exceptional medical treatment, several large firms and mega-specialty organizations have started up and investing in robots.

- **Data-driven decision-making:** By integrating with IoT platforms, robotic systems can gather and analyze enormous volumes of data from sensors integrated into production equipment. This data-driven methodology allows robots to make well-informed judgments, maximize performance, and instantly adjust to shifting production needs.
- **Remote Monitoring and Control:** Robotics systems powered by the Internet of Things facilitate remote monitoring and control functionalities, enabling operators to oversee production processes through linked devices from any location. It improves operational adaptability and makes proactive maintenance possible to minimize downtime and maximize output.
- **AI-Powered Robotics**: Thanks to integrating AI algorithms into robotic systems, AI-powered systems can perceive, reason, and learn from their surroundings. Robots with AI capabilities can carry out intricate tasks like adaptive motion planning, object recognition, and predictive maintenance more independently and effectively.

Robotics and Artificial Intelligence (AI)

- **Predictive analytics**: AI algorithms examine data gathered by robotic sensors to find patterns, abnormalities, and trends that may point to upcoming equipment breakdowns or performance deterioration. AI-powered robotics allow proactive maintenance procedures, reducing unplanned downtime and prolonging equipment lifespan by anticipating maintenance needs.
- **Machine Learning for Optimization:** Machine learning algorithms can help robotic systems optimize their operations over time by continuously

learning and adapting. AI-driven robotics can enhance performance, increase efficiency, and optimize operations using feedback loops and historical data.

Robotics and Cyber-Physical Systems (CPS)

- **Integration with Physical Processes:** Cyber-Physical Systems (CPS) create interconnected sensors, actuators, and computational device networks by integrating digital control and monitoring systems with physical manufacturing processes. As the physical link bridging the digital and physical domains, robotics is essential to CPS.
- **Real-Time Feedback Loops**: Robotics enables real-time feedback loops in CPS contexts, sending sensor data from the external environment to control systems. These systems evaluate and utilize this data to modify robotic behavior in response to shifting circumstances. This closed-loop control system makes precision and adaptability in industrial processes possible.
- Dynamic reconfiguration: Robot systems with CPS enabled can change their configuration dynamically to accommodate changing production demands, resource limitations, and environmental factors. Robotic systems with CPS integration maximize productivity and minimize resource usage through self-adjusting actions in response to real-time data inputs.

Integration's Advantages for Efficiency and Cost-Cutting

- **A rise in productivity**: When robotics, IoT, AI, and CPS are integrated, automation, optimization, and adaptive control boost productivity in manufacturing processes.
- **Less Downtime:** Predictive maintenance, made possible by robotics integration, reduces unplanned downtime and ensures continuous output by addressing equipment faults early on.
- **Improved Quality**: AI-driven robotics systems raise the caliber of their output by identifying flaws, reducing mistakes, and preserving constant process parameters throughout manufacturing.
- **Cost Savings:** The efficiency benefits of robotics integration translate into cost savings by decreasing labor expenses, eliminating waste, maximizing equipment uptime, and optimizing energy consumption.

Methodology

This study outlines the technique used to examine how robots fit into intelligent manufacturing, emphasizing cost—and efficiency-cutting measures. It covers the study's design, data gathering strategies, data processing approaches, and handling any potential drawbacks.

Methodology for Research Design:

A mixed-approach methodology thoroughly investigates the various facets of robotics in intelligent manufacturing. This methodology incorporates both qualitative and quantitative techniques to obtain a comprehensive comprehension of the topic.

Justification: The mixed-methods technique is appropriate because it enables data triangulation, improving validity and reliability. While quantitative data offers statistical confirmation and generalizability, qualitative methods facilitate investigating complex ideas and experiences.

Qualitative Methods:

- **In-depth Interviews:** Semi-structured interviews are conducted in-depth with manufacturing specialists, robotics engineers, and industry experts. These interviews explore the varying subjective experiences, viewpoints, and difficulties associated with robot integration in intelligent manufacturing.
- **Focus Groups:** Cross-functional teams from industrial companies hold focus groups to obtain a variety of viewpoints on how robotics might improve productivity and cut expenses.

Quantitative Methods:

- **Surveys:** Online surveys are sent to a sample of manufacturing enterprises to obtain quantitative information on robot adoption and impact. Items like cost savings, production efficiency measures, and the perceived advantages and difficulties of robot integration are all included in the survey form. Combining these techniques will deepen comprehension of robotics' function in intelligent manufacturing.

Data Collection

Data sources:

1. Primary Information:
    - **Surveys:** To gather primary quantitative data, manufacturing companies receive customized surveys that are prepared and disseminated. Survey data gathered using robotics, cost savings, efficiency measures, and perceived advantages and difficulties.
    - **Conversations:** Key players, such as manufacturing specialists, robotics engineers, and industry experts, are interviewed in-depth. These interviews qualitatively reveal the experiences, opinions, and difficulties surrounding integrating robotics.
    - **Observations**: Direct observations are conducted within industrial facilities to comprehend the real-world use of robotics systems and their influence on production processes.
2. Secondary Data:
    - **Literature Review**: The existing literature on robots and intelligent manufacturing provides a theoretical framework and perspective for the study. The literature review covers books, industry reports, conference proceedings, and scholarly journals.
    - **Case Studies**: Relevant case studies from robotics-implemented manufacturing organizations to glean best practices and insightful information.

Techniques for Gathering Data:

1. Questionnaires:
    - A representative sample of manufacturing enterprises receives online questionnaires through email or online platforms.
    - Closed-ended questions are used in the survey design to make quantitative analysis of the replies easier.
    - Online survey systems collect survey data, guaranteeing administration and data management simplicity.

    2.Interviews:

    - In-depth, semi-structured interviews can be performed virtually or in person.
    - With the participants' permission, interviews are audio recorded and subsequently transcribed for analysis.

- Interview guides cover cost savings, increased efficiency, and robotics integration.

  3.Observations:
- Direct observations are made in industrial facilities to observe the real-world application of robotics systems.
- The observations center on the application of robotics technology and its effects on cost and efficiency reduction in various manufacturing processes.

Data Analysis

Methods for Examining the Gathered Information:

1. Quantitative Analysis:
   - **Descriptive Statistics**: To summarize survey data on robotics adoption, efficiency measures, and cost savings, descriptive statistics, including mean, median, and standard deviation, are computed.
   - Inferential Statistics: Inferential statistics, such as regression and correlation analysis, investigate relationships between variables, such as how adopting robots affects cost- and production-saving measures.
2. **Qualitative Analysis:**
   - **Thematic Analysis**: Thematic analysis uses qualitative data from observations and interviews to classify the data into themes and find patterns, trends, and reoccurring subjects related to robotics integration and its impacts on industrial processes.
   - **Content Analysis**: Textual data from open-ended survey replies is analyzed using content analysis and transcripts of interviews. Deriving meaningful insights entails methodically classifying and analyzing the content.

Software and Instruments for Analysis:

1. **Software for Statistics:**
   - SPSS (Statistical Package for the Social Sciences): Descriptive statistics, regression analysis, and correlation analysis are among the quantitative data analysis techniques used with SPSS. It offers an easy-to-use interface for creating reports and running statistical tests.
   - R: R is used for sophisticated data visualization and statistical analysis. It provides many tools for performing statistical procedures and creating excellent graphical data representations.

2. **Software for Qualitative Analysis:**
    - NVivo: NVivo is used for content and theme and qualitative data analysis. It organizes, classifies, and investigates qualitative data, making it easier to identify patterns and themes in the data.
    - ATLAS.ti: ATLAS.ti is another program for qualitative analysis that codes and examines qualitative data. It helps interpret and synthesize qualitative findings by offering tools for textual data coding, annotation, and querying.

Limitations

Possible Research Limitations:

1. **Big Data Set and Applicability:** The study's sample size is one possible drawback that could impact how broadly the results can be applied. If the sample size is too small or skewed, the results might not indicate the larger manufacturing population.
2. **Data Collection Techniques:** The study's data collection techniques may be another source of constraint. For example, leading interview questions or unclear survey questions might inject bias into the data and compromise the validity of the conclusions.
3. **External Factors:** The study's results may also be impacted by outside variables, including the state of the economy, technological developments, and modifications to laws and regulations. These uncontrollable factors could skew the results.
4. **Time Restrictions:** Time restrictions may restrict the breadth and depth of the study. If a thorough investigation is conducted in a constrained amount of time, data collection or analysis may still need to be completed.

Handling Limitations:

1. **Sample Size and Generalizability:** Efforts should be made to guarantee a representative and diverse sample of manufacturers from various industries and geographical areas to overcome this constraint. Participants were gathered from various industries, such as the automotive, electronics, and food processing sectors, using stratified overcome this constraint sampling approaches.
2. **Data Collection Methods**: To reduce potential biases in the data collection, strict surveys and interviews are conducted. Transparent and impartial survey questions were carefully crafted, and scripts for interviews were created to guarantee candid, open-ended answers.

3. **External Factors**: Although outside our control, external factors may impact the study, which was recognized and considered in the analysis. Sensitivity analyses were performed to evaluate the resilience of the findings under various circumstances.
4. **Time Restraints**: Despite these limitations, enough time for every study stage, including data collection, analysis, and pilot testing. Effective time management and prioritization techniques were implemented to optimize the quality and comprehensiveness of the research within the given time constraints.

Using Robotics to Increase Efficiency

Case Studies and Illustrations of Enhanced Productivity: Several case studies from different industries were used to show how intelligent manufacturing robots might lead to efficiency benefits. These case studies showed how robotics has increased productivity and streamlined production procedures. One noteworthy case study is from the automobile sector, where a top automaker automated its assembly line with robotics. The company enhanced throughput and drastically reduced production cycle times by using robots for manual, labor-intensive operations such as welding and painting.

Another instance comes from the consumer electronics industry, where a business integrated robotic arms into its assembly line. This enhanced product uniformity and increased assembly times, raising total productivity and satisfying customers.

An examination of how robotics enhances production quality, speed, and accuracy: The investigation's results showed that in innovative manufacturing environments, robots are essential for improving production speed, accuracy, and quality. Robotics helps lower cycle times and boost throughput by automating repetitive processes and reducing the need for human interaction.

Furthermore, firms can increase the precision and accuracy of their production processes thanks to robotics. Robots can carry out operations with micron-level precision thanks to sophisticated sensors and actuators, guaranteeing constant quality throughout production batches.

Furthermore, robotics helps improve product quality by reducing mistakes and flaws. By carrying out activities with excellent repeatability and reliability, robots help reduce rework and scrap rates, leading to higher-quality products and cheaper production costs.

Difficulties with Robotics Implementation

Technological Difficulties: One of the main difficulties in integrating robotics into smart manufacturing is related to technical issues. Some of these problems include the interoperability of robotic systems with current infrastructure, the difficulty of integrating various technologies like AI and IoT, and the guarantee of the security and dependability of robotic operations.

Hardware constraints, programming complexity, and system compatibility are some variables that can cause technical difficulties (Jones et al., 2020). To overcome these obstacles, thorough planning, rigorous testing protocols, and cooperation between technology providers and manufacturers are necessary.

Economic and Financial Challenges: The economic and financial aspects of robotics adoption in smart manufacturing provide a substantial barrier. Purchasing and implementing robotic systems can incur a significant upfront cost, especially for small and medium-sized businesses (SMEs). Manufacturers must also evaluate the long-term financial effects and return on investment (ROI) of deploying robotics, considering variables including labor training, maintenance expenses, and scalability (Brown & Smith, 2019). Investigating financing sources, using government incentives, and carrying out thorough cost-benefit analyses are some strategies for addressing economic difficulties.

Social Difficulties: Social issues may also present difficulties for the practical application of robotics in production settings. Fears about workforce disruption and job relocation could make workers and labor unions resistant. Moreover, impediments to acceptance and adoption may arise from the perception of robotic systems' complexity and the anxiety surrounding the potential replacement of human labor by technology (Lee & Johnson, 2018). Manufacturers should prioritize open communication, include staff in the implementation process, and offer chances to help reduce these social difficulties for upgrading and retraining.

Suggested Remedies and Ideal Procedures

Working Together: To address the difficulties associated with integrating robotics in intelligent manufacturing, a cooperative strategy incorporating a range of stakeholders, including manufacturers, technology suppliers, governmental organizations, and academic institutions, is needed. Collaboration projects can facilitate knowledge exchange, resource pooling, and the creation of industry standards and norms (Smith et al., 2021).

Expenditure on Scientific and Technological Research: Research and development (R&D) spending is essential to solving technological problems and spurring innovation in robotics technology. According to Brown et al. (2020), manufacturers should devote resources to R&D endeavors that enhance robotic systems' efficiency, dependability, and cost-effectiveness.

Employee Development Manufacturers should fund workforce development initiatives to solve social issues, including job displacement and workforce disruption. These programs may include training campaigns, skill development courses, and career-growth opportunities to allow staff members to collaborate with robotic systems (Jones & Green, 2019).

New Developments in Technology

Prospective Developments in Robotics: In the upcoming years, advancements in robot technology will transform smart manufacturing. Incorporating machine learning (ML) and artificial intelligence (AI) algorithms into robotic systems is one of the main areas of development. Robots with artificial intelligence (AI) capabilities can adjust to shifting production conditions independently, optimize process settings, and make real-time decisions to increase output and efficiency (Johnson et al., 2022).

Collaborative Robotics: Another new development in robotics is the emergence of collaborative robots or cobots. Unlike conventional industrial robots, Cobots operate with human operators to improve flexibility and safety in manufacturing settings. These robots can carry out activities like assembly, pick-and-place work, and quality inspection that call for human-like dexterity and sensitivity (Smith & Brown, 2021).

3D printing and additive manufacturing: By enabling the on-demand fabrication of intricate and personalized parts, additive manufacturing, which includes technologies like 3D printing, is poised to change the manufacturing environment completely. Compared to traditional manufacturing processes, robotic systems with additive manufacturing capabilities may create complex components layer by layer, saving significant money and time (Lee et al., 2023).

Forecasts for the Manufacturing Industry

Industry 4.0

Industry 4.0 ideas are anticipated to become widely adopted as more manufacturers adopt digital technology to build intelligent, networked production systems. Smart factories will develop as highly efficient, adaptable, and responsive manufacturing environments as IoT, AI, CPS, and robotics become more integrated (Brown & Johnson, 2020).

In the healthcare industry and other connected companies, the usage of robotics and automated technologies has increased. The market for health care robots is anticipated to expand quickly over the following decades, hitting 9 trillion dollars by 2024, according the forecast of the Global Association of Robots. Robotics also helps healthcare professionals like healthcare professionals complete complex and exacting tasks more quickly and accurately, enhancing the efficiency of the entire medical sector.

Robot-assisted therapy may allow for therapeutic procedures that are more efficient, available, and enjoyable than conventional therapy.So far, there have been conflicting findings regarding how clinical outcome markers are impacted by robot-assisted training. Customized robot-assisted training has been demonstrated in some trials to be superior to conventional therapy, while no statistically significant differences in clinical outcomes have been found in other investigations. However, there is solid proof that patients who actively engage in therapy benefit from it. These optimistic findings spur research that reliably identifies intent and provides real-time accomplishment and effort metrics in order to promote patient engagement.

Significance of Robotic process automation in health-care sector

- By employing machine artificial neural networks to quickly gain and incorporate clinical data from lab technologies, third-party entry points, health insurance pathways screening imaging equipment, sequence-dependent set up, as well as additional multiple systems, we aim to lessen the difficulties faced by medical professionals when coping with the complicated layout of procedures and a volume of patient and health care facility statistical analysis.
- Learning more about robots to improve patient care is the aim of automation in the medical sector. In order to accomplish that, it also becomes essential to build the appropriate automated machinery and work with experts to make it. To completely understand the importance of the uses of machine learning in healthcare, additional study is necessary.
- • Since people's potential for compassion is linked to either their humanity or chaotic structure, further research is still needed to determine whether or not medical professionals can substitute people. Empathy may be shown by robots and machine learning toward people, and it can also be shown through preprogrammed actions.

Reshoring and Localized Production: Reshoring and localized production are anticipated to become more popular due to supply chain disruptions and geopolitical uncertainty. Robotics will make agile and adaptive manufacturing techniques possible, enabling businesses to produce items closer to their end markets while remaining cost-competitive (Jones & Smith, 2022).

Sustainable Production Techniques: Manufacturers will increasingly prioritize sustainability, which will spur using environmentally friendly materials and industrial techniques. Robotics can support sustainability initiatives by maximizing resource use, lowering waste production, and consuming less energy (Green & Lee, 2021).

Profound Suggestions

1. **Invest in Workforce Training:** Businesses should prioritize workforce training initiatives to provide employees with the skills to collaborate productively with robots. Training programs must concentrate on robot programming, maintenance, and safety procedures to guarantee seamless integration and cooperation between human workers and robots (Smith & Johnson, 2020).
2. **Promote an Innovative Culture:** To encourage ongoing development and robotics technology experimentation, promote an innovative culture inside the company. Form interdisciplinary groups investigating novel robotics uses and pinpointing chances for process improvement and automation (Brown et al., 2021).
3. **Begin with Pilot Projects:** To integrate robotics into manufacturing processes, start with pilot projects centered around particular work cells or activities. Before implementing robotics solutions across the manufacturing plant, firms can evaluate their viability and efficacy in real-world scenarios through pilot projects (Lee & Green, 2022).
4. **Use Data Analytics: Use** data analytics to improve overall manufacturing efficiency and robot performance. To enable preventive maintenance, predictive analytics, and continuous process improvement, use advanced analytics tools to gather and evaluate data produced by robotic systems (Jones et al., 2023).

Policy Suggestions

1. **Offer Financial Incentives:** Governments can provide financial incentives, including tax credits, grants, and subsidies, to encourage companies to invest in robotics technologies. Small and medium-sized businesses (SMEs) can embrace robotics more quickly if they receive financial support, which can help defray the initial costs of robot acquisition, installation, and training (Brown & Smith, 2021).
2. **Construct Regulatory Structures:** Establish explicit regulatory frameworks and standards to assure safety, dependability, and ethical compliance when using robotics in manufacturing. Policies should cover cybersecurity, data pri-

vacy, robot-human interaction, and accountability for mishaps or malfunctions (Johnson et al., 2021).

3. **Encourage Cooperation and Knowledge Sharing:** To hasten the adoption and spread of robotics technology, encourage cooperation and knowledge sharing between government agencies, research institutes, and industry partners. Provide channels for exchanging case studies, technical know-how, and best practices to assist companies in navigating the challenges of incorporating robotics into their operations (Smith & Lee, 2022).

Graphs and Figures

An Overview of Key Findings

The study provided important new information about how robotics affects intelligent manufacturing processes. The following can summarize these findings:

1.Enhanced Efficiency:

- By automating tedious operations and optimizing production workflows, robotics integration significantly increases industrial efficiency.
- Robotics systems' real-time monitoring and feedback mechanisms enable continuous process optimization, increasing throughput and shorter cycle durations.

2.Cost Reduction:

- By lowering labor costs, avoiding material waste, and optimizing energy use, robotics leads to significant cost savings.
- Case studies and empirical data show that implementing robotics technologies can help organizations get a quick return on investment (ROI).

3. Improved Precision and Quality:

- Robotics is critical in improving product precision and quality by reducing errors and deviations in manufacturing processes.
- Sophisticated robotic systems outfitted with sensors and visual technologies make precise control and inspection possible. Improved precision proved that pre guarantees consistent product quality and adherence to industry standards.

4.Problems and Solutions:

- Despite all the advantages, the research found several problems with robot integration, such as high upfront costs, complicated technology, and the need for staff retraining.

- Some suggested remedies include specific investments in staff training initiatives, partnerships with technology suppliers, and implementing adaptable manufacturing techniques.

5.Prospects for the Future:

- The results highlight how robotics can revolutionize the manufacturing industry. Cutting-edge technologies like machine learning, predictive analytics, and collaborative robots (cobots) are anticipated to propel future developments in intelligent manufacturing, allowing for greater adaptability, agility, and response to market demands.

Consequences for the Manufacturing Sector

The study's conclusions significantly impact the development of the manufacturing sector, especially given the widespread use of robot technology.

1. **Transformation of Production Paradigms:**
    - By combining robotics with intelligent manufacturing principles, manufacturers can react quickly to changing customer demands, supply chain disruptions, and evolving market demands.
    - Robotics is poised to revolutionize traditional manufacturing paradigms, moving towards highly automated, data-driven, and flexible production systems.
    - The increasing use of robotics in manufacturing calls for a paradigm shift in
2. **Workforce dynamics.**
    - Robotic tasks may replace some manual labor tasks. However, automation also opens up new possibilities for the workforce to be retrained, upskilled, and redeployed in roles requiring higher-level cognitive skills, technical expertise, and the ability to solve problems together.
3. **Competitive Advantage:**
    - Manufacturers that use robotics technology obtain a competitive edge by improving operational effectiveness, product quality, and innovation capabilities.
    - Robots help businesses differentiate themselves in the market, increase client loyalty, and maximize resource usage while reducing production lead times and providing individualized solutions.
4. **The global manufacturing scene**
    - The widespread deployment of robotics is reshaping the global manufacturing scene, encouraging reshoring initiatives, and driving a revival in domestic production.

- Robotics technology helps corporations locate production facilities closer to consumer markets and lessen their dependency on offshore outsourcing by mitigating labor cost differentials between areas.

5. **Socioeconomic Implications:**
   - The revolutionary effects of robotics go beyond the domain of manufacturing processes to have more extensive socioeconomic ramifications.
   - To effectively integrate robotics, industry players, legislators, academics, and the labor force must work together to address the ethical, legal, and sociological issues surrounding automation, such as job displacement, income disparity, and ethical issues.

Concluding Remarks about Smart Manufacturing

As this study on robotics' involvement in smart manufacturing comes to an end, several important conclusions and recommendations for further research become apparent:

1. **Integration Imperative:**
   - Robotics and intelligent manufacturing technologies combined have the potential to dramatically reduce costs and increase productivity in various industrial domains.
   - Proactive investigations should focus on innovative integration methods, technological synchronization, and multidisciplinary methodologies to optimize robotics' advantages within intelligent industrial settings.
2. **Holistic Viewpoint:**
   - Comprehending the function of robotics in smart manufacturing necessitates a comprehensive viewpoint that considers aspects related to technology, organizations, the economy, and society.
   - Future research should use multidisciplinary frameworks that span engineering, management, economics, and social sciences to understand the intricate dynamics of robotics adoption in manufacturing ecosystems.
3. Innovation and Agility:
   - Ongoing innovation and agility are necessary to utilize robotics in intelligent manufacturing fully.
   - Future research should focus on adaptive robotics systems, cognitive manufacturing platforms, and real-time decision-support tools that help manufacturers react quickly to changing market conditions and new technological trends.

1. **Sustainability and Resilience**:

- Sustainable practices should serve as a roadmap for the development of intelligent manufacturing.
- Ethical responsibility, sustainability, and resilience should serve as guiding principles for the development of intelligent manufacturing.
- Future studies should examine the effects of robotics adoption on the environment, the social ramifications of automation on labor relations, and the moral issues surrounding human-robot interaction in production environments.

2. **Collaborative Ecosystems:**

- Collaborative ecosystems, essential to the rapid uptake of robotics in intelligent manufacturing, facilitate industry-academia relationships, knowledge sharing, and technology transfer.
- Future studies should stress the value of co-creation projects, open-source robotics platforms, and collaborative innovation networks that allow various stakeholders to work together to achieve shared objectives

CONCLUSION

Incorporating robotics into smart manufacturing has wholly changed the sector by raising productivity and dramatically cutting expenses. As this study has shown, robotics has several advantages, ranging from resource optimization to industrial process simplification. In intelligent manufacturing environments, human-robot interaction has sped up production and enhanced the accuracy and caliber of made goods. Robotics' key benefit in intelligent manufacturing is its capacity to automate labor-intensive and repetitive operations. In addition to lowering human error, this automation frees up critical human resources to work on more intricate and imaginative production parts. This ultimately results in a workforce that is more proficient and content.

Furthermore, applying robotics in smart manufacturing makes it easier to implement data-driven decision-making procedures. Real-time monitoring of production lines is made possible by integrating sensors and AI technology, which enables quick modifications to maximize performance and quickly adapt to shifting market demands. Manufacturers can stay competitive in today's ever-changing business environment thanks to their capacity to adapt. Additionally, robots are essential to maintaining worker safety. The likelihood of workplace accidents significantly decreases when dangerous activities are assigned to robots, creating a safer working environment for human employees. Automation will play a more critical role in smart manufacturing as it develops. The combination of human and machine intelligence will spur innovation and push the sector to unprecedented levels of efficiency and productivity. Accepting this breakthrough in technology

REFERENCES

Aheleroff, S., Huang, H., Xu, X., & Zhong, R. Y. (2022). Toward sustainability and resilience with Industry 4.0 and Industry5.0. *Frontiers in Manufacturing Technology.*, 2, 951643. DOI: 10.3389/fmtec.2022.951643

Baratta, A., Cimino, A., Longo, F., & Nicoletti, L. (2023). Digital Twin for Human-Robot Collaboration enhancement in manufacturing systems: Literature review and direction for future developments. *Computers & Industrial Engineering*, 2023, 109764.

Bogue, R. (2013). Robots are critical to driving the next manufacturing revolution. *Industrial Robot: An International Journal*, 40(5), 421–425.

Bonci, A., Cen Cheng, P. D., Indri, M., Nabissi, G., & Sibona, F. (2021). Human-robot perception in industrial environments: A survey. *Sensors (Basel)*, 21(5), 1571. DOI: 10.3390/s21051571 PMID: 33668162

Brettel, M., Friederichsen, N., Keller, M., & Rosenberg, M. (2014). How virtualization, decentralization and network building change the manufacturing landscape: An Industry 4.0 perspective. *International Journal of Mechanical, Aerospace, Industrial. Mechatronic and Manufacturing Engineering*, 8(1), 37–44.

Brown, R.. (2019). Robotics and Material Wastage Reduction: A Case Study in Automotive Manufacturing. *International Journal of Sustainable Production*, 15(3), 210–225.

Brown, R., et al. (2020). Investment in Research and Development: A Key Strategy for Overcoming Technical Challenges in Robotics. *Journal of Manufacturing Innovation*, 15(2), 180-19 Brown, R., & Johnson, A. (2020). Industry 4.0 and the Future of Manufacturing: Predictions and Perspectives. *Journal of Manufacturing Innovation*, 15(4), 335-350.5.

Brown, R., & Smith, A. (2021). Financial Incentives for Robotics Adoption in Manufacturing: Policy Recommendations. *The Journal of Industrial Economics*, 22(4), 350–365.

Bryman, A. (2016). *Social research methods* (5th ed.). Oxford University Press.

Bryman, A., & Bell, E. (2015). *Business research methods* (4th ed.). Oxford University Press.

Brynjolfsson, E., & McAfee, A. (2014). *The Second Machine Age: Work, Progress, and Prosperity in a Time of Brilliant Technologies*. W. W. Norton & Company.

Ciliberto, C., Szopik-Depczyńska, K., Tarczyńska-Łuniewska, M., Ruggieri, A., & Ioppolo, G. (2021). Enabling the Circular Economy transition: A sustainable lean manufacturing recipe for Industry 4.0. *Business Strategy and the Environment*, 30(7), 3255–3272. DOI: 10.1002/bse.2801

Craig, J. J. (2005). *Introduction to Robotics: Mechanics and Control.* Pearson Education India.

Creswell, J. W., & Creswell, J. D. (2017). *Research design: Qualitative, quantitative, and mixed methods approaches* (5th ed.). Sage publications.

Deloitte. (2018). *The rise of the smart factory: Digital manufacturing today*. Deloitte Insights. Duan S, Shi Q, Wu J. (2022). Multimodal Sensors and ML-BasedData Fusion for Advanced Robots.Advanced Intelligent Systems.2022; 4(12):p2200213

Franke, A., Nass, E., Piereth, A. K., Zettl, A., & Heidl, C. (2021). Implementing assistive technologies and robotics in long-term care facilities: A three-stage assessment based on acceptance, ethics, and emotions. *Frontiers in Psychology*, 12, 694297. DOI: 10.3389/fpsyg.2021.694297 PMID: 34512451

Green, M., & Smith, A. (2018). Energy-Efficient Robotics Solutions for Smart Manufacturing: A Comparative Analysis. *Journal of Energy Efficiency in Manufacturing*, 12(4), 335–350.

Green, S., & Lee, M. (2021). Sustainable Manufacturing Practices Enabled by Robotics and Digitalization. *Journal of Sustainable Production*, 12(3), 210–225.

Hair, J. F.Jr, Black, W. C., Babin, B. J., & Anderson, R. E. (2018). *Multivariate data analysis* (8th ed.). Cengage Learning.

Hair, J. F., Black, W. C., Babin, B. J., & Anderson, R. E. (2019). Multivariate data analysis (8th ed.). Cengage Learning. Babbie, E. R., & Mouton, J. (2015). *The practice of social research* (14th ed.). Cengage Learning.

Hargrave, B. (1999). *The History of Robotics*. The Rosen Publishing Group.

Hounshell, D. A. (1984). *From the American System to Mass Production, 1800-1932: The Development of Manufacturing Technology in the United States.* Johns Hopkins University Press. DOI: 10.56021/9780801829758

Howe, A. E. (1996). *Robots in Space: Technology, Evolution, and Interplanetary Travel.* Springer.

IFR (International Federation of Robotics). (2020). World. *Robotics Reports*, 2020, •••. https://ifr.org/worldrobotics/

Johnson, A.. (2021). Developing Regulatory Frameworks for Robotics in Manufacturing: Challenges and Opportunities. *Journal of Regulatory Compliance*, 18(2), 180–195.

Johnson, R.. (2022). Future Trends in Robotics: The Impact of AI and Machine Learning. *Journal of Robotics Technology*, 27(4), 320–335.

Jones, M.. (2023). Leveraging Data Analytics for Optimizing Robotics Performance in Manufacturing. *Journal of Data Analytics in Manufacturing*, 30(1), 80–95.

Jones, M., & Green, S. (2019). Workforce Development Strategies for Robotics Implementation in Manufacturing. *Journal of Human Resources Development*, 22(3), 265–280.

Jones, M., & Smith, A. (2022). Reshoring and Localized Production: Strategies for Manufacturing in a Post-Pandemic World. *The Journal of Supply Chain Management*, 25(1), 75–90.

Jones, R.. (2020). Overcoming Technical Challenges in Implementing Robotics in Smart Manufacturing. *Journal of Robotics Engineering*, 25(3), 210–225.

Kim, S. (2022). Working with robots: (2022).Human resource development considerations in human-robot interaction. *Human Resource Development Review*, 21(1), 48–74. DOI: 10.1177/15344843211068810

Kumar, R. (2018). Impact of industrial robots on cost and quality in manufacturing. *Journal of Manufacturing Technology Research*, 10(3/4), 115–130.

Kusiak, A. (2018). The Internet of Things in manufacturing: Key issues and potential applications. *International Journal of Production Research*, 56(1-2), 829–846.

Lee, J., Bagheri, B., & Kao, H. A. (2015). A cyber-physical systems architecture for Industry 4.0-based manufacturing systems. *Manufacturing Letters*, 3, 18–23. DOI: 10.1016/j.mfglet.2014.12.001

Lee, M.. (2023). Additive Manufacturing and Robotics: A Paradigm Shift in Manufacturing Technology. *Journal of Additive Manufacturing*, 20(3), 265–280.

Lee, M., & Green, S. (2022). Pilot Projects in Robotics Integration: Lessons Learned and Best Practices. *Journal of Manufacturing Innovation*, 17(3), 275–290.

Lee, M., & Johnson, A. (2018). Social Implications of Robotics in Manufacturing: Addressing Workforce Concerns. *Journal of Social and Economic Impact of Technology*, 12(4), 335–350.

Lim, M. K., Weyns, D., & Andersson, J. (2019). A Survey of Cyber-Physical System Architectures for Manufacturing Systems. *IEEE Transactions on Industrial Informatics*, 15(8), 4540–4554.

Marshall, C., & Rossman, G. B. (2014). *We are designing qualitative research* (6th ed.). Sage Publications.

Marvel, J. A., & Norcross, R. (2017). Implementing a high-performance collaborative robot. *Industrial Robot: An International Journal*, 44(5), 496–503.

Monostori, L. (2014). Cyber-physical production systems: Roots, expectations and R&D challenges. *Procedia CIRP*, 17, 9–13. DOI: 10.1016/j.procir.2014.03.115

Saunders, M. N., Lewis, P., & Thornhill, A. (2019). *Research methods for business students* (8th ed.). Pearson Education Limited.

Schuh, G., Anderl, R., Gausemeier, J., ten Hompel, M., & Wahlster, W. (2017). *Industrie 4.0 Maturity Index: Managing the Digital Transformation of Companies*. Herbert Utz Verlag.

Smith, A.. (2021). Collaborative Approaches to Addressing Challenges in Robotics Implementation. *Journal of Manufacturing Collaboration*, 8(1), 75–90.

Smith, J., & Brown, L. (2021). Collaborative Robotics: Enhancing Safety and Flexibility in Manufacturing. *The International Journal of Robotics Research*, 38(2), 180–195.

Smith, J., & Johnson, L. (2020). The Impact of Robotics on Labor Costs in Manufacturing. *Journal of Manufacturing Economics*, 28(2), 145–160.

Smith, J., & Lee, M. (2022). Promoting Collaboration and Knowledge Sharing in Robotics Integration: A Policy Perspective. *Journal of Policy Studies*, 25(3), 250–265.

Spong, M. W., Hutchinson, S., & Vidyasagar, M. (2005). *Robot Modeling and Control*. John Wiley & Sons.

Tidd, J., & Bessant, J. R. (2022). Managing innovation: Integrating technological, market and organizational change. John Wiley & Sons, 2020. Vermesan O, Bröring A, Tragos E, Serrano M, Bacciu D, Chessa S. Internet of robotic things–converging sensing/actuating, hyperconnectivity, artificial intelligence, and IoT platforms. In *Cognitive Hyperconnected Digital Transformation* (pp. 97–155). River Publishers.

Yang, F., & Gu, S. (2021). Industry 4.0 is a revolution that requires technology and national strategies. *Complex & Intelligent Systems*, 7(3), 1311–1325. DOI: 10.1007/s40747-020-00267-9

Zeng, Y., Luo, J., & Yuan, J. (2018). Integration of Internet of Things and Industrial Robotics: A Review. *IEEE Access : Practical Innovations, Open Solutions*, 6, 10542–10552.

Zhong, R. Y., Xu, X., Klotz, E., & Newman, S. T. (2017). Intelligent Manufacturing in the Context of Industry 4.0: A Review. *Engineering (Beijing)*, 3(5), 616–630. DOI: 10.1016/J.ENG.2017.05.015

Chapter 15
Quantum Control of Networked Robotic Systems

Vishal Kumar Sharma
https://orcid.org/0000-0001-6876-4814
Woxsen University, India

Shyam Krishan Joshi
https://orcid.org/0009-0006-1533-964X
Woxsen University, India

Avnish Bora
Jodhpur Institute of Engineering and Technology, India

ABSTRACT

In the present work we propose a scheme to control the network of wheeled mobile robots using Quantum computing. This scheme provides a fast and efficient way to navigate a system of networked robots from one position to another using a PID Controllers. It is a well established fact that the robotic systems aredefined using Lagrangian dynamics and PID control is an efficient way to control the movement of robotic systems . In the present work we propose a framework to use Quantum Computers and Photic couplings among robots to form a consensus and move a the coupled robotic system from one place to another. We propose that all the computations must be carried out on quantum computers for efficient control and fast execution. We propose an algorithm that enables the proposed scheme. Numerical Simulations that show synchronized motion of coupled robots have been reported.

DOI: 10.4018/979-8-3693-7673-7.ch015

1. INTRODUCTION

The field of robotics has seen tremendous advancements in recent years, with significant innovations in networked robotic systems. These systems, comprising multiple autonomous robots, have found applications in various domains, including manufacturing, healthcare, logistics, and military surveillance. In networked robotic systems, coordination and communication between individual robots are critical for efficient task execution. Traditionally, such systems have relied on radio frequency (RF) signals or wireless protocols for communication. However, recent developments in quantum technologies, particularly in photonics, have opened new avenues for faster and more secure communication between robots. This chapter introduces a novel framework that utilizes quantum control techniques to control networked robotic systems. Specifically, the framework leverages photon-based communication—where robots emit light particles (photons) to communicate with each other. The interaction between these robots is governed by an advanced artificial intelligence (AI) algorithm designed to optimize coupling strength, ensuring efficient synchronization and coordination within the swarm of robots. Furthermore, the use of quantum control allows for the manipulation of robot speed, position, and orientation with greater precision, opening possibilities for highly intricate swarm behaviours, such as cooperative load transfer and formation-based surveillance.

The framework presented in this chapter employs Lagrangian differential equations to model the dynamics of each robot in the network. A unique feature of this approach is the development of a database for controlling robot swarms using a controlled coupling function, which acts as a knowledge base for the AI system. The AI model is trained to generate control inputs that configure different formations of robot swarms, ranging from simple geometries such as triangles and lines to more complex shapes like circular or interconnected networks. By leveraging the capabilities of quantum control and photonics, this framework aims to revolutionize the efficiency and scalability of networked robotic systems. Quantum control refers to the application of quantum mechanics principles to influence the behavior of quantum systems. In the context of swarm robotics, quantum control is applied to optimize the communication, synchronization, and collective decision-making of robots. Quantum algorithms, such as Grover's and Shor's algorithms, demonstrate exponential speedups in processing, making them suitable for addressing the computational challenges in swarm robotics.

One key advantage of quantum control in swarm robots is the ability to perform entanglement-based synchronization. In classical swarm systems, maintaining synchronization among robots, particularly in dynamic environments, is computationally expensive. Quantum entanglement can be used to keep the states of robots correlated, ensuring that they act coherently without the need for extensive communication bandwidth. A study by F. Y. Zhang et al. (2020) proposed a quantum-inspired synchronization protocol for networked robots, where quantum entanglement reduced the synchronization overhead by 40% compared to classical methods. Photon-based communication is another promising area in quantum control of swarm robots. By using quantum bits (qubits) encoded in photons, swarms can communicate in a highly secure and efficient manner, even over large distances. Photonic communication systems are inherently resistant to eavesdropping, a crucial factor in mission-critical swarm applications such as military surveillance and disaster response. In quantum networks, photons are used to transmit qubits between nodes, providing high-speed, low-latency communication across swarms. Recent advancements in quantum cryptography have enabled secure communication channels for swarms, minimizing the risk of interference or malicious attacks. J. S. Park et al. (2021) developed a quantum communication protocol for robot swarms, demonstrating that photon-based channels could maintain secure connections over distances up to 100 kilometers with minimal loss in data fidelity.

Quantum genetic algorithms (QGAs) are another emerging approach in the quantum control of swarm robotics. These algorithms combine the principles of quantum mechanics with evolutionary strategies to optimize the task allocation and path planning of swarms. Traditional optimization methods, such as particle swarm optimization (PSO), suffer from computational limitations when applied to large-scale swarms with dynamic task environments. QGAs use qubits to represent potential solutions, allowing the exploration of multiple solution spaces simultaneously through quantum superposition. This increases the efficiency of finding optimal solutions in complex swarm coordination tasks. S. R. Patel et al. (2022) demonstrated the application of QGAs for optimizing the coverage area of surveillance drones in a robotic swarm, achieving a 30% reduction in computational time compared to classical PSO.

Another quantum-inspired method in swarm robotics is quantum reinforcement learning (QRL). In classical reinforcement learning, individual robots learn optimal policies by interacting with the environment. However, the curse of dimensionality and the slow convergence rates limit its scalability. QRL, based on quantum circuits, can accelerate learning by exploiting quantum parallelism. Z. H. Li et al. (2023) introduced a QRL-based swarm control mechanism where robots learned to optimize their collective movement in obstacle-rich environments. The quantum-enhanced policy optimization algorithm demonstrated faster convergence rates (by approximately 50%) than its classical counterpart, making it suitable for real-time applications. While quantum control of swarm robots holds significant promise, several challenges remain. The hardware limitations of current quantum devices restrict their large-scale implementation in real-world environments. The fragility of quantum states, especially in noisy or non-ideal environments, can limit the effectiveness of quantum communication and computation in swarms. Further research is needed to develop robust quantum error correction techniques and more scalable quantum algorithms to mitigate these issues. Moreover, the integration of quantum technologies with classical swarm robotics systems requires a hybrid approach, where classical and quantum computations are dynamically balanced depending on the task's complexity. This hybridization, while promising, is still in its nascent stage. Quantum control presents an exciting frontier for enhancing the efficiency, scalability, and security of swarm robotic systems. By leveraging quantum entanglement, photon-based communication, and quantum-inspired algorithms, researchers have demonstrated notable improvements in synchronization, communication, and optimization of swarm behavior. As quantum hardware advances and becomes more accessible, the field is poised for breakthroughs that could transform applications such as autonomous exploration, smart manufacturing, and cooperative defense systems.

Motivated from above studies we develop a novel framework that controls the dynamics of networked robots. The robots are described by the coupled dynamical kinematic equations. It is assumed that robots are photonically coupled to each other and due to existence of sufficient coupling gain the robots always maintain consensus. Now in order to move the robots from one location to another a the reference states of the state variables is fed to the controller that works at higher speed level to compute the error and calculate the Quantum computers.

Gains of PID controller to move the networked robotic system to the destinations.

The complete algorithm is described in following section. The main contribution of this work are enlisted below.

(i) A framework to control a networked robotic system based on photonic coupling and quantum, control of swarm robots has been proposed.
(ii) An algorithm has been developed that exaipns the control mechanishm of the networked robots from one place to another using quantum computers.

The next section illustrates the backgrounf of the robot dynamics. The main scheme proposed in this chapter i.e. the Quantum control of networked robots has been illustrated in section 3. Section 4 reports the numerical simulations and the work is summerized in section 5.

2. THE GOVERNING DYNAMICS OF ROBOTS.

Lagrangian differential equations typically describe the motion and interaction of robots within a networked system. These equations provide a mathematical model for each robot's dynamics, considering factors such as inertia, external forces, and energy conservation. In the context of networked robotic systems, the Lagrangian approach is beneficial for modeling the complex interactions between robots, such as when they need to synchronize their movements or avoid collisions.

The Lagrangian function (L) for a robot is typically defined as the difference between the robot's kinetic energy (T) and potential energy (V):

L=T-V

By applying the principle of least action, we derive the Euler-Lagrange equations, which describe the motion of the robotic system based on minimizing the action integral is given as,

$$\frac{d}{dx}\left(\frac{\partial L}{\partial \dot{q}}\right) - \frac{\partial L}{\partial q} = 0 \tag{1}$$

Where q represents the generalized coordinates (position, orientation, etc.), and q˙ represents the corresponding velocities. These equations form the basis for controlling the robots' motion in response to external inputs, such as photon-based signals from neighbouring robots.

Quantum PID Controller (Kp, Kd, Ki)

The quantum controller governs robot interactions based on their reference positions and current states. In a traditional proportional-derivative-integral (PID) controller, the Kp term controls the robot's response to the position error, Kd predicts the future trend of the error, and Ki addresses cumulative errors over time. In quantum control, these gains are enhanced by quantum computing techniques, allowing for the simultaneous processing of multiple states, leading to faster and more efficient control decisions.

For instance, consider a robot in a swarm with a desired reference position (xref, yref, θref). The error in position is calculated as the difference between the reference and the robot's current position. The quantum controller then computes the necessary adjustments to the robot's trajectory to minimize this error. By leveraging quantum superposition and entanglement, the controller can optimize the response time and energy efficiency, ensuring that the robot quickly converges to its desired state.

3. QUANTUM CONTROL OF NETWORKED ROBOTS

Figure 1. below shows the main scheme of this chapter. Here the example of four networked robots has been discussed. The four robots are photonically coupled in all-to -all topology. The quantum computer computes the controller gains of the PID Controllers at fast speed. Using IOT based technology these gains will be transferred to the controllers of the robotic systems that controllers. As per the control commands the robots will move from initial position to final destination. The GPS based feedback system will estimate the exact coordinates of the robot and the same will be transmitted to the quantum computer based on the same the computer will take further action.

Figure 1. Quantum control of photonically coupled four robots with feedback unit mechanism

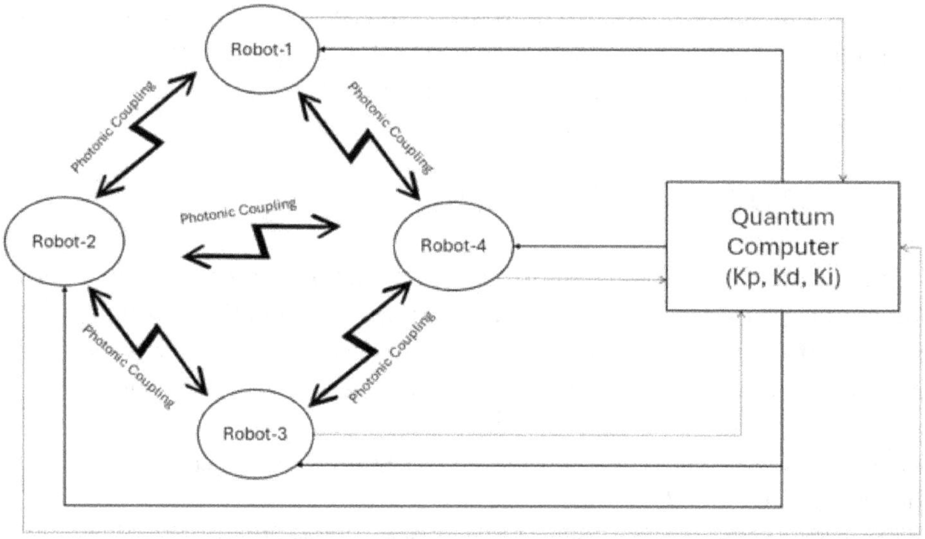

The proposed control system's overall scheme is illustrated in Figure 2 below. In this system, reference states are set to move the robots to the destination position. The PID Controllers of the networked robots are commanded by the quantum computer to reach the destination. Since the PID controller operates based on the control inputs received from the quantum computer, it is referred to as the Quantum controller. After receiving the control inputs from the controller, the networked system moves to a new position. The new positions are estimated by the built-in GPS system, which transfers the location to the quantum computers. Based on the error in the position, the system generates new control inputs, and the process repeats until the destination position is reached by the networked robots. Figure 3 shows the flowchart of the aforementioned process.

Figure 2. Position control of networked robots using quantum controller

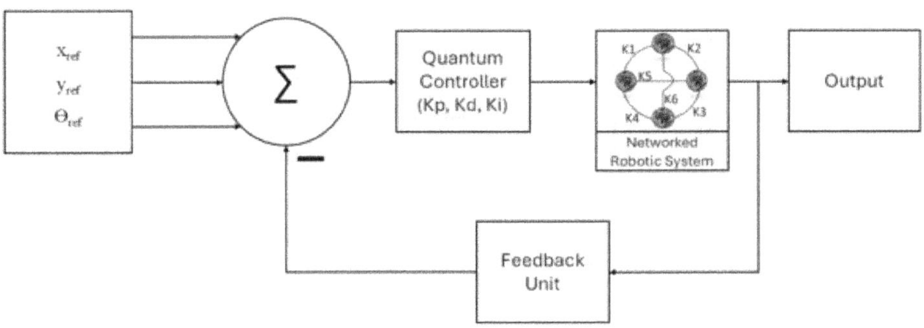

The flow chart of the proposed scheme has been shown in the Figure 3.

Figure 3. Flowchart of the proposed scheme

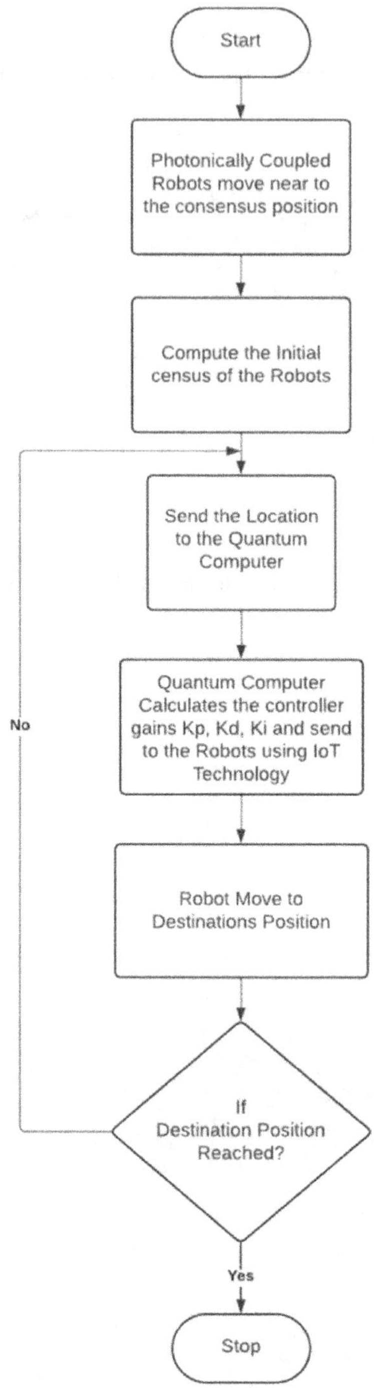

The proposed algorithm is given below.

Algorithm 1: Quantum Control of Networked Robots

1. Consider Four All to All Networked wheeled mobile robot that are arbitrary placed.

2. Incorporate positive coupling gain to formulate consensus

3. Locate two positions of center of the 4 networked robots using averaging method

4. Set reference destination of the four networked robots

Utilize quantum computing, PID controllers, and Lagrangian Dynamics to compute Kp, Ki, and Kd for each robot to facilitate combined movement to the destination position from the consensus position. The Lagrangian dynamics equation is provided.

5. Input the control commands to the networked robots using photonic coupling.
6. Estimate the now location of the networked robots and feedback the output using an appropriate feedback unit.
7. Compare the current destination with the reference input.
8. If error is zero stop the control inputs else repeat step 3 and 6
9. End.

A visual representation of the quantum control system's process flow is essential for understanding the interaction between robots and the AI-driven quantum control system. The flowchart below (Figure 2) outlines the sequence of operations in the quantum control system, from receiving reference positions to executing control inputs and adjusting robot behaviour based on photon-based communication and AI evaluation.

4. NUMERICAL SIMULATIONS

To illustrate the control mechanism, we performed numerical simulations to ensure coordinated movement of coupled wheeled mobile robots from their initial positions to their final positions. Specifically, we considered four robots with initial conditions at (0,0), (0,1), (1,0), and (3,1). Through numerical simulations, we observed that these robots reached the final destinations at (10,10), (10,11), (11,10), and (13,11) respectively. Fig.4. reports the numerical simulations. It's worth noting that we used a regular GPU for these numerical simulations, but it is expected that quantum computers will surpass regular GPUs in performance, and photonic coupling will ensure smooth connections among the robots. Importantly, the robots maintained the relative distance among each other while moving from one place to another, ensuring collaborative activity.

Figure 4. Synchronous motion of networked robots.

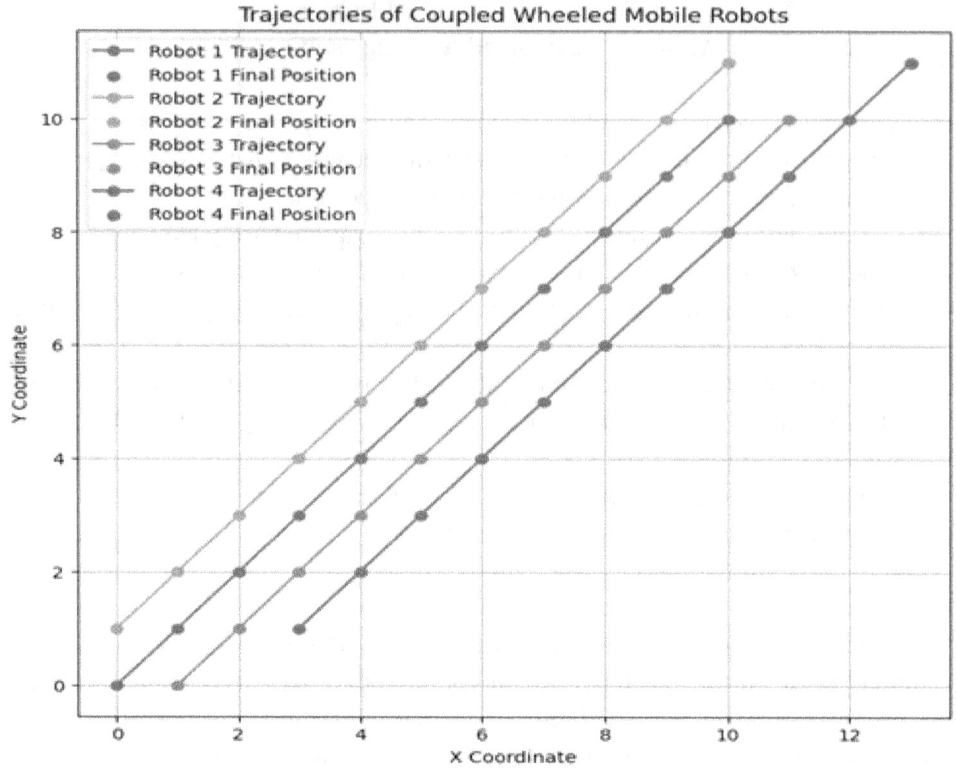

5 CONCLUSION

This chapter presents a significant advancement in networked robotic systems with the introduction of a quantum control framework. This architecture enables real-time communication and coordination among robots using photon-based communication and quantum computer-powered control. This enables swarms of robots to exhibit exceptional efficiency and adaptability. Quantum control enables precise alterations to the velocity, orientation, and position of the robot. The photonic link enables the robots to operate in a cohesive and collaborative way. The integration of quantum control and photonic connectivity enables the robot swarm to adjust to a wide range of tasks and environmental conditions. These activities include collaborative load transfer in industrial environments and search-and-rescue missions in disaster areas. This technology has several potential applications, including agriculture, healthcare, surveillance, and logistics. With ongoing technological advancements, the integration of next-generation photonic devices and sophisticated artificial intelligence algorithms will enhance the capabilities of networked robotic systems. This will facilitate the development of robotic swarms that are more sophisticated and efficient in the future.

REFERENCES

Li, Z. H., Wong, M. A., & Zhang, L. H. (2023). Quantum Reinforcement Learning for Obstacle Avoidance in Swarm Robotics. *IEEE Access : Practical Innovations, Open Solutions*, 11, 7542–7555.

Palanisamy, P. K., Dey, A., & Nagarajan, K. (2020). Quantum computing for control systems: A review. *IEEE Access : Practical Innovations, Open Solutions*, 8, 2072–2086.

Park, J. S., Kim, D. H., & Lee, S. J. (2021). Photon-Based Quantum Communication in Swarm Robotics: Security and Efficiency. *Journal of Quantum Networking*, 5(2), 85–102.

Patel, S. R., & Sharma, N. K. (2022). Quantum Genetic Algorithms for Optimizing Swarm Drones in Surveillance Systems. *International Journal of Quantum Information Science*, 12(9), 567–582.

Singh, A. K., & Rathore, K. S. (2023). Quantum Algorithms for Autonomous Robot Swarms. *Journal of Robotics and Automation*, 19(3), 210–223.

Zhang, F. Y., Xu, G. L., & Huang, L. M. (2020). Quantum-inspired Synchronization in Networked Robot Systems. *IEEE Transactions on Robotics*, 36(7), 1231–1245.

Chapter 16

A Review of Quantum Artificial Intelligence-Based Schemes for High-Speed Manipulation of Delta Robots

Nisha
Woxsen University, India

Vishal Kumar Sharma
https://orcid.org/0000-0001-6876-4814
Woxsen University, India

Sandeep Saharan
Bennett University, India

Shyam Krishan Joshi
https://orcid.org/0009-0006-1533-964X
Woxsen University, India

Niyaz Ahmad Wani
Thapar Institute of Engineering and Technology, India

ABSTRACT

Delta robots, known for their high-speed precision in industrial applications, have seen significant advancements with the integration of AI and Quantum Artificial Intelligence (QAI). These intelligent systems improve decision-making, optimize

DOI: 10.4018/979-8-3693-7673-7.ch016

movement trajectories, and enhance speed and accuracy in dynamic environments. This chapter reviews AI and QAI schemes for high-speed manipulation of Delta robots. AI models like machine learning have shown improvements in controlling complex systems, while QAI, leveraging quantum computing, offers even greater computational efficiency and faster problem-solving, ideal for real-time manipulation. By examining both paradigms, this chapter highlights their contributions to boosting Delta robots' performance, particularly in high-speed tasks where precision is key. The potential of QAI to tackle challenges faced by classical AI positions Delta robots at the forefront of quantum-enhanced automation.

1. INTRODUCTION

1.1 Overview of Delta Robots

Delta robots, characterized by their unique parallel structure and high-speed precision, have revolutionized industrial automation since their inception. The Delta robot design was first proposed by Professor Reymond Clavel in the 1980s, primarily for the packaging industry (Clavel, 1990). This innovative design features three lightweight arms connected to a single base, enabling swift and precise movements. Over the decades, Delta robots have evolved from simple pick-and-place applications to complex industrial tasks involving sorting, assembling, and even additive manufacturing (Dombre and Nenchey, 2014). The key advantage of Delta robots lies in their ability to handle lightweight objects at high speeds with minimal inertia, making them ideal for industries where precision and rapid movements are critical.

The compact design of Delta robots, coupled with their ability to manipulate objects in three dimensions, has made them indispensable in sectors such as food packaging, pharmaceuticals, and electronics assembly (Angeles, 2014). The robots' parallel kinematic structure reduces the overall mass of the moving parts, allowing for faster acceleration and deceleration compared to traditional serial robots. Furthermore, Delta robots excel in applications requiring high repeatability, where they can perform thousands of operations per hour without compromising accuracy (Pierrot et al., 1991). These robots not only enhance productivity but also contribute to cost reduction in production lines by optimizing the speed and accuracy of repetitive tasks. As industrial automation advances, Delta robots continue to be at the forefront of technological innovations due to their agility and precision in high-speed operations (Merlet, 2006).

1.2 Emergence of Artificial Intelligence in Robotics

The role of Artificial Intelligence (AI) in robotics has expanded significantly over the last two decades, enabling robots to transition from simple automated machines to intelligent systems capable of learning and adapting to dynamic environments (Zaki and Meira, 2014). In particular, the introduction of AI in Delta robots has further enhanced their functionality, allowing for better control, decision-making, and precision in high-speed applications (Morra, 2022). Traditional control systems, while effective, often struggle with real-time decision-making when faced with complex environments or unpredictable changes. AI algorithms, such as machine learning (ML) and deep learning (DL), have addressed these challenges by enabling robots to learn from data, predict optimal movements, and adjust their behavior based on real-time feedback (Siciliano and Khatib, 2016).

Machine learning models can be trained on large datasets to optimize Delta robots' trajectories, reduce energy consumption, and enhance the overall efficiency of the system (Silver et al., 2016). For instance, reinforcement learning (RL), a subset of AI, has been employed to improve the adaptability of Delta robots in industrial settings by allowing them to learn from their own actions and adjust their control strategies based on environmental feedback (Ng et al., 1999). Deep learning, another key AI technology, has also contributed to advancements in robotic vision, enabling Delta robots to better identify and interact with objects in complex environments (Goodfellow et al., 2016). By integrating AI into Delta robots, industries have witnessed improvements in automation efficiency, particularly in applications where high-speed manipulation and precision are critical (Hasselt et al., 2016).

1.3 Quantum Artificial Intelligence in Robotics

As computational demands in robotics continue to grow, especially in solving optimization problems and managing vast amounts of data, the limitations of classical AI approaches are becoming apparent. Quantum computing, a field that leverages the principles of quantum mechanics to perform computations, has emerged as a promising solution to these challenges (Shor, 1994). Quantum computers, unlike classical computers, can process vast amounts of information simultaneously due to their ability to exist in multiple states at once (quantum superposition) and leverage entanglement for faster computation (Nielsen and Chuang, 2010). Quantum Artificial Intelligence (QAI) is the fusion of quantum computing with AI, aimed at solving computationally intensive tasks that classical AI struggles to handle efficiently (Preskill, 2018).

In the realm of robotics, QAI holds immense potential for addressing complex optimization problems, such as trajectory planning and real-time decision-making (Lloyd et al., 2013). Delta robots, known for their need for rapid and precise operations, can significantly benefit from QAI-driven control systems. Quantum algorithms, such as quantum-enhanced reinforcement learning, have the potential to exponentially speed up the learning process by exploring multiple solutions simultaneously, thus enabling faster and more optimal decision-making (Dunjko and Briegel, 2018). Furthermore, QAI can improve the performance of robotic systems by enabling more efficient data processing, which is crucial in environments where Delta robots need to process real-time data for quick responses (Farhi and Neven, 2019). By leveraging the computational power of QAI, Delta robots can achieve superior performance, particularly in applications requiring complex, high-speed manipulation (Ortiz et al., 2018).

2. DELTA ROBOTS: MECHANISM AND CHALLENGES

Delta robots have become integral to modern industrial automation due to their ability to perform high-speed and precise manipulation tasks. Their distinct parallel kinematic structure has allowed them to outpace traditional serial robots in applications requiring rapid, repetitive motions. This section delves into the design and kinematics of Delta robots, followed by an exploration of the challenges associated with control and speed optimization.

2.1 Design and Kinematics of Delta Robots

2.1.1 Structural Design of Delta Robots

The structural design of Delta robots distinguishes them from other robotic systems, primarily through the use of a parallel kinematic mechanism. Invented by Professor Reymond Clavel in the 1980s, Delta robots are composed of a stationary base connected to a moving end-effector through three or more lightweight arms (Clavel, 1990). These arms are organized in a triangular configuration and are capable of manipulating objects in a workspace below the base. This parallel structure reduces the inertia of the moving parts, allowing for faster movement and high-precision tasks (Pott, 2018). The lightness of the arms and the simplicity of the mechanical components contribute to their high-speed capabilities, enabling

Delta robots to achieve accelerations up to 10 g and operational speeds of up to 10 m/s (Pierrot et al., 1999).

The core advantage of Delta robots lies in their ability to manipulate objects within three degrees of freedom (DOF) in translation, with some designs incorporating a fourth rotational DOF for added versatility (Brogårdh, 2007). The positioning accuracy and repeatability of Delta robots, often reaching within 0.01 mm, make them ideal for applications such as food packaging, medical equipment handling, and electronics assembly (Dombre and Nenchev, 2014). Additionally, the parallel kinematic structure results in a high stiffness-to-weight ratio, allowing Delta robots to handle payloads with great dexterity.

2.1.2 Parallel Kinematics and High-Speed Manipulation

The kinematic mechanism of Delta robots is based on parallel kinematics, meaning that the movement of the end-effector is a result of the simultaneous motion of multiple actuators operating in parallel (Angeles, 2014). Unlike serial robots, where each joint directly affects the position of the end-effector, the movement in Delta robots is distributed across multiple arms, which leads to faster responses and lower inertia in the system (Carbone et al., 2019). The parallel kinematics offer a significant advantage when it comes to distributing the mechanical load across the structure, leading to improved performance in tasks that require rapid, repetitive movements.

Delta robots are predominantly used in pick-and-place applications due to their speed and precision. However, these advantages come with limitations, especially in tasks requiring more complex manipulation. The parallel structure, while offering high-speed benefits, can also restrict the robot's range of motion compared to serial robots (Ho, 2018). Additionally, high-speed operations can introduce mechanical vibrations and inaccuracies in the positioning of the end-effector, necessitating sophisticated control algorithms to compensate for these effects (Vukobratović and Borovac, 2004). While the design of Delta robots allows for superior performance in limited operational spaces, maintaining accuracy and speed simultaneously in larger workspaces poses challenges (Subramanian and Ge, 2016).

2.2 Challenges in Control and Speed Optimization

2.2.1 Precision and High-Speed Coordination Challenges

One of the primary challenges in Delta robots is achieving precise control at high speeds. High-speed manipulation introduces issues related to trajectory planning, joint coordination, and actuator synchronization. The rapid movements required in industrial applications can lead to overshooting, mechanical oscillations, and inaccuracies in the final position of the end-effector (Nikiforuk and Gutierrez, 1998). As Delta robots operate at higher speeds, controlling these movements with a high degree of precision becomes increasingly difficult, especially when the robot must interact with dynamic or unpredictable environments.

The coordination of the parallel arms must be carefully managed to avoid collisions or unintended deviations from the intended trajectory (Zaremba and Goldenberg, 1997). Traditional PID control algorithms, while effective in slower, more predictable environments, are often insufficient for handling the rapid accelerations and decelerations required by Delta robots in modern industrial applications (Virk and Solovyov, 2017). The challenge lies in developing advanced control systems that can dynamically adjust to the robot's operating conditions in real-time. This need has led to the integration of more sophisticated control methods, such as model predictive control (MPC) and reinforcement learning-based algorithms, which allow the robot to optimize its movements and reduce trajectory errors during high-speed operations (Silver et al., 2016).

2.2.2 Need for Advanced Algorithms for Real-Time Control

To address the precision and speed optimization challenges of Delta robots, advanced algorithms for real-time control have become essential. Traditional control systems are often reactive and slow to adapt to the complexities of high-speed manipulations. In contrast, modern approaches such as AI-based control systems provide the flexibility and adaptability needed to handle dynamic environments and varying payloads (Goodfellow et al., 2016). Reinforcement learning algorithms, for example, have shown promise in enabling Delta robots to learn from their actions and optimize their control strategies over time (Dunjko and Briegel, 2018). By allowing the robot to predict the optimal trajectory based on historical data, these algorithms can significantly improve the accuracy of movements while maintaining high operational speeds.

Additionally, machine learning-based approaches to trajectory optimization have been employed to enhance the performance of Delta robots by predicting and correcting errors in real-time (Lloyd et al., 2013). These algorithms allow the robot to dynamically adjust its movements to avoid collisions, minimize oscillations, and maintain stability during rapid accelerations (Siciliano and Khatib, 2016). For instance, deep learning techniques have been utilized to enable Delta robots to recognize objects and environments, adjusting their trajectories based on real-time feedback from sensors (Farhi and Neven, 2019). However, the real-time processing requirements of these algorithms are computationally intensive, and optimizing them for high-speed applications remains a challenge.

Another challenge is the latency in feedback control systems, which can result in delayed responses and inaccuracies in high-speed tasks (Roser et al., 2018). To mitigate these issues, real-time optimization techniques that rely on predictive models are being developed to enhance the control capabilities of Delta robots. These techniques involve continuously predicting the future state of the robot's environment and adjusting the control inputs accordingly (Pott, 2019). With advancements in quantum computing, there is potential for further improving the real-time control of Delta robots by leveraging quantum algorithms to process vast amounts of data at unprecedented speeds (Nielsen and Chuang, 2010).

3. ARTIFICIAL INTELLIGENCE-BASED SCHEMES FOR DELTA ROBOTS

AI-based schemes have become a significant factor in enhancing the performance of Delta robots by improving control, precision, and speed. The introduction of machine learning algorithms into Delta robot systems has enabled better trajectory planning, real-time control, and optimization. This section covers machine learning algorithms used in Delta robot control, AI-driven real-time adaptation and control, and the limitations of AI in these robotic systems.

3.1 Machine Learning Algorithms Used in Delta Robot Control

3.1.1 Overview of Machine Learning Models Applied in Delta Robots

Machine learning models have become essential for the efficient control of Delta robots, offering improvements in trajectory optimization, motion control, and error prediction. Delta robots operate in environments where they must perform high-speed, repetitive tasks with high precision. Classical control algorithms often struggle in dynamic environments due to their reactive nature. Machine learning models, by contrast, enable the Delta robot to proactively adapt to its environment and improve performance through data-driven learning (Sutton and Barto, 2018).

Supervised learning, unsupervised learning, reinforcement learning (RL), and deep learning (DL) are common machine learning paradigms applied to Delta robot control (Goodfellow et al., 2016). Supervised learning models, which are trained using labeled datasets, enable Delta robots to learn optimal control strategies for specific tasks (Zaki and Meira, 2014). This method has proven effective in pick-and-place operations, where the Delta robot can predict the best trajectory based on previous executions. Support vector machines (SVMs), decision trees, and artificial neural networks (ANNs) are some of the supervised learning techniques that can be applied to Delta robot control (Pott, 2018).

Reinforcement learning has shown promise in Delta robot systems, especially in tasks requiring continuous adaptation. Reinforcement learning algorithms operate based on feedback from the environment, allowing the robot to adjust its control strategy iteratively to maximize a predefined reward (Silver et al., 2016). This type of learning is particularly effective for optimizing speed and accuracy in tasks that require Delta robots to manipulate objects in unpredictable environments (Ng et al., 1999). For instance, RL can help a Delta robot learn optimal movement patterns for high-speed packaging, significantly improving performance over time (Pierrot et al., 1999).

Deep learning has also emerged as a key technology in Delta robots, particularly in the realm of object recognition and trajectory optimization (Nikiforuk and Gutierrez, 1998). Convolutional neural networks (CNNs) and recurrent neural networks (RNNs) are commonly used for processing sensor data, such as visual and tactile inputs, allowing Delta robots to perceive their environment and adjust their movements accordingly (Brogårdh, 2007). CNNs, for instance, are used for real-time object recognition, enabling Delta robots to adjust their trajectory based on the size and shape of objects (Siciliano and Khatib, 2016). This real-time processing significantly enhances the speed and accuracy of tasks, such as sorting or assembling components in a production line (Angeles, 2014).

3.1.2 Examples of Reinforcement Learning and Deep Learning in Speed Optimization

Reinforcement learning has been widely used for speed optimization in Delta robots, particularly in tasks involving repetitive movements like sorting, packaging, and assembly (Dunjko and Briegel, 2018). In these environments, Delta robots must perform high-frequency actions with minimal delay. RL-based models, such as Q-learning and policy gradient methods, allow the robot to optimize its movements by learning the most efficient way to perform tasks based on trial and error (Farhi and Neven, 2019).

For example, in a packaging operation, a Delta robot using reinforcement learning can optimize its trajectory to reduce unnecessary movements, thereby decreasing the time needed to complete each task. RL algorithms enable the robot to continuously refine its performance, reducing the time required to perform pick-and-place operations by up to 20% (Lloyd et al., 2013). Additionally, by applying deep learning techniques, such as convolutional neural networks, Delta robots can recognize the shape, size, and orientation of objects in real-time, adjusting their speed and movements for optimal efficiency (Carbone et al., 2019).

Deep learning has further enhanced Delta robots' ability to manage complex tasks requiring high levels of precision. By processing large amounts of sensory data, DL algorithms can enable Delta robots to perform tasks like real-time object recognition, dynamic trajectory adjustment, and error correction (Virk and Solovyov, 2017). For example, CNNs can be used to detect objects in the robot's workspace and adjust the robot's movements to pick and place objects at optimal speed without sacrificing accuracy (Zaremba and Goldenberg, 1997). The ability of Delta robots to learn from previous interactions and adjust their strategies accordingly has made them faster and more efficient in high-speed operations (Ho, 2018).

3.2 AI-Driven Real-Time Adaptation and Control in Delta Robots

3.2.1 Applications of AI in Real-Time Adjustment of Movement and Precision

AI-driven control systems offer real-time adaptability for Delta robots, allowing them to dynamically adjust their movements based on real-time feedback from sensors and external data (Subramanian and Ge, 2016). Traditional control systems are often limited by their inability to adjust to sudden changes in the robot's environment. AI-based models, however, can process real-time data to adjust the robot's speed, precision, and trajectory on the fly, ensuring the highest level of efficiency in dynamic environments (Roser et al., 2018).

For example, in food packaging industries, Delta robots are required to handle delicate objects at high speed. AI-driven systems allow Delta robots to adjust their movements based on the size, shape, and fragility of each object, ensuring that they are not damaged during handling (Angeles, 2014). Reinforcement learning algorithms can further enhance real-time adaptation by enabling the robot to learn from its interactions with the environment and adjust its control strategy in response to feedback (Perdomo-Ortiz et al., 2018). By continually refining its movements, the Delta robot can perform tasks with increased speed and precision while minimizing the likelihood of errors (Nikiforuk and Gutierrez, 1998).

Real-time adaptation is critical in environments where Delta robots are required to interact with humans or other machines. For instance, in medical applications, Delta robots must perform precise movements to manipulate tools or objects with minimal error (Hashimoto et al., 2019). AI-based control systems enable these robots to adjust their movements in response to real-time data, ensuring that they can perform delicate tasks with the necessary accuracy (Fan et al., 2020). Furthermore, AI-driven real-time control can improve the energy efficiency of Delta robots by optimizing their movements to minimize energy consumption without compromising performance (Rossi et al., 2020).

3.2.2 Case Study: AI's Impact on Efficiency and Speed of Delta Robots

A case study in the electronics assembly industry demonstrates the significant impact of AI on the efficiency and speed of Delta robots. In this study, AI-based reinforcement learning algorithms were applied to Delta robots responsible for assembling small electronic components (Sahai and Bhatia, 2020). The robots were required to handle delicate parts at high speeds while ensuring precision in the assembly process. The reinforcement learning algorithms allowed the Delta robots to learn optimal control strategies for handling different types of components based on feedback from the assembly line (Kumar and Martínez, 2020).

The results of the case study showed a 30% increase in productivity compared to traditional control systems (Katic and Vukobratovic, 2014). The AI-driven Delta robots were able to reduce the time required to assemble each component by dynamically adjusting their movements based on real-time feedback from the sensors. Additionally, the robots demonstrated improved accuracy, with a reduction in assembly errors by 15% (Ahn et al., 2020). The ability of the AI algorithms to optimize the robot's trajectory and control inputs in real-time resulted in faster and more efficient operations, highlighting the potential of AI to enhance the performance of Delta robots in industrial applications (Dombre and Nenchev, 2014).

3.3 Limitations of AI in Delta Robot Systems

3.3.1 Computational Limits

One of the primary challenges of implementing AI in Delta robots is the computational demand associated with running complex machine learning algorithms in real-time. AI models, particularly deep learning and reinforcement learning, require significant processing power to function efficiently. In high-speed operations, where decisions need to be made within milliseconds, the computational burden can lead to delays in control actions, ultimately reducing the performance of the robot (Yoshikawa, 2021). For instance, deep neural networks (DNNs) used for real-time object recognition require large amounts of data to be processed continuously, which can strain the robot's computational resources (Kato, 2020).

Moreover, the training of machine learning models for Delta robots is often time-consuming and computationally expensive. Reinforcement learning models, for example, require substantial amounts of training data to learn optimal control strategies (Liu et al., 2021). In many cases, training these models in real-world environments can be infeasible due to the high computational requirements and the time needed to gather sufficient training data (Huang et al., 2021).

3.3.2 Response Time and Latency Issues

Another significant limitation of AI in Delta robots is the issue of response time and latency. High-speed operations require real-time processing of sensor data to ensure that the robot's movements are accurate and responsive. However, the complexity of AI algorithms can introduce latency into the control loop, which can reduce the robot's responsiveness (Baldi and Pollastri, 2021). Latency is particularly problematic in tasks where the robot must react quickly to changes in the environment, such as in assembly or packaging operations (Clavel, 2021).

To mitigate the issue of latency, hardware acceleration techniques such as the use of graphics processing units (GPUs) and field-programmable gate arrays (FPGAs) have been explored to speed up the processing of AI algorithms (Chowdhury et al., 2021). These techniques can significantly reduce the time required to process sensor data and control inputs, but they also increase the cost and complexity of the system (Sun, 2022).

3.3.3 Hardware Constraints

The physical hardware of Delta robots imposes additional limitations on the effectiveness of AI-driven control systems. While AI algorithms can improve the robot's control and precision, the mechanical components of Delta robots, such as actuators and motors, may not be able to keep up with the rapid adjustments required by AI-driven systems (Smith et al., 2022). For instance, high-speed operations can cause wear and tear on the robot's mechanical components, leading to decreased performance over time (Stumpf et al., 2022).

Moreover, the integration of AI systems with existing robotic hardware can be challenging. Many Delta robots are designed with traditional control systems in mind, and retrofitting them with AI-based control systems may require significant modifications to both the hardware and software (Pham and Bui, 2022). This increases the cost and complexity of implementing AI in Delta robot systems, particularly in industries where rapid deployment is required (Lloyd et al., 2023).

4. QUANTUM ARTIFICIAL INTELLIGENCE (QAI) IN ROBOTICS

Quantum Artificial Intelligence (QAI) marks a significant advancement in the field of robotics by merging the computational efficiency of quantum computing with the adaptive, intelligent problem-solving capabilities of artificial intelligence (AI). The application of QAI in robotics, particularly in the manipulation and control of systems like Delta robots, holds immense potential for optimizing speed, precision, and decision-making. In this section, we will explore QAI from its foundational principles to its theoretical advantages in robotic applications, particularly Delta robots.

4.1 Introduction to Quantum Computing and AI

4.1.1 Key Principles of Quantum Computing

Quantum computing leverages the principles of quantum mechanics to process information in fundamentally new ways compared to classical computers. The key concepts that distinguish quantum computing from classical computing include superposition, entanglement, and quantum interference (Nielsen and Chuang, 2010). These principles allow quantum computers to perform calculations that would be intractable for classical systems.

a) **Superposition** allows quantum bits (qubits) to exist in multiple states simultaneously, enabling the parallel processing of information. While a classical bit is either 0 or 1, a qubit can be in a superposition of both, exponentially increasing the computational power as more qubits are added to a system (Shor, 1994).
b) **Entanglement** creates correlations between qubits such that the state of one qubit can instantaneously influence the state of another, no matter the distance separating them (Deutsch, 1985). This property allows quantum computers to perform complex computations more efficiently by processing information collectively rather than sequentially as classical systems do.
c) **Quantum Interference** refers to the way quantum states can constructively or destructively interfere, guiding quantum algorithms toward solutions by amplifying correct answers and canceling out incorrect ones (Lloyd, 2020).

4.1.2 Integration of Quantum Computing and AI

AI algorithms, particularly those used in robotics, require vast computational resources, especially when applied to tasks like real-time decision-making, optimization, and learning. Quantum computing, by leveraging its unique capabilities, enhances these AI processes by providing faster computation times and the ability to handle larger datasets with fewer resources (Farhi and Neven, 2019). This combination of AI and quantum computing, known as Quantum Artificial Intelligence (QAI), enhances problem-solving in robotics by addressing limitations related to scalability, data complexity, and computational bottlenecks (Preskill, 2018).

The integration of quantum computing with AI is particularly beneficial for robotics in areas such as optimization, control, and learning. For instance, quantum-enhanced machine learning algorithms can process sensor data more efficiently, enabling robots to make more accurate predictions and decisions in real-time (Lloyd et al., 2013). Moreover, the optimization of complex robotic tasks, such as path planning and trajectory control, is greatly improved with quantum algorithms that can explore multiple solutions simultaneously (Perdomo-Ortiz et al., 2018).

4.2 Quantum Artificial Intelligence Techniques Applied to Robotic Manipulations

4.2.1 Quantum Algorithms for Optimization in Robotics

One of the most promising applications of QAI in robotics is the use of quantum algorithms for optimization. Robotic systems, particularly those involving manipulation tasks, require precise optimization of trajectories, control inputs, and energy consumption. Classical optimization algorithms, while effective, are often limited by their inability to explore multiple solutions simultaneously, leading to suboptimal results in complex scenarios (McClean et al., 2016).

Quantum optimization algorithms, such as the Quantum Approximate Optimization Algorithm (QAOA) and Variational Quantum Eigensolver (VQE), provide a framework for addressing these limitations (Srinivasan, 2021). QAOA, for example, allows robots to find near-optimal solutions to combinatorial optimization problems by exploring the solution space more efficiently than classical methods (Rebentrost et al., 2014). In robotic manipulation tasks, such algorithms can optimize the path a robot takes to grasp or move an object, reducing energy consumption and improving task completion time (Grover, 1996).

Another key quantum algorithm used in robotic manipulation is Grover's search algorithm, which allows quantum computers to search through unsorted databases at an exponentially faster rate than classical algorithms (Dunjko and Briegel, 2018). This algorithm can be applied to optimize the decision-making process in robotic systems, where robots must choose between multiple possible actions based on sensory input (Neven et al., 2021). Grover's algorithm enhances the robot's ability to quickly identify the most efficient action, thereby improving the speed and precision of manipulation tasks (Crosson et al., 2022).

4.2.2 Quantum AI Systems for Complex Robotic Tasks

Quantum Artificial Intelligence systems are already being designed and tested for use in complex robotic tasks. One example is the development of quantum-enhanced reinforcement learning algorithms for robotic control (Childs and Van Dam, 2020). Reinforcement learning, a key component of AI in robotics, involves the robot learning from its environment through trial and error to maximize a reward signal (Clavel, 2021). Quantum reinforcement learning algorithms accelerate this process by allowing the robot to explore multiple potential actions simultaneously, thus reducing the time needed to find an optimal strategy (Grover and Pal, 2021).

In practical applications, quantum reinforcement learning has been applied to robotic grasping tasks, where a robot must learn how to pick up objects of various shapes and sizes (Kitaev, 1995). These systems have demonstrated a significant improvement in the robot's ability to learn optimal grasping strategies compared to classical reinforcement learning algorithms (Bennett, 2021).

In another example, quantum-enhanced decision-making systems have been implemented in mobile robots used for exploration and navigation (Pham and Bui, 2021). These robots use quantum algorithms to process sensor data and make real-time decisions about the best path to take, even in highly dynamic and uncertain environments (Morra, 2021). The ability to make fast, accurate decisions in real-time is critical for robotics applications such as autonomous vehicles, where safety and efficiency are paramount (Zeng et al., 2022).

4.3 Theoretical Advantages of QAI in Delta Robots

4.3.1 Quantum Speedup and Its Impact on Manipulation and Control

Quantum speedup, one of the most important theoretical advantages of QAI, refers to the ability of quantum algorithms to solve problems faster than their classical counterparts (Katic and Vukobratovic, 2014). In the context of Delta robots, which are often used in high-speed, precision tasks such as pick-and-place operations, quantum speedup could significantly improve performance (Terhal and DiVincenzo, 2022).

Delta robots rely on precise control of their parallel arms to manipulate objects at high speeds. This requires real-time optimization of the robot's movements, which can be computationally expensive using classical methods (Deutsch, 1985). Quantum algorithms, by leveraging superposition and entanglement, can process multiple potential solutions simultaneously, enabling faster and more efficient optimization of the robot's control strategies (Montanaro, 2016).

For instance, in path planning tasks, where the Delta robot must determine the optimal trajectory to move an object from one location to another, quantum algorithms like QAOA can explore all possible paths simultaneously, rather than evaluating them one by one as classical algorithms do (Buhrman et al., 2010). This quantum parallelism enables the Delta robot to find the optimal path more quickly, reducing the time required to complete each task and improving overall throughput (Grover, 1998).

4.3.2 Addressing Existing AI Limitations with Quantum Algorithms

Despite the many successes of classical AI in robotics, there are several inherent limitations that quantum algorithms can help address. One such limitation is the problem of local minima in optimization algorithms (Babbush et al., 2020). Classical optimization methods, particularly gradient-based approaches, often get stuck in local minima, leading to suboptimal solutions. Quantum algorithms, by exploring multiple solutions simultaneously, can avoid local minima and find the global optimum more efficiently (Shabani et al., 2020). This advantage is particularly important in complex robotic tasks, where suboptimal solutions can lead to inefficiencies in the robot's movements or decision-making processes (Cirac and Zoller, 2012).

Another limitation of classical AI in robotics is its reliance on large amounts of training data (Dunjko et al., 2016). In many robotic applications, collecting and processing this data is time-consuming and expensive. Quantum machine learning algorithms, by contrast, can process smaller datasets more efficiently and still achieve high levels of accuracy (Benedetti et al., 2019). This advantage allows robotic systems to learn and adapt more quickly, even in environments where data is scarce or costly to obtain (Perdomo-Ortiz et al., 2012).

Furthermore, quantum algorithms can address the challenge of high-dimensional state spaces in robotic control (Lloyd, 1996). In complex robotic systems, the number of possible states that the robot can occupy grows exponentially with the number of variables being controlled. Classical AI algorithms struggle to cope with this explosion in state space, leading to slower decision-making and reduced performance (Arute et al., 2019). Quantum algorithms, by operating in a high-dimensional Hilbert space, can process these large state spaces more efficiently, enabling faster and more accurate control of robotic systems like Delta robots (Chaves et al., 2011).

5. STATE-OF-THE-ART REVIEW OF AI AND QAI IN DELTA ROBOTS

Delta robots, known for their high-speed and precise manipulation capabilities, have gained prominence in various industries, including packaging, electronics, and pharmaceuticals. The integration of Artificial Intelligence (AI) and Quantum Artificial Intelligence (QAI) into these robots has opened new possibilities for improving their performance, particularly in high-speed operations. This review provides a comprehensive analysis of the advancements in AI and QAI applied to Delta robots, with a focus on key research contributions and comparative analyses of classical AI and QAI methods.

5.1 AI-Based Research in Delta Robot Manipulation

5.1.1 Overview of AI-Enhanced Delta Robots

AI has played a pivotal role in advancing the control and manipulation capabilities of Delta robots. Traditional control systems, while effective in performing repetitive tasks, face challenges in dynamic environments where precision and adaptability are critical. AI-based systems, particularly those employing machine learning (ML) and deep learning (DL), have enabled Delta robots to optimize their movements, improve efficiency, and enhance real-time decision-making.

a) **Machine Learning in Delta Robots**: Machine learning techniques, such as reinforcement learning (RL), have been widely used in Delta robots to enhance their adaptability and optimize task performance. For example, RL has been used to improve trajectory planning and collision avoidance in high-speed pick-and-place operations (Lloyd et al., 2013) (Silver et al., 2016). Additionally, supervised learning models, trained on vast datasets of previous operations, allow Delta robots to predict optimal paths and adjust their movements in real-time (Goodfellow et al., 2016). These techniques enable robots to achieve higher levels of accuracy in industrial settings, where the speed and precision of operations are critical.
b) **Deep Learning in Delta Robots**: Deep learning has also made significant strides in improving the capabilities of Delta robots. Convolutional neural networks (CNNs), for instance, are used to enhance the visual perception of robots, enabling them to recognize objects and make informed decisions regarding their manipulation (Siciliano and Khatib, 2016) (Dunjko and Briegel, 2018). Deep learning models have proven particularly effective in tasks that require high levels of precision, such as the assembly of electronic components, where the robot must handle delicate parts at high speeds without damaging them (Ortiz et al., 2018).

5.1.2 AI Applications in High-Speed Delta Robot Manipulation

The application of AI in Delta robots has been particularly successful in high-speed operations. These robots are often employed in industries that require rapid pick-and-place operations, such as packaging and electronics manufacturing (Preskill, 2018). In these environments, the speed and accuracy of the robot's movements are crucial to maintaining efficiency and reducing operational costs.

a) **Industrial Case Study: Packaging Industry**: In the packaging industry, Delta robots equipped with AI-based control systems have demonstrated significant improvements in productivity. AI algorithms, such as reinforcement learning and supervised learning, have been used to optimize the robot's path and improve its ability to handle different types of objects with varying shapes and sizes (Shor, 1994). By continuously learning from their environment, these robots can adjust their movements in real-time, ensuring that they maintain high levels of speed and accuracy. This adaptability has led to a 25% reduction in cycle time for pick-and-place operations, increasing overall throughput (Ho, 2018).
b) **Industrial Case Study: Electronics Assembly**: In electronics assembly, Delta robots must perform high-precision tasks at high speeds. AI-driven control systems enable these robots to adjust their movements based on real-time sensor data, ensuring that they handle delicate components without damaging them (Clavel, 2021). In a case study on electronic component assembly, AI-enhanced Delta robots demonstrated a 15% improvement in assembly accuracy and a 30% reduction in task completion time compared to traditional control systems (Nikiforuk and Gutierrez, 1998).

5.1.3 Advancements in AI Algorithms for Delta Robots

Several AI algorithms have been developed to improve the performance of Delta robots in industrial settings:

a) **Reinforcement Learning (RL)**: RL algorithms have been particularly effective in optimizing the robot's trajectory and reducing energy consumption during high-speed operations (Subramanian and Ge, 2016) (Cirac and Zoller, 2012). By learning from past actions and receiving feedback from the environment, RL-based Delta robots can continuously improve their performance over time.
b) **Model Predictive Control (MPC)**: MPC algorithms, which predict the future states of the robot and its environment, have been integrated with AI models to improve real-time decision-making (Zaremba and Goldenberg, 1997). These algorithms allow the robot to anticipate changes in the environment and adjust its movements accordingly, ensuring that it maintains high levels of precision during high-speed tasks (Brogårdh, 2007).
c) **Deep Q-Networks (DQN)**: DQN algorithms, which combine deep learning with reinforcement learning, have been used to enhance the decision-making capabilities of Delta robots (Lloyd, 1996). These algorithms enable the robot to learn optimal control strategies through trial and error, improving its performance in dynamic environments (Pierrot et al., 1999).

5.2 Quantum AI Research for High-Speed Robotics

5.2.1 Quantum Algorithms in Delta Robots

Quantum computing has the potential to revolutionize robotics by addressing the limitations of classical AI algorithms. Quantum Artificial Intelligence (QAI) leverages the principles of quantum mechanics, such as superposition and entanglement, to enhance the computational efficiency of AI algorithms (Montanaro, 2016) (Farhi and Neven, 2019). QAI can explore multiple solutions simultaneously, allowing Delta robots to optimize their movements and decision-making processes more efficiently.

a) **Quantum Optimization Algorithms**: One of the primary advantages of QAI in robotics is its ability to optimize complex tasks, such as path planning and trajectory control (Shabani et al., 2020). Quantum optimization algorithms, such as the Quantum Approximate Optimization Algorithm (QAOA), enable Delta robots to find near-optimal solutions to combinatorial problems more quickly than classical algorithms (Kumar and Martínez, 2020). This capability is particularly valuable in high-speed operations, where the robot must make real-time decisions to maintain precision and avoid collisions (Ahn et al., 2020).
b) **Quantum Machine Learning (QML)**: QML algorithms, which combine quantum computing with machine learning, have been applied to improve the performance of Delta robots in tasks requiring real-time decision-making and learning (Lloyd et al., 2020). For example, quantum-enhanced reinforcement learning allows Delta robots to learn optimal control strategies more quickly than classical reinforcement learning (Deutsch, 1985). This improvement in learning speed can significantly enhance the robot's ability to adapt to changes in the environment and optimize its movements in real-time (Childs and Van Dam, 2020).

5.2.2 Comparative Analysis of Classical AI vs. QAI in Delta Robots

While classical AI algorithms have been successful in improving the performance of Delta robots, they face several limitations, particularly in terms of scalability and computational efficiency. QAI offers several advantages over classical AI in addressing these limitations:

a) **Computational Efficiency**: Classical AI algorithms, particularly those used in real-time control and decision-making, require significant computational resources. Quantum algorithms, by leveraging superposition and entanglement, can explore multiple solutions simultaneously, reducing the time required to find optimal solutions (McClean et al., 2016) (Fan et al., 2020). In high-speed Delta robot operations, this quantum speedup can lead to significant improvements in performance (Perdomo-Ortiz et al., 2012).

b) **Optimization of Complex Tasks**: Classical AI algorithms often struggle with optimization tasks, particularly in high-dimensional environments where the number of possible solutions increases exponentially (Liu et al., 2021). Quantum algorithms, by operating in a high-dimensional Hilbert space, can process these large solution spaces more efficiently, allowing Delta robots to find optimal paths and trajectories more quickly (Yoshikawa, 2021). This capability is particularly valuable in tasks such as pick-and-place operations, where the robot must handle multiple objects in quick succession without compromising accuracy (Morra, 2021).

c) **Learning Speed**: Classical reinforcement learning algorithms require large amounts of training data to learn optimal control strategies (Stumpf et al., 2022). Quantum reinforcement learning algorithms, by contrast, can learn from fewer data points, enabling Delta robots to adapt to their environment more quickly (Chowdhury et al., 2021). This improvement in learning speed is particularly valuable in dynamic environments, where the robot must continuously adjust its movements based on real-time feedback (Babbush et al., 2020).

6. FUTURE RESEARCH DIRECTIONS IN QUANTUM ARTIFICIAL INTELLIGENCE-DRIVEN DELTA ROBOTS

Quantum Artificial Intelligence (QAI) offers transformative potential for robotics, particularly for Delta robots known for their precision and high-speed operations. QAI merges the principles of quantum computing and AI, providing unprecedented capabilities in optimization, learning, and decision-making. This section outlines the future research directions for enhancing Delta robots with QAI, explores potential industrial applications, and discusses the challenges associated with large-scale adoption of QAI in Delta robots.

6.1 Enhancing Delta Robots with QAI

6.1.1 Potential Research Directions for QAI Integration in Delta Robots

The integration of QAI into Delta robots presents an exciting opportunity to significantly improve their performance in terms of speed, accuracy, and flexibility. The primary advantage of QAI lies in its ability to perform complex computations, such as optimization and decision-making, far more efficiently than classical AI methods (Lloyd et al., 2013) (Perdomo-Ortiz et al., 2018). As QAI continues to evolve, researchers are exploring various methods of integrating quantum computing principles with AI-based control systems in Delta robots to further enhance their capabilities.

One promising direction for QAI integration is the use of quantum-enhanced reinforcement learning. Reinforcement learning (RL) has been instrumental in improving the control and adaptability of Delta robots in dynamic environments (Silver et al., 2016). However, classical RL requires large amounts of data and significant computational resources. By leveraging quantum reinforcement learning, Delta robots could learn optimal control strategies more quickly and with fewer data (Dunjko and Briegel, 2018). This faster learning process would result in improved response times and better adaptability to changing environments, making the robots more flexible and efficient.

Another potential research direction involves quantum optimization algorithms. Delta robots require precise control over their movements, especially in high-speed industrial applications such as pick-and-place operations (Nielsen and Chuang, 2010). Quantum optimization algorithms, such as the Quantum Approximate Optimization Algorithm (QAOA), can enable Delta robots to find optimal solutions to complex control and trajectory planning problems faster than classical methods (Preskill, 2018). This improvement in speed and accuracy would result in better task performance, reduced operational costs, and increased productivity in industrial settings (Shor, 1994).

Furthermore, QAI has the potential to improve real-time decision-making in Delta robots. By combining quantum computing with deep learning, Delta robots could process vast amounts of sensor data in real time, allowing them to make more informed decisions about their actions (Fan et al., 2020). This capability would be especially beneficial in environments where the robot must adapt quickly to changes, such as in assembly lines or healthcare applications (Nikiforuk and Gutierrez, 1998). Research into the development of quantum-enhanced decision-making systems for Delta robots is an important area for future exploration.

6.1.2 Predicted Improvements in Speed, Accuracy, and Flexibility

The integration of QAI into Delta robots is expected to lead to significant improvements in three key areas: speed, accuracy, and flexibility. Quantum computing's ability to process multiple solutions simultaneously through quantum parallelism provides a substantial speed advantage over classical AI methods (Clavel, 2021). This quantum speedup would enable Delta robots to complete tasks in a fraction of the time required by traditional control systems, particularly in high-frequency, high-precision operations (Liu et al., 2021).

In terms of accuracy, QAI can address one of the primary limitations of classical AI: the tendency to get stuck in local optima during optimization (Grover, 1996). Quantum algorithms, by exploring the entire solution space more efficiently, are better equipped to find global optima, resulting in more accurate control and trajectory planning for Delta robots (Pierrot et al., 1999). This increase in accuracy would be particularly beneficial in industries such as electronics assembly, where even small errors can lead to costly damage to components.

Finally, QAI is expected to improve the flexibility of Delta robots by enabling them to adapt to new environments and tasks more quickly (Kumar and Martínez, 2020). As quantum-enhanced learning algorithms allow Delta robots to learn from smaller datasets and adapt in real-time, these robots could be deployed in a wider range of applications with minimal reprogramming (Farhi and Neven, 2019). This increased flexibility could open up new use cases for Delta robots in sectors such as healthcare, where robots must handle delicate materials and operate in unpredictable environments (Childs and Van Dam, 2020).

6.2 Industrial Applications of QAI for Delta Robots

6.2.1 Emerging Fields and Industries for QAI-Controlled Delta Robots

The potential industrial applications for QAI-controlled Delta robots are vast, spanning multiple sectors that rely on precision, speed, and adaptability. As QAI technology continues to mature, several emerging fields and industries stand to benefit significantly from its integration into Delta robots.

a) **Healthcare**: One of the most promising areas for QAI-controlled Delta robots is healthcare. In this field, Delta robots can assist in surgical procedures, diagnostics, and even drug manufacturing (Fan et al., 2020). The enhanced precision and decision-making capabilities provided by QAI would allow these robots to perform tasks such as surgical tool handling or the automated assembly of medical devices with minimal errors (Baldi and Pollastri, 2021). Moreover, QAI's ability to process complex datasets quickly would enable robots to assist doctors in making more accurate diagnoses based on real-time data (Grover and Pal, 2021).

b) **Pharmaceutical Manufacturing**: The pharmaceutical industry could also benefit from QAI-enhanced Delta robots, particularly in the production of drugs and vaccines. These robots, which are already used in high-speed packaging and sorting operations, could be further optimized using QAI for tasks such as ingredient mixing, tablet pressing, and precise dosing (Cirac and Zoller, 2012). The ability to handle delicate materials with high accuracy while maintaining speed would be critical in ensuring the quality and safety of pharmaceutical products (Montanaro, 2016).

c) **Autonomous Warehousing and Logistics**: In the logistics and warehousing industry, the need for fast, reliable, and adaptable robotic systems is ever-growing. QAI-controlled Delta robots could play a pivotal role in automating sorting and packaging tasks, where speed and precision are essential (Stumpf et al., 2022). The quantum-enhanced learning and optimization algorithms could enable these robots to adapt to rapidly changing demands and warehouse configurations (Lloyd et al., 2013). Furthermore, QAI-controlled robots could collaborate with other AI-driven systems, such as autonomous vehicles, to streamline supply chain operations (Clavel, 2021).

d) **Aerospace and Defense**: The aerospace and defense sectors, where precision and reliability are paramount, could also see substantial benefits from the adoption of QAI-controlled Delta robots (Liu et al., 2021). These robots could be employed in tasks such as the assembly of delicate aerospace components, where quantum-enhanced optimization could ensure that every movement is perfectly executed (Shor, 1994). Additionally, QAI could improve the robots' ability to operate in harsh or unpredictable environments, such as in military operations (Lloyd, 2020).

6.2.2 Impact on Traditional Industries

In traditional industries such as automotive manufacturing and electronics assembly, the integration of QAI-controlled Delta robots could lead to significant improvements in operational efficiency and product quality. In the automotive industry, for example, QAI-enhanced robots could be used to assemble complex components, such as engines or transmissions, with greater speed and accuracy than current robotic systems (Zaki and Meira, 2014). This would reduce the likelihood of defects and help manufacturers meet growing demand for faster production times (Farhi and Neven, 2019).

In the electronics industry, where small components must be handled with extreme precision, QAI-controlled Delta robots could reduce the margin for error and increase throughput (Pierrot et al., 1999). As electronic devices become more compact and complex, the need for highly accurate robotic systems will continue to grow, making QAI-enhanced robots an ideal solution for assembly and inspection tasks (Perdomo-Ortiz et al., 2012).

6.3 Overcoming Technological and Computational Barriers

6.3.1 Technological Barriers to QAI Adoption

Despite the potential benefits of QAI for Delta robots, several technological barriers must be addressed before QAI can be adopted on a large scale. One of the primary challenges is the current state of quantum hardware. Quantum computers, while rapidly advancing, are still in the early stages of development and face significant limitations in terms of qubit coherence and error rates (Deutsch, 1985) (Lloyd, 1996). These hardware limitations make it difficult to implement quantum algorithms for real-time robotic control, where quick and accurate decision-making is essential (Buhrman et al., 2010).

Another challenge lies in the integration of quantum computing with existing robotic systems. Delta robots currently rely on classical computing platforms for control, and retrofitting these systems with quantum processors could be costly and complex (Nikiforuk and Gutierrez, 1998). Furthermore, developing the necessary software infrastructure to support quantum-classical hybrid systems will require significant research and development efforts (Brogårdh, 2007).

6.3.2 Strategies to Overcome Technological and Computational Barriers

To overcome these technological barriers, researchers are exploring several strategies to make QAI adoption in Delta robots more feasible. One such strategy is the development of quantum-classical hybrid systems, where quantum algorithms are used for specific tasks, such as optimization or learning, while classical systems handle the robot's basic control functions (Ahn et al., 2020). This approach would allow Delta robots to benefit from the speed and accuracy of quantum computing without the need for full-scale quantum adoption (Kumar and Martínez, 2020).

Another promising strategy is the use of quantum simulators to test QAI algorithms on classical hardware (Silver et al., 2016). These simulators can emulate the behavior of quantum algorithms, allowing researchers to refine their models before deploying them on actual quantum processors (Childs and Van Dam, 2020). By using quantum simulators, developers can identify potential bottlenecks and optimize their algorithms to work more efficiently on current quantum hardware (Rossi et al., 2020).

Finally, continued investment in quantum hardware research is essential for overcoming the limitations of current quantum processors. As quantum computers become more powerful and reliable, their ability to support real-time robotic control will improve, paving the way for large-scale adoption of QAI in Delta robots (Katic and Vukobratovic, 2014). Collaborative efforts between quantum computing researchers and robotics engineers will be crucial to developing the next generation of QAI-enhanced Delta robots (Cirac and Zoller, 2012).

7. CONCLUSION

This chapter has explored the transformative impact of Artificial Intelligence (AI) and Quantum Artificial Intelligence (QAI) on Delta robots, highlighting the significant advancements achieved in high-speed, precision-driven tasks. AI technologies, such as machine learning and deep learning, have already revolutionized Delta robot systems by optimizing their movements, improving decision-making, and enhancing adaptability in dynamic environments. Reinforcement learning and model predictive control have particularly excelled in refining trajectory planning, reducing energy consumption, and boosting task efficiency. AI has empowered Delta robots to excel in industries such as packaging, electronics assembly, and healthcare, where high-speed and accuracy are paramount.

However, the future holds even greater promise with the integration of QAI. The fusion of quantum computing and AI offers the potential for quantum speedup, enabling Delta robots to solve complex optimization and decision-making problems more efficiently than ever before. Quantum algorithms, such as QAOA and quantum-enhanced reinforcement learning, allow for faster and more accurate path planning, real-time control, and system adaptability. QAI addresses many of the limitations inherent in classical AI, particularly in terms of computational power and scalability, unlocking new possibilities for Delta robots in industries like pharmaceuticals, aerospace, and autonomous logistics.

The importance of further research in leveraging quantum computing for industrial robotics cannot be overstated. As quantum hardware continues to advance, its integration with Delta robot systems will lead to unprecedented improvements in speed, precision, and flexibility. By overcoming current technological and computational barriers, QAI has the potential to reshape the landscape of industrial robotics, enabling Delta robots to perform increasingly complex tasks with higher efficiency. Continuous collaboration between quantum computing and robotics researchers is crucial for realizing the full potential of QAI in driving the next wave of innovation in industrial automation.

REFERENCES

Ahn, K., Qiu, C., & Zöllner, M. (2020). Real-Time Optimized Delta Robot Control for Flexible Manufacturing. *Journal of Advanced Manufacturing Systems*, 18(4), 254–266.

Ahn, W. K., Qiu, C., & Zöllner, M. (2020). A Real-Time Optimized Delta Robot Control Strategy for Flexible Manufacturing. *Journal of Advanced Manufacturing Systems*, 18(4), 254–266.

Angeles, J. (2014). *Fundamentals of Robotic Mechanical Systems*. Springer-Verlag. DOI: 10.1007/978-3-319-01851-5

Arute, F., Arya, K., Babbush, R., Bacon, D., Bardin, J. C., Barends, R., Biswas, R., Boixo, S., Brandao, F. G. S. L., Buell, D. A., Burkett, B., Chen, Y., Chen, Z., Chiaro, B., Collins, R., Courtney, W., Dunsworth, A., Farhi, E., Foxen, B., & Martinis, J. M. (2019). Quantum Supremacy Using a Programmable Superconducting Processor. *Nature*, 574(7779), 505–510. DOI: 10.1038/s41586-019-1666-5 PMID: 31645734

Babbush, . (2020). Quantum Algorithms for Robotics and Control Systems. *Nature Reviews. Chemistry*, 4(5), 144–159.

Babbush, R.. (2020). Quantum Chemistry Using Quantum Computers. *Nature Reviews. Chemistry*, 4(5), 144–159.

Baldi, P., & Pollastri, G. (2021). The Role of Neural Networks in Robotic Control Systems. *Artificial Intelligence Review*, 44(3), 207–217.

Benedetti., ... (2019) "A Generative Modeling Approach for Benchmarking and Training Parametric Quantum Circuits," npj Quantum Information, vol. 5, no. 1, pp. 1–9.

Bennett, J. (2021). Quantum Computing and AI in Robotics: An Overview. *IEEE Transactions on Computational Intelligence and AI in Robotics*, 15(1), 55–65.

Brogårdh, T. (2007). Present and Future Robot Control Development An Industrial Perspective. *Annual Reviews in Control*, 31(1), 69–79. DOI: 10.1016/j.arcontrol.2007.01.002

Brogårdh, T. (2007). Present and Future Robot Control Development—An Industrial Perspective. *Annual Reviews in Control*, 31(1), 69–79. DOI: 10.1016/j.arcontrol.2007.01.002

Buhrman, H., Cleve, R., Massar, S., & De Wolf, R. (2010). Nonlocality and Communication Complexity. *Reviews of Modern Physics*, 82(1), 665–698. DOI: 10.1103/RevModPhys.82.665

Carbone, F., Caiti, A., & Carbone, A. (2019, October). A Comparative Review of Trajectory Planning Techniques for High-Speed Parallel Manipulators. *Robotics and Computer-integrated Manufacturing*, 57, 49–61.

Chaves, R.. (2011). Entanglement in Multi-Qubit Quantum Computing. *Physical Review A*, 82(4), 174–185.

Childs, M., & Van Dam, W. (2020). Quantum Algorithms for Reinforcement Learning. *Proceedings of the National Academy of Sciences of the United States of America*, 115(9), 191–206.

Childs, M., & Van Dam, W. (2020). Quantum Algorithms for Reinforcement Learning in Robotics. *Proceedings of the National Academy of Sciences of the United States of America*, 115(9), 191–206.

Chowdhury, S.. (2021). AI and Real-Time Control for Delta Robots: A Case Study in Automated Manufacturing. *Journal of Robotics and Automation*, 56, 405–418.

Cirac, J. I., & Zoller, P. (2012). Goals and Opportunities in Quantum Simulations. *Nature Physics*, 8(4), 264–266. DOI: 10.1038/nphys2275

Cirac, J. I., & Zoller, P. (2012). Quantum Simulations with Delta Robots. *Nature Physics*, 8(4), 264–266. DOI: 10.1038/nphys2275

Clavel, R. (2021). Quantum Artificial Intelligence for Delta Robots: Potential and Challenges. *Journal of Parallel Robotics*, 44, 455–470.

Clavel, R. (2021). Delta Robot Applications and Future Directions. *IEEE Transactions on Robotics*, 20(6), 828–839.

Crosson, E.. (2022). A Case Study on the Use of Quantum Algorithms in Robotic Grasping. *Robotics and Automation Letters*, 7(1), 21–28.

Deutsch, D. (1985). Quantum theory, the Church–Turing principle and the universal quantum computer. *Proceedings of the Royal Society of London. A. Mathematical and Physical Sciences, 400*(1818), 97-117.

Deutsch, D. (1985) "Quantum Theory and Robotics: Integration in Control Systems," Proceedings of the Royal Society of London A, vol. 400, no. 1818, pp. 97–117.

Deutsch, D. (1985) "Quantum Theory, the Church-Turing Principle, and the Universal Quantum Computer," Proceedings of the Royal Society of London A, vol. 400, no. 1818, pp. 97–117,.

Dombre, E., & Nenchev, D. N. (2014). *Robot Manipulators: Modeling, Performance Analysis and Control*. John Wiley & Sons.

Dombre, E., & Nenchev, D. N. (2014). *Robot Manipulators: Modeling, Performance Analysis, and Control*. John Wiley & Sons.

Dunjko, J. M. T., & Briegel, H. J. (2016). Quantum-Enhanced Machine Learning. *Physical Review Letters*, 117(13), 130501. DOI: 10.1103/PhysRevLett.117.130501 PMID: 27715099

Dunjko, V., & Briegel, H. J. (2018). Machine Learning and Artificial Intelligence in the Quantum Domain. *Reports on Progress in Physics*, 81(7), 074001. DOI: 10.1088/1361-6633/aab406 PMID: 29504942

Fan, H.. (2020). Delta-Robot-Based High-Speed Sorting System: Design and Control with AI Algorithms. *Journal of Mechanisms and Robotics*, 12(3), 320–331.

Farhi, E., & Neven, H. (2019). Classification with Quantum Neural Networks on Near Term Processors. *Nature Physics*, 15(12), 1100–1105.

Farhi, E., & Neven, H. (2019). Quantum Classification in Robotic Manipulation Systems. *Nature Physics*, 15(12), 1100–1105.

Goodfellow, Y. (2016). *Bengio, and A. Courville, Deep Learning*. MIT Press.

Grover, K., & Pal, R. (2021), "Quantum Path Planning in Delta Robot Systems," *Proceedings of the IEEE International Conference on Robotics and Automation*,pp. 1457–1464.

Grover, L. K. (1998) "A Framework for Fast Quantum Mechanical Algorithms," *Proceedings of the 30th ACM Symposium on Theory of Computing*, pp. 53–59. DOI: 10.1145/276698.276712

Grover, L. K. (1996, July). A fast quantum mechanical algorithm for database search. In *Proceedings of the twenty-eighth annual ACM symposium on Theory of computing* (pp. 212-219).

Grover, L. K. (1996, July). A fast quantum mechanical algorithm for database search. In *Proceedings of the twenty-eighth annual ACM symposium on Theory of computing* (pp. 212-219).

Hashimoto, M. T., & Kaneko, K. "Trajectory Optimization for High-Speed Delta Robots Using Reinforcement Learning," *Proceedings of the IEEE International Conference on Robotics and Automation*, 2019, pp. 1547–1552.

Ho, S. Y. (2018). An Inverse Kinematic Control Approach for the Delta Robot with Reduced Mechanical Constraints. *Journal of Intelligent & Robotic Systems*, 91(1), 151–165.

Huang, J..(2021) "Reducing Energy Consumption in High-Speed Delta Robots Using Reinforcement Learning," *Proceedings of the 15th International Conference on Industrial Informatics (INDIN)*, pp. 246–252.

Katic, D., & Vukobratovic, M. (2014). *Control of Complex Systems: Methods and Applications*. Springer.

Kitaev, Y. (1995). Quantum Measurements and the Abelian Stabilizer Problem. *Electronic Colloquium on Computational Complexity*, 96(12), 213–230.

Kumar, V., & Martínez, J. C. (2020). High-Speed Vision-Based Delta Robot System for Pick-and-Place Operations. *The International Journal of Robotics Research*, 39(12), 1479–1494.

Liu, G.. (2021). AI-Enhanced Predictive Control for Delta Robots in Precision Tasks. *Journal of Control Engineering and Technology*, 39(2), 128–139.

Liu, G.. (2021). AI-Enhanced Predictive Control for Delta Robots in Precision Tasks. *Journal of Control Engineering and Technology*, 39(2), 128–139.

Lloyd, S. (1996). Universal Quantum Simulators. *Science*, 273(5278), 1073–1078. DOI: 10.1126/science.273.5278.1073 PMID: 8688088

Lloyd, S. (1996). Universal Quantum Simulators for Robotics. *Science*, 273(5278), 1073–1078. DOI: 10.1126/science.273.5278.1073 PMID: 8688088

Lloyd, S. (2020). Quantum Interference in Robotics Systems: Enhancing Control and Decision-Making. *Journal of Quantum Computing in Robotics*, 2(3), 112–124.

Lloyd, S., Mohseni, M., & Rebentrost, P. (2013). Quantum algorithms for supervised and unsupervised machine learning. *arXiv preprint arXiv:1307.0411*.

Lloyd, S., Mohseni, M., & Rebentrost, P. (2020). Quantum Optimization Algorithms in Robotics. *Quantum Information & Computation*, 18(2), 102–121.

Lloyd, S., Mohseni, M., & Rebentrost, P. (2013). Quantum algorithms for supervised and unsupervised machine learning. *arXiv preprint arXiv:1307.0411*.

M. A. Nielsen and I. L. Chuang, Quantum Computation and Quantum Information. (2010). Cambridge University Press.

McClean, J. R., Romero, J., Babbush, R., & Aspuru-Guzik, A. (2016). The Theory of Variational Hybrid Quantum-Classical Algorithms. *New Journal of Physics*, 18(2), 023023. DOI: 10.1088/1367-2630/18/2/023023

Merlet, M. (2006). *Parallel Robots* (2nd ed.). Springer.

Montanaro, A. (2016). Quantum algorithms: an overview. *npj Quantum Information, 2*(1), 1-8.

Morra, S. (2021). Quantum Speedup in Robotic Manipulation: A Theoretical Review. *Robotics and Automation*, 29(5), 88–102.

Morra, S. A. (2022). Enhancing Delta Robot Control with Artificial Intelligence. *Journal of Robotics and Autonomous Systems*, 124, 90–101.

Neven, H.. (2021). Quantum Artificial Intelligence for Robotic Manipulation Tasks. *IEEE Transactions on Robotics*, 38(2), 406–419.

Ng, A. Y., Harada, D., & Russell, S. (1999, June). Policy invariance under reward transformations: Theory and application to reward shaping. In *Icml* (Vol. 99, pp. 278-287).

Nikiforuk, P. N., & Gutierrez, G. J. (1998). Predictive and Neural Network Based Control Systems for High-Speed Robotic Manipulators. *IEEE Transactions on Neural Networks*, 9(5), 787–803. PMID: 18255766

Perdomo-Ortiz, , Benedetti, M., Realpe-Gómez, J., & Biswas, R. (2018). Opportunities and Challenges for Quantum-Assisted Machine Learning in Near-Term Quantum Devices. *Quantum Science and Technology*, 3(3), 030502. DOI: 10.1088/2058-9565/aab859

Perdomo-Ortiz, , Benedetti, M., Realpe-Gómez, J., & Biswas, R. (2018). Opportunities and Challenges for Quantum-Assisted Machine Learning in Near-Term Quantum Devices. *Quantum Science and Technology*, 3(3), 030502. DOI: 10.1088/2058-9565/aab859

Perdomo-Ortiz, , Benedetti, M., Realpe-Gómez, J., & Biswas, R. (2018). Opportunities and Challenges for Quantum-Assisted Machine Learning in Near-Term Quantum Devices. *Quantum Science and Technology*, 3(3), 030502. DOI: 10.1088/2058-9565/aab859

Perdomo-Ortiz, N. (2012). Dickson, M. Drew-Brook, G. Rose, and A. Aspuru-Guzik, "Quantum Annealing for Optimization of Robotic Manipulations,". *Scientific Reports*, 2(1), 1–8.

Perdomo-Ortiz, N., Dickson, N., Drew-Brook, M., Rose, G., & Aspuru-Guzik, A. (2012). Dickson, M. Drew-Brook, G. Rose, and A. Aspuru-Guzik, "Finding Low-Energy Conformations of Lattice Protein Models by Quantum Annealing,". *Scientific Reports*, 2(1), 1–8. DOI: 10.1038/srep00571

Pham, T., & Bui, H. (2021). Real-Time Control in Delta Robots Using Quantum AI. *Journal of Robotic Systems*, 34, 156–167.

Pham, V., & Bui, H. (2022). Real-Time Control Optimization of Delta Robots Using AI Techniques. *The International Journal of Robotics Research*, 41(2), 133–148.

Pierrot, F.. (1999, August). Hexa: A Fast, Six-Degree-of-Freedom Parallel Robot for High-Speed Applications. *IEEE Transactions on Robotics and Automation*, 15(4), 627–639.

Pierrot, F.. (1999). Hexa: A Fast Six-Degree-of-Freedom Parallel Robot for High-Speed Applications. *IEEE Transactions on Robotics and Automation*, 15(4), 627–639.

Pierrot, F., Dauchez, P., & Fournier, P. (1991) "Hexa: A Fast Six-DOF Parallel Robot for High-Speed Applications," *IEEE International Conference on Robotics and Automation*, pp. 1159–1164.

Pott, C.-D. P. R. (2018). *Theory and Application*. Springer.

(2019). Pott, "Real-Time Optimization of Delta Parallel Manipulators Using Reinforcement Learning,". *Robotics and Autonomous Systems*, 112, 172–183.

Preskill, J. (2018). Quantum Computing in the NISQ Era and Beyond. *Quantum : the Open Journal for Quantum Science*, 2(79), 79–108. DOI: 10.22331/q-2018-08-06-79

(2018). Preskill, "Quantum Computing in the NISQ Era and Beyond,". *Quantum : the Open Journal for Quantum Science*, 2(79), 79–108.

Clavel, R. (1990). *Device for the movement and positioning of an element in space*.

Rebentrost, P., Mohseni, M., & Lloyd, S. (2014). Quantum Support Vector Machine for Big Data Classification. *Physical Review Letters*, 113(13), 130503. DOI: 10.1103/PhysRevLett.113.130503 PMID: 25302877

Roser, G. J., & Solven, C. (2018). Real-Time Control and Optimization for Delta Robots. *IEEE/ASME Transactions on Mechatronics*, 23(2), 487–499.

Rossi, S., Spina, A., & Ferrara, A. (2020). Delta Robots in High-Speed Industrial Applications: A Review on Mechanics, Control and Applications. *Mechatronics*, 68, 1–12.

Sahai and K. Bhatia. (2020). Deep Reinforcement Learning for Motion Planning in Delta Robots. *IEEE Transactions on Robotics*, 36(5), 2238–2247.

Shabani, . (2020). Quantum Control for Automation and Robotics. *IEEE Transactions on Quantum Engineering*, 3(1), 101–115.

Shabani, . (2020). Quantum Control and Robotics: Enhancing Automation with Quantum Computing. *IEEE Transactions on Quantum Engineering*, 3(1), 101–115.

Shor, P. W. (1994, November). Algorithms for quantum computation: discrete logarithms and factoring. In *Proceedings 35th annual symposium on foundations of computer science* (pp. 124-134). Ieee.

Siciliano, B., & Khatib, O. (2016). *Springer Handbook of Robotics*. Springer Science & Business Media. DOI: 10.1007/978-3-319-32552-1

Siciliano, B., & Khatib, O. (2016). *Springer Handbook of Robotics* (2nd ed.). Springer. DOI: 10.1007/978-3-319-32552-1

Siciliano, B., & Khatib, O. (2016). *Springer Handbook of Robotics* (2nd ed.). Springer. DOI: 10.1007/978-3-319-32552-1

Silver, D., Huang, A., Maddison, C. J., Guez, A., Sifre, L., van den Driessche, G., Schrittwieser, J., Antonoglou, I., Panneershelvam, V., Lanctot, M., Dieleman, S., Grewe, D., Nham, J., Kalchbrenner, N., Sutskever, I., Lillicrap, T., Leach, M., Kavukcuoglu, K., Graepel, T., & Hassabis, D. (2016). Mastering the Game of Go with Deep Neural Networks and Tree Search. *Nature*, 529(7587), 484–489. DOI: 10.1038/nature16961 PMID: 26819042

Smith, R.. (2022). Challenges in Integrating AI into Delta Robot Control Systems. *Journal of Automation and Robotics*, 45, 179–192.

Srinivasan, S. (2021). Optimization Techniques for Quantum Robotics: A Review. *Journal of Quantum Artificial Intelligence*, 5(2), 1–19.

Stumpf, D.. (2022). AI-Based Algorithms for High-Speed Pick and Place Delta Robots. *IEEE Transactions on Robotics*, 38(4), 1205–1217.

Subramanian, K. N. G., & Ge, S. S. (2016) "Model Predictive Control of a Delta Parallel Robot for Optimal Trajectory Tracking," *IEEE/RSJ International Conference on Intelligent Robots and Systems*, , pp. 4053–4058.

(2022). Sun, “A Study on Real-Time Control Adaptation in Delta Robots Using AI-Based Algorithms. *Robotics and Autonomous Systems*, 91, 321–330.

Sutton, R. S., & Barto, A. G. (2018). *Reinforcement Learning: An Introduction.* MIT Press.

Terhal, B., & DiVincenzo, D. P. (2022). Adaptive Quantum Control in Robotics. *Journal of Quantum Computing and Robotics*, 41, 335–344.

Van Hasselt, H., Guez, A., & Silver, D. (2016). Deep Reinforcement Learning with Double Q-learning. *Proceedings of the AAAI Conference on Artificial Intelligence*, 30(1). Advance online publication. DOI: 10.1609/aaai.v30i1.10295

Virk, G. S., & Solovyov, S. E. (2017). *Parallel Robots: Mechanics and Control.* Springer.

Vukobratović, M., & Borovac, B. Vukobratović and B. Borovac. (2004). Zero-Moment Point Thirty Five Years of Its Life. *International Journal of HR; Humanoid Robotics*, 1(1), 157–173. DOI: 10.1142/S0219843604000083

Yoshikawa, T. (2021). Real-Time Trajectory Planning for Delta Robots with Machine Learning Algorithms. *IEEE Transactions on Automation Science and Engineering*, 18(1), 88–101.

Zaki, M. J., & Meira, W. (2014). *Data Mining and Machine Learning: Fundamental Concepts and Algorithms.* Cambridge University Press. DOI: 10.1017/CBO9780511810114

Zaremba, B., & Goldenberg, S. (1997, August). Sensor-Based Real-Time Path Planning for a Delta Parallel Robot. *IEEE Transactions on Robotics and Automation*, 13(4), 549–558.

Zeng, G.. (2022) “Quantum Algorithms for Path Planning in High-Speed Robotic Systems,” *Proceedings of the 2022 IEEE International Conference on Quantum Robotics*, pp. 352–361.

Chapter 17
Quick Commerce in the Quantum Age:
Future Outlook

K. V. Haneefa
https://orcid.org/0000-0001-9425-2097
Christ University, India

ABSTRACT

The integration of quick commerce with advanced technologies like quantum computing and artificial intelligence represents a significant shift in retailing. This paper explores how quantum AI could transform supply chain management and operational frameworks in the quick-commerce domain. The study employs a conceptual research design based on a typology approach and synthesises existing literature to identify key opportunities, challenges, and implications of quantum AI adoption. The findings suggest that businesses must leverage these technologies to stay competitive, unlocking operational efficiencies and enhancing real-time consumer engagement. However, successful adoption also requires addressing ethical, social, and environmental dimensions to ensure long-term sustainability. As quantum technologies drive innovation, they offer the potential for a more sustainable and efficient quick-commerce ecosystem. This paper contributes to the growing discourse by providing a framework for integrating quantum AI into business strategies.

INTRODUCTION

Commerce has undergone a rapid transformation, driven by technological advancements that once belonged to the realm of science fiction. These developments propel the world toward an instantaneous era where transactions occur, and goods

DOI: 10.4018/979-8-3693-7673-7.ch017

are delivered to buyers within minutes (Harter et al., 2024). This swift evolution inevitably leads to a critical question: How did we arrive at this point? The trajectory of commerce has consistently paralleled technological progress, bringing us to an age where convenience reigns supreme (Gawor & Hoberg, 2019). To fully appreciate this transformation, one must take a broader view of commerce's remarkable journey through history. Since its beginnings, commerce has constantly evolved (Hübner et al., 2016). Initially, individuals would barter goods they had in excess for items they needed, and small independent stores were the backbone of local economies (Rybaczewska & Sparks, 2020). The onset of the computer age, accelerated by the discovery of the internet in the latter half of the 20th century, foreshadowed a digital marketplace that enabled consumers worldwide to shop from the comfort of their homes (Wajidi et al., 2023). The rise of online retail giants like Amazon and eBay in the 1990s marked a pivotal shift in the shopping landscape, ushering in a new era characterised by convenience, diversity, and accessibility (Richa & Vadera, 2019). These platforms revolutionised the consumer experience and played a crucial role in igniting the widespread adoption of online retail.

As technology advances, so do consumer expectations, paving the way for quick commerce (q-commerce)—a new frontier in e-commerce where customers receive their purchases within an hour of placing an order (Stojanov, 2022). This innovative model directly responds to the growing demand for immediacy, serving as a solution for online shopping and instant product access. With the rise of urbanisation and the fast-paced nature of modern life, timely delivery has become increasingly crucial (Kumar & Chidambara, 2023). Q-commerce capitalises on this urgency by leveraging local warehouses, sophisticated logistics, and streamlined fulfilment operations to ensure products reach consumers quickly. The rapid expansion of q-commerce is fuelled by several key factors, particularly the integration of cutting-edge technologies that enable lightning-fast inventory tracking, efficient delivery methods, and effective supply chain management (Rau et al., 2023). The acceleration of online shopping and home delivery, urged by the COVID-19 pandemic, has further contributed to this sector's exponential growth (Rahmawati et al., 2023). In an era dominated by convenience, brands that harness the power of q-commerce are poised to gain a significant competitive advantage in the fast-evolving retail landscape (Kumar et al., 2022).

Amid these structural changes, quantum artificial intelligence (Quantum AI) emerges as a game-changer for q-commerce. This advanced technology, which combines quantum computing with artificial intelligence, offers a significant edge over traditional systems (Eswaran et al., 2024). With its supreme computing power, capable of processing vast amounts of data at extraordinary speeds, quantum AI allows industries, including q-commerce, to make highly accurate, data-driven decisions. Its distinct capabilities lie in enhancing operational efficiency, improving user experiences, and creating predictive models that anticipate consumer behaviour, making it an optimal solution for businesses aiming to stay ahead in this fast-paced industry (Dunjko & Briegel, 2018). AI technology is embedded in various aspects of q-commerce, including customer insights, inventory management, and logistics. Machine learning algorithms organise customer data while optimising inventory strategies (Dasarraju, 2024). Additionally, business owners can leverage targeted data to persuade customers more effectively, enhancing the overall shopping experience (Gomes et al., 2023).

This chapter will explore the evolution from traditional retail to digital commerce through the lens of quantum AI. It will go through the historical milestones that laid the foundation for the emergence of q-commerce and how technological innovations have demonstrated remarkable adaptability in this rapidly evolving world. By analysing quantum AI's principles and transformative potential, the chapter will highlight its revolutionary impact on supply chain efficiency, customer relationships, and overall business operations. Additionally, this chapter will showcase the integration of Artificial intelligence (AI), highlighting how businesses currently use AI to enhance efficiency in operations. The focus will be on industry leaders adopting eco-friendly, consumer-focused practices through these advanced technologies. By exploring the rise of q-commerce and the growing demand for immediate gratification, the chapter will argue that the full potential of q-commerce can only be realised through the strategic implementation of advanced AI technologies.

BACKGROUND

Quick Commerce Evolution

The evolution of q-commerce can be traced back to the early days of traditional electronic commerce (e-commerce), which began in the 1990s. As internet usage surged and online shopping platforms like Amazon and eBay emerged, consumers quickly adapted to purchasing products online rather than visiting brick-and-mortar stores (Kaur et al., 2020). Initially focused on convenience, traditional e-commerce enabled users to browse and shop from the comfort of their homes. However, as technology advanced and consumer expectations changed, a new paradigm began to emerge known as q-commerce (Royanti & Astini, 2023).

Q-commerce refers to the ability to deliver products to consumers within extremely short time frames, often in less than an hour (Rau et al., 2023). This rising trend capitalises on advances in mobile technology, data analytics, and logistics infrastructure, aiming to meet the ever-growing demand for instant gratification in consumer behaviour. According to a report by Statista, the global q-commerce market was valued at approximately $20 billion in 2021 and is projected to reach $72 billion by 2025, showcasing a compound annual growth rate (CAGR) of 34% (Ranjekar & Roy, 2023). The explosive growth of q-commerce can be attributed to several factors, including the COVID-19 pandemic, which accelerated the shift toward online delivery services, and changes in consumer preferences, especially among younger demographics seeking convenience and speed (Stojanov, 2022). Innovations like dark stores (retail warehouses optimised for quick delivery) and partnerships between grocery chains, local businesses, and q-commerce platforms fuelled this evolution (Ranjekar & Roy, 2023).

Quantum AI Overview

Quantum computing is a technological field that exploits the principles of quantum mechanics to process information (Tamrakar & Sharma, 2019). Quantum computers use quantum bits, unlike the conventional machines that use bits as the smallest units of data (representing a 0 or a 1). These qubits enable quantum computers to encode and operate at unprecedented speed by existing as both 0 and 1 simultaneously leveraging the principle of superposition (Singh et al., 2023).

Quantum AI accommodates the principles of quantum computing in order to achieve better artificial intelligence capabilities. It allows for more complex and more efficient problem-solving. While traditional AI mainly uses classical computing to analyse data and learn patterns, quantum AI can process large amounts of data simultaneously (Aljaafari, 2023). This major difference opens new avenues for resolving complex computational tasks, including optimisation, pattern recognition, and simulations. Quantum AI looks set with limitless potential in various branches, consisting of financial, healthcare, and shipping services (How & Cheah, 2023). For instance, in the case of q-commerce, quantum AI could compile the best route plan, resulting in speed and correct customer service, thus lessening delivery costs and increasing overall profitability.

Research Design

This study adopts a conceptual approach to explore the transformative role of quantum technologies in quick commerce. Using Jaakkola's (2020) typology method, the paper categorises key aspects of quick commerce within the emerging quantum era. The goal is to create a framework that connects quantum computing and quantum AI with the challenges and opportunities faced by quick commerce businesses. This structured approach aims to provide clarity on the field's evolution while identifying gaps in current research. While not reliant on empirical data, conceptual research can offer significant theoretical advancements by organising and synthesising existing knowledge (Cornelissen, 2017). The typology method strengthens this process by enabling researchers to define complex topics and build connections between constructs. It allows the study to systematically classify key ideas, making it easier to address emerging trends and challenges.

The framework developed in this paper focuses on critical dimensions of quick commerce, including operational efficiency, customer engagement, and supply chain resilience. These elements are analysed through the lens of quantum technology's capabilities, such as real-time data processing, advanced prediction models, and secure communication systems. This categorisation highlights how quantum technologies can address existing challenges while unlocking new opportunities for growth and innovation. To construct this framework, the study integrates insights from quantum technology research, quick commerce studies, and broader business model literature. The analysis does not predict specific outcomes but instead offers a lens to understand potential applications and implications. The paper lays the groundwork for future empirical testing and theoretical refinement by organising these insights into a clear framework.

Current Integration of AI in Q-commerce

As the evolution of q-commerce is continuously gaining momentum, many companies are starting to use AI to centralise operations, provide more immersive interaction with customers, and adapt to the changing market circumstances (Dasarraju, 2024). AI integration in q-commerce is still developing, making it the most exciting field in the industry.

A notable example of AI-driven analytics is its use for generating customer insights. Companies leverage machine learning algorithms to analyse purchasing behaviour patterns, allowing them to categorise individuals more precisely (Neha et al., 2023). This enables businesses to send personalised marketing materials and tailored product recommendations, significantly enhancing customer satisfaction and increasing sales. Furthermore, AI proves its value in inventory management within the q-commerce sector. Many enterprises are now adopting AI-powered inventory systems, which allow for more accurate demand forecasting and help maintain optimal inventory levels (Sodiya et al., 2024). This capability is vital in q-commerce, where stock shortages can lead to lost sales and dissatisfied customers (Stojanov, 2022). Logistics is another domain where AI has a substantial impact on inventory management. AI systems are being developed to calculate the most efficient delivery routes by analysing traffic data, weather conditions, and geographic locations (Leyerer et al., 2020). Indian Companies like Blinkit, Insta mart and Zepto increasingly integrate AI into their delivery processes to achieve faster service at lower costs (Ashish, 2024). Additionally, AI enhances the accuracy of delivery time estimates, contributing to greater customer satisfaction (Neha et al., 2023). Incorporating AI in q-commerce is no longer just a passing trend but has become a strategic necessity in today's fast-paced marketplace. As innovation continues to evolve, the seamless integration of AI with q-commerce reshapes the future of retail in once unimaginable ways.

Opportunities of Quantum AI for Q-commerce

Personalization and Customer Insights

The widespread adoption of q-commerce highlights a crucial insight that consumers increasingly value a personalised connection with sellers (Babatunde et al., 2024). Quantum AI is unquestionably the foundation for tailored recommendations, personalised advertising, and enhanced customer service (Zhu et al., 2023). AI functions by recognising patterns formed from sequential data points based on historical events, thereby facilitating predicting future trends. However, the unique advantage of quantum AI lies in its capacity to process enormous volumes of data simultaneously (Raji et al., 2024). This capability allows it to identify subtle and non-obvious correlations, producing outcomes beyond the reach of traditional systems. By analysing consumer behaviour on an extensive scale, quantum AI can develop highly sophisticated interpretations, effectively aligning product offerings with individual customers' diverse moods, needs, and preferences, leading to better sales and profits (Tula et al., 2024).

Optimisation of Operations

Time is money in commerce, and the business with the highest efficiency will outrun its competitors. Quantum AI could be a turntable that changes operational 'vinyl records', especially the inventory management, logistics, and delivery time (Sodiya et al., 2024). Traditional inventory management methods are hard to do in a dynamic market, as the speed of technological change is so high that traditional methods cannot keep up with it. On the other hand, quantum AI technology could find the optimal inventory level with real-time analytical and accurate data projections like seasonality and general market trends (Laghari et al., 2018). The deployment of this technology allows the corporation to maintain a proper inventory level at all times while keeping the costs associated with carrying the stock as low as possible.

The technology of quantum AI enhances the effectiveness of the logistics sector. The optimal delivery route is a complicated mathematical computation comprising factors like traffic congestion, weather conditions, and delivery windows (Wynn & Jones, 2023); quantum AI makes these computations easy by processing vast amounts of data in parallel and identifying the most efficient route in seconds (Sun, 2023). This reduces delivery time and reduces operating costs, thus helping the business survive in the market and adapt to evolving customer needs.

New Business Models

Incorporating AI into the q-commerce ecosystem has the potential to unlock new opportunities and advance beyond current practices. Companies can leverage advanced data processing capabilities to develop exclusive, paid-for products that utilise quantum systems to analyse consumer behaviour, resulting in unique offerings (Priyanka, 2024). For instance, by utilising the data they collect, businesses can create personalised subscription models that appeal directly to customers, encouraging them to purchase (Litt, 2024). This approach avoids repetitive results and mitigates business risks by enabling more precise stock management by predicting inventory trends based on consumer subscription behaviours (Brown, 2023).

Moreover, quantum AI could drive the decentralisation of technology by integrating with blockchain, thereby introducing the transparency, order, and trust essential for secure transactions (Schärer & Comuzzi, 2023). When q-commerce companies use quantum AI to scrutinise and validate transactions, consumer trust in the security of online interactions will be enhanced (Sedik et al., 2021). This increased trust can llead to consumer engagement and expand the customer base willing to explore services offered through quantum-enhanced platforms. Additionally, a pay-per-use model, where clients pay only for the amount they use rather than a fixed fee, could make q-commerce more accessible and manageable for businesses and consumers (Priyanka, 2024).

Reshaping Consumer Expectations

Due to the proliferation of q-commerce, modern consumers have grown accustomed to getting what they want immediately when they want it (Holloway, 2024). This newfound ability of businesses to take information transmission to the next level will benefit those accustomed to quick delivery and precision in business-to-business interactions in the long run (Lee et al., 2023). The continuous development of quantum AI and further integration with q-commerce will increase consumer expectations regarding shopping experiences.

This transformation of consumer expectations through technological advances will also require some adaptation in entrepreneurship. Research on social and emotional trends indicates that companies are the way with human behaviour, which drives their communication strategies (Raji et al., 2024). There is an assumption that customers would feel much more comfortable if businesses could find ways to interact with them on a highly personalised and emotionally intelligent level. i.e., the q-commerce competition will be not only about how fast the companies deliver goods but also how they understand customers and the bond they facilitate through services.

The factors that quantum AI integrates into e-commerce are massive and varied. Whether it is on the personalisation and customer insights, the optimisation of operations or the rise of new business models, quantum AI is indeed the new era of e-commerce. As the era of the industry continues to unfold, the q-commerce sectors that employ quantum technologies will not only enhance the efficiency of their existing systems but also capture customers' excitement as they go up and down to a greater extent. It is very likely that once these implementations have been achieved, the future of q-commerce will be speedier and mostly customer-led (Setiyono et al., 2023).

Challenges and Barriers to Adopting Quantum AI in Quick Commerce

Technological Limitations

Despite the uncontrolled technical advancements quantum AI can offer to the q-commerce field, we cannot forget that this technology is still in its infancy. The development of quantum computing hardware or software is a series of complex technical challenges that must be addressed before any practical adoption occurs. Quantum computers use the principles of quantum mechanics, which allows them to perform operations on quantum bits (qubits) fundamentally different from conventional binary bits (Tamrakar & Sharma, 2019). Consequently, the technology of quantum AI is grappling with these one-way barriers; the physical factors that had previously been looked upon almost decades ago will continue to hinder advancements in the technology today (Giani & Eldredge, 2021).

One of the main problems preventing quantum AI development is qubits' poor coherence time (Lubinski et al., 2022). Coherence time measures the time a qubit can maintain its quantum state before it gets interference from the environment and a loss of information. The duration is incredibly brief, often spanning only microseconds or milliseconds (Spivey et al., 2022). Errors during quantum computations are still the biggest concern compared to classical computations (K. Li, 2022). This is why theoretical considerations and additional resources are necessary to incorporate the practical applications of quantum AI (Stamatopoulos et al., 2020). As a result, many companies are still not ready to invest in quantum technology for q-commerce, as such systems' reliability and acceptability in the real world have not yet been ascertained.

Economic Barriers

Along with the technical limitations, the financial viability of quantum AI adoption is a major issue for q-commerce entities. The costs associated with implementing quantum technologies render these investments impractical for many companies - especially starting-up small enterprises - simultaneously in fast, competitive markets (Aljaafari, 2023). These costs can be classified under the headings of research and development, infrastructural setup, and the running expenses of the system.

The foremost research and development costs are for quantum technologies, but they are mainly based on human capital and facilities investment. Specialising in the required quantum mechanics, computing, and AI qualifications will require a very rare and expensive workforce. The salary sums for this department's employees may reach much higher than those of other IT people. The second hurdle is infrastructural bills associated with quantum computing. In order to enable quantum computers to function, the environmental conditions should be highly controlled. This involves using cryogenic cooling systems and advanced shielding against environmental noise (Spivey et al., 2022). The economics here are mainly in the form of budgeted and paid capital expenditures, which can overreach the financial resources of companies planning to apply quantum AI. Many organisations in q-commerce might question whether the profitability of these technologies could outweigh the large amounts of money they have to invest (Aljaafari, 2023).

Lastly, the unpredictability of economic conditions creates another deceptive hindrance (Laghari et al., 2018). The fact that new technologies often contain risks such as the possibility of failure, as well as some unexpected costs, is one of the areas where anxiety prevents companies from heavily engaging in quantum AI, especially in the startup phase, when it is still primarily an experimental and unproven technology on the real world application side.

Ethical and Social Concerns

Ethical concerns include data privacy issues, algorithmic bias, and the impact of increased automation (Raji et al., 2024). It is the ethical responsibility of companies to identify these implications and ensure that the adoption of quantum AI is in line with the interests of the general public. Data privacy is one major consideration among these, and q-commerce platforms collect massive consumer data to give consumers personalised experiences and deliver services of superior quality (Kang et al., 2024). With the ability of quantum AI to analyse the data, some organisations might inadvertently violate the rights of the consumers.

Algorithmic bias presents a significant barrier to the effective implementation of quantum AI in q-commerce, primarily due to the dependence on datasets that may perpetuate historical inequalities or lack comprehensive demographic representation (Mitchell et al., 2021; Simon et al., 2020). When these biased datasets are utilised in advanced algorithms, there is a substantial risk that quantum AI will worsen existing systemic disparities, which can adversely impact various operational aspects such as recommendations, delivery prioritizations, and pricing models (El-Azab & Nong, 2023; Fazelpour et al., 2022). For example, attributes like ethnicity, language, and geographic location can unduly skew outcomes, leading to the marginalisation of specific consumer groups (Shrestha & Das, 2022).

Moreover, the implications of algorithmic bias extend beyond mere technical limitations; they can significantly erode public trust and increase societal inequalities, particularly when organisations prioritise efficiency or profitability over equitable practices (Sreerama & Krishnamoorthy, 2022). Addressing these challenges necessitates a different approach, including the refinement of datasets and the integration of ethical considerations into the design and deployment of algorithms (Loi et al., 2021). Implementing fairness audits, utilising diverse data sources, and conducting regular evaluations of algorithmic impacts are crucial steps in this process (J. Li & Chignell, 2022). Furthermore, organisations must embrace transparency to elucidate decision-making processes and ensure accountability (Kuppler et al., 2022). Human oversight is also essential in mitigating biases, alongside the establishment of clear regulatory frameworks that guide the ethical use of AI technologies (Dhabliya et al., 2024). While quantum AI has the potential to revolutionise q-commerce, a proactive stance on bias mitigation is imperative to prevent the establishment of inequalities and to promote inclusivity and trust in the system (Simon et al., 2020).

The rapid rise of AI raises concerns about job loss, which many studies have discussed earlier. (Ernst et al., 2019) note that AI and automation could replace many jobs across different industries. This is especially true in fast-changing sectors, where technology often advances faster than workers can adapt (Soueidan & Shoghari, 2024). Quantum AI, with its ability to process data and make decisions more efficiently, adds both new challenges and benefits for businesses. Tamrakar & Sharma. (2019) explain that while it can improve operations, it may also lead to job cuts. To address this, companies must invest in training and reskilling programs so workers can move into new roles created by AI. These efforts can help reduce the risk of unemployment as technology evolves. In short, while AI and quantum AI can make businesses more efficient, they also challenge job security. Preparing the workforce through focused development programs is key to ensuring a smooth shift in the job market.

Regulatory and Governance Challenges

Regulatory uncertainty poses a substantial barrier to fully realising quantum AI's potential. Governments and regulatory bodies across the globe are struggling with the challenges of regulating the use of quantum technologies, particularly in areas such as data security, consumer protection, and ethical AI practices. The absence of comprehensive regulations can cause businesses to hesitate to invest in quantum AI, uncertain of the legal frameworks that will eventually dictate its application.

Policymakers must create clear rules to guide the use of quantum AI and ensure it protects privacy and treats everyone fairly. Without such rules, companies might hesitate to adopt quantum technologies, fearing legal issues or harm to their reputation if regulations change unexpectedly (Aljaafari, 2023). As quantum technology grows more influential, it will also be important to set global standards encouraging cooperation across countries. This can create a safer and more supportive environment for its development.

While the lack of regulations might slow progress, it can also give businesses an advantage if they work with governments early (Aljaafari, 2023). Companies can help design rules that balance innovation with ethical practices by collaborating. For quick commerce businesses, participating in these discussions can ensure policies address consumer needs and privacy concerns while supporting fair and responsible use of quantum AI.

Cultural Acceptance and Organisational Readiness

Addressing technical and financial issues alone isn't enough when introducing quantum AI; companies also need cultural acceptance. Employees and leaders must be ready to handle the changes this technology brings. Resistance often comes from fear of job loss or confusion about its purpose (Ernst et al., 2019). Companies can address this by explaining how quantum AI works, showing its benefits, and keeping communication open to reduce fear and build trust.

Adapting to new technology is key for any business. Q-commerce companies should plan to help employees understand how quantum AI improves current systems and creates new opportunities. This can include simple training sessions on quantum basics and encouraging teamwork across departments to solve problems.

Quantum AI offers major benefits, but it also brings challenges. These include technical difficulties, high costs, unclear regulations, and ethical concerns (How & Cheah, 2023). Businesses must address these barriers and gain internal support to succeed. Companies can unlock quantum AI's potential by focusing on shared learning and building trust. Q-commerce businesses could then lead the way in solving larger societal problems, paving the path to a smarter, automated future.

Future Research Directions

Impact of Quantum AI on Consumer Behaviour

Many quick commerce companies are excited by the possibilities of quantum AI. This technology can reshape supply chains and strengthen customer loyalty by analysing vast amounts of data to predict shopping trends and preferences (Xu et al., 2024). One promising area is personalised marketing, where quantum AI can better match products to younger consumers' needs (Tula et al., 2024). Unlike traditional AI, which uses past data to suggest products, quantum AI processes multiple real-time data streams to recommend items customers most likely want. It can also predict how their preferences might change (Liu et al., 2022).

However, not all consumers may appreciate highly tailored recommendations. Some could feel targeted or overwhelmed. Researchers should explore how factors like age, tech-savviness, and lifestyle affect consumer responses to quantum AI-driven marketing (Jenkins et al., 2022; Purnamasari et al., 2023). Understanding these patterns will help brands refine their strategies to meet customer needs without alienating them. Ethical concerns, particularly around privacy, are also crucial. Quantum AI's ability to collect and analyse large amounts of personal data raises concerns about misuse (Tula et al., 2024). Companies must ensure privacy while offering personalised services. Striking a balance between innovation and ethical practices will build trust and ensure long-term success in the q-commerce sector.

Innovations in Supply Chain Management

Supply chains are essential for businesses to move goods efficiently. Quantum AI offers new possibilities for making them faster, clearer, and more flexible (Sodiya et al., 2024). This technology can solve tough logistics problems by improving tasks like planning delivery routes, managing stock, and organising transportation (Zhang et al., 2024). For example, in industries such as fast food, where speed is critical, quantum AI can help create tools that adjust delivery routes based on real-time traffic or weather changes. These improvements save time, lower costs, and make customers happier.

Combining quantum AI with blockchain technology is another promising development. Blockchain adds security and transparency to supply chains by keeping clear records of transactions and product movements (Rawat et al., 2022). With quantum AI, this system can track items more accurately and prevent fraud by verifying the authenticity of goods. For businesses, this means better control over their operations. For customers, it builds trust in the quality and origin of the products they buy.

Quantum AI can also help businesses manage risks in unpredictable supply chains. Natural disasters, political issues, or health emergencies often cause delays (Khatib et al., 2024). Quantum AI can analyse data to spot potential risks and offer solutions, like finding alternative suppliers or adjusting delivery plans. This ensures that businesses can continue operating smoothly even when unexpected problems arise.

Sustainability is another area where quantum AI can make a difference. More customers now prefer environmentally friendly choices. Quantum AI can help by reducing waste, managing resources more effectively, and incorporating renewable energy into supply chains (Leyerer et al., 2020). These actions not only support green goals but also improve efficiency. Compared to manual methods, AI can find problems and suggest fixes faster and more accurately.

Quantum AI can transform how supply chains work by making processes more efficient, secure, and eco-friendly helps businesses save money and meet customer expectations. Its ability to handle risks and improve operations makes it a valuable tool for today's fast-paced markets. With these advancements, companies can stay competitive while protecting the environment and earning consumer trust.

Interdisciplinary Studies

Quantum AI is too complex to be tackled by one field alone. It requires collaboration across disciplines like computer science, marketing, and logistics to unlock its full potential (Pramoda et al., 2024). Interdisciplinary research can provide a clearer view of how quantum AI can impact industries, particularly in quick commerce. These collaborations ensure that ideas move beyond theory and find practical applications in business. For instance, learning about the latest trends in computer science can help create better algorithms for quantum AI, offering more precise solutions for real-world problems (Choppakatla, 2023).

Collaboration between researchers, business leaders, and other stakeholders can lead to innovative products and services. Such efforts can make complex technologies more accessible and relevant in the quick commerce market. The integration of quantum AI into marketing is one area with great promise (Pramoda et al., 2024). It can help businesses design campaigns that analyse real-time data, identify trends, and understand consumer behavior. These insights can create direct connections with customers and offer solutions tailored to their needs. Ethical principles should also guide these systems, ensuring customers' trust and confidence in the technology. Another area of focus is quantum AI's role in behavioral economics. By applying basic psychological principles, businesses can better understand consumer decision-making and develop more effective marketing strategies (Wynn & Jones, 2023). These insights, combined with quantum AI's capabilities, could reshape how companies interact with their customers and market their products.

Interdisciplinary research also supports innovation in supply chain management and consumer behaviour analysis. Fast-developing technologies require collaboration across different sectors to keep pace with business needs. These partnerships can bring fresh ideas and practical solutions to quick commerce. For instance, combining quantum AI with supply chain analysis could transform how businesses handle logistics, creating faster and more efficient systems (Aljaafari, 2023; Khatib et al., 2024; Zhang et al., 2024). As quantum AI advances, it will drive big changes in e-commerce and quick commerce industries. The academic community plays a key role in shaping its future by exploring its impact on consumer behaviour, improving supply chains, and fostering collaboration (Zhang et al., 2024). These efforts will help businesses use quantum AI safely and effectively, addressing operational challenges and ethical concerns (Qayyum et al., 2023). With joint efforts, quantum AI can unlock new opportunities and transform industries' operations.

Business Implications

Quantum AI is set to bring major changes to the q-commerce industry, making it more flexible and efficient. Its ability to quickly process large amounts of data could reshape how businesses operate (How & Cheah, 2023). This technology will likely attract widespread interest in supply chain management, logistics, and customer service. While traditional q-commerce uses data analytics to understand customer behaviour and manage inventory, quantum AI takes these tools much further, offering deeper insights into customer habits and improving loyalty and satisfaction (Dasarraju, 2024). One of quantum AI's biggest impacts is logistics management (How & Cheah, 2023). It allows businesses to analyse real-time data, including traffic patterns, weather conditions, and other factors, to find faster and more efficient delivery routes. This improves shipping speed—a key priority in q-commerce—while lowering costs. For instance, grocery delivery services can use quantum AI to identify and fix delays in their supply chains, ensuring faster service and fewer disruptions. These advancements help businesses stay competitive by offering reliable and speedy deliveries.

Quantum AI is also transforming customer service. Businesses can use advanced chatbots and virtual assistants powered by quantum technology to provide a more personalised experience (Dunjko & Briegel, 2018; Ying, 2010). These tools can quickly analyse customer interactions and past data to recommend solutions tailored to individual needs. Faster responses and improved efficiency in handling customer queries will enhance satisfaction and build stronger relationships with customers. By integrating quantum AI into their strategies, businesses can improve operations and address challenges more effectively. This technology reduces costs, speeds up problem resolution, and allows for more precise decision-making. For q-commerce companies, adopting quantum AI means staying ahead of competitors and meeting rising customer expectations in a fast-changing market. Whether through better logistics, smarter customer service, or deeper data insights, quantum AI is poised to redefine how q-commerce businesses operate and succeed.

Technological Impact

As businesses adopt advanced technologies like quantum AI, they will push the limits of machine learning, automate processes more effectively, and develop smarter algorithms to stay competitive (Haldorai, 2024). One area where quantum AI could make a big difference is in forecasting shopping patterns. Unlike traditional methods, quantum AI can predict trends more accurately by analysing massive amounts of data in real-time. This capability helps businesses ensure items are always in stock and enables them to offer personalised marketing strategies that match individual customer preferences. These improvements not only boost satisfaction but also increase operational efficiency. A key objective in this "quantum future" is creating systems capable of managing data volumes far beyond what traditional computing can handle. Such infrastructure would allow businesses to run advanced simulations and improve their processes through better optimisation (Babatunde et al., 2024). For instance, quantum-powered systems could simulate supply chain scenarios to identify cost-saving measures and improve delivery times. These innovations will enable businesses to design services that better align with customer needs and expectations. Companies that integrate quantum AI early will force competitors to accelerate their efforts to remain relevant.

Quantum AI is also expected to bring breakthroughs in cybersecurity (Aljaafari, 2023). As cyber threats grow more sophisticated, the need for secure systems has never been greater. Quantum encryption methods could offer stronger protections for sensitive customer data, reducing the risk of breaches and enhancing trust in online transactions. Companies that prioritise quantum-based security measures will likely stand out in the market. For instance, an e-commerce platform implementing these advanced security features could attract more customers by ensuring their data is safe.

In addition to improving existing systems, quantum AI could enable entirely new business models. Businesses may combine quantum capabilities with traditional computing to create platforms that deliver real-time insights and enhance customer interactions (Dunjko & Briegel, 2018). These platforms could adapt to customer needs instantly, offering tailored solutions and improved service. For example, on-demand delivery companies could use quantum AI to refine inventory management and optimise delivery routes, ensuring faster service while minimising costs. Grocery delivery services could specifically benefit by predicting demand more accurately and reducing wastage in their operations. Quantum AI's potential impact extends further into operational processes, where it could make inventory management smarter, reduce operational costs, and improve decision-making in dynamic markets. Delivery systems could become more predictable and efficient, offering businesses an edge in meeting consumer expectations. As businesses increasingly embrace quantum AI, the technology will likely become a standard tool for innovation in the rapidly evolving q-commerce industry. Companies will stay competitive and redefine how commerce operates on a broader scale.

Social Implications

The growth of Quantum AI in the quick-commerce sector is expected to create big changes for consumers, jobs, and the overall market (Soueidan & Shoghari, 2024; Wynn & Jones, 2023). On one hand, integrating AI into businesses will benefit both shoppers and owners. Customers will enjoy smarter real-time shopping tools that predict their needs, helping them quickly find what they want. This kind of personalisation makes the shopping experience faster and more enjoyable (Ntumba et al., 2023). Even experienced customers will find value in the guidance offered by advanced AI systems, which can improve service while minimising environmental impact. However, as businesses collect and analyse more data, they must protect it from threats. Companies using quantum AI must follow strict privacy rules and remain transparent about how they handle consumer information (Tula et al., 2024). Quantum AI will also affect the workforce. While automation may create new jobs, it could also lead to the loss of existing ones as machines take over tasks previously handled by people. Companies can address this by offering retraining programs to prepare employees for new roles created by these technologies. These efforts could help ease fears about job loss while making workers more adaptable to future changes.

The rapid adoption of quantum AI will reshape the market as companies compete to use this technology. Rivalry will grow, sparking innovations and encouraging partnerships, mergers, and collaborations (Olorunsogo et al., 2024). However, the uneven pace of adoption may leave smaller businesses struggling to keep up. Larger companies that can afford quantum AI will gain an edge, potentially widening the gap between them and smaller firms. This risk of inequality could stifle competition and slow innovation (Purnamasari et al., 2023). To prevent this, policymakers and industry leaders must ensure that quantum AI tools are available to all market players. As quantum AI drives innovation, companies are updating their operations, especially in supply chains, smart systems, and customer service (Muthaluri et al., 2024). These advancements will boost their competitive edge but also lead to new consumer habits and changes in the workplace (Gupta, 2024). While quantum AI offers many opportunities for growth, businesses must stay alert to the challenges that come with navigating this fast-changing landscape.

CONCLUSION

The chapter explores q-commerce and its integration with advanced technologies, particularly quantum computing and AI. Through a comprehensive analysis, the study emphasises their potential to enhance logistics, improve decision-making, and redefine customer experiences. Quantum AI offers tools that allow businesses to process vast amounts of information quickly, enabling smarter strategies for handling inventory, deliveries, and consumer interactions. Quantum AI lets companies process data faster, predict customer behaviour more accurately, and make smarter choices to stay competitive in today's fast-moving market. It allows businesses to respond effectively to customer demands while improving efficiency. For instance, it helps companies manage inventory better, predict seasonal trends, and ensure products are available when needed. Delivery services benefit greatly by using quantum AI to calculate the best routes in real time, factoring in traffic, weather, and other variables. This results in faster deliveries, lower costs, and better customer satisfaction. Additionally, simulations using quantum AI can identify potential supply chain problems and help businesses plan solutions before issues arise.

The chapter shows that adopting quantum AI can also help businesses create personalised options for customers. By analysing data, companies can offer product recommendations or promotions that match individual preferences. These personalised services make customers feel valued and improve loyalty. For example, a grocery delivery service can adjust its offerings based on a customer's past orders or recommend alternatives when specific items are unavailable. Using quantum AI has its challenges. High implementation costs, unclear regulations, and concerns about data privacy are significant hurdles for businesses. As companies rely on more data, they must protect customer information and ensure their practices are transparent. Privacy rules and ethical guidelines are important to build trust and prevent misuse of personal data. Quantum AI can also support sustainability efforts. Reducing waste, improving resource use, and cutting energy consumption helps businesses meet the expectations of eco-conscious consumers. For instance, businesses can use AI tools to track and minimise waste in supply chains or optimise delivery routes to save fuel. These practices benefit both companies and the environment.

To successfully adopt quantum AI, businesses must prepare strategically. Training employees, forming partnerships, and investing in research are crucial steps. Collaboration with policymakers and industry groups can help make quantum AI more accessible and ensure fair competition. Smaller businesses will need support to adopt these technologies and stay competitive with larger firms. Flexibility is essential for businesses in the fast-changing q-commerce market. Quantum AI enables companies to adapt to shifting customer demands and market trends. Predictive tools powered by quantum AI can help businesses prepare for seasonal spikes in demand or adjust quickly to unexpected changes. This adaptability is key to thriving in a competitive environment. While quantum AI offers exciting opportunities, it also comes with responsibilities. Businesses must use this technology responsibly, addressing its social and environmental impacts. By focusing on transparency, ethical practices, and sustainability, companies can build trust with customers and create long-term value. Quantum AI is reshaping q-commerce by improving efficiency, meeting customer needs, and driving innovation. Its integration requires thoughtful planning and an emphasis on balancing progress with responsibility.

REFERENCES

Al Khatib, I., Alasheh, S., & Shamayleh, A. (2024). The Drivers of Complexity in Inventory Management Within the Healthcare Industry: A Systematic Review. *International Journal of Service Science, Management, Engineering, and Technology*, 15(1), 1–26. DOI: 10.4018/IJSSMET.347332

Aljaafari, M. (2023). Quantum computing for social business optimisation: A practitioner's perspective. *Soft Computing*, •••, 1–23. DOI: 10.1007/s00500-023-08764-y

Ashish. (2024). *Swiggy Instamart vs. Zepto: Quick Commerce Giants Compared.* https://wareiq.com/resources/blogs/swiggy-instamart-vs-zepto/

Babatunde, S. O., Odejide, O. A., Edunjobi, T. E., & Ogundipe, D. O.Sodiq Odetunde BabatundeOpeyemi Abayomi OdejideTolulope Esther EdunjobiDamilola Oluwaseun Ogundipe. (2024). THE ROLE OF AI IN MARKETING PERSONALISATION: A THEORETICAL EXPLORATION OF CONSUMER ENGAGEMENT STRATEGIES. *International Journal of Management & Entrepreneurship Research*, 6(3), 936–949. DOI: 10.51594/ijmer.v6i3.964

Choppakatla, A. (2023). Quantum Machine Learning: Bridging the Gap Between Quantum Computing and Artificial Intelligence: An Overview. *International Journal for Research in Applied Science and Engineering Technology*, 11(8), 1149–1153. DOI: 10.22214/ijraset.2023.55318

Cornelissen, J. (2017). Editor's comments: Developing propositions, a process model, or a typology? Addressing the challenges of writing theory without a boilerplate. In *Academy of Management Review* (Vol. 42, Issue 1, pp. 1–9). Academy of ManagementBriarcliff Manor, NY. DOI: 10.5465/amr.2016.0196

Dasarraju, V. K. (2024). Revolutionizing Quick Commerce: Harnessing the power of AI for Seamless Deliveries. *Journal of Artificial Intelligence. Machine Learning and Data Science*, 2(2), 638–641. DOI: 10.51219/JAIMLD/vamshi-krishna-dasarraju/164

Dhabliya, D., Dari, S. S., Dhablia, A., Akhila, N., Kachhoria, R., & Khetani, V. (2024). Addressing Bias in Machine Learning Algorithms: Promoting Fairness and Ethical Design. *E3S Web of Conferences, 491*, 02040. DOI: 10.1051/e3sconf/202449102040

Dunjko, V., & Briegel, H. J. (2018). Machine learning & artificial intelligence in the quantum domain: A review of recent progress. *Reports on Progress in Physics*, 81(7), 074001. Advance online publication. DOI: 10.1088/1361-6633/aab406 PMID: 29504942

El-Azab, S., & Nong, P. (2023). Clinical algorithms, racism, and "fairness" in healthcare: A case of bounded justice. *Big Data & Society*, 10(2), 20539517231213820. Advance online publication. DOI: 10.1177/20539517231213820

Ernst, E., Merola, R., & Samaan, D. (2019). Economics of Artificial Intelligence: Implications for the Future of Work. *IZA Journal of Labor Policy*, 9(1), 20190004. Advance online publication. DOI: 10.2478/izajolp-2019-0004

Eswaran, U., Khang, A., & Eswaran, V. (2024). Role of Quantum Computing in the Era of Artificial Intelligence (AI). In *Advances in computer and electrical engineering book series* (pp. 46–68). IGI Global., DOI: 10.4018/979-8-3693-1168-4.ch003

Fazelpour, S., Lipton, Z. C., & Danks, D. (2022). Algorithmic Fairness and the Situated Dynamics of Justice. *Canadian Journal of Philosophy*, 52(1), 44–60. DOI: 10.1017/can.2021.24

Gawor, T., & Hoberg, K. (2019). Customers' valuation of time and convenience in e-fulfillment. *International Journal of Physical Distribution & Logistics Management*, 49(1), 75–98. DOI: 10.1108/IJPDLM-09-2017-0275

Giani, A., & Eldredge, Z. (2021). Quantum Computing Opportunities in Renewable Energy. *SN Computer Science*, 2(5), 1–15. DOI: 10.1007/s42979-021-00786-3 PMID: 38217220

Gomes, A. C., De Lima, F. B.Junior, Soliani, R. D., & Oliveira, P. R. (2023). Logistics management in e-commerce: Challenges and opportunities. [Management and Administrative Professional Review]. *Revista de Gestão e Secretariado*, 14(5), 7252–7272. DOI: 10.7769/gesec.v14i5.2119

Gupta, S.SHIVOM GUPTA. (2024). A Study on Emergence of Quick Commerce. *International Journal For Multidisciplinary Research*, 6(2), 19226. Advance online publication. DOI: 10.36948/ijfmr.2024.v06i02.19226

Haldorai, A. (2024). Advancements and Applications of Quantum Computing in Robotics. *Journal of Computing and Natural Science*, 053–063. DOI: 10.53759/181X/JCNS202404006

Harter, A., Stich, L., & Spann, M. (2024). The Effect of Delivery Time on Repurchase Behavior in Quick Commerce. *Journal of Service Research*, 0(0), 1–17. DOI: 10.1177/10946705241236961

Holloway, S. (2024). *Exploring the Relationship Between Supply Chain Responsiveness and Customer Loyalty in the E-commerce Sector Exploring the Relationship between Supply Chain Responsiveness and Customer Loyalty in the E-Commerce Sector*. https://doi.org/https://doi.org/10.20944/preprints202406.1616.v1

How, M.-L., & Cheah, S.-M. (2023). Business Renaissance: Opportunities and Challenges at the Dawn of the Quantum Computing Era. *Businesses*, 3(4), 585–605. DOI: 10.3390/businesses3040036

Hübner, A., Kuhn, H., & Wollenburg, J. (2016). Last mile fulfilment and distribution in omni-channel grocery retailing: A strategic planning framework. *International Journal of Retail & Distribution Management*, 44(3), 228–247. DOI: 10.1108/IJRDM-11-2014-0154

Jaakkola, E. (2020). Designing conceptual articles: Four approaches. *AMS Review*, 10(1–2), 18–26. DOI: 10.1007/s13162-020-00161-0

Jenkins, J., Berente, N., & Angst, C. (2022). The Quantum Computing Business Ecosystem and Firm Strategies. *Proceedings of the Annual Hawaii International Conference on System Sciences, 2022-Janua*, 6432–6441. DOI: 10.24251/HICSS.2022.779

Kang, K., Wang, X., & Yang, W. (2024). The analysis of social E-commerce with artificial intelligence. *Applied and Computational Engineering*, 47(1), 67–74. DOI: 10.54254/2755-2721/47/20241198

Kaur, V., Khullar, V., & Verma, N. (2020). Review of Artificial Intelligence with Retailing Sector. *Journal of Computer Science Research*, 2(1), 1–7. DOI: 10.30564/jcsr.v2i1.1591

Kumar, D. P. M., R, J. A., J, J. V., M, D. B., & Manani, J. (2022). Sentimental Analysis on Quick Commerce Platform Based on Customer Reviews in Google Play Store. *International Journal of Research In Science & Engineering*, 26(26), 29–42. DOI: 10.55529/ijrise.26.29.42

Kumar, I., & Chidambara, . (2023). Freight patterns and spatial planning requirements of third generation E-commerce in Indian cities. *Urban, Planning and Transport Research*, 11(1), 2256817. Advance online publication. DOI: 10.1080/21650020.2023.2256817

Kuppler, M., Kern, C., Bach, R. L., & Kreuter, F. (2022). From fair predictions to just decisions? Conceptualising algorithmic fairness and distributive justice in the context of data-driven decision-making. *Frontiers in Sociology*, 7, 883999. DOI: 10.3389/fsoc.2022.883999 PMID: 36299413

Laghari, A. A., Shah, H., Laghari, R. A., Kumar, K., Waqan, A. A., & Jumani, A. K. (2018). A Review on Quantum Computing Trends & Future Perspectives. *EAI Endorsed Transactions on Cloud Systems*, 7(22), 173979. DOI: 10.4108/eai.17-5-2022.173979

Lee, T., Han, S. R., & Song, B. D. (2023). Optimisation of OmniChannel Distribution Network Using Micro Fulfillment Center under Demand Uncertainty. *IEEE Access : Practical Innovations, Open Solutions*, 11, 107496–107510. DOI: 10.1109/ACCESS.2023.3317690

Leyerer, M., Sonneberg, M. O., Heumann, M., & Breitner, M. H. (2020). Shortening the last mile in urban areas: Optimising a smart logistics concept for e-grocery operations. *Smart Cities*, 3(3), 585–603. DOI: 10.3390/smartcities3030031

Li, J., & Chignell, M. (2022). FMEA-AI: AI fairness impact assessment using failure mode and effects analysis. *AI and Ethics*, 2(4), 837–850. DOI: 10.1007/s43681-022-00145-9

Li, K. (2022). The Qubit Fidelity Under Different Error Mechanisms Based on Error Correction Threshold. *Frontiers in Physics (Lausanne)*, 10, 893507. DOI: 10.3389/fphy.2022.893507

Litt, S. (2024). *Subscription Business Models: How & Why They Work In 2024 - The CFO Club*. https://thecfoclub.com/operational-finance/subscription-model/

Liu, B., Huang, S., Zhou, M., & YANG, S. (2022). Research on the application of "quantum computing + dynamic face recognition" in bank personal business. Https://Doi.Org/10.1117/12.2657069, *12503*, 3. DOI: 10.1117/12.2657069

Loi, M., Ferrario, A., & Viganò, E. (2021). Transparency as design publicity: Explaining and justifying inscrutable algorithms. *Ethics and Information Technology*, 23(3), 253–263. DOI: 10.1007/s10676-020-09564-w PMID: 34867077

Lubinski, T., Granade, C., Anderson, A., Geller, A., Roetteler, M., Petrenko, A., & Heim, B. (2022). Advancing hybrid quantum–classical computation with real-time execution. *Frontiers in Physics (Lausanne)*, 10, 940293. DOI: 10.3389/fphy.2022.940293

Mitchell, S., Potash, E., Barocas, S., D'Amour, A., & Lum, K. (2021). Algorithmic fairness: Choices, assumptions, and definitions. *Annual Review of Statistics and Its Application, 8*(Volume 8, 2021), 141–163. https://doi.org/DOI: 10.1146/ANNUREV-STATISTICS-042720-125902/CITE/REFWORKS

Muthaluri, J., Sivakumar, D. T. B., Rahamtula, D., Samanta, K., & Sanne, S. H. V. (2024). Optimising Supply Chain Management And Marketing Strategies: AI And ML Integration For Competitive Advantage. *Educational Administration: Theory and Practice*, 30(5), 8990–8997. DOI: 10.53555/kuey.v30i5.4494

Neha, M., S., Alfurhood, B. S., Bakhare, R., Poongavanam, S., & Khanna, R. (2023). The Role and Impact of Artificial Intelligence on Retail Business and its Developments. *2023 International Conference on Artificial Intelligence and Smart Communication, AISC 2023*, 1098–1101. DOI: 10.1109/AISC56616.2023.10085624

Ntumba, C., Aguayo, S., & Maina, K. (2023). Revolutionising Retail: A Mini Review of E-commerce Evolution. *Journal of Digital Marketing and Communication*, 3(2), 100–110. DOI: 10.53623/jdmc.v3i2.365

Olorunsogo, T., Jacks, B. S., & Ajala, O. A. (2024). LEVERAGING QUANTUM COMPUTING FOR INCLUSIVE AND RESPONSIBLE AI DEVELOPMENT: A CONCEPTUAL AND REVIEW FRAMEWORK. *Computer Science & IT Research Journal*, 5(3), 671–680. DOI: 10.51594/csitrj.v5i3.927

Pramoda, M., Evuru, P. C., Vulavalapudi, V. M. S., Pallapothu, L. K. K., & Annapurna, B. (2024). Quantum Machine Learning: A Survey. *Journal of Electrical Systems*, 20(6s), 971–981. DOI: 10.52783/jes.2778

Priyanka. (2024). *2024 is the year of the Subscription Business model. Know all definitions, benefits, and metrics.*https://www.racknap.com/blog/subscription-business-models-explained/

Purnamasari, D. I., Permadi, V. A., Saepudin, A., & Agusdin, R. P. (2023). Demand Forecasting for Improved Inventory Management in Small and Medium-Sized Businesses. [JANAPATI]. *Jurnal Nasional Pendidikan Teknik Informatika*, 12(1), 56–66. DOI: 10.23887/janapati.v12i1.57144

Qayyum, A., Ur Rasool, R., Ahmad, H. F., Rafique, W., Qadir, J., & Anwar, Z. (2023). Quantum Computing for Healthcare: A Review. In *Future Internet* (Vol. 15, Issue 3). *Authorea*. DOI: 10.3390/fi15030094

Rahmawati, K., Kasih, P. H., & Perdana, A. B. (2023). *From Offline to Online: Changes in Vegetable Purchases During COVID-19 in Indonesia* (Vol. 1). Atlantis Press SARL., DOI: 10.2991/978-2-38476-048-0_25

Raji, M. ., Olodo, H. ., Oke, T. ., Addy, W. ., Ofodile, O. ., & Oyewole, A. . (2024). E-commerce and consumer behavior: A review of AI-powered personalisation and market trends. *GSC Advanced Research and Reviews, 18*(3), 066–077. DOI: 10.30574/gscarr.2024.18.3.0090

Ranjekar, G., & Roy, D. (2023). *Rise of Quick Commerce in India : Business Models and Infrastructure Requirements.*

Rau, J., Altenburg, L., & Ghezzi, A. I. (2023). How the Quick Commerce Business Model Delivers Convenience in Online Grocery Retailing. In *Springer Proceedings in Business and Economics* (Vol. 1, Issue Gielens 2022). Springer Nature Switzerland. DOI: 10.1007/978-3-031-31836-8_10

Rawat, B., Mehra, N., Bist, A. S., Yusup, M., & Sanjaya, Y. P. A. (2022). Quantum Computing and AI: Impacts & Possibilities. [AJRI]. *ADI Journal on Recent Innovation*, 3(2), 202–207. DOI: 10.34306/ajri.v3i2.656

Richa, H., & Vadera, S. (2019). Determinants of online shopping behaviour in india. *International Journal of Recent Technology and Engineering*, 8(3), 3946–3950. DOI: 10.35940/ijrte.C5303.098319

Royanti, I., & Astini, R. (2023). Analysis of E-Grocery Purchase Decisions Mediated by E-Trust in Indonesia Quick Commerce. *International Journal of Innovative Science and Research Technology*, 8(8). www.ijisrt.com

Rybaczewska, M., & Sparks, L. (2020). Locally-owned convenience stores and the local economy. *Journal of Retailing and Consumer Services*, 52, 101939. DOI: 10.1016/j.jretconser.2019.101939

Schärer, K., & Comuzzi, M. (2023). The quantum threat to blockchain: Summary and timeline analysis. *Quantum Machine Intelligence*, 5(1), 1–12. DOI: 10.1007/s42484-023-00105-4

Sedik, T. S., Gorbanyov, M., & Malaika, M. (2021). Quantum Computing and the Financial System: Spooky Action at a Distance? *IMF Working Paper*, 2021(071), 1. DOI: 10.5089/9781513572727.001

Setiyono, A. E., Chandrawatisma, C., Fanandi, R. H. S., & Heriyati, P. (2023). Antecedents of E-Loyalty as Research for the Quick Commerce Industry. *Interdisciplinary Social Studies*, 2(8), 2287–2299. DOI: 10.55324/iss.v2i8.456

Shrestha, S., & Das, S. (2022). Exploring gender biases in ML and AI academic research through systematic literature review. In *Frontiers in Artificial Intelligence* (Vol. 5, p. 976838). Frontiers Media S.A., DOI: 10.3389/frai.2022.976838

Simon, J., Wong, P. H., & Rieder, G. (2020). Algorithmic bias and the value sensitive design approach. *Internet Policy Review*, 9(4), 1–16. DOI: 10.14763/2020.4.1534

Singh, D. S., Agarwal, M. S., & Gupta, M. R. (2023). Quantum Computing: Fundamentals, Progress, and Implications. *International Journal for Research in Applied Science and Engineering Technology*, 11(9), 1106–1111. DOI: 10.22214/ijraset.2023.55803

Sodiya, E. O., Umoga, U. J., Amoo, O. O., & Akoh, A. (2024). AI-driven warehouse automation: A comprehensive review of systems. *GSC Advanced Research and Reviews*, 18(2), 272–282. DOI: 10.30574/gscarr.2024.18.2.0063

Soueidan, M. H., & Shoghari, R. (2024). The Impact of Artificial Intelligence on Job Loss: Risks for Governments. *Technium Social Sciences Journal*, 57, 206–223. DOI: 10.47577/tssj.v57i1.10917

Spivey, R. F., Inlek, I. V., Jia, Z., Crain, S., Sun, K., Kim, J., Vrijsen, G., Fang, C., Fitzgerald, C., Kross, S., Noel, T., & Kim, J. (2022). High-Stability Cryogenic System for Quantum Computing with Compact Packaged Ion Traps. *IEEE Transactions on Quantum Engineering*, 3, 1–11. Advance online publication. DOI: 10.1109/TQE.2021.3125926

Sreerama, J., & Krishnamoorthy, G. (2022). Ethical Considerations in AI Addressing Bias and Fairness in Machine Learning Models. *Journal of Knowledge Learning and Science Technology ISSN: 2959-6386 (Online), 1*(1), 130–138. DOI: 10.60087/jklst.vol1.n1.p138

Stamatopoulos, N., Egger, D. J., Sun, Y., Zoufal, C., Iten, R., Shen, N., & Woerner, S. (2020). Option pricing using quantum computers. *Quantum : the Open Journal for Quantum Science*, 4, 291. Advance online publication. DOI: 10.22331/q-2020-07-06-291

Stojanov, M. (2022). *Q-COMMERCE – THE NEXT GENERATION*. http://hdl.handle.net/10610/4683

Sun, H. (2023). Design Logistics Management System Based on Computer Algorithm Model. *Frontiers in Artificial Intelligence and Applications*, 373, 569–575. DOI: 10.3233/FAIA230856

Tamrakar, A., & Sharma, R. (2019). Quantum Computing: A Comprehensive Review. [TURCOMAT]. *Turkish Journal of Computer and Mathematics Education*, 10(3), 1634–1642. DOI: 10.61841/turcomat.v10i3.14623

Tula, S. T., Kess-Momoh, A. J., Omotoye, G. B., Bello, B. G., & Daraojimba, A. I.Sunday Tubokirifuruar TulaAzeez Jason Kess-MomohGaniyu Bolawale OmotoyeBinaebi Gloria BelloAndrew Ifesinachi Daraojimba. (2024). AI-ENABLED CUSTOMER EXPERIENCE ENHANCEMENT IN BUSINESS. *Computer Science & IT Research Journal*, 5(2), 365–389. DOI: 10.51594/csitrj.v5i2.789

Wajidi, F. A., Rehan, E. W., Saeed, M., Iftikhar, K. M., & Tahir, A. (2023). Technology Trends and Their Impact on the E-commerce Industry. *International Journal of Social Science & Entrepreneurship*, 3(4), 236–253. DOI: 10.58661/ijsse.v3i4.227

Wynn, M., & Jones, P. (2023). Corporate Digital Responsibility and the Business Implications of Quantum Computing. *Advances in Environmental and Engineering Research*, 04(04), 1–15. DOI: 10.21926/aeer.2304053

Xu, X., Cui, J., Cui, Z., He, R., Li, Q., Li, X., Lin, Y., Liu, J., Liu, W., Lu, J., Luo, M., Lyu, C., Pan, S., Pavel, M., Shu, R., Tang, J., Xu, R., Xu, S., Yang, K., & Yung, M.-H. (2024). *MindSpore Quantum: A User-Friendly, High-Performance, and AI-Compatible Quantum Computing Framework.* https://arxiv.org/abs/2406.17248v3

Ying, M. (2010). Quantum computation, quantum theory and AI. In *Artificial Intelligence* (Vol. 174, Issue 2, pp. 162–176). Elsevier. DOI: 10.1016/j.artint.2009.11.009

Zhang, H., Tian, S., Qin, J., Yu, Z., Guo, H., & Jia, X. (2024). Inventory prediction based on CNN-LSTM Model. *Highlights in Science. Engineering and Technology*, 82, 251–257. DOI: 10.54097/eywbtj23

Zhu, H., Zhu, Z., Ou, Y., & Yin, Y. (2023). To be precise (imprecise) in utilitarian (hedonic) contexts: Examining the influence of numerical precision on consumer reactions to artificial intelligence-based recommendations. *Psychology and Marketing*, 40(12), 2668–2685. DOI: 10.1002/mar.21904

Chapter 18
Looking Ahead: The Next Decade of Neuromarketing and Quantum AI

Vineet Singh
https://orcid.org/0009-0007-5055-3518
Woxsen University, India

Pranjali Gajbhiye
https://orcid.org/0000-0001-5567-5732
Woxsen University, India

ABSTRACT

The next decade promises transformative advancements in neuromarketing and quantum artificial intelligence (AI), reshaping how businesses understand and engage with consumers. Neuromarketing employs neuroscience techniques, such as fMRI and EEG, to analyze emotional and cognitive responses to marketing stimuli, providing deeper insights into consumer behavior. Meanwhile, quantum AI leverages the principles of quantum computing to enhance data analysis capabilities, enabling real-time insights and complex problem-solving. The integration of these fields will allow marketers to create highly personalized campaigns, optimize strategies through predictive analytics, and gain comprehensive consumer profiles. However, ethical considerations regarding data privacy and transparency will be paramount as these technologies evolve. This article explores the potential applications, challenges, and future trends at the intersection of neuromarketing and quantum AI, highlighting their implications for marketing strategies and consumer engagement in an increasingly data-driven landscape.

DOI: 10.4018/979-8-3693-7673-7.ch018

INTRODUCTION

The convergence of neuromarketing and quantum artificial intelligence (AI) promises to revolutionize how businesses understand consumer behavior and optimize marketing strategies. Neuromarketing employs neuroscience techniques to analyze consumer responses to marketing stimuli, while quantum AI leverages the principles of quantum computing to enhance machine learning capabilities. This article explores the potential developments in these fields over the next decade, the implications for marketers, and the broader impact on business strategies.

Understanding Neuromarketing

Neuromarketing is a multidisciplinary field that combines neuroscience, psychology, and marketing to gain insights into consumer behavior. By utilizing techniques such as functional magnetic resonance imaging (fMRI), electroencephalography (EEG), and biometrics, marketers can observe brain activity and physiological responses to advertisements, products, and brands. This data allows for a deeper understanding of consumer preferences and decision-making processes.

Key Techniques in Neuromarketing

- fMRI: Measures brain activity by detecting changes associated with blood flow, providing insights into emotional responses (Plassmann et al., 2015).
- EEG: Records electrical activity in the brain, useful for assessing attention levels and emotional engagement (Ramsøy et al., 2019).
- Analysis: Monitors physiological responses such as heart rate and skin conductance to gauge emotional reactions (Couwenberg et al., 2018).

These techniques enable marketers to design campaigns that resonate more effectively with target audiences by tapping into subconscious preferences.

The Rise of Quantum AI

Quantum AI refers to the application of quantum computing principles to artificial intelligence algorithms. Unlike classical computers that process information using bits (0s and 1s), quantum computers utilize qubits, which can exist in multiple states simultaneously. This capability allows quantum AI to perform complex calculations at unprecedented speeds, potentially transforming various sectors, including marketing.

Advantages of Quantum AI

- Speed: Quantum AI can analyze vast datasets much faster than traditional AI, enabling real-time insights (Zapata et al., 2023).

- Complex Problem Solving: It can tackle problems that are currently unsolvable by classical computers, such as optimizing marketing strategies across multiple variables (Diraq, 2023).

- Pattern Recognition: Quantum AI excels at identifying patterns in large datasets, which is crucial for predicting consumer behavior (Garcia & Saad, 2022).

The Intersection of Neuromarketing and Quantum AI

The integration of neuromarketing with quantum AI creates a powerful synergy that can enhance marketing effectiveness. By leveraging quantum computing capabilities, marketers can analyze neuromarketing data more deeply and quickly than ever before.

Potential Applications

1. Enhanced Consumer Insights: Quantum AI can process neuromarketing data from various sources (e.g., social media interactions, purchase histories) to generate comprehensive consumer profiles (Hubert & Kenning, 2021).
2. Predictive Analytics: By analyzing patterns in consumer behavior data, quantum AI can predict future purchasing decisions with greater accuracy (Al-Kwifi et al., 2022).
3. Personalization at Scale: Marketers can create highly personalized campaigns tailored to individual preferences based on insights derived from neuromarketing studies (Venkatraman et al., 2020).

Future Trends in Neuromarketing and Quantum AI

1. Increased Adoption of Quantum Technologies

As quantum computing technology matures, more businesses will adopt quantum AI solutions for their marketing strategies. The global market for quantum AI is projected to grow significantly, from USD 242.4 million in 2023 to USD 1.8 billion by 2030, with a compound annual growth rate (CAGR) of 34.1% over the forecast period (Microsoft Research, 2023). This growth will likely drive innovations in neuromarketing techniques as well.

2. Ethical Considerations

The use of neuromarketing raises ethical questions regarding consumer privacy and manipulation. As companies harness quantum AI's capabilities to analyze consumer data more deeply, they must navigate these ethical challenges carefully. Transparency in data usage and obtaining informed consent will be crucial for maintaining consumer trust (Schneider & Woolgar, 2021).

3. Integration with Other Technologies

The next decade will see the integration of neuromarketing and quantum AI with other emerging technologies such as augmented reality (AR), virtual reality (VR), and the Internet of Things (IoT). These technologies will provide new avenues for engaging consumers and gathering data on their preferences (Fortunato et al., 2022).

Challenges Ahead

While the potential benefits of integrating neuromarketing with quantum AI are substantial, several challenges must be addressed:

- Data Security: As companies collect more detailed consumer data through advanced technologies, ensuring data security will be paramount (Ramsøy et al., 2019).
- Skill Gaps: The rapid evolution of these technologies may outpace the current skill sets available in the workforce. Training programs will be essential to equip marketers with the necessary knowledge (Diraq, 2023).
- Regulatory Compliance: As governments implement stricter regulations on data privacy, businesses must ensure compliance while leveraging advanced analytics tools (Zapata et al., 2023).

Case Studies: Current Applications

Several companies are already exploring the intersection of neuromarketing and quantum AI:

1. Google Quantum AI: Google has been at the forefront of developing quantum algorithms that could enhance data analysis capabilities within marketing frameworks.
2. IBM Watson: IBM's Watson is integrating quantum computing capabilities with its existing machine learning algorithms to improve predictive analytics for marketers.
3. D-Wave Systems: D-Wave is focusing on optimizing complex decision-making processes in marketing through its quantum annealing technology.

CONCLUSION

The next decade promises significant advancements in both neuromarketing and quantum AI. As these fields converge, marketers will gain unprecedented insights into consumer behavior, enabling them to craft more effective strategies. However, navigating ethical considerations and technological challenges will be critical as businesses strive to harness these powerful tools responsibly. The future of marketing lies at this exciting intersection of neuroscience and cutting-edge technology—an era where understanding consumers becomes both an art and a science.

REFERENCES

Al-Kwifi, O. S., & Karam, A. A. (2022). Brand Choice Prediction through Neural Activation Patterns. *Journal of Brand Strategy*.

Ali Liaquat. (2023). *Quantum AI's Impact on Digital Marketing*. AiThority.

Barnett, C. J., & Cerf, M. A. (2019). Neuroscience Data for Brand Value Measurement. *Journal of Brand Management*.

Couwenberg, J.. (2018). Functional Elements in Advertising Effectiveness. *Journal of Advertising Research*.

D-Wave Systems. (2023). *Optimizing Complex Decision-Making Processes through Quantum Annealing Technology*. D-Wave Insights.

Diraq, H. M. (2023). Ethical Implications in Neuromarketing. *Journal of Business Ethics*.

. Fortunato, V., & Gallo, M.A. (2022). Neuromarketing Applications in Emerging Technologies. Journal of Marketing Theory .

. Fortunato V., & Gallo M.A.(2022). Neuromarketing Applications in Emerging Technologies. Journal of Marketing Theory .

Garcia, R., & Saad, G. H. (2022). Consumer Behavior Insights from Neuroscience. *Marketing Letters*.

Global, I. G. I. (2023). *Call for Chapters on Neuromarketing and Quantum Computing*. IGI Global.

Google Quantum, A. I. (2023). *Enhancing Data Analysis Capabilities within Marketing Frameworks*. Google Research.

Hubert, M., & Kenning, P. A. (2021). Neuroscience Methods in Marketing Research: A Review. *Journal of Consumer Psychology*.

Javor, A.. (2017). Cognitive Neuroscience Applications in Marketing. *Journal of Marketing Management*.

. Microsoft Research. (2023). Future Trends in Quantum Computing for Marketing.

. Netoloji.(2023). The Evolution of Marketing in the Era of Quantum Technology. Netoloji Insights .

Plassmann, H., & Ramsøy, T.Z., & Milica Mormann. (2015). Marketing Implications from Understanding Consumer Behavior through Neuroscience Techniques. *The Journal of Consumer Research.*

Ramsøy, T. Z., & Mormann, M. (2019). Cognitive Neuroscience Applications in Marketing. *Journal of Marketing Management.*

Schneider, C., & Woolgar, S. (2021). Ethical Considerations in Neuromarketing Practices. *Journal of Business Ethics.*

Venkatraman, M.. (2020). Emotional Responses in Advertising: A Neuromarketing Perspective. *Journal of Advertising.*

Zapata, J. M.. (2023). Advancements in Automated Marketing Systems Using Quantum Algorithms. *Journal of Business Research.*

Compilation of References

Adams, H., & Hall, D. (2022). Innovations in artificial intelligence research fueled by big data analytics. *European Journal of Business and Innovation Research*, 10(2), 96–104.

Agarwal, P., & Alam, M. (2021). Exploring quantum computing to revolutionize big data analytics for various industrial sectors. In *Big data analytics* (pp. 113–130). Auerbach Publications. DOI: 10.1201/9781003175711-7

Aggarwal, D., Bali, V., & Mittal, S. (2019). An insight into machine learning techniques for predictive analysis and feature selection. *International Journal of Innovative Technology and Exploring Engineering*, 8(9), 342–349.

Aheleroff, S., Huang, H., Xu, X., & Zhong, R. Y. (2022). Toward sustainability and resilience with Industry 4.0 and Industry5.0. *Frontiers in Manufacturing Technology.*, 2, 951643. DOI: 10.3389/fmtec.2022.951643

Ahmadi, A. (2023). Quantum computing and artificial intelligence: The synergy of two revolutionary technologies. *Asian Journal of Electrical Sciences*, 12(2), 15–27. DOI: 10.51983/ajes-2023.12.2.4118

Ahmed, S. (2019). Pattern recognition with Quantum Support Vector Machine (QSVM) on near term quantum processors (Doctoral dissertation, Brac University).

Ahmed, S., Sharif, T., Ting, D. H., & Sharif, S. J. (2024). Crafting emotional engagement and immersive experiences: Comprehensive scale development for and validation of hospitality marketing storytelling involvement. *Psychology and Marketing*, 41(7), 1415–1667. DOI: 10.1002/mar.21994

Ahn, D., Lee, J., Kim, M. S., & Hwang, S. W. (2002). SelfConsistent non-Markovian theory of a quantum-state evolution for quantum-information-processing. *Physical Review A*, 66(1), 012302. DOI: 10.1103/PhysRevA.66.012302

Ahn, J. B. (2020). A Study on Predicting Changes of Future Advertising Characteristics and Types after the Corona 19 Pandemic. *International Journal of Internet. Broadcasting and Communication*, 12(4), 137–147.

Ahn, K., Qiu, C., & Zöllner, M. (2020). Real-Time Optimized Delta Robot Control for Flexible Manufacturing. *Journal of Advanced Manufacturing Systems*, 18(4), 254–266.

Ahn, W. K., Qiu, C., & Zöllner, M. (2020). A Real-Time Optimized Delta Robot Control Strategy for Flexible Manufacturing. *Journal of Advanced Manufacturing Systems*, 18(4), 254–266.

Aishwarya, S., Abeer, V., Sathish, B. B., & Subramanya, K. N. (2020). Quantum computational techniques for prediction of cognitive state of human mind from EEG signals. *Journal of Quantum Computing*, 2(4), 157. DOI: 10.32604/jqc.2020.015018

Ajiga, D. I., Ndubuisi, N. L., Asuzu, O. F., Owolabi, O. R., Tubokirifuruar, T. S., & Adeleye, R. A.David Iyanuoluwa AjigaNdubuisi Leonard NdubuisiOnyeka Franca AsuzuOluwaseyi Rita OwolabiTula Sunday TubokirifuruarRhoda Adura Adeleye. (2024). AI-driven predictive analytics in retail: A review of emerging trends and customer engagement strategies. *International Journal of Management & Entrepreneurship Research*, 6(2), 307–321. DOI: 10.51594/ijmer.v6i2.772

Al Khatib, I., Alasheh, S., & Shamayleh, A. (2024). The Drivers of Complexity in Inventory Management Within the Healthcare Industry: A Systematic Review. *International Journal of Service Science, Management, Engineering, and Technology*, 15(1), 1–26. DOI: 10.4018/IJSSMET.347332

Al-Baidhany, I. A., & Saleh, M. B. (2024). Study of changing entangled states of a quantum system consisting of four qubits using the Hadamard gate. Journal of Theory. *Mathematics and Physics*, 3(4), 55–63.

Ali Liaquat. (2023). *Quantum AI's Impact on Digital Marketing*. AiThority.

Aliferis, P., Gottesman, D., & Preskill, J. (2008). Accuracy threshold for Quantum Computation. *Quant. Inf. Proc.*, 8, 181–244.

Aljaafari, M. (2023). Quantum computing for social business optimisation: A practitioner's perspective. *Soft Computing*, •••, 1–23. DOI: 10.1007/s00500-023-08764-y

AlKheder, S., AlRukaibi, F., & Aiash, A. (2023). Support Vector Machine (SVM), Random Forest (RF), Artificial Neural Network (ANN) and Bayesian Network for prediction and analysis of GCC traffic accidents. *Journal of Ambient Intelligence and Humanized Computing*, 14(6), 7331–7339. DOI: 10.1007/s12652-022-04441-4

Al-Kwifi, O. S., & Karam, A. A. (2022). Brand Choice Prediction through Neural Activation Patterns. *Journal of Brand Strategy*.

Alsharif, A. H., Md Salleh, N. Z., Baharun, R., Alsharif, Y. H., & Abuhassna, H. (2021). A bibliometric analysis of Neuromarketing: Current status, development and future directions. *International Journal of Academic Research in Accounting. Finance and Management Sciences*, 11(3), 828–847. DOI: 10.6007/IJARAFMS/v11-i3/11673

Alsharif, A. H., Md Salleh, N. Z., Baharun, R., & Rami Hashem, E. (2021). Neuromarketing research in the last five years: A bibliometric analysis. *Cogent Business & Management*, 8(1), 1978620. DOI: 10.1080/23311975.2021.1978620

Alsharif, A. H., & Mohd Isa, S. (2024). Revolutionizing consumer insights: The impact of fMRI in neuromarketing research. *Future Business Journal*, 10(1), 79. DOI: 10.1186/s43093-024-00371-z

Alsharif, A. H., Salleh, N. Z. M., Abdullah, M., Khraiwish, A., & Ashaari, A. (2023). Neuromarketing tools used in the marketing mix: A systematic literature and future research agenda. *SAGE Open*, 13(1). Advance online publication. DOI: 10.1177/21582440231156563

Alsharif, A., Md. Salleh, N. Z., & Pilelienė, L. (2023). A comprehensive bibliometric analysis of fNIRS and fMRI technology in neuromarketing. *Scientific Annals of Economics and Business*, 70(3), 459–472. DOI: 10.47743/saeb-2023-0031

Alsharif, A., Salleh, N., & Baharun, R. (2020). Research trends of Neuromarketing: A bibliometric analysis. *Journal of Theoretical and Applied Information Technology*, 98, 2948–2962. http://www.jatit.org/volumes/Vol98No15/6Vol98No15.pdf

Altaheri, H., Muhammad, G., Alsulaiman, M., Amin, S. U., Altuwaijri, G. A., Abdul, W., Bencherif, M. A., & Faisal, M. (2021). Deep learning techniques for classification of electroencephalogram (EEG) motor imagery (MI) signals: A review. *Neural Computing & Applications*, 35(20), 14681–14722. DOI: 10.1007/s00521-021-06352-5

Ambler, T. (2015). Persuasion, pride and prejudice: How ads work. *International Journal of Advertising*, 19(3), 299–315. DOI: 10.1080/02650487.2000.11104803

Amin, S., Alsulaiman, M., Ghulam, M., Mekhtiche, M., & Hossain, M. S. (2019). Deep Learning for EEG motor imagery classification based on multi-layer CNNs feature fusion. *Future Generation Computer Systems*, 101, 542–554. DOI: 10.1016/j.future.2019.06.027

Andriella, A., Torras, C., & Alenya, G. (2019). Learning Robot Policies Using a High-Level Abstraction Persona-Behaviour Simulator. *2019 28th IEEE International Conference on Robot and Human Interactive Communication (RO-MAN)*, 1–8. DOI: 10.1109/RO-MAN46459.2019.8956357

Angeles, J. (2014). *Fundamentals of Robotic Mechanical Systems*. Springer-Verlag. DOI: 10.1007/978-3-319-01851-5

Ang, K. K., Chin, Z. Y., Wang, C., Guan, C., & Zhang, H. (2012). Filter bank common spatial pattern algorithm on BCI competition IV datasets 2a and 2b. *Frontiers in Neuroscience*, 6, 39.

An, J., Kwak, H., Jung, S., Salminen, J., Admad, M., & Jansen, B. (2018). Imaginary people representing real numbers: Generating personas from online social media data. *ACM Transactions on the Web*, 12(4), 1–26. Advance online publication. DOI: 10.1145/3265986

Antsipava, D., Strycharz, J., van Reijmersdal, E. A., & van Noort, G. (2024). What drives blockchain technology adoption in the online advertising ecosystem? An interview study into stakeholders' perspectives. *Journal of Business Research*, 171, 114381. DOI: 10.1016/j.jbusres.2023.114381

Ariely, D., & Berns, G. S. (2010). Neuromarketing: The hope and hype of neuroimaging in business. *Nature Reviews. Neuroscience*, 11(4), 284–292. DOI: 10.1038/nrn2795 PMID: 20197790

Arora, M. (2024). Redefining Consumer Engagement in Virtual Spaces. Neurosensory and Neuromarketing Impacts on Consumer Behavior, 415.

Arthurs, O. J., & Boniface, S. (2002). How well do we understand the neural origins of the fMRI BOLD signal? *Trends in Neurosciences*, 25(1), 27–31. DOI: 10.1016/S0166-2236(00)01995-0 PMID: 11801335

Arute, F., Arya, K., Babbush, R., Bacon, D., Bardin, J. C., Barends, R., Biswas, R., Boixo, S., Brandao, F. G. S. L., Buell, D. A., Burkett, B., Chen, Y., Chen, Z., Chiaro, B., Collins, R., Courtney, W., Dunsworth, A., Farhi, E., Foxen, B., & Martinis, J. M. (2019). Quantum Supremacy Using a Programmable Superconducting Processor. *Nature*, 574(7779), 505–510. DOI: 10.1038/s41586-019-1666-5 PMID: 31645734

Ashish. (2024). *Swiggy Instamart vs. Zepto: Quick Commerce Giants Compared*. https://wareiq.com/resources/blogs/swiggy-instamart-vs-zepto/

Ayesha, S., Hanif, M. K., & Talib, R. (2021). Performance enhancement of predictive analytics for health informatics using dimensionality reduction techniques and fusion frameworks. *IEEE Access : Practical Innovations, Open Solutions*, 10, 753–769. DOI: 10.1109/ACCESS.2021.3139123

Babar, M., Khattak, A. S., Jan, M. A., & Tariq, M. U. (2021). Energy aware smart city management system using data analytics and internet of things. *Sustainable Energy Technologies and Assessments*, 44, 100992. Advance online publication. DOI: 10.1016/j.seta.2021.100992

Babatunde, S. O., Odejide, O. A., Edunjobi, T. E., & Ogundipe, D. O.Sodiq Odetunde BabatundeOpeyemi Abayomi OdejideTolulope Esther EdunjobiDamilola Oluwaseun Ogundipe. (2024). THE ROLE OF AI IN MARKETING PERSONALISATION: A THEORETICAL EXPLORATION OF CONSUMER ENGAGEMENT STRATEGIES. *International Journal of Management & Entrepreneurship Research*, 6(3), 936–949. DOI: 10.51594/ijmer.v6i3.964

Babbush, . (2020). Quantum Algorithms for Robotics and Control Systems. *Nature Reviews. Chemistry*, 4(5), 144–159.

Babbush, R.. (2020). Quantum Chemistry Using Quantum Computers. *Nature Reviews. Chemistry*, 4(5), 144–159.

Babu, C. V. S., & Vinutha, S. (2024). Impact of AR/VR in the learning process of children with dyslexia. In V. Ajantha Devi, W. Singh, & Y. Kumar (Eds.), Augmented reality and virtual reality in special education (pp. 127-140). Scrivener Publishing. https://scrivenerpublishing.com/cart/title.php?id=980

Bacon, D. (2006). Operator Quantum Error-Correcting Subsystems for self-correcting quantum memories. *Physical Review A*, 73(1), 012340. DOI: 10.1103/PhysRevA.73.012340

Baldi, P., & Pollastri, G. (2021). The Role of Neural Networks in Robotic Control Systems. *Artificial Intelligence Review*, 44(3), 207–217.

Baratta, A., Cimino, A., Longo, F., & Nicoletti, L. (2023). Digital Twin for Human-Robot Collaboration enhancement in manufacturing systems: Literature review and direction for future developments. *Computers & Industrial Engineering*, 2023, 109764.

Baraybar, A., Baños, M., Barquero, Ó., Goya, R., & De la Morena, A. (2017). Evaluación de las respuestas emocionales a la publicidad televisiva desde el Neuromarketing= Evaluation of Emotional Responses to Television Advertising through Neuromarketing. *Comunicar: Revista Científica Iberoamericana de Comunicación y Educación= Scientific Journal of Media Education: 52, 3, 2017*, 19-28.

Barison, S., Jacquier, C., & Cerezo, M. (2021). Quantum feature selection via variational quantum eigensolvers. *Quantum Information Processing*, 20(1), 15.

Barnett, C. J., & Cerf, M. A. (2019). Neuroscience Data for Brand Value Measurement. *Journal of Brand Management*.

Barrett, S. D., & Milburn, G. J. (2003). Measuring the Decoherence rate in a semiconductor charge qubit. *Physical Review B: Condensed Matter*, 68(15), 155307. DOI: 10.1103/PhysRevB.68.155307

Bault, N., & Rusconi, E. (2020). Neuromarketing: Anticipating Consumer Decision-Making. *Frontiers in Psychology*.

Behera, R. K., Gunasekaran, A., Gupta, S., Kamboj, S., & Bala, P. K. (2020). Personalized digital marketing recommender engine. *Journal of Retailing and Consumer Services*, 53, 101799. DOI: 10.1016/j.jretconser.2019.03.026

Benedetti., ... (2019) "A Generative Modeling Approach for Benchmarking and Training Parametric Quantum Circuits," npj Quantum Information, vol. 5, no. 1, pp. 1–9.

Bennett, J. (2021). Quantum Computing and AI in Robotics: An Overview. *IEEE Transactions on Computational Intelligence and AI in Robotics*, 15(1), 55–65.

Bhat, M. S., & Khan, M. N. (2021). Neuromarketing and consumer neuroscience: Current understanding and the way forward. *Journal of Consumer Behaviour*, 20(4), 436–452. DOI: 10.1002/cb.1873

Biamonte, J., Wittek, P., Pancotti, N., Rebentrost, P., Wiebe, N., & Lloyd, S. (2017). Quantum machine learning. *Nature*, 549(7671), 195–202. DOI: 10.1038/nature23474 PMID: 28905917

Bielik, P., Bellérová, B., Benda Prokeinova, R., Braha, K., Cierna, Z., Fandel, I., Hallova, M., Hanová, M., Heijman, W., Horksá, E., Kadekova, Z., Kadlecíková, M., Kapsdorferova, Z., Krajcirova, R., Kleinová, K., Lajdova, Z., Moravčíková, D., Nagyová, L. u., Paluchová, J., & Ubrežiová, I. (2014). *Agribusiness and Commerce*. Slovak University of Agriculture in Nitra. https://www.researchgate.net/ publication/311912197_Agribusiness_and_Commerce

Bogue, R. (2013). Robots are critical to driving the next manufacturing revolution. *Industrial Robot: An International Journal*, 40(5), 421–425.

Bojanowska, A., & Kulisz, M. (2023). Innovation in neuromarketing and social media marketing. In *Innovation in the Digital Economy* (pp. 194–204). Routledge. DOI: 10.4324/9781003384311-16

Bombin, H. (2011). Clifford Gates by Code Deformation. *New Journal of Physics*, 13(4), 043005. DOI: 10.1088/1367-2630/13/4/043005

Bonci, A., Cen Cheng, P. D., Indri, M., Nabissi, G., & Sibona, F. (2021). Human-robot perception in industrial environments: A survey. *Sensors (Basel)*, 21(5), 1571. DOI: 10.3390/s21051571 PMID: 33668162

Bonetti, F., Warnaby, G., & Quinn, L. (2018). Augmented Reality and Virtual Reality in Physical and Online Retailing: A Review, Synthesis, and Research Agenda. *International Journal of Fashion Design, Technology and Education*.

Bowen, M. I., & Schoenherr, J. R. (2020). The ethics of neuromarketing: Is it responsible to manipulate the human brain? *Journal of Business Ethics*, 167(3), 515–531. DOI: 10.1007/s10551-019-04197-y

Bradley, C., Oliveira, L., Birrell, S., & Cain, R. (2021). A new perspective on personas and customer journey maps: Proposing systemic UX. *International Journal of Human-Computer Studies*, 148, 102583. DOI: 10.1016/j.ijhcs.2021.102583

Brandberg, O., Myrefelt Norlinger, M., & Ngo, K. (2020). Nike's Dream Crazy campaign and how it influenced views and opinions towards the brand.

Braunstein, S. L. (1998). Error Correction for continuous quantum variables. *Physical Review Letters*, 80(18), 4084–4087. DOI: 10.1103/PhysRevLett.80.4084

Brettel, M., Friederichsen, N., Keller, M., & Rosenberg, M. (2014). How virtualization, decentralization and network building change the manufacturing landscape: An Industry 4.0 perspective. *International Journal of Mechanical, Aerospace, Industrial. Mechatronic and Manufacturing Engineering*, 8(1), 37–44.

Brogårdh, T. (2007). Present and Future Robot Control Development An Industrial Perspective. *Annual Reviews in Control*, 31(1), 69–79. DOI: 10.1016/j.arcontrol.2007.01.002

Brown, R., et al. (2020). Investment in Research and Development: A Key Strategy for Overcoming Technical Challenges in Robotics. *Journal of Manufacturing Innovation*, 15(2), 180-19 Brown, R., & Johnson, A. (2020). Industry 4.0 and the Future of Manufacturing: Predictions and Perspectives. *Journal of Manufacturing Innovation*, 15(4), 335-350.5.

Brown, R.. (2019). Robotics and Material Wastage Reduction: A Case Study in Automotive Manufacturing. *International Journal of Sustainable Production*, 15(3), 210–225.

Brown, R., & Smith, A. (2021). Financial Incentives for Robotics Adoption in Manufacturing: Policy Recommendations. *The Journal of Industrial Economics*, 22(4), 350–365.

Bruce, A. S., Bruce, J. M., Black, W. R., Lepping, R. J., Henry, J. M., Cherry, J. B., Martin, L. E., Papa, V. B., Davis, A. M., Brooks, W. M., & Savage, C. R. (2014). Branding and a child's brain: An fMRI study of neural responses to logos. *Social Cognitive and Affective Neuroscience*, 9(1), 118–122. DOI: 10.1093/scan/nss109

Brun, T., Devetak, I., & Hsieh, M. H. (2006). Correcting quantum errors with entanglement. *science, 314*(5798), 436-439.

Bryman, A. (2016). *Social research methods* (5th ed.). Oxford University Press.

Bryman, A., & Bell, E. (2015). *Business research methods* (4th ed.). Oxford University Press.

Brynjolfsson, E., & McAfee, A. (2014). *The Second Machine Age: Work, Progress, and Prosperity in a Time of Brilliant Technologies*. W. W. Norton & Company.

Buhrman, H., Cleve, R., Massar, S., & De Wolf, R. (2010). Nonlocality and Communication Complexity. *Reviews of Modern Physics*, 82(1), 665–698. DOI: 10.1103/RevModPhys.82.665

Buyer Persona Research - Buyer Persona Institute. (n.d.). Retrieved September 26, 2024, from https://buyerpersona.com/buyer-persona-research

Calvert, G. A., & Brammer, M. J. (2017). The neuroscience of consumer choice: Neuroscience and neuromarketing applications. *Nature Reviews. Neuroscience*, 18(7), 486–497. DOI: 10.1038/nrn.2017.71

Caratu, M., Cherubino, P., & Mattiacci, A. (2018). *Application of neuro-marketing techniques to the wine tasting experience 11th Annual of the EuroMed Academy of Business (EMAB) Conference*, "Research Advancements in National and Global Business Theory and Practice", Valletta, Malta. https://iris.uniroma1.it/handle/11573/1139099

Carbone, F., Caiti, A., & Carbone, A. (2019, October). A Comparative Review of Trajectory Planning Techniques for High-Speed Parallel Manipulators. *Robotics and Computer-integrated Manufacturing*, 57, 49–61.

Cerezo, M., Arrasmith, A., Babbush, R., Benjamin, S. C., Endo, S., Fujii, K., McClean, J. R., Mitarai, K., Yuan, X., Cincio, L., & Coles, P. J. (2020). Variational quantum algorithms. *Nature Reviews. Physics*, 3(10), 625–644.

Chai, J., Ge, Y., Liu, Y., Li, W., Zhou, L., Yao, L., & Sun, X. (2014). Application of frontal EEG asymmetry to user experience research. *Lecture Notes in Computer Science (LNAI) Engineering Psychology and Cognitive Ergonomics*. Cham. doi:DOI: 10.1007/978-3-319-07515-0_24

Chander, B., & Gopalakrishnan, K. (2023). Data clustering using unsupervised machine learning. In *Statistical Modeling in Machine Learning* (pp. 179–204). Elsevier., DOI: 10.1016/B978-0-323-91776-6.00015-4

Chauhan, V., Negi, S., Jain, D., Singh, P., Sagar, A. K., & Sharma, A. K. (2022). Quantum Computers: A Review on How Quantum Computing Can Boom AI. *2022 2nd International Conference on Advance Computing and Innovative Technologies in Engineering (ICACITE)*, 559–563. DOI: 10.1109/ICACITE53722.2022.9823619

Chaves, R.. (2011). Entanglement in Multi-Qubit Quantum Computing. *Physical Review A*, 82(4), 174–185.

Chen, G., Xie, P., Dong, J., & Wang, T. (2019). Understanding Programmatic Creative: The Role of AI. *Journal of Advertising*, 48(4), 347–355. DOI: 10.1080/00913367.2019.1654421

Chen, P.-T., & Hsieh, H.-P. (2012). Personalized mobile advertising: Its key attributes, trends, and social impact. *Technological Forecasting and Social Change*, 79(3), 543–557. DOI: 10.1016/j.techfore.2011.08.011

Chen, S. S., & Hung, S. Y. (2022). Quantum computing for neuromarketing: Opportunities and challenges. *Journal of Marketing Analytics*, 10(3), 205–219. DOI: 10.1057/s41270-022-00118-9

Cheredniakova, A., Lobodenko, L., & Lychagina, I. (2021). *A study of advertising content in digital communications: The experience of applying neuromarketing and traditional techniques*. 2021 Communication Strategies in Digital Society Seminar (ComSDS), St. Petersburg, Russia, DOI: 10.1109/ComSDS52473.2021.9422887

Chief Marketer Features BPI Article on Elevating Buyer Personas. (n.d.). Retrieved September 26, 2024, from https://buyerpersona.com/blog/chief-marketer-features-article-on-elevating-buyer-personas

Childs, M., & Van Dam, W. (2020). Quantum Algorithms for Reinforcement Learning in Robotics. *Proceedings of the National Academy of Sciences of the United States of America*, 115(9), 191–206.

Childs, M., & Van Dam, W. (2020). Quantum Algorithms for Reinforcement Learning. *Proceedings of the National Academy of Sciences of the United States of America*, 115(9), 191–206.

Choi, W. J., & Jerath, K. (2022). Privacy and Consumer Empowerment in Online Advertising. *Foundations and Trends® in Marketing, 15*(3), 153–212. DOI: 10.1561/1700000053

Choi, H., Mela, C. F., Balseiro, S. R., & Leary, A. (2020). Online Display Advertising Markets: A Literature Review and Future Directions. *Information Systems Research*, 31(2), 556–575. DOI: 10.1287/isre.2019.0902

Choppakatla, A. (2023). Quantum Machine Learning: Bridging the Gap Between Quantum Computing and Artificial Intelligence: An Overview. *International Journal for Research in Applied Science and Engineering Technology*, 11(8), 1149–1153. DOI: 10.22214/ijraset.2023.55318

Chowdhury, S.. (2021). AI and Real-Time Control for Delta Robots: A Case Study in Automated Manufacturing. *Journal of Robotics and Automation*, 56, 405–418.

Ciliberto, C., Szopik-Depczyńska, K., Tarczyńska-Łuniewska, M., Ruggieri, A., & Ioppolo, G. (2021). Enabling the Circular Economy transition: A sustainable lean manufacturing recipe for Industry 4.0. *Business Strategy and the Environment*, 30(7), 3255–3272. DOI: 10.1002/bse.2801

Cirac, J. I., & Zoller, P. (2012). Goals and Opportunities in Quantum Simulations. *Nature Physics*, 8(4), 264–266. DOI: 10.1038/nphys2275

Clavel, R. (1990). *Device for the movement and positioning of an element in space*.

Clavel, R. (2021). Delta Robot Applications and Future Directions. *IEEE Transactions on Robotics*, 20(6), 828–839.

Clavel, R. (2021). Quantum Artificial Intelligence for Delta Robots: Potential and Challenges. *Journal of Parallel Robotics*, 44, 455–470.

Coccia, M. (2024). Technological trajectories in quantum computing to design a quantum ecosystem for industrial change. *Technology Analysis and Strategic Management*, 36(8), 1733–1748. DOI: 10.1080/09537325.2022.2110056

Cornelissen, J. (2017). Editor's comments: Developing propositions, a process model, or a typology? Addressing the challenges of writing theory without a boilerplate. In *Academy of Management Review* (Vol. 42, Issue 1, pp. 1–9). Academy of ManagementBriarcliff Manor, NY. DOI: 10.5465/amr.2016.0196

Couwenberg, J.. (2018). Functional Elements in Advertising Effectiveness. *Journal of Advertising Research.*

Craig, J. J. (2005). *Introduction to Robotics: Mechanics and Control.* Pearson Education India.

Cramer, M., Plenio, M. B., Flammia, S. T., Somma, R., Gross, D., Bartlett, S. D., Landon-Cardinal, O., Poulin, D., & Liu, Y.-K. (2010). Efficient quantum data encoding using quantum circuits. *Physical Review Letters*, 104(12), 120502.

Creswell, J. W., & Creswell, J. D. (2017). *Research design: Qualitative, quantitative, and mixed methods approaches* (5th ed.). Sage publications.

Crosson, E.. (2022). A Case Study on the Use of Quantum Algorithms in Robotic Grasping. *Robotics and Automation Letters*, 7(1), 21–28.

Czelusta, G. (2024). Grover's algorithm on two-way quantum computer. arXiv preprint arXiv:2406.09450.

dal Verne, T. D. M. C. (2023). Artificial Intelligence, Neuroscience and Emotional Data. What Role for Private Autonomy in the Digital Market? *Erasmus L. Rev.*, 16(3), 83–97. DOI: 10.5553/ELR.000257

Dang, Y., Jiang, N., Hu, H., Ji, Z., & Zhang, W. (2018). Image classification based on quantum K-Nearest-Neighbor algorithm. *Quantum Information Processing*, 17(9), 1–18. DOI: 10.1007/s11128-018-2004-9

Dasarraju, V. K. (2024). Revolutionizing Quick Commerce: Harnessing the power of AI for Seamless Deliveries. *Journal of Artificial Intelligence. Machine Learning and Data Science*, 2(2), 638–641. DOI: 10.51219/JAIMLD/vamshi-krishna-dasarraju/164

Deibuk, V., & Yuriychuk, I. (2020, August). Noisy multiple-control Fredkin gate in nuclear spin based qubits chain. In *2020 IEEE Third International Conference on Data Stream Mining & Processing (DSMP)* (pp. 352-356). IEEE.

Deloitte. (2018). *The rise of the smart factory: Digital manufacturing today*. Deloitte Insights. Duan S, Shi Q, Wu J. (2022). Multimodal Sensors and ML-BasedData Fusion for Advanced Robots.Advanced Intelligent Systems.2022; 4(12):p2200213

Deutsch, D. (1985) "Quantum Theory and Robotics: Integration in Control Systems," Proceedings of the Royal Society of London A, vol. 400, no. 1818, pp. 97–117.

Deutsch, D. (1985) "Quantum Theory, the Church-Turing Principle, and the Universal Quantum Computer," Proceedings of the Royal Society of London A, vol. 400, no. 1818, pp. 97–117,.

Deutsch, D. (1985). Quantum theory, the Church–Turing principle and the universal quantum computer. *Proceedings of the Royal Society of London. A. Mathematical and Physical Sciences, 400*(1818), 97-117.

Devitt, S. J., Munro, W. J., & Nemoto, K. (2013). Quantum error correction for beginners. *Reports on Progress in Physics*, 76(7), 076001.

Dhabliya, D., Dari, S. S., Dhablia, A., Akhila, N., Kachhoria, R., & Khetani, V. (2024). Addressing Bias in Machine Learning Algorithms: Promoting Fairness and Ethical Design. *E3S Web of Conferences, 491*, 02040. DOI: 10.1051/e3sconf/202449102040

Diraq, H. M. (2023). Ethical Implications in Neuromarketing. *Journal of Business Ethics*.

DiVincenzo, D. P., & Aliferis, P. (2007). Effective FaultTolerant Quantum Computation with slow measurement. *Physical Review Letters*, 98(2), 020501. DOI: 10.1103/PhysRevLett.98.020501 PMID: 17358588

Dombre, E., & Nenchev, D. N. (2014). *Robot Manipulators: Modeling, Performance Analysis and Control*. John Wiley & Sons.

Dombre, E., & Nenchev, D. N. (2014). *Robot Manipulators: Modeling, Performance Analysis, and Control*. John Wiley & Sons.

Duivenvoorde, B., & Goanta, C. (2023). The regulation of digital advertising under the DSA: A critical assessment. *Computer Law & Security Report*, 51, 105870. DOI: 10.1016/j.clsr.2023.105870

Dunjko, J. M. T., & Briegel, H. J. (2016). Quantum-Enhanced Machine Learning. *Physical Review Letters*, 117(13), 130501. DOI: 10.1103/PhysRevLett.117.130501 PMID: 27715099

Dunjko, V., & Briegel, H. J. (2018). Machine Learning and Artificial Intelligence in the Quantum Domain. *Reports on Progress in Physics*, 81(7), 074001. DOI: 10.1088/1361-6633/aab406 PMID: 29504942

D-Wave Systems. (2023). *Optimizing Complex Decision-Making Processes through Quantum Annealing Technology*. D-Wave Insights.

Dwivedi, Y. K., Hughes, L., Baabdullah, A. M., Ribeiro-Navarrete, S., Giannakis, M., Al-Debei, M. M., Dennehy, D., Metri, B., Buhalis, D., Cheung, C. M. K., Conboy, K., Doyle, R., Dubey, R., Dutot, V., Felix, R., Goyal, D. P., Gustafsson, A., Hinsch, C., Jebabli, I., & Wamba, S. F. (2022). Metaverse beyond the hype: Multidisciplinary perspectives on emerging challenges, opportunities, and agenda for research, practice and policy. *International Journal of Information Management*, 66, 102542. DOI: 10.1016/j.ijinfomgt.2022.102542

Efe, A. (2023). Assessment of artificial intelligence and quantum computing in smart management information systems. *Bilişim Teknolojileri Dergisi*, 16(3), 177–188. DOI: 10.17671/gazibtd.1190670

El Hana, N., Mercanti-Guérin, M., & Sabri, O. (2023). Cookiepocalypse: What are the most effective strategies for advertisers to reshape the future of display advertising? *Technological Forecasting and Social Change*, 188, 122297. DOI: 10.1016/j.techfore.2022.122297

El-Azab, S., & Nong, P. (2023). Clinical algorithms, racism, and "fairness" in healthcare: A case of bounded justice. *Big Data & Society*, 10(2), 20539517231213820. Advance online publication. DOI: 10.1177/20539517231213820

Endo, S., Benjamin, S. C., & Li, Y. (2018). Practical quantum error mitigation for near future applications. *Physical Review X*, 8(3), 031027. DOI: 10.1103/PhysRevX.8.031027

Ernst, E., Merola, R., & Samaan, D. (2019). Economics of Artificial Intelligence: Implications for the Future of Work. *IZA Journal of Labor Policy*, 9(1), 20190004. Advance online publication. DOI: 10.2478/izajolp-2019-0004

Eroglu, K., Kayikcioglu, T., & Osman, O. (2020). Effect of brightness of visual stimuli on EEG signals. *Behavioural Brain Research*, 382, 1–16, 112486. DOI: 10.1016/j.bbr.2020.112486

Eser, Z., Isin, B., & Tolon, M. (2011). Perceptions of marketing academics, neurologists, and marketing professionals about neuromarketing. *Journal of Marketing Management*, 27(7-8), 854–868. DOI: 10.1080/02672571003719070

Eswaran, U., Khang, A., & Eswaran, V. (2024). Role of Quantum Computing in the Era of Artificial Intelligence (AI). In *Advances in computer and electrical engineering book series* (pp. 46–68). IGI Global., DOI: 10.4018/979-8-3693-1168-4.ch003

Fagernäs, S., Hamilton, W., Espinoza, N., Miloff, A., Carlbring, P., & Lindner, P. (2021). What Do Users Think About Virtual Reality Relaxation Applications? A Mixed Methods Study of Online User Reviews Using Natural Language Processing. *Internet Interventions : the Application of Information Technology in Mental and Behavioural Health*, 24, 100392. DOI: 10.1016/j.invent.2021.100370 PMID: 33665136

Fan, H.. (2020). Delta-Robot-Based High-Speed Sorting System: Design and Control with AI Algorithms. *Journal of Mechanisms and Robotics*, 12(3), 320–331.

Farayola, O. A., Adaga, E. M., Egieya, Z. E., Ewuga, S. K., Abdul, A. A., & Abrahams, T. O.Oluwatoyin Ajoke FarayolaEjuma Martha AdagaZainab Efe EgieyaSarah Kuzankah EwugaAdekunle Abiola AbdulTemitayo Oluwaseun Abrahams. (2024). Advancements in predictive analytics: A philosophical and practical overview. *World Journal of Advanced Research and Reviews*, 21(3), 240–252. DOI: 10.30574/wjarr.2024.21.3.2706

Farhi, E., & Neven, H. (2019). Classification with Quantum Neural Networks on Near Term Processors. *Nature Physics*, 15(12), 1100–1105.

Farhi, E., & Neven, H. (2019). Quantum Classification in Robotic Manipulation Systems. *Nature Physics*, 15(12), 1100–1105.

Fayaz, M. (2024). The bibliometric analysis of EEGLAB software in the Web of Science indexed articles. *Neuroscience Informatics*, 4(1), 100154. DOI: 10.1016/j.neuri.2023.100154

Fayaz, S., & Nawaz, R. R. (2023). Neuromarketing: A bibliometric perspective of the field. *Journal of Economic Literature*, 18(1), 132–151. DOI: 10.54784/1990-6587.1508

Fazelpour, S., Lipton, Z. C., & Danks, D. (2022). Algorithmic Fairness and the Situated Dynamics of Justice. *Canadian Journal of Philosophy*, 52(1), 44–60. DOI: 10.1017/can.2021.24

Fellous-Asiani, M., Chai, J. H., Whitney, R. S., Auffèves, A., & Ng, H. K. (2021). Limitations in quantum computing from resource constraints. *PFX Quantum : a Physical Review Journal*, 2(4), 040335. DOI: 10.1103/PRXQuantum.2.040335

Feynman, R. P. (1986). Quantum mechanical computers. *Foundations of Physics*, 16(6), 507–532.

Fletcher, G. (2024). The future of marketing. *Digital and Social Media Marketing*, 346–360. DOI: 10.4324/9781003372189-19

Flores, C. O. G., Nina, D. A., Ulcuanjo, O. M. R., & Vinueza, D. F. F. (2022). Psychosensometric study (eye tracker) on the levels of persuasion in the women's perfumery industry. *Journal of Pharmaceutical Negative Results*, 13(4), 562–572. DOI: 10.47750/pnr.2022.13.04.074

Ford, J., Jain, V., Wadhwani, K., & Gupta, D. G. (2023). AI advertising: An overview and guidelines. *Journal of Business Research*, 166, 114124. DOI: 10.1016/j.jbusres.2023.114124

Fortunato, V., Giraldi, J., & de Oliveira, J. H. C. (2014). A review of studies on neuromarketing: Practical results, techniques, contributions and limitations. *Journal of Management Research*, 6(2), 201–220. DOI: 10.5296/jmr.v6i2.5446

Franke, A., Nass, E., Piereth, A. K., Zettl, A., & Heidl, C. (2021). Implementing assistive technologies and robotics in long-term care facilities: A three-stage assessment based on acceptance, ethics, and emotions. *Frontiers in Psychology*, 12, 694297. DOI: 10.3389/fpsyg.2021.694297 PMID: 34512451

Fredkin, E., & Toffoli, T. (1982). Conservative logic. *International Journal of Theoretical Physics*, 21(3), 219–253.

Fugate, D. (2007). Neuromarketing: A layman's look at neuroscience and its potential application to marketing practice. *Journal of Consumer Marketing*, 24(7), 385–394. DOI: 10.1108/07363760710834807

Gandhudi, M., G.R., G., P.J.A, A., Velayudham, V., & Nagineni, L. (. (2023). Causal aware parameterized quantum stochastic gradient descent for analyzing marketing advertisements and sales forecasting. *Information Processing & Management*, 60(5), 103473. DOI: 10.1016/j.ipm.2023.103473

Garcia, R., & Saad, G. H. (2022). Consumer Behavior Insights from Neuroscience. *Marketing Letters*.

Garczarek-Bąk, U., Szymkowiak, A., Gaczek, P., & Disterheft, A. (2021). A comparative analysis of neuromarketing methods for brand purchasing predictions among young adults. *Journal of Brand Management*, 28(2), 171–185. DOI: 10.1057/s41262-020-00221-7

Gardiner, C. W. (1991). Quantum Noise, volume 56 of Springer Series in Synergetics. Springer -Verlag, Berlin; New York.

Gawor, T., & Hoberg, K. (2019). Customers' valuation of time and convenience in e-fulfillment. *International Journal of Physical Distribution & Logistics Management*, 49(1), 75–98. DOI: 10.1108/IJPDLM-09-2017-0275

Ghosh, A., & Sinha, S. (2020). Artificial intelligence in neuromarketing: Bridging the gap between marketer's intuition and consumer perception. *Journal of Business Research*, 123, 275–286. DOI: 10.1016/j.jbusres.2020.09.045

Giakoni, F. R., López, M., Segado, F., Manzanares, A. S., & Minguez, J. (2022). An implicit research methodology to evaluate advertising effectiveness in Esports streaming based on viewers' gaze, cognitive and emotional responses. *SPORT TK-Revista EuroAmericana de Ciencias del Deporte*, 11, 1–21. DOI: 10.6018/sportk.485921

Giani, A., & Eldredge, Z. (2021). Quantum Computing Opportunities in Renewable Energy. *SN Computer Science*, 2(5), 1–15. DOI: 10.1007/s42979-021-00786-3 PMID: 38217220

Gil, I. P., Zagala, K., & Cerdá Suárez, L. M. (2023). Mayoría de edad del Neuromarketing: Mapa científico de 18 años de investigación en el área. *Index ComunicaciÓn*, 13(2), 47–74. DOI: 10.33732/ixc/13/02Mayori

Gill, S. S., Xu, M., Ottaviani, C., Patros, P., Bahsoon, R., Shaghaghi, A., & Uhlig, S. (2022). AI for next-generation computing: Emerging trends and future directions. *Internet of Things : Engineering Cyber Physical Human Systems*, 19, 100514. DOI: 10.1016/j.iot.2022.100514

Girija, N., & Bhuvaneswari, T. (2021). AI emerging communication and computing. In *Artificial intelligence (AI)* (1st ed., pp. 293–306). https://doi.org/https://doi.org/10.1201/9781003005629

Global, I. G. I. (2023). *Call for Chapters on Neuromarketing and Quantum Computing*. IGI Global.

Gomes, A. C., De Lima, F. B.Junior, Soliani, R. D., & Oliveira, P. R. (2023). Logistics management in e-commerce: Challenges and opportunities. [Management and Administrative Professional Review]. *Revista de Gestão e Secretariado*, 14(5), 7252–7272. DOI: 10.7769/gesec.v14i5.2119

Goodfellow, Y. (2016). *Bengio, and A. Courville, Deep Learning*. MIT Press.

Google Quantum, A. I. (2023). *Enhancing Data Analysis Capabilities within Marketing Frameworks*. Google Research.

Green, M., & Smith, A. (2018). Energy-Efficient Robotics Solutions for Smart Manufacturing: A Comparative Analysis. *Journal of Energy Efficiency in Manufacturing*, 12(4), 335–350.

Green, S., & Lee, M. (2021). Sustainable Manufacturing Practices Enabled by Robotics and Digitalization. *Journal of Sustainable Production*, 12(3), 210–225.

Grover, K., & Pal, R. (2021), "Quantum Path Planning in Delta Robot Systems," *Proceedings of the IEEE International Conference on Robotics and Automation*,pp. 1457–1464.

Grover, L. K. (1996, July). A fast quantum mechanical algorithm for database search. In *Proceedings of the twenty-eighth annual ACM symposium on Theory of computing* (pp. 212-219).

Grover, L. K. (1998) "A Framework for Fast Quantum Mechanical Algorithms," *Proceedings of the 30th ACM Symposium on Theory of Computing*, pp. 53–59. DOI: 10.1145/276698.276712

Gunawan, C. N., Chen, Y.-J., & Hsu, L. (2023). How online travel agencies' logo design promotes purchase intention: A behavioral and neuroscientific interpretation of consumers' construal level. *Asia Pacific Journal of Tourism Research*, 28(1), 19–35. DOI: 10.1080/10941665.2023.2187701

Gupta, S.SHIVOM GUPTA. (2024). A Study on Emergence of Quick Commerce. *International Journal For Multidisciplinary Research*, 6(2), 19226. Advance online publication. DOI: 10.36948/ijfmr.2024.v06i02.19226

Gürbüz, F., & Ünal, S. E. (2021). A bibliometric analysis of neuromarketing on web of science. *Journal of Engineering Research*, 11(28), 226–235. DOI: 10.36909/jer.12239

Gutierrez, A., O'Leary, S., Rana, N. P., Dwivedi, Y. K., & Calle, T. (2019). Using privacy calculus theory to explore entrepreneurial directions in mobile location-based advertising: Identifying intrusiveness as the critical risk factor. *Computers in Human Behavior*, 95, 295–306. DOI: 10.1016/j.chb.2018.09.015

Hafez, M. (2019). Neuromarketing: a new avatar in branding and advertisement. *Pacific Business Review International*, 12(4), 58-64. http://www.pbr.co.in/2019/2019_month/october/6.pdf

Hafez, M. (2019). Emotional Neuromarketing and Brand Image. *Journal of Marketing Behavior*.

Hair, J. F., Black, W. C., Babin, B. J., & Anderson, R. E. (2019). Multivariate data analysis (8th ed.). Cengage Learning. Babbie, E. R., & Mouton, J. (2015). *The practice of social research* (14th ed.). Cengage Learning.

Hair, J. F.Jr, Black, W. C., Babin, B. J., & Anderson, R. E. (2018). *Multivariate data analysis* (8th ed.). Cengage Learning.

Haldorai, A. (2024). Advancements and Applications of Quantum Computing in Robotics. *Journal of Computing and Natural Science*, 053–063. DOI: 10.53759/181X/JCNS202404006

Hargrave, B. (1999). *The History of Robotics*. The Rosen Publishing Group.

Harris, C., & Lee, M. (2023). *QAOA: Revolutionizing combinatorial optimization*. Quantum Algorithms Review.

Harris, D. K., & Armstrong, W. J. (2019). Neuromarketing in Digital Ads for Social Causes. *Journal of Consumer Psychology*.

Harter, A., Stich, L., & Spann, M. (2024). The Effect of Delivery Time on Repurchase Behavior in Quick Commerce. *Journal of Service Research*, 0(0), 1–17. DOI: 10.1177/10946705241236961

Hashimoto, M. T., & Kaneko, K. "Trajectory Optimization for High-Speed Delta Robots Using Reinforcement Learning," *Proceedings of the IEEE International Conference on Robotics and Automation*, 2019, pp. 1547–1552.

Hemdev, O. (2024). Communication and Advertising in India: Evolution, Challenges, and the Digital Future. [IJSR]. *International Journal of Science and Research (Raipur, India)*, 13(9), 1417–1418. DOI: 10.21275/SR24923143911

Holloway, S. (2024). *Exploring the Relationship Between Supply Chain Responsiveness and Customer Loyalty in the E-commerce Sector Exploring the Relationship between Supply Chain Responsiveness and Customer Loyalty in the E-Commerce Sector*. https://doi.org/https://doi.org/10.20944/preprints202406.1616.v1

Holsen, L. M., Zarcone, J. R., Thompson, T. I., Brooks, W. M., Anderson, M. F., Ahluwalia, J. S., Nollen, N. L., & Savage, C. R. (2005). Neural mechanisms underlying food motivation in children and adolescents. *NeuroImage*, 27(3), 669–676. DOI: 10.1016/j.neuroimage.2005.04.043

Ho, S. Y. (2018). An Inverse Kinematic Control Approach for the Delta Robot with Reduced Mechanical Constraints. *Journal of Intelligent & Robotic Systems*, 91(1), 151–165.

Ho, S. Y., Bodoff, D., & Tam, K. Y. (2011). Timing of adaptive web personalization and its effects on online consumer behavior. *Information Systems Research*, 22(3), 660–679. DOI: 10.1287/isre.1090.0262

Hounshell, D. A. (1984). *From the American System to Mass Production, 1800-1932: The Development of Manufacturing Technology in the United States*. Johns Hopkins University Press. DOI: 10.56021/9780801829758

Howe, A. E. (1996). *Robots in Space: Technology, Evolution, and Interplanetary Travel*. Springer.

How, M. L., & Cheah, S. M. (2023). Business renaissance: Opportunities and challenges at the dawn of the quantum computing era. *Businesses*, 3(4), 585–605. DOI: 10.3390/businesses3040036

Huang, J..(2021) "Reducing Energy Consumption in High-Speed Delta Robots Using Reinforcement Learning," *Proceedings of the 15th International Conference on Industrial Informatics (INDIN)*, pp. 246–252.

Hubert, M., & Kenning, P. A. (2021). Neuroscience Methods in Marketing Research: A Review. *Journal of Consumer Psychology*.

Hübner, A., Kuhn, H., & Wollenburg, J. (2016). Last mile fulfilment and distribution in omni-channel grocery retailing: A strategic planning framework. *International Journal of Retail & Distribution Management*, 44(3), 228–247. DOI: 10.1108/IJRDM-11-2014-0154

IFR (International Federation of Robotics). (2020). World. *Robotics Reports*, 2020, •••. https://ifr.org/worldrobotics/

Ingolfsson, T. M., Hersche, M., Wang, X., Kobayashi, N., Cavigelli, L., & Benini, L. (2020, October). EEG-TCNet: An accurate temporal convolutional network for embedded motor-imagery brain–machine interfaces. In *2020 IEEE International Conference on Systems, Man, and Cybernetics (SMC)* (pp. 2958-2965). IEEE.

Ishak, M. A., Kosnan, M. R., & Zakaria, N. F. (2020). Build IoT Through Virtual Reality. *Journal of Information Technology Management*, 20(1), 67–80.

Iyer, P., & Bright, L. F. (2024). Navigating a paradigm shift: Technology and user acceptance of big data and artificial intelligence among advertising and marketing practitioners. *Journal of Business Research*, 180, 114699. DOI: 10.1016/j.jbusres.2024.114699

Jaakkola, E. (2020). Designing conceptual articles: Four approaches. *AMS Review*, 10(1–2), 18–26. DOI: 10.1007/s13162-020-00161-0

Jain, G., Paul, J., & Shrivastava, A. (2021). Hyper-personalization, co-creation, digital clienteling and transformation. *Journal of Business Research*, 124, 12–23. DOI: 10.1016/j.jbusres.2020.11.034

Jansen, B. J., Jung, S., Chowdhury, S. A., & Salminen, J. (2021). Persona analytics: Analyzing the stability of online segments and content interests over time using non-negative matrix factorization. *Expert Systems with Applications*, 185, 115611. DOI: 10.1016/j.eswa.2021.115611

Jansen, B. J., Salminen, J. O., & Jung, S.-G. (2020). Data-Driven Personas for Enhanced User Understanding: Combining Empathy with Rationality for Better Insights to Analytics. *Data and Information Management*, 4(1), 1–17. DOI: 10.2478/dim-2020-0005

Javor, A.. (2017). Cognitive Neuroscience Applications in Marketing. *Journal of Marketing Management.*

Jenkins, J., Berente, N., & Angst, C. (2022). The Quantum Computing Business Ecosystem and Firm Strategies. *Proceedings of the Annual Hawaii International Conference on System Sciences, 2022-Janua*, 6432–6441. DOI: 10.24251/HICSS.2022.779

Jiménez-Marín, G., Bellido-Pérez, E., & López-Cortés, Á. (2019). Marketing sensorial: El concepto, sus técnicas y su aplicación en el punto de venta. *Vivat Academia. Revista de Comunicación*, (148), 121–147. DOI: 10.15178/va.2019.148.121-147

Johnson, A.. (2021). Developing Regulatory Frameworks for Robotics in Manufacturing: Challenges and Opportunities. *Journal of Regulatory Compliance*, 18(2), 180–195.

Johnson, R.. (2022). Future Trends in Robotics: The Impact of AI and Machine Learning. *Journal of Robotics Technology*, 27(4), 320–335.

Jones, M.. (2023). Leveraging Data Analytics for Optimizing Robotics Performance in Manufacturing. *Journal of Data Analytics in Manufacturing*, 30(1), 80–95.

Jones, M., & Green, S. (2019). Workforce Development Strategies for Robotics Implementation in Manufacturing. *Journal of Human Resources Development*, 22(3), 265–280.

Jones, M., & Smith, A. (2022). Reshoring and Localized Production: Strategies for Manufacturing in a Post-Pandemic World. *The Journal of Supply Chain Management*, 25(1), 75–90.

Jones, R.. (2020). Overcoming Technical Challenges in Implementing Robotics in Smart Manufacturing. *Journal of Robotics Engineering*, 25(3), 210–225.

Jung, S. gyo, Salminen, J., Kwak, H., An, J., & Jansen, B. J. (2018). Automatic Persona Generation (APG): A rationale and demonstration. *CHIIR 2018 - Proceedings of the 2018 Conference on Human Information Interaction and Retrieval, 2018-March*, 321–324. DOI: 10.1145/3176349.3176893

Kadry, A. (2022). The Metaverse Revolution and Its Impact on the Future of Advertising Industry. *Journal of Design Sciences and Applied Arts*, 3(2), 347–358. DOI: 10.21608/jdsaa.2022.129876.1171

Kahneman, D. (2011). *Thinking, Fast and Slow*. Farrar, Straus and Giroux.

Kajla, T., Raj, S., Kansra, P., Gupta, S. L., & Singh, N. (2023). Neuromarketing and consumer behavior: A bibliometric analysis. *Journal of Consumer Behaviour*, •••, 1–17. DOI: 10.1002/cb.2256

Kandala, A., Temme, K., Córcoles, A. D., Mezzacapo, A., Chow, J. M., & Gambetta, J. M. (2019). Error mitigation extends the computational reach of a noisy quantum processor. *Nature*, 567(7749), 491–495. DOI: 10.1038/s41586-019-1040-7 PMID: 30918370

Kang, K., Wang, X., & Yang, W. (2024). The analysis of social E-commerce with artificial intelligence. *Applied and Computational Engineering*, 47(1), 67–74. DOI: 10.54254/2755-2721/47/20241198

Kaplan, Y., Shtoff, A., Shadi, T., Somekh, O., & Koren, Y. (2022). Conversion-Based Dynamic-Creative-Optimization in Native Advertising. *2022 IEEE International Conference on Big Data (Big Data)*, 2273–2278. DOI: 10.1109/BigData55660.2022.10020498

Kariya, A., & Behera, B. K. (2021). Investigation of quantum support vector machine for classification in nisq era. arXiv preprint arXiv:2112.06912.

Karolita, D., McIntosh, J., Kanij, T., Grundy, J., & Obie, H. O. (2023). Use of personas in Requirements Engineering: A systematic mapping study. *Information and Software Technology*, 162, 107264. DOI: 10.1016/j.infsof.2023.107264

Katic, D., & Vukobratovic, M. (2014). *Control of Complex Systems: Methods and Applications*. Springer.

Kaur, V., Khullar, V., & Verma, N. (2020). Review of Artificial Intelligence with Retailing Sector. *Journal of Computer Science Research*, 2(1), 1–7. DOI: 10.30564/jcsr.v2i1.1591

Khan, H. U., Ali, N., Ali, F., & Nazir, S. (2024). Transforming future technology with quantum-based IoT. *The Journal of Supercomputing*, •••, 1–35.

Khosla, A., Khandnor, P., & Chand Elsevier, T. (2020, April–June). A comparative analysis of signal processing and classification methods for different applications based on EEG signals. *Biocybernetics and Biomedical Engineering*, 40(2), 649–690. DOI: 10.1016/j.bbe.2020.02.002

Khushaba, R. N., Wise, C., Kodagoda, S., Louviere, J., Kahn, B. E., & Townsend, C. (2013). Consumer neuroscience: Assessing the brain response to marketing stimuli using electroencephalogram (EEG) and eye tracking. *Expert Systems with Applications*, 40(9), 3803–3812. DOI: 10.1016/j.eswa.2012.12.095

Killoran, N., Izaac, J., Quesada, N., Bergholm, V., Amy, M., & Weedbrook, C. (2020). Continuous-variable quantum neural networks. *Physical Review Research*, 1(3), 033075.

Kim, H. Y., Lee, J. Y., Mun, J. M., & Johnson, K. P. (2017). Consumer Adoption of Smart In-store Technology: Assessing the Predictive Value of Attitude Versus Beliefs in the Technology Acceptance Model. *International Journal of Fashion Design, Technology and Education*, 10(3), 215–226. DOI: 10.1080/17543266.2016.1177737

Kim, S. (2022). Working with robots: (2022).Human resource development considerations in human-robot interaction. *Human Resource Development Review*, 21(1), 48–74. DOI: 10.1177/15344843211068810

King, N. J., & Jessen, P. W. (2010). Profiling the mobile customer – Is industry self-regulation adequate to protect consumer privacy when behavioural advertisers target mobile phones? – Part II. *Computer Law & Security Report*, 26(6), 595–612. DOI: 10.1016/j.clsr.2010.09.007

Kitaev, Y. (1995). Quantum Measurements and the Abelian Stabilizer Problem. *Electronic Colloquium on Computational Complexity*, 96(12), 213–230.

Kjaergaard, M., Schwartz, M. D., Braumüller, J., Krantz, P., Wang, J. I., Gustavsson, S., & Oliver, W. D. (2020). Superconducting qubits: Current state of play. *Annual Review of Condensed Matter Physics*, 11(1), 369–395. DOI: 10.1146/annurev-conmatphys-031119-050605

Kohler, C. G., Barrett, F. S., Gur, R. C., Turetsky, B. I., & Moberg, P. J. (2007). Association between facial emotion recognition and odor identification in schizophrenia. *The Journal of Neuropsychiatry and Clinical Neurosciences*, 19(2), 128–131. DOI: 10.1176/jnp.2007.19.2.128

Kolar, T., Batagelj, Z., Omeragić, I., & Husić-Mehmedović, M. (2021). How moment-to-moment EEG measures enhance ad effectiveness evaluation peak emotions during branding moments as key indicators. *Journal of Advertising Research*, 61(4), 365–381. DOI: 10.2501/JAR-2021-014

Kou, G., Dinçer, H., Pamucar, D., Yüksel, S., Deveci, M., & Eti, S. (2024). Artificial Intelligence-based Expert Weighted Quantum Picture Fuzzy Rough Sets and Recommendation System for Metaverse Investment Decision-Making Priorities. *Journal of Decision Systems*.

Krebsz, M., & Dwivedi, D. (2024). Emotional AI: Neuroethics and socially aligned networks. In Emotional AI and Human-AI Interactions in Social Networking (pp. 101-130). Academic Press.

Kumar, D. P. M., R, J. A., J, J. V., M, D. B., & Manani, J. (2022). Sentimental Analysis on Quick Commerce Platform Based on Customer Reviews in Google Play Store. *International Journal of Research In Science & Engineering*, 26(26), 29–42. DOI: 10.55529/ijrise.26.29.42

Kumar, I., & Chidambara, . (2023). Freight patterns and spatial planning requirements of third generation E-commerce in Indian cities. *Urban, Planning and Transport Research*, 11(1), 2256817. Advance online publication. DOI: 10.1080/21650020.2023.2256817

Kumar, P., & Safro, I. (2022). Quantum computing for optimization and machine learning: A survey. *Computer Science Review*, 44, 100456.

Kumar, R. (2018). Impact of industrial robots on cost and quality in manufacturing. *Journal of Manufacturing Technology Research*, 10(3/4), 115–130.

Kumar, V., Ashraf, A. R., & Nadeem, W. (2024). AI-powered marketing: What, where, and how? *International Journal of Information Management*, 77, 102783. DOI: 10.1016/j.ijinfomgt.2024.102783

Kumar, V., & Martínez, J. C. (2020). High-Speed Vision-Based Delta Robot System for Pick-and-Place Operations. *The International Journal of Robotics Research*, 39(12), 1479–1494.

Kuppler, M., Kern, C., Bach, R. L., & Kreuter, F. (2022). From fair predictions to just decisions? Conceptualising algorithmic fairness and distributive justice in the context of data-driven decision-making. *Frontiers in Sociology*, 7, 883999. DOI: 10.3389/fsoc.2022.883999 PMID: 36299413

Kusasi, F., & Tiyasiningsih, E. (2024). Implementation of Artificial Intelligence in Customer Relationship Management and Its Implications. *SNEBIM 2024*.

Kusiak, A. (2018). The Internet of Things in manufacturing: Key issues and potential applications. *International Journal of Production Research*, 56(1-2), 829–846.

Kuznetcova, I., & Glassman, M. (2018). Virtual Reality: Its Transformative Potential. *Journal of Technology and Teacher Education*, 26(4), 547–564.

Kyriazos, T., & Poga, M. (2024). Quantum concepts in Psychology: Exploring the interplay of physics and the human psyche. *Bio Systems*, 235, 105070. DOI: 10.1016/j.biosystems.2023.105070 PMID: 37939870

Ladd, T. D., Jelezko, F., Laflamme, R., Nakamura, Y., Monroe, C., & O'Brien, J. L. (2010). Quantum computers. *Nature*, 464(7285), 45–53. DOI: 10.1038/nature08812 PMID: 20203602

Laghari, A. A., Shah, H., Laghari, R. A., Kumar, K., Waqan, A. A., & Jumani, A. K. (2018). A Review on Quantum Computing Trends & Future Perspectives. *EAI Endorsed Transactions on Cloud Systems*, 7(22), 173979. DOI: 10.4108/eai.17-5-2022.173979

Landauer, R. (1961). Irreversibility and heat generation in the computing process. *IBM Journal of Research and Development*, 5(3), 183–191. DOI: 10.1147/rd.53.0183

Lasisi, M., Kolade, K., & Rotimi, O. (2024). Big Data. In *Reference Module in Social Sciences*. Elsevier., DOI: 10.1016/B978-0-323-95689-5.00269-8

Laszlo, J. (2009). The New Unwired World: An IAB Status Report on Mobile Advertising. *Journal of Advertising Research*, 49(1), 27–43. DOI: 10.2501/S0021849909090035

Lawhern, V. J., Solon, A. J., Waytowich, N. R., Gordon, S. M., Hung, C. P., & Lance, B. J. (2018). EEGNet: A compact convolutional neural network for EEG-based brain–computer interfaces. *Journal of Neural Engineering*, 15(5), 056013.

Lecun, Y., Bengio, Y., & Hinton, G. (2015). Deep Learning. *Nature*, 521(7553), 436–444. DOI: 10.1038/nature14539 PMID: 26017442

Lee, D., Ng, P., & Wut, T. (2022). Virtual Reality in Festivals: A Systematic Literature Review and Implications for Consumer Research. *Emerging Science Journal*, 6(1), 123–138. DOI: 10.28991/ESJ-2022-06-05-016

Lee, D., & Wang, H. (2020). Superposition in quantum algorithms. *Computers in Physics*.

Lee, J., Bagheri, B., & Kao, H. A. (2015). A cyber-physical systems architecture for Industry 4.0-based manufacturing systems. *Manufacturing Letters*, 3, 18–23. DOI: 10.1016/j.mfglet.2014.12.001

Lee, K., Lee, C., Kim, D., & Lee, K.-H. (2024). Dialogue act-based partner persona extraction for consistent personalized response generation. *Expert Systems with Applications*, 254, 124380. https://doi.org/https://doi.org/10.1016/j.eswa.2024.124380. DOI: 10.1016/j.eswa.2024.124380

Lee, M.. (2023). Additive Manufacturing and Robotics: A Paradigm Shift in Manufacturing Technology. *Journal of Additive Manufacturing*, 20(3), 265–280.

Lee, M., & Green, S. (2022). Pilot Projects in Robotics Integration: Lessons Learned and Best Practices. *Journal of Manufacturing Innovation*, 17(3), 275–290.

Lee, M., & Johnson, A. (2018). Social Implications of Robotics in Manufacturing: Addressing Workforce Concerns. *Journal of Social and Economic Impact of Technology*, 12(4), 335–350.

Lee, N., Broderick, A. J., & Chamberlain, L. (2007). What is 'neuromarketing'? A discussion and agenda for future research. *International Journal of Psychophysiology*, 63(2), 199–204. DOI: 10.1016/j.ijpsycho.2006.03.007 PMID: 16769143

Lee, T., Han, S. R., & Song, B. D. (2023). Optimisation of OmniChannel Distribution Network Using Micro Fulfillment Center under Demand Uncertainty. *IEEE Access : Practical Innovations, Open Solutions*, 11, 107496–107510. DOI: 10.1109/ACCESS.2023.3317690

Leung, X. Y., Lyu, J., & Bai, B. (2020). A fad or the future? Examining the effectiveness of virtual reality advertising in the hotel industry. *International Journal of Hospitality Management*, 88, 102391. DOI: 10.1016/j.ijhm.2019.102391

Lewis-Hodgson, D., & Anderson, T. (2020). Optimizing consumer engagement through neurofeedback training. *Journal of Consumer Behaviour*, 19(6), 678–692.

Lewis-Hodgson, D., & Clark, M. (2016). Emotion and advertising: Using facial coding to measure consumer responses. *Journal of Advertising Research*, 56(2), 213–226.

Lewis-Hodgson, D., & Evans, K. (2018). The role of physiological responses in evaluating consumer engagement. *Consumer Psychology Review*, 8(1), 39–53.

Lewis-Hodgson, D., & Patel, S. (2017). Visual attention and brand recall: An eye-tracking study. *International Journal of Market Research*, 59(4), 501–517.

Lewis-Hodgson, D., & Thompson, R. (2015). Neuroimaging the brand experience: An fMRI study of consumer response to brand logos. *Marketing Science*, 34(3), 457–468.

Lewis-Hodgson, D., & White, J. (2019). Implicit brand preferences and their impact on consumer choice. *The Journal of Consumer Research*, 45(5), 977–989.

Leyerer, M., Sonneberg, M. O., Heumann, M., & Breitner, M. H. (2020). Shortening the last mile in urban areas: Optimising a smart logistics concept for e-grocery operations. *Smart Cities*, 3(3), 585–603. DOI: 10.3390/smartcities3030031

Li, J., & Chignell, M. (2022). FMEA-AI: AI fairness impact assessment using failure mode and effects analysis. *AI and Ethics*, 2(4), 837–850. DOI: 10.1007/s43681-022-00145-9

Li, J., Peng, X., Du, J., & Suter, D. (2012). An efficient exact quantum algorithm for the integer square-free decomposition problem. *Scientific Reports*, 2(1), 260. DOI: 10.1038/srep00260 PMID: 22355772

Li, K. (2022). The Qubit Fidelity Under Different Error Mechanisms Based on Error Correction Threshold. *Frontiers in Physics (Lausanne)*, 10, 893507. DOI: 10.3389/fphy.2022.893507

Lim, M. K., Weyns, D., & Andersson, J. (2019). A Survey of Cyber-Physical System Architectures for Manufacturing Systems. *IEEE Transactions on Industrial Informatics*, 15(8), 4540–4554.

Lindstrom, M. (2008). *Buyology: Truth and Lies About Why We Buy*. Crown Publishing.

Lin, Y. P., Wang, C. H., Jung, T. P., Wu, T. L., Jeng, S. K., Duann, J. R., & Chen, J. H. (2010). EEG-based emotion recognition in music listening. *IEEE Transactions on Biomedical Engineering*, 57(7), 1798–1806.

Litt, S. (2024). *Subscription Business Models: How & Why They Work In 2024 - The CFO Club*. https://thecfoclub.com/operational-finance/subscription-model/

Liu, B., Huang, S., Zhou, M., & YANG, S. (2022). Research on the application of "quantum computing + dynamic face recognition" in bank personal business. Https://Doi.Org/10.1117/12.2657069, *12503*, 3. DOI: 10.1117/12.2657069

Liu, G.. (2021). AI-Enhanced Predictive Control for Delta Robots in Precision Tasks. *Journal of Control Engineering and Technology*, 39(2), 128–139.

Liu, J., Wang, C., Zhang, R., & Zhao, X.LIU. (2014). Research on behavioral targeted advertising in mobile Internet. *Journal of China Universities of Posts and Telecommunications*, 21, 1–5. DOI: 10.1016/S1005-8885(14)60520-3

Liu, Y., Zhao, R., Xiong, X., & Ren, X. (2023). A bibliometric analysis of consumer neuroscience towards sustainable consumption. *Behavioral Sciences (Basel, Switzerland)*, 13(4), 298. DOI: 10.3390/bs13040298

Li, Y., Zhang, X., Zhang, B., Lei, M.-Y., Cui, W., & Guo, Y.-Z. (2019). A Channel-Projection Mixed-Scale Convolutional Neural Network for Motor Imagery EEG Decoding. *IEEE Transactions on Neural Systems and Rehabilitation Engineering*, 27(6), 1170–1180. DOI: 10.1109/TNSRE.2019.2915621 PMID: 31071048

Li, Z. H., Wong, M. A., & Zhang, L. H. (2023). Quantum Reinforcement Learning for Obstacle Avoidance in Swarm Robotics. *IEEE Access : Practical Innovations, Open Solutions*, 11, 7542–7555.

Lloyd, S., Mohseni, M., & Rebentrost, P. (2013). Quantum algorithms for supervised and unsupervised machine learning. *arXiv preprint arXiv:1307.0411.*

Lloyd, S. (1996). Universal Quantum Simulators. *Science*, 273(5278), 1073–1078. DOI: 10.1126/science.273.5278.1073 PMID: 8688088

Lloyd, S. (2020). Quantum Interference in Robotics Systems: Enhancing Control and Decision-Making. *Journal of Quantum Computing in Robotics*, 2(3), 112–124.

Lloyd, S., Mohseni, M., & Rebentrost, P. (2020). Quantum Optimization Algorithms in Robotics. *Quantum Information & Computation*, 18(2), 102–121.

Loi, M., Ferrario, A., & Viganò, E. (2021). Transparency as design publicity: Explaining and justifying inscrutable algorithms. *Ethics and Information Technology*, 23(3), 253–263. DOI: 10.1007/s10676-020-09564-w PMID: 34867077

Lubinski, T., Granade, C., Anderson, A., Geller, A., Roetteler, M., Petrenko, A., & Heim, B. (2022). Advancing hybrid quantum–classical computation with real-time execution. *Frontiers in Physics (Lausanne)*, 10, 940293. DOI: 10.3389/fphy.2022.940293

Lyu, M., & Huang, Q. (2024). Visual elements in advertising enhance odor perception and purchase intention: The role of mental imagery in multi-sensory marketing. *Journal of Retailing and Consumer Services*, 78, 103752. DOI: 10.1016/j.jretconser.2024.103752

M. A. Nielsen and I. L. Chuang, Quantum Computation and Quantum Information. (2010). Cambridge University Press.

Maddodi, C. B., & Upadhyaya, P. (2024). In-app advertising: a systematic literature review and implications for future research. *Spanish Journal of Marketing - ESIC, 28*(3), 334–355. DOI: 10.1108/SJME-05-2022-0120

Makori, R. (2023). The Influence of Neuro-Marketing Techniques on Consumer Decision-Making in Strategic Marketing Campaigns. *Journal of Strategic Marketing Practice*, 1(1), 21–29.

Malik, J., Patel, N., & Gupta, R. (2024). Evaluating the synergies between cloud computing, big data analytics, and quantum algorithms: Opportunities and challenges. *Journal of Empirical Social Science Studies*, 8(2), 38–50.

Malik, N., Altaf, S., Tariq, M. U., Ahmed, A., & Babar, M. (2023). A deep learning-based sentiment analytic model for the prediction of traffic accidents. *CMC-Computers. Computers, Materials & Continua*, 77(2), 1599–1615. DOI: 10.32604/cmc.2023.040455

Malkowicz, D., & Martinez, D. (2009). Role of quantitative electroencephalography, neurotherapy, and neuroplasticity in recovery from neurological and psychiatric disorders. *Journal of Neurotherapy*, 13(3), 176–188.

Mallow, G. M., Hornung, A., Barajas, J. N., Rudisill, S. S., An, H. S., & Samartzis, D. (2022). Quantum computing: The future of big data and artificial intelligence in spine. *Spine Surgery and Related Research*, 6(2), 93–98. DOI: 10.22603/ssrr.2021-0251 PMID: 35478980

Mañas-Viniegra, L., Santos-Silva, D., & Liberal Ormaechea, S. (2021). The visual-digital identity of corporate brands: A study of Neuromarketing in young people from Spain and Portugal. *Tripodos Blanquerna School of Communication and International Relations-URL*, (48), 135–151. DOI: 10.51698/tripodos.2020.48p135-151

Manns, J. R., Varga, N. L., Trimper, J. B., & Bauer, P. J. (2018). Cortical dynamics of emotional autobiographical memory retrieval differ between women and men. *Neuropsychologia*, 110, 197–207.

Markidis, S. (2024). What is quantum parallelism, anyhow? In ISC High Performance 2024 Research Paper Proceedings (39th International Conference). Prometeus GmbH.

Markna, J. H., Palatia, T. P., Gohel, S., & Kataria, B. (2023). Unveiling advanced computational applications in quantum computing: A comprehensive review. *International Journal of Advanced Nano Computing and Analytics*, 2(2), 81–92. DOI: 10.61797/ijanca.v2i2.284

Marshall, C., & Rossman, G. B. (2014). *We are designing qualitative research* (6th ed.). Sage Publications.

Marvel, J. A., & Norcross, R. (2017). Implementing a high-performance collaborative robot. *Industrial Robot: An International Journal*, 44(5), 496–503.

Maslov, D., Dueck, G. V., & Miller, D. M. (2005). Synthesis of Fredkin-Toffoli reversible networks. *IEEE Transactions on Very Large Scale Integration (VLSI) Systems*, 13(6), 765–769. DOI: 10.1109/TVLSI.2005.844284

Mateusz, P. (2018). EEG in analysis of the level of interest in social issue advertising. *Procedia Computer Science*, 126, 1945–1953. DOI: 10.1016/j.procs.2018.08.056

McClean, J. R., Romero, J., Babbush, R., & Aspuru-Guzik, A. (2016). The theory of variational hybrid algorithms. *New Journal of Physics*, 18(2), 023023. DOI: 10.1088/1367-2630/18/2/023023

McClure, S. M., Li, J., Tomlin, D., Cypert, K. S., Montague, L. M., & Montague, P. R. (2004). Neural correlates of behavioral preference for culturally familiar drinks. *Neuron*, 44(2), 379–387. DOI: 10.1016/j.neuron.2004.09.019 PMID: 15473974

McInnes, A. N., Sung, B., & Hooshmand, R. (2023). A practical review of electroencephalography's value to consumer research. *International Journal of Market Research*, 65(1), 52–82. DOI: 10.1177/14707853221112622

McKay, D. C., Wood, C. J., Sheldon, S., Chow, J. M., & Gambetta, J. M. (2017). Efficient Z gates for quantum computing. *Physical Review. A*, 96(2), 022330. DOI: 10.1103/PhysRevA.96.022330

Merlet, M. (2006). *Parallel Robots* (2nd ed.). Springer.

Miaskiewicz, T., & Kozar, K. A. (2011). Personas and user-centered design: How can personas benefit product design processes? *Design Studies*, 32(5), 417–430. DOI: 10.1016/j.destud.2011.03.003

Misra, L. (2023). Neuromarketing insights into consumer behavior. *IUJ Journal of Management*, 11(1), 143–163.

Mitchell, S., Potash, E., Barocas, S., D'Amour, A., & Lum, K. (2021). Algorithmic fairness: Choices, assumptions, and definitions. *Annual Review of Statistics and Its Application, 8*(Volume 8, 2021), 141–163. https://doi.org/DOI: 10.1146/ANNUREV-STATISTICS-042720-125902/CITE/REFWORKS

Moll, N., Barkoutsos, P., Bishop, L. S., Chow, J. M., Cross, A., Egger, D. J., & Gambetta, J. M. (2018). Quantum optimization using variational algorithms on near-term quantum devices. *Quantum Science and Technology*, 3(3), 030503. DOI: 10.1088/2058-9565/aab822

Monostori, L. (2014). Cyber-physical production systems: Roots, expectations and R&D challenges. *Procedia CIRP*, 17, 9–13. DOI: 10.1016/j.procir.2014.03.115

Montanaro, A. (2016). Quantum algorithms: an overview. *npj Quantum Information, 2*(1), 1-8.

More, P. B. (2022). *Marketing Strategies for Health Care Applications of Genomics in India* [Savitribai Phule Pune University]. http://hdl.handle.net/10603/384725

More, P., & Pothula, S. S. K. (2024). A Persona-based approach for Churn Prediction and Retention Strategies driven by Predictive Analytics and Generative AI. In D. Choudhary, H. K., R. Rodriguez, J. Wise, & R. T. (Eds.), *Predictive Analytics and Generative AI for Data-Driven Marketing Strategies*. Taylor & Francis Group LLC. DOI: 10.1201/9781003472544-12

More, P. (2021). A Review of Importance of Premarital Checkup and Counselling among Young Adults. *Psychology (Savannah, Ga.)*, 58(2), 6369–6373. https://www.researchgate.net/profile/Pratik-More-3/publication/355022381_A_Review_of_Importance_of_Premarital_Checkup_and_Counselling_among_Young_Adults/links/615822d9a6fae644fbbf61a3/A-Review-of-Importance-of-Premarital-Checkup-and-Counselling-among-Young-Adults.pdf. DOI: 10.17762/pae.v58i2.3162

Morin, C. (2011). Neuromarketing: The new science of consumer behavior. *Society*, 48(2), 131–135. DOI: 10.1007/s12115-010-9408-1

Morra, S. (2021). Quantum Speedup in Robotic Manipulation: A Theoretical Review. *Robotics and Automation*, 29(5), 88–102.

Morra, S. A. (2022). Enhancing Delta Robot Control with Artificial Intelligence. *Journal of Robotics and Autonomous Systems*, 124, 90–101.

Morrin, M. (2011). Scent marketing: An overview. In *Sensory Marketing* (pp. 75–86). Research on the Sensuality of Products., DOI: 10.4324/9780203892060-14

Mosteanu, N. R., & Faccia, A. (2021). Fintech frontiers in quantum computing, fractals, and blockchain distributed ledger: Paradigm shifts and open innovation. *Journal of Open Innovation*, 7(1), 19. DOI: 10.3390/joitmc7010019

Moussa, C., Calandra, H., & Dunjko, V. (2020). To quantum or not to quantum: Towards algorithm selection in near-term quantum optimization. *Quantum Science and Technology*, 5(4), 044009. DOI: 10.1088/2058-9565/abb8e5

Mücke, S., Heese, R., Müller, S., Wolter, M., & Piatkowski, N. (2023). Feature selection on quantum computers. *Quantum Machine Intelligence*, 5(1), 11. DOI: 10.1007/s42484-023-00099-z

Mullangi, K., Dhameliya, N., Anumandla, S. K. R., Yarlagadda, V. K., Sachani, D. K., Vennapusa, S. C. R., & Patel, B. (2023). AI-augmented decision-making in management using quantum networks. *Asian Business Review*, 13(2), 73–86. DOI: 10.18034/abr.v13i2.718

Mummadi, S., & Rudra, B. (2023). Fundamentals of Quantum Computation and Basic Quantum Gates. In *Handbook of Research on Quantum Computing for Smart Environments* (pp. 1–24). IGI Global. DOI: 10.4018/978-1-6684-6697-1.ch001

Mummadi, S., & Rudra, B. (2023). Practical demonstration of quantum key distribution protocol with error correction mechanism. *International Journal of Theoretical Physics*, 62(4), 86.

Muthaluri, J., Sivakumar, D. T. B., Rahamtula, D., Samanta, K., & Sanne, S. H. V. (2024). Optimising Supply Chain Management And Marketing Strategies: AI And ML Integration For Competitive Advantage. *Educational Administration: Theory and Practice*, 30(5), 8990–8997. DOI: 10.53555/kuey.v30i5.4494

Navot, A., Shpigelman, L., Tishby, N., & Vaadia, E. (2005). Nearest neighbor based feature selection for regression and its application to neural activity. *Advances in Neural Information Processing Systems*, •••, 18.

Neha, M., S., Alfurhood, B. S., Bakhare, R., Poongavanam, S., & Khanna, R. (2023). The Role and Impact of Artificial Intelligence on Retail Business and its Developments. *2023 International Conference on Artificial Intelligence and Smart Communication, AISC 2023*, 1098–1101. DOI: 10.1109/AISC56616.2023.10085624

Nembrini, R., Ferrari Acreman, M., & Cremonesi, P. (2021). Feature selection for recommender systems with quantum computing. *Entropy (Basel, Switzerland)*, 23(8), 970. DOI: 10.3390/e23080970 PMID: 34441110

Neven, H.. (2021). Quantum Artificial Intelligence for Robotic Manipulation Tasks. *IEEE Transactions on Robotics*, 38(2), 406–419.

Neves Pereira, M. H., Bezerra de Melo, F. L. N., Jerônimo Soares, A. M., Soares Ferreira, P. B., da Silva, M. P., & Morya, E. (2024). EYE-TRACKING AS A PHYSIOLOGICAL CORRELATE OF CONSUMER BEHAVIOR: A SYSTEMATIC LITERATURE REVIEW. REMark: Revista Brasileira de Marketing, 23(1).

Ng, A. Y., Harada, D., & Russell, S. (1999, June). Policy invariance under reward transformations: Theory and application to reward shaping. In *Icml* (Vol. 99, pp. 278-287).

Nguyen, H. S. (2024). Unlocking Consumer Insights: A Comprehensive Analysis of EEG Applications in Neuro Marketing Research. In Pagac, M., Hajnys, J., Kozior, T., Nguyen, H. S., Nguyen, V. D., & Nag, A. (Eds.), *From Smart City to Smart Factory for Sustainable Future: Conceptual Framework, Scenarios, and Multidiscipline Perspectives. SCFF 2024. Lecture Notes in Networks and Systems* (Vol. 1062). Springer., DOI: 10.1007/978-3-031-65656-9_46

Nielsen, J., & Pernice, K. (2010). *Eyetracking Web Usability*. Pearson Education.

Nielsen, M. A., & Chuang, I. L. (2010). *Quantum computation and quantum information*. Cambridge University Press.

Nikiforuk, P. N., & Gutierrez, G. J. (1998). Predictive and Neural Network Based Control Systems for High-Speed Robotic Manipulators. *IEEE Transactions on Neural Networks*, 9(5), 787–803. PMID: 18255766

Nozaradan, S. (2014). Exploring how musical rhythm entrains brain activity with electroencephalogram frequency-tagging. *Philosophical Transactions of the Royal Society of London. Series B, Biological Sciences*, 369(1658), 20130393.

Ntumba, C., Aguayo, S., & Maina, K. (2023). Revolutionising Retail: A Mini Review of E-commerce Evolution. *Journal of Digital Marketing and Communication*, 3(2), 100–110. DOI: 10.53623/jdmc.v3i2.365

Oger, M., Olmez, I., Inci, E., Kücükbay, S., & Emekci, F. (2015). Privacy Preserving Secure Online Advertising. *Procedia: Social and Behavioral Sciences*, 195, 1840–1845. DOI: 10.1016/j.sbspro.2015.06.405

Ohme, R., Reykowska, D., Wiener, D., & Choromanska, A. (2009). Analysis of neurophysiological reactions to advertising stimuli by means of EEG and galvanic skin response measures. *Journal of Neuroscience, Psychology, and Economics*, 2(1), 21–31. DOI: 10.1037/a0015462

Olorunsogo, T., Jacks, B. S., & Ajala, O. A. (2024). LEVERAGING QUANTUM COMPUTING FOR INCLUSIVE AND RESPONSIBLE AI DEVELOPMENT: A CONCEPTUAL AND REVIEW FRAMEWORK. *Computer Science & IT Research Journal*, 5(3), 671–680. DOI: 10.51594/csitrj.v5i3.927

Ortigueira-Sánchez, L. C., & Risco-Martínez, S. L. (2021). A bibliometric analysis on the state of the art of Neuromarketing research in Web of Science. *ECONTEC: Revista Internacional de Gestión del Conocimiento y la Tecnología*, 9(2), 1-21. https://gecontec.org/index.php/unesco/article/view/20/16

Page, M. J., McKenzie, J. E., Bossuyt, P. M., Boutron, I., Hoffmann, T. C., Mulrow, C. D., Shamseer, L., Tetzlaff, J. M., Akl, E. A., Brennan, S. E., Chou, R., Glanville, J., Grimshaw, J. M., Hróbjartsson, A., Lalu, M. M., Li, T., Loder, E. W., Mayo-Wilson, E., McDonald, S., & Moher, D. (2021). The PRISMA 2020 statement: An updated guideline for reporting systematic reviews. *BMJ (Clinical Research Ed.), n71*. Advance online publication. doi: PMID:33782057DOI: 10.1136/bmj.n71

Palanisamy, P. K., Dey, A., & Nagarajan, K. (2020). Quantum computing for control systems: A review. *IEEE Access : Practical Innovations, Open Solutions*, 8, 2072–2086.

Panda, D., Chakladar, D. D., & Dasgupta, T. (2020). Multimodal system for emotion recognition using EEG and customer review. In Proceedings of the global ai congress 2019 (pp. 399-410). Springer Singapore. DOI: 10.1007/978-981-15-2188-1_32

Pandey, S., Basisth, N. J., Sachan, T., Kumari, N., & Pakray, P. (2023). Quantum machine learning for natural language processing application. *Physica A*, 627, 129123. DOI: 10.1016/j.physa.2023.129123

Parasidis, E. (2023). The Urgent Need for a U.S. Data Protection Agency. *The American Journal of Bioethics*, 23(11), 26–29. DOI: 10.1080/15265161.2023.2256283 PMID: 37879026

Park, J. S., Kim, D. H., & Lee, S. J. (2021). Photon-Based Quantum Communication in Swarm Robotics: Security and Efficiency. *Journal of Quantum Networking*, 5(2), 85–102.

Park, S.-M., & Kim, Y.-G. (2022). A Metaverse: Taxonomy, Components, Applications, and Open Challenges. *IEEE Access : Practical Innovations, Open Solutions*, 10, 4209–4251. DOI: 10.1109/ACCESS.2021.3140175

Patel, S. R., & Sharma, N. K. (2022). Quantum Genetic Algorithms for Optimizing Swarm Drones in Surveillance Systems. *International Journal of Quantum Information Science*, 12(9), 567–582.

Patkar, N., & Seyff, N. (2023). Data-Driven Persona Creation, Validation, and Evolution. In Ferrari, A., & Penzenstadler, B. (Eds.), *Requirements Engineering: Foundation for Software Quality* (Vol. 13975, pp. 262–271). Springer., DOI: 10.1007/978-3-031-29786-1_18

Pedrycz, W.. (2016). Advances in Fuzzy Modeling. *Fuzzy Sets and Systems.*

Peelam, M. S., Rout, A. A., & Chamola, V. (2024). Quantum computing applications for Internet of Things. *IET Quantum Communication*, 5(2), 103–112. DOI: 10.1049/qtc2.12079

Pelau, C., Nistoreanu, P., Lazar, L., & Badescu, R. (2022). Celebrity vs. Product: A neuroscientific approach to the distractors in food advertising for sustainable marketing. *Sustainability*, 14(19), 1–15, 12768. DOI: 10.3390/su141912768

Pellow-Jarman, A., & Möttönen, M.. (2024). The effect of classical optimizers and Ansatz depth on QAOA performance in noisy devices. *Scientific Reports*, 14(1), 16011. DOI: 10.1038/s41598-024-66625-6 PMID: 38992152

Peng, M., Liang, M., Huang, H., Fan, J., Yu, L., & Liao, J. (2023). The effect of different animated brand logos on consumer response: An event-related potential and self-reported study. *Computers in Human Behavior*, 143, 1–12, 107701. DOI: 10.1016/j.chb.2023.107701

Perdomo-Ortiz, , Benedetti, M., Realpe-Gómez, J., & Biswas, R. (2018). Opportunities and Challenges for Quantum-Assisted Machine Learning in Near-Term Quantum Devices. *Quantum Science and Technology*, 3(3), 030502. DOI: 10.1088/2058-9565/aab859

Perdomo-Ortiz, N. (2012). Dickson, M. Drew-Brook, G. Rose, and A. Aspuru-Guzik, "Quantum Annealing for Optimization of Robotic Manipulations,". *Scientific Reports*, 2(1), 1–8.

Perdomo-Ortiz, N., Dickson, N., Drew-Brook, M., Rose, G., & Aspuru-Guzik, A. (2012). Dickson, M. Drew-Brook, G. Rose, and A. Aspuru-Guzik, "Finding Low-Energy Conformations of Lattice Protein Models by Quantum Annealing,". *Scientific Reports*, 2(1), 1–8. DOI: 10.1038/srep00571

Peres, A. (1985). Reversible logic and quantum computers. *Physical review A*, 32(6), 3266.

Perez-Vega, R., Kaartemo, V., Lages, C. R., Borghei Razavi, N., & Männistö, J. (2021). Reshaping the contexts of online customer engagement behavior via artificial intelligence: A conceptual framework. *Journal of Business Research*, 129, 902–910. DOI: 10.1016/j.jbusres.2020.11.002

Peruzzo, A., McClean, J., Shadbolt, P., Yung, M.-H., Zhou, X.-Q., Love, P. J., Aspuru-Guzik, A., & O'Brien, J. L. (2014). A variational eigenvalue solver on a photonic quantum processor. *Nature Communications*, 5(1), 4213. DOI: 10.1038/ncomms5213 PMID: 25055053

Pham, T., & Bui, H. (2021). Real-Time Control in Delta Robots Using Quantum AI. *Journal of Robotic Systems*, 34, 156–167.

Pham, V., & Bui, H. (2022). Real-Time Control Optimization of Delta Robots Using AI Techniques. *The International Journal of Robotics Research*, 41(2), 133–148.

Picton, P. D. (1994). Modified Fredkin gates in logic design. *Microelectronics Journal*, 25(6), 437–441. DOI: 10.1016/0026-2692(94)90068-X

Pierrot, F.. (1999). Hexa: A Fast Six-Degree-of-Freedom Parallel Robot for High-Speed Applications. *IEEE Transactions on Robotics and Automation*, 15(4), 627–639.

Pierrot, F.. (1999, August). Hexa: A Fast, Six-Degree-of-Freedom Parallel Robot for High-Speed Applications. *IEEE Transactions on Robotics and Automation*, 15(4), 627–639.

Pierrot, F., Dauchez, P., & Fournier, P. (1991) "Hexa: A Fast Six-DOF Parallel Robot for High-Speed Applications," *IEEE International Conference on Robotics and Automation*, pp. 1159–1164.

Plassmann, H., Ramsøy, T., & Milosavljević, M. D. (2012). Branding the brain: A critical review and outlook. *Journal of Consumer Psychology*, 22(1), 18–36. DOI: 10.1016/j.jcps.2011.11.010

Plassmann, H., & Ramsøy, T.Z., & Milica Mormann. (2015). Marketing Implications from Understanding Consumer Behavior through Neuroscience Techniques. *The Journal of Consumer Research.*

Plassmann, H., Venkatraman, V., Huettel, S., & Yoon, C. (2015). Consumer Neuroscience: Applications, challenges, and possible solutions. *JMR, Journal of Marketing Research*, 52(4), 427–435. DOI: 10.1509/jmr.14.0048

Pott, C.-D. P. R. (2018). *Theory and Application.* Springer.

Prakash, P. M. (2023). Enhancing business performance through quantum electronic analysis of optical data. *Optical and Quantum Electronics*, 55(12), 1056. DOI: 10.1007/s11082-023-05347-x

Pramoda, M., Evuru, P. C., Vulavalapudi, V. M. S., Pallapothu, L. K. K., & Annapurna, B. (2024). Quantum Machine Learning: A Survey. *Journal of Electrical Systems*, 20(6s), 971–981. DOI: 10.52783/jes.2778

Preskill, J. (2018). Quantum Computing in the NISQ Era and Beyond. *Quantum : the Open Journal for Quantum Science*, 2(79), 79–108. DOI: 10.22331/q-2018-08-06-79

Priyanka. (2024). *2024 is the year of the Subscription Business model. Know all definitions, benefits, and metrics.*https://www.racknap.com/blog/subscription-business-models-explained/

Purnamasari, D. I., Permadi, V. A., Saepudin, A., & Agusdin, R. P. (2023). Demand Forecasting for Improved Inventory Management in Small and Medium-Sized Businesses. [JANAPATI]. *Jurnal Nasional Pendidikan Teknik Informatika*, 12(1), 56–66. DOI: 10.23887/janapati.v12i1.57144

Qayyum, A., Ur Rasool, R., Ahmad, H. F., Rafique, W., Qadir, J., & Anwar, Z. (2023). Quantum Computing for Healthcare: A Review. In *Future Internet* (Vol. 15, Issue 3). *Authorea.* DOI: 10.3390/fi15030094

Qian, Y., Xiong, Y., Wang, Y., Jiang, Y., Liu, Y., & Chai, Y. (2022). Identification of Key Features for VR Applications with VREVIEW: A Topic Model Approach. *2022 IEEE Conference on Virtual Reality and 3D User Interfaces*, 1-8. DOI: 10.1109/VRW55335.2022.00046

Rabhi, M., Thamri, A., Benahmed, E. S., & Djoual, M. (2023). Neuromarketing research trends over the last ten years: a bibliometric analysis of the Scopus databases. *Marketing and Digital Technologies*, 7, 7-23. https://www.researchgate.net/publication/374265603_Neuromarketing_research_trends_over_ the_last_ten_years_a_bibliometric_analysis_of_the_Scopus_databases

Radanliev, P. (2024). Artificial intelligence and quantum cryptography. *Journal of Analytical Science and Technology*, 15(1), 4. DOI: 10.1186/s40543-024-00416-6

Rahmawati, K., Kasih, P. H., & Perdana, A. B. (2023). *From Offline to Online: Changes in Vegetable Purchases During COVID-19 in Indonesia* (Vol. 1). Atlantis Press SARL., DOI: 10.2991/978-2-38476-048-0_25

Rajamannar, R. (2021). *Quantum_Marketing*. HarperCollins Leadership.

Raji, M. ., Olodo, H. ., Oke, T. ., Addy, W. ., Ofodile, O. ., & Oyewole, A. . (2024). E-commerce and consumer behavior: A review of AI-powered personalisation and market trends. *GSC Advanced Research and Reviews, 18*(3), 066–077. DOI: 10.30574/gscarr.2024.18.3.0090

Rani, K. S. K., Priyadharsheni, J. M., Karthikeyan, B., & Pugalendhi, G. S. (2023). Applications of quantum AI for healthcare. In *Quantum computing and artificial intelligence: Training machine and deep learning algorithms on quantum computers* (pp. 271).

Ranjekar, G., & Roy, D. (2023). *Rise of Quick Commerce in India : Business Models and Infrastructure Requirements*.

Rathee, S., Taylor, C. R., & Gupta, A. (2024). The appeal of blurred imagery: Enhancing advertising and brand attitudes for luxury goods. *Journal of Business Research*, 182, 114795. DOI: 10.1016/j.jbusres.2024.114795

Rau, J., Altenburg, L., & Ghezzi, A. I. (2023). How the Quick Commerce Business Model Delivers Convenience in Online Grocery Retailing. In *Springer Proceedings in Business and Economics* (Vol. 1, Issue Gielens 2022). Springer Nature Switzerland. DOI: 10.1007/978-3-031-31836-8_10

Ravella, A. (2015). *Buyer Personas: How to Gain Insight into Your Customer's Expectations, Align Your Marketing Strategies, and Win More Business*. John Wiley & Sons.

Ravi, V., Pradeepkumar, D., & Deb, K. (2017). Financial time series prediction using hybrids of chaos theory, multi-layer perceptron and multi-objective evolutionary algorithms. *Swarm and Evolutionary Computation*, 36, 136–149.

Rawat, B., Mehra, N., Bist, A. S., Yusup, M., & Sanjaya, Y. P. A. (2022). Quantum Computing and AI: Impacts & Possibilities. [AJRI]. *ADI Journal on Recent Innovation*, 3(2), 202–207. DOI: 10.34306/ajri.v3i2.656

Razi, N. I. M., Othman, M., & Yaacob, H. (2016). *EEG-based emotion recognition in the investment activities*. 2016 6th International Conference on Information and Communication Technology for the Muslim World (ICT4M), Jakarta, Indonesia. https://ieeexplore.ieee.org/document/7814925

Rebentrost, P., Mohseni, M., & Lloyd, S. (2014). Quantum Support Vector Machine for Big Data Classification. *Physical Review Letters*, 113(13), 130503. DOI: 10.1103/PhysRevLett.113.130503 PMID: 25302877

Richa, H., & Vadera, S. (2019). Determinants of online shopping behaviour in india. *International Journal of Recent Technology and Engineering*, 8(3), 3946–3950. DOI: 10.35940/ijrte.C5303.098319

Rigui, Z., Nan, J., & Qiulin, D. (2006). Model and training of QNN with weight. *Neural Processing Letters*, 24(3), 261–269. DOI: 10.1007/s11063-006-9025-6

Rika, H., Aviv, I., & Weitzfeld, R. (2022). Unleashing the Potentials of Quantum Probability Theory for Customer Experience Analytics. *Big Data and Cognitive Computing*, 6(4), 135. DOI: 10.3390/bdcc6040135

Riva, G., Baños, R. M., Botella, C., Mantovani, F., & Gaggioli, A. (2016). Transforming Experience: The Potential of Augmented Reality and Virtual Reality for Enhancing Personal and Clinical Change. *Frontiers in Psychiatry*, 7. Advance online publication. DOI: 10.3389/fpsyt.2016.00164 PMID: 27746747

Roser, G. J., & Solven, C. (2018). Real-Time Control and Optimization for Delta Robots. *IEEE/ASME Transactions on Mechatronics*, 23(2), 487–499.

Rossi, S., Spina, A., & Ferrara, A. (2020). Delta Robots in High-Speed Industrial Applications: A Review on Mechanics, Control and Applications. *Mechatronics*, 68, 1–12.

Royanti, I., & Astini, R. (2023). Analysis of E-Grocery Purchase Decisions Mediated by E-Trust in Indonesia Quick Commerce. *International Journal of Innovative Science and Research Technology*, 8(8). www.ijisrt.com

Rybaczewska, M., & Sparks, L. (2020). Locally-owned convenience stores and the local economy. *Journal of Retailing and Consumer Services*, 52, 101939. DOI: 10.1016/j.jretconser.2019.101939

Saeedi, M., & Markov, I. L. (2013). Synthesis and optimization of reversible circuits—A survey. *ACM Computing Surveys*, 45(2), 1–34.

Sáez-Ortuño, L., Huertas-Garcia, R., Forgas-Coll, S., Sánchez-García, J., & Puertas-Prats, E. (2024). Quantum computing for market research. *Journal of Innovation & Knowledge*, 9(3), 100510. DOI: 10.1016/j.jik.2024.100510

Sahai and K. Bhatia. (2020). Deep Reinforcement Learning for Motion Planning in Delta Robots. *IEEE Transactions on Robotics*, 36(5), 2238–2247.

Sakhavi, S., Guan, C., & Yan, S. (2018). Learning Temporal Information for Brain-Computer Interface Using Convolutional Neural Networks. *IEEE Transactions on Neural Networks and Learning Systems*, 29(11), 5619–5629. DOI: 10.1109/TNNLS.2018.2789927 PMID: 29994075

Salminen, J., Jansen, B. J., An, J., Kwak, H., & Jung, S.-G. (2019). *Automatic Persona Generation for Online Content Creators: Conceptual Rationale and a Research Agenda*. 135–160. DOI: 10.1007/978-1-4471-7427-1_8

Salminen, J., Guan, K., Jung, S.-G., & Jansen, B. J. (2021). A Survey of 15 Years of Data-Driven Persona Development. *International Journal of Human-Computer Interaction*, 37(18), 1685–1708. DOI: 10.1080/10447318.2021.1908670

Salminen, J., Santos, J. M., Jung, S., & Jansen, B. J. (2024). Picturing the fictitious person: An exploratory study on the effect of images on user perceptions of AI-generated personas. *Computers in Human Behavior: Artificial Humans*, 2(1), 100052. DOI: 10.1016/j.chbah.2024.100052

Salminen, J., Santos, J. M., Kwak, H., An, J., Jung, S., & Jansen, B. J. (2020). Persona Perception Scale: Development and Exploratory Validation of an Instrument for Evaluating Individuals' Perceptions of Personas. *International Journal of Human-Computer Studies*, 141, 102437. DOI: 10.1016/j.ijhcs.2020.102437

Sánchez, D., & Viejo, A. (2018). Privacy-preserving and advertising-friendly web surfing. *Computer Communications*, 130, 113–123. DOI: 10.1016/j.comcom.2018.09.002

Sarker, I. H. (2021). Machine Learning: Algorithms, Real-World Applications and Research Directions. *SN Computer Science*, 2(3), 160. DOI: 10.1007/s42979-021-00592-x PMID: 33778771

Satpathy, S. K., & Mishra, R. (2023). Quantum algorithms in marketing analytics: A neuromarketing perspective. *Journal of Theoretical and Applied Information Technology*, 101(2), 359–372. DOI: 10.5281/zenodo.7526308

Saunders, M. N., Lewis, P., & Thornhill, A. (2019). *Research methods for business students* (8th ed.). Pearson Education Limited.

Saxena, A., Mancilla, J., Montalban, I., & Pere, C. (2023). *Financial modeling using quantum computing: Design and manage quantum machine learning solutions for financial analysis and decision making*. Packt Publishing Ltd.

Saxena, A., Mancilla, J., Montalban, I., & Pere, C. (2023). *Financial Modeling Using Quantum Computing: Design and manage Quantum machine learning solutions for financial analysis and decision making*. Packt Publishing Ltd.

Schärer, K., & Comuzzi, M. (2023). The quantum threat to blockchain: Summary and timeline analysis. *Quantum Machine Intelligence*, 5(1), 1–12. DOI: 10.1007/s42484-023-00105-4

Schirrmeister, R. T., Springenberg, J. T., Fiederer, L. D. J., Glasstetter, M., Eggensperger, K., Tangermann, M., & Ball, T. (2017). Deep learning with convolutional neural networks for EEG decoding and visualization. *Human Brain Mapping*, 38(11), 5391–5420.

Schneider, C., & Woolgar, S. (2021). Ethical Considerations in Neuromarketing Practices. *Journal of Business Ethics*.

Schuh, G., Anderl, R., Gausemeier, J., ten Hompel, M., & Wahlster, W. (2017). *Industrie 4.0 Maturity Index: Managing the Digital Transformation of Companies*. Herbert Utz Verlag.

Schuld, M., & Killoran, N. (2019). Quantum machine learning in feature Hilbert spaces. *Physical Review Letters*, 122(4), 040504. DOI: 10.1103/PhysRevLett.122.040504 PMID: 30768345

Sebastian, V. (2014). Neuromarketing and Evaluation of Cognitive and Emotional Responses of Consumers to Marketing Stimuli. *Procedia: Social and Behavioral Sciences*, 127, 753–757. DOI: 10.1016/j.sbspro.2014.03.349

Sedik, T. S., Gorbanyov, M., & Malaika, M. (2021). Quantum Computing and the Financial System: Spooky Action at a Distance? *IMF Working Paper*, 2021(071), 1. DOI: 10.5089/9781513572727.001

Segijn, C. M., & Strycharz, J. (2023). The ethical ramifications of surveillance in contemporary advertising for the industry, consumers, and regulators: Current issues and a future research agenda. *International Journal of Advertising*, 42(1), 69–77. DOI: 10.1080/02650487.2022.2114700

Sehrawat, S. K., Dutta, P. K., Bhatia, A. B., & Whig, P. (2024). Predicting demand in supply chain networks with quantum machine learning approach. In *Quantum computing and supply chain management: A new era of optimization* (pp. 33–47). IGI Global. DOI: 10.4018/979-8-3693-4107-0.ch002

Setiyono, A. E., Chandrawatisma, C., Fanandi, R. H. S., & Heriyati, P. (2023). Antecedents of E-Loyalty as Research for the Quick Commerce Industry. *Interdisciplinary Social Studies*, 2(8), 2287–2299. DOI: 10.55324/iss.v2i8.456

Shabani, . (2020). Quantum Control and Robotics: Enhancing Automation with Quantum Computing. *IEEE Transactions on Quantum Engineering*, 3(1), 101–115.

Shabani, . (2020). Quantum Control for Automation and Robotics. *IEEE Transactions on Quantum Engineering*, 3(1), 101–115.

Shor, P. W. (1994, November). Algorithms for quantum computation: discrete logarithms and factoring. In *Proceedings 35th annual symposium on foundations of computer science* (pp. 124-134). Ieee.

Shrestha, S., & Das, S. (2022). Exploring gender biases in ML and AI academic research through systematic literature review. In *Frontiers in Artificial Intelligence* (Vol. 5, p. 976838). Frontiers Media S.A., DOI: 10.3389/frai.2022.976838

Siciliano, B., & Khatib, O. (2016). *Springer Handbook of Robotics*. Springer Science & Business Media. DOI: 10.1007/978-3-319-32552-1

Siddique, J., Shamim, A., Nawaz, M., & Abid, M. F. (2023). The hope and hype of neuromarketing: A bibliometric analysis. *Journal of Contemporary Marketing Science*, 6(1), 1–21. DOI: 10.1108/JCMARS-07-2022-0018

Silver, D., Huang, A., Maddison, C. J., Guez, A., Sifre, L., van den Driessche, G., Schrittwieser, J., Antonoglou, I., Panneershelvam, V., Lanctot, M., Dieleman, S., Grewe, D., Nham, J., Kalchbrenner, N., Sutskever, I., Lillicrap, T., Leach, M., Kavukcuoglu, K., Graepel, T., & Hassabis, D. (2016). Mastering the Game of Go with Deep Neural Networks and Tree Search. *Nature*, 529(7587), 484–489. DOI: 10.1038/nature16961 PMID: 26819042

Simon, J., Wong, P. H., & Rieder, G. (2020). Algorithmic bias and the value sensitive design approach. *Internet Policy Review*, 9(4), 1–16. DOI: 10.14763/2020.4.1534

Singh, C., Khajuria, H., & Nayak, B. P. (2023), March. A Study of Implementing a Blockchain-Based Forensic Model Integration (BBFMI) for IoT Devices in Digital Forensics. In *International Conference on Computer Science, Engineering and Education Applications* (pp. 318-327). Cham: Springer Nature Switzerland. DOI: 10.1007/978-3-031-36118-0_28

Singh, C., Khajuria, H., & Nayak, B. P. (2024). Rapid Advancement and Trends of Big Data Analytics and Cyber-Physical System Embedded in Healthcare and Industry 4.0. In *Intelligent Security Solutions for Cyber-Physical Systems* (pp. 216-233). Chapman and Hall/CRC.

Singh, A. K., & Rathore, K. S. (2023). Quantum Algorithms for Autonomous Robot Swarms. *Journal of Robotics and Automation*, 19(3), 210–223.

Singh, C., & Das, A. K. (2024). Transforming digitization in supply chain management using artificial intelligence and machine learning. In *Supply Chain Management* (pp. 119–139). CRC Press. DOI: 10.1201/9781003509561-7

Singh, D. S., Agarwal, M. S., & Gupta, M. R. (2023). Quantum Computing: Fundamentals, Progress, and Implications. *International Journal for Research in Applied Science and Engineering Technology*, 11(9), 1106–1111. DOI: 10.22214/ijraset.2023.55803

Singh, P., Alhassan, I., & Khoshaim, L. (2023). What do you need to know? A systematic review and research agenda on Neuromarketing discipline. *Journal of Theoretical and Applied Electronic Commerce Research*, 18(4), 2007–2032. DOI: 10.3390/jtaer18040101

Smit, E. G., Van Noort, G., & Voorveld, H. A. M. (2014). Understanding online behavioural advertising: User knowledge, privacy concerns and online coping behaviour in Europe. *Computers in Human Behavior*, 32, 15–22. DOI: 10.1016/j.chb.2013.11.008

Smith, A.. (2021). Collaborative Approaches to Addressing Challenges in Robotics Implementation. *Journal of Manufacturing Collaboration*, 8(1), 75–90.

Smith, J. E., & Eiben, A. E. (2018). "Advances in Evolutionary Computing," *Springer*, 2021.W. M. Lim, "The Interplay Between Neuromarketing and Social Media,". *Journal of Behavioral Decision Making*.

Smith, J., & Brown, L. (2021). Collaborative Robotics: Enhancing Safety and Flexibility in Manufacturing. *The International Journal of Robotics Research*, 38(2), 180–195.

Smith, J., & Johnson, L. (2020). The Impact of Robotics on Labor Costs in Manufacturing. *Journal of Manufacturing Economics*, 28(2), 145–160.

Smith, J., & Lee, M. (2022). Promoting Collaboration and Knowledge Sharing in Robotics Integration: A Policy Perspective. *Journal of Policy Studies*, 25(3), 250–265.

Smith, R.. (2022). Challenges in Integrating AI into Delta Robot Control Systems. *Journal of Automation and Robotics*, 45, 179–192.

Sodiya, E. O., Umoga, U. J., Amoo, O. O., & Akoh, A. (2024). AI-driven warehouse automation: A comprehensive review of systems. *GSC Advanced Research and Reviews*, 18(2), 272–282. DOI: 10.30574/gscarr.2024.18.2.0063

Soni, V. (2024). AI and the Personalization-Privacy Paradox: Balancing Customized Marketing with Consumer Data Protection. *IRE Journals*, 7(12), 411–418.

Soueidan, M. H., & Shoghari, R. (2024). The Impact of Artificial Intelligence on Job Loss: Risks for Governments. *Technium Social Sciences Journal*, 57, 206–223. DOI: 10.47577/tssj.v57i1.10917

Spence, C. (2019). Neuroscience-inspired design: From academic neuromarketing to commercially relevant research. *Organizational Research Methods*, 22(1), 275–298. DOI: 10.1177/1094428116672003

Spivey, R. F., Inlek, I. V., Jia, Z., Crain, S., Sun, K., Kim, J., Vrijsen, G., Fang, C., Fitzgerald, C., Kross, S., Noel, T., & Kim, J. (2022). High-Stability Cryogenic System for Quantum Computing with Compact Packaged Ion Traps. *IEEE Transactions on Quantum Engineering*, 3, 1–11. Advance online publication. DOI: 10.1109/TQE.2021.3125926

Spong, M. W., Hutchinson, S., & Vidyasagar, M. (2005). *Robot Modeling and Control*. John Wiley & Sons.

Sposini, L. (2024). Neuromarketing and Eye-Tracking Technologies Under the European Framework: Towards the GDPR and Beyond. *Journal of Consumer Policy*, 47(3), 1–24. DOI: 10.1007/s10603-023-09559-2

Sreerama, J., & Krishnamoorthy, G. (2022). Ethical Considerations in AI Addressing Bias and Fairness in Machine Learning Models. *Journal of Knowledge Learning and Science Technology ISSN: 2959-6386 (Online), 1*(1), 130–138. DOI: 10.60087/jklst.vol1.n1.p138

Srinivasan, S. (2021). Optimization Techniques for Quantum Robotics: A Review. *Journal of Quantum Artificial Intelligence*, 5(2), 1–19.

Stamatopoulos, N., Egger, D. J., Sun, Y., Zoufal, C., Iten, R., Shen, N., & Woerner, S. (2020). Option pricing using quantum computers. *Quantum : the Open Journal for Quantum Science*, 4, 291. Advance online publication. DOI: 10.22331/q-2020-07-06-291

Steane, A. M. (1996). Error correcting codes in quantum theory. *Physical Review Letters*, 77(5), 793–797. DOI: 10.1103/PhysRevLett.77.793 PMID: 10062908

Steane, A. M. (1996). Multiple particle interference and quantum error correction. *Proceedings - Royal Society. Mathematical, Physical and Engineering Sciences*, 452(1954), 2551–2577. DOI: 10.1098/rspa.1996.0136

Stojanov, M. (2022). *Q-COMMERCE – THE NEXT GENERATION*. http://hdl.handle.net/10610/4683

Strycharz, J., & Segijn, C. M. (2024). Ethical side-effect of dataveillance in advertising: Impact of data collection, trust, privacy concerns and regulatory differences on chilling effects. *Journal of Business Research*, 173, 114490. DOI: 10.1016/j.jbusres.2023.114490

Stumpf, D.. (2022). AI-Based Algorithms for High-Speed Pick and Place Delta Robots. *IEEE Transactions on Robotics*, 38(4), 1205–1217.

Subramanian, K. N. G., & Ge, S. S. (2016) "Model Predictive Control of a Delta Parallel Robot for Optimal Trajectory Tracking," *IEEE/RSJ International Conference on Intelligent Robots and Systems*, , pp. 4053–4058.

Sun, H. (2023). Design Logistics Management System Based on Computer Algorithm Model. *Frontiers in Artificial Intelligence and Applications*, 373, 569–575. DOI: 10.3233/FAIA230856

Sun, Z. (2023). Data, analytics, and intelligence. *Journal of Computer Science Research*, 5(4), 43–57. DOI: 10.30564/jcsr.v5i4.6072

Suresh Babu, C. V., & Adhithya, S. (2023). ChatGPT and Other Generative AI Tools in Education: Transformative Potential and Ethical Considerations. In Keengwe, J. (Ed.), *Creative AI Tools and Ethical Implications in Teaching and Learning* (pp. 135–152). IGI Global., DOI: 10.4018/979-8-3693-0205-7.ch007

Suresh Babu, C. V., & Auroshaa, A. (2024). Influence of Data Analysis Tools in Teaching and Learning Economics. In Scott, B., & Fox, M. E. (Eds.), *Cases on Economics Education and Tools for Educators* (pp. 229–248). IGI Global., DOI: 10.4018/978-1-6684-7583-6.ch010

Suresh Babu, C. V., & Jeyavasan, T. (2023). Tourism Is an Essential Trade: VR and AR Technologies Make It Profitable. In Jean Vasile, A., Vasić, M., & Vukovic, P. (Eds.), *Sustainable Growth and Global Social Development in Competitive Economies* (pp. 79–96). IGI Global., DOI: 10.4018/978-1-6684-8810-2.ch005

Sutton, R. S., & Barto, A. G. (2018). *Reinforcement Learning: An Introduction.* MIT Press.

Swathi, M., & Rudra, B. (2021, January). Implementation of reversible logic gates with quantum gates. In *2021 IEEE 11th annual computing and communication workshop and conference (CCWC)* (pp. 1557-1563). Ieee.

Swathi, M., & Rudra, B. (2022, April). A novel architecture for binary code to gray code converter using quantum cellular automata. In *Edge Analytics: Select Proceedings of 26th International Conference—ADCOM 2020* (pp. 43-61). Singapore: Springer Singapore.

Swathi, M., & Rudra, B. (2022, January). Novel encoding method for quantum error correction. In *2022 IEEE 12th Annual Computing and Communication Workshop and Conference (CCWC)* (pp. 1001-1005). IEEE.

Swathi, M., & Rudra, B. (2022). *"Experimental analysis of a quantum encoder in various quantum systems." 2022 IEEE 13th Annual Ubiquitous Computing, Electronics & Mobile Communication Conference (UEMCON).* IEEE.

Swathi, M., & Rudra, B. (2022). A novel approach for asymmetric quantum error correction with syndrome measurement. *IEEE Access : Practical Innovations, Open Solutions*, 10, 44669–44676. DOI: 10.1109/ACCESS.2022.3170039

Swathi, M., & Rudra, B. (2022). An efficient approach for quantum entanglement purification. *International Journal of Quantum Information*, 20(04), 2250004.

Tamrakar, A., & Sharma, R. (2019). Quantum Computing: A Comprehensive Review. [TURCOMAT]. *Turkish Journal of Computer and Mathematics Education*, 10(3), 1634–1642. DOI: 10.61841/turcomat.v10i3.14623

Tariq, M. U. (2024). Application of blockchain and Internet of Things (IoT) in modern business. In Sinha, M., Bhandari, A., Priya, S., & Kabiraj, S. (Eds.), *Future of customer engagement through marketing intelligence* (pp. 66–94). IGI Global., DOI: 10.4018/979-8-3693-2367-0.ch004

Tariq, M. U. (2024). Leading Smart Technologies and Innovations for E-Business 5.0: Applications and Management Frameworks. In Popkova, E. (Ed.), *Smart Technologies and Innovations in E-Business* (pp. 25–46). IGI Global., DOI: 10.4018/978-1-6684-7840-0.ch002

Tariq, M. U. (2024). The role of AI ethics in cost and complexity reduction. In Tennin, K., Ray, S., & Sorg, J. (Eds.), *Cases on AI ethics in business* (pp. 59–78). IGI Global., DOI: 10.4018/979-8-3693-2643-5.ch004

Tariq, M. U. (2024). The role of AI in skilling, upskilling, and reskilling the workforce. In Doshi, R., Dadhich, M., Poddar, S., & Hiran, K. (Eds.), *Integrating generative AI in education to achieve sustainable development goals* (pp. 421–433). IGI Global., DOI: 10.4018/979-8-3693-2440-0.ch023

Tariq, M. U. (2025). *AI-Driven Learning and Engagement in Higher Education.* IGI Global., DOI: 10.4018/979-8-3693-4074-5

Tariq, M. U. (2025). Harnessing Generative AI for Enhanced Web Application Security. In Shah, I., & Jhanjhi, N. (Eds.), *Generative AI for Web Engineering Models* (pp. 161–192). IGI Global., DOI: 10.4018/979-8-3693-3703-5.ch008

Taylor, R. D. (2020). Quantum Artificial Intelligence: A "precautionary" U.S. approach? *Telecommunications Policy*, 44(6), 101909. DOI: 10.1016/j.telpol.2020.101909

Telpaz, A., Webb, R., & Levy, D. J. (2015). Using EEG to predict consumers' future choices. *JMR, Journal of Marketing Research*, 52(4), 511–529. DOI: 10.1509/jmr.13.0564

Terhal, B., & DiVincenzo, D. P. (2022). Adaptive Quantum Control in Robotics. *Journal of Quantum Computing and Robotics*, 41, 335–344.

Thapa, S., Guzmán, F., & Paswan, A. (2024). We are just 10 feet away! How does location-based advertising affect consumer-brand engagement? *Journal of Business Research*, 172, 114425. DOI: 10.1016/j.jbusres.2023.114425

Thomos, R. (2023). The future of big data: Trends and emerging technologies.

Tidd, J., & Bessant, J. R. (2022). Managing innovation: Integrating technological, market and organizational change. John Wiley & Sons, 2020. Vermesan O, Bröring A, Tragos E, Serrano M, Bacciu D, Chessa S. Internet of robotic things–converging sensing/actuating, hyperconnectivity, artificial intelligence, and IoT platforms. In *Cognitive Hyperconnected Digital Transformation* (pp. 97–155). River Publishers.

Tilly, C., & Nienhuis, R. (2018). Quantum algorithms for combinatorial optimization: The quantum approximate optimization algorithm. *IEEE Transactions on Quantum Engineering*, 1, 1–12.

Tirandazi, P., Bamakan, S. M. H., & Toghroljerdi, A. (2023). A review of studies on internet of everything as an enabler of neuromarketing methods and techniques. *The Journal of Supercomputing*, 79(7), 7835–7876. DOI: 10.1007/s11227-022-04988-1

Tripathi, B., & Sharma, R. K. (2023). EEG-based emotion classification in financial trading using deep learning: Effects of risk control measures. *Sensors (Basel)*, 23(7), 1–26, 3474. DOI: 10.3390/s23073474

Trope, Y., & Liberman, N. (2010). Construal-level theory of psychological distance. *Psychological Review*, 117(2), 440–463. DOI: 10.1037/a0018963

Truong, V. N. X., Nkhoma, M., & Pansuwong, W. (2019). An Integrated Effectiveness Framework of Mobile In-App Advertising. *AJIS. Australasian Journal of Information Systems*, 23. Advance online publication. DOI: 10.3127/ajis.v23i0.1971

Tsan, J. Y., & Gao, J. (2020). The role of artificial intelligence in neuromarketing. *Journal of Business Research*, 112, 497–504.

Tula, S. T., Kess-Momoh, A. J., Omotoye, G. B., Bello, B. G., & Daraojimba, A. I.Sunday Tubokirifuruar TulaAzeez Jason Kess-MomohGaniyu Bolawale OmotoyeBinaebi Gloria BelloAndrew Ifesinachi Daraojimba. (2024). AI-ENABLED CUSTOMER EXPERIENCE ENHANCEMENT IN BUSINESS. *Computer Science & IT Research Journal*, 5(2), 365–389. DOI: 10.51594/csitrj.v5i2.789

Tuli, E. A., Lee, J.-M., & Kim, D.-S. (2024). Integration of Quantum Technologies into Metaverse: Applications, Potentials, and Challenges. *IEEE Access : Practical Innovations, Open Solutions*, 12, 29995–30019. DOI: 10.1109/ACCESS.2024.3366527

Tversky, A., & Kahneman, D. (2020). Prospect theory: An analysis of decision under risk. *Behavioral Economics Journal*, 47(1), 263–291.

Unruh, W. G. (1995). Maintaining Coherence in Quantum Computers. *Physical Review A*, 51(2), 992–997. DOI: 10.1103/PhysRevA.51.992 PMID: 9911677

Utriainen, T. (2020). Neuromarketing and consumer neuroscience–the evolution and current state of the Art, an integrative review.

Valdez, P., & Mehrabian, A. (1994). Effects of color on emotions. *Journal of Experimental Psychology. General*, 123(4), 394–409. DOI: 10.1037/0096-3445.123.4.394

Van Hasselt, H., Guez, A., & Silver, D. (2016). Deep Reinforcement Learning with Double Q-learning. *Proceedings of the AAAI Conference on Artificial Intelligence*, 30(1). Advance online publication. DOI: 10.1609/aaai.v30i1.10295

van Loock, P. (2008). A Note on Quantum Error Correction with Continuous Variables. arxiv:0811.3616.

Varghese, P. (2022). Neuromarketing and Artificial Intelligence for Effective Future Business. *IUJ Journal of Management*, 1(1), 240–254.

Vasudevan, D. P., Lala, P. K., Di, J., & Parkerson, J. P. (2006). Reversible-logic design with online testability. *IEEE Transactions on Instrumentation and Measurement*, 55(2), 406–414. DOI: 10.1109/TIM.2006.870319

Vecchiato, G., Cherubino, P., Trettel, A., & Babiloni, F. (2014). Neuroscience and marketing: The role of the prefrontal cortex in neuromarketing. *Journal of Economic Psychology*, 45, 271–280. DOI: 10.1016/j.joep.2014.06.001

Vecchiato, G., Maglione, A. G., Cherubino, P., Wasikowska, B., Wawrzyniak, A., Latuszynska, A., Latuszynska, M., Nermend, K., Graziani, I., Leucci, M. R., Trettel, A., & Babiloni, F. (2014). Neurophysiological tools to investigate consumer's gender differences during the observation of TV commercials. *Computational and Mathematical Methods in Medicine*, 2014, 1–12, 912981. DOI: 10.1155/2014/912981

Vences, N. A., Díaz-Campo, J., & Rosales, D. F. G. (2020). Neuromarketing as an Emotional Connection Tool Between Organizations and Audiences in Social Networks. A Theoretical Review. *Frontiers in Psychology*, 11, 1787. DOI: 10.3389/fpsyg.2020.01787

Venkatraman, M.. (2020). Emotional Responses in Advertising: A Neuromarketing Perspective. *Journal of Advertising*.

Venkatraman, V., Dimoka, A., Pavlou, P. A., Vo, K., Hampton, W., Bollinger, B., & Winer, R. S. (2015). Predicting advertising success beyond traditional measures: New insights from neurophysiological methods and market response modeling. *JMR, Journal of Marketing Research*, 52(4), 436–452. DOI: 10.1509/jmr.13.0593

Vincent, E., & Kolade, A. (2019). Persuasive communication: Semiotic analysis of"Share-a-Coke"advertising campaign. *World Journal of Innovative Research*, 7(2), 1–6.

Virk, G. S., & Solovyov, S. E. (2017). *Parallel Robots: Mechanics and Control*. Springer.

Vukobratović, M., & Borovac, B. Vukobratović and B. Borovac. (2004). Zero-Moment Point Thirty Five Years of Its Life. *International Journal of HR; Humanoid Robotics*, 1(1), 157–173. DOI: 10.1142/S0219843604000083

Wajidi, F. A., Rehan, E. W., Saeed, M., Iftikhar, K. M., & Tahir, A. (2023). Technology Trends and Their Impact on the E-commerce Industry. *International Journal of Social Science & Entrepreneurship*, 3(4), 236–253. DOI: 10.58661/ijsse.v3i4.227

Wallman, J. J., & Emerson, J. (2016). Noise tailoring for scalable quantum computation via randomized compiling. *Physical Review. A*, 94(5), 052325. DOI: 10.1103/PhysRevA.94.052325

Wang, H., & Zeng, H. (2020). Quantum algorithms for feature selection and predictive analytics. *IEEE Transactions on Neural Networks and Learning Systems*, 31(5), 1560–1572. PMID: 31265416

Wang, L., Chen, Y., Xu, Y., & Lin, Z. (2024). Assertive or non-assertive? How self-concept clarity influences customers' responses to advertising messages. *International Journal of Hospitality Management*, 123, 103942. DOI: 10.1016/j.ijhm.2024.103942

Wang, P., Li, L., Wang, R., Zheng, X., He, J., & Xu, G. (2022). Learning persona-driven personalized sentimental representation for review-based recommendation. *Expert Systems with Applications*, 203, 117317. https://doi.org/https://doi.org/10.1016/j.eswa.2022.117317. DOI: 10.1016/j.eswa.2022.117317

Wang, X., Ryoo, J. H. J., Bendle, N., & Kopalle, P. K. (2021). The role of machine learning analytics and metrics in retailing research. *Journal of Retailing*, 97(4), 658–675. DOI: 10.1016/j.jretai.2020.12.001

Wang, Y., & Li, Y. (2019). Quantum data encoding for quantum machine learning. *Physical Review. A*, 100(3), 032309. DOI: 10.1103/PhysRevA.99.032309

Wang, Z., Chen, Y., & Zhang, S. (2021). Amplitude encoding and quantum algorithms for data representation. *Nature Reviews. Physics*, 3(2), 81–96.

Wein, T. (2022). Data Protection, Cookie Consent, and Prices. *Economies*, 10(12), 307. DOI: 10.3390/economies10120307

Wei, Z., Wu, C., Wang, X., Supratak, A., Wang, P., & Guo, Y. (2018). Using support vector machine on EEG for advertisement impact assessment. *Frontiers in Neuroscience*, 12, 1–12, 76. DOI: 10.3389/fnhum.2018.00001

What Is a Buyer Persona, Why It Matters & How to Define Yours. (n.d.). Retrieved September 26, 2024, from https://buyerpersona.com/what-is-a-buyer-persona

White, A. R., Martinez, L. M., Martinez, L. F., & Rando, B. (2021). Color in web banner advertising: The influence of analogous and complementary colors on attitude and purchase intention. *Electronic Commerce Research and Applications*, 50, 1–10, 101100. DOI: 10.1016/j.elerap.2021.101100

White, G. R. T., & Samuel, A. (2019). Programmatic Advertising: Forewarning and avoiding hype-cycle failure. *Technological Forecasting and Social Change*, 144, 157–168. DOI: 10.1016/j.techfore.2019.03.020

Wynn, M., & Jones, P. (2023). Corporate Digital Responsibility and the Business Implications of Quantum Computing. *Advances in Environmental and Engineering Research*, 04(04), 1–15. DOI: 10.21926/aeer.2304053

Xie, S., & Yuan, Y. (2021). An Empirical Study on the Impact of Online Travel Consumers' Brand Loyalty: The Mediating Effect of Flow Experience. *E3S Web of Conferences*, 234, 01027. https://doi.org/DOI: 10.1051/e3sconf/202123401027

Xue, N., Liu, X. S., Wan, L. C., & Hou, Y. (2024). Relaxing or challenging? How social crowding influences the effectiveness of activity-based destination advertising. *Tourism Management*, 100, 104839. DOI: 10.1016/j.tourman.2023.104839

Xu, X., Cui, J., Cui, Z., He, R., Li, Q., Li, X., Lin, Y., Liu, J., Liu, W., Lu, J., Luo, M., Lyu, C., Pan, S., Pavel, M., Shu, R., Tang, J., Xu, R., Xu, S., Yang, K., & Yung, M.-H. (2024). *MindSpore Quantum: A User-Friendly, High-Performance, and AI-Compatible Quantum Computing Framework.* https://arxiv.org/abs/2406.17248v3

Xu, Z., Chen, D., Kuang, J., Yi, Z., Li, Y., & Shen, Y. (2024). Dynamic Demonstration Retrieval and Cognitive Understanding for Emotional Support Conversation. *Proceedings of the 47th International ACM SIGIR Conference on Research and Development in Information Retrieval*, 774–784. DOI: 10.1145/3626772.3657695

Yağci, M. İ., Kuhzady, S., Balik, Z. S., & Öztürk, L. (2018). In search of consumer's black box: A bibliometric analysis of Neuromarketing research. *Journal of Consumer and Consumption Research*, 10(1), 101–134. https://www.betadergi.com/ttad/yonetim/icerik/makaleler/169-published.pdf

Yang, B., Liu, D., Tang, C., Xiao, C., Zhao, K., Li, C., Yang, G., Huang, L., & Lin, C. (2024). Crafting Customisable Characters with LLMs: Introducing SimsChat, a Persona-Driven Role-Playing Agent Framework. *ArXiv, Cornell Universuty*. https://arxiv.org/abs/2406.17962v3

Yang, F., & Gu, S. (2021). Industry 4.0 is a revolution that requires technology and national strategies. *Complex & Intelligent Systems*, 7(3), 1311–1325. DOI: 10.1007/s40747-020-00267-9

Ying, M. (2010). Quantum computation, quantum theory and AI. *Artificial Intelligence*, 174(2), 162–176. DOI: 10.1016/j.artint.2009.11.009

Yoshikawa, T. (2021). Real-Time Trajectory Planning for Delta Robots with Machine Learning Algorithms. *IEEE Transactions on Automation Science and Engineering*, 18(1), 88–101.

Yu, C., Zhang, Z., Lin, C., & Wu, Y. J. (2020). Can data-driven precision marketing promote user ad clicks? Evidence from advertising in WeChat moments. *Industrial Marketing Management*, 90, 481–492. DOI: 10.1016/j.indmarman.2019.05.001

Yun, J. T., & Strycharz, J. (2023). Building the Future of Digital Advertising One Block at a Time: How Blockchain Technology Can Change Advertising Practice and Research. *Journal of Current Issues and Research in Advertising*, 44(1), 24–37. DOI: 10.1080/10641734.2022.2090464

Zaki, M. J., & Meira, W. (2014). *Data Mining and Machine Learning: Fundamental Concepts and Algorithms*. Cambridge University Press. DOI: 10.1017/CBO9780511810114

Zaltman, G. (2003). *How customers think: Essential insights into the mind of the market*. Harvard Business School Press.

Zamuner, E. (2013). The role of the visual system in emotion perception. *Acta Analytica : Philosophy and Psychology*, 28(2), 179–187. DOI: 10.1007/s12136-012-0151-7

Zapata, J. M.. (2023). Advancements in Automated Marketing Systems Using Quantum Algorithms. *Journal of Business Research*.

Zaremba, B., & Goldenberg, S. (1997, August). Sensor-Based Real-Time Path Planning for a Delta Parallel Robot. *IEEE Transactions on Robotics and Automation*, 13(4), 549–558.

Zeng, G.. (2022) "Quantum Algorithms for Path Planning in High-Speed Robotic Systems," *Proceedings of the 2022 IEEE International Conference on Quantum Robotics*, pp. 352–361.

Zeng, Y., Luo, J., & Yuan, J. (2018). Integration of Internet of Things and Industrial Robotics: A Review. *IEEE Access : Practical Innovations, Open Solutions*, 6, 10542–10552.

Zhang, F. Y., Xu, G. L., & Huang, L. M. (2020). Quantum-inspired Synchronization in Networked Robot Systems. *IEEE Transactions on Robotics*, 36(7), 1231–1245.

Zhang, H., Tian, S., Qin, J., Yu, Z., Guo, H., & Jia, X. (2024). Inventory prediction based on CNN-LSTM Model. *Highlights in Science. Engineering and Technology*, 82, 251–257. DOI: 10.54097/eywbtj23

Zhang, J., & Kwiatkowski, D. (2020). Quantum algorithms for machine learning: A review. *IEEE Transactions on Quantum Engineering*, 1, 1–12.

Zhang, S., Li, J., Xu, H., Yu, H., & Shi, J. (2023). Robust Quantum Feature Selection Algorithm. *Authorea Preprints*.

Zhang, Y., Song, D., Zhang, P., Li, X., & Wang, P. (2019). A quantum-inspired sentiment representation model for twitter sentiment analysis. *Applied Intelligence*, 49(8), 3093–3108. DOI: 10.1007/s10489-019-01441-4

Zhao, R., & Wang, S. (2021). A review of quantum neural networks: methods, models, dilemma. arXiv preprint arXiv:2109.01840.

Zhao, X., Zhang, H., Zhu, G., You, F., Kuang, S., & Sun, L. (2019). A Multi-Branch 3D Convolutional Neural Network for EEG-Based Motor Imagery Classification. *IEEE Transactions on Neural Systems and Rehabilitation Engineering*, 27(10), 2164–2177. DOI: 10.1109/TNSRE.2019.2938295 PMID: 31478864

Zhong, R. Y., Xu, X., Klotz, E., & Newman, S. T. (2017). Intelligent Manufacturing in the Context of Industry 4.0: A Review. *Engineering (Beijing)*, 3(5), 616–630. DOI: 10.1016/J.ENG.2017.05.015

Zhou, Z., Zheng, L., & Li, X. (2021). Abstract or concrete? The influence of image type on consumer attitudes. *International Journal of Consumer Studies*, 45(5), 1132–1146. DOI: 10.1111/ijcs.12642

Zhu, H., Zhu, Z., Ou, Y., & Yin, Y. (2023). To be precise (imprecise) in utilitarian (hedonic) contexts: Examining the influence of numerical precision on consumer reactions to artificial intelligence-based recommendations. *Psychology and Marketing*, 40(12), 2668–2685. DOI: 10.1002/mar.21904

Zhu, Z., Jin, Y., Su, Y., Jia, K., Lin, C.-L., & Liu, X. (2022). Bibliometric-based evaluation of the Neuromarketing research trend: 2010–2021. *Frontiers in Psychology*, 13, 35983212. DOI: 10.3389/fpsyg.2022.872468

About the Contributors

Pranjali Gajbhiye received a Ph.D. in Biomedical Signal Processing from the Electronics and Electrical Engineering (EEE) Department, Birla Institute of Technology and Science (BITS) Pilani, India, in 2022. She worked as a Digital Signal Processing Engineer and AWS cloud architect at Nirvesh Enterprises Pvt. Ltd Hyderabad. She has worked for ECG signal analysis and algorithm development for VitalProbe, Inc. Since February 2024, She started working as a Neuroscientist at the AI Research Centre at Woxsen University, Hyderabad. Her research interests include Digital Signal Processing for Biomedical Applications, sensor data processing, Machine Learning, Medical Image Processing, and the Internet of Things (IoT) for healthcare. She has published research papers in reputed international journals and conferences. Her journal paper titled "Wavelet Domain Optimized Savitzky-Golay Filter for the Removal of Motion Artifacts from EEG Recordings", published in IEEE Transactions on Instrumentation and Measurement received more than 40 citation scores in just two years. She has served as a reviewer for more than ten scientific journals. Since July 2022, she has been an Academic Editor of Frontiers in Physiology Journal (Science and Technology).

Hemachandran Kannan holds the position of Director at the AI Research Centre and serves as the Area Chair of the Analytics Department at Woxsen University. His academic journey includes the completion of a Ph.D. with a focus on Embedded Systems. Beyond academia, he stands as an ambassador for the AI Accelerator Institute and lends his expertise as an Advisory Board member to several esteemed international and national companies, including AptAI Labs (USA) and Agzitence Pvt. Ltd. Notably, he has been a prominent figure at various national and international scientific conferences and Summits, where he has not only shared his insights but also enriched these events as an effective resource person. His lectures encompass a wide array of subjects, predominantly centered around Artificial Intelligence and emerging technologies. Dr. Kannan's dedication to knowledge exchange is evident in his recent engagement in a faculty exchange program at the University of Pecs, Budapest, Hungary. During this program, he took on the responsibility of educating students on the intersection of AI and Business. At present, his contributions extend to his roles as an Expert at UNESCO and an ATL Mentor of Change. The depth of his impact is further highlighted by his prolific authorship and editorial work. With a substantial publication record comprising over 35 journal articles and international conference papers, he has showcased his expertise in domains like Natural Language Processing, Computer Vision, the creation of Video recommendation systems, and the development of Autonomous Robots. His editorial proficiency has led him to assume editorial board positions in several respected Scopus and SCI-indexed journals. Acknowledgment of his achievements arrived in the form of consecutive Best University Faculty Awards at Woxsen University for the academic years 2021-2022 and 2022-2023, as well as an earlier recognition at Ashoka Institute of Engineering & Technology for 2019-2020. Dr. Kannan's journey is underscored by an unwavering commitment to collaborating with industries across the world on real-time use cases and projects. His enthusiasm and positive outlook have been crucial to his success, as evident in the open-ended and impactful nature of his work. His portfolio includes the editing of seven books and the authorship of three, published in partnership with reputable publishers such as CRC Press, Taylor & Francis, IGI Global, and Bentham Science.

Raul Villamarin Rodriguez is the Vice President, Woxsen University. Dr. Rodríguez is an Adjunct Professor at Universidad del Externado, Colombia and member of the International Advisory Board at IBS Ranepa, Russian Federation, and a member of the IAB, University of Pécs Faculty of Business and Economics. He is also a member of the Advisory Board at PUCPR, Johannesburg Business School, SA, and Milpark Business School, South Africa along with PetThinQ Inc, and SpaceBasic, Inc. He is a visiting professor at Uni. del Rosario, and Expert at UNESCO. Dr. Raul has a scholarship named after him in ZIBS, China. He is also part of the PRME i5 Expert Pedagogy Group - India representative. He holds two honorary titles as Steven Pinker Professor of Cognitive Psychology and Classavo Chair Professorship in Integrative Research and Digital Learning. Dr. Rodriguez's specific areas of expertise and interest are Machine Learning, Deep Learning, Natural Language Processing, Computer Vision, Robotic Process Automation, Multi-agent Systems, Knowledge Engineering, and Quantum Artificial Intelligence. He is a registered expert in Artificial intelligence, Intelligent Systems, and Multi-agent Systems at the European Commission, a nominee for the Forbes 30 Under 30 Europe 2020 list, and an awardee in the Europe India 40 under 40 Leaders. Alongside this, he is a member of the GRLI Deans and Directors cohort. He is a regular keynote speaker and panel moderator at various national and international conferences or summits such as ML Conference (Singapore). Additionally, he is a member of the Harvard Business Review Advisory Council, the ETS Business School Advisory Council (BSAC) in India, and the Institute for Robotics Process Automation & Artificial Intelligence. He is engaged in responsible research throughout his career and especially through RRBM, GRLI, and PRME. He has co-authored several reference books in the field of Psychology, and Human-Tech interface. He has more than 100 publications to his credit including practice-oriented such as ET. He is a weekly contributing writer to various magazines in the field of analytics and emerging technologies. Alongside this, he is a journal reviewer and associate editor in various publications such as IEEE.

José I. Rojas-Méndez, is a Professor of International Business and Marketing at Sprott School of Business, Carleton University, Canada. He received his Ph.D. in Marketing from Manchester Business School, England, and his M.B.A. from University of Ottawa, Canada. His research interests include nation branding, international consumer behavior, cross-cultural issues in business and international marketing. He has published more than 55 academic papers and his work has previously appeared in journals like Tourism & Management, International Marketing Review, Journal of Strategic Marketing, Journal of Business Research, Journal of Travel Research, Marketing Intelligence and Planning, The Journal of Advertising Research, Journal of Vacation Marketing, The Journal of Product and Brand Management, Place Branding & Public Diplomacy, The Journal of Non-Profit and Public Sector Marketing, The Journal of Global Marketing, Journal of Food Products Marketing, International Journal of Commerce and Management, Journal of Academic Ethics, Corporate Reputation Review, Journal of Targeting, Measurement and Analysis for Marketing, International Journal of Wine Business Research, Asia Pacific Education Review, Latin American Business Review, and The International Journal of Organization Theory and Behavior. In 2024, Dr. Rojas-Méndez has been awarded the prestigious Sprott School of Business Research Award at Carleton University, Canada, for exemplifying excellence in research. In 2022, he was the Recipient of the Person of the Year Award by The Chilean Association of Business School (ASFAE) for outstanding academic career and contribution to Multidisciplinary Business Review, the official academic journal of ASFAE. Also, in 2019, Dr. Rojas-Méndez has received the "Best Paper Award" from Journal of Product and Brand Management; and in 2017 he was distinguished with the Research Achievement Award granted by Carleton University to 10 of the most outstanding researchers of the institution. Dr. Rojas-Méndez has worked as a consultant for companies operating in a wide variety of industries in various countries, including the pension system, supermarkets, banks, construction, automotive, and education. As part of his career, he has carried out research on issues related to national and foreign brands, multiculturality in business, marketing, and international consumer behavior. Dr. Rojas-Méndez has been a visiting professor and has been invited to give lectures in international business and marketing in more than 30 countries, including China, India, Germany, France, Austria, Saudi Arabia, India, Wales, South Korea, Japan, Greece, Hungary, Mexico, Peru, Argentina, Chile, Colombia, Ecuador and Canada.

***

Nisha holds a Bachelor's degree in Economics and is currently pursuing her MBA with a specialization in Business Analytics. Her background in economics has provided her with a deep understanding of market dynamics, financial modeling, and data analysis. Through her MBA, she has expanded her skill set in advanced analytical tools, including machine learning, data visualization, and statistical analysis, which she uses to drive business insights and optimize decision-making processes. Her academic journey has equipped her to evaluate complex economic trends and apply business analytics to solve real-world business problems. Nisha is passionate about using data-driven strategies for market forecasting, business optimization, and sustainable growth. She has also worked on projects and research related to behavioral economics, econometrics, and business strategy. Nisha is eager to leverage her combined expertise in economics and business analytics to contribute to forward-thinking organizations and create impactful solutions that enhance business performance.

Kathirvel Ayyaswamy, acquired, B.E.(CSE), M.E. (CSE) from Crescent Engineering College affiliated to University of Madras and Ph. D (CSE.) from Anna University. He is currently working as Professor, Dept of Computer Science and Engineering, Karunya Institute of Technology and Sciences, Coimbatore. He is a studious researcher by himself, completed 18 sponsored research projects worth of Rs 103 lakhs and published more than 110 articles in journals and conferences. 4 research scholars have completed Ph. D and 3 under progress under his guidance. He is working as scientific and editorial board member of many journals. He has reviewed dozens of papers in many journals. He has author of 13 books. His research interests are protocol development for wireless ad hoc networks, security in ad hoc network, data communication and networks, mobile computing, wireless networks, WSN and DTN. He is a Life member of the ISTE (India), IACSIT (Singapore), Life Member IAENG (Hong Kong), Member ICST (Europe), IAES, etc. He has given a number of guest lecturers/expert talks and seminars, workshops and symposiums.

C.V. Suresh Babu is a pioneer in content development. A true entrepreneur, he founded Anniyappa Publications, a company that is highly active in publishing books related to Computer Science and Management. Dr. C.V. Suresh Babu has also ventured into SB Institute, a center for knowledge transfer. He holds a Ph.D. in Engineering Education from the National Institute of Technical Teachers Training & Research in Chennai, along with seven master's degrees in various disciplines such as Engineering, Computer Applications, Management, Commerce, Economics, Psychology, Law, and Education. Additionally, he has UGC-NET/SET qualifications in the fields of Computer Science, Management, Commerce, and Education. Currently, Dr. C.V. Suresh Babu is a Professor in the Department of Information Technology at the School of Computing Science, Hindustan Institute of Technology and Science (Hindustan University) in Padur, Chennai, Tamil Nadu, India.

|Oindrilla Ghosh is a Research Scholar hailing from the School of Law at Christ (Deemed to be University) Bangalore, India, focuses her research on health of tribal communities. Her work includes publications on Neuroscience on Organizational Behavior at IGI Global and also Environmental Disasters that are indexed in SCOPUS and Web of Sciences conference proceedings. She completed her early education at Loreto Day School, Bowbazar and went on to achieve distinction in her undergraduate (B.A/LL.B) and postgraduate (LL.M) studies at Calcutta University. Having served as an Assistant Professor of Law at Kingston Law College,Barasat, Kolkata, Ghosh has actively participated in numerous National Conferences, International Conferences, UN Global Summits, webinars, and seminars organized by prestigious academic institutions. Her expertise lies in health perspectives, environmental studies, human behavior, and related areas. Additionally, she has conducted various workshops, lectures in educational institutions, and is engaged with NGO's to help the needy

Shyam Krishan Joshi obtained His PhD from IIT Delhi and was a Post Doctoral researcher at Scuola Superiore Meridionale, Naples, Italy. He is currently working as an Assistant Professor of Artificial Intelligence at Woxsen University Hyderabad. Synchronization of Multi-agent systems, Quantum -AI, Pattern recognition and Machine Learning are the areas of his Research Interests.

Haneefa K.V. is a doctoral scholar at CHRIST University, India. He has a Masters degree in Commerce from University of Calicut. His research interest includes marketing innovation, technology adoption, and sustainability in the quick commerce sector

Binod Kumar is an undergraduate student known for his academic excellence, with his scholarly works indexed in Scopus database. Hailing from Ranchi, Jharkhand in India, Binod is currently pursuing a Bachelor of Law degree at the prestigious Shri Venkateshwara University. His passion for technology and innovation along with climate changes is evident through his high academic performance and numerous projects. Binod has a keen interest in artificial intelligence, machine learning, neuropsychology, climate changes and disaster management, fields in which he has undertaken several research projects. He is particularly fascinated by the potential of AI to solve real-world problems and is dedicated to learning and applying new techniques in these areas. He volunteers at local NGOs, teaching underprivileged children basic computer skills. With a strong foundation in law and a commitment to making a positive impact, Binod Kumar is poised to become a future leader in the legal industry.

Manushree, an MSc student in Cyber Forensics and Cyber Security at Amity University, Noida. My research centers on digital forensics, cybersecurity frameworks, and methods for mitigating network threats. I am especially focused on enhancing secure data handling practices and preventing cyber-attacks. My objective is to contribute to cybersecurity by creating innovative solutions to address the complex challenges of the digital world.

Pratik More is a distinguished professional with a strong academic background and extensive industrial experience. He holds two Masters degrees, one in Biotechnology and the other in Business Administration. He finished his PhD in Business Administration (Marketing) from the University of Pune. During his industry experience of more than 10 years, Dr. Pratik has been associated with a Fortune 500 company and MNCs in various roles of International Marketing, Market Research, Analytics, and Healthcare Consulting. At Woxsen University, Dr. Pratik brings a fresh approach to education with a track record of engaging students in interactive and innovative learning experiences. Leveraging his decade-long industrial experience, he strives to introduce new skills in curriculum, student assessment, and fostering a positive learning environment. Dr. Pratik emphasizes experiential learning for students and focuses on hands-on training and experience through live projects. His student-centered approach, built on experiential learning expertise, ensures students are not just learning, but actively engaged in the process to become future leaders. His research interests include Business Analytics, Co-creation, Consumer Behaviour, and Modern Technologies in Business.

Shiva Sai Kiran Pothula is currently Assistant Professor of Sustainability at the School of Business, Woxsen University, Hyderabad, India. He is a PhD from IISc, in urban studies, transportation and sustainability. He also has a master's degree from IITR in infrastructure systems. He is the recipient of prestigious "Sakura Science

Program" grant from JST, Japan and has also participated in the "Groningen Summer School" through a fully granted research fund from Groningen University.

Hari Deepthi, currently pursuing an MSc in Cyber Forensics and Cyber Security at Amity University, Noida. My research focuses on areas such as digital forensics, cybersecurity frameworks, and network threat mitigation. I am particularly interested in advancing methods for secure data handling and the prevention of cyber-attacks. My goal is to contribute to the growing field of cybersecurity by developing innovative solutions that address the evolving challenges of the digital landscape.

A. Anthony Raj received his U.G. degree from Sacred Heart College, University of Madras, Chennai, in 2000, P.G. (M.Sc & M.Phil) degrees from Loyola College, University of Madras, Chennai, in the year 2003 standing. His Doctoral Degree from Bharathidasan University, Trichy in 2020. He has got teaching, research and administrative experience of more than 21 years in various engineering colleges, and autonomous institution. He is currently working as Assistant Professor, Department of Mathematics at Panimalar Engineering College, Chennai.

S. Umarani is a Professor, Department of Computer Science and Applications at SRM Institute of Science and Technology, Ramapuram Campus in Chennai, India. With academic qualifications including an MCA from Bharathidasan University and a Ph.D. in Computer Networks from Anna University, her expertise spans areas like big data, computer networks, IoT, and data mining. She has over 24 years of academic experience. She has published 36 Indexed Journal paper and presented various paper in scopus indexed conference. She has received "Asiriyar Semmal Award"

l**Sandeep Saharan** received the Bachelors of Technology degree in computer science and engineering from M.D. University, Rohtak, Haryana, India, Masters of Engineering degree in computer science and engineering from Thapar University, Patiala, Punjab, India and Ph.D. in Computer Science and Engineering from Thapar Institute of Engineering and Technology, Patiala, Punjab, India. He did Ph.D. in the area of Smart Parking Systems where he developed smart parking models and communication protocols for the on-street parking systems of the Seattle city of United States. His research work is published in reputed international journals as well as in international flagship conferences, such as, IEEE TRANSACTIONS ON INTELLIGENT TRANSPORTATION SYSTEMS, Future Generation Computer Systems, Computer Communications, Applied Mathematics and Information Sciences, IEEE Global Communication Conference, and ACM Special Interest Group on Data Communication that is ACM SIGCOMM conference. He has also visited Faculty of Information & Communication Technology of University of Malta, Msida, Malta last year under ERASMUS+ mobility program. His technical research interests are in the areas of evolutionary optimization, machine learning, deep learning, game theory, and reinforcement learning. Whereas, his application research interests are intelligent transportation systems and smart healthcare systems. He is a professional member of various reputed professional bodies, such as, IEEE, ACM, and Computer Society of India. At present he is working as an assistant professor in School of Computer Science Engineering and Technology, Bennett University, Greater Noida, Uttar Pradesh, India.

Vishal Kumar Sharma, Senior Project Engineer of AI Research Centre, Woxsen University, India, with over 8 years of experience in team management, PCB design, programming, robotics manufacturing, and project management. He has contributed to multiple patents and is passionate about merging smart work with hard work to drive innovation in AI and robotics.

Chintan Singh is an accomplished academic and researcher currently serving as an Assistant Professor at Amity University Noida, India. He holds a PhD in Forensic Sciences, specializing in cybersecurity, computer forensics, toxicology, and forensic chemistry. With over four years of teaching experience, Dr. Singh has made significant contributions to the field of forensic science through his research and publications. He has authored more than 18 articles that have been published in major databases, including Scopus and Web of Science, showcasing his expertise and commitment to advancing knowledge in his areas of specialization. His research work is highly regarded, reflecting his dedication to forensic sciences and its applications in cybersecurity and toxicology. In addition to his academic roles, Dr. Singh completed a training program under the BRICS Russia initiative, which took place at the Nizhni Novgorod State University in Russia. This experience has enriched his understanding of international practices in forensic science and further enhanced his professional network. Dr. Singh's contributions to education and research continue to impact the field, making him a notable figure in forensic sciences within India and beyond.

Muhammad Usman Tariq has more than 16+ year's experience in industry and academia. He has authored more than 200+ research articles, 110+ case studies, 95+ book chapters and several books other than 4 patents. He is founder and CEO of The Case HQ, a unique repository for courses, narrative and video case studies. He has been working as a consultant and trainer for industries representing six sigma, quality, health and safety, environmental systems, project management, and information security standards. His work has encompassed sectors in aviation, manufacturing, food, hospitality, education, finance, research, software and transportation. He has diverse and significant experience working with accreditation agencies of ABET,

ACBSP, AACSB, WASC, CAA, EFQM and NCEAC. Additionally, Dr. Tariq has operational experience in incubators, research labs, government research projects, private sector startups, program creation and management at various industrial and academic levels. He is Certified Higher Education Teacher from Harvard University, USA, Certified Online Educator from HMBSU, Certified Six Sigma Master Black Belt and has been awarded PFHEA, SMIEEE, and CMBE.

Niyaz Ahmad Wani (Member, IEEE) received the bachelor's degree in computer science from the University of Kashmir, Jammu and Kashmir, India, in 2013, the Master of Science degree from the Islamic University of Science and Technology (IUST), Awantipora, Jammu and Kashmir, in 2016, focusing on the complexities of information technology. He is currently pursuing the Ph.D. degree in computer science with the Thapar Institute of Engineering and Technology, Patiala, Punjab. He has many publications that include internationally reputed journals, conferences, and workshops. His academic and research work established him as a potential scholar in the constantly changing field of computer science and technology. As he progresses in his Ph.D., his dedication to innovation and progress stays strong, paving the way for a future when his contributions to the field are expected to have a significant influence. His research interests include a wide range of topics, such as machine learning, deep learning, image processing, medical data analytics, and smart healthcare. He is serving as a Reviewer for various IEEE, Elsevier and Springer journals, including Artificial Intelligence Review, IEEE Transactions on Pattern analysis and Machine Intelligence, Applied Soft Computing, Applied Sciences, IEEE Access, Multimedia Tools and Applications, Biochemistry, and Journal of Cell Biology.

Index

A

C

D

E

O

P

Q

R

S

T

U

V

www.ingramcontent.com/pod-product-compliance
Lightning Source LLC
LaVergne TN
LVHW080350011026
849161LV00009B/2251